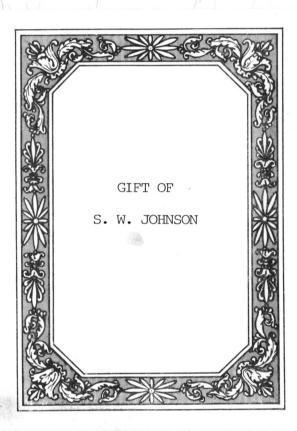

Personality:

Theory,
Research,
and Applications

Personality:
Theory, Research, and Applications

Charles R. Potkay
and
Bem P. Allen

Western Illinois University

Brooks/Cole Publishing Company
Monterey, California

Brooks/Cole Publishing Company
A Division of Wadsworth, Inc.

Printed in the United States of America
10   9   8   7   6   5   4   3   2   1

Library of Congress Cataloging-in-Publication Data

Potkay, Charles R., [date]
    Personality : theory, research, and applications.

    Includes index.
    1. Personality.   2. Personality—Research.
3. Adjustment (Psychology)   I. Allen, Bem P.,
[date].   II. Title.
BF698.P655   1986   155.2   85-19477
ISBN 0-534-05634-2

Sponsoring Editor: *Claire Verduin*
Project Development Editor: *John Bergez*
Marketing Representative: *Catherine Konradt, Thomas L. Braden*
Editorial Assistant: *Pat Carnahan, Linda Wright*
Production Editor: *Candyce Cameron*
Production Assistant: *Louise Rixey*
Manuscript Editor: *Margaret C. Tropp*
Permissions Editor: *Carline Haga*
Interior Design: *Jamie Sue Brooks*
Cover Design and Illustration: *Joyce C. Weston*
Cover Photos: *Courtesy of B. F. Skinner, Carl Rogers (front); Courtesy of Culver Pictures, Inc. (back).*
Part Opening Illustrations: *Joyce C. Weston*
Art Coordinator: *Judith Macdonald*
Interior Illustration: *Maggie Stevens*
Photo Editor: *Judy Blamer*
Photo Researcher: *Marquita Flemming*
Typesetting: *Progressive Typographers, Emigsville, Pennsylvania*
Cover Printing: *Lehigh Press Lithographers, Pennsauken, New Jersey*
Printing and Binding: *R. R. Donnelley & Sons Co., Crawfordsville, Indiana*
Credits continue on page C1.

To Cathy and Paula,
Bem III, Kathleen, Margaret, Sandy, Sue,
and Families;

and, to Their Children, and Yours.

May they live in peace and love.

Preface

A textbook reviewer once concluded that "choosing a textbook for a basic under-graduate course in personality psychology is, these days, a little like a rerun of Solomon's decision to cut the baby in half" (Hochreich, 1979). That is, instructors were compelled to choose either a book on personality theories or a book on empirical research for their students. Books on theories emphasized psychologists such as Freud, Rogers, Skinner, and Kelly. Books on empirical research empha-sized topics such as introversion-extraversion, aggression, authoritarianism, and factor analysis. Likewise, personality textbooks have tended to be either academic or applied in their approaches. The academic approach has dwelled on abstract concepts, theoretical controversies, and complexities of personality study. The applied approach has emphasized practical aspects of personality, including solu-tions to personal adjustment problems. Yet all of these are important pieces of the puzzle of personality.

Although that is the way it has been with personality textbooks, that is not the way it has to be. We have endeavored to write a book that presents theories and research as complementary and that relates the academic study of personality to real-life personal and social issues. In short, we have adopted Solomon's decision to keep the baby whole. Above all, we have tried to present this complex field in a way that will be representative and comprehensible, as well as interesting to the introductory student.

Given that some recent "comprehensive" books have similar aims, what is different about this one? There are three major aspects of our approach that we believe distinguish this book as a vehicle for introducing personality: balanced coverage, the organization of the text, and an orientation to the needs of students.

Balanced Coverage

Our guiding principle in writing this book has been *balance*. Our assumption is that no one personality theorist, researcher, or concept holds the corner on "truth." Various points of view are important and potentially compatible with one another. Classical theories and contemporary research, empirical and clinical approaches, scientific rigor and personal applications all have a place in the field of personality. Furthermore, our backgrounds helped to make possible a fruitful interplay of person orientation and scientific-mindedness. One author is a practicing clinical psychologist and the other an active experimental psychologist. Both are professors of psychology who have published regularly in the personality and personality assessment fields.

Although we have generally sought to maintain a stance of theoretical neutrality, in the concluding portions of this book we do present a sympathetic view of the interactionist approach to personality. This approach is grounded in the assumption that internal characteristics, such as traits and self, and external influences, such as social situations, operate jointly to determine behavior. Our evaluation of this reorientation as being on the leading edge of the personality field is supported by the psychology literature of the past two decades. As a psychological tool, interactionism can serve as a conceptual bridge between the long and honored histories of personality theory (Lewin, 1936; Murray, 1943) and empirical research (Rabin, Aronoff, Barclay, & Zucker, 1981). It also points the way toward the field's exciting future by linking a variety of theoretical and experimental approaches (Mischel, 1973, 1984).

Organization

A clear organization is a must if undergraduate students are not to be overwhelmed by the multiple approaches and facets of the field of personality. The organization of this book reflects two basic goals: first, to present systematic coverage of major personality theories, accompanied by empirical findings and applications; second, to show how contemporary research addresses fundamental questions about personality. In this way we hope to provide students with complementary frameworks for absorbing new information about personality from diverse sources.

OVERVIEW OF THE TEXT

Part 1 introduces the major themes and techniques of personality study. The first chapter offers a preliminary working definition of personality in terms of individual differences along many behavioral dimensions. We believe this device is useful for teaching purposes because it provides a concrete framework for an initial understanding of the field. In subsequent chapters we return to the working definition, showing how specific personologists would either accept the definition or qualify it according to their own points of view. The chapter also reviews central questions and issues that characterize the field.

The second chapter introduces the methods by which personality is studied and measured. We consider how theory, clinical observation, correlational research, and experimental research complement one another. We also review the background of personality assessment techniques and the important role they play in personologists' attempts to understand the individual. The strengths and limitations of these techniques are illustrated by examples involving real individuals.

Part 2 presents major theoretical approaches to personality, including classical psychoanalysis (Freud, Jung), social psychoanalysis (Horney, Sullivan, Adler, Fromm), behaviorism (Skinner), and the more modern perspectives of social learning (Rotter, Bandura), humanism (Rogers, Maslow), and cognition (Kelly). The sequence in which we present these approaches reflects the general pattern of their historical development. To help students make sense of the multiplicity of theories, we try to show how these approaches grow out of, complement, or vie with one another.

We have taken special care in this part of the book to follow a systematic outline in our coverage, to integrate related ideas, and to facilitate comparisons across theories. Toward this end, similar headings are used across chapters. Each chapter includes a *biographical sketch* of the theorist whose ideas are being highlighted. These sketches go beyond the brief factual introductions typical of many personality texts. Often, knowing something about the life experiences of a particular theorist can give students a head start in learning a theory, because they can see why a particular thinker came to emphasize certain aspects of personality. Next, we discuss the theorist's *view of the person* — the basic philosophical orientation the theorist assumes in approaching individuals and their personalities. For example, some theorists believe that people exhibit "free will" in their behavior (Rogers, Maslow), while other theorists disclaim such a capacity (Freud) and still others argue that people have free will only in a qualified sense (Skinner, Kelly). Knowledge of these beliefs about human nature will help students understand the implications of different theories.

With this foundation, we next present the *basic concepts* of each theorist, following with sections devoted to *supporting evidence* and *applications* of the theory. As Kurt Lewin stated, "There is nothing so practical as a good theory." The applications sections place special emphasis on assessment and the practical meaning of theoretical ideas. Finally, each chapter concludes with evaluations of the *contributions* and *limitations* of the theory.

Part 3 centers on modern empirical research as an approach to understanding personality. Although we emphasize that theoretical and empirical approaches are intimately related, the researchers reviewed in Part 3 generally have followed a more inductive method than the classical personality theorists. These researchers also have tended to focus on specific topics or concepts rather than on very broad theoretical speculations. Accordingly, this part of the book stresses such topics as specific personality traits and the explanations of particular kinds of behavior.

The number and variety of important topics in contemporary personality research can present a real stumbling block to introductory students who are trying to gain an overall understanding of the field. To help students conceptualize the wealth of modern empirical research, we have organized this part of the book around the theme of three major approaches to personality — the trait approach, the situational approach, and the interactionist approach. This theme enables students to see how different emphases result from the varying perspectives that researchers adopt toward personality. At the same time, it is broad enough to permit discussion of several topics that are of interest in their own right.

The first two chapters in Part 3 are devoted to research emphasizing *traits,* focusing on the past assumption that internal factors are of primary importance in determining people's behaviors. After considering how traits can be identified and measured — for example, by Eysenck's scientific model that uses factor analysis — we look at four specific traits "in action": authoritarianism (and dogmatism), anxiety, achievement motivation, and sensation seeking.

The next two chapters consider research that tends to emphasize *situational influences* on personality and behavior. Once again we begin with a survey of how situational influences may be identified and studied and then follow with a chapter of illustration — in this case, using aggression as the clearest example of a behavior that is significantly influenced by factors external to the individual.

The next step is to focus on an approach that considers the mutual influence of both internal and external factors. Accordingly, the final two chapters in Part 3 consider the recent elaboration of *interactionism.* Our first chapter on this topic explains how Endler derives interactionism from the questions raised earlier in the book and examines Mischel's theory in some detail. The second chapter provides a number of examples of an interactionist analysis of behavior, with special emphasis on questions related to sex roles and purported sex differences.

In Part 4, the book "closes the loop" by identifying concepts that cut across various theoretical and research approaches and by looking to the future of personality study. The discussion of self-concept and personality development provides a useful basis for returning to the whole person and addressing questions often raised by students, such as "Who am I? How did I get to be the way I am? How am I changing? How can I have a well-adjusted personality?" The views of Allport, Erikson, and Kohlberg are considered here, together with the implications of major personality theories for effective adjustment.

Our concluding chapter contains a unique feature. Here we take a look backward in order to see forward with greater acuity. We summarize and compare the various approaches, to leave students with a coherent review of what they have learned and to present points of integration. We also try to pull together different trends and overlapping concepts in personality theory and research, ending with some suggestions for further study and a brief forecast of how the study of personality might be enhanced in the future.

ALTERNATIVE USES OF THE BOOK

We have put together a comprehensive book so that those who wish to cover all aspects of the field of personality can do so. However, in our experience as instructors, we have found that we sometimes choose a book that "covers everything" so we can select what we think is most important. Such a choice allows us the flexibility to sample areas that our professional experience identifies as central and to choose considerations that are commensurate with our expertise and interests. Having made our choices, we then feel free to de-emphasize parts of the chosen book that we deem to be less relevant. Only a relatively complete book can allow this kind of adaptability. After all, one can't select all those topics and issues one wishes to emphasize from a book that has a limited scope.

Knowing that some instructors will wish to adopt the selective approach, we have a few suggestions. Consider Chapter 1 as an introduction to the field, and Chapter 16 as a concluding overview of the book. Chapter 2 covers research and assessment. You may find you wish to omit one or more of these chapters, or make them optional reading.

For those who stress personality *theory* in their courses, we recommend coverage of Part 2 in its entirety as well as a selection of sections from the chapters in Parts 3 and 4 that contain coverage of important theories. For example, the sections on trait theory (Chapters 9 and 10) and on the theories of Endler, Mischel, Allport, Erikson, and Kohlberg (Chapters 13 and 15) can be read with understanding even if other chapters are omitted. Such a selection would not neglect the empirical approach, as each of the "theory" chapters in Part 2 includes discussion of relevant research.

For instructors who wish to emphasize *empirical* approaches and current research, some basic theory could be considered by covering selected chapters of Part 2. More detailed attention could then be given to Part 3, where research on such topics as authoritarianism and anxiety, aggression, interactionism, and sex differences is reviewed. This strategy would not neglect theory, as Part 3 delves into several important points of view.

Still other instructors will want to "follow their noses." The broad field of personality certainly permits professional discretion in the selection of topics to emphasize. In general, we have tried to include enough basic information for instructors of different persuasions to choose from. No one knows better than you what your students need.

An Orientation to Students

In the ultimate analysis, textbooks are for students. Students enrolled in a personality course rely on us, their professors, to guide their discoveries. With this in mind, we have made every effort to present the field in such a way that students can achieve an understanding that will be useful to them now and in years to come. We want to interest students not only in personality, but more generally in the discipline of psychology.

WRITING STYLE

First, the text is written in straightforward and, we hope, appealing English. In communicating with students, it is important to introduce needed vocabulary while minimizing the pomposity of abstruse jargon that often characterizes presentations of any scientific discipline. Accordingly, we have avoided using words like "pomposity" and "abstruse." One of our primary goals has been to make the material readable and interesting.

At the same time, we have tried to give students solid, well-researched material—something they can sink their teeth into. We believe strongly in scientific rigor and academic scholarship, and we have tried to build these values into the text. However, intelligent laypeople also appreciate everyday examples, concrete illustrations, and questions whose meaning they can relate to readily. We have been careful to define basic concepts and key terms in clear and direct language and to give frequent examples of abstract ideas.

INTEGRATION OF CONCEPTS

To help students absorb an imposing quantity of information, we have tried throughout the book to link specific ideas and findings to the larger questions that motivate personality theory and research. The final chapter's integrative review highlights points of similarity as well as differences among theorists and researchers. Thus, end-of-course comparisons and evaluations are not left entirely up to the student, but are presented directly by the authors. The goal is to enable students to come away from the course with substantial notions of what personality is about, rather than with some fuzzy ideas crammed hastily into short-term memory.

APPLICATIONS

To further enhance the meaning of the material presented, the book includes a variety of personal applications and demonstrations clearly tied to the text discussion. For example, a number of exercises are presented in boxed format and then "revisited" in the text. Students are asked to record their early memories, write down self-descriptions, respond to "mini" personality measures, and observe their own behavior. In this way, they will see support for the idea endorsed by personality psychologists over many decades that individuals do have capacities for understanding their own behaviors, directly and simply (Allport, 1942; Mischel, 1977; Rogers, 1950). They also will gain an understanding of why some aspects of personal experience have been seen as inaccessible to conscious self-report (Freud, 1900; Skinner, 1971). In one unique highlight (Chapter 7), readers can see how a renowned psychologist, Carl Rogers, responded to a self-description technique. In short, students are encouraged to become active participants in their learning.

LEARNING AIDS

The learning aids built into the text are carefully designed to support our goal of making the field of personality comprehensible and interesting. Each chapter begins with *teaser questions* designed to arouse curiosity and preview the chapter contents. Carefully selected *boxed inserts* present concrete previews and illustrations of topics and are always discussed in the text. *Key concepts* are highlighted in the margin as they are introduced and listed for review at the end of the chapter. In this way students can readily identify the important concepts they should master, as well as locate discussion of them in the text. In addition to a prose summary, each chapter ends with a brief section of *review questions,* many of which ask students to make comparisons and applications, and to address critical issues about personality. A *glossary* at the end of the book provides a dictionary of new and technical language. Collectively, these features constitute a built-in "study guide" for the text.

In sum, here is an attempt at balance and integration in the coverage of the complex field of personality. We hope you — students and instructors — both like it. Most important, we hope that the book will enable students to share our sense of fascination and excitement about the study of personality. To present a comprehensive yet comprehensible overview of this rapidly changing and diversifying field is an ambitious task. For this reason, we welcome your reactions to the book and your suggestions for its improvement.

Acknowledgments

We would like to thank the following psychologists who offered advice or contributed materials for the book: Albert Bandura, T. X. Barber, Robert A. Baron, James Bieri, John Black, Theodore M. Dembroski, Edward Donnerstein, Norman Endler, Hans J. Eysenck, Harrison Gough, James P. James, Neil Malamuth, Carl R. Rogers, Julian Rotter, B. F. Skinner, and Mark Snyder.

We also would like to acknowledge those who reviewed the manuscript at various stages. They include:

Robert Arkin
University of Missouri-Columbia

Frank Brotherton
Xavier University

Mike Brown
Gonzaga University

Gerald S. Clack
Loyola University

Georgette Daugherty
Miami Dade Community College

Michael J. Dougher
University of New Mexico

Peter Dowrick
University of Alaska

Lawrence A. Fehr
Widener University

Larry Froman
Towson State University

Kirby Gilliland
University of Oklahoma

Sharon Herzberger
Trinity College

Richard High
Leigh University

Joseph Istvan
Oregon Health Sciences University

John A. Johnson
Penn State University, DuBois Campus

Rhoda Lindner
California State University, Long Beach

Marilyn P. Mindingall
Auburn University at Montgomery

Richard L. Moreland
University of Pittsburgh

John Moritsugu
Pacific Lutheran University

Richard P. Rakos
Cleveland State University

Steve Slone
Cleveland State University

Francis Terrell
North Texas State University

Norris D. Vestre
Arizona State University

We incorporated many of their helpful suggestions as best we could.

We are grateful to a number of colleagues who were generous enough to read parts of the manuscript, provide information, and otherwise offer assistance and support: Paula Allen, Dave Budinger, Rita Clark, Frank E. Fulkerson, Steve George, Holly Head, Vernon Joy, Paul and Pat Kennedy, Nick and Ben Kubasak, Donna Leach, Eugene Mathes, Sue Moriearty, Stewart Nyi, Don Oitker, Cathy Potkay, Carolyn Prueter, Roderick Pugh, Gene Smith, and Eric Ward.

We also wish to express our appreciation and indebtedness to the Brooks/Cole family, especially to Claire Verduin, our editor, "taskmaster," and patiently special person, and John Bergez, our creative developmental specialist and indispensable third member of the writing team. Special mention also should be given to our super production editor, Candy Cameron, and copy editor, Peggy Tropp. Finally, the efficiency and consideration of members of the production staff also merit recognition. They include Jamie Brooks, Judy Blamer, Judith Macdonald, Carline Haga, and Pat Carnahan.

Thanks to you all!

Charles R. Potkay
Bem P. Allen

Contents

CHAPTER TWO   *How Personality Is Studied:*
The Field, the Person   21

PART TWO
Theoretical Approaches to Personality

63

Box 5.1   170
Baby in a Box

Box 6.1   193
The P & A I-E Scale

Box 7.1   234
Adjective Descriptions of Your Actual and Desired Self

Box 7.2   239
"Dear Dr. Rogers"

Box 7.1   254
Revisited:
Rogers Describes "Carl Rogers"

PART THREE
Contemporary Empirical Approaches to Personality

293

Box 9.1   296
Which Traits Best
Describe You?

Box 9.2   304
Maudsley Personal-
ity Inventory, Short
Form

Box 10.1   329
Modified F Scale

Box 10.2 343
Anxiety Experi-
enced by a College
Student

Box 10.3 355
Sensation-Seeking
Exercise

CHAPTER ELEVEN *Identifying Situational Influences*
on Behavior

Box 11.1 364
What Is Your
College Like?

Box 11.2 392
Identifying
Stressors in Your
Own Life

CHAPTER TWELVE *Situations and Behavior:*
Aggression

Box 12.1 398
Woman Raped
While Bar Patrons
Cheer

PART FOUR
Integrating Perspectives

493

Personality:

Theory,
Research,
and Applications

PART ONE

The Study of Personality

PART 1 introduces you to the concept of personality and to the approaches psychologists have taken in seeking to understand it. In the initial chapter, "personality" is defined and is related to what you already know about it. This chapter also introduces the issues and themes that psychologists have emphasized in studying personality. In Chapter 2, you will find answers to the questions "What is a theory?" and "How does it differ from research?" You will also learn how professionals make observations of people in a psychotherapy session and how they measure personality. We expect that you will come away from Part 1 with a reasonable appreciation of how personality is studied and how knowledge about it is applied. You will then be ready to consider various theories of personality and methods of investigating it scientifically.

1

What Is Personality?

How well do psychologists' views of personality coincide with those of the "person on the street"?

Can personality be defined so as to accommodate the views of many psychologists and the layperson too?

What are the issues and themes of interest to psychologists who study personality?

I N THIS FIRST chapter, we will introduce you to some major considerations that form the foundation for much of what follows. In order to profit by what you already know, the chapter opens with a discussion of commonsense notions about personality. These ideas are then used to bridge the gap between your conception of personality and the one that we will use in this book. Next, we review Sheryl Wilson's and Theodore X. Barber's (1983) study of "fantasizers." Consideration of these unique and interesting individuals provides the opportunity to raise several questions that have been of continuing interest to psychologists who study personality. The chapter closes with an overview of controversies about personality.

Commonsense Notions about Personality

All of us talk about personality and act as if we know what it is, often without even attempting to define it. You probably know many of the commonsense notions about personality. For example, "personality" is credited to an individual who is not very attractive. "It's what's inside that counts" refers to personality, suggesting that internal traits are what matter, not superficial characteristics. "She has a good personality" reflects our need to distribute personalities along a "good—bad" scale. People with "good" personalities are assumed to be socially skilled, friendly, outgoing, and witty, the kind of individuals who are fun to be with. Those with personalities located at the opposite end of the scale lack these desirable attributes.

Some people talk about personality as if it can vary in amount from "a great deal" to "very little." In fact, you've probably heard the rather extreme statement "So-and-so has no personality." As a case in point, consider the basketball coach at a prominent university. Because his team had made the play-offs, sports writers were very interested in him. However, the coach just wasn't giving them anything to write about. Never once did he demand that the referees be subjected to psychiatric examinations. Neither did he question their ancestry. Writers just couldn't pin him down on anything. He said little and had no prominent characteristics. They couldn't call him a "battler" or "a thinking man's coach" or "skilled at psyching out his players." Therefore, he was accused of having "no personality." Evidently, if your traits are not "worn on your sleeve," people may think you have little or no personality.

If there are people with "no personality," there must be people with "lots of personality." People with "lots of personality" have a number of prominent traits that are easy to appreciate. Thus, journalists are fond of Ronald Reagan partly because, unlike other U.S. presidents in recent history, he has definite traits that are easy to spot and easy to write or talk about. He's percieved by most as a grandfatherly, friendly person with a good sense of humor.

Some people speak of personality as if it can be healthy or sick, like a vital organ. This notion implies that just as the heart and the liver are located in the body, so also is the personality. Like a weak heart or a deteriorated liver, a personality can go bad. An example of this notion would be the case of Lenny Bruce, the late comedian who liked to tell "dirty jokes" back in the 1950s when such humor was taboo. He also defied authority and social convention. Bruce was in trouble with the law on several occasions and was known to have attempted lovemaking at public gatherings. The label "sick personality" was often applied to this defiant funnyman. The technical description of such people is *antisocial personality*. Often called *sociopaths*, these people are characterized by poor social relationships and are unable or unwilling to honor social rules. More generally, people who are unconventional, whether they are antisocial or not, may be accused of having a "sick personality."

Other commonsense notions have to do with people's relationships with one another. The saying "birds of a feather flock together" expresses one of these ideas. It implies that people with similar traits will like one another, get along well, and, consequently, spend a good deal of time together. An example would be the famous bandits Bonnie and Clyde. The other side of the coin is the "personality clash." Sometimes the personalities of two people are so out of tune that they can't be in the same room with each other. It might be said that newscaster Dan Rather and former president Richard Nixon had a "personality clash." During one of Nixon's last presidential news conferences, he took offense at every question asked by Rather. Finally, he asked the network reporter "What are you running for?" Rather faced the man who was soon to be forced from the presidency and replied "Nothing, sir, what about you?" It was the last of several clashes.

COMMON SENSE: WHAT'S IN COMMON?

Several trends can be extracted from these commonsense notions about personality. One of them emerges from all the rest: "It's what's inside that counts." Those who hold this belief assume that personality is internal and consists of relatively deep-seated traits, rather than superficial characteristics. The notions of "good personality," "sick personality," and "birds of a feather flocking together" have interesting implications. First, these beliefs lead to the assumption that different people are likely to have different personalities. Some people have "good personalities"; others have "sick personalities"; the personalities of some persons are so different that they "clash." In sum, there are differences among people in their personalities.

Second, these same notions imply that certain categories of people have a number of traits in common, even though their personalities are not identical. Members of the "good personality" class are all friendly, outgoing, and witty.

Those who belong to the "sick personality" category share antisocial orientation, unconventionality, and disobedience. Although "persons on the street" believe that there are individual differences in personality, they also think that it is possible to group together those people who have traits in common.

Finally, the notions of "no personality" and "lots of personality" imply that, even though personality is internal, it has readily observable external manifestations, commonly called *behaviors*. Behaviors are actions involving the muscles of the body or the mechanisms of thinking and feeling. It is by observing other people's behaviors that one is able to draw conclusions about their personalities. Behaviors corresponding to traits stand out for all to see.

There are a number of important considerations here. First, internal traits are the source of external behaviors that logically correspond to the traits. If a person frequently offers aid and comfort to others, we conclude that he or she has the trait "helpfulness." Second, people cannot make valid inferences unless they see frequent performances of a behavior corresponding to a trait. Observing a person being flirtatious once or twice in the same situation isn't enough to allow the inference that he or she is "a flirtatious person." Only after witnessing the performance of flirtatious behaviors on a number of occasions in several situations is it reasonable to infer that the person has the trait "flirtatiousness." Third, commonsense notions make it seem that personality can be assessed fairly easily. If it is possible to tell a great deal about an individual's personality just through casual observation, psychologists with their sophisticated tests should be able to describe an individual's personality in great detail.

Psychologists' View of Personality: A Working Definition

Although commonsense notions about personality are obviously imprecise, they are not so far off base as you might think. Just how well do these everyday ideas match the view of personality developed by psychologists?

As you might expect, there are disagreements among *personologists*— psychologists who specialize in the study of personality. Thus, it is practically impossible to provide a definition that would be accepted by all personologists. Nevertheless, it would be useful to have a working definition, one that includes the most common areas of agreement among those who study personality. Such a definition would provide a standard against which we could compare the specific ideas of the several theorists and researchers covered in this book. It will be evident that some theorists follow the definition rather closely, while others do not. Finally, in the last part of this text, we examine how modern theory and research suggest alterations to the "working definition." In the meantime, you are about to see that the commonsense notions just reviewed are in some cases quite similar to the ideas of the many personologists who have inspired our "working definition" (Bem & Allen, 1974; Lamiell, 1981).

personologist*

---

* Key concepts are listed in the margin when they first occur. You can review these terms when you reach the Chapter Review at the end of the chapter.

ELEMENTS OF THE WORKING DEFINITION: INDIVIDUAL DIFFERENCES, BEHAVIORAL DIMENSIONS, TRAITS, AND PROFILES

individual differences

Individual differences generally refer to the observation that people differ in a variety of ways. More specifically, individual differences are reflected in the tendency for the behaviors of different people to fall at different points along various behavioral dimensions.

behavioral dimension

The term *behavioral dimension* requires a bit of explanation. Recall that traits have corresponding behaviors. Each such behavior can be placed along a behavioral dimension. A dimension is a continuum, like a yardstick. Just as one end of a yardstick is anchored by 0 inches and the other end by 36 inches, one end of a behavioral dimension is anchored by one extreme of a behavior and the other end is anchored by the opposite extreme. For example, *affiliativeness, assertiveness,* and *conscientiousness* are labels of behavioral dimensions. Each has anchors representing behavioral extremes. The following diagram illustrates a behavioral dimension.

1 2 3 4 5 6 7

assertive ▪ ▪ ▪ ▪ ▪ ▪ ▪ unassertive

One end of the assertiveness dimension is anchored by *assertive* — showing a strong tendency to stand up for one's rights and to say no when it seems appropriate to do so. The other end is anchored by *unassertive* — tending to allow one's rights to be trampled on by others. Similarly, *affiliative* means desiring social relations with others, while *unaffiliative* refers to shunning relations with others.

As common sense suggests, even people who are similar in many ways have distinct personalities.

Conscientious means giving careful attention to duties and obligations, and *unconscientious* means failing to meet obligations and to perform duties.

For the sake of convenience and simplicity, we will define dimensions as having only seven degrees. Actually, the number of degrees of a dimension is difficult or impossible to determine. In any case, only behaviors falling at the extremes of dimensions have much meaning for personality; degrees near the middle of dimensions are too ambiguous to allow inferences in which one can be confident.

In sum, a *behavioral dimension* is a continuum having end points representing behavioral extremes. Because most people, including personologists, agree that traits have corresponding behaviors, it is possible to define traits in terms of behavioral dimensions. A *trait* is an internal characteristic that corresponds to an   trait
extreme position on a behavioral dimension. If a person's behavior can be represented on the assertiveness dimension by a degree close to the anchor *assertive,* the person can be said to possess the trait *assertive.* On the other hand, if an individual displays behavior indicative of the other extreme, he or she is labeled *unassertive.*

Traits are directly related to profiles. An individual possesses many different traits in various combinations. For example, a person may be assertive, conscientious, and unaffiliative. Such a combination of traits is called a personality *profile.*   profile
A personality profile can be represented visually by the line that connects the degrees on the behavioral dimensions associated with various traits that a person possesses. In a real sense, a profile is a graphic summary of an individual's personality.

Having defined the parts of the working definition, let's consider the whole. *A personality of an individual is a set of points falling along several behavioral dimen-*   personality
sions, each corresponding to a trait, resulting in a unique profile, different from that of other individuals. Note that although some people may share a particular trait, there are individual differences in possession of the trait. Some people have it, and others don't. However, sharing does apply to profiles. There are individual differences in profiles, such that no two are exactly alike.

A PORTRAIT OF THREE PERSONALITIES

Now we're ready for a concrete illustration of our working definition. We'll paint a picture of personalities belonging to three imaginary people: Jane, John, and Julie. To see what traits are possessed by these people, it is necessary to observe behaviors reflecting some sample trait dimensions across three different social situations. However, remember that no individual's personality is limited to traits corresponding to just three dimensions, nor are corresponding behaviors performed in just three social situations. We must simplify. "Classroom," "work," and "party" have been chosen as our sample social situations, and it is assumed that observations of behavior have been made in each situation on a number of different occasions.

Now turn to Table 1.1 and look at the "Jane" entries under *assertiveness.* Her behavior is extremely assertive across occasions in the classroom (degree 1), less so across occasions at work (degree 2), and extreme again at parties (degree 1). The average assertiveness (see *mean* column) across situations is 1.33. One can make

TABLE 1.1   Behavioral Dimensions

	Assertiveness (1 = assertive)					Affiliativeness (1 = affiliative)			
	Classroom	Work	Party	Mean		Classroom	Work	Party	Mean
Jane	1	2	1	1.33	Jane	5	5	5	5.00
John	6	6	6	6.00	John	1	1	1	1.00
Julie	4	3	4	3.67	Julie	1	1	1	1.00

	Conscientiousness (1 = conscientious)			
	Classroom	Work	Party	Mean
Jane	6	7	7	6.33
John	2	1	2	1.67
Julie	5	6	5	5.33

the strong inference that Jane possesses the trait *assertive.* In fact, one could say "Jane is really a very assertive person." John is clearly unassertive, and Julie is so neutral on the assertiveness dimension that she cannot be meaningfully characterized in terms of this trait.

Turning to the other behavioral dimensions, one can see that Jane possesses the trait *unaffiliative.* On the other hand, John and Julie are both clearly affiliative. John is conscientious, but Jane and Julie are not. In examining Table 1.1, please remember that you are looking at a simplified picture. Real people's behaviors don't fall so neatly at the extremes or in the middle of behavioral dimensions.

Next let's consider concrete examples of John's, Jane's, and Julie's profiles. Figure 1.1 shows the personality profiles of Jane, John, and Julie. For each person, the line connecting points on the behavioral dimensions represents a summary of the individual's personality. It is clear that the line is different for each person. You can literally see that different personalities are reflected in individual differences along several behavioral dimensions, each corresponding to a trait, resulting in individual differences in profiles. Picturing Figure 1.1 in your "mind's eye" will allow you to remember the working definition of personality and, more important, to understand it thoroughly.

IMPLICATIONS AND CAUTIONS

Our simplified illustrations in Table 1.1 and Figure 1.1 highlight the coincidence of personologists' beliefs about personality and the commonsense notions held by most nonprofessionals or laypersons. First, as represented in Table 1.1, many personologists and laypersons believe that people are quite consistent across different situations (remember, the consistency is exaggerated here for the purpose of illustration). Second, where single dimensions are involved, individuals can be very similar or even identical. That is, two or more people can exhibit about the same degree of a behavior, on the average, and thus possess the same trait. Julie and Jane are unconscientious to a similar extent, while John and Julie

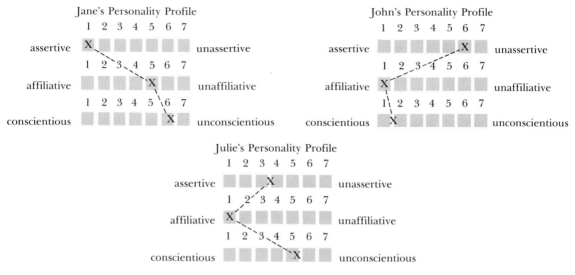

Figure 1.1   Personality profiles.

are affiliative to the same degree. Therefore, Julie and Jane both possess the trait *unconscientious,* and John and Julie both possess the trait *affiliative.*

Third, an overriding point of agreement between personologists and the people they study is the shared belief in individual differences. That belief is at the core of conceptions about personality (Lamiell, 1981). Our working definition specifies that a large group of people will display behaviors fitting both extremes and the midpoints of a given behavioral dimension. There are individual differences in placement of behaviors along any dimension. True, some people have traits in common, but given enough dimensions, no two people would share the same profiles and thus the same personalities. One estimate has put the number of traits and corresponding dimensions at nearly 18,000 (Allport & Odbert, 1936).

Even though professionals and laypersons seem to agree on the nature of personality, previous experience along with the first part of this chapter may have given you the impression that it is the professionals who decide for you what your personality is like. Such may seem to be the case in practice, because professionals may have already attempted to assess your personality with the use of some tests. However, you do have your own rendition of your personality. It is called your *self-concept.* Your self-concept can be thought of as your own perception of your personality. It is not only important to your understanding of you and your daily functioning, but it is also valuable to professionals who wish to understand and help you. We will return to self-concept at several points in the book.

Issues and Themes in the Study of Personality

The purpose of this section is to discuss some themes and issues that recur throughout the book. In order to make these considerations more concrete and lifelike, they are illustrated by reference to some unusual and interesting people.

Read about these individuals first. Then we will use them to preview the major concerns of personologists that are taken up in the remainder of the book.

FANTASIZERS

Sheryl Wilson and Theodore X. Barber (1983) have discovered some excellent hypnotic subjects. These individuals are able to take any of those suggestions that we associate with hypnosis — for example, age regression, anesthesia, amnesia, or blindness. They are able to perform behaviors associated with suggestions as expertly and convincingly as they can be done. Also, they take suggestions equally well when not under hypnosis.

The factor that is most common to excellent hypnotic subjects, and the trait that has been used to label their personalities, is that almost all are *fantasizers*. Fantasizers are individuals who spend huge portions of their daylight hours engaging in vivid fantasies, more vivid than the most engrossing movie or the most lifelike dream. To them, their fantasies are "as real as real" (Wilson & Barber, 1983). Twenty-six of Wilson's and Barber's 27 excellent hypnotic subjects clearly fit the *fantasizer* label. Perhaps the lone exception was simply a reflection of the failure to precisely define "excellent hypnotic subject," "fantasizer," or both. If so, future research may show that "excellent hypnotic subject" is synonymous with "fantasizer." In any case, fully 92% of the fantasizers spend more than 50% of their time in fantasy, the highest estimate being 90% of the time. The incidence of fantasizers is estimated by Wilson and Barber at 4% of the female population. These are rare people.

While Wilson and Barber (1983) are quick to point out that their 26 fantasizers differed quite markedly in personality, with some extraverted and others introverted, some high and others low in self-esteem (p. 6), they were remarkably similar in many ways. First, all were women. This fact could be due to happenstance. Wilson and Barber pointed out that the pool of individuals from which they drew their subjects contained mostly women. However, it cannot be entirely written off as coincidence. Further research may reveal that women outnumber men in the fantasizer category. At this point, Barber (personal communication) has no explanation for the possible sex difference.

The first question that comes to your mind is probably "How can these people possibly function on a day-to-day basis, if they so often leave our reality for their own?" The answer is straightforward: they quickly learn that they must keep an ear tuned to the "other reality," the one they share with us. Please note that the fantasy world of these people is, in most cases, just as real as everyone else's reality. For example, one of the 26 fantasizers recalled the day of her childhood in which she learned to always know what is happening in the reality she shared with others. She was tripping through a fantasy meadow, high-stepping over the tall grass, while leading her "pet lamb." Suddenly the honking automobile horns awakened her to the other reality, the middle of a busy street. Another subject, who in childhood viewed herself as a princess playing the role of a regular child, began to separate her realities when several friends derided her upon being shown her "castle" — actually her middle-class home.

Excellent hypnotic subjects are usually also fantasizers.

Personality development of fantasizers. How do the unusual personalities of fantasizers develop? *Personality development* refers to the process by which children are shaped and formed by their social and physical environment, and their genetic makeup, until they emerge as unique adults having distinctive personalities. An assumption implicit in the phrase "personality development" is that the way a child is reared determines, to a great extent, what traits he or she will possess. It follows from this assumption that the degree to which people are reared alike is the degree to which they will share the same traits. Of course, this statement does not contradict the belief that no two people have exactly the same personality. No two people are subjected to exactly the same child-rearing practices.

There is an unusual degree of overlap among the childhood experiences reported by fantasizers. As children, 80% of Wilson's and Barber's fantasizers believed that their dolls and stuffed animals were living beings with feelings and personalities. This may not seem unusual, because almost all children sometimes treat their stuffed toys as real beings. The difference lies in the duration and intensity of the fantasy. A typical child treats playthings as real only during play, and only to a moderate degree. Fantasizers considered their dolls and stuffed toys to be real all the time. They worried when dolls were left home, and were careful not to place their stuffed toys in a draft because "they might catch cold." Also, since the toys, in effect, were real living beings, they tended not to be relinquished until each had disintegrated from age and wear.

Fantasizers, as children, believed in fairies, leprechauns, elves, guardian angels, and the like. Nearly 60% spent time playing with imaginary companions, people or animals. Often these creatures were substitutes for toys and unavailable

personality development

playmates. Sometimes imaginary playmates corresponded to a character in a childhood myth. For example, during childhood, one fantasizer joined the characters in the Peter Pan story and, along with Tinker Bell, enjoyed many adventures. A few even had God or Jesus as imaginary companions. Others had imaginary playmates who were children just like themselves. For example, in one actual case not included in the Wilson/Barber sample, a child accompanied her mother and "Jackie," her imaginary friend, aboard a bus. Mother and child separated, because an empty seat for two was occupied by the child and "Jackie." At the next stop, a rather large individual boarded and sat next to the child, on "Jackie." The youngster became very distressed and recruited her mother to rescue "Jackie." Ninety-two percent of the fantasizers at one time or another during childhood had become someone else, such as a princess. These childhood behaviors must contribute greatly to adult fantasy-proneness.

How much of the similarity among fantasizers can be attributed to similarity in their childhood environments? There appear to be four child-rearing practices or childhood conditions that produce the traits of fantasizers. First, Wilson and Barber report that 70% of their subjects were encouraged to fantasize by a parent or other significant adult. Fantasizers tended to be read fairy tales, praised for engaging in fantasy and imagination, and assisted in their fantasy by adults who also treated dolls and stuffed toys as living beings. Second, 62% of the fantasizers were isolated from others, spending much of their time alone during childhood, and thus had need of imaginary companions and fantasy. Third, 35% of the fantasizers were subjected to stress during childhood. Some of this group were physically or psychologically abused, and some had parents with emotional problems. Others were deserted by their parents or were shuttled about among relatives or foster homes. Fourth, another 35% were involved in piano lessons, ballet dancing, dramatic acting, or other childhood activities that encouraged fantasy. For example, a ballet dancer had to imagine her musical accompaniment, and a student of piano resorted to fantasy to pass the long hours of practice. Since the percentages add up to more than 100%, it is obvious that a number of fantasizers were subjected to more than one of the four circumstances.

The adult personalities of fantasizers.   As you might expect, similarities in childhood experiences and in child-rearing practices yield similarities in adult personality. In adulthood, fantasizers share the tendency to improve a boring social gathering by seeing, hearing, and smelling what is being discussed, by imagining the participants as clowns or other entertaining figures, and by escaping into fantasy altogether. They also tend to use actual stimuli in their environment as cues for a fantasy (a shower becomes a waterfall in the Caribbean), to fantasize during ordinary or undesirable tasks (doing the dishes), and to complete a movie, TV show, or book enjoyed before bedtime by continuing the plots with themselves as main characters.

Seventy-five percent of Wilson's and Barber's fantasizers reported orgasms produced solely by sexual fantasy. Some of them reported "better" orgasms during fantasy than those achieved with husbands or boyfriends. These fantasies tended to occur anytime or at any place. One fantasizer imagined sexual interaction with a male co-worker while casually working and talking with him. The vividness of these fantasies can be appreciated by the fact that some fantasizers who imagined sexual interactions with absent lovers had trouble distinguishing between imagined and actual sexual episodes.

Fantasizers may be very attractive to men. One of these individuals related that she had been pursued by men to the point of distraction (not reported by Wilson and Barber). The "problem" became so disruptive that she purposely gained weight to appear unattractive. When this ploy failed, she just resigned herself to her status. At a conference on hypnosis, another fantasizer was continually followed by an entourage of admiring men. While, objectively, she is very pretty, her looks cannot completely account for the number of men surrounding her or the observation that they seemed totally entranced by every word she uttered.

Sixty-five percent of the Wilson/Barber sample hallucinate in all sense modalities. With their eyes wide open, they can see, hear, touch, and smell beings and objects that are "as real as real," but for which there are no corresponding physical representations in their environment. Some fantasizers report that they have trouble driving. For example, if they think of a child running into the street, they are apt to see a child dart in front of them with such realism that a screeching halt is liable to result in a collision.

Sixty-four percent of the sample have "become someone else." Fantasizers tend to become much more engrossed in being someone else than do other people. For example, one fantasizer who has revealed her status to her husband will one day be Lady Godiva when he returns from work, the next day a Gypsy, the next a businesswoman, the next a teenager, and so on. Another enjoys trying out her fantasies on people she will never see again. So skilled is she at "becoming someone else" that she convinced a fellow passenger on a bus that she was an Eskimo, fresh from Alaska.

Almost all of Wilson's and Barber's fantasizers have extraordinarily vivid memories (96% of the sample). When asked about a previous experience, they don't just recall it, they reexperience it. Remembered sights, sounds, smells, and tastes become as intense and real as were the originals. One fantasizer, as a child, had such total memory that she could turn the pages of a storybook and recite the text perfectly, before she could read. She simply used the picture on each page as a stimulus for recalling the words spoken by her parents when they read the story to her. As an adult, she took no notes in her art history class. On test day, when she was asked to describe the content of some slides, she used each slide as a stimulus for recollections of the professor's voice when he had discussed the slide in class.

Seventy-three percent of the fantasizers showed strong physical effects corresponding to their fantasies. One spent a year in pain when she was told by her dentist that children her age develop painful cavities. Another developed a wart upon touching a frog, because she believed the myth about the amphibious creatures. All could make a part of their anatomy rise or lower in temperature. Fully 60% reported having had false pregnancies, complete with termination of menstruation, breast changes, abdominal enlargement, morning sickness, unusual food cravings, and "fetal" movements. As the reader might expect, these people are "naturals" for *biofeedback*—a method for learning to control physiological responses, such as heart rate.

Finally, let's return to the link between hypnotic suggestibility and fantasy-proneness. As you recall, the overlap between excellence at accepting suggestions and tendency to fantasize is almost complete. Although an occasional excellent hypnotic subject may not also be a fantasizer, Wilson and Barber imply that fantasizers apparently all are excellent hypnotic subjects. Wilson and Barber suggest that such is the case because fantasizers have actually experienced, during their lifetime, all of the phenomena typically associated with acceptance of hypnotic suggestions. They have age-regressed (gone back in time to become themselves at an earlier age), reincarnated, experienced analgesia (loss of pain sensation), suffered amnesia, and so on. Thus, when they are asked to take these suggestions under hypnosis, or even while wide awake, it is easy for them.

Wilson's and Barber's observation has led them to contend that hypnosis — or suggestion in general — succeeds in creating extraordinary suggested behaviors only to the extent that subjects have previously experienced the same behaviors. Thus, hypnosis may boil down to reliving unusual experiences from suggestees' past lives. For example, Barber (1978) reports a study in which only one subject successfully developed a blister when raising a blister was suggested to her. She was the only subject who had previously developed a blister on the area to which the suggestion was directed. Since many of us have had at least a few very unusual experiences, the reader may wonder why fantasizers are unique in being almost universally able to conjure up previous experiences while under suggestion. Wilson and Barber (1983) and Barber (personal communication) suggest that fantasizers' remarkable ability to concentrate totally on experiences — savoring every delicious taste, "photographing" every special scene — creates total memory for them. In turn, that ability enables them to relive experiences under suggestion, as if these were occurring all over again. Hypnosis just supplies them with the stimulus and the license; they do the rest.

ISSUES

Considering fantasizers raises a number of issues that are important to personologists. By *issues*, we mean relatively specific concerns that are of general interest. Now that you are familiar with Wilson's and Barber's (1983) work, we consider those issues and illustrate them by using information about fantasizers.

Childhood experiences.   One crucial issue that has been of continuing interest to personologists is the relative importance for personality of childhood or early experiences compared to more contemporary experiences. Wilson and Barber (1983; and personal communication) indicate that fantasizers tend to be somewhat withdrawn into themselves and secretive about their special skills and abilities. They have gotten that way because of early experiences. Recall that one of them found herself humiliated when peers didn't see a "castle" instead of her middle-class house. You can imagine that this kind of embarrassing early experience is fairly common among fantasizers and may lead them to become drawn into themselves and usually unwilling to talk about their fantasies. The psychoanalysts, led by Sigmund Freud, are among those personologists who emphasize early experience. You'll find out more about this orientation in Chapters 3 and 4.

However, some personologists deemphasize early experience, casting personality in terms of more current experience. These include the humanists (Chapter 7). In Chapters 5, 6, and 8, you will encounter other theorists who focus either on the present or on the future (Skinner, Bandura, and Kelly).

Types.   Are there really people who are so much alike that they can be grouped together and called *types*? A *type* is a category of individuals who share a number of traits or characteristics in common. Obviously, fantasizers fit the notion of type. Most tend to be secretive, creative (artistic), able to concentrate totally on specific events, unusually good at recalling events, and able to develop rare conditions such as false pregnancy. Personologists have a long-standing interest in types. You will learn more about types later in this book (Chapters 9 and 14).

personality type

Nature versus nurture.   What is the underlying determinant of personality —nature (biological factors, including those that are inherited) or nurture (environmental factors)? If you have had any other course in psychology, you know that the nature/nurture issue is one that concerns many kinds of psychologists, not just personologists. It is embedded in the theme of personality development, to which we will return shortly. For now, recall the orientation taken in describing the personalities of fantasizers. Basically, it was assumed that fantasizers' personalities were largely the product of environmental events. Fantasizers' unusual childhood experiences — for example, long hours of practice in the arts — undoubtedly had an important influence on the development of their rather extraordinary personalities. So did the somewhat uniform and peculiar child-rearing practices they faced. Throughout this book, you will see emphasis on the environment in development of personality (especially by the social psychoanalysts, Chapter 4, and the contemporary social personologists, Erikson and Allport, covered in Chapter 15). However, the other side of the coin, nature, should not be neglected. Perhaps some characteristics of fantasizers, such as excellent memory and extraordinary ability to concentrate, are products more of biology than of environment. You will also find that extraversion-introversion, concepts you've probably heard of before, may develop in part because of biological dispositions. In any case, it seems that both nature and nurture play a role in the development of personality.

Interpersonal relations.   Humans, and perhaps other primates (for example, chimpanzees), apparently have a strong need for relations with members of their own species. Fantasizers manifest this need in the extreme. If they have no one available with whom they can interact, they literally manufacture companions by creating imaginary playmates or bringing mythical characters to life. Interpersonal relations — sustained interactions among humans — form the core of some approaches to personality. As we explore personality in the pages of this book, we will often refer to people's critical need for interpersonal relations.

Reinforcement, cognition, emotion.   In the area of personality, and in psychology more generally, there exist three basic orientations toward studying and understanding human beings: reinforcement, cognition, and emotion. These orientations amount to rival ways of explaining human behavior.

For our present purposes, *reinforcement* can be taken to mean the processes involving the delivery of rewards, called *reinforcers*. Food is a reinforcer. However, reinforcers can be more abstract. For example, praise is a common, everyday reinforcer. You will recall that fantasizers were actively taught to create another reality by parents who offered praise to reinforce flights of fancy. In one way or another, reinforcement is assumed at several points in this book, especially in Chapters 5 and 6 (Pavlov, Watson, Skinner, Rotter, and Bandura).

Cognition refers to thinking, imagining, and reasoning processes. Right now in psychology, the cognitive revolution is under way (Baron & Byrne, 1984). There is an apparent shift toward what is happening inside people's heads, in terms of thinking, reasoning, or imagining, as opposed to what is happening outside of them or in their past or in their physiological processes (emotions). Fantasizers demonstrate the power of cognition when they achieve better and more frequent orgasms in imagination than in a sexual exchange with another person. Researcher Byrne (Chapter 14) has repeatedly found that imagination is a potent sexual stimulant. The more general utilization of the cognitive orientation is considered in Chapter 8, where Kelly's ideas are reviewed. Mischel (Chapter 13) and Bandura (Chapter 6) also emphasize cognition.

Emotion roughly and generally has to do with sensations coming from the body's tissues—that is, the physiology of the individual. It involves feeling as opposed to thinking. Emotions come from within the body, although they may be provoked from without. Fantasizers' lives are often dominated by pure feelings. They are able to conjure up the cold of Alaska, the warmth of the Caribbean, the pain of a "bad tooth," or relief of pain (analgesia). As you will see, the psychoanalysts discuss how feelings, such as those related to sex, discomfort (wet diaper), and hunger, dominate humans rather totally early in life and continue to partially control them even as adults (Chapter 3). The humanists (Chapter 7) stress the expression of feeling, but focus on more complex emotions such as joy, fulfillment, and despair. You will see that it is a rare theorist or investigator of personality who attempts to embrace all three—reinforcement, cognition, and emotion—equally.

Sex differences.   The observation that fantasizers tend to be women suggests the idea of sex differences. Perhaps fantasizers reflect a real sex difference, but, as you have seen, it is too early to tell. More generally, the degree to which the sexes may differ has been a matter of some concern to personologists. Sometimes the picture of the sexes has been virtually that of two distinct personality types. Karen Horney (Chapter 4) is rare in not taking the alleged differences between males and females for granted. In terms of research, sex similarities and differences have been heavily investigated. Chapter 14 covers the topic in some detail.

Subjective reality.   Fantasizers construct a reality that is, for them, as real as the one they share with others. Thus, their subjective reality, the one that is peculiar to them, is as important to them as objective reality, the one shared with others and tied to physical events. People's subjective interpretation of what happens to them is perhaps more important in understanding them than what objectively occurs to them. Throughout this book, you will encounter a number of personologists who are more concerned about what people say has happened in their lives than an account of what "actually" took place.

THEMES

A *theme* is broader and more general than an issue, and often points to goals in the study of personality.

Personality development.   One important theme emphasized in the account of fantasizers is personality development. The study of history illustrates that it is possible to understand the present by appreciating the chain of events leading to the here and now. Likewise, a personality can be better understood if the sequence of events leading to its current status are known. Personality development is so important that virtually all personologists have something to say about it. We recognize its critical nature by devoting some space to it in each theoretical chapter to follow.

Personality assessment.   Without the ability to measure personality, little could be known about it. No science could proceed in the absence of measurement; without it, the area of personality would have the status of astrology. Theories would lack credibility, because a worthwhile scientific theory must produce hypotheses that researchers can test via measurement. Assessment of personality is critical for another reason. Aside from allowing research to support theories, measurement tells clinical psychologists, psychiatrists, and counselors about the personalities of people who need help. Accordingly, we have devoted part of the next chapter and portions of the theoretical chapters to personality assessment.

Uniqueness.   Another critical theme is embodied in the question, "What makes people unique?" In effect, discovering the uniqueness of people is what the discipline of personality is all about. Showing that some people can really stand out in contrast to others was part of the reason for including the section on fantasizers. For the area of personality to be legitimate, it must be possible to say that people differ in other than physical ways, such as appearance and mannerism. The whole idea of personality implies that people are unique psychologically — in their thoughts, feelings, experiences, traits, and other such characteristics that are not readily apparent to the naked eye. We hope and expect that you will come away from this book believing that, indeed, people are unique.

Wholeness.   Wilson and Barber did not just consider one aspect of fantasizers, such as their ability to take hypnotic suggestions; they looked at their subjects thoroughly, from childhood to adulthood. Focusing on the whole person is possibly more true of personologists than of any other kind of psychologist. Personologists rarely are content to examine just one or a few aspects of people. They typically are interested in the entire range of activities in which people engage. In essence, personologists tend to believe that isolating parts of people is not meaningful, because no aspect of a person can be understood aside from its relationship to the whole.

Discovery.   The thrill of discovery is just as much a part of studying personality as it is integral to examining other objects of science. Wilson and Barber probably experienced the "Aha!" effect when, in the course of studying fantasizers, they discovered that accepting suggestions to perform a certain behavior may be facilitated by having behaved in that way before. Likewise, Endler may have had a similar reaction when he first came upon the idea that people are better understood when both their traits and the situation in which they operate are considered (Chapter 13). You will see other examples of the "Aha!" effect throughout this book.

Prediction and application.   The very heart and soul of science is *prediction*. It does little good to merely describe an individual's personality after the person has committed some profound act, such as an assassination. If enough is known about the personality of an individual to predict what he or she will do on future occasions, it is possible to say that a scientific understanding of the person exists. Furthermore, the ability to predict opens up the possibility of promoting beneficial behaviors and preventing detrimental ones.

Application is another important part of the field of personality. If it is known what a person is likely to do, one can actively encourage the performance of beneficial behaviors and steer the person away from detrimental behaviors. Describing why persons did what they did after they've done it may make us all feel better, but after-the-fact "explanation" has little scientific or practical significance. The importance of applying what is known about personality is recognized in each theoretical chapter by including a special section on application.

CONTROVERSIES

Aside from but related to the issues and themes that have occupied personologists are certain enduring controversies. Among these is the question of *behavioral consistency*. According to our working definition, personality consists of traits. Traits, in turn, imply consistency of behavior from situation to situation. Yet certain personologists, such as Mischel (Chapter 13), argue that consistency of behavior across situations is largely an illusion. Others stoutly defend the existence of behavioral consistency. The controversy remains unresolved. There is research to support the contention that people's behavior can be controlled by the situation in which they operate (Chapters 11 and 12), while other investigations support the assertion that people behave according to the dictates of their traits, regardless of the situations in which they find themselves (Chapters 9 and 10).

An obvious way to approach resolution of the trait-situation controversy is to suggest that understanding people requires knowledge of their traits *and* the situations in which they operate. Chapters 13 and 14 take this position. You probably will come away from those chapters thinking that one can have more confidence in statements about persons if both sources of information are used. Nevertheless, the *interactionist* position is itself controversial. As Chapters 10 and

12 indicate, it is often possible to predict some behavior of individuals based on certain of their traits *or* on knowledge of the situations in which they operate.

Finally, a long-standing controversy exists concerning whether conscious or unconscious processes control people. The psychoanalysts (Chapter 3) believe that most of the psychological processes of people are unconscious. Others actively promote the importance of conscious processes (Chapter 7). Theorists who emphasize principles of learning and conditioning hold that people may not be aware of the connections between events in their environment and the consequences of their reactions to those events (Chapters 5 and 6). However, those same individuals do not believe that inaccessible, unconscious forces control behavior.

Looking Ahead

Now you have a working definition of personality and some idea of the themes and issues that concern personologists. To help you further understand the orientations of personologists, you will have an opportunity in the next chapter to express where you stand on the various issues and themes, as these are presented in more common and general terms. Then it is on to theories of and research into personality. By the time you reach the end of the book, you will have a more informed understanding of personality. Then, in the last chapter, you will be given an opportunity to review your stand on the basic issues and themes. So keep them firmly in mind as you read the book. They can be the framework upon which you construct your own more enlightened view of personality.

CHAPTER REVIEW

Various commonsense notions about personality, such as "good personality" and "lots of personality," coincide rather well with the notions of personality advanced by a number of personologists. These everyday ideas provide a bridge between the layperson's view of personality and that of the professional. Building on that connection, it is possible to offer a working definition of personality: the personality of an individual is a set of points falling along several behavioral dimensions, each corresponding to a trait, resulting in a unique profile, different from that of other individuals.

Fantasizers are individuals who spend huge portions of their daylight hours engaging in vivid fantasies. These individuals have had early experiences and faced child-rearing practices that have shaped them into unique persons, distinct from most other people. An account of how their personalities have developed and what they are like as adults raises many of the issues and themes that concern personologists. For example, personologists focus on whether early or contemporary experience best reveals the workings of personalities, whether nature or nurture forms the basis of personality, and whether emphasis on reinforcement, cognition, or emotion provides the most fruitful orientation to personality. They also pursue the themes of personality assessment, prediction, uniqueness, and the "whole person." Finally, certain controversies, such as conscious versus unconscious and trait versus situation, are also matters of concern to personologists.

KEY CONCEPTS

Personologist

Behaviors

Individual differences

Behavioral dimension

Trait

Profile

Personality

Personality development

Type

REVIEW QUESTIONS

1. What are some implications of commonsense notions about personality?
2. Explain the three elements of the working definition of personality.
3. How is the idea of personality development illustrated by the early experiences of fantasizers and by the child-rearing practices adopted by their parents?
4. What is the adult personality of a fantasizer like?
5. What are the major themes and issues of concern to personologists?
6. What controversies continue to exist in the area of personality?

2

How Personality Is Studied: The Field, the Person

What is the value of personality theories?

What are the principal observation and research methods used in the study of personality?

How can individuals' personalities be assessed?

Can psychologists really tell all about you from personality tests?

Did Nazi war criminals have abnormal personalities?

T HE GOAL of this chapter is to answer the general question "How is personality studied?" Our answers to this question are divided into two parts, focusing on the field of personality and the individual person. The *field* includes the major approaches taken in personality theory and research. We consider the nature and uses of personality theory, and the kinds of evidence that have been used to support theoretical ideas. In the process, you are asked to explore some of your own basic ideas about personality. Our discussion of the *person* centers on assessing personality and behavior in individual persons. We look at what personality assessment is, how it is accomplished, and the purposes and limits of the major assessment strategies. Two assessment applications are detailed, one involving the administration of a psychological test battery to a college student, and the other involving interpretations of Rorschach inkblot results obtained from a group of Nazi war criminals. Also, you will be encouraged to explore an interpretation of your own personality.

The Field of Personality: Theory and Methods of Study

WHAT IS PERSONALITY THEORY?

Historically, the psychology of personality has been grounded in theory. A *theory* is a set of interrelated assumptions, ideas, and principles proposed by a person to explain certain observations of reality. A theory is speculative and tentative in nature. It requires support and verification before it can be accepted as valid or credible. Theory, therefore, differs from established facts. Facts are actual findings resulting from observations of reality using uniformly accepted procedures. Facts may be observed repeatedly under the same conditions by many workers, as usually occurs with data from formal experiments that support accurate predictions. However, facts seldom speak for themselves and typically are open to interpretation, as you likely have noted in reports of jury trials. Facts often become connected with theory in an attempt to explain their overall "meaning." Examples of factual evidence include fingerprints found on a murder weapon, the current number of car sales or housing starts in a particular economy, and the length of time it takes light from distant stars to reach the planet Earth. Examples of theories related to such facts encompass Sherlock Holmes' deductions as to "whodunit," economists' assumptions about the best way to promote a nation's monetary growth, and Einstein's revolutionary ideas about the relativity of time and space.

As suggested by the working definition of personality introduced in Chapter 1, a *personality theory* is a related, internally consistent set of ideas and assumptions about why people show individual differences. Theoretical ideas about personality date to 350 B.C., the time of Greek philosophers such as Aristotle and Plato. However, most currently accepted theories of personality were developed during the early decades of the 20th century, a time of rapid growth in psychology (Reisman, 1966). The names of some types of theories may already be familiar to you, including psychoanalytic, learning, humanistic, and cognitive theories.

personality theory

WHY HAVE PERSONALITY THEORIES BEEN IMPORTANT?

Since all theories are tentative by definition, personality theories are seldom considered "true" or "false." Thus, no personality theory has ever been totally accepted or rejected by psychologists. Personality theories are always in various stages of being supported or not supported, and most have offered some supporting, factual evidence on their behalf, however incomplete. This may be quite puzzling, even frustrating, to students seeking true answers to questions about personality. How can personality theory be neither true or false and yet make valuable contributions to psychology? These contributions may include:

1. Directing attention to important aspects of human behavior and experience
2. Organizing thinking
3. Guiding understanding
4. Offering tentative explanations
5. Suggesting methods of measurement
6. Stimulating research

Thus, a personality theory can have value if it gains the attention of psychologists by suggesting new ideas, stimulating thinking, or generating research, even out of disbelief and skepticism. To illustrate, Freud's psychoanalytic theory led psychologists to organize their thinking about human behavior around such concepts as unconscious motivation, id/ego/superego, and early childhood stages of personality development. Karen Horney's revisions of psychoanalytic theory offered alternatives to Freud's concepts of instinctual aggression and penis envy, and added new concepts of basic anxiety and neurotic needs. Humanistic theories have emphasized the wholeness of personality and a striving toward self-actualization, while influencing psychologists to pay greater attention to positive aspects of human experience, such as love, joy, and creativity. Learning theories have added concepts of stimulus and response, reinforcement, drive reduction, habit, and environmental influences.

In brief, it is difficult for any one theory to account for the enormous range of facts and observations associated with the concept of personality. For this reason, theories of personality have been important to psychologists by formally pointing out major aspects of human experience. This contribution is especially significant considering obvious historical limitations in understanding human behavior well enough to predict it. While civilization is now able to predict the paths of missiles in space over hundreds of days and millions of miles, it has not yet been able to predict often basic aspects of human behavior, such as criminal aggression, stability of love relationships, outstanding creativity, leadership, abnormality, and occupational success. Theories of personality represent small but progressive steps toward increasing our understanding of real people in everyday, clinical, and research settings.

MODELS AS A SUBSTITUTE FOR THEORIES

model

During the second half of the 20th century, many psychologists have preferred to talk of models rather than theories. A *model* is an analogy or partial similarity between two aspects of reality. In short, one way of viewing reality is used to represent another. Examples of models include "people behave like animals," "the brain functions as a computer," and "political assassins must be mentally sick."

Some interesting computer models of personality were introduced in a book by John Loehlin (1968). Loehlin named his own model "Aldous," after Aldous Huxley, author of *Brave New World.* Aldous was designed to display a number of features of human behavior, in very simplified form: recognizing situations, acting, learning from past experience, and reacting emotionally, but with limited introspection and symbolic-planning capacities. Several versions of Aldous were programmed and tested under different conditions. One version was called Abstract Aldous, because of the heavy weight placed on higher-order memory classifications. Another was Decisive Aldous, which was programmed to act strongly on slight emotion. This contrasted with Hesitant Aldous, which acted only weakly on emotion. Radical and Conservative Aldouses differed from Standard Aldous on two dimensions—current mood and quickness of memory change. Radical Aldous was highly reactive to current conditions, while Conservative Aldous was governed by the past.

What functions do computer models such as Aldous serve? Asssuming that computer models could be accurately programmed to represent real people, Loehlin identified several possibilities. First, suppose you want to see if individual A will get along with individual B. Build a model of A and one of B, allow them to interact in a computer, and see what happens. Second, suppose you are training people for a role requiring interpersonal skills, such as auto salesman or psychotherapist. Let them do some of their initial practicing on computer models. Third, suppose you are a psychologist who has developed a new therapy technique. Try it out on a model simulating persons with different behavioral problems to see if it might be likely to work better with some kinds of problems than others.

The major advantage of models over theories is that models do not attempt to account for reality in grand, comprehensive ways. In the case of Aldous, only a few variables were manipulated. The more limited scope of models makes it easier for them to be revised, or even abandoned, as soon as their usefulness has run their course, especially in the face of new information.

In a 17th-century play by French playright Jean Molière (1670/1728), a middle-class gentleman exclaims "Good heavens! For more than forty years I have been speaking prose without knowing it." It hadn't occurred to him that a sophisticated label such as "prose" could refer to something as ordinary as everyday language. In a parallel vein, you might find yourself exclaiming "Good heavens! For close to two decades I have been viewing people from the perspective of my own personality theory without even knowing it." While all of us have the informal beginnings of a personality theory, few of us actually identify it by paying it close attention. (In fact, the idea that everyone has a personal theory of human behavior has been developed into a formal theory of personality by George Kelly, whom we discuss in Chapter 8. Kelly believed all people had to be "scientists" of personality just to get through the business of everyday social interaction.)

The assumption that each of us has a miniature personality theory can be explored through the following exercise.

Instructions: For each of the following statements, circle the number that corresponds most closely to your point of view.

1. Human behavior results primarily from *heredity,* what has been genetically transmitted by parents, or from *environment,* the external circumstances and experiences that shape a person after conception has occurred.

                 1   2   3   4   5   6   7
    heredity   –   –   –   –   –   –   –   environment

2. An important part of every person is a *self,* some central aspect of personality referred to as "I" or "me," or there really is *no self* in personality.

                 1   2   3   4   5   6   7
    self   –   –   –   –   –   –   –   no self

3. Personality is relatively *unchanging,* with each person showing the same behavior throughout a lifetime, or personality is relatively *changing,* with each person showing different behavior throughout a lifetime.

                 1   2   3   4   5   6   7
    unchanging   –   –   –   –   –   –   –   changing

4. The most important influences on behavior are *past* events, what has previously occurred to a person, or *future* events, what a person seeks to bring about by striving to meet certain goals.

                 1   2   3   4   5   6   7
    past   –   –   –   –   –   –   –   future

5. The most important characteristics about people are *general* ones, those commonly shared by many people, or *unique* ones, those that make each person different from every other person.

                 1   2   3   4   5   6   7
    general   –   –   –   –   –   –   –   unique

continued

BOX 2.1
continued

6. People are motivated to cooperate with others mainly because they are *self-centered*, expecting to receive some personal gain, or mainly because they are *altruistic*, seeking to work with others only for the benefit of doing things with and for others.

	1	2	3	4	5	6	7	
self-centered	–	–	–	–	–	–	–	altruistic

7. People learn best when they are motivated by *reward*, involving pleasure, or by *punishment*, involving pain.

	1	2	3	4	5	6	7	
reward	–	–	–	–	–	–	–	punishment

8. The main reason you behave as you do (for example, attend college) is because of conscious *personal* decisions to do so, or because *social* factors outside your control leave you little real choice in the matter.

	1	2	3	4	5	6	7	
personal	–	–	–	–	–	–	–	social

9. Human nature is essentially *constructive*, with people showing positive, personal growth and a desire to help others fulfill their potentials, or *destructive*, with people showing behavior that is ultimately self-defeating and a desire to keep others from improving themselves.

	1	2	3	4	5	6	7	
constructive	–	–	–	–	–	–	–	destructive

10. Human beings have *no purpose* or reason for their existence other than what they experience on a day-to-day basis, or human beings have some *purpose* for living that is outside themselves.

	1	2	3	4	5	6	7	
no purpose	–	–	–	–	–	–	–	purpose

11. An additional characteristic about people that I have found helpful for understanding or predicting their behavior is _____.

Each rating you made represents an important part of your own, existing "theory" of personality. What patterns do you see in your answers to these basic questions about personality? How do your answers compare with those of other students in class? As you proceed through the book, compare your beliefs with those of major personality theorists.

SOURCES OF SUPPORT FOR PERSONALITY THEORIES

methods of study

One way to evaluate a theory is to examine the evidence that has been accumulated to support or disconfirm it. Three main methods of study have been used as bases of support for personality theories. They include personal observation, clinical observation, and formal research.

Personal observation.   Personal observation refers to gathering information about oneself and other people on an informal, everyday basis. In the words
of former New York Yankee baseball player Yogi Berra, "You can observe a lot
just by watchin'." All of us make use of personal observation as a regular part of
daily living. We seek to understand ourselves through *introspection,* the process of
examining and exploring our own experiences, thoughts, and reactions. We may
ask ourselves "Why did I say that?" or "What effect is this situation having on
me?" Introspection is a fundamental psychological method of looking within,
different from inspecting events from the outside or physically. We also use
methods of informal observation socially, to better understand other people
(Hastorf, Schneider, & Polefka, 1970). We size up other people by forming
impressions of them in different situations and validating earlier impressions of
them. We may ask "Do my childhood friends have the same personality today?" or
"What is my professor really like?"

Personal observation has been used by all personality theorists, although to
varying degrees. When used, it has always involved the theorist's experiences as a
person. Early works of Freud (1900/1958, 1901/1965) were based on a high
degree of personal observation. Freud reported detailed analyses of his own
behavior, including dreams, memories, and "slips of the tongue." Humanistic
theories of personality, including phenomenology and existentialism, have placed
a high value on reports of personal experience. These theories have sought to
understand individuals from their own frames of reference and experiences.
Individuals have been encouraged to become highly aware of themselves as persons, to identify their personal perceptions, and to get closely in touch with their
inner being. Carl Rogers (1961) linked this "experiencing of experience" to the
process of becoming a person, which he saw as very different from viewing oneself
impersonally as an object of scientific study. On the other hand, behaviorists have
made relatively little use of personal observation. However, B. F. Skinner's (1979)
autobiography contained examples linking Skinner the scientist with Skinner the
person. To illustrate, one of Skinner's technological contributions to psychology
was to develop new, objective, and permanent ways of recording animal behavior.
This contribution actually reflects an important personal value for Skinner, who
has made a lifelong practice of keeping systematic, written records of his own
behavior for regular review and evaluation.

The main limitation of introspection is subjectivity. Self-reports are influenced by selectivity in what we experience and subjective biases in what we
report about our experiences. However, certain information about human experience is not always available through other methods. Only self-reports can disclose toothaches, experiencing oneself as being outside one's body, fantasy
images induced by drugs, and perceptions of apparent movement of a stationary
white light in otherwise total darkness (the autokinetic effect).

Clinical observation.   Clinical observation refers to considerations of
human behavior derived from professional situations, such as offices, clinics, and
hospitals, where people seek psychological help for personal problems. This kind
of evidence is more structured and systematic than personal observation but less

personal
observation

clinical
observation

so than formal research. Much of Freud's theoretical work was based on clinical observations of neurotic patients treated in private practice. Similarly, Carl Rogers' (1942) person-centered theory evolved from counseling experiences with children and families in child-guidance clinics, and with college students in campus counseling centers. Freud and Rogers would probably observe different aspects of personality and arrive at strikingly different conclusions about the same individual. This is because each theorist's clinical observations are selectively influenced by differences in samples of clients, client problems, and work settings. Like personal observation, clinical observations are also limited by subjective influences. The close relationship between the psychologist as a theorist and as a person may be due to "biological bents" or "social learning experiences" (Ellis, 1974a). Some of the personal factors affecting theorists will be seen in the biographical histories presented in later chapters.

formal research

Formal research.   Formal research refers to the systematic use of scientific methods to discover or confirm facts in ways that are relatively impersonal and objective. Over time, psychologists have increased their reliance on scientific research methods as a preferred foundation of support for growth in their field. This emphasis was clearly reflected in a 1957 address by Lee Cronbach, then president of the American Psychological Association:

> The job of science is to ask questions of Nature. A discipline is a method of asking questions and of testing answers to determine whether they are sound. Scientific psychology is still young, and there is rapid turnover in our interests, our experimental apparatus and our tests, and our theoretical concepts. But our methods of inquiry have become increasingly stable, and it is these methods which qualify us as scientists rather than philosophers or artists. (p. 671)

Because of the importance of formal research, the next section will look more closely at how this kind of investigation is used in the field of personality.

Nomothetic versus idiographic approaches.   We can further characterize kinds of support for personality theories in terms of a useful distinction introduced by Gordon Allport (1937, 1968). The distinction is between *nomothetic* and *idiographic* approaches to human behavior.

nomothetic approach

In the nomothetic approach, emphasis is directed to the study of general principles. This approach seeks to understand and predict human behavior in general, by identifying universal characteristics of people and broad principles governing the development and maintenance of people's behaviors over time. In psychology, the nomothetic approach has been most closely associated with the use of formal scientific research methods. This is because formal research methods typically (1) gather information from groups of people rather than individuals, under controlled conditions; (2) rely on analyses of numerical data rather than verbal descriptions; and (3) aim at establishing general laws that apply to most people rather than one person.

idiographic approach

In the idiographic approach, emphasis is directed to the study of the individual case. This approach seeks to understand and predict the behavior of a single person by identifying what is particular and unique about that person. According to Allport, the idiographic approach is characteristic of biography, history, and literature. A novelist, for example, is concerned with depicting individuals in their uniqueness, not with deriving abstract and general laws of human behavior. Within psychology, investigators using the idiographic approach have typically gathered information through informal observations, autobiographical histories, personal diaries and letters, dream reports, psychological-test results, and case studies. These techniques can reveal a wealth of information about an individual. However, compared with the formal methods associated with the nomothetic approach, they entail a greater risk that the psychologist will influence the findings by becoming subjectively involved in gathering and interpreting the information.

David McClelland (1957) explained his view of the two approaches by contrasting the work of psychoanalyst Freud with that of learning theorist Clark Hull. Freud's interest was to understand an individual, whereas Hull's was to predict behavior. Hull's work was represented by a page of "definitions, axioms, deductions and equations," whereas Freud's was represented by a page of "closely reasoned analysis of inner mental life." To McClelland, "it is small wonder that people have doubted whether they were in the same field" (1957, p. 38).

Which approach is more fruitful for studying personality? The answer is that the two are complementary. In fact, as Allport acknowledged, the distinction between them is far from absolute. Some research combines elements of both approaches (Allen & Potkay, 1977a, 1977b; D. J. Bem, 1977), and the number of experimental studies focusing on single cases is increasing (Davidson & Costello, 1969; Hersen & Barlow, 1976; Kratochwill, 1978). Furthermore, formal research has served as a source of support for many, diverse theories of personality, even those beginning with informal observation. An example of constructive interplay between the two approaches is Carl Rogers' person-oriented theory of personality. Developed largely in counseling settings involving clinical observations of single individuals, this viewpoint pioneered the use of mechanical recordings in formal research. Through use of this technique with individual clients, "many vaguely formulated ideas became crystallized" (Rogers, 1942, p. 17), and it was possible to identify naturally occurring stages of therapy progress for clients in general (Curran, 1945). Thus, both idiographic and nomothetic methods have a role to play in enhancing our understanding of personality.

Formal Research in Personality

As psychology attempts to become a truly scientific discipline, informal methods of investigation and broad theoretical speculations are yielding their place to carefully controlled studies. Formal research is an increasingly significant aspect of the field of personality.

There are two general types of formal research conducted to study personality. In *experimental research,* experimenters create changes *(manipulations)* in the environments of participants *(subjects)* and then observe whether the participants' behaviors show any subsequent change. Julian Rotter's social-learning theory has relied heavily on experimental research as a basis of support. The theory allows for predictions of college students' behaviors, based on theoretical ideas that have

experimental research

Formal research makes use of objective techniques to measure behavior, often to assess the influence of controlled environmental changes on behavior.

correlational research

been tested by gathering findings from a large number of laboratory and field studies. *Correlational research* involves no attempt at environmental change, but does seek to determine whether two or more events (*variables* or *factors*) tend to "go together" when undisturbed by any environmental manipulation or intervention. Hans Eysenck's and Raymond Cattell's factor theories of personality have used this approach, in conjunction with decades of systematic collection and analysis of numerical data. Cattell's data have been obtained from countless administrations of personality tests to groups of people in laboratory, educational, clinical, and industrial settings.

Each of these types of research has its benefits and limitations. Let us consider them in turn.

EXPERIMENTAL RESEARCH

All scientists deal with variables. A *variable* is anything that can assume different values. The values fall along a *continuum,* a continuous series of steps indicating the amount or degree of something. For example, weight is a variable whose values can vary from person to person (*between-subject variance*) or for the same person at different times (*within-subject variance*). To appreciate some of your own within-subject variance, step on a scale before and after your next Thanksgiving dinner.

It is hard to imagine any aspect of reality that doesn't vary in values along some continuum or another. Scientists who engage in experimental research treat variables in one of two ways: as independent or dependent variables. The variation in *independent variables* is created through manipulations by an experimenter. For psychological science, the variation created by the experimenter is usually some form of environmental manipulation. Any variation in the *dependent variables* is then assumed to be created by the manipulations of the independent variables. In this way, the experimenter tries to discover whether and how the independent and dependent variables are related. For psychological science, variation in dependent variables is usually variation in behavior, defined broadly to encompass thoughts and feelings as well as actions. Thus, variation in a dependent variable is measured by changes in the behaviors of the experimental subjects under different conditions of manipulation.

What is an experiment? An *experiment,* then, consists of creating change in one or more independent variables and observing whether variation in dependent variables follows in close order. If so, the experimenter's next step is to determine whether or not the variation is statistically significant. *Statistical significance* means that variation of the dependent variable is greater than one would expect on the basis of pure chance. By way of illustration, let's consider an example of an experiment in the psychology of personality.

An experiment about honesty. Edward Diener and Mark Wallbom (1976) wanted to investigate an aspect of personality, honesty. They believed that people are likely to be dishonest only if they fail to focus on their own standards of honesty. Diener and Wallbom made a prediction based on the theory of Duval and Wicklund (1972): if people are made aware of themselves, they will focus on their own standards, and this will be followed by honesty in their behavior. Diener and Wallbom also expected that a lack of self-awareness would be followed by dishonest behavior. Their experiment involved one independent variable, self-awareness, with two values: high self-awareness and low self-awareness. The experiment had two dependent variables: presence of cheating and amount of cheating.

To vary the independent variable, self-awareness, Diener and Wallbom placed half of their subjects in front of a mirror in such a way that the subjects could not help but see themselves, repeatedly. These same subjects had previously made an audio tape in which they described themselves. The tape was played over and over during the experiment. The other half of the subjects were placed in such a way that they could not see their reflections. They also listened to a tape, over and over again, but it was of someone else describing himself. The first group of subjects was exposed to conditions designed to create a high degree of self-awareness, whereas the second group experienced a low degree of self-awareness.

All subjects were told that they would be completing an intelligence test during the course of the experiment. Actually, subjects were given an impossible task. They were given a series of word problems to complete in 5 minutes. The problems were so tough that the typical person would be only halfway through at the end of 5 minutes. After explaining about the "intelligence test," the experimenter placed a timer with a loud alarm in front of the subject. Before setting the timer for 5 minutes, the experimenter warned each subject to stop working when the alarm sounded. As he was leaving, he indicated that he would be detained for 10 minutes.

You probably have guessed the rest. Subjects could cheat by continuing to work after the alarm sounded. The large mirror that subjects were placed in front of, or turned away from, was in fact a one-way mirror. An experimenter stationed in an adjoining room on the other side of the mirror could see through it and observe the subjects. For subjects in both conditions, the two dependent variables were: (1) the percentage of subjects who cheated to some degree in each condition of self-awareness; and (2) the number of responses made after the alarm sounded.

The results were, well, "alarming." Fully 71% of subjects in the low-self-awareness condition cheated, while only 7% of those in the high-self-awareness condition did so. The difference was statistically significant. That is, the probability that this result was due solely to chance was quite low. Subjects in the low-self-awareness condition also made more responses after the alarm had sounded than did subjects in the high-self-awareness condition. The difference was again statistically significant. (On the next test day in this course, if your professor should say "While taking the test, please repeatedly think of yourself and look at yourself using the pocket mirrors I am now passing out," you'll know what's up.) Diener and Wallbom's study is important because it shows that if people are aware of themselves, they will focus on their personal standards of honesty and will be likely to behave in an honest manner. This is the outcome predicted by Duval and Wicklund's (1972) theory. Although the findings do not "prove" the theory, they do offer experimental evidence in support of the theory.

CORRELATIONAL RESEARCH

Like experimental research, correlation also involves variables, but it does not distinguish between independent and dependent variables. Instead, correlational research seeks to determine whether, and to what degree, variations in the variables tend to occur together. Do changes in variable *X* and variable *Y* show any relationship with one another, or are the two variables unrelated?

With correlation, the interest is usually in a particular kind of relationship called a *linear* or *straight-line relationship*. In the simplest case of two variables, a perfect linear relationship exists if the values of the two variables correspond exactly in one-to-one fashion. The values don't have to be the same in both cases, but their patterns of high and low values must show mutual, systematic change. In the case of perfect *positive correlation*, if values of variable *X* increase, then there is an exactly corresponding increase in the values of variable *Y*, and if values of *X* decrease, then there is a corresponding decrease in values of *Y*. In the case of perfect *negative* or *inverse correlation*, if values of variable *X* increase, then those in variable *Y* decrease correspondingly, and if values of *X* decrease, then those of *Y* correspondingly increase.

As an example, we could ask the question "Are the heights of husbands and wives correlated?" The answer to this question is "Yes, in general." Take a look at the hypothetical findings in Figure 2.1. Height of husbands appears on the vertical axis of the graph and height of wives on the horizontal axis. The degree of linear relationship is represented by the solid line. In general, the taller the husband is, the taller is the wife. Because there are exceptions, the line is not perfectly straight. If there were no exceptions to the rule, knowing the height of one spouse would allow us to predict, exactly, the height of the other. In this case, a perfect straight-line or linear relationship would exist between the heights of husbands and wives. Such a perfect relationship is represented in Figure 2.1 by the dotted line.

Correlations are matters of degree, not all or nothing. The index of a linear relationship is called the *coefficient of correlation (r)*, a number representing the degree of linear relationship between two variables. This number may be positive or negative. Thus, coefficients for linear relationships may range from $+1.00$ (representing a perfect positive correlation between variables), through 0.00 (no relationship whatsoever), to -1.00 (representing a perfect negative or inverse correlation). In practice, coefficients are not as extreme as -1.00 or $+1.00$. Typical correlation coefficients reported in psychological research are seldom greater than the low .90s. In Figure 2.1, the line of open circles represents a perfect negative linear relationship. If this correlation existed between the heights of spouses, then the taller a wife was, the shorter her husband would be. Marriage between the world's tallest woman and shortest man would be consistent with this pattern.

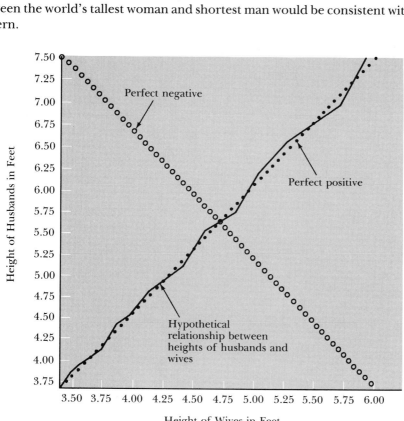

Figure 2.1 Hypothetical relationships between heights of husbands and wives.

A correlational study of consistency in children's behaviors.   A good example of correlational research is provided by Swedish psychologists Gunnar Backteman and David Magnusson (1981). They wanted to show that behaviors relating to traits can be stable, or constant, over time.

To reach their goal, Backteman and Magnusson had Swedish schoolteachers observe their pupils for three years, between ages 7 and 10, and then rate the pupils on several behavioral dimensions corresponding to traits. Other teachers observed the same pupils for three years, between ages 10 and 13, and rated them on the same dimensions. Seven-point rating scales were used for this purpose. The six dimensions rated by teachers are summarized in Table 2.1, along with the correlation coefficients (r's) averaged across boys and girls.

All of the coefficients were positive and statistically significant, even when those for boys and girls were considered separately. Thus, the pupils' behaviors were relatively consistent over a three-year period, supporting the researchers' hypothesis. In effect, when individual pupils were ordered relative to one another on a given dimension, they generally were ordered the same on both occasions. The most aggressive pupils at age 10 tended to be rated the most aggressive at age 13, and the least timid pupils at age 13 also had been the least timid at age 10. Taken together, these findings suggest there were individual differences on each of the behavioral dimensions, and that these differences persisted over time. In the terms used in Chapter 1, the pupils had distinct and enduring personality profiles.

Correlation is not causation.   It is easy to confuse correlation with causation. However, the fact that changes in two variables are correlated does *not* mean that one causes the other, as a few examples will illustrate. There is a high, positive correlation between inseam length of pants and height of wearers, but buying longer jeans won't change your height. Nor will changes in your height cause your jeans to grow with you. Similarly, a researcher once found a high, positive correlation between the amount of rainfall in Arizona and the rate of suicide in Canada. However, no one was willing to argue that the rain caused suicides, or that the suicides caused rain.

It often happens that when one of two correlated variables seems to have caused the other, a third or fourth variable actually is a more likely candidate as the cause. One winter in another country, there was a high correlation between the presence of storks on roofs and the births of babies the following summer and

TABLE 2.1   Correlations between Ratings of Pupils' Behaviors at Ages 10 and 13

Traits	Behaviors	r
Aggressiveness	Rebellious, obstructive	.44
Motor disturbance	Talkative, fidgety	.55
Timidity	Shy, low self-esteem	.43
Disharmony	Unhappy	.46
Distraction	Unable to concentrate	.58
Lack of school motivation	Disinterested in school	.53

fall. Assuming that storks don't bring babies, perhaps a third variable accounted for the observed relationship. One hypothesis centers on the fact that the winter was very cold. The storks roosted on the roofs near chimneys to keep warm, and the people, having no TV and tiring of card games, resorted to other forms of evening recreation (Baron & Byrne, 1981).

In general, cautious statements about cause and effect may be made on the basis of carefully controlled experiments, because experimental research does distinguish between independent and dependent variables. It also is true that new correlational techniques can sometimes allow cautious statements to be made about cause and effect. However, many scientific psychologists agree with philosophers of science who argue that cause-and-effect language should be eliminated (Danto & Morgenbesser, 1960). For this reason, when *experiments* are under discussion, we are likely to say only that variation in a dependent variable *follows* variation in an independent variable, rather than "was caused by" the independent variable. In the case of *correlations,* we generally will say only that changes in the variables showed a positive, a negative, or no relationship with each other.

The Person in Particular: Personality Assessment

A popular belief about psychologists is that they have the ability to know a person's true personality, including hidden thoughts, feelings, and motivations. This belief has at least three different origins. The first is social expectation. As specialists in the study of behavior, psychologists are expected to be "experts" in understanding people and their personalities (J. D. Frank, 1961; Sullivan, 1954). If you are a psychology major, you may have experienced such social expectations already. Friends or relatives may have indicated you are "always observing" what they do or "analyzing" what they say. Perhaps they have asked you to interpret a dream or tell them something about themselves on the basis of their handwriting style or color preferences. Unfortunately, many expectations about psychologists' ability to "tell all about" people's personalities are naive. Human behaviors are far too complex, especially for the current state of psychological knowledge.

A second reason for the popular belief in psychologists' powers is the beliefs of psychologists themselves. Psychologists have met their own professional expectations by publishing explanations of unusual human events, reports of case studies, and idiographic analyses of famous religious, historical, political, and courtroom figures (Freud, 1910/1957, 1939; Erikson, 1975; R. J. Lifton, 1974; Elms, 1976). Important historical figures who have been subjects of published psychological analyses include Moses, Leonardo da Vinci, Martin Luther, Gandhi, Adolf Hitler, Woodrow Wilson, and Richard Nixon. A striking example of this kind of analysis was undertaken in 1943 at the request of the United States Office of Strategic Services (OSS), a forerunner of the Central Intelligence Agency. "What do you make of Hitler?" asked General Bill Donovan. Walter Langer (1972) recalled that "as a psychologist I could not help but be interested" in the people who were leading the incredible Nazi regime.

Langer's analysis of Hitler's personality actually was an application of *psychohistory,* a type of personality assessment that combines both psychological and historical techniques. The major limitation of psychohistorical analyses is that they are developed in retrospect. They look backward at a person's past life and mainly offer explanations of experiences and behaviors that have already occurred, similar to psychological autopsies on suicide victims (Shneidman, Farberow, & Litman, 1970). It is much more difficult to actually predict an individual's *future* behavior. Langer's analysis was unusual in this regard, since it contained a discussion of Hitler's probable future behavior if the tide of battle were to turn against him. Of eight alternatives considered, including Hitler's seeking refuge in another country or going insane, "the most plausible outcome" was that Hitler would commit suicide. His prediction proved accurate.

A third reason supporting popular belief in the ability of psychologists to understand true personality is related to the development of psychological tests. Psychological tests have been used to understand many facets of a person: intelligence, abilities, interests, and personality characteristics. Administering and interpreting tests have been major activities of psychologists in clinical, school, industrial, and research settings (American Psychological Association, 1980). In fact, "psychological testing was once the primary, if not sole, activity of clinical psychologists" (Korchin, 1976, p. 194). Testing continues to play an important role in understanding personality and has become "big business" in America.

To what extent is the popular faith in psychologists' ability to interpret personality justified? The answer to this question depends on an understanding of the processes and techniques of personality assessment. The remainder of this chapter explores this fascinating area of personality study, in which psychological knowledge is brought to bear directly on individual persons.

WHAT IS PERSONALITY ASSESSMENT?

personality
assessment

five-stage process

Personality assessment is a process in which a psychologist uses systematic procedures to gather and organize information about a person to aid understanding, prediction, or the making of decisions about that person. It is considered a *process* because it is characterized by a sequence of identifiable stages. Sundberg (1977) has identified five such stages:

1. Establishing the reason for assessment
2. Selecting the assessment techniques
3. Gathering the information
4. Organizing and interpreting the information
5. Communicating conclusions and making decisions

Since the final goal of personality assessment is to contribute valid conclusions and decisions about an individual, it is logical for the psychologist to begin by asking some relevant questions: "Why is this assessment being undertaken? What exactly needs to be understood or decided in relation to the person being assessed?" Knowing the specific purpose of the assessment, including a clear comprehension of the referral question, enables the psychologist to proceed more realistically and efficiently, with a minimum of error in direction and interpretation (Levine, 1981). Referring to our earlier example, Langer's (1972) assessment of Hitler's personality did not address itself to General Donovan's vague question, "What do you make of Hitler?" Rather, Langer was directed by a number of more specific questions, which actually served as organizing chapters in his final report. As clarified by Donovan,

> What we need . . . is a realistic appraisal of the German situation. If Hitler is running the show, what kind of person is he? What are his ambitions? How does he appear to the German people? What is he like with his associates? What is his background? And most of all, we want to know as much as possible about his psychological make-up—the things that make him tick. In addition, we ought to know what he might do if things begin to go against him. Do you suppose you could come up with something along these lines? (Langer, 1972, p. 19)

Psychologists who devote the greatest amount of professional activity to understanding individual behavior using psychological tests are sometimes referred to as *personality assessors*. Their approach differs from that of untrained persons, whose commonsense personal opinions about people are derived largely from informal observations. Personality assessors value a more scientific and objective approach to understanding people. They study individual behavior by means of formal, systematic procedures that combine psychological theory, research findings, and clinical experience (Shakow, 1947). Among these procedures are interviewing, administering psychological tests, observing and monitoring behavior, analyzing fantasies such as dreams, exploring self-reports, measuring physiological responses, and reviewing biographical and personal documents (Allport, 1942). Personality assessors also place a high value on detailing what they do and how they do it, within the limits of technical possibility (Potkay, 1971). This more explicit approach increases the likelihood that their professional procedures can be repeated by other assessors, and their conclusions demonstrated to be accurate or inaccurate.

PERSONALITY ASSESSMENT AND PSYCHOLOGICAL TESTS

Personality assessment has been closely identified with the administration and interpretation of psychological tests. One reason for this is that tests are intentionally developed as standardized and systematic procedures for gathering information from people and summarizing that information. The same tasks are administered in the same way to all persons. An individual's responses are samples of behavior which may then be assigned scores for use in making comparisons with those of other people and categorizing the individual's behavior (for example, if IQ = 100, then intellectual functioning falls within the average range). Specific standards have been established by the American Psychological Association (1974) for use in designing, standardizing, validating, scoring, and interpreting tests.

A second reason is more historical in nature. Psychologists traditionally have been interested in individual differences—in observing how people vary. Intelligence testing has gone hand in hand with the study of individual differences. The first tests developed for widespread use were the Stanford-Binet Intelligence Scale, the Wechsler Adult Intelligence Scale, and the Army Alpha and Beta group intelligence tests. In fact, during the first quarter of this century, applied psychologists were identified as "intelligence testers"—specialists who administered intelligence tests. By midcentury, personality measures had gained prominence, and a number of psychologists became identified as "personality testers." They earned their occupational keep by asking other people to report what they saw in inkblots, make up stories to go with pictures, write endings to incomplete sentences, and choose answers to paper-and-pencil questions that best represented their personal experiences—thoughts, values, feelings, and actions. They journeyed "an avenue into the fascinating private world of the individual, where he was continuously engaged in creating, maintaining, and defending his perceptions and beliefs" (Reisman, 1966, p. 278). Tests, including personality tests, were seen as a useful tool for psychologists in identifying patterns of individual differences.

Third, a "tests" approach to understanding various aspects of personality has been an important part of the history of *clinical psychology,* the branch of psychology most involved in assessing and treating behavioral difficulties (American Psychological Association, 1980). During World War II, clinical psychologists became active in administering personality tests so as to enhance the efficiency of psychiatric screening. Up to that time, the primary method of obtaining data from recruits was for psychiatrists to conduct brief interviews with them. *Interviews* are a type of professional conversation undertaken for a predetermined purpose. Interviewing is the most common form of assessment and cuts across many professions—psychology, psychiatry, social work, medicine, business management, and personnel selection. It differs from therapy because its goal is to assess or evaluate behavior, not to change it.

interviews

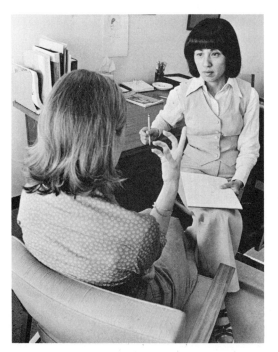

Interviewing is the most universal form of individual assessment. The interviewer obtains information by directing a person's conversation to meet a predetermined purpose.

During World War II, the goal of screening interviews was to evaluate a recruit's emotional adjustment by quickly reviewing and evaluating the recruit's past life, present experiences, and future goals. Psychiatrists were scheduled to spend 10 – 15 minutes interviewing each military inductee, up to a maximum of 50 inductees per day. However, the numbers of inductees needing evaluation sometimes went as high as 100 – 500 per day (W. C. Menninger, 1948). Paper-and-pencil tests were adopted as reasonable alternatives to interviews because tests could be administered to large groups of inductees in a single session.

The use of psychological tests for military screening in World War II was aimed not only at the intellectual and ability characteristics of recruits, as in World War I, but at mental-health adjustment and personality characteristics as well. At the time of the Vietnam conflict, psychological assessments were helpful in reducing the incidence of immediate combat-stress reactions to 2%, down from 39% of medical discharges in World War II (Coleman, Butcher, & Carson, 1984).

RELIABILITY AND VALIDITY

Assessment techniques must meet important technical standards before they can be considered scientifically acceptable measures for making inferences about characteristics of people (American Psychological Association, 1974). Two critical standards are reliability and validity.   test standards

Reliability.   First, tests must demonstrate *reliability,* which means that   reliability
their results must be repeatable. If you were to take the same test twice, in rapid succession and under ordinary conditions, your test scores should be about the same. If so, the test displays acceptable *test-retest reliability.* If you took a second or third version of a particular test, your scores on these different forms should also be about the same. If so, the test displays *reliability of parallel forms.* Although a slight difference in scores might occur, the two results would be considered equivalent if past use of the test had demonstrated it to be a reliable measure of behavior.

Statistical calculations help determine a test's expected range of measurement error and, thus, the significance of possible differences in test scores. If your scores at two different times show a large difference, that difference should not be due to errors in the test or chance factors, but to systematic influences or characteristics of your behavior. Perhaps the time interval between tests was long enough for you to have undergone gradual changes in your behavior, related to experiences of everyday living, personal growth, or situational influences such as psychotherapy or college education. Or, if the time interval was short, perhaps conditions were not so ordinary. You may have won a large sum of money, fallen in or out of love, learned of a death in your family, or experienced an earthquake.

Validity.   A second test standard is *validity*—the degree to which a test   validity
actually measures what it was designed to measure. Although a test may result in similar scores every time the same person takes it, thereby reflecting reliability, it is possible that no meaningful inferences or conclusions can be drawn about the person. *Content validity* refers to the quality of a test whose items actually sample

the behaviors of interest, such as typing skills or arithmetic computation. If you were to take a personality test measuring introversion and extraversion, you would expect the results to indicate whether you tend to be preoccupied with inner events and withdraw from social situations, or to focus on events outside yourself and behave in socially outgoing ways. Since the content of this course emphasizes the psychology of personality, you certainly wouldn't expect examinations to test your knowledge of the Roman Empire.

Criterion-related validity is an alternative to the one just described. It means that a test shows the capacity to make predictions about a person's behavior, by demonstrating a statistical relationship with scores obtained on a second test or with some specific behavior in a given situation. A test could display this type of validity without showing obvious content validity. Suppose your score on Test A could be used to statistically predict your score on Test B, administered sequentially, or to predict how many friends you have at the present time. Test A would then be reflecting a type of criterion-related validity called *concurrent validity*. Suppose your score on Test A could be used to estimate how many friends you will have five years from now, or whether you will be successful in the future as a business executive. Test A then would be reflecting another type of criterion-related validity called *predictive validity*. In this case, validity is demonstrated if the predicted outcomes actually occur. Such validity would be illustrated, for example, if freshmen who achieve higher scores on a college-entrance examination actually show higher grade-point averages as seniors compared with freshmen who achieve lower scores. Concurrent (present) and predictive (future) validity are subtypes of criterion-related validity.

Your introversion-extraversion score might even allow a psychologist to make an indirect, theoretical inference about your personality. If you scored high in extraversion, you would also be likely to show greater tolerance for certain types of physical pain than persons scoring low in extraversion. This conclusion reflects yet another type of validity, known as *construct validity*. Construct validity occurs when support for a hypothesis based on theory is demonstrated. For example, Eysenck's (1962b) finding of a relationship between extraversion and pain tolerance was guided by Ivan Pavlov's (1927) theory of physiology of behavior (discussed in Chapters 5 and 9).

A construct-validity strategy has been recommended for joint validation of personality-assessment techniques and hypothetical constructs, using groups of persons rather than single individuals. In an important paper, Campbell and Fiske (1959) presented a convincing rationale for using different types of assessment methods in personality research. They recommended adoption of a research design termed "multitrait-multimethod." The *multitrait* procedure entails measuring two or more personality dimensions at the same time, and the *multimethod* procedure involves using two or more assessment methods or "modes" of measurement at the same time. The goal is to enhance the likelihood of achieving research results that stem from characteristics of persons, not from artificial reliance on a single aspect of personality and a single technique of measurement. Similar traits measured by different modes would be expected to show close relationships with one another *(convergent validity)*, whereas different traits measured by similar modes would be expected to show low interrelationships *(diver-*

gent validity). Fiske (1971) has identified six typical modes of personality measurement. Each mode has its own pattern of characteristics related to source of information, task to be met, and representative assessment methods:

1. Person reports picture of self:
   objective questionnaires, self-ratings, biographies
2. Person reports immediate experience:
   tests of perceived movement and figure preference
3. Person gives correct answer:
   tests of achievement, ability, and knowledge
4. Observer extracts impression of person from materials:
   ratings based on records
5. Observer gives impression of person:
   interviews, projective techniques, situational tests
6. Instrument measures physiologic responses:
   biofeedback machines

Types of Assessment Techniques

Assessment techniques come in a variety of forms. They include inkblots, drawings, checklists, true/false statements and behavior rating scales. Each has special strengths and limitations regarding the kinds of responses obtained, scoring, interpretation, reliability, and validity. In this section, we will look at three basic types of assessment techniques: projective, objective, and behavioral.

assessment techniques

PROJECTIVE TECHNIQUES

Projective techniques are measures of personality whose stimulus features are so unstructured, ambiguous, or open-ended that they allow people a wide range of freedom in making highly personal responses. In theory, respondents "project" themselves onto "blank screens" of neutral test stimuli in ways that reflect their individual backgrounds, perceptions, and fantasies (L. K. Frank, 1939). There are no right or wrong answers, and as with fingerprints, no two personalities are expected to be exactly alike. All responses are considered to be reflections of one's personality. Examples of minimally structured stimuli include blank sheets of paper on which persons are asked to write or draw something, pictures of cloud formations, inkblots, and vague sketches or drawings aimed at eliciting a variety of personally meaningful responses.

projective techniques

Two examples of projective techniques are the Rorschach inkblot technique and the Thematic Apperception Test (TAT). Both were developed as comprehensive measures of personality, especially at an unconscious level. Both base their understanding of personality on an individual's *apperceptions* or unique perceptual interpretations of ambiguous stimuli resulting from past experiences (Abt & Bellak, 1950).

The Rorschach (1942/1951) consists of ten cards on which there are inkblots, five in black and white and five in color. A person is asked to look at each inkblot and say what it looks like or what it might be. Responses are then scored for various categories of content, location, use of shape and color determinants, popularity or originality, and level of organization (Beck, 1952; Exner, 1978; Klopfer, Meyer, & Brawer, 1970). An inkblot similar to Rorschach inkblots appears in Figure 2.2.

The TAT was developed as a method of "revealing to the trained interpreter some of the dominant drives, emotions, sentiments, complexes and conflicts of a personality" (Murray, 1943, p. 1). It consists of a set of picture cards on which there are black-and-white drawings, paintings, or photographs of "classic" human situations, along with one blank card. A person is asked to look at each of 20 cards and make up a short story about it, which the assessor writes down. These stories are then analyzed to identify dominant themes or patterns of inner needs and external forces important for understanding the individual's personality. The stories usually are interpreted subjectively, guided by general expectancies (Henry, 1956/1974). However, normative or typical responses have been reported (Murstein, 1963, 1972; Potkay, Merrens, & Allen, 1979), and some useful scoring systems have been developed (M. B. Arnold, 1962; McClelland, Atkinson, Clark, & Lowell, 1958). A picture similar to those found in the TAT appears in Figure 2.3.

OBJECTIVE TESTS

objective tests

Objective tests are highly structured paper-and-pencil questionnaires of the true/false or multiple-choice variety. They are considered "structured" because they allow people very little freedom of response in answering items. Persons

Figure 2.2   Example of a Rorschach inkblot. "It's a big, black bat flapping its wings."

Figure 2.3
Picture similar to TAT. "They're talking about a job they have to finish. She's confident they'll meet their deadline. He's not so sure."

typically are instructed to read a number of statements and indicate whether each statement is best answered True or False, Yes or No, or Agree or Disagree in relation to themselves. Few other responses are possible, except for occasional options such as Uncertain or giving no answer at all. To appreciate the difference in structure between objective and projective techniques, contrast the format and degree of response freedom you have in answering true/false and multiple-choice examinations with those of open-ended, essay exams. The scoring of objective tests is straightforward, typically aided by stencils for use in tallying answers relevant to a given dimension. Scoring also may be done by computer, which, along with computer administration and interpretation, represents a rapidly developing trend in personality assessment. Kleinmuntz (1982) reports "no fewer than seven" commercial, computerized scoring and interpretation services for a single test, the MMPI.

The "relevance" of items appearing on an objective test is often established empirically. That is, responses of different groups to test items may be compared statistically to determine whether frequencies of particular answers for any items differentiate the groups. For example, groups of psychologists might differ from groups of forest rangers in responses to items such as "I enjoy spending most of my time with people" and "I would avoid living in the forest by myself." Psychologists might be more likely to answer Yes, as a group, and forest rangers to answer No. Researchers don't decide this ahead of time. Results must be determined empirically, by objective data. (Would psychologists and forest rangers differ in answers to "I spend lots of time thinking about myself"?) Any differences between groups must be large enough to be statistically significant.

One example of an empirically derived, objective assessment technique is the Minnesota Multiphasic Personality Inventory (MMPI) (Hathaway & McKinley, 1943, 1967). The MMPI is the most popular paper-and-pencil test of personality in clinical and research settings. It provides scores on nine scales of abnormality, including depression, anxiety, antisocial behavior, and psychotic experiences. Each scale is made up of items known to differentiate between groups of normal adults and clinical patients. In effect, the MMPI matches a test-taker's pattern of true/false responses with those of previously defined patient groups. The Strong Vocational Interest Blank (SVIB) (D. P. Campbell, 1977) follows a similar strategy, except that the test-taker's responses are matched with those of successful persons from various occupational groups: accountants, X-ray technicians, office managers, artists, police officers, and business executives.

The Sixteen Personality Factor Questionnaire (16 PF) (Cattell, Eber, & Tatsuoka, 1970) is another objective assessment technique. However, its items were determined to be "relevant" using a different statistical technique, factor analysis, that computes the degree to which subgroups of test items are intercorrelated, or internally consistent with one another. This technique is discussed in Chapter 9.

BEHAVIORAL MEASURES

behavioral
measures

Behavioral measures assess a person's direct actions in response to particular situations, rather than attitudes and feelings. Observers may be trained to record the frequency of certain behaviors or their duration. In one application, Mariotto and Paul (1974) developed a Time Sample Behavioral Checklist for use by hospital staff trained to observe the behaviors of patients in psychiatric wards. Brief but systematic observations of every patient were made, 2 seconds every hour, thereby providing daily records of the patients' behaviors in a natural, real-life setting. Results were used to identify trends in patient behaviors—such as speaking incoherently, pacing the floor, reading and talking to others—analyzed by time of day, week, or month.

The Bender Visual-Motor Gestalt Test (Bender, 1938) was originally developed as a behavioral "performance test for children" (p. 112) and has primary usefulness as such a measure (Koppitz, 1975). Nine cards containing geometrical designs are presented individually to a child who is then asked to copy them using pencil and paper. The technique is partly *visual* because the child first looks at the design, and partly *motor* because the child must physically reproduce the design using fine muscle coordination. Thus, the Bender provides a direct sampling of copy-drawing behavior. The assessor scores each reproduction for predetermined errors, and a total score is computed for estimating the child's normative level of perceptual-motor maturity (Koppitz, 1975). Examples of mature and immature Bender-type drawings appear in Figure 2.4.

Systematic *self-monitoring* also has been used, with people serving as observers of their own behavior (Ciminero, Calhoun, & Adams, 1977). Wrist counters and the writing of ongoing activity logs help people keep track of many behaviors: saying "hello" to others, smoking, cracking one's knuckles, reading pages in a textbook, feeling rejected, and complimenting people (Watson & Tharp, 1977).

Compared with projective and objective approaches, behavioral assessment places higher value on obtaining information about possible relationships between behavior and environmental conditions present every time the target behavior occurs, even when self-report methods are used. If a person reports experiences of anxiety or hostility, behavioral assessors are interested in identifying specific situations in which these experiences do and do not appear: when, where, with whom, reason, and outcome (Wolpe, 1982). The S-R Inventory of General Trait Anxiousness (Endler & Okada, 1975) was developed on the assumption that

Ben, 5 years old

Figure 2.4
Drawings of overlapping circles and
diamonds done by a younger and an
older brother, similar to those seen
on the Bender Gestalt Test.

Nick, 8 years old

"general anxiousness" is not a single trait but has multiple dimensions, each related to a different situation. People are asked to indicate their reactions to four general situations: physical danger, social interaction, new situations, and daily routine. For each situation, nine items are to be rated on a five-point scale, from "very much" (1) to "not at all" (5). Items include "perspire," "heart beats faster," and "enjoy these situations." The same items are used for all four situations. Endler and Okada observed different ratings by the same person to these items, depending on the situation. This enabled them to "more adequately assess the interaction of persons and situations on behavioral states" (p. 328), an idea discussed more fully in Chapter 13.

Finally, biofeedback machines may be used as direct measures of behavior. *Biofeedback* refers to "any technique that uses instrumentation to provide a person with immediate and continuing signals concerning bodily functions of which that person is not normally conscious" (Kanfer & Goldstein, 1980, p. 537). These machines record such ongoing physiological responses as forehead tension, blood pressure, penile erection, body temperature, and brain waves (L. H. Epstein, 1976).

WHICH ASSESSMENT TECHNIQUES ARE BEST?

Psychologists are periodically surveyed to determine what tests they use most frequently. The "Top Ten" (actually, top eleven) results of two recent surveys are summarized in Tables 2.2 and 2.3, accompanied by examples of instructions and items similar to those used in the tests listed. The Rorschach inkblot technique, Thematic Apperception Test, and Bender Test overlap both surveys. These three techniques also appeared on lists of popularly used tests reported earlier by Norman Sundberg (1961) and Lubin, Wallis, and Paine (1971). However, differences in results across various surveys highlight the impossibility of identifying any "best" tests, for many reasons.

First, tests may be popular for a decade or two and then decline in use as professional and research needs change or new techniques are developed. When

TABLE 2.2   Personality Assessment Techniques Often Used with Adults
(Adapted from Reynolds & Sundberg, 1976)

Objective Techniques

Minnesota Multiphasic Personality Inventory
  True or False: "I am a person who never sleeps."
California Psychological Inventory
  True or False: "I enjoy telling jokes."
Edwards Personal Preference Schedule
  Choose A or B: A. "I would like to be a good friend."
                   B. "I would like to be a famous writer."
Sixteen Personality Factor Questionnaire
  Yes, Uncertain, or No: "People consider me successful."
Strong Vocational Interest Blank
  Like, Indifferent, or Dislike: "Selling cars."
Kuder Vocational Preference Record
  Like Most and Like Least: "Play basketball."
                              "Go bird watching."
                              "Read a book."
Allport-Vernon-Lindzey Study of Values
  Assign up to 3 points for total agreement: "Factories are more important than museums."
Maudsley Personality Inventory
  Yes, ?, or No: "I like to be alone."

Projective Techniques

Rorschach Inkblot Technique
  "Tell what this inkblot looks like."
Thematic Apperception Test
  "Tell a story about this picture."

Behavioral Techniques

Bender Visual-Motor Gestalt Test
  "Copy this design."

Sundberg (1961) compared his results with those of earlier researchers (Louttit & Browne, 1947), he noted a number of interesting patterns over time. Between 1935 and 1959, there was a turnover of 76% among the top 20 tests. Intelligence tests represented 55% of the total number of responses in 1935 but dropped to 24% in 1959. Why? Sundberg discovered two reasons: psychologists had (1) increased their testing of adults compared with children and (2) dramatically increased the number of personality tests they administered. Their use of projective techniques alone increased from close to 0% in 1935 to 23% in 1959. Recent surveys have shown less dramatic changes in test use, although psychologists are increasing their reliance on objective tests of personality (Reynolds & Sundberg, 1976) and on direct behavioral observations (Hersen & Bellack, 1976).

Second, no technique holds a monopoly on personality assessment. Goh, Teslow, and Fuller (1981) noted no clear preference for any single personality or behavioral instrument among 274 school-psychologist respondents. A large num-

TABLE 2.3   Personality Assessment Techniques Often Used with Children
(Adapted from Goh, Teslow, & Fuller, 1981)

Projective Techniques

Sentence Completion Tests
   Finish this sentence: "I do best at school when . . ."
House-Tree-Person Test
   "Draw a picture of a house . . . a tree . . . a person."
Thematic Apperception Test
   "Tell a story about this picture."
Children's Apperception Test
   "Tell a story about this picture of animals."
Draw-a-Person Test
   "Draw a picture of a person."
Rorschach Inkblot Technique
   "Tell what this inkblot looks like."

Behavioral Techniques

Behavior Rating Scales
   Parent rates child's behavior: "Has temper tantrums."
      (0) No problem
      (1) Minor problem
      (2) Serious problem
Devereaux Behavior Rating Scale
   Teacher rates child's behavior: "Hits other children."
      (1) Never
      (2) Quarterly
      (3) Monthly
      (4) Weekly
      (5) Daily
Walker Behavior Problem Checklist
   "Put a check mark next to any behavior that is a problem for the child."
Bender Visual-Motor Gestalt Test
   "Copy this design."

Objective Techniques

Self-Concept Scales
   Point to one picture: "Is your team the one that wins, or the one that loses?"

ber of techniques were used equally often, but frequency of listing was low for all, indicating the presence of many personal favorites among psychologists.

   Third, the potential usefulness of a technique depends on the assessment question being asked. Different tests have strengths for measuring some personality dimensions, but not others. No assessment technique measures all dimensions (Woody, 1980). The Maudsley Personality Inventory (Eysenck, 1962b) taps two personality dimensions, whereas the 16 PF (Cattell, Eber, & Tatsuoka, 1970) taps 16. The 16 PF measures normal personality experiences, whereas the MMPI measures abnormal ones. Although behavioral measures share a common focus on observable behaviors, the behaviors to be rated often differ across instruments. The Devereaux Child Behavior Rating Scale assesses a child's toilet-training behavior and need for adult contact (Spivack & Levine, 1964), but related scales do not (Burks, 1971). The Rorschach (1942/1951) and TAT (Murray, 1943) cover the total range of personality structure, development, and motivation in a "wide band" fashion, but at the cost of precision.

Fourth, individual differences are as much a part of professional behavior as they are of personal behavior (Thorne, 1961). Psychologists tend to use techniques most compatible with their assessment orientations and training experiences, whether projective (Rabin, 1981), objective (Butcher, 1972), or behavioral (Hersen & Bellack, 1976). Some psychologists purposely avoid using any formal assessment techniques whatsoever. Carl Rogers, the founder of person-centered theory, long ago disclaimed the need to administer tests to clients in counseling. "In 1928," he wryly notes, "I developed an inventory of the inner world of childhood which — may Heaven forgive me — is still being sold by the thousands" (Rogers, 1974, p. 115). Rogers believes important information will always be made known by people as they talk about themselves and their experiences. Other humanistic (Maslow, 1966) and existential (May, Angel, & Ellenberger, 1958) psychologists support this point of view.

ASSESSMENT BATTERIES

assessment
batteries

Personality assessors often resolve the "best test" issue by using a combination of assessment techniques, referred to as a *psychological test battery*. Instead of relying on a single method for obtaining information about a person, they use several techniques, each reflecting a different perspective. This approach is illustrated later in the chapter, in the assessment of a college student's personality. Nay (1979) has written in favor of such a comprehensive view of persons. In a similar vein, Cautela and Upper (1976) have introduced a standardized behavioral-analysis procedure called the Behavioral Inventory Battery (BIB). Four primary, four secondary, and any number of additional scales are administered "to provide the type of information which is useful in planning treatment for virtually every client" (p. 82). Information is gathered about a person's life history, present behaviors, enjoyments, fears, assertiveness, thoughts, physical tensions, images, and specific problem behaviors related to alcohol, sex, smoking, eating habits, social skills, and so on. The BIB is similar to most objective assessment techniques in its reliance on *self-reports* or self-descriptions. However, it differs by focusing on what a person *does* rather than on what characteristics or traits the person *has*. Development of the BIB occurred within the framework of social-learning theory, discussed in Chapter 6.

Assessing Individuals

One of the most interesting characteristics of the personality field is its *applied* nature. Indeed, personality assessment lends itself to a variety of practical applications. In what follows, personality assessment is illustrated by excerpts from psychologists' reports, the step-by-step process of assessing a college art major, and an empirical study based on Rorschach records of a group of Nazi officials. There is even an attempt at "interpreting" your own personality. Let us begin by discussing how psychologists formulate ideas about individuals whose personalities they seek to understand.

Use of personality tests is closely tied to the development of working images of people (Sundberg & Tyler, 1962). A *working image* is defined as "a set of hypotheses about the person and his situation, or potential situations" (Sundberg, 1977, p. 22). It is a tentative, descriptive model of an individual's personality. It considers the environmental setting in which the person's behavior occurs, including what is physical, social, and psychological (Endler, 1981; Lewin, 1936). Sundberg considers image-making to be a major purpose of personality assessment, along with decision-making and theory-building. Working images reflect the psychologist's best understanding of the person assessed and offer the assessor's most informed answers to questions about personality. Here, for example, is Langer's (1972) working image of Adolf Hitler: "It is Hitler's ability to play upon the unconscious tendencies of the German people and to act as their spokesman that has enabled him to mobilize their energies and direct them into the same channels through which he believed he had found a solution to his own personal conflicts" (p. 209).

working image

THE IMPORTANCE OF ASSESSMENT SKILLS

Some personality assessors are exceptionally skillful at developing working images of an individual's personality. They sometimes portray the individuality of personality in near-literary detail, complete with psychological explanations of past causes of the person's behavior and predictions about future behavior. Samuel Beck (1960) was one such expert assessor. Consider his interpretation of the responses made by a 10-year-old schizophrenic boy who was asked to look at Rorschach inkblots (Figure 2.2) and tell what he saw in them:

> The all-absorbing insecurity and violence have already been noted. The "house on fire" appears early and recurs. It is a frequent motif in very anxious or panicky children. The "Korean War" theme is the focus of many related associations. The interest in destruction also emerges in "slaughtered, killed, animals," "skeletons," "person from Korea," "intestines." Recurrent themes are "a big war gun shooting in all directions," "clouding over," and "bullets." A very regressive content is: "looks like someone made a mess all over the bed (laughs), it's black; someone had diarrhea and had a bowel movement on the bed." . . . [T]he essential lack of ego in the sense of central motivation and of standards must make for pessimism in predicting the ultimate personality structure. A benign environment will help, but love will not be enough. The critical therapeutic problem will be that of planting the seed of an ego. (p. 161)

Other assessors prefer less literary interpretations, favoring straightforward statements of rules and empirical findings. For example, Gilberstadt and Duker (1965) offer a collective personality description based on a subgroup of MMPI profiles. Their approach to assessment emphasizes descriptive statements having a high probability of applying to persons who obtain a similar pattern of scores. The "1-2-3-4 type" in the following example refers to persons who receive above-average scores on the first four of nine MMPI scales (see Figure 2.5). Past research findings have identified common characteristics among persons making up the

The Minnesota Multiphasic Personality Inventory

Starke R. Hathaway and J. Charnley McKinley

Scorer's Initials_____

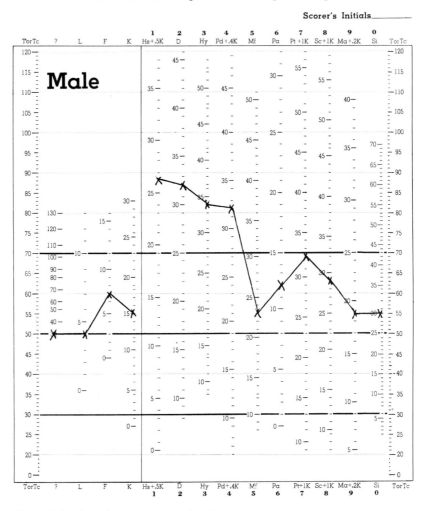

Figure 2.5 "1-2-3-4" MMPI profile from Gilberstadt and Duker (1965). Rule: 1, 2, 3, and 4 are higher than scores on all other scales.

1-2-3-4 MMPI group, especially if they have a medical history of stomach problems. Findings in this instance imply the development of psychological reactions caused by physical problems.

> The case histories of the 1-2-3-4 type offer support for the hypothesis that there may be a genetic basis for their physiological stomach disturbances. Fathers and siblings [frequently reported stomach problems and alcoholism.] The most frequent symptom at the time of hospitalization was severe alcoholism. About one-half of the patients complained of stomach distress or had a history of ulcers. (Gilberstadt & Duker, 1965, pp. 28–30)

While tests "are not the X-ray of the person once extravagantly claimed" by psychologists and publishing houses, they certainly have offered skilled interpreters important frameworks "for observing people and testing hypotheses about their behavior" (Korchin & Schuldberg, 1981, p. 1156). The popularity of testing has declined over time, especially during the second half of this century (Korchin, 1976). Too often, the correspondence between test use and supporting research has been "discouraging" (Reynolds & Sundberg, 1976). This has been particularly true of projective techniques in which people are instructed to "draw a house . . . a tree . . . a person . . . people doing something" (Murstein, 1965; Wise & Potkay, 1983). The most favorable correspondence found by Reynolds and Sundberg between tests popularly in use and published research reports occurred with the Rorschach and MMPI techniques, which averaged 92 and 132 publications per year, respectively, between 1951 and 1971. Nevertheless, assessment skills remain an essential part of most psychologists' professional training and employment activities (Levy & Fox, 1975; Wade & Baker, 1977). Millon (1984), in fact, believes that a Renaissance in personality assessment is under way.

Assessment currently is moving in new directions, linked to developments in behavioral and cognitive psychology. In 1971, the venerable *Journal of Projective Techniques* was renamed the *Journal of Personality Assessment* to encompass a "wider range of assessment procedures" (Farberow, 1970). New journals are placing greater emphasis on assessing behavior rather than personality and on demonstrating the effectiveness of such techniques. They include *Behavioral Assessment* and the *Journal of Behavioral Assessment*. As summarized by Walter Mischel (1977), writing about the future of personality measurement, there is "a growing synthesis" of several research and theoretical influences that views the person as (1) so complex and multifaceted as to defy easy classification and comparisons on any single or simple common dimension; (2) as influenced by a host of interacting determinants; (3) as uniquely organized on the basis of prior experiences and future expectations; and yet (4) as rule-guided in systematic, potentially comprehensive ways that are open to study by the methods of science (p. 253).

THE PROCESS OF ASSESSING A PERSON: MARTIN FACIE

The personality-assessment process has been illustrated in a film entitled *Personality,* which is available to instructors for classroom use (McGraw-Hill Films, 1971). The film demonstrates how personality assessment is conducted, along with some of the techniques used to gather psychological information. It focuses on a college art major, Martin Facie, who responded to a newspaper ad calling for volunteers to take a battery of psychological tests. Martin had no specific clinical problem or personal need to be assessed. Purposes of the film were to demonstrate personality-assessment procedures and convey general psychological understanding of Martin by developing "working image" hypotheses of his personality and behavior. The assessment was conducted by clinical psychologist Ira Nathanson.

Table 2.4 summarizes the process of Martin's assessment, following Sundberg's (1977) five stages. Note the wide variety of techniques selected by Dr. Nathanson as aids to understanding Martin's personality. They encompass all of

TABLE 2.4   The Process of Personality Assessment with Martin Facie

Step 1. Establishing the Reason for Assessment
To demonstrate use of a personality assessment battery
To develop "working image" hypotheses about Martin
Not to answer a specific clinical or personal question

Step 2. Selecting the Assessment Techniques
Psychological interviews
Objective techniques
Projective techniques
Observations of behavior in natural settings

Step 3. Gathering the Information
Psychological interviews
    Parents
    Female friend
    Martin
Behavioral observations
    Naturalistic observations
        On campus: interacting with female friend
        During art class: painting
        In apartment: interacting with male friend
    Professional observations
        In office: interacting with Dr. Nathanson
Personality assessment
    Objective techniques
        Wechsler Adult Intelligence Scale
        Minnesota Multiphasic Personality Inventory
        Personality Research Form
    Projective techniques
        Draw-a-Person Technique
        Rotter Incomplete Sentences Blank
        Holtzman Inkblot Technique
        Thematic Apperception Test

Step 4. Organizing and Interpreting the Information
Scoring tests
Comparing scores with norms
Identifying themes
Incorporating observations
Forming hypotheses
Cross-checking results
Interpreting results
Confirming and eliminating hypotheses
Summarizing findings
Integrating and organizing findings

Step 5. Communicating Conclusions and Making Decisions
Writing report
Informing Martin of results and recommendations
Conveying understanding
Answering questions
Concluding that no predictions or decisions are necessary

the major categories of assessment techniques identified earlier: interviews, behavioral observations, projective techniques, and objective tests.

Psychological interviews.   In gathering the information, Dr. Nathanson first conducted psychological interviews, not only with Martin but also with his parents and friends. Mr. and Mrs. Facie were interviewed to provide personal-history and background information on their son, including their perceptions of Martin's typical personality characteristics. Martin's friends offered observations about Martin's recent behaviors outside the family setting, based on their own observations and relationships with him. Finally, Martin was asked to express his own reactions, feelings, attitudes, and beliefs.

Observations of behavior.   Martin's behaviors were observed in natural life settings, with the camera making a permanent record. *Naturalistic observation* refers to viewing a person's behaviors in everyday surroundings and situations, in contrast to unfamiliar laboratory or office circumstances, which may place artificial restrictions on what the person feels free to say or do. You will readily understand the importance of obtaining assessment information about behavior in real-life settings if you simply think about ways in which your own behavior changes depending on the situation you are in — where you are, who is with you, and what your reason is for being there. Martin was observed in a variety of daily activities and relationships: walking and talking with a female friend outdoors on the university campus, attending art class, reviewing the day's events with a male friend in an apartment at mealtime, and working alone in the evening on an art project.

Psychological test situations.   Several sources of psychological information figured in Martin's assessment, including interactions with the psychologist, findings from objective tests, and results from projective techniques. Martin's natural behaviors and social interactions likely did appear in the "artificial" setting of the testing office. They would have included Martin's verbal comments before, during, and after the testing, along with his nonverbal behavior, such as speed of work, efficiency over time, changes in body posture, and his developing relationship with Dr. Nathanson. As a personality assessor, Dr. Nathanson observed and interpreted these events. At one point in the film, Martin is viewed through the lens of Dr. Nathanson's eyeglasses, highlighting the importance of the assessor as a measuring instrument, however imperfect (Potkay, 1982).

Personality assessors place greatest value on normative comparisons and interpretations derived from objective-test findings. Many numerical scores were available to Dr. Nathanson in assessing Martin's personality. Results from the Wechsler Adult Intelligence Scale (WAIS) indicated above-average intellectual potential for Martin. At the same time, Dr. Nathanson saw Martin's functioning as being slightly lowered because of emotional tensions that Martin was not facing squarely. Results pointed out Martin's "perfectionism," which could have been reflected in scores from the two objective personality questionnaires administered to Martin. Included among the 15 dimensions of normal personality functioning measured by the Personality Research Form (PRF) (D. N. Jackson, 1967) are needs for precise and orderly structure in life, and for achieving success. Included among the nine dimensions of abnormal personality functioning measured by the Minnesota Multiphasic Personality Inventory (MMPI) (Hathaway & McKinley, 1967) are experiences of excessive worry and anxiety.

Martin's responses to the unstructured tests, such as the Draw-a-Person Technique, Incomplete Sentences Blank, Holtzman Inkblot Test, and Thematic Apperception Test, offered a number of hypotheses about his personality. Martin performed well in perceiving and handling reality, was able to use his inner resources constructively, and showed a variety of interests. His personality also showed patterns of holding spontaneous feelings in check, using intellectual controls, and experiencing mild tensions that made it difficult for him to relax and be at ease. Martin's drawing of a woman, and the "Clark Gable" story he told in response to the picture of a man and woman, suggested some emotional distance in close interpersonal relationships, a need to emphasize the masculine side of himself, and attitudes toward women as sex objects.

Martin's reactions.   Martin's comments at the end of the film generally were supportive of Dr. Nathanson's hypotheses, although some "jumping to conclusions" was noted, possibly related to the limited testing time of only a few hours. Martin also noted that he was willing to reveal himself as a person "in ways that a lot of people wouldn't." While indicating that certain areas of his personality were touched only lightly, he concluded "I'll go along with whatever you say."

How about putting yourself in Martin's place? Take a moment to complete the exercise in Box 2.2 before reading further.

BOX 2.2	*The Mystery Assessor*
	Interprets Your Personality

Unbeknownst to you, our crackerjack personality assessor has observed your behavior during the time you have been a student in this course. Would you like to know the results? Remember that psychologists have been trained to explore *all* aspects of human behavior, including unconscious conflicts and abnormalities. Will the assessment results identify some skeleton hidden in your personal closet?

What follows is our mystery assessor's interpretations of your personality. To help us evaluate the assessor's accuracy, you are asked to make ratings regarding the degree to which you believe the interpretation actually fits your personality. For each of the five areas covered, circle the number that best corresponds to how well the interpretation fits you.

ABILITIES

You are a person who is above average in intelligence or mental alertness. You also are above average in accuracy, which may be rather painstaking at times. You deserve a reputation for neatness. In fact, you dislike turning out sloppy work.

continued

BOX 2.2
continued

You have good initiative. That is, you have the ability to make suggestions and to develop new ideas in an open-minded way.

          1   2   3   4   5   6   7
low fit   –   –   –   –   –   –   –   high fit

EMOTIONS

You have a tendency to worry at times, but not to excess. Although you do find yourself getting depressed at times, you couldn't be called a moody person because you are generally cheerful and rather optimistic. You have a good disposition. However, earlier in your life you have had a struggle with yourself to control your impulses and temper.

          1   2   3   4   5   6   7
low fit   –   –   –   –   –   –   –   high fit

INTERESTS

You are strongly socially inclined. You like to meet people, but especially like to mix with people you know well. You appreciate music, art, and painting, but you will never be a success as a composer of music or as an artist or creator. Although you like sports and athletic events, you devote more of your attention to reading about them in the sporting pages of newspapers than to actual participation.

          1   2   3   4   5   6   7
low fit   –   –   –   –   –   –   –   high fit

AMBITIONS

You are ambitious and deserve credit for wanting to be well thought of by your family, friends, and associates. These ambitions come out most strongly in your tendency to indulge in daydreams, in building air-castles, but this does not mean that you fail to get into the game of life actively.

          1   2   3   4   5   6   7
low fit   –   –   –   –   –   –   –   high fit

VOCATIONAL

You ought to continue to be successful so long as you stay in a social vocation. That is, you need to keep yourself in work that brings you in contact with people. Just what type of work you pick out isn't as important as the fact that it must be work bringing you in touch with people. On the negative side, you would never have been a success at strictly theoretical work or in pure research work, such as in physics or neurology.

          1   2   3   4   5   6   7
low fit   –   –   –   –   –   –   –   high fit

That's it!

How did our personality assessor do in understanding your personality, using his hidden technique? How do your results compare with those of other students in the class?

GENERALIZED INTERPRETATIONS OF PERSONALITY

Assuming that you have completed the exercise in Box 2.2, it is quite likely that you rated some of the interpretations as fitting your personality to a high degree. This would be supported by your having selected points 5, 6, or 7 on the rating scales. If so, how could such matching have occurred? You did not take any personality tests, and you certainly were not given a battery of psychological assessment techniques such as Martin Facie was given.

The originator of the personality interpretations in Box 2.2 was showman P. T. Barnum. Barnum prepared these interpretations as guidelines for use by his circus employees whose job it was to do "character readings" of visitors to the midway (Thorne, 1961, pp. 30–31). You may now see that the purpose of the exercise is to alert you to some necessary cautions regarding the use of personality-assessment techniques in understanding individual persons (Nicholls, Licht, & Pearl, 1982). The *Barnum effect* refers to the phenomenon in which people readily accept generalized descriptions of personality as accurately applying to themselves, on the false assumption that the interpretations are individualized (Meehl, 1956).

A number of influences contribute to the Barnum effect. First, all individuals are in many ways similar to all other individuals because of the sharing of common human experiences. The same conclusions about personality will apply to more than one person. We all "worry at times" and want to be "well thought of" by people who are important to us. Second, some interpretations are so general or commonplace that they could apply to almost everyone (Ulrich, Stachnik, & Stainton, 1963). Nearly all of us are involved in work settings that bring us "in contact with people," and few of us are interested in work that is "pure research" such as "physics or neurology." Third, we are quite willing to accept positive information about ourselves, especially when it comes from respected sources of authority (Baillargeon & Danis, 1984; Merrens & Richards, 1970). It delights us to be considered "above average in intelligence" and "open-minded." Fourth, in situations where we are the focus of attention, especially social demonstrations involving an expert, we are motivated to help things work out as expected. Despite our ability to differentiate trivial and relevant information (Harris & Greene, 1984), we will search for some circumstance or time in our past life in which a generalized statement really has applied to us. You may have observed this in demonstrations of stage hypnosis or while reading about your "personality" in newspaper astrology columns. Martin Facie made a comment consistent with this idea at the end of the film when he said "I'll go along with whatever you say," partly because he recognized his role as "a guinea pig for your film." Fifth, along with being so generalized and trivial that they apply to anyone's Aunt Fanny, personality interpretations may avoid being too specific, by beating around the bush. If not above average "in intelligence," then perhaps the person is above average in "mental alertness" or "accuracy." Also, Barnum's guidelines were intended to be modified according to the age, sex, manner of dress, and reactions of customers whose personalities were being interpreted.

Barnum effect

Assessing Individual Differences: A Group Application

We close this chapter with a concrete illustration of some of the key ideas presented so far in the text. In Chapter 1, a definition of personality was presented that emphasized individual differences, tied to different psychological profiles for different people. In this chapter, we added a definition of "personality assessment," a process of gathering information about people in a systematic way in order to better understand, predict, and make decisions about their behavior. In this section, individual differences are illustrated using information obtained from Nazi war criminals following the Second World War. Personality assessment is illustrated because the Rorschach inkblot technique was used to gather and organize information about these individuals in a systematic way. The making of decisions is apparent in Molly Harrower's clinical judgments about the degree of psychological adjustment present in each Nazi's Rorschach record, on eight behavioral dimensions comprising their psychological profiles.

NAZI LEADERS: BANAL AND ORDINARY PERSONS?

Karl Adolf Eichmann was a Nazi leader in charge of the Office for Jewish Emigration. This agency had direct responsibility for the extermination of millions of Jews, a program Hitler saw as the "final solution to the Jewish question." Although Eichmann was identified as a major war criminal, his escape from an American internment camp allowed him to avoid immediate prosecution for "crimes against humanity" at the postwar Nuremberg trials. Hannah Arendt (1964), an historian, studied Eichmann's personal life and observed him during his 1961 trial in Jerusalem. She concluded that Eichmann and earlier Nazi defendants at Nuremberg were quite ordinary and normal in their personalities. In her view, their implementation of Hitler's ideas reflected a "banal" or commonplace form of evil rather than any extraordinary sadism or cruelty that might make them different from most other persons. In effect, Arendt accepted the Nuremberg defense of these leaders that they were "only obeying orders," similar to highly obedient participants in Stanley Milgram's (1974) psychology experiments. (In the most representative experiment, nearly two-thirds of Milgram's American subjects obediently administered "fatal" electric shocks to other people.)

HARROWER: INDIVIDUAL DIFFERENCES GREATER THAN ABNORMALITY

Molly Harrower (1976), a clinical psychologist, also studied the Nuremberg group. Her conclusion, similar to Arendt's, was based on psychological analyses of the Nuremberg defendants' pretrial responses to the Rorschach. Harrower found that Rorschach results for the group of 17 defendants generally fell within normal ranges of expectancy, with little evidence of outstanding abnormality for the group as a whole. Most clearly, the Rorschach records showed much individual variability across defendants, ranging from highly disturbed to highly superior in personality functioning. Harrower presented some preliminary information to support her clinical judgment that the records were characterized by "basic individual differences . . . differences which greatly outweighed any similarities" (p. 344). She reported having made consistently favorable ratings of Rorschach results for Hjalmar Schacht, Nazi Minister of Economics, and unfavorable ratings for Joachim von Ribbentrop, Foreign Minister, on eight personality dimensions: productivity, contact with reality, thought content, constructive fantasy, drive, emotions, anxiety, and overall evaluation. Results pointed to marked disturbances in personality functioning for von Ribbentrop, but superior personality functioning for Schacht.

Harrower recognized that these early assessment results were based on the judgment of only one psychologist, herself. Her approach was one of *clinical observation,* discussed previously, in which one assessor observes or interprets the psychological findings on one or more clients. Harrower's awareness of the scientific limitations of this approach led her to undertake a more systematic study, to determine whether other professionals would reach similar conclusions under more controlled conditions. Convinced in her own mind of the individual differences characterizing the Nazi Rorschachs, she sought to validate her personal impressions by obtaining independent judgments from other psychologists of "unquestioned" clinical experience and competence. The psychologists also had to be unaware that these were Nazi records, so that they would not be biased in their interpretations, especially considering the horror of the Holocaust and the intensity of public reaction to it.

The experts were mailed groups of Rorschach records along with instructions to decide whether there were any common denominators present in the records. The specialists were given no information as to whose records they were examining or how the Rorschachs had been obtained. Each specialist received the same 16 Rorschach records, which included the responses of 8 Nazi defendants (Groups A and C), 4 members of the clergy (Group B), and 4 psychiatric patients (Group D). Four levels of personality functioning were represented, equally, in the four groups: superior, normal, mediocre, and disturbed.

All ten specialists failed to correctly identify the eight Nazi Rorschach records. They grouped the records by higher and lower quality of personality functioning, not by "group characteristic." This outcome supported Harrower's original clinical observations, that no underlying common "Nazi" denominator could be identified by a sample of independent Rorschach experts.

Harrower's explanation of the unexpected discrepancy between the observed extraordinary behaviors of Nazi leaders and their ordinary range of personality functioning was that a well-integrated personality was no protection against being influenced by Nazi ideas and war-criminal behaviors. In addition, Harrower had evaluated the later Rorschach record of Adolf Eichmann as being so ordinary as to serve as an example of normal personality among Nazi officials (McCully, 1980), no different from that of "the man next door" (Harel, 1975; Ritzler, 1978). Conclusions of this kind run counter to the popularly held stereotype that persons who commit unusual crimes must be mentally "sick." In addition, it is worthwhile to note that evidence against the stereotype has been established on theoretical grounds by knowledgeable mental-health professionals

(Szasz, 1960, 1963), as well as by recent court proceedings regarding the legal sanity of mass murderer John Gacy and political assassin Sirhan Sirhan.

PERHAPS NOT SO ORDINARY

Since Harrower (1976), questions have been raised as to whether the Nazi Rorschachs really evidenced "ordinary" personality characteristics. In a book addressed more to general readers than professional workers, Miale and Selzer (1975) reexamined and published 16 of the Rorschach records. They concluded that "the Nazis were not psychologically normal or healthy individuals" (p. 287). However, the basis of the conclusion was subjective interpretation of the records, with minimal use of scores and with prior knowledge that the Rorschachs were of Nazi origin. This may be contrasted with the more neutral and controlled circumstances of interpretation established for Harrower's Rorschach experts, who relied more on group comparisons and classifications.

Although Miale and Selzer did not offer an interpretation of Eichmann's Rorschach, one later was provided by Robert McCully (1980). McCully concluded that Eichmann's personality "was not so commonplace or ordinary as was generally supposed" (p. 318). However, this too was based on subjective interpretation and prior knowledge of the Rorschach subject's identity.

Allen (1984) has questioned Harrower's and Miale and Selzer's identification of Hjalmar Schacht as "a typical Nazi." Schacht was the Nuremberg defendant whose Rorschach record pointed to superior personality functioning (Harrower, 1976). Allen's "most conservative conclusion" was that Schacht "was not a Nazi, just an opportunist who used the Nazis, and then later turned on them, joining the plot against Hitler's life" (p. 2). During the Nuremberg trial, Schacht was identified as one of the anti-Hitler conspirators (Shirer, 1960). The Nuremberg jury was convinced of his innocence, and he was acquitted (Jarman, 1961).

A definitive answer to the question of whether Eichmann and other Nazi officials were ordinary or extraordinary persons may be difficult to establish. Ritzler (1978) saw the answer as falling in middle ground. Miale and Selzer's thematic interpretations involved high levels of inference and were done subjectively. It should be noted that single items of personal-history information—including "previous experience," "middle class," and "psychiatric patient"—are often powerful sources of inference when judgments are made about people (Potkay, 1973). The label "Nazi" may have a similar effect. On the other hand, Harrower's assessors, in grouping Rorschachs into categories, may have failed to detect subtle distinctions in personality styles. Ritzler (1978), using only numerical Rorschach scores, found some deviation by the Nazi group from other groups of normal subjects matched for age, era of testing, depression, and anxiety, "but not as much as might have been expected from the discussions of Miale and Selzer" (p. 352).

More generally, the study of Nazi Rorschach records illustrates some of the limitations involved in relying on a single personality-assessment technique when making decisions about people. It also reflects (1) the complexity and contradictoriness of human behavior; (2) the need to consider possible influences on test-taking by the special circumstances of trial defendants accused of serious crimes; and (3) the uncertainty that psychologists face when lacking a normative frame of reference for evaluating such extraordinary behaviors as those endorsed by leaders of the Third Reich. Differences in psychological-test interpretation appear highly dependent upon the assessment methods used, and on the particular psychologists doing the interpreting (Potkay, 1971, 1982). It is always important to consider the situations in which psychological information is gathered and the circumstances under which it is interpreted (Rosenhan, 1973).

CHAPTER   REVIEW

This chapter has provided a variety of answers to the question "How is personality studied?" The question has been approached at two different levels.

At one level, the *field* of personality often makes use of theories and models. Supporting evidence has come from personal observations, clinical observations, and formal research. Formal research, including both experimental and correlational research, was illustrated by Diener and Wallbom's (1976) experiment on honesty and by Backteman and Magnusson's (1981) study of trait stability. Methods of studying personality also encompass idiographic and nomothetic approaches, which are complementary to each other. Nomothetic approaches seek to establish general laws applicable to groups of people in general, while idiographic approaches seek to understand a person's uniqueness.

At a second level, the study of a particular *person* has often been linked to the applied area of personality assessment. This process of obtaining information about a person leads to informed understanding, prediction, and decision making about that person. Five stages of the assessment process have been identified by Sundberg (1977): establishing the reason for assessment, selecting assessment techniques, gathering information, organizing and interpreting the information, and communicating conclusions and making decisions. The most common assessment technique is the interview, which cuts across many disciplines. However, there are three major types of psycho-

logical techniques used to assess individual personality: projective, objective, and behavioral. Measures of each type often are part of an assessment battery. It is not possible to indicate which specific techniques are "best" because many considerations need to be taken into account. These considerations include historical developments in the study of individual differences, technical standards of reliability and validity, relatively rapid changes in the popularity of specific techniques over time, factors related to a professional's training and theoretical framework, personal preferences of psychologists, application to adults or children, and the kinds of questions that need to be answered. Despite evidence of recent decline in traditional uses of psychological tests, assessment remains an important aspect of personality study.

In evaluating the effectiveness of personality theories and assessment strategies, it is important to recognize that an understanding of personality depends on information not only from "inside" the person (traits, perceptions, attitudes) but from "outside" the person as well (environmental circumstances, social situations). These ideas are developed most fully in Part 3, which discusses traits, situations, and interactions between the two. More immediately, we shall turn our attention to Part 2, which elaborates a number of major theories of personality, most of which tend to emphasize either internal (Freud) or external (Skinner) influences.

KEY CONCEPTS

Personality theory
   Model
Methods of study
   Personal observation
   Clinical observation
   Formal research
      Experimental research
      Correlational research
   Nomothetic approach
   Idiographic approach
Personality assessment
   Five-stage process
   Working image

Test standards
   Reliability
   Validity
Barnum effect
Assessment techniques
   Interviews
   Projective techniques
   Objective tests
   Behavioral measures
   Assessment batteries

REVIEW QUESTIONS

1. Distinguish theories from models, and both of these from facts. In what ways are theories and models useful in the study of personality?
2. What are the idiographic and nomothetic approaches to personality? How do they complement each other?
3. Explain the difference between experimental and correlational research.
4. Define personality assessment, and explain its five-stage process.
5. What are the three major types of assessment techniques? Give examples of each, and compare their advantages and disadvantages.

PART TWO

Theoretical Approaches to Personality

PART 2 EMPHASIZES theoretical approaches to personality—broad interpretations psychologists have offered to explain and predict observations. We examine several varieties of personality theory: psychoanalytic (Chapter 3), social-psychoanalytic (Chapter 4), behavioral (Chapter 5), social-learning (Chapter 6), humanistic (Chapter 7), and cognitive (Chapter 8). As you will see, each theory is based on somewhat different assumptions and tends to highlight particular facets of people's behavior.

Each chapter also discusses applications and research associated with the theory. There is a natural feedback mechanism built into the relationship between theory and supporting research. First, theory guides research. Just as a play needs a plot so that the dialogue doesn't go off in all directions at once, the observations that constitute research must have a theoretical base so that investigations of personality aren't random snapshots of the irrelevant as well as the relevant. At the same time, what is found in the course of research often requires theorists to modify their viewpoints, thus changing theory for the better.

3

Classical Psychoanalysis: Freud and Jung

How rational are "normal" people?

Is most of personality unconscious?

How important are childhood experiences for later personality development?

What is the true meaning and purpose of dreams?

Can a "talking therapy" change personality?

S TUDENTS SOMETIMES FEEL disappointed when psychologists fail to provide clear-cut answers to apparently simple questions about human behavior. Such disappointments have been less frequent in students exposed to the ideas of early personality theorists. These theorists took professional, even personal, pride in offering definite answers to basic questions about personality. If anything, students in personality courses have found themselves questioning or disagreeing with many of the answers offered, much as psychologists themselves did during early-20th-century decades of great debate and rivalry among different schools of personality theory (Reisman, 1966).

Sigmund Freud is among the most definite theorists in providing answers to questions about personality. In fact, his dogmatism led him to reject persons unwilling to agree with his beliefs. During a 1905 trip to the United States, to speak at Clark University, he went so far as to accuse one of his most ardent followers—Carl Jung—of being interested in the dead past of archeology because of an unconscious wish that Freud, the father figure, be dead. Jung and many other early followers soon split with Freud as their ideas began to deviate in new directions.

This chapter emphasizes the views of Freud, the founder of classical psychoanalysis. It also presents Jung's ideas about personality, referred to as "analytical psychology." Although Jung's ideas departed from those of Freud, he still adhered to Freud's basic framework. Commonalities between Freud and Jung include assumptions about the biological origins of personality, the functioning of personality as an energy system, and the major role of *internal,* unconscious influences on human behavior. Jung's adherence to classical psychoanalysis certainly is greater than that of the social psychoanalysts, a group of important thinkers who extended Freudian notions by stressing the importance of *external* influences on personality, as discussed in the next chapter.

As you read about the different theories of personality, we invite you to keep a running list of your own questions, disagreements, and agreements. This will help you identify your personal assumptions and beliefs as a beginning personality theorist and can provide a framework for exchanging ideas with your classmates.

Freud, the Person

Sigmund Freud was born on May 6, 1856, in Moravia, a Germanic area that is now central Czechoslovakia. He was the oldest of eight children born to Amalie and

Jakob Freud. Amalie was Jakob's second wife, 20 years his junior, who bore her "golden Sigi" at age 21. She had a lively personality and sharp-witted intelligence. Jakob, a wool merchant, had a close attachment to his wife and a good sense of humor, and was a liberal thinker.

At age 17, Sigmund entered medical school at the University of Vienna to study neurology. He was an excellent student, with a photographic memory. The teacher who influenced him most was Ernst Brucke, a respected and disciplined physiologist with an uncompromising spirit and a terrible gaze. Brucke believed that the only active forces in living organisms were physical-chemical ones interacting in a closed energy system, a viewpoint Freud later adapted when theorizing about psychological forces.

Freud's preoccupation during medical school was to make a name for himself by discovering something important (E. Jones, 1953). His student research included dissecting 400 male eels to verify the existence of testes in them, an observation not previously confirmed; establishing new characteristics of nerve cells in fish; and developing the gold-chloride technique of staining nervous tissue. However, his most important discovery was that cocaine could be used as an anesthetic. He arrived at this discovery by directly observing the effects of cocaine on himself. The episode highlights one of Freud's most significant char-

SIGMUND FREUD.   Freud is the founder of psychoanalysis, the dominant theory of personality during the first half of the 20th century. He pioneered discoveries of the unconscious, dream interpretation, Oedipus complex, and the treatment of neurotic disturbances.

acteristics. Confronted with an isolated fact or observation, Freud "could not dismiss it from his mind" until he had found an explanation (E. Jones, 1953, p. 97).

Jones linked the cocaine method to Freud's most unique, momentous, and heroic discovery—the psychoanalysis of his own unconscious. Throughout his life, Freud never ceased self-analysis, using himself as "the single fact," and reserving the last half-hour of each day for this purpose. He found it uncanny when he was unable to understand someone else's behavior in terms of himself. His most important book, *The Interpretation of Dreams* (1900/1958), was based on analyses of his own dreams. His *Psychopathology of Everyday Life* (1901/1965) also was derived from analyses of personal experiences. It dealt with the psychological meanings of apparent "mistakes" in memory, speech, reading, and writing. Both works assumed the influence of *psychological determinism,* a philosophical belief that nothing about human behavior occurs by accident or chance. For Freud, everything about personality "is determined" or has a psychological cause. One need only explore, trace, and uncover these causes.

Freud was an admirably courageous individual, able to confront his own personal experiences, secrets, and conflicts through self-analysis. Using himself as a primary subject, he traced his own behaviors back to their hidden origins. John Huston's popular film, *Freud,* portrayed him as a theoretical pioneer whose psychological bravery enabled him to overcome intense personal fears as he explored the closeness of his relationship with his mother, as well as hostile feelings toward his father. In fact, Freud's explorations of his own childhood experiences were important contributors to his belief in the Oedipus complex, a psychological process in which boys are seen as wanting to "kill" their father in order to "marry" their mother. Among Freud's earliest memories, "one was of penetrating into his parents' bedroom out of (sexual) curiosity and being ordered out by an irate father" (E. Jones, 1953, p. 7).

Paradoxically, Freud often controlled and hid important aspects of himself from others, including his family and closest followers, who in turn aided the cover-up of his private life. He actively promoted positive biases about himself by destroying hundreds of his personal letters and some early professional works that would have shed new light on himself and the development of his ideas. In his brief autobiography (1925/1952), he indicated that the public does not appreciate learning the truth about things and thus "has no claim" to learn more of his personal affairs.

Recent biographies have added "warts and all" to some of the more positive, legendary images of "the master" (Gelman & Hager, 1981). A 1979 book by Frank Sulloway goes "beyond the psychoanalytic legend" by tackling some of the myths and cultism developed about Freud by Freud and his followers. Sulloway believes that Freud borrowed more ideas from an early confessor and father figure, Wilhelm Fleiss, than has been recognized or admitted. Another critic, Jeffrey Masson, was fired from his post as projects director of the Sigmund Freud Archives because of an announcement that could upend classical psychoanalysis. Masson states that Freud decided to ignore the reality of reports by female patients that they had been victims of childhood sexual abuse by their fathers, substituting the alternative idea that such accounts were wishful fantasies of imagination, even though he had evidence to the contrary (Gelman & Hager, 1981). Freud did write a despairing letter to Fleiss regarding the impossibility of believing that so many fathers might be sexual perverts (Lauzun, 1965, p. 49).

Freud lived 80 of his 83 years in Vienna, where he established a private practice for the treatment of nervous disorders. His home and offices were located at the famed address, Berggasse 19. He enjoyed his role as father to six children, one of whom, Anna, became an important psychoanalyst, specializing in the treatment of children. Shortly after the Nazi invasion in 1938, Freud had to be persuaded by friends to leave Vienna because of the oppression of Jews. In fact, Freud never identified himself as an avid believer in Judaism, considering all religion an illusion used by civilization to cope with feelings of infantile helplessness. At the time of his departure, the Gestapo attempted to obtain an endorsement from him, which was something Freud said he could "hardly" do (they believed he had said "heartily").

Freud died in London on September 23, 1939, from cancer of the jaw and mouth. The malignancy undoubtedly stemmed from his lifelong addiction to cigars, which he chain-smoked from early morning to late evening. During his last 16 years, he experienced pain, fatigue, and difficulties in speaking and eating because of repeated surgery and the wearing of a mechanical device that separated his nasal cavity from his mouth. Essayist Stefan Zweig (1933/1962) wrote of Freud's "gloomy" perspective, which became all the more evident during the autumn of Freud's years:

> gloomy because the eyes have seen so much gloom. The men and the women who, during these fifty years, have come bringing their troubles, their needs, their distresses, and their disturbances; they have come complaining, questioning, eager and excited, hysterical and irate; always the sick, the oppressed, the tormented, the mentally disordered; and throughout these five decades it has been the unhappy, the ineffective aspect of humanity which has been disclosed to this observer. . . . So long and so abundantly has Sigmund Freud been a physician that he has gradually come to look upon mankind at large as ailing. His first impression, therefore, when he looks forth from his consulting-room into the outer world, is a pessimistic one, wherein a gloomy diagnosis anticipates examination. "Just as for the individual, so also for all mankind, life is hard to bear." (p. 208)

However, to the very end, Freud's instinct for life still was greater than that for death: "I prefer a mechanical jaw to no jaw at all. I still prefer existence to extinction" (quoted in Golub, 1981, p. 195).

Freud's View of the Person

Probably you are already familiar with some of the fundamental notions of Freudian theory. Freud painted a vivid and distressing portrait of human nature as dominated by instinctual, unconscious, and irrational forces. The human organism is selfish, at war internally and externally, aggressive, and sexual even during years of what had been thought to be childhood innocence. Determined by events outside of conscious control, the person is civilized but constantly frustrated, and religious out of fearfulness and illusion.

To get a preliminary view of some of the ideas discussed in this chapter, we invite you to complete the pretest in Box 3.1. The items are based on Freudian concepts, although they are somewhat simplified for teaching purposes. By indicating your agreement or disagreement, you can begin to identify some of your own basic assumptions about human nature. Later in the chapter, you will be asked to compare your answers with those that Freud would have given.

Preliminary Self-Test: **BOX 3.1**
Freud's View of the Person

Answer each question true or false according to your own point of view.

1. My basic personality is the same today as when I was about 5 years old.
   TRUE   FALSE

2. I have little knowledge of my real personality or its development.
   TRUE   FALSE

3. I choose to lead my life in a self-directed manner.
   TRUE   FALSE

4. My basic motivations are sex and aggression.
   TRUE   FALSE

5. Many of my behaviors are irrational, in that I repeatedly do things that make little logical sense.
   TRUE   FALSE

6. I have had few inner conflicts in my life.
   TRUE   FALSE

7. I have had abnormal experiences during my lifetime, including psychotic ones.
   TRUE   FALSE

8. I am afraid to know my true self, and I keep unpleasant aspects of my personality hidden from myself.
   TRUE   FALSE

9. As a child, I had sexual wishes and feelings toward my opposite-sex parent.
   TRUE   FALSE

10. Women and men are psychological equals.
    TRUE   FALSE

11. The best way for me to change my personality is to enter long-term therapy with a trained expert who will provide insight into my early childhood experiences.
    TRUE   FALSE

Basic Concepts: Freud

PERSONALITY STRUCTURE: THREE INTERACTING SYSTEMS

personality
structure

Structure refers to how something is put together—the parts that are included, and how these parts are arranged and relate to one another. Most things have a readily definable structure: atoms, clarinets, dormitories, families, and business organizations. For Freud, personality also has a definable structure, comprising three aspects: id, ego, and superego. *Id* represents the biological aspect of personality, *ego* the psychological aspect, and *superego* the social aspect. These are not "parts" of personality in a physical sense, nor do they have any specific, physical location in the person. Rather, they are *psychic*—inner psychological processes or systems of the mind that organize mental life and interact with one another in a dynamic way through continuous activity, changes, and influence on the personality.

id

Id.   For Freud, the origin of personality is biological, represented by id, the most basic of the three systems. Id comprises whatever is present in the organism at the time of birth, including everything inherited. Personality operates through id in the manner of a closed energy system. Food provides the organism with a powerhouse of energy that can be discharged in two ways: (1) physically, through innate, automatic reactions termed *reflexes,* and (2) psychologically, through infantile images and wishes termed *primary-process* events. Id is the reservoir of *instincts,* inborn forces whose characteristics are both physical (bodily needs) and psychological (wishes).

After career-long deliberation, Freud (1940/1949) assumed the existence of only two basic categories of instinct, those of life and those of death. Instincts toward life, called *Eros,* represent energy for preserving oneself (love of self) and one's species (love of others). The most important aspect of Eros is *libido,* a generalized pleasure drive. The instinct toward destructiveness and death, called *Thanatos,* is aimed at returning living things to their original inorganic state. The most important aspect of Thanatos is its aggressive drive. Life and death instincts may fuse together or work against each other, giving rise to "vicissitudes" or constant changes in a single personality, as well as to individual differences across personalities.

To understand the operation of id, think of the behaviors of a baby just a few days old. What does the baby do? It sleeps, it awakens, it cries for milk and comfort, it sucks firmly on a nipple, it urinates and defecates, it fusses, it reflexively moves its head toward the cheek you touch, it grasps your finger tightly, it startles, or its hand finds its mouth, which might even form a smile. Now ask yourself, "What does this baby do for me? For its parents? For anyone?" It does nothing at all for you, nor anyone for that matter, at least not intentionally. Since the baby's personality is dominated by id, its natural preoccupation is with itself and its inner, primarily physical, needs and comfort. Its behavior is determined by what Freud termed the *pleasure principle*—the reducing of pain (any increase in energy or tension), resulting in pleasure, as quickly and immediately as possible. The behavior of the infant corresponds with a popular song lyric, "I want what I want when I want it."

Ego.   Why are infant behaviors so one-sided and preoccupied with inner states of tension? It is because id is entirely isolated from the external world. Id has no means of directly establishing contact with the world outside itself. While able to detect changes in internal tension, such as hunger or cold, it has no way of satisfying these needs. It experiences only pain and pleasure.

Consider a baby fussing because of hunger. The baby can be temporarily "fooled" into calm when something other than food or a nipple is placed in its mouth. This is because it has no way of telling the difference between sucking a thumb, pacifier, toy, or breast. In fact, the functioning of id occurs on an entirely unconscious level; it has no conscious awareness of anything. Id obviously requires "a little help from a friend" in receiving and making sense of information from stimuli outside itself. It gets this help from ego, the second major system in Freudian personality theory.

Ego develops out of id as a special energy system, taking form as a coherent organization of mental processes to which consciousness is attached. Ego's purpose is to allow the personality to adapt to the world outside itself. Whereas id is subjective, directed internally toward itself in its wants and demands, ego is objective, or directed outside itself. Ego can determine whether id pleasures may be satisfied safely, in a manner of self-preservation.   **ego**

Whereas id is governed by the pleasure principle, ego operates according to the *reality principle*. That is, ego has the capacity to delay id's pressing demands for immediate tension reduction until an appropriate object of gratification is available. Ego is guided by a higher level of mental functioning, called *secondary process*. Secondary process includes such intellectual operations as thinking, evaluating, planning, and decision making that test reality to determine whether certain behaviors will benefit the personality. Ego thus serves as a mediator or liaison, planning for actions in the real world that will satisfy id. Unlike id, ego has the capacity to accurately differentiate and remember true food-producing breasts from thumbs, toys, and pacifiers. Ego's functioning increases the likelihood that id's instinctual striving toward pleasure and away from pain will occur in relation to the outside environment, appropriately and without danger.

While obviously of critical importance as a personality system, ego's secondary status may be seen in Freud's analogy that the conscious aspect of personality is just the tip of a floating iceberg whose bulk is hidden beneath the water (see Figure 3.1). In fact, even ego's functioning is not totally conscious. Ego's mediating role, along with its secondary status, makes it vulnerable to stresses from both internal and external sources of danger. For this reason, ego constantly has to be on protective guard. External dangers include inadequate food, water, and physical comfort for sustaining life, threats of physical or psychological injury, and loss of parental love. Parents typically help children combat these dangers. Internal dangers include uncontrollable increases of instinctual energies, particularly sex and aggression. Freud (1923/1961b) liked to use the metaphor of horse and rider: the superior strength of the horse (id) must be held in check by its rider (ego).

Ego's reaction to threatening surges of instinct is to experience *anxiety*, a state of extremely unpleasant emotional discomfort. To minimize this anxiety, ego calls upon various *defense mechanisms* — internal, unconscious, and automatic psychological strategies for coping with or regaining control over threatening id   **unconscious defense mechanisms**

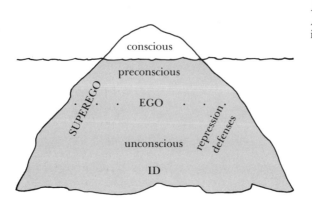

Figure 3.1
Analogy of personality as an
iceberg.

instincts. Defense mechanisms protect the personality by keeping unacceptable
urges or ideas from ever reaching conscious awareness. Freud believed that exaggerated use of such defense mechanisms results in *neuroses,* patterns of abnormal
behavior related to an overcontrol of instincts. One such pattern is *hysterical
neurosis,* in which a person who feels angry may develop a "paralyzed" arm to
lessen the chances of hitting someone. Freud's ability to trace neurotic symptoms
to their unconscious sources, thereby unraveling their meaning, showed his creative genius as a psychoanalyst.

superego

Superego.   The third major force in personality is superego, which carries
both conscience and ego ideal. Superego operates according to the *morality principle,* thereby representing society's values of right and wrong. Like ego, superego
develops from id energy and is irrational in its influence. Although it is a specialized system within ego, it often operates below the level of ego's awareness.
Superego's most important function is to help control id impulses by directing
energy toward reducing or inhibiting entirely id's expression of its sexual and
aggressive instincts.

The specific content of each personality's superego results from *introjection*
—a process by which personality incorporates the norms and standards of its
culture through identification with parents or other admired persons in society,
such as clergy and teachers. As the primary interpreters of society's rules of
proper conduct, parents convey these values to their children by showing them
love for being "good" and punishing them for being "bad." A child's immature
ego is especially sensitive to potential losses of love when parental standards are
not being assimilated, or adopted internally. The lengthy dependency of children
on parents contributes to this uniquely human phenomenon.

Superego can become an independent and dominating force in personality,
as occurs in neuroses. Superego can work against both id and ego by making
personality excessively conforming to social norms, resulting in oversocialized
patterns of neurotic behavior such as illogically striving for 100% perfection in
absolutely everything one does. It can observe and influence ego directly, taking it
to task, giving it orders, correcting it, and threatening it with unpleasant emotional experiences when its subsystem of perfectionistic, parental standards *(con-*

science) is not being satisfied. These unpleasant emotions include guilt, an intense feeling of regret over having done something wrong or out of character, and lowered self-worth, or unfavorable evaluations of oneself as an undeserving or inadequate person. It is as if an adult's personality never outgrows its role of child in relation to its parents, substituting self-statements for those once made by parents: "That's a bad feeling. It's wrong to think that. You'll be punished. Always do what your parents have told you to do. Be perfect in everything."

On the other hand, superego can offer the personality positive emotional experiences when its standards of "doing what's right," or *ego ideal,* are met. Feelings of pride and self-respect take the form of substitute self-statements such as "Good child. You make us proud. We are happy. We love you."

Freud's concept of personality can be seen as an internal battleground. Superego is yet another force that ego has to contend with in its struggle to satisfy id without endangering the personality. Forces of id, ego, and superego are constantly on the march to dominate the personality by taking whatever extra energy they can from competing systems, sometimes forming temporary alliances with one system against another. Table 3.1 compares the three major structural systems of personality identified by Freud.

TABLE 3.1   Comparisons of Freud's Three Systems of Personality

	Id	Ego	Superego
Nature	Biological	Psychological	Social
Origin	Heredity	Experience	Culture
Contribution	Instincts	Self	Conscience
Orientation	Past	Present	Past
Level	Unconscious	Conscious and unconscious	Unconscious
Principle	Pleasure	Reality	Morality
Purpose	Seek pleasure	Adapt to reality	Represent right and wrong
	Avoid pain	Know true and false	
Aim	Immediate gratification	Safety and compromise	Perfection
Rationality	Irrational	Rational	Illogical
Reality	Subjective	Objective	Subjective

PERSONALITY DEVELOPMENT: FIVE SEQUENTIAL STAGES

Development refers to the processes by which something grows from a beginning state to a later one. Development is seen in plants, animals, solar systems, the constructing of college dormitories, and the planning of careers. Personality also

five stages of
personality
development

develops over time, from states of early childhood immaturity to those of later adult maturity. Freud hypothesized a series of five sequential stages of personality development: oral, anal, phallic, latency, and genital. Consistent with Freud's emphasis on biology, four of the stages are closely associated with *erogenous zones,* sensitive areas of the body from which instinctual satisfactions can be obtained. These zones are the mouth, anus, penis or clitoris, and penis or vagina. Freud assumed the clitoris to be a miniature penis, because both are outer sexual organs that become erect during sexual stimulation.

Although Freud identified the satisfactions as sexual, he defined "sexual" very generally to encompass *any* pleasurable feeling associated with stimulation of the erogenous zones, whether or not the stimulation is directed toward genital sex. *Libido* is a substitute term for sexual cravings or satisfactions, which also are reflections of Eros, the instinct toward life. One example of libidinous satisfaction is the release of tension associated with urination. This broader view of sexuality makes understandable Freud's references to the developmental stages as "psychosexual."

Freud's statement that "the child is father to the man" represents his firm belief that every person's basic personality is established by the age of 5. In short, important psychological aspects of the personality you have today are basically the same as those you had when you were just entering kindergarten. This idea is grounded in Freud's philosophical determinism, which allows no room for personal freedom, conscious purpose, or routine changes in one's personality or behavior.

Suppose you were asked to think of the name of a person, any person. Would you feel you were making a free choice or decision about the name you came up with? Freud would say your feeling is simply an illusion. No mental activity occurs in an arbitrary, free-choice manner. Freud's psychic determinism means that every single behavior you display during your lifetime—from your "choice" of hobbies to your selection of a mate—results totally from energies and influences present in your unconscious personality, related to your early childhood experiences.

Oral stage.   According to Freud, the first stage in personality development is the *oral stage.* From the time of birth, all of the organism's psychic activity is directed toward satisfying the needs of the mouth, an erogenous zone that includes the tongue and lips and is associated with the organism's intestinal system. Eros' aim of self-preservation is met by the production of energy, made possible by nourishment received through the mouth. Independent of nourishment, an infant's sucking movements also provide it with pleasure. "Thumbsucking shows that the pleasure gained from breast or bottle is based not alone on the gratification of hunger but on the stimulation of the erogenous oral mucous membrane as well; otherwise the infant would disappointedly remove his thumb, since it produces no milk" (Fenichel, 1945, p. 63).

fixation

The importance of stages in understanding adult personality is manifested in Freud's concept of fixation. *Fixation* refers to a person's being developmentally arrested or stopped at a particular stage because of excessive satisfaction, frustration, or anxiety. Because libidinal energy is permanently invested in such a stage, the person is likely to show periodic regression to this earlier stage as a psychological retreat under stress. Freud traced two types of personality traits to fixation at the oral stage.

The *oral-receptive* trait is derived from childhood pleasures of receiving and ingesting food. Persons with this trait form dependent relationships on others who feed and care for them. Psychologically, such persons are more suggestible and gullible than others, as if "swallowing" whatever is given them. They are also interested in receiving information and knowledge, learning from others, and acquiring material goods. Persons especially fond of candy, sweets, smoking, and oral sex, and those who are obese, are often identified in psychoanalytic literature as oral-receptive.

The *oral-aggressive* trait is also derived from childhood pleasures associated with the mouth, food, and eating, but with greater chewing, biting, and use of teeth. Persons of this character type would be expected to favor rock candy and jawbreakers to gumdrops and marshmallows, and hard-stemmed pipes to cigarettes. They are orally aggressive in their relationships with others, as if to bite the hand (or maternal breast) that feeds them. Their manner of talking is sarcastic and argumentative. They also seek to hold firmly onto others, as if to possess them or incorporate them internally.

Anal stage. Freud's second phase of personality development is the *anal stage*. Around the age of 2–3 years, libidinal gratifications are met through the region of the anus, with tensions and discomforts created by a full bowel relieved through defecation. "There are many people who retain a voluptuous feeling in defecating all through their lives and describe it as being far from small" (Freud, 1920/1977, p. 316). The pleasure of elimination can be increased by the child's "holding in" the feces. Recall your own experience of needing "to go" while driving down an isolated highway and the accompanying sense of relief you felt when you finally located a toilet and "just made it."

An important aspect of the anal stage is toilet training, which involves child and parents in issues of social interaction and conflict. From the parents' point of view, the issue is social control: "Will my child 'go' in this potty or not?" The child's point of view, on the other hand, is power: "Should I do what *I* want to do or what *they* want me to do?" Individual differences are shown in the manner in which parents and children answer these questions behaviorally. Some parents are rigid and demanding, expecting their child to "Go potty! Right here! Right now!" These interactions can lead to a struggle of wills, with the child experiencing conflict and social pressures to perform for Mommy and Daddy. Such experiences can carry over to later situations in life, even building to rebellion against other authority figures in society—schoolteachers, principals, police, and bosses. On the other hand, some parents are highly permissive in accepting their child's preferences and schedule, reacting favorably to the child's personal needs and self-expressions: "Take as long as you want. Look what you made! Isn't that wonderful! We're so happy and proud." Such reactions can foster positive self-esteem in the child and even lead the child to develop artistic and creative tendencies because of the "fun" of "going potty" and parental recognition of defecation "gifts."

Fixation at the anal stage produces the *anal-retentive* personality, which seeks to delay final satisfactions to the last possible moment. Persons with this personality might always eat their desserts last, after others have finished theirs, and constantly "save" for the future. Traits related to this "constipated" type of personality include orderliness, stinginess, and stubbornness. In a famous case study called *The Wolf Man* (1963b), Freud traced an adult's interests in gifts and money to childhood defecation experiences. In contrast, the *anal-expulsive* type of personality exhibits a "diarrhetic" type of fixation. People with anal-expulsive personalities react against parental strictness by "defecating" whenever and wherever they want. Traits associated with this type include messiness, aggressive destructiveness, temper tantrums, explosive emotional outbursts, and even sadistic cruelty.

Phallic stage.   Freud's third stage of personality development occurs at around 4–5 years of age. During the *phallic stage,* satisfaction is gained primarily through stimulation of the penis or clitoris, through masturbation. The phallic stage is central to Freud's theoretical ideas for several reasons:

1. It is the last of the pregenital or infantile stages of psychosexual development.
2. It provides the context in which the important Oedipus, Electra, castration, and penis-envy complexes operate.
3. It forms the basis of psychological and social identification for all children.
4. It results in psychological and sex-role differences between boys and girls.
5. It determines the development of superego, or conscience.

Physical and fantasy pleasures experienced through masturbation are important aspects of the phallic stage. However, satisfaction of libidinous needs is only one part of this developmental experience, because the phallic stage is dominated by the realization that boys have penises whereas girls do not. Freud maintained that this realization is startling to both boys and girls because of their assumption that all persons are supposed to have penises.

"Why don't girls have penises?" According to Freud, answers to this question are accompanied by negative emotions of fear in boys, jealousy in girls, and changes in all children's relationships with their parents. He theorized that boys, up to this stage of development, have feelings of possessive love for their mothers and see their fathers as rivals. His thinking was influenced by the Greek myth of Oedipus Rex, immortalized by Sophocles. In this tragedy, fate determines that Oedipus will kill his father and marry his mother. To Freud, the scenario reflects an internal psychological process characteristic of everyone. Freud termed this

Oedipus complex

Electra complex

dynamic the *Oedipus complex.* (The reverse dynamic for girls, involving love of father and hatred of mother, is called the *Electra complex* by Anna Freud.) The significance Freud attached to the Oedipus complex is evident in his famous assessertion that "if psychoanalysis could boast of no other achievement than the discovery of the repressed Oedipus complex, that alone would give it a claim to be counted among the precious new acquisitions of mankind" (1940/1949, p. 97).

Freud saw boys as experiencing *castration anxiety*, a generalized fear that they might lose their highly prized organ of pleasure (see Box 3.2). Paraphrased in everyday language, the unconscious process runs something like this:

castration anxiety

> Sister used to have a penis, but father got mad and cut it off when he found her playing with it and thinking about having mother all to herself. The same will happen to me when father finds out I don't want him around and want to marry mother. I'd better give mother up, be like father and then marry someone else, who is like mother, when I am older.

Girls, on the other hand, experience *penis envy* — feelings of inferiority over not having the male organ and compensatory wishes to someday obtain one of their own. Again, to paraphrase:

penis envy

> Brother has a penis but I don't, which must be mother's fault because she doesn't have one either. From now on I'm not going to care so much about mother. Father has a penis, so maybe I can get one from him. Or, I'll have a baby boy and it'll be just like having my own penis. Meanwhile, I'm going to stop playing with my clitoris because it's so small and can't be as much fun as boys have when they play with their penises.

The Case of Little Hans   **BOX 3.2**

Freud's (1909/1963a) case study of Little Hans provided the cornerstone for his ideas about the Oedipus complex.

Hans was a 5-year-old boy who was afraid to go outdoors because of a phobia, an exaggerated fear that a horse would bite him. The phobia developed after Hans had seen a large horse fall down in the street. Freud agreed that Hans was afraid, but not about horses. For Freud, the origin of all phobias is unconscious anxiety whose target is different from the more obvious, conscious one. Through the ego defense mechanism of *displacement,* Hans' anxiety had been redirected away from its original source onto horses. Freud hypothesized that Hans actually was afraid of his sexual feelings toward his mother and aggressive wishes toward his father. Freud supported this hypothesis with the following observations:

1. Hans said he wanted to sleep in his mother's bed, "coax with" or caress her, be married to her, and have children "just like daddy." He thus had a repressed, or unconscious, erotic longing for his mother.
2. Hans experienced castration anxiety. His parents had told him that if he continued to play with his "widdler" (penis), it would be cut off. He saw that his younger sister had no "widdler."
3. Hans wanted his mother all to himself, was jealous of his father, and feared that his mother would prefer father's bigger widdler, which was "like a horse." Hans had dreamed of two giraffes, a "big" one and a "crumpled" one. Freud inferred that Hans had a death wish regarding his father.

continued

BOX 3.2
continued

4. Hans showed greatest fear of horses with black muzzles, similar to his father's black mustache. Hans "accidentally" knocked a statue of a horse from its stand. When Hans saw a real horse fall down, he sensed his own aggressive wish that father fall down and die, an idea that frightened Hans because it was too ego-threatening to recognize. Thus, horses were symbolic substitutes for Hans's father.

5. Psychoanalysis helped remove Hans's phobia. Hans's resistances were overcome by "enlightening" conversation. Unconscious fears were brought into the open, and through the process of insight, the unconscious was made conscious. As stated by Freud (1909/1963a), "Hans was really a little Oedipus who wanted to have his father 'out of the way,' to get rid of him, so that he might be alone with his handsome mother and sleep with her" (p. 148).

It should be noted that Freud's analysis of Little Hans was indirect, arrived at mainly through letters received from the boy's father, who served as Hans's "psychoanalyst." The father was biased in favor of Freud's theory, and his questioning of Hans was often quite leading. Several alternatives to Freud's interpretation of Little Hans have been suggested. Marsha Garrison (1978) observes that Hans seemed to fear castration more from his mother than from his father and likely had more of a death wish toward his younger sister. Joseph Wolpe and Stanley Rachman (1960) offer a detailed reinterpretation of Little Hans from a behavior-modification point of view. They conclude that Hans's "cure" was simply desensitization, resulting from repeated discussing of his obvious fear, horses. Maurer (1964) sees Hans as "occupied with the problem of existence," fearing death and wishing "first of all to remain alive, unhurt, safe" (p. 147).

The validity of Freud's Oedipus concept is presently in doubt. While it may fit the interaction patterns of some families, its universality has been seriously questioned by the social psychoanalysts, and simpler, behavioral explanations have been well received.

At this point, the foundations of socialization are set. Faced with fantasized threats of either "losing my penis" or "giving up Mama," boys choose the latter. They react to the imagined threat of castration by accepting their father's dominant status and power. For safety's sake, they identify with father, becoming "just like Dad," introjecting or accepting his values and rules, even though these might be opposite to their previous wishes and feelings. Thus, the superego or conscience is formed as an inner moral code based on the father's translation of society's taboos, rights, and wrongs. The formation of the superego resolves the Oedipal complex and cements the ego ideal.

If libidinous feelings toward mother, the first object of childhood phallic pleasure, are not entirely eliminated, they will be actively kept buried deep in the unconscious aspect of personality. This occurs through the ego defense mechanisms, which operate automatically, without any conscious awareness on the part of the person involved. The most important defense mechanism in this process is *repression,* a selective type of memory. Repression protects the personality by allowing ego to be conscious only of those thoughts and urges that it finds acceptable or that actively push threatening experiences out of consciousness. Other defense mechanisms can be called upon as well, modifying instincts and wishes and distorting subjective reality through denial, fantasy, displacement, and projection. Examples of some defense mechanisms appear in Table 3.2.

Freud saw the socialization process as different for girls, with the result that girls' superego development is inferior to that of boys. He saw girls as being less motivated to adopt society's standards because of their already "castrated" condition. Girls don't have anything to lose. Identification with the same-sex parent also is more difficult for girls, for two reasons. First, girls experience ambivalence toward mother. Pre-Oedipal love mixes with Oedipal hostility feelings because girls blame mother for their missing penis and devalue her for not having a penis of her own. Second, girls' Electra complex turns them toward father in hopes of obtaining the missing penis from him, perhaps by having him all to themselves. Mother not only has too little with which girls might identify, she is also the object of her daughter's jealousy in relation to father.

TABLE 3.2   Examples of Ego Defense Mechanisms

Defense mechanisms	Popular examples
Denial	"President Kennedy was assassinated? Don't joke about things like that. You can't expect me to believe that."
Rationalization	"So what if I did take a box of pencils home? I've spent 37 years working for this crummy company. It's the least they could do for me. Besides, it's no big deal."
Fantasy	Tevye's song, from *Fiddler on the Roof:* "If I were a rich man . . . I wouldn't have to work hard . . . I'd build a real tall house. . . ."
Projection	"It's the Prof's fault I flunked that test! She just didn't want me to do well. She spent a lot of time figuring out questions I wouldn't know the answers to. She tricked me by asking questions that were so simple and obvious that only her favorite students would know the right answers. She's so dumb and stupid."
Introjection	Song Lyric: "I want a girl just like the girl that married dear old dad."
Displacement	A researcher's grant proposal is rejected for funding. She tells her lab assistant he's been goofing off, who tells his wife she's been ignoring the kids, who tells their 6-year-old to pick up all the toys, who throws a shoe at the family dog, which pees on the kitchen floor.
Repression	Song lyric: "I don't know why I love you like I do, I don't know why, I just do."
Intellectualization	"I know smoking is bad for my health. It just means I'll get lung cancer or die earlier than other people. That's OK. I don't care one way or the other."
Undoing	Lady Macbeth, wringing her hands to atone for guilt over her husband's murder: "Out, damned spot!"

Note: The authoritative work on defense mechanisms was written by Anna Freud (1936/1967).

Latency stage.　Freud's fourth stage of psychosexual development is notable for its absence of dominant erogenous zones and readily visible events or outcomes. As its name implies, *latency* is a quiet period of transition from pregenital to genital stages, between ages 6 and 12. Libidinous instincts previously seeking expression are reduced in intensity or more deeply buried in the unconscious through repression. They are transformed, through *sublimation,* and redirected away from their original instinctual aims in new directions that are more personally and culturally acceptable. For example, an adolescent psychologically fixated at the anal stage of development might, unconsciously, become interested in sculpting with clay. This would be an acceptable substitute (sublimation) for earlier desires to make or play with feces. Similarly, a person who is fearful of intimate sexual contact might find personal and social satisfactions "from a distance" by becoming a centerfold photographer for *Playboy* or *Playgirl.*

Genital stage.　Freud's final stage of development is the *genital* or mature stage of psychosexuality, which begins during puberty. It differs from the first three (pregenital) stages by the type of cathexes that accompany it. *Cathexes* are investments or attachments of the personality's libidinous energy either to real objects in the external world or to fantasized images in the inner world. Pregenital cathexes are typified by the self-centered quality of maximizing pleasure from one's own body, supported by one-sided "me first" relationships with parents or

In psychoanalytic theory, a person's capacities to love and to work are the major indicators of mature personality functioning.

peers. In contrast, genital-stage cathexes are directed less selfishly and more altruistically toward something other than oneself.

These externally directed energies are represented by two psychoanalytic ideals of mature, normal personality functioning: to love and to work. Thus, loving and caring relationships with other people develop during adolescence and young adulthood, along with interests and activities related to productive, cooperative work within society. The successful pursuit of these goals contributes to the fulfillment of Eros' instinctual aim—preservation of self and species. Earlier cathexes do not disappear entirely but are rechanneled and integrated, through sublimation, with those occurring during the genital stage. Persons unable to make psychological attachments during their early years will show abnormal personality patterns later on: immaturity, sexual deviation, neurosis.

Another characteristic of this stage is the final resolution of the phallic-stage identification difficulties theorized for women. Mature women accept the absence of a penis and identify with the vagina. With this change to "femininity," the clitoris "should wholly or in part hand over its sensitivity, and at the same time its importance, to the vagina" (Freud, 1901/1965, p. 118). This viewpoint supported Freud's belief in vaginal orgasm as the standard of mature, normal sexual experience for women. The standard of vaginal orgasm generated much controversy (Rohrbaugh, 1979) and has been brought into question by experimental findings on female sexual response. For example, Masters and Johnson (1966) report that vaginal and clitoral orgasm are not distinct, as Freud believed, and that the clitoris participates in orgasm even when not stimulated directly.

Table 3.3 summarizes the five stages of psychosexual development identified by Freud.

FREUD AND SEXISM

Because of the different socialization processes for girls and boys, Freud believed that both the sexual identity and the superego of girls are likely to be weaker than boys', more dependent on the defense mechanism of repression, and more long-term in development. Freud's startling conclusion was that "for

TABLE 3.3   Summary of Freud's Stages of Psychosexual Development

Stages	Ages	Zones	Activities	Task
Pregenital (infantile)				
Oral	0–1	Mouth	Sucking Biting	Weaning
Anal	2–3	Anus	Expelling Retaining	Toilet training
Phallic	4–5	Penis Clitoris	Masturbating	Identifying
Latency	6–12		Repressing	Transforming
Genital	13+	Penis Vagina	Being sexually intimate Sublimating	Loving another Working

women the level of what is ethically normal is different from what it is in men" (Freud, 1925/1959, p. 196). Another psychological consequence is that women switch from an active sexual role of clitoral masturbation to a passive, submissive role of vaginal intercourse, in which satisfaction requires the presence of a male organ. Freud adhered strongly to these beliefs, not allowing himself "to be deflected from such conclusions by the denials of the feminists, who are anxious to force us to regard the two sexes as completely equal in position and worth" (1925/1959, p. 197).

Freud clearly placed high importance on physical sexual organs as determining different developmental processes and personality characteristics for men and women. The implications of the belief that "anatomy is destiny" (Erikson, 1968b) went far beyond biological differences in sex organs to psychological identities and sociocultural sex roles as well. In fact, Freud's theory of personality development was biased by the primary emphasis he placed on the male sexual organ as the starting point of his ideas, and he meant what he said (Fliegel, 1982), despite later attempts to suggest otherwise. As stated by Joanna Rohrbaugh (1979), "Freud takes the male as the basic pattern for health and normality" (p. 108).

This male bias was questioned by later psychoanalysts who proposed revisions of Freud's ideas. For example, Karen Horney (1926) and Clara Thompson (1943) presented alternative, cultural perspectives to Freud's biological, "boy's-eye" point of view. If a concept such as penis envy does influence childhood development among girls, Horney and Thompson maintained, its origins can be traced to social rather than anatomical factors. Penis envy could only be a symbolic reflection of men's comparatively greater cultural and economic advantages, including social prestige and power. Anthropologist Margaret Mead (1974) went further by offering a parallel, female-oriented concept of womb envy. This concept would account for compensatory rituals observed among men, cross-culturally, who obviously desired but were missing childbearing organs. For Mead, as boys began to accept the fact that they could not have children, they would learn to place a very high value on achievement. Freud, in fact, did claim that men are more often professionally creative because of their inability to bear children.

BOX 3.1 REVISITED	*Freud's "Answers" to the Preliminary Self-Test*

Now that we have reviewed Freud's basic concepts, you may find it interesting to compare your assumptions about personality with those of Freud. How closely do your answers in Box 3.1 agree with those of Freud, indicated below? Are you surprised by any of the similarities or differences? Count the number of matches as your score and compare your results with those of other students in class.

1. My basic personality is the same today as when I was about 5 years old.
   TRUE: "The child is father to the man."

continued

BOX 3.1
REVISITED
continued

2. I have little knowledge of my real personality or its development.
   TRUE: Personality is largely unconscious, similar to an iceberg submerged in water.

3. I choose to lead my life in a self-directed manner.
   FALSE: We are not in control of our own fates. "Man is not master in his own house."

4. My basic motivations are sex and aggression.
   TRUE: Human behavior is governed by the two basic instincts of life (generalized "sexual" pleasure) and death (destructiveness).

5. Many of my behaviors are irrational, in that I repeatedly do things that make little logical sense.
   TRUE: People are dominated by their instincts and emotions, not by logic and intellect, and they compulsively relive their past.

6. I have had few inner conflicts in my life.
   FALSE: Psychological conflict is a fact of life. Only the dead have no conflicts.

7. I have had abnormal experiences during my lifetime, including psychotic ones.
   TRUE: Abnormal behaviors are simply exaggerations of normal ones, and dreams share all the absurdities and delusions of psychoses.

8. I am afraid to know my true self, and I keep unpleasant aspects of my personality hidden from myself.
   TRUE: Personality is a complicated system of psychological avoidance and defense, triggered by feelings of anxiety.

9. As a child, I had sexual wishes and feelings toward my opposite-sex parent.
   TRUE: Inevitably, all sons live through the Oedipus complex of "killing" father and "marrying" mother, and all daughters live through the Electra complex of "wanting" father's baby.

10. Women and men are psychological equals.
    FALSE: Women cherish the hope of someday getting a penis and differ from men in their weaker ethical development.

11. The best way for me to change my personality is to enter long-term therapy with a trained expert who will provide insight into my early childhood experiences.
    TRUE: There is nothing better than psychoanalysis for making conscious that which is unconscious, thereby minimizing personality conflicts and problems.

Basic Concepts: Jung

A number of early-20th-century psychiatrists developed the revolutionary framework initially established by Freud. Foremost among them was Carl Gustav Jung, who extended Freud's "discovery" of the unconscious beyond the individual to the "collective unconscious" of humanity, manifested in art, literature, myths, folklore, and dreams. Jung adhered to Freud's assumption about the biological

CARL JUNG.
"I am a solitary, because I know things and must hint at things which other people do not know, and usually do not even want to know."

origins of personality, believing that the collective unconscious is transmitted genetically. Jung also believed it essential that each person "listen to" the wisdom of the collective unconscious.

Jung was born in Wesswill, Switzerland, in 1875. As a boy, he seemed always frightened and sickly, suffering unexplained fainting spells (which he was quite willing to make use of to avoid school and homework). He had "anxiety dreams," experienced overpowering visions, and was fearful of his mother, whose intense moods were unpredictable. He recalled running at the sight of a Jesuit priest walking down the road, whom Jung mistakenly believed was "wearing women's clothes." This event terrified Jung for days. Another event, a recurrent dream, haunted Jung for years. It had to do with what he called "the man-eater," a ceremonial phallus 12–15 feet in height. Jung steadfastly resisted the temptation to mention this dream to anyone until he was 65 years old.

Jung spent much of his youth by himself, in "extreme loneliness," talking out his innermost thoughts to a small mannequin he had carved and secreted away under the floorboards of the family's "forbidden attic."

> I am a solitary, because I know things and must hint at things which other people do not know, and usually do not even want to know [Jung, 1963, p. 42]. Loneliness does not come from having no people about one, but from being unable to communicate the things that seem important to oneself, or from holding certain views which others find inadmissible. (p. 356)

Following medical training at the University of Basel, Jung had his first meeting with a person of "real importance," Sigmund Freud, in 1907. This meeting resulted in a 13-hour conversation that went on, virtually without pause, until three o'clock in the morning. Freud was struck with Jung's intellectualism and believed Jung might aid general acceptance of psychoanalysis because he was not Jewish. Jung was adopted as a beloved "eldest son," dubbed Freud's "crown prince" successor, and chosen first president of the International Psychoanalytic Association, which Freud founded in 1910.

In 1911, Jung broke with Freud. Wracked by anguish and uncertainty, Jung decided to open himself up to the depths of his unconscious (as had Freud), surviving by "brute strength" a voluntary three-year confrontation that would have "shattered" the personalities of others. This personal encounter provided him with primary material for a lifetime's work. He traced all later writings and creative activity to these initial fantasies, dreams, emotions, and inner images. Jung's interesting orientation to his autobiography (1963) is summarized in its title, *Memories, Dreams, Reflections*. It begins with a characteristically subjective approach to personality: "My life is a story of the self-realization of the unconscious" (p. 3). He directs readers interested in a more external, objective story of his life and time to look elsewhere.

THE COLLECTIVE UNCONSCIOUS: "THE MIND OF OUR ANCIENT ANCESTORS"

One of Freud's greatest contributions was to demonstrate the influence of dynamic, unconscious influences on personality. Jung expanded this contribution by hypothesizing two levels of unconscious influence: personal and collective.

Jung's *personal unconscious* is very similar to Freud's concept of the unconscious. Ideas once conscious have since been forgotten or repressed. However, Jung emphasizes feeling-toned *complexes,* or clusters of emotionally related ideas, feelings, and memories acquired by each person during a lifetime. Complexes may become strong enough to dominate personality, appearing and disappearing according to their own laws and behaving "like independent beings." They often interfere with conscious functioning and willful intentions. Jung (1910) demonstrated this by detecting a thief whose verbal responses to emotionally relevant stimulus words on the Word Association Test ("steal," "money," "guilty") showed uncommon answers, delayed reaction times, inability to remember earlier answers, and nervous behaviors.

personal unconscious

complexes

By contrast, Jung's *collective unconscious* refers to universally shared thoughts and feelings that have existed since ancient times and are not peculiar to any single individual. The collective unconscious contains dynamic psychic forces that are identical in all individuals, in all societies, and for all of humankind. It is a sort of living "museum" of distilled memories of the human species, which goes back to the time of "grey antiquity." This archaic heritage has arisen from recurrent, identical human situations in which "patterns of instinctual behavior" predominate. Thus, the collective unconscious does not owe its existence to acquired personal experience, but is inborn, universal, and impersonal.

collective unconscious

What led Jung to the hypothesis of a collective unconscious? Jung was an avid and scholarly reader. He had broad, sometimes esoteric interests in many fields: archeology, history, religion, mythology, and even alchemy, a now discredited precursor of science prevalent during the Middle Ages. Jung was struck by remarkable consistencies in comparative studies of different cultures, religions, literature, and art forms, spanning thousands of years. Despite differences in time, geography, race, culture, and historical development, people everywhere seemed to express their life experiences in highly similar ways. The similarities encompassed many forms of human experience: attitudes, ideas, feelings, actions, fantasies, and dreams. Jung saw much of human experience as being communicated through common, age-old symbols, artistic figures, myths, legends, fairy tales, and folklore. Jung attributed these motives and images which he believed could "spring anew in every age and clime without historical tradition or migration" to the collective unconscious.

ARCHETYPES

archetypes

The contents of the collective unconscious are called *archetypes,* primitive forces or "pre-existent forms." Archetypes are innate psychic predispositions that lead people to apprehend, experience, and respond to the world in certain ways. Jung explains their nature as *psychoid* — analogous to Freud's biological instincts, but more psychological. The existence of archetypes is due "exclusively to heredity," linked especially to the brain and autonomic nervous system. Therefore, the mind of the newborn infant is not a *tabula rasa,* or blank slate, but is imprinted with forms of past experience. What is inherited are not specific ideas or images but potential, general types of inner patterns and functioning. Table 3.4 identifies examples of archetypal constellations of ancestral experience, revolving around some central themes.

TABLE 3.4   Examples of Jungian Archetypes

Archetypes	Symbols	Definitions
Self	Mandala or "magic circle"	Organizing core of personality, as wholeness and unity
Persona	Mask	Public, conforming, artificial self
Shadow	Monster	Darker aspects of self, repressed animal instincts, inferiorities
Anima	Woman	Feminine component in men
Animus	Man	Masculine component in women
Wise old man	Prophet	Spiritual principle in men
Magna mater	Fertility goddess	Material principle in women, of nature and earth
God	Eye of the sun	A psychic reality, projected final realization on external reality
Quaternity	Squared circle with cross	Natural fourfold division of ideal completeness

According to Jung, masks are symbolic of an individual's persona, or public self.

Jung likened the process by which archetypes exert their force to falling in love at first sight. This experience has its own autonomy and "can suddenly seize you." It may be that the person in love has been carrying "a certain eternal image" of a potential partner, without necessarily knowing it. Another person then appears who meets that inner image and "instantly you get the seizure; you are caught" (quoted in Evans, 1964, p. 51). Jung believed every personality contains an opposite-sex component in the form of unconscious archetypes, thereby making all persons psychologically androgenous, or unisexual. The *anima* archetype is the feminine aspect present in all men, while *animus* is the masculine aspect present in all women. Positive attraction indicates that one's potential love partner has the same qualities present in one's opposite-sex archetype. Aversion indicates just the opposite. Difficulties arise when the person in love relates to the other not according to reality but primarily according to unconscious archetypal influences, as in the relationship of one's anima to the other's animus. In a sense, persons are "forced" into love, not by personal choice, but by deterministic, unconscious influences that originated thousands of years ago! One's matchmaker is an internal template.

In another context, Jung (1958/1978) speculated that 20th-century interest in unidentified flying objects (UFOs) may reflect the archetype of wholeness or totality. He noted that the "visionary rumor" about flying saucers began toward the end of World War II, a time of intense conflict and strife. The psychic basis of such a rumor is collective emotional tension, distress, or danger, which is then projected outward. Wholeness is often symbolized by a *mandala,* or "magic circle." Thus, the "many thousands of individual testimonies" involving round flying bodies may be a compensation on the part of the collective unconscious seeking to bring about order and "heal the split in our apocalyptic age by means of the symbol of the circle" (Jung, 1964, p. 285). UFOs are frequently reported as luminous disks that come to earth from another planet (the unconscious) and contain strange creatures (archetypes) (Hall & Nordby, 1973).

Archetypes seem present always and everywhere in the psyche. While predominantly emotional, they also have intellectual elements. However, no archetype has ever been present in an individual's conscious awareness. Archetypes manifest themselves only secondarily, through symbols and behavior. The form of their appearance is more primitive in dreams than in myths, whose greater complexity is due to the operation of conscious elaboration. Like complexes, it is possible for archetypes to become so powerful that they constitute a separate personality system, as sometimes occurs in schizophrenia.

Synchronicity.   It is important to understand that archetypes do not cause behavior. Their existence, while simultaneous with behavior, only parallels it. In this context, Jung introduced a unique principle of acausality called *synchronicity* —the simultaneous occurrence of two events that are related but have no direct cause-and-effect connection. The phenomenon is one of meaningful coincidence, involving co-occurrences of psychological and physical realities that are independent of each other. Jung used the concept of synchronicity to explain simultaneous occurrences of inner images (archetypes) and outer events (behaviors), without implying causality. Inner, psychological realities also include dreams, visions, forebodings, and hunches. Outer, physical realities include any observable events from the past, present, or future. A few everyday examples are: "It's strange that you telephoned, because I was just thinking about you." "I would have been in that plane crash if I hadn't canceled my reservation at the last moment." "Speak of the Devil, and he appears."

Jung also linked synchronicity to the area of parapsychology, a subfield of psychology in search of acceptable scientific explanations for extrasensory perception (ESP), mental telepathy, and clairvoyance. Arthur Koestler (1972) has popularized the synchronicity principle in his book *The Roots of Coincidence,* which addresses paradoxes in physics as well as parapsychology.

DREAMS AS MESSAGES FROM A WISE UNCONSCIOUS

Jung was highly respectful of dreams and fantasies. Dreams were the primary vehicle of his approach to therapy. "I have spent more than half a century in investigating natural symbols, and I have come to the conclusion that dreams and their symbols are not stupid and meaningless" (Jung, 1964, p. 93). He was convinced dreams contained important messages from the "wise" unconscious. The task was simply to decipher these messages, which Jung was willing to take the trouble to understand.

One type of message, mentioned earlier in relation to flying saucers, is *compensation.* This basic law of psychic behavior refers to observations that a dream's meaning is often just the opposite of the person's conscious experience. In this sense, the collective unconscious represents the second of "two sides to every story," reflecting functions that are autonomous and compensatory. Jacobi (1962) offers an example and interpretation of a compensation dream:

> Someone dreams that it is spring, but that his favourite tree in the garden has only dry branches. This year it bears no leaves or blossoms. What the dream is trying to communicate is this: Can you see yourself in this tree? That is how you are, although you don't want to recognize it. Your nature has dried up, no green grows within you. Such dreams are a lesson to persons whose consciousness has become autonomous and overemphasized. Of course the dreams of an unusually unconscious person, living entirely by his instincts, would correspondingly emphasize his "other side." Irresponsible scoundrels often have moralizing dreams while paragons of virtue frequently have immoral dream images. (p. 76)

Another type of message is *anticipation,* through which dreams may "foretell" future events and outcomes. A personal illustration may be given. The father of one of the authors told of a dream he had during his high school years. He was riding a bicycle, with his brother on the handlebars, when a hole suddenly opened in the street, toppling both of them. The sudden appearance of the hole was unexplained. Such an incident occurred two days following the dream.

PERSONALITY TYPOLOGY

Two psychological attitudes: extraversion and introversion. After 20 years of observing people "of all classes from all the great nations," Jung (1921/ 1971) theorized that human beings could be divided into two groups based on "two fundamentally different general attitudes," extraversion and introversion (p. 549). He defined *attitude* as "a readiness of the psyche to act or react in a certain way" to experience (p. 414). He defined *type* as a habitual attitude, or a person's "characteristic way." Although extraversion and introversion are discussed at length in Chapter 9, we would be remiss not to introduce Jung's version of these two *psychological types,* which many psychologists consider his best-known contribution to personality theory (Evans, 1964).

psychological types

According to Jung (1921/1971), *extraversion* is an "outward-turning" of libido or psychic energy. It involves a positive movement of interest away from one's inner experience toward outer experience. The extravert is characterized by

extraversion

> interest in the external object, responsiveness, and a ready acceptance of external happenings, a desire to influence and be influenced by events, a need to join in and get "with it," the capacity to endure bustle and noise of every kind, and actually find them enjoyable, constant attention to the surrounding world, the cultivation of friends and acquaintances, none too carefully selected, and finally by the great importance attached to the figure one cuts, and hence by a strong tendency to make a show of oneself. (p. 549)

introversion

Introversion is an "inward-turning" of psychic energy. It involves a negative movement or withdrawal of subjective interest away from outer objects and toward one's inner subject. Jung believed that introverts are less well adjusted than extraverts. The introvert

> holds aloof from external happenings, does not join in, has a distinct dislike of society as soon as he finds himself among too many people. In a large gathering he feels lonely and lost. The more crowded it is, the greater becomes his resistance. He is not in the least "with it," and has no love of enthusiastic get-togethers. He is not a good mixer. What he does, he does in his own way, barricading himself against influences from outside. He is apt to appear awkward, often seeming inhibited. . . . His own world is a safe harbour, a carefully tended and walled-in garden, closed to the public and hidden from prying eyes. His own company is the best. He feels at home in his world, where the only changes are made by himself. His best work is done with his own resources, on his own initiative, and in his own way. (Jung, 1921/1971, pp. 550–551)

Four psychological functions: sensing, thinking, feeling, and intuiting.   Jung also theorized that there are four orientations, or basic psychological functions, in personality: sensing, thinking, feeling, and intuiting. The first and last are considered "irrational," while the middle two are "rational." Personality is often dominated by one of the functions, which may be found either in introverts or extraverts, making eight combinations possible. *Sensation* determines *that* something is present. It is the same as sensory perceptions of sight, sound, smell, taste, and touch. It is especially characteristic of children, with emphasis placed on actual observations or "facts." *Thinking* understands *what* is present and what it means. It brings the contents of ideation into conceptual connection with one another to form intellectual concepts or reach solutions. *Feeling* evaluates *how* experiences strike us, whether they are suitable to us or not. Feeling is a kind of judgment that is an entirely subjective process. It imparts a definite value, of acceptance-rejection or of like-dislike. It also includes mood. *Intuition* suggests *where* something seems to have come from and where it may be going. It is a kind of "instinctive apprehension," of unconscious origin, with no tangible basis.

It should be noted that Jung was not primarily interested in classifying people into distinct categories. His aims were to (1) understand dimensions of individual differences, (2) guide research, and (3) aid clinical evaluation of patients.

PERSONALITY DEVELOPMENT

individuation

Individuation: differentiating oneself from the collective.   For Jung, the direction of personality development is *individuation*—"the process by which a person becomes a psychological 'in-dividual,' that is, a separate, indivisible unity or 'whole' " (Jung, 1936/1959, p. 275). The individual's realization of a whole self or personality develops out of the general, undifferentiated collective. At first, the person becomes an individual by refusing to accept the total collective that is within. However, the person eventually begins to accept what is within as part of his or her personality, rather than "projecting" it outside the self, onto others, as "not me." Thus, personality development is expressed through the archetypes, as the person comes to terms with each, in sequence (Hogan, 1976): (1) The persona dissolves when the person recognizes the artificiality of society's goals. (2) The shadow is assimilated when there is awareness of one's selfish and destructive "dark side" (Freud's "id"). (3) Acceptance of the anima or animus requires recognition of opposite-sex components in one's personality. (4) Commitment to an archetype symbolic of spiritual or creative meaning allows one to tackle the final stage of individuation (which Hogan sees as "telescoped" during Jungian therapy). *Recognition* serves to integrate archetypes from the collective unconscious, resulting in self-knowledge (Freud's "insight"). Recognition allows projections to be withdrawn from the external world, thereby releasing energy for continued personal development.

The process of individuation proceeds slowly, in stages covering the entire life span. Fulfillment of individuation is "a favor that must be paid for dearly." This is because separation from the unconscious, undifferentiated herd is unavoidable, as is the expansion of one's consciousness. Archetypes need to be recognized every step of the way, which is no easy task. However, the process is not simply one of antagonism to the collective, but a continuing adaptation to collective standards. Think of a plant that must first be able to grow in soil (collective unconscious) before it can unfold its own particular fullness (personality). In its ultimate form, individuation shows three characteristics not found in children: definiteness, fullness, and maturity.

Four stages of life-span development. Jung discussed four stages of personality development: childhood, youth, middle age, and old age (Hall & Nordby, 1973).

four stages of personality development

Childhood, which begins at birth, is relatively problem-free. It is dominated by instincts, dependency, and a psychological atmosphere provided by parents. Development of a conscious ego occurs gradually, as does one's separation from the protective "psychic womb" of home when schooling starts.

Youth—which includes adolescence and youth adulthood—begins at puberty, at which time physiological changes are accompanied by "psychic revolution." The demands of life require more independent decision making, and the person finds it difficult but necessary to give up the illusions and fantasies of childhood. "Psychic birth" occurs as the psyche begins to take on its own character, although experiences of sexuality and inferiority may create problems. The person begins to establish vocational, marital, and community places in the world.

Middle age begins around age 40, marking the "second half" of life. One's task during this stage is to build a whole personality. Jung observed many of his adult patients dealing with issues of lost zest and meaning in life. Their focus was on inner, spiritual values, different from earlier adaptations that were more external, extraverted, and materialistic. Contemplation becomes more important than activity. Opposite psychological processes, such as introversion-extraversion or feeling-thinking, may be synthesized through symbols of spiritual transcendence. One example is the symbol of yang and yin, representing universal male/ female principles in Chinese philosophy.

The period of extreme *old age* parallels childhood because of a return to submersion in the unconscious. The mandala of a snake biting its own tail is symbolic of life coming full circle. Death is as important as birth. Jung found belief in a hereafter so universal that he considered it to be a manifestation of the unconscious (see D. T. Campbell, 1975). Perhaps psychic life continues after bodily death because the psyche has not yet attained complete self-realization.

One aspect of Jung's view of interpersonal relationships differs quite markedly from those of Freud and the social psychoanalysts discussed in the next chapter. Jung sees individuals as relating psychologically to others more on the basis of universal, inner archetypes than on others' individual characteristics. Jung attributes only "limited etiological significance" to a child's personal mother and father. The influences mothers reportedly have on their children "do not come from the mother herself, but rather from the archetype projected upon her" (1959, p. 83). In effect, children respond less to their parents than to the archetypes they have of "Mother" or "Father." The Mother archetype is a composite of experiences with *all* mothers down through the ages for all of humankind. It has "an almost infinite variety of aspects": mother, grandmother, stepmother, mother-in-law, nurse, governess, "good" mother, "bad" mother, Mother of God, Great Mother, fertility, fruitfulness, cooking vessels, rose, cow, witch, dragon, deep water, and so on. On the other hand, parents do have an influence on the child's development of other archetypes. A boy's interactions with his personal mother and father influence the development of his anima and shadow, respectively. The pattern is reversed for girls, indicating the importance of sex differences.

These ideas are in keeping with Jung's assumption of the collective unconscious. Remember that during the childhood stage of development, the infant has no real consciousness, ego, or separate identity, and is almost totally dependent on its parents. The infant's unconscious is not personal, only collective.

self-realization

Personality as self-realization. Jung treats personality as the highest realization of the inborn distinctiveness of the individual. Its core is the *self,* the central archetype or fullest expression of the person's individuality. The symbol of self is the mandala, the completeness of which is symbolized by a circle or sphere. Personality does not necessarily imply consciousness. The self is both unconscious and conscious, as is *ego,* an aspect of the self that serves as the "centrum" or center of consciousness. Even without consciousness, the self is purposive and contains the life goal of the individual. "Consciousness grows out of an unconscious psyche which is older than it, and which goes on functioning together with it or even in spite of it" (Jung, 1959, p. 281).

Supporting Evidence

This section reviews some of the research relevant to selected concepts of Freud and Jung. Both theories have stimulated research, although with mixed results.

FREUD: PSYCHOSEXUAL CONFLICTS AND DEFENSES

J. McVicker Hunt (1979) assessed evidence from different streams of investigation flowing from Freud's ideas. He found that the studies "lent support" to Freud's general proposition about "the special importance of early experience" (p. 119), but not to the specific psychosexual experiences hypothesized by Freud. The historical contributions of classical psychoanalysis are reflected in Hunt's observation that until the 20th century, the special importance of early experience on psychological development "was only an opinion held by occasional philosophers" (p. 135).

Salvatore Maddi's (1968) review of empirical studies led him to conclude that there was qualified support for two Freudian concepts. First, while not all behavior is defensive, the general concept of ego defense is "tenable," supported by a "rather convincing" number of studies related to repression. Second, "there is more evidence of castration anxiety among men than women" (p. 392).

Lloyd Silverman (1976) summarized two 10-year research programs bearing on specific Freudian concepts. Results of these independent, laboratory studies support the relationship between certain types of abnormal behavior and certain types of unconscious conflict over libidinal and aggressive wishes. One series of studies involved 39 groups, each comprised of 24–46 subjects: stutterers, depressives, homosexuals, and schizophrenics. Subjects were asked to view flickers of light through the eyepiece of a tachistoscope, a machine that exposes visual stimuli for fractions of a second. Visual information relevant to the participants' psychological conflicts was presented to subjects *subliminally,* below their level of conscious awareness (Dixon, 1971). As predicted by Freudian theory, levels of psychopathology could be increased or decreased, as measured by personality tests (Silverman, 1971), by manipulating psychologically relevant information. Persons with oral-aggressive conflicts were stirred up by the message "Cannibal eats person" but not by "Murderer stabs victim." Persons with oral-receptive conflicts showed decreased anxiety with the wishful message "Mommy and I are one" but not with "I am losing Mommy." In the latter case, the fantasy of oneness may have implied greater availability of "oral supplies" from mother, thereby reducing aggressive reactions to feeling deprived by a possible loss of mother.

A number of research studies on castration anxiety in men and penis envy in women have been reported. Blum (1949, 1950, 1962) assessed psychosexual fantasies in college students who were asked to tell stories to the Blacky Test, a series of cartoon pictures about a dog named Blacky. In the 1949 study, differences in test responses of 119 men and 90 women agreed with "some aspects" of psychoanalytic theory. In the 1962 study, men who were high and low in castration conflict told contrasting stories in response to a picture of Blacky looking on as a knife falls toward sibling Tippy's tail. One example of a "low castration anxiety" response is as follows:

> Tippy, Blacky's little brother, is about to have his tail chopped off unknowingly. Blacky is about to bark and warn him of his danger. Physically there is nothing he can actually do, but he will also try to push him away from the block. (p. 135)

Compare the preceding with the following example of a "strong castration anxiety" response:

> Blacky doesn't like the looks of this at all, and he's very conscious of his big black tail out behind him. But his big worry is to see if this new thing that his sister is undergoing will hurt much. The expression on Tippy's face is worried, and Blacky's beginning to think that way. (p. 135)

Another study by Hall and Van de Castle (1965) found that men report more dreams related to castration anxiety (CA) than to castration wishes (CW) and penis envy (PE), while women show the reverse pattern. Three groups of college students, 20 men and 20 women per group, recorded their dreams as part of a class project. All of the 1,909 dreams were scored by two judges to determine the presence of CA, CW, and PE. The majority of male dreamers had higher CA scores, and the majority of female dreamers had higher CW and PE scores. Zero CA scores were observed for 50% of the women but only 13% of the men. Findings for men were replicated using an additional sample of men aged 37–54, suggesting a stable rate of castration anxiety from young adulthood to middle age.

A major review of research studies related to psychoanalysis was reported by Paul Kline (1972). It updated Sears' (1943) earlier, negative review, citing more than 700 references. Kline offered a positive view. Wholesale rejection of psychoanalytic theory is not possible, he concluded, because "too much that is distinctively Freudian has been verified [and] there are few good experiments which actually refute the theory" (p. 350).

Overall, although research reports have supported some general aspects of classical psychoanalytic theory, they have been enmeshed in criticism and controversy. Lindzey and Hall (1965) have been among those least pessimistic about the status of psychoanalysis, expressing their belief that "the situation is far from bleak today" (p. 1). However, experimental support for Freud's theory generally remains weak.

JUNG: PSYCHOLOGICAL TYPES

Recall that Jung's typology is based on combinations of the two attitudes of extraversion and introversion with the four functions of thinking, feeling, sensing, and intuiting. These ideas about personality types have been the focus of a number of research studies.

Jung's typology was investigated empirically by Gorlow, Simonson, and Krauss (1966). The subjects were 98 introductory psychology students at the Pennsylvania State University, two-thirds of whom were male. The results supported the hypothesis that subjects using a self-report technique would order themselves into the eight types postulated by Jung. However, extraverted types emerged much more clearly than introverted types in the population studied. Evidence was strongest for the extraverted-feeling type, followed by the extraverted-thinking type. The significant relationship observed between extraverted-feeling type and sex of subjects supported Jung's assertion that this type of personality is more commonly female than male.

The most popular psychological measure of Jung's typology is the Myers-Briggs Type Indicator (MBTI) (Myers, 1962). The MBTI is a self-report questionnaire that has been used in 400–500 studies (Carlyn, 1977; Carskadon, 1978). Although some MBTI types are "quite similar" to those postulated by Jung, significant correlations between two of four MBTI scales suggest there may be fewer types than those theorized by Jung.

Carskadon (1978) has used the MBTI to predict the quality of contributions made by students to discussions in undergraduate psychology classes at Mississippi State University. Carskadon noticed that self-described MBTI extraverts made "very infrequent discussion contributions," whereas introverts made "frequent and thought-provoking contributions." However, this pattern seemed to be related less to the extraversion-introversion dimension and more to the sensation-intuition dimension. Carskadon tested the hypothesis that the best classroom contributions come from intuitive types. At the end of a semester, 65 students in three psychology courses were asked to rate every class member on quality of discussion contributions during the course. A 3-point rating scale was used (3 = excellent, 2 = good, and 1 = fair to poor). Carskadon also rated the students, independently. The correlation of .84 between class means and instructor ratings was highly significant ($p < .001$). Results for both sets of rating data also proved significant. Students with high intuitive scores obtained the highest discussion ratings, while students with high sensation scores obtained the lowest ratings (peer ratings = 2.05 and 1.62, respectively; instructor ratings = 2.06 and 1.26, respectively). All other MBTI types showed equivalent mid-range ratings, including extraversion and introversion types (peer ratings = 1.86 and 1.84, respectively; instructor ratings = 1.66 and 1.69, respectively). In suggesting that instructors ensure a balance of types in discussion groups, Carskadon noted:

> Too many extraverts can give all action but little thought; too many introverts, all thought and no action. Too many thinking types can use all logic and no human values; too many feeling types, all subjective values and no critical analysis. Too many judging types tend to produce lots of decisions and conclusions based on too few data; and too many perceptive types, lots of data but no decisions or conclusions. (p. 141)

In brief, empirical support has been greatest for Jung's concept of the extraverted personality type. At the same time, a large number of studies are complicated by the fact that the most popular measure of types, the MBTI, departs from Jung's original schema of eight types by assuming the existence of 16 personality types, some of which are not independent of one another.

Applications

Psychoanalysis developed in a clinical setting and is intimately tied to questions about how people's personalities might be changed for the better. These origins are reflected in two major applications of psychoanalytic theory: personality-assessment techniques and procedures for changing personality.

PERSONALITY-ASSESSMENT TECHNIQUES

To talk of unconscious aspects of personality is one thing; to observe or measure such phenomena is quite another. How can psychologists possibly get at something that, by definition, is not directly available to consciousness? Freud and Jung suggested a number of avenues: free association, word association, slips of the tongue, certain events occurring during psychoanalytic therapy, waking fantasy, and interpretation of dreams. Here we consider some of these revolutionary techniques for exploring the unconscious.

free association

Free association.   Freud's primary assessment technique for getting at the unconscious was free association. *Association* is another term for "idea," and Freud considered associations *free* when they appear during a "preconscious" mental state of nonreflection that allows inner events to surface from what is only temporarily unconscious. In *free association,* the person adopts a mental orientation in which ideas, images, memories, and feelings are permitted to flow spontaneously on their own, without external guidance or suppression. The person goes beyond what is usually expressed willingly and intentionally. The fundamental rule of free association is to allow anything and everything to come to mind, no matter how senseless, illogical, unimportant, embarrassing, unpleasant, or absurd. Freud followed this rule in his own dream analysis by recalling, thinking about, being reminded of, and otherwise connecting (associating) anything with anything.

Why was free association important? It allowed Freud to discover what was in a person's unconscious. As discussed earlier in this chapter regarding Freud's assumption of determinism, he believed that nothing psychological ever happens by accident or chance. Every idea has meaning in relation to every other idea. One need only trace the connections.

Word Association Test

Word Association Test.   In the same vein, Carl Jung (1910) sought to get at the unconscious by developing the Word Association Test (WAT), one of the first personality tests used in clinical settings. Jung instructed persons to say the first word that came to mind after hearing each of 100 words from a standardized list. He then analyzed these associations according to content, commonality or uniqueness, reaction time, later recall, and accompanying behavior (facial expressions, postural shifts, voice changes, laughing, crying). He paid particular attention to responses given to emotionally arousing words. Jung found it helpful to interpret results in the context of *emotional complexes,* in which ideas that seem illogical on the surface can be understood by their links to similar feelings, conflicts, or experiences likely to be present in the deeper unconscious.

dream interpretation

Interpretation of dreams.   For Freud (1900/1958), dreams are "the royal road to a knowledge of the unconscious activities of the mind" (p. 608). It is not simply dreams in and of themselves that are important, but their interpretation. Freud believed that the *manifest content* of dreams — what the dreamer remembers about the dream when awakened — is deceptive and should not be taken at face

Psychoanalysts view staircases in dreams as sexual symbols and the climbing of staircases as symbolic of sexual arousal or intercourse.

value. Dreams originate in unconscious, primary processes of the id. Id forces gain strength during sleep, when conscious suppression is less than during wakefulness. Through dream work, the ego lessens the threat of id's instinctual impulses and images breaking into consciousness by modifying and distorting them, using such mechanisms as censorship, symbolic substitution, and defensive elaboration. Consequently, the true content of dreams is seldom what it appears to be on the surface; everything is disguise and mystery. To get at the underlying meaning of each dream, called the *latent content,* skilled interpretation is required. Interestingly, Freud believed that the *affect,* or feeling, present in dreams remains undisguised and is represented fairly directly.

dream work

Freud assumed that every dream has a meaning that can be interpreted either symbolically or through decoding. *Symbolic interpretation* focuses on the dream as a whole and seeks to replace disguised manifest content with some reasonable parallel. For example, in a biblical account from Genesis, a Pharaoh dreamed of seeing seven fat cows come out of the Nile River, followed by seven lean cows that then ate the fat ones. Pharaoh also dreamed of seven plump ears of corn on a single stalk, followed by seven diseased ears that devoured the first seven. What did these perplexing dreams mean? Joseph offered a symbolic interpretation: the cows and ears of corn were substitute or disguised representations that stood for seven future years of good harvest for Egypt, followed by seven of famine.

Freud agreed that symbols can sometimes have common meanings for people in general. Table 3.5 illustrates this point. However, his stronger belief was that symbols are more highly personal than universal. All symbols need to be interpreted individually, because they are determined by unconscious forces in the individual's own personality: "The same piece of content may conceal a different meaning when it occurs in various people or in various contexts" (Freud, 1900/1958, p. 105).

Typically, Freud preferred a *decoding* method of dream interpretation. In this method, each part of the dream is analyzed separately from the others. His method of decoding is far more sophisticated than that found nowadays in popular guides to dream interpretation. Correct analysis deciphers all dream elements, including symbols, that are then put together to uncover each dream's hidden meaning. The final result is certain to involve the discovery of some *wish fulfillment* for the dreamer, which Freud saw as the primary purpose of dreaming. Other functions served by dreams include guarding sleep (keeping the dreamer from waking), releasing emotional energy, lessening the shock of traumatic events, and aiding problem-solving.

Interpreting dreams in a series.   Unlike Freud, Jung generally saw dreams as having little to do with worldly concerns and much to do with the meaning of life. Jung's approach to dream interpretation was one of *amplification* — broadening and enriching dream content through a process of "directed association." Jung's interpretations were guided by images and analogies related to the dream's emotional nucleus or hub. His method differs from Freud's free association in three ways: (1) Instead of deducing meaning by working backward from present to past, Jung sought to understand meaning by progressing forward, from present to future. (2) Jung provided dreamers with his vast knowledge of universal archetypal symbols and meanings, orienting them in certain directions and ac-

TABLE 3.5   Some Freudian Dream Symbols

Dream contents	Symbolic meanings
Knife, umbrella, snake	Penis
Box, oven, ship	Uterus
Room, table with food	Woman
Staircase, ladder	Sexual intercourse
Water	Birth, mother
Baldness, tooth removal	Castration
Left (direction)	Crime, sexual deviation
Children playing	Masturbation
Fire	Bed-wetting
Robber	Father
Falling	Anxiety

tively guiding their interpretations. (3) Jung offered his own associations to dream content. Jung did not use any standard, cookbook approach to interpreting dream symbols. His approach was also highly individualized, taking into account different personalities, circumstances, and contexts. He sought to increase his patients' ability to interpret dreams by encouraging them to keep a log of all dreams and interpretations, and to pursue their own interpretations whenever possible.

Jung was the first theorist to investigate large numbers of dreams in succession, or *dream series* (Jacobi, 1962). Jung did not find interpretations of single dreams generally representative of the dreamer, and he found later dreams helpful in correcting misinterpretations of earlier ones. He also recognized that the meaning of dreams in a sequence is not necessarily chronological, but radial. Imagine a wagon wheel whose spokes extend outward from a central hub. Different dreams would be represented by the spokes, but all would be related to the dreamer's psychic core, or emotional complex. Thus, Jung's dream-series method is an alternative to Freud's therapy technique of free association.

Waking-dream fantasy.   Jung's second alternative to free association is the technique of *waking-dream fantasy*, through which patients are encouraged to simulate dream experiences by actively engaging in imagination while fully awake (Watkins, 1976). For example, a patient may be asked to close his eyes in a darkened room and imagine himself descending a succession of stairways. While so doing (symbolically going down into the unconscious), the patient is also asked to detail his sensations, perceptions, experiences, thoughts, and behaviors as vividly as possible. It frequently happens that the patient finds himself next to water, perhaps a lake, the most common symbol of unconscious psychological spirit. Thereafter, ascent may occur.

PROCEDURES FOR CHANGING PERSONALITY: PSYCHOANALYSIS

Free association quickly became the basic technique of Freud's "talking treatment" for exploring the unconscious (Breuer & Freud, 1895/1950). As a treatment technique, *psychoanalysis* refers to Freud's systematic procedures for   psychoanalysis
providing a patient with the insight necessary to rid the personality of its neurotic conflicts. The recall of childhood experiences is central to these procedures, especially involving memories of sex and aggression in relation to one's parents. Through *insight,* personally unacceptable and socially "taboo" experiences buried in the person's unconscious can be made conscious. Id is then replaced with ego.

Free association substituted for Freud's earlier use of hypnosis as a treatment technique. Unlike the seemingly unconscious "trance" state traditionally linked to hypnosis, it enabled patients to consciously recall everything they said. Free association was one reason Freud decided to use a couch in psychoanalysis, to help patients settle into the mental state needed for effective free association. Use of the couch led patients to adopt a passive posture and relaxed attitude for experiencing a more preconscious state of fantasy and recall than usually occurs during alert consciousness. Freud sat behind his patients, away from their direct view, to minimize his influence on their psychological explorations. He wanted to be like "a neutral, blank screen," so that his patients would feel free to verbalize their associations without looking for his facial reactions or fearing criticism or disapproval.

Eventually, patients would not only project their unconscious images onto Freud, "the mirror," they would relate to him as if he were some other person from their past with whom they were continuing to experience psychological conflict. Freud termed this reaction *transference*—the process by which patients distort the analyst's personality by making it different from what it really is. The origin of these unrealistic transformations is the patient's unconscious. It is as if the patient needs to remake the analyst in the image of the patient's father, mother, or some other significant person in order to work through the psychological fixations of childhood. Freud's use of the couch partly contributed to this phenomenon by fostering the patient's dependent, childlike relationship with the analyst, who quickly became a more superior parent-expert. When untrained analysts project their own unconscious needs onto their patients, the result is termed *countertransference*.

Jung's approach to therapy was flexible, open-minded, and *eclectic*, showing a willingness to use whatever methods seem most workable with individual patients, including the methods of other therapists (Hall & Nordby, 1973). Roazen (1974) writes that Jung "successfully pioneered in short-term psychotherapy" and inspired the development of self-help programs such as Alcoholics Anonymous (p. 284). Jung also initiated the use of projective tests during therapy. He often encouraged patients to express their experiences through drawing and painting, a technique that has been adopted by others, especially therapists who work with children. The waking-imagery techniques he developed have become popular with current-day professionals working with terminally ill cancer patients (Achterberg & Lawlis, 1978; Simonton & Simonton, 1975).

Freudian and Jungian approaches to treatment continue to have special followings, supported by training institutes in a number of major cities and some 15–20 professional journals. Corsini (1984) reports that there are 2500 Freudian analysts affiliated with the American Psychoanalytic Association, all members of the medical profession, along with 26 training institutes in the United States. He also reports that there are 400 qualified Jungian analysts, all members of the International Association for Analytic Psychology, with three training institutes in the United States. Many of the treatment techniques originated by Freud and Jung continue to be used by psychiatrists and psychologists whose therapy frameworks are more general than psychoanalytic. However, the once-dominant influence of psychoanalytic treatment has declined markedly during the second half of the 20th century. Alternative approaches have increased in popularity over time, especially humanistic, behavioral, and crisis-intervention strategies. These approaches typically take a less "comprehensive" view of personality, require no medical degrees or lengthy personal analyses as part of training, and have demonstrated their effectiveness while devoting briefer periods of time to each client.

Evaluation

THREE CONTRIBUTIONS: THEORY, THERAPY, AND A PHILOSOPHY OF HUMAN NATURE

Freud summarized his contributions to psychology in a brief, recorded statement, the year before he died (Lawrence, 1938):

> I started my professional activity as a neurologist trying to bring relief to my neurotic patients. Under the influence of an older friend, and by my own efforts, I discovered some important new facts about the unconscious in psychic life, the role of instinctual urges, and so on. Out of these findings produced a new science, psychoanalysis, a part of psychology, and a new method of treatment of the neuroses. I had to pay handily for this bit of good luck. People did not believe in my facts and thought my theories unsavory. Resistance was strong. . . . In the end I succeeded in acquiring . . . an international psychoanalytic association. But the struggle is not yet over.

Freud's statement identifies the three major contributions of psychoanalysis to psychology: a theory of personality, a method of treatment, and a philosophy of human nature.

A theory of personality.   Freud's contributions to personality theory have been detailed in this chapter. You need only recall his basic theoretical concepts of unconscious motivation in personality, the three-part structure of personality, the five psychosexual stages of personality development, the Oedipus complex, ego defense mechanisms, and the importance of early childhood experiences in normal and abnormal behavior. Freud's ideas set the stage for much creative thinking during the first half of the 20th century, which may have been his greatest contribution to psychology. To illustrate, Jung and all of the personality theorists reviewed in the next chapter grounded their ideas in the psychodynamic framework pioneered by Freud. Although these theorists departed from Freud by questioning certain of his concepts and introducing new ones, their ideas still were heavily influenced by Freud. Other theorists who have disagreed sharply with classic psychoanalytic thinking have nevertheless had to reckon with Freud's ideas.

A method of treatment.   Psychoanalysis was not only able to offer a theoretical way of understanding personality, it provided a practical means of actually changing personality. Freud's clinical work demonstrated that insight into the unconscious, instinctual, and childhood aspects of one's personality could free a person from inner defenses and conflicts. Abnormal symptoms of neurosis could be made to disappear, thereby heightening the person's capacities for cooperation, love, and productivity. Freud's translation of theoretical ideas about the psychological causes of human behavior into psychological treatment that brought about changes in behavior was an enormous contribution to the field of abnormal psychology, without historical parallel. In fact, it is difficult to identify a therapy whose origin is earlier than psychoanalysis. Freud was the first to demonstrate to other professionals that personality can be changed through systematic application of psychological assumptions, concepts, and principles. As stated by psychoanalyst Anna Freud (1976), Sigmund's daughter who died in 1982, "apart from suggestion and hypnosis, we had no rivals in the field of mental treatment" (p. 257).

A philosophy of human nature.   Freud's summary statement refers indirectly to psychoanalysis' third contribution: a philosophy of human nature. Freud "had to pay" for his discovery of "important new facts" because the pessimistic and unpopular picture his ideas painted of human nature served to diminish human stature, away from the romanticized ideals of religious free will and scientific rationality popular in his time. In the 16th century, observations by Copernicus had removed humankind from the physical center of the universe to the periphery. In the 19th century, Darwin's theory of evolution had removed humankind from a category of special creation to one of natural selection, with a line of development no different from those of related species. Then, in the 20th century, Freud removed humankind from the psychological center of its own personal universe to one in which unconscious biology dominated over illusions of personal freedom and rational choice. No wonder public resistance was high.

LIMITATIONS: HOW SCIENTIFIC IS PSYCHOANALYTIC THEORY?

Freud's view of psychoanalysis as "a new science" may have been partly justified during psychology's youth at the turn of the century. It certainly was Freud's intent to make psychoanalysis the basis of an experimental psychology that would integrate, once and for all, the psychological and physical events of mind and body. However, after three-quarters of a century, the scientific potential of psychoanalysis has not been realized, despite occasionally supportive research and attempts to integrate psychoanalysis with other areas of psychology such as learning (Dollard & Miller, 1950), development (Wolff, 1960), and cognition (G. Klein, 1970). It is not that psychoanalysis is "bad science," as once concluded by Sears (1943), but that it "is not and cannot be" a *natural* science in the manner of physics or chemistry (McIntosh, 1979). Many factors have contributed to this limitation, some of which are characteristic of personality theories in general.

Difficult concepts to measure.   The concepts of psychoanalysis, even when clearly defined, are not open to direct observation. Thus, they are hard to test experimentally. How is a researcher to measure energy that is "psychological" or get at events that are "unconscious" and "repressed"? Jung's concept of the "collective unconscious" involves hundreds of generations of human beings, spanning centuries of human existence. At what point does one begin to measure the influence of an "archetype," or assess the "compensatory" role it plays in personality functioning? Understanding Jung's ideas is further complicated by a writing style that is notoriously obscure and sometimes mystical. Schafer's development of *A New Language for Psychoanalysis* (1976) is one attempt to overcome this kind of limitation. It highlights the observation that, beginning with Freud, there is no fixed or final form of psychoanalytic theory.

Low predictive ability.   Psychoanalytic theory has shown little ability to predict behavior and has no universal laws — problems that also apply to other personality theories. Psychoanalysis works best when it is applied backward, accounting for an individual's past behavior after the facts have been gathered. It seldom indicates the person's future behavior — a limitation that, by definition, places the theory outside the category of science.

Uncontrolled clinical settings.   The primary setting for gathering data has been the clinic, not the experimental laboratory. Many influences acting on patients and analysts cannot be controlled: family life, work, money, social relationships, health, life-and-death events, moods, interruptions, and so on. One of Freud's patients, a psychiatrist, wrote that during treatment sessions Freud's dog was "sitting quietly on his haunches at the foot of the bed . . . a big chow" (Wortis, 1954, p. 23).

Participation in observations.   The analyst, as data gatherer, is a participant in the "experiment," not just an observer. Analysts influence the very processes they wish to record objectively (Joseph, 1980). Attempts have been made to overcome this limitation by requiring a training analysis or personal psychoanalytic treatment for all analysts, so that they may better understand their own personalities and influences on patients. However, total objectivity in human relationships is much more ideal than real. Returning to the previous example, Wortis (1954) noted on one occasion that Freud "did not approve" of his dog licking her genitals "and tried to make her stop" (p. 76). Other analysts, even those allowing a dog in the office, might react in different ways to their dog's behavior.

Overreliance on the case-study method.   The typical research method of psychoanalysis is the case study. This approach, with its focus on a single individual, differs from the nomothetic, group focus of experimental methods discussed in Chapter 2. In psychoanalysis, emphasis is placed on a particular person's early background and development, responses to diagnostic interviews and tests, and personal ideas, feelings, and experiences. Much of what the analyst values in this clinical work is not accessible in any objective or reliable way. Because the individual's experiences are so private, reliance is placed on the person's ability and willingness to communicate internal events that often are well hidden or disguised. In turn, these events are interpreted by yet another individual, the psychoanalyst, who, though trained, is still subject to limitations in personal ability and willingness to make interpretations. In all cases, the important reality is subjective or personal rather than objective or verifiable.

Sampling biases.   Samples of subjects used by Freud and other psychoanalysts as the basis of their observations are unrepresentative of people in general. For example, persons seen in clinical settings typically share the bias of being in psychoanalysis precisely because they are having problems in their lives. As summarized by Brody (1970), Freud's major case studies were of persons seen in Victorian Vienna (probably 100%) between the years 1889 and 1900 (50%) who showed abnormal behaviors (50% hysterical neuroses). This sample was heavily biased in favor of upper-class (100%) women (67%) between the ages of 18 and 20 (75%) who were single (75%). Such a selective sampling is clearly unrepresentative of people in general, biasing the theory and calling into question the generalizability of Freud's observations.

Limited experience with children.   Freud's theoretical ideas relied heavily on experiences related to early childhood development: psychosexual stages, Oedipus and Electra complexes, castration anxiety, penis envy, real or fantasized sexual seductions, and so on. However, Freud actually had few patients who were children. He obtained most of his information about children through everyday experience, reading, and the childhood recollections of adult patients who were well aware of Freud's belief in the sexual origins of maladaptive behavior. Freud (1909/1963a) recognized but dismissed the objection that the case of Little Hans was "an analysis of a child conducted by its father, who went to work instilled with *my* theoretical views and infected with *my* prejudices" (p. 139). However, a number of Freud's assumptions about children have been called into question by later research.

In two separate studies, only 50% of children between 4 and 6 years of age showed knowledge of genital sex differences, and those who did showed little evidence of emotional trauma. Results were obtained in two ways—interviews with children (Conn & Kanner, 1947) and having children complete puzzle pictures of people (Katcher, 1955). According to Kohlberg (1966), a "more plausible" alternative to castration anxiety is children's "uncertainty about anatomical constancy," with children fearing bodily injury much more generally than loss of a sex organ. Social-learning explanations of sex roles also have offered supportable alternatives to Freud's overemphasis on physical anatomy as the basis of sex differences (Rohrbaugh, 1979). Referring to the research example of castration anxiety in dreams, discussed earlier, Hall and Van de Castle (1965) recognize that "other explanations" than penis envy can account for women dreaming of weddings and babies more often than men.

CONCLUSION

Freud.   Despite the limitations of psychoanalysis as a scientific theory, Freud's genius is commonly accepted. No history of psychology could be written "in the next three hundred years" without mentioning him, "a man with the attributes of greatness" (Boring, 1957, p. 706). He was the right person at the right time, a synthesizer with strong leadership ability. As psychological detective, he left no stone unturned and no thread unraveled in arriving at analytic conclusions of certainty to himself. He was a detailed, thorough observer of his own experience and that of his Victorian community. His professional integrity led him to pursue original and unpopular ideas even when under harsh, personal attack by colleagues. He not only identified important psychological causes of abnormal behavior arising during childhood, he was the leader in showing how abnormal behaviors could be systematically changed. Freud was one of the most influential thinkers of the early 20th century, along with Charles Darwin and Albert Einstein. The theoretical ideas he developed have had major impact in the fields of psychiatry, social work, psychology, literature, history, and advertising. His ideas have had a direct impact on each and every one of us, by increasing our awareness of childhood influences on our behavior and our understanding of our own expressions of unconscious and irrational behavior.

Jung. Although Jung's contributions to the psychology of personality have had much less impact than those of Freud, appreciation of his ideas is likely to increase over time. Jung did not happen to be a theorist in the right place at the right time. He was often overshadowed by the dominating presence of Freud, a circumstance he shared with the social psychoanalysts discussed in the next chapter. Following his break with Freud, Jung (1963) found even his professional acquaintances dropping away — "I was a mystic, and that settled the matter" (p. 167). However, the breadth of Jung's perspective on personality remains unrivaled. It encompasses the collective unconscious of ancient antiquity as well as futuristic ideas about acausal synchronicity and extrasensory perception.

Clinically, Jung worked more with normal persons than did Freud, covering the full range of life-span development, including adults undergoing midlife crises. Also, his therapeutic work was undertaken not only with neurotic patients, but with more seriously disturbed schizophrenics. Thus, ideas derived from his clinical experience are likely to be more generally representative than those of Freud, and his flexibility more realistic. Other workers would endorse Jung's assumptions about dream-series interpretation (Perls, 1969), self-realization (Horney, 1950), the holistic nature of human experience (Rogers, 1961), and the biological origin of spiritual meaning (Maslow, 1967). Experimentally, there is support for Jung's concepts of introversion and extraversion, and for applications of the Word Association Test (Cramer, 1968). Although Jung's popularity is greater in Europe than the United States, the *Journal of Analytical Psychology* has an American as well as a British version. Jung's collected works total some 20 volumes.

CHAPTER REVIEW

Classical psychoanalysis is the theory of personality developed by Sigmund Freud. It was the first comprehensive theory of its kind, and also became a historically important treatment method for changing neurotic behavior.

For Freud, the structure of personality comprises three interacting systems: id, ego, and superego. Id is the biological aspect of personality and operates according to the pleasure principle. Id is the reservoir of all instinctual energy, including the two basic instincts of life (Eros, or libido) and death (Thanatos). Ego is the psychological or conscious aspect of personality, a kind of "self," and operates according to the reality principle. Superego is the social aspect of personality, and operates according to the morality principle. People have little knowledge of their personalities, because personality is largely unconscious, analogous to an iceberg submerged in water. Personality also functions as an inner battleground of energy forces, defenses, repressions, and anxieties.

The development of personality is essentially determined by the time a person is 5 years old. Five stages are involved: oral, anal, phallic, latency, and genital. Freud termed these stages "psychosexual" because of their close association with biological pleasure zones of the body, referred to as sexual or "erogenous" zones: mouth, anus, penis or clitoris, and penis or vagina. The phallic stage is the last of three pregenital stages, and provides the context in which important Oedipus, Electra, castration, and penis-envy complexes operate. Freud considered the Oedipus complex a universal psychological experience, with boys wishing to "kill" their father so as to "marry" their mother. He cited the case of Little Hans as the clinical cornerstone supporting this idea. The phallic stage also accounts for psychological and sex-role differences, especially in the development of superego or "conscience," which Freud saw as stronger in boys than in girls. Freud's belief in physical anatomy as the basis of psychological and moral differences between the sexes has been viewed as naive and sexist in its male bias. The final, genital stage of personality development occurs when the Oedipus complex in boys and Electra complex in girls is successfully resolved through identification with the parent of the same sex. This resolution leads to the fulfillment of mature goals of loving and working.

Jung, in his analytical psychology, hypothesized two levels of unconscious influence on personality—the personal (Freudian) and the collective (Jungian). Each layer has its own type of content (complexes versus archetypes), and each has its own mode of transmission (acquired experience versus hereditary preexistence). Archetypes in the collective unconscious represent universal experiences of our ancient human ancestors, and need to be wisely heeded and accepted. Each person becomes separated from the collective through individuation, the direction of which is self-realization. Self-realization develops throughout the entire life span, beginning with one's childhood dependency on parents, going through youth and middle age, followed by a return to the collective in old age.

Freud developed two major assessment techniques for uncovering the unconscious. First, free association was employed to encourage persons to say anything and everything that came to mind. This technique became the fundamental rule of psychoanalysis as a "talking" therapy. Freud made extensive use of free association in his own self-analysis, a method he relied on heavily for coming up with theoretical ideas. Second, the "royal road" to the unconscious was dream interpretation. Freud interpreted his own dreams, experiences, and everyday "mistakes." For him, nothing psychological ever occurred by accident. Everything was determined.

Jung also developed some major assessment techniques for uncovering what was unconscious. First, the Word Association Test allowed access to emotional complexes hidden in the personal unconscious. Second, Jung interpreted dreams in a series rather than singly. He also preferred to amplify dream content in a future direction, sharing his knowledge of universal symbols and archetypes, rather than decoding them as Freud did. Third, Jung encouraged his patients to simulate dream experiences through waking-dream fantasy.

Classical psychoanalysis has made contributions to psychology as a theory of personality, a method of treatment for changing behavior through insight, and a philosophy of human nature. Freud identified important psychological causes of abnormal behavior arising during childhood and showed how abnormal behaviors could be systematically changed. Some research studies supportive of Freudian and Jungian ideas have been reported. However, criticisms of psychoanalysis have been frequent, particularly regarding the limitations of psychoanalysis as a science and the acceptability of alternative explanations of factual data.

KEY CONCEPTS

Freud
    Personality structure
        Id
        Ego
        Superego
    Unconscious
        Defense mechanisms
    Five stages of personality development
        Fixation
        Oedipus complex/Electra complex
        Castration anxiety/penis envy
Jung
    Personal unconscious
        Complexes

    Collective unconscious
        Archetypes
    Psychological types
        Extraversion
        Introversion
    Self-realization
        Individuation
        Four stages of personality development
Psychoanalysis
    Free association
    Word Association Test
    Dream interpretation

REVIEW QUESTIONS

1. What is psychic determinism? What role does it play in psychoanalytic theory?
2. Compare the personality types hypothesized by Freud and Jung, and contrast their development.
3. Identify the various assessment techniques developed by Freud and Jung, and explain how they "get at" unconscious aspects of personality.
4. Why would Freud's theory of personality meet resistance from his contemporaries? To what extent do you think that resistance exists today?
5. What are some of the issues involved in evaluating whether psychoanalysis is scientific?

4

Social Psychoanalysis:
Horney, Sullivan, Adler, and Fromm

Did Freud overestimate the importance of biological factors in personality?

What role do family and social relationships play in the development of personality?

Is a sense of inferiority a blessing in disguise?

Do whole societies have personalities?

A LTHOUGH FREUD stands by himself in pioneering new ideas and methods for understanding personality, one of his continuing contributions has been to show others how to think in new ways about personality. It wasn't just a matter of the content of Freud's ideas — *what* to think. It was also a matter of procedure — *how* to think. Some of Freud's psychiatric followers adhered closely to his orthodox tradition (Deutsch, 1945; Fenichel, 1945). Others began to elaborate entirely new concepts, to question and even abandon some of the tenets of classical psychoanalysis. These *neo-Freudians* include the theorists covered in this chapter: Karen Horney, Harry Stack Sullivan, Alfred Adler, and Erich Fromm. Because all four theorists emphasized social factors over biological ones, they can be called *social psychoanalysts*. Although these theorists were heavily influenced by Freud and maintained a general psychoanalytic framework, they all departed from Freud's ideas. They abandoned Freud's "overemphasis" on infantile sexuality and elaborated new concepts about parent-child relationships, social experiences, and cultural patterns of behavior.

social psychoanalysts

Recall that Freud saw personality largely as a function of biological influences. Jung's "collective unconscious" also was intimately tied to biology. As you proceed through this chapter, you will see a general pattern of decreasing biological influences and broadening social influences on personality. Horney's "basic anxiety" originates in close parent/child relationships. Sullivan's "interpersonal theory" emphasizes a sequence of two-person social relationships, at six different stages of personality development; for him, personality *is* interpersonal relationships. Adler's "social feeling" encompasses interests in family, society, work, and love. Finally, Fromm's broad cultural approach presents the strongest case for individual differences among societies as a whole.

Before going further, we would like you to complete the exercise in Box 4.1. It will be discussed later in the chapter.

| *What Is Your Earliest Memory?* | BOX 4.1 |

Think back to the earliest time in your life that you can remember. Write down this earliest recollection, as completely as you can.

Social-Psychoanalytic Views of the Person

SIMILARITIES WITH FREUD

All of the theorists in this chapter acknowledged their indebtedness to Freud, especially his assumptions about the unconscious and dreams. Adler, for example, recommended that his students become thoroughly acquainted with Freud's attempt to establish a scientific theory of dreams—"a lasting merit that no one can lessen" (1939/1964, p. 252). The social psychoanalysts also agreed with Freud on the importance of childhood experiences in psychological adjustment and maladjustment. For them, anxiety remains a useful concept, accounting for the operation of various defensive and security operations in personality. With Freud, they saw neuroses as the predominant form of maladjustment of the early 20th century.

There are other similarities as well. Like Freud, the social psychoanalysts saw motivation as active and dynamic. They agreed that personality is changeable through psychoanalytic treatment that provides insight into the development and maintenance of problem behaviors. As support for their theories, they drew on clinical observation and case-study analyses rather than experimental research. Finally, all four theorists believed that human nature and values merit discussion.

IRRECONCILABLE DIFFERENCES: NOT SEX, NOT OEDIPUS

At the same time, there are irreconcilable differences. The social psychoanalysts discarded Freud's theory of instincts as the explanation of human behavior. Adler believed that Freud was wrong in interpreting all psychological events according to "the single ruling principle" of sexual libido. Adler also saw little direct influence of heredity on the development of personality traits. Horney pointed out that oral, anal, genital, and aggressive drives do not exist in all human beings. The aim of compulsive drives is not to satisfy sexual instincts but to provide safety from feelings of isolation, helplessness, fear, and hostility. Her (1939) conviction, "expressed in a nutshell," is that psychoanalysis should outgrow the one-sided limitations set by an instinctivistic and genetic psychology. Sullivan's advice to psychoanalysts was to "see if you can't find something besides the sexual problem" in those who come seeking help (1953, p. 296).

Adler also believed that Freud was wrong in fixing attention only on "mischievous" instincts. Sullivan agreed, arguing that the assumption that humankind is essentially evil has little support, even among persons who are most psychologically disturbed, schizophrenics. People are not innately aggressive, destructive, and sadistic. They have no actual need to be cruel and hurtful to one another. Nor is society the only thing preventing everybody from tearing everybody else to bits. If anything, society contributes its own "deviltry" to human living. The malevolent attitude of harmfulness to others is conspicuous only in children whose experiences of excessive social anxiety and being made fun of have taught them that they are living among enemies. What these childen learn from authoritative figures is that it is "highly disadvantageous to show any need for tender cooperation" (Sullivan, 1953, p. 214). Adler would concur, adding that children who do not acquire the necessary degree of social sense will not develop it as adults, except under special conditions such as therapy.

The social psychoanalysts abandoned Freud's concept of the Oedipus complex, which they did not accept as universal or even central to understanding personality. At best, it is relevant to some cases of neurotic jealousy in parent/child relationships (Horney, 1937) or of overindulgent pampering that leads a child to relate exclusively to one parent (Adler, 1964). Jung had already argued that if the Oedipus complex were as predominant as Freud claimed, civilization would have been "suffocated in incest half a million years ago" (Jung, in Evans, 1964, p. 36).

The social psychoanalysts also took issue with Freud's view of the differences between the sexes. Horney (1937) began her questioning in response to Freud's biased postulations about the psychology of women, especially his concept of "penis envy." Adler and Fromm were directly supportive of Horney's cultural orientation to sex differences. Sullivan openly expressed greater caution than Freud about confining his remarks to male patients because of the absence of material on the "complicated" female experience.

With the preceding as background, it may not be surprising that the social psychoanalysts sometimes experienced jolting disbelief and lifelong disappointments over Freud's lack of openness to independent ideas, as once manifested in his plea "My dear Jung, promise me never to abandon the sexual theory. . . . we must make a dogma of it" (Jung, 1963, p. 150). Freud would never accept a symbolic, rather than a literal, interpretation of the Oedipus complex. His rigidity explains Adler's comment that he, Adler, had profited from never having been psychoanalyzed. It kept him from the required rigorous acceptance of Freud's doctrine, which "destroys scientific impartiality" (1964, p. 254).

CONSTRUCTIVE ALTERNATIVES: CULTURAL AND INTERPERSONAL RELATIONSHIPS

Most important, the social psychoanalysts saw Freud as lacking a sociological orientation. To them, he showed a total disregard of cultural factors as influences on personality. As Horney (1937) remarked:

> Freud sees a culture not as the result of a complex social process but primarily as the product of biological drives which are repressed or sublimated, with the result that reaction formations are built up against them. The more complete the suppression of these drives, the higher the cultural development. . . . Historical and anthropological findings do not confirm such a direct relation between height of culture and the suppression of sexual or aggressive drives. (pp. 282–283)

Freud's view was contrary to social-psychoanalytic experience. For example, when Horney (1945) first came to the United States, in 1932, she noted important differences between the behaviors of persons in this country and in European countries that "only the difference in civilizations" could account for. Adler believed that the tasks human beings must meet in life "are conceived and formulated within the framework of society" (1930, p. 402). Fromm referred to progress in psychoanalytic theory as leading to a new concept founded not on the idea of isolated individuals but on "the *relationship* of man to others, to nature, and to himself" (1947, p. 57). Sullivan's distinction between humankind and lower animals was based on the fact that humankind "requires interchange with an environ-ment which includes culture" (1953, p. 32). Sullivan, in fact, redefined psychiatry as the study of interpersonal relationships. He saw abundant evidence that the human animal is simply unable to look after itself for a long time after birth. He also saw that a critical component of the process of human maturation is the development of language — a purely human, non-instinctive method of communicating with voluntarily produced symbols (Sapir, 1921, p. 7).

Working independently, the social psychoanalysts developed alternative, social concepts. The real forces motivating human attitudes and actions, they concluded, are social ones: dependency, cooperation, interpersonal anxiety, hostility, love, jealousy, competitiveness, inferiority, work. Sexual love is a task for two persons that requires social feeling. Even a newborn's first experience, feeding, is one of social cooperation. The collective emphasis of these theorists is clearly on human interactions in cultural and interpersonal contexts: parents, siblings, peers, significant social figures, and one's total society. Their perspective compensated for Freud's theoretical deficit.

In general, the social psychoanalysts also placed greater emphasis than Freud on ego, the more conscious and purposive aspect of personality. Adler and Fromm, like Jung, viewed personality as having a forward aim that is goal-directed, both consciously and unconsciously. For Adler, especially, all children make use of their situation in life and the impressions derived from it as the basic material for creating a personality — their unifying "style of life" or characteristic traits. This process of creative self-construction "leaves little room for the assumption that character traits are hereditary" (1964, p. 240). Thus, id influences recede into the background of social-psychoanalytic theories. Superego influences remain important, but they are tied to the process of socialization. The primary vehicle of socialization is the family, with results transmitted from one generation to the next (Fromm, 1947). The neurotic "stepchild of our culture" is the person whose early experiences involve culturally determined difficulties in their most extreme form (Horney, 1939).

WHAT OF HUMAN VALUES?

The social psychoanalysts do show some differences in regard to the origin of human values. The major issue involves the degree to which values are built into human nature or are culturally relative. You will recall that Jung (1963) believed in innate, archetypal forms of human experience that included possibilities of values, spirituality, God, and life after death. However, judgments about these "ethically neutral" experiences often are reflections of contemporary times, places, and cultural contexts. Fromm (1947) believed there is a built-in human nature, comprised of five existential needs, that would rise up against cultural influences too strongly opposed to its display. "Sane" societies support this human nature, whereas "sick" societies thwart it. On the other hand, Horney believed there is "no such thing" as a universal trend in human nature or a "normal" psychology that holds true for all humankind. Nevertheless, she did endorse a view of healthy persons as having the capacity to bestow "a good deal of genuine friendliness and confidence" on people (1937, p. 95). The most important aspect of individual self-realization is self-knowledge.

For present purposes, Adler may be viewed as the most direct representative of the social-psychoanalytic theorists regarding questions of human nature:

> However we may judge people, whatever we try to understand about them, what we aim at when we educate, heal, improve, condemn—we base it always on the same principle: social feeling! cooperation! Anything that we estimate as valuable, good, right, and normal, we estimate simply in so far as it is "virtue" from the point of view of an ideal society. The individual, ranged in a community which can preserve itself only through cooperation as a human society, becomes a part of this great whole through socially enforced division of labor, through association with a member of the opposite sex, and finds his task prescribed by this society. And not only his task, but also his preparation and ability to perform it. (Adler, 1930, p. 401)

In short, from both a psychological and an ethical point of view, the individual cannot be separated from the social community. Healthy development occurs when the individual strives to become "part of the whole," without seeking to destroy fellowship with others. Indeed, those who contribute nothing to the general welfare disappear completely. It is as though a questioning universe commands "Away with you! You have not grasped the meaning of life. You cannot endure into the future!" (Adler 1964, p. 279). Kal's (1972) survey of Adlerian therapists confirms their continuing commitment to views of people as social, purposeful in their behavior, and partly free to make choices ("soft determinism").

Basic Concepts: Horney

Born in Hamburg, Germany, in 1885, Karen Horney displayed an early concern for human relationships and the role of women. In her adolescent diaries, she portrayed herself as often intensely satisfied with life, a person who had lived and loved: "I think very highly of men who can bear to love a woman just as she is without demanding that she be in one certain uniform" (1980, p. 177).

Horney's goal to study medicine was clear to her at age 14, encouraged by her intelligent and freethinking mother, but unconventional for a woman of her day. However, Karen proved to be in the right place at the right time. Social changes in Germany allowed her to move to the forefront of new circumstances favorable to women's rights: secondary education and medical training. She received her medical degree at the University of Berlin in 1913 and underwent personal psychoanalysis with Karl Abraham and Hans Sachs. Abraham also served as training analyst for Erich Fromm who, like Horney, never had a personal relationship with Freud.

Karen had married Oskar Horney, a lawyer and economist, in 1910. Her early letters to Oskar reflect much personal questioning and deep exploration of Alfred Adler's concepts of inferiority and self-confidence, especially regarding women in social relationships. When her marriage began to dissolve in 1926, "writing—the search for truth—became her passion" (Eckardt, 1980). She

KAREN HORNEY.
Horney's concept of basic anxiety and helplessness in children contributed a social dimension to psychoanalysis. She saw neurosis as due to disturbances in human relationships. Horney continues to be recognized as an important leader in developing a psychology of women.

could think of nothing more unbearable than "disappearing quietly in the great mass of the average" or "of being told one is a nice, friendly, average person" (Horney, 1980, p. 245).

After immigrating to the United States, Horney was associated with the Psychoanalytic Institute in Chicago and New York. She later founded her own Association for the Advancement of Psychoanalysis and a training institute, the American Institute of Psychoanalysis. Horney was also editor of the *American Journal of Psychoanalysis*. She died in 1952. Kelman (1967) describes Horney's personal philosophy as growth-oriented, life-affirming, and freedom-seeking.

BASIC ANXIETY: INFANTILE HELPLESSNESS IN A PARENTAL WORLD

According to Horney (1950), normal personality development occurs when factors in the social environment allow children to develop "basic confidence" in themselves and other people. This is most likely to result when parents convey genuine and predictable warmth, interest, and respect toward their child. Abnormal development occurs when environmental conditions obstruct a child's natural psychological growth. Instead of developing confidence in self and others, the child develops *basic anxiety,* "a feeling of being isolated and helpless toward a world potentially hostile" (Horney, 1950, p. 366). The child feels "small, insignificant, helpless, deserted, endangered, in a world that is out to abuse, cheat, attack, humiliate, betray, envy" (Horney, 1937, p. 92). Basic anxiety is an irrational, emotional experience involving a pervasive, unpleasant feeling of extreme discomfort.

basic anxiety

A wide range of factors in the family environment contribute to this basic insecurity: parental domination, belittling attitudes, indifference, unkept promises, overprotection, a hostile home atmosphere, encouraging the child to take sides in parental disagreements, isolation from other children, and lack of respect for the child's individual needs (Horney, 1945). However, "the basic evil is invariably a lack of genuine warmth and affection" because of the parents' own neurotic incapacity to give it (Horney, 1937, p. 80). Horney saw neurotic persons as requiring excessive amounts of reassurance, and as incapable of loving. At bottom, all neuroses are expressions of a disturbance in human relationships.

COPING BY WAY OF TEN NEUROTIC NEEDS

The child's methods of adjusting to basic anxiety form enduring motivational patterns, or neurotic needs, which crystallize into important aspects of personality. *Neurotic needs* are the child's coping techniques — excessive, insatiable, and unrealistic demands developed in response to basic anxiety — which then dominate the person. Their aim is not instinctual satisfaction, as Freud believed, but social safety or security.

neurotic needs

Needs are considered neurotic when a person (1) adheres to them more rigidly than do other people in the culture and (2) shows a discrepancy between his or her potentialities and actual accomplishments. Neurotic persons lack flexibility in reacting to different situations. For example, most people in our culture are likely to react indecisively or suspiciously when there are appropriate reasons for doing so, perhaps in response to having to make a difficult choice or to evidence of insincerity from another person. However, neurotic individuals tend to be undecided or suspicious at all times, regardless of the circumstances and persons involved. They always seem unable to make up their mind, or repeatedly indicate how impossible it is to trust anyone because "everyone" is out to get whatever they can. They experience a discrepancy between their potential — personal gifts and the support of favorable circumstances — and their actual productivity or enjoyment. Even though they seem to have everything going for them, their feelings point to an inappropriate sense of inferiority and an absence of happiness. They sense that they stand in their own way. Table 4.1 presents ten neurotic needs discussed by Horney (1942), together with some illustrative behaviors.

MOVING TOWARD, AGAINST, AND AWAY FROM PEOPLE

According to Horney, identifying the characteristics of an individual's dominant needs can reveal the relative direction the person is likely to take in relationships with other people. The overall pattern also suggests the form "basic conflict" would take in the individual's personality. For Horney (1945), neurotic conflict stems from "contradictory attitudes" the person holds toward other people. She called attention to the dramatization of one such contradiction, the story of Dr. Jekyll and Mr. Hyde. One side of Dr. Jekyll is "delicate, sensitive, sympathetic, helpful," while a second side is "brutal, callous, and egotistical." Horney did not imply that the Jekyll/Hyde story is the precise form that neurotic

TABLE 4.1   Ten Neurotic Needs Identified by Horney

Excessive needs for	Shown in behaviors
1. Affection and approval	Striving to be liked and pleasing to others, to live up to the expectations of others; dreading self-assertion and hostility
2. Having a "partner"	Seeking to be taken over by another, through "love"; dreading being left alone
3. Narrowly restricting one's life	Trying to be inconspicuous, undemanding, and modest; contented with little
4. Power	Seeking domination and control over others; dreading weakness
5. Exploiting others	Taking advantage of others, using others; dreading being "stupid"
6. Social recognition or prestige	Seeking public acceptance; dreading "humiliation"
7. Personal admiration	Being self-inflating; seeking to be valued according to one's self-image
8. Personal achievement	Striving to be best; ambitious; dreading failure
9. Self-sufficiency and independence	Trying to not need others; maintaining distance; dreading closeness
10. Perfection and unassailability	Being driven toward superiority; dreading flaws and criticism

conflict takes, only that the central character shows a basic incompatibility of attitudes in relation to other people.

The idea of incompatible attitudes is an essential aspect of Horney's description of neurosis, "a psychic disturbance brought about by fears and defenses against these fears, and by attempts to find compromise solutions for conflicting tendencies" (1937, pp. 28–29). Their function is to reduce anxiety, to make the person feel better emotionally. Since all persons experience conflicting attitudes, neurotic conflict is a matter of degree—an *excessive* deviation from the cultural norm. Eventually, neurotic attitudes are brought to bear on the self, pervading the entire personality "as a malignant tumor."

Horney (1945) has discussed three generalized attitudes that individuals typically hold toward others and themselves. Each attitude is "a whole way of life," including thinking, feeling, and acting: (1) moving toward people, (2) moving against people, and (3) moving away from people. Each attitude results from different combinations of the ten needs summarized in Table 4.1.

Moving toward people reflects neurotic needs for affection and a partner, as well as compulsive modesty. This attitude is associated with the first three needs listed in the table. The predominant direction is one of *helplessness* and *compliance*. The person

moving
toward. . .

accepts his own helplessness, and in spite of his estrangement and fears tries to win the affection of others and to lean on them. Only in this way can he feel safe with them. If there are dissenting parties in the family, he will attach himself to the most powerful person or group. By complying with them, he gains a feeling of belonging and support which makes him feel less weak and less isolated. (p. 42)

Moving against people is associated with needs 4, 5, 6, and 8. This attitude reflects compulsive cravings for power and prestige, as well as personal ambition. There is an overemphasis on *hostility* and *aggressiveness.* The person

> accepts and takes for granted the hostility around him, and determines, consciously or unconsciously, to fight. He implicitly distrusts the feelings and intentions of others toward himself. He rebels in whatever ways are open to him. He wants to be the stronger and defeat them, partly for his own protection, partly for revenge. (p. 43)

. . . against . . .

Moving away from people reflects a person's concern with self, as seen in needs for admiration and perfectionism. This attitude is associated with needs 7, 9, and 10 in Table 4.1. The predominant direction is one of *isolation* and *detachment.* The person

. . . and away from people

> wants neither to belong nor to fight, but keeps apart. He feels he has not much in common with them, they do not understand him anyhow. He builds up a world of his own—with nature, with his dolls, his books, his dreams. (p. 43)

DEVELOPING AN IDEALIZED VERSUS A REAL SELF

Once established, basic anxiety gives rise to additional feelings of alienation toward one's real self and growing self-hatred. Genuine self-realization is sacrificed to an *idealized self,* an artificial pride system that the person creates to give the personality a sense of unity that does not exist. Horney (1945) refers to a cartoon she once saw in *The New Yorker.* A heavyset, middle-aged adult is depicted as looking in a mirror and seeing the image of a trim, young adult. Such an idealized self serves five functions: (1) It substitutes for the absence of realistic self-confidence and pride, through an inflated but ungrounded feeling of significance and power. (2) It counteracts the presence of inner weakness and self-contempt, by falsely allowing the person to feel better or more worthy than others. (3) It compensates for the absence of genuine ideals, which otherwise would lead the person to feel quite lost. (4) Reliance on an idealized, private mirror causes one's most blatant faults and handicaps to disappear or take on an attractive coloration. (5) Creation of an idealized self offers the appearance of reconciled conflicts and inconsistencies in personality, even though such is not the case.

real versus idealized self

Creation of an idealized self takes place unconsciously. It also may be accompanied by other forms of pretense, such as *externalization*—the tendency to experience internal processes as if they occurred outside oneself and to hold these "external" factors responsible for one's difficulties. Externalization serves to eliminate oneself as the cause of difficulties by allowing the person to project or shift blame onto other people, identify with "underdogs," or focus on physical symptoms rather than psychological ones. The central inner conflict is "between the constructive forces of the real self and the obstructive forces of the pride system, between healthy growth and the drive to prove in actuality the perfection of the idealized self" (Horney, 1950, p. 368).

Horney (1937) discusses four maladaptive ways people in our culture seek to escape from anxiety (and maintain idealized pictures of themselves). First, people may *rationalize* anxiety by coming up with any "good" justification that makes their fear appear reasonable or explains it away. Second, people may *deny* anxiety by excluding it from consciousness, in an "out of sight, out of mind" manner. Third, it is possible to *narcotize* anxiety by overusing alcohol, drugs, sex, and sleep, or by keeping overly "busy" with work and social activities. Fourth, people may simply *avoid* all situations, thoughts, or feelings that arouse anxiety. This includes procrastinating, falsely pretending that things are not important or liked when they really are, and inhibiting certain thoughts or feelings so that they will not occur. However, these common methods of maladjusted coping often prove ineffective.

A PSYCHOLOGY OF WOMEN

psychology of
women

Horney made significant contributions to the psychology of women, questioning Freudian assumptions about women. She was an influential critic of Freud's "boy's eye" view of physical anatomy as the basis of psychological differences between men and women. She challenged Freud's theoretical speculations that the absence of a penis led women to (1) envy men for their penises; (2) feel shame over biological "deficiency"; (3) resent their mothers, who were to blame for their not having a penis; (4) overvalue relationships with men, including having male babies as a way of obtaining a substitute penis; (5) become jealous of other women as competitors for male penises; (6) seek sexual stimulation through the penis-like clitoris rather than through the vagina; (7) experience uniquely feminine desires for submissiveness, dependency, and masochistic abuse; and (8) be generally motivated by the ultimate driving force of wishing for a penis of their own.

Why were Freud's underlying assumptions open to question? First, Horney considered it illogical that persons built for specific biological functions should be psychologically determined to wish for the biological attributes of the other sex. "It would require tremendous evidence to make it plausible" (1939, p. 104). Second, Horney saw no evidence of innate, universal support for Freud's conjectures. Cross-cultural investigations failed to demonstrate the universality of "penis envy" or of the Oedipus complex (the supposed cornerstone of child development), while indicating that some societies actually showed "womb envy." In effect, Freud had overgeneralized his observations from a limited sample of persons, many of whom were neurotic. Third, Horney (1926) addressed the issue of male bias as a source of observer error. Psychoanalysis was created by "a male genius," almost all of whose followers were men. It is understandable that a masculine psychology would evolve more easily than a psychology of women, especially considering the generally masculine context of the whole civilization. "Like all sciences and all valuations, the psychology of women has hitherto been considered only from the point of view of men" (Horney, 1967, p. 56).

Horney recast Freud's biologically-based interpretations in terms of cultural, social, and psychological influences. Culturally, she endorsed philosopher Georg Simmel's view of western civilization as predominantly masculine in ideology. For centuries, women have been enmeshed in social systems that have promoted a "too exclusive" concentration on, and "overvaluation" of, men. Women's lives have been structured around political, economic, and psychological dependency on men. The specific social vehicle contributing to female dependency is the development of "love" relationships, based on the woman's belief "I must have a man." Horney saw this belief as unconsciously motivating women to adapt themselves to the wishes of men and then assume, erroneously, that these adaptations represented true feminine nature.

Socially, Horney saw women's adaptations as "cultivated" through a process of systematic selection by men. Male selectivity fostered the development of relationships with certain types of conforming women, those whose willingness to please would compensate for male deficiencies in self-esteem and would offer evidence of dependency, inconspicuousness, frailty, suffering, emotionality, and jealousy of women, through a kind of self-fulfilling prophecy.

Psychologically, society's "masculine tendency" conveys demeaning attitudes toward women. Women are then led to compensate for this socially heightened sense of inferiority and lack of confidence by further increasing their overvaluation of relationships with "superior" men.

Horney's reconceptualization is a clear alternative to Freud's. It redirects attention away from previously assumed biological origins of observed personality and social differences between the sexes, to origins more sociocultural in nature. Horney's impact was important, then as well as now. Then, it was great enough to elicit Freud's (1925/1959) direct opposition, and the support of Adler and Fromm. Adler, for example, addressed the myth of women's inferiority, and indicated that issues of birth control and abortion should "best be left entirely to the woman" (1982, p. 63). He also saw society's "overestimation of the masculine principle" as encouraging the development of *masculine protest,* or women's striving for success as an overcompensatory reaction against stereotypic feminine roles (1930). Now, there is renewed interest in the work of Horney, associated with ongoing development of the women's movement and specific interest in the psychology of women (Rohrbaugh, 1979; Williams, 1983). She continues to be cited as an important figure on the issue of culture and sex roles.

Basic Concepts: Sullivan

Harry Stack Sullivan is sometimes considered "America's psychiatrist" (Perry, 1982). He was born in the rural New York town of Norwich in 1892 and raised on a nearby farm. Harry was an only child, idealized by his mother but considered by his father "no good to work, for he has his nose stuck in a book all the time" (Perry, 1982, p. 85). He graduated valedictorian of his high school class at age 16.

Suggestions of psychological difficulties were present throughout Sullivan's life. He had an isolated childhood, was a loner at school, and often conveyed a sense of ambiguous, preadolescent sexuality. He was suspended from Cornell as a

H. S. SULLIVAN.
"America's psychiatrist" theorized that personality does not exist in the absence of other people and that all of us are reflections of the relationships we have had with significant other people.

freshman for illegally obtaining drugs. During his medical-school years, he began to rely on alcohol as a way of handling anxiety. A schizophrenic breakdown may have led him to seek personal psychoanalysis and develop a professional interest in psychiatry. There were also rumors of possible suicide surrounding Sullivan's death in Paris, in 1949.

Sullivan attended the Chicago College of Medicine and Surgery and received psychiatric training at St. Elizabeth's Hospital in Washington, D.C. As a clinician, he is probably best known for his work with schizophrenic men, for whom he established a successful residential treatment program grounded in experiences of interpersonal trust through development of "preadolescent" friendships. He believed in the principle "like cures like," which guided his selection of "sensitive, shy" ward staff. Sullivan was also editor of the journal *Psychiatry,* sponsored by the William Alanson White Psychiatric Foundation for preventive psychiatry.

PERSONALITY AS PATTERNS OF INTERPERSONAL RELATIONSHIPS

interpersonal
relationships

Sullivan's theory revolves around the idea that a person's needs and developmental tasks are met in a series of two-person relationships, beginning with "a mothering one" and ending with a sexual partner. Sullivan believed we have as many personalities as we have interpersonal relationships. However, he formally defined *personality* as "the relatively enduring pattern of recurrent interpersonal situations which characterize a human life" (1953, pp. 110–111).

In essence, personality does not exist in the absence of other people. Without other people, there can be no development of a self-system, "that part of personality which is born entirely out of the influences of significant others upon one's feeling of well-being" (Sullivan, 1954, p. 101). Nor can there be any sense of self-esteem, which originates in the positive and negative evaluations we receive about ourselves from other people ("reflected appraisals"). *Significant others* are those people who are most meaningful to us in our lives. Interestingly, our relationships with them may be fantasied as well as real, including imaginary playmates, literary characters, and idealized public figures with whom we have never had face-to-face contact. An example is John Hinckley's fantasized infatuation with movie actress Jodie Foster, whom he tried to impress by attempting to assassinate President Ronald Reagan.

significant others

AN INTERPERSONAL NEED FOR TENDERNESS

For Sullivan, personality is derived from human experience, all of which is comprised of alternating tensions and satisfactions. Tensions are of two kinds: physical needs and interpersonal anxiety. Needs seek satisfaction (oxygen, water, sugar, body temperature), whereas anxiety seeks interpersonal security or feelings of well-being. Anxiety is the "first of all learning," signifying a felt danger to biological existence (Sullivan, 1953).

Like Horney, Sullivan saw infants as being totally powerless and at the mercy of other people for their security. However, Sullivan further theorized that the infant's nearly absolute dependency effects a *need for tenderness* which, different from "love," refers to relief from various tensions that can only be met in a relationship with a "mothering one"—some cooperative adult who is able to aid the infant's survival by providing outside help. Observations of tension in the infant create a reciprocal tension in the mothering one, which is experienced as tenderness and leads to activities aimed at relieving the infant's needs. Thus, tenderness is an *interpersonal* need, "ingrained from the very beginning of things" (Sullivan, 1953). The outer-directed, social implications of this need set Sullivan apart from Freud, whose theory places greater emphasis on intrapsychic events occurring within the individual.

need for tenderness

EMPATHY, ANXIETY, AND SECURITY

One of Sullivan's theorems is: "The tension of anxiety, when present in the mothering one, induces anxiety in the infant" (1953, p. 41). The transfer of anxiety to the infant may be brought about by rough attitudes or behaviors in the mothering one, which convey to the infant a sense that something, somehow, is "bad," "disapproved of," or "wrong." This occurs even though the origin of tension in the mothering one has no direct connection with the infant. It may be due to the caregiver's personality, uncertainty about the parenting role, or circumstances entirely unrelated to the infant, such as a parent's being ill, tired, or upset by bad news. However, the infant has no way of knowing this. The infant simply senses or participates in the other person's tension or discomfort, through a global type of emotional reaction termed *empathy*. Anxiety can interfere with the

anxiety

empathy

satisfaction of physical and tenderness needs. For example, it may produce crying or vomiting, thereby disrupting the infant's feeding behavior and further increasing anxiety in both infant and mothering one. Since the infant has no systematic capacity for removing, destroying, or escaping from the anxiety, the infant is totally dependent on a cooperative other person for relief. The only relief is freedom from anxiety, which is interpersonal security.

SIX STAGES OF DEVELOPMENT

six
developmental
epochs

Sullivan (1953) conceptualized personality development as consisting of six stages or *developmental epochs,* spanning infancy through late adolescence. Table 4.2 summarizes these six stages, along with their corresponding benchmarks. A brief review of the six stages will show that each stage has a corresponding kind of interpersonal relationship.

Before discussing the six stages, we need to introduce three *modes of experience* Sullivan associated with them, called the prototaxic, parataxic, and syntaxic. The *prototaxic* mode is the earliest, most primitive type of experience, a state of generalized sensation or feeling, in the absence of thought. The infant knows only what William James called a "big, blooming, buzzing confusion"—vague perceptions of momentary states having no "before" or "after." There is no awareness of self as separate from the world. The *parataxic* mode is experienced as the infant enters childhood and begins to use symbolic speech. However, the child makes few orderly or logical connections about the sequence of its experiences (as when dreaming), and understanding remains minimal. There is a sense of "magic" in which things "just happen," as in seeing colorful Christmas lights suddenly appear with the simple flip of a switch. In adults, parataxic experience may serve as a rough basis of generalized memory, related to habits. Examples include routine activities that often occur without conscious decision making, such as dressing, walking to class, eating, or doing repetitive piecework. The *syntaxic* mode becomes

TABLE 4.2   Sullivan's Six Developmental Epochs

Epochs	Characteristics	Capacities for
Infancy	Need for contact with caregiver Prototaxic experience	Beginning speech
Childhood	Need for adult participation in activities Parataxic experience	Language
Juvenile Era	Need for acceptance by compeers Syntaxic experience	Compeer or playmate relationship
Preadolescence	Need for intimate exchange with a loved one	Close, same-sex relationship (chum)
Early Adolescence		Close, opposite-sex relationship Patterning of lustful or genital behavior

Late Adolescence		Mature and independent development
		  of love relationships in which
		  another person is as important as
		  oneself

important during the juvenile stage, at which time the meaning of words becomes shared with most other people in society. Individuals become able to communicate syntaxic experiences with others because both parties define the symbols alike. This is the stage of "consensual validation," in which the child has learned "the precisely right word for a situation" (Sullivan, 1953).

As you can see, the direction of development as reflected by the three modes is toward increased socialization. Over time, the social "majority" rules over personal interpretations. With this as background, we can now turn our attention to Sullivan's six developmental stages.

Infancy: prototaxic feelings about "good" and "bad" caregivers.   The *infancy* stage starts at birth and continues until the appearance of speech. The development of personality begins with feeding. This is because the infant's initial interpersonal situation is the "nipple-in-lips" experience, which evolves around the infant's oral zone and the mother's mammary zone. The experience integrates the infant's need for water, food, and contact, and the caregiver's need to show tenderness. The infant's accompanying hand and foot movements—touching, grasping, pulling, pushing, rubbing, patting, cuddling—become an increasingly important part of this first interpersonal situation because they help the infant differentiate experiences and objects. That is, when the infant's interactions with mothering ones are experienced as satisfying, warm, and comforting, it forms early impressions about the existence of "good nipple" or "good mother." This empathic sensory image is not of the real mother, but of the infant's vague, prototaxic sense of feeding experiences as good because they result in relaxations of tensions. If the same caregiver, or a substitute, interacts with the infant in ways that are "rough, sound unpleasant, hurt the baby, and generally discompose him," the infant will be led to form a second rudimentary personification, that of "bad mother" (Sullivan, 1953, p. 116).

It is from these early experiences with other persons that the infant begins to differentiate its own *self-system*. Experiences of positive satisfactions, in which the mothering one is pleased, are organized around a personification of "good me." Interpersonal security prevails. On the other hand, experiences of anxiety in caregiver relationships are organized around a personification of "bad me." Insecurity prevails. In this way, the undifferentiated nature of early experience begins to break down into parts. The infant has learned to make some distinctions between itself and the world.

self-system

Childhood: parataxic learning of social habits and self.   The *childhood* stage emerges with articulate speech and ends with the appearance of the need for peers. A number of important developmental tasks are met during this stage.

First, there is rapid social acculturation in what is "proper." Children largely accept their parents' lessons in cleanliness, feeding habits, toilet training, obedience, oughts, and musts.

Second, language is acquired as a communication tool for manipulating the outside social world into satisfying one's tensions.

Third, there is continuing development of the self-system, an organization of experience of "stupendous importance" in personality. Having come into being by incorporating the "bad mother" personification, the function of the self-system is to avoid or minimize incidents of anxiety. Through trial and error, the child skillfully learns to read the "forbidding gestures" of significant others, the anxiety-arousing signs that precede or accompany their disapprovals and withholdings of tenderness. In this sense, the self-system is somewhat parallel to Freud's concept of ego in seeking to secure necessary satisfactions without incurring much anxiety. The self-system minimizes anxiety through selective inattention and by anticipating what to avoid by way of experiences that are incompatible with its past development. Also, it is through our self-systems that we psychologically carry our parents around with us throughout our lives, as a continuing frame of reference regarding what is "approved" and "disapproved." In this sense, the self-system is partly analogous to Freud's concept of superego.

Fourth, there is learning of such negative emotions as disgust, shame, anger, and resentment. "Willie, I told you not to do that. Now say you are sorry" (Sullivan, 1953, p. 200). There also is learning of such negative forms of social interaction as malevolence, hatred, and isolation. Sullivan (1953) considers the learning of malevolence as "perhaps the greatest disaster" to happen during the childhood phase of personality development.

Juvenile era: syntaxic experiences of finding playmates and questioning parents.   The *juvenile era* is ushered in with the child's need for peer companions, or "playmates rather like oneself." It coincides with the elementary school years, during which the child has many opportunities to learn the ways of other children and show social subordination to new authority figures such as teachers, coaches, and club leaders. The juvenile develops an appreciation of differences in living never conceived of before, some "right" and some "wrong." Ideas and social operations learned at home may be found not to apply at school or with friends, and are reformulated. Authorities, including one's parents, are reduced "from godlike figures to people." Along with cooperation are experiences of competition, stereotyping, ostracism, and compromise. References are made to "our team" and "our teacher." Social accommodation is partly motivated by peer pressure. A personally meaningful orientation in living begins to take form, based on growing understanding of one's needs, appropriate social circumstances, and future goals. Sullivan likens the juvenile stage to Freud's latency period of development.

Preadolescence: collaborating happily with a chum.   The period of *preadolescence* is brief, beginning with the need for interpersonal intimacy in the form of a close relationship with another person "of comparable status." Somewhere between the ages of 8½ and 10, the child "begins to develop a real sensitivity to what matters to another person" (Sullivan, 1953, p. 245). One's predominant interest is in establishing a relationship with a chum, a particular member of the same sex who becomes a close friend. Juveniles contribute to the happiness of their pals through collaboration, making personal adjustments aimed at providing mutual satisfactions. When two young people become mutually important to each other, the process of consensual validation supports the personal worth of both. Preadolescents may spend hours with one another in mutual daydreaming. Participation in cliques or gangs may be traced to interlocking, two-person relationships in which persons A and B also have individual relationships with persons C and D, respectively. Loneliness resulting from the absence of close peer relationships may be overcome by the "profound need for dealings with others," which is sufficiently powerful to lead people to seek companionship despite experiences of fear and anxiety.

Early adolescence: experiencing lust toward a sexual partner. The eruption of puberty and genital sexuality during *early adolescence* results in a shift in the need for intimacy toward more lustful feelings of closeness and tenderness with a sexual partner. Interest in a member of one's own sex is replaced by interest in a member of the opposite sex. The object of interest is no longer a person quite like oneself, but one who is "very different." The epoch continues until there is a patterning of some type of performance that satisfies lust, Sullivan's term for "certain tensions of or pertaining to the genitals," culminating in orgasm (1953, p. 109). He identifies some 50 patterns of "sexual and friendly" relationships with others. Sullivan considers lust a *dynamism*, the smallest subsystem of integrating tendencies within the personality. Because dynamisms organize and channel physical energy, they have the power to dominate personality and cause it to follow one developmental direction rather than another. Other dynamisms include the self-system and the intimacy of closeness and tenderness.

Late adolescence: establishing love relationships. What separates early and late adolescence is not biological maturation but an achievement. Partially developed aspects of personality fall into place. The person is able to tolerate some previously avoided anxiety, which allows favorable changes to be made in the self-system. *Late adolescence* begins when the person discovers his or her preference with regard to genital behavior and how to fit this into the rest of life. It ends with "the establishment of a fully human or mature repertory of interpersonal relations, as permitted by available opportunity, personal and cultural" (Sullivan, 1953, p. 297). Into adulthood, one is able to "establish relationships of love for some other person, in which relationship the other person is as significant, or nearly as significant, as one's self" (p. 34).

Basic Concepts: Adler

Alfred Adler was born in Vienna in 1870. He was the second of six children in a middle-class Jewish family, and converted to Protestantism in his youth. In a lecture given when he was more than 60 years old, Adler talked about the importance of his early physical ailments and handicaps:

> I was born a very weak child suffering from certain weaknesses, especially from rickets which prevented me from moving very well. Despite this obstacle, now, nearly at the end of my life, I am standing before you in America. You can see how I have overcome this difficulty. Also, I could not speak very well early in my life; I spoke very slowly. Now, though you are probably not aware of it in my English, I am supposed to be a very good orator in German. I have also overcome this difficulty. (Stepansky, 1983, p.9)

ALFRED ADLER.
Adler loved to lecture to groups of parents and teachers about the importance of social interest in personality development. He believed that a person's style of life results from unique ways of overcoming inferiority by striving for superiority, and that the essential goals in life are social ones—society, work, and love.

Adler received his medical degree from the University of Vienna in 1895. His first important theoretical work (1907/1917) was on the inferiority of physical organs and psychological attempts to compensate for them. However, he was also interested in practical applications of knowledge, and was sympathetic to the socialist movement. His earlier *Health Book for the Tailoring Trade* (1898) called for a politicized medical profession. Adler wanted physicians to actively improve community hygiene through education and psychotherapy. One of Adler's own social contributions was to introduce child-guidance centers, which were housed in public schools, into Viennese society.

Adler was the first psychoanalyst to break with Freud, maintaining that sexual difficulties were *symbolic* of social problems. Freud's attack on this "deviant" position was unsparing. Later, Adler vehemently denied ever having been a disciple of Freud's—an equal, yes, but never a student. For his part, Freud claimed Adler was "a defector" who was too proud to live in the shadow of a giant.

After coming to the United States in 1935, Adler became known as an "indefatigable lecturer" to parents and teachers, as well as a "constant advisor" to child-guidance clinics (Alexander & Selesnick, 1966) until his death in 1937. His life combined great energy, enjoyment, and capacity for work. He has been described as "a most democratic, friendly, hospitable person with a love for informal sociability, music, and all the arts, including gardening" (Ansbacher, 1964, p. xxii). Two of his four children, Alexandra and Kurt, became psychiatrists in their father's tradition. Ellenberger (1970) believes it would be hard to find another theorist from whom "so much has been borrowed" without acknowledgment.

DEVELOPING SOCIAL INTEREST: SOCIETY, WORK, AND LOVE

Alfred Adler's commitment to the concept of individual differences in personality is captured in the designation of his theory as *individual psychology*. "Every single case represents something unique, something that will never occur again" (1964, p. 188). Even the same situations, experiences, dreams, and life problems have different psychological and physical effects on every person. While recognizing the factual existence of constitutional differences among people, Adler warned against overstressing them: the important thing is "not what one is born with, but what use one makes of that equipment" (1956, p. 176). He viewed the basis of individual differences as psychosocial, not hereditary.

The cornerstone of individual psychology is Adler's belief that there are three unavoidable tasks each person must meet in life: society, work, and love. The solution to all three tasks requires childhood preparation for *social interest* — the   social interest
development of social feeling related to association and cooperation with other people. For Adler, social feeling is the ultimate norm of civilization.

First, social feeling toward *society* shows itself in the individual's capacity to retain friendship. It involves preparation for cooperation in school, sports, and choice of a partner, as well as the development of interest in state, country, race, and humanity. Second, the individual must show an ability to be interested in *work.* Social feeling here takes the form of cooperative activity for the benefit of others. Individuals who perform useful work not only provide themselves with a livelihood but obtain a sense of worth to society, which values industry over laziness. It is through work that individuals assist in the progress of their self-developing community. Third, in *love,* individuals show the ability to be more interested in a partner than in themselves. Social feeling here is concerned with a task that requires the cooperation of two persons, as both help perpetuate the human species by caring for offspring. Prerequisites of love include childhood preparation for a two-person task, continuing consciousness of the equal worth of both partners, and a capacity for mutual devotion.

PERSONALITY AS CREATING A STYLE OF LIFE

According to Adler, an individual's attitudes toward society, work, and love are summarized in a *style of life* — the individual's unique but consistent movement   style of life
toward self-created goals and ideals developed during childhood. The style of life is an original, psychological "type" that contains the individual's relatively permanent "law of movement" in the world. Adler gives the illustration of two pine trees, one growing in a valley and one growing on a mountaintop. Although both are the same kind of tree, each shows a distinct style of life, with individuality "expressing itself and molding itself in an environment" (1956, p. 173). In human terms, the style of life is the vehicle through which each of us interprets the facts of our existence. The style of life dominates personal experience. It guides one's dreams, fantasies, games, and early recollections, and even selects images for its own purpose. It determines thinking, feeling, willing, and acting.

In forming a style of life, we are not passively molded by our environment. Personality results from the activity of the *creative self* — the process by which we   creative self
each make original constructions of ourselves and our world as we develop a style of life for solving the three great problems of life. Thus, interpretation is fundamental to a person's view of the world, making each of us "the artist" of our own personality. Childhood beliefs are particularly influential in this process, typically created between the ages of 3 and 5, as part of the style of life. Once these beliefs

have been held for a short time, later experiences of a different kind "scarcely count." Behavior springs from a person's ideas about self and life.

FUTURE GOALS VERSUS PAST EVENTS

It is also during childhood that each person establishes a *finalism*—a fictional goal toward which all psychological currents flow, thereby unifying the personality. Development of this concept was influenced by Hans Vaihinger's (1925) philosophy that people create fictional ideas for themselves "as if" they were objectively true. Examples of such hypothetical, convenient fictions include "All men are created equal," "Climb every mountain," and "I am an average person." Fictional ideas, nevertheless, may be quite useful. A finalistic goal orients the individual's personality toward future expectations, not the past. It provides direction for promised security, power, and perfection, and awakens feelings consistent with one's anticipations. Freudian instincts, mechanisms, impulses, and childhood traumas are far less important in this process than Adlerian *teleology*, the intentional directedness of human behavior toward a future goal or purpose of its own making. One's finalistic goal

> appears in one's attitude toward others, toward one's vocation, toward the opposite sex. Thus we find concrete single purposes, such as: to operate as a member of the community or to dominate it, to attain security and triumph in one's chosen career, to approach the other sex or to avoid it. We may always trace in these special purposes *what sort of meaning the individual has found in his existence,* and how he proposes to realize that meaning. (Adler, 1930, p. 400)

The attitude we adopt toward solving the "three great problems of existence" is necessarily reflected in our personality. Because personality is a unity, the direction of our capacity for living life in common with others is manifested even in the "slightest" of our expressive movements. Our beliefs, misconceptions, social interest, or lack of social interest characterize all forms of personal expression, including our memories, dreams, bodily postures, and physical ailments. This framework underlies Adler's personality-assessment technique of interpreting early recollections (see Applications).

Further, an individual's style of life is best seen in new situations, especially those that confront the person with difficulties. This is because one's stylistic "gait" is more clearly displayed during "storms of life" and other "serious tests" demanded by reality. Problems result when the individual's fictions clash with reality, thereby "disclosing his wrong meaning—the mistaken significance he has foisted on life" (Adler, 1964, pp. 40–41). A type of psychological *shock* or failure may be experienced, resulting in a narrowing of the person's field of action or path of advance, an exclusion of threatening tasks, and a retreat from problems for which the person is not prepared. Disillusionment, disappointment, and isolation may occur. In fact, Adler defines *neurosis* as an extreme form of reaction to shock, "a person's automatic, unknowing exploitation of the symptoms resulting from the effects of a shock" (1964, p. 180). The general level of social feeling is not high among neurotics, who likely have been pampered as children. At bottom, negative personality traits such as shyness, anxiety, reserve, and pessimism are marks of a longstanding "defective inclination and preparation of the whole personality" in contacts with other persons (p. 112). The essence of Adlerian therapy is to increase the neurotic's awareness of this lack of cooperative power, traced to early childhood maladjustments. A technique he found helpful in working with neurotics is to bring out the "courage" and "optimism" aspects of social feeling still existing within the neurotic personality.

OVERCOMING INFERIORITY

Adler believed in the thesis that to be human means to feel inferior, insufficient, helpless. This universal human experience is grounded in a struggle for perfection. Individuals are "always possessed and spurred on by a feeling of inferiority," brought about by their perpetual comparisons of themselves with unattainable ideals of perfection (Adler, 1964, p. 37). As evidenced in evolution, there is a "great upward drive" or "compulsion" to carry out a better adaptation. In essence, all personality develops from *inferiority*—"the persistence of the consequences of the feeling of inferiority and the retention of that feeling" (1964, p. 115). The individual's movement in life is "from a minus to a plus situation."

inferiority

Inferiority complex is Adler's term for a more exaggerated, personal, and abnormal form of weakness that is partly explained by a deficiency in social feeling. Adler discussed three childhood handicaps contributing to a lack of social feeling: inferior organs, neglect, and overindulgence.

First, there is the child's possession of inferior physical organs. Adler's (1907/1917) study of organic inferiority led him to conclude that feelings of psychological inferiority might be due to a person's physical limitations. This is because children born with organic weaknesses are necessarily required to compensate for them. They may even "overcompensate." The Greek orator, Demosthenes, had weak lungs and a weak voice. Pianist Klara Schumann had hearing problems as a child, and composer Beethoven was too deaf to hear his magnificent Ninth Symphony. Closer to home, we are reminded of a blind college student who ended a classroom talk about personal career plans by indicating all possibilities were open to him, including that of becoming an astronomer. Adler saw human development as "blessed with inferior organs" (1930, p. 395) because of the achievements that can be traced to the effort taken to overcome physical inferiorities.

The second childhood handicap is parental neglect—the unwanted or hated child. Such a child does not experience love, cooperation, and friendly forces, and seldom finds a trustworthy other person. Throughout life, personal resources are often underrated as being too limited to meet life's problems which, in turn, are overrated as being too difficult. Neglected children may be described as cold, suspicious, untrusting, hard, envious, and hateful.

Third, there is parental overindulgence—a harmful practice often producing a pampered or spoiled child. Adler proposed this framework as an alternative to Freud's "misinterpretation" of observations surrounding the Oedipus complex. The Oedipus complex is not a universal fact but something that occurs infrequently. It is an abnormality, the unnatural outcome of overindulgence by the child's opposite-sex parent. The basic pattern is one in which the pampered child is allowed contact mainly with the person doing the spoiling, thereby excluding others.

STRIVING FOR SUPERIORITY

striving for superiority

If one fundamental law of life is that to be human is to feel inferior, a second law is that to be human is to overcome one's constantly pressing sense of inferiority. "To live means to develop oneself" (Adler, 1964, p. 269). This *striving for superiority* is a universal psychological phenomenon that parallels physical growth. Its goal is to bring about perfection, security, or strength, as represented by the dictates "Achieve! Arise! Conquer!" Specific paths to conquest are as different "in a thousand ways" as the chosen goals. *Superiority complex* is Adler's term for a more exaggerated, abnormal form of striving or "overcompensation" for personal weakness that, again, is partly explained by an unaccepted deficiency in social feeling. The neurotic person presents a false front of superiority as a method of escaping from social difficulties. Normal persons do not have superiority complexes. Their strivings for superiority are aimed at common ambitions for success, expressed through cooperation in society, work, and love. By contrast, a superiority complex "invariably" stands in opposition to social cooperation.

FAMILY INFLUENCES ON PERSONALITY DEVELOPMENT

birth order

Several family influences on personality development are discussed by Adler (1964). The most important influence is that of the mother, whose contact probably contributes the largest part of human social feeling to the child. Two tasks are involved: encouraging social interest by providing "the greatest experience of love and fellowship" the child will ever have; and spreading this connectedness, trust, and friendship onto others as an attitude of working cooperatively with others in life. Adlerian therapists assume this role when working with persons who are deficient in social feeling, first winning the patient's goodwill and then transferring it to others in the environment. The second phase of development is experience with the father, toward whom Adler directed a number of specific suggestions: allow children freedom to speak and ask questions; encourage children to pursue their own interests; do not ridicule or belittle; do not seek to supplant the mother; make mealtimes pleasant; be supportive. Adler stated that the authority of paternal leadership in family organization "rests only to a very slight degree on social interest" (1964, p. 174). Third in importance is *birth order* — the child's position relative to other siblings (see Table 4.3). Adler deemed it a "superstition" to believe that a given family situation is the same for each individual child. It is not birth order itself that accounts for differences among siblings, but the psychological situation resulting from it. This clarification helps account for exceptions to Adler's hypotheses about sibling positions, since situations may be psychologically similar for children in seemingly inconsistent birth-order positions. Additional developmental factors discussed by Adler include illness, school entry, and sex.

TABLE 4.3   Some Adlerian Hypotheses about Birth Order

Birth order	Hypotheses
Only child	The center of attention, dominant, often spoiled because of excessive parental timidity and anxiety
First-born	Dethroned from a central position, with negative attitudes and feelings toward the second child, often a problem child, but protective and helpful toward others
Second-born	Actively struggling to surpass others, with success, related to competition with the first-born, restless
Last-born	The most pampered because the smallest and weakest, not unhappy, able to excel over others by being different, often a problem child
Only girl/boy	Extreme feminine or masculine orientation

Basic Concepts: Fromm

Erich Fromm was born in Frankfurt, Germany, in 1900, the only child of Orthodox Jewish parents. He characterized his parents as "highly neurotic" and himself as an "unbearable, neurotic child" (Funk, 1982).

Fromm's professional life was marked by interests in two major figures of the 20th century, Sigmund Freud and Karl Marx, whose ideas he tried to synthe-

ERICH FROMM.
How is it possible for people to give up the freedom of life or support the destructiveness of war? Fromm's sociocultural perspective extended social psychoanalytic ideas to their fullest. He wrote of differences among entire societies, some productive, others nonproductive, some "sane," and some "sick."

size. His interest in psychoanalysis was triggered by an incident that occurred during his adolescence. A 25-year-old friend of the family, a painter, killed herself following the death of her widowed father, with whom she had spent nearly all of her time.

> I had never heard of an Oedipus complex or of incestuous fixations between daughter and father. But I was deeply touched. I had been quite attracted to the young woman; I had loathed the unattractive father; never before had I known anyone to commit suicide. I was hit by the thought "How is it possible?" How is it possible that a beautiful young woman should be so in love with her father, that she prefers to be buried with him to being alive to the pleasures of life and of painting? (Fromm, 1962, p. 4)

Fromm arrived at his interest in Marx—"the key" to understanding human events—through multiple avenues. First, the religious atmosphere in his childhood home led to intensive study of the Old Testament. He was particularly taken with the prophets who wrote of universal peace and harmony among all nations. Second, as a Jewish boy in a Christian community, he experienced feelings of "clannishness" on both sides, along with occasional episodes of anti-Semitism. Third, there was World War I, "the event that determined more than anything else my development" (1962, p. 6). He could not fathom the jubilation of an admired teacher over the outbreak of war, and was equally struck by a national hysteria of hate against the British. Amidst doubletalk of "strategic retreats" and "victorious defenses," he found that a number of uncles, cousins, and schoolmates had been killed. He again asked himself "How is it possible?" These adolescent experiences produced a deeply troubled young man who was moved to seek understanding of the irrationality of human mass behavior. He also became "deeply suspicious of all official ideologies and declarations" (1962, p. 9).

Fromm studied philosophy, sociology, and psychology at the universities of Heidelberg, Frankfurt, and Munich. He came to the United States in 1933, settling in New York City, where he became acquainted with Horney and Sullivan. A lecturer and practicing psychoanalyst, Fromm joined the American Socialist Party, became active in the peace movement, and was a cofounder of SANE (the Organization for a Sane Nuclear Policy). He later established the Department of Psychoanalysis at the National University of Mexico. He died in 1980.

A SOCIOCULTURAL, PSYCHOANALYTIC, AND HUMANISTIC FRAMEWORK

Fromm's perspective on social influences was very broad. He discussed such cultural influences on personality as the feudal system of the Medieval Age, the Protestant Reformation, 19th-century industrialization, and 20th-century nazism, fascism, communism, and capitalism. His discussions nevertheless occurred within a psychoanalytic context. As a humanistic psychologist, Fromm was quite comfortable talking about human values, ethics, and meaning (as was Jung). He was convinced that psychology cannot be divorced from philosophy, ethics, sociology, or economics. He saw psychology as having the potential to debunk false ethical judgments and build objective and valid norms of conduct. His theory may be described as *sociopsychoanalytic humanism*.

FIVE EXISTENTIAL NEEDS

According to Fromm, people are alike in that they all experience the same fundamental facts of human existence, which are inherently contradictory and troublesome. This is because the human situation is grounded in dichotomies, or opposites, that are *existential* — biologically rooted in the very existence of humankind, somewhere "between missing instincts and self-awareness" (Fromm, 1973). Thus, all persons find themselves part of, yet alone; living, yet dying; free, yet responsible; conscious of their potentialities, yet powerless over their limitations.

People also are alike in sharing *five existential needs:* a frame of orientation and object of devotion, rootedness, unity, effectiveness, and excitation and stimulation. If any of these needs is not met, abnormality results.

five existential
needs

Frame of orientation and object of devotion.   First, all persons need a *frame of orientation* — a cognitive "map" of their natural and social world that enables them to organize and make rational sense of puzzling phenomena and place themselves in a context of intellectual understanding. A frame of orientation is important regardless of its being true or false, as with a person's belief "in the power of a totem animal, in a rain god, or in the superiority and destiny of his race" (Fromm, 1959, p. 160). This vital need for a cohesive frame of orientation partly explains the ease with which people fall under the spell of irrational political and religious doctrines. "The more an ideology pretends to give answers to all questions, the more attractive it is" (Fromm, 1973, p. 231). In addition, people need some *object of devotion* — a goal that gives meaning to their existence and position in the world. Such an "ultimate concern" provides direction in life, reduces isolation, and permits transcendence beyond one's immediate self.

Rootedness.   The second need, rootedness, is a deep craving to maintain one's natural ties and not be "separated." Without roots we would have to stand alone, in isolation and helplessness, not knowing where or who we are. Most persons show progress in life by substituting new roots for old. When biological separation occurs, through birth and maturation, substitute attachments are sought, both symbolically (god, mother, country) and emotionally (love, community).

Those who fight too strongly against life's process of continuous birth exhibit severe abnormalities. They regress by psychologically fixating themselves on the protection of their parents, home, or past, unable to give them up. Although people may relate to others through submission or domination, these are forms of dependency that, unlike love, destroy personal integrity and freedom. Such a "symbiotic" form of relatedness was shown by the young woman discussed in Fromm's biography who committed suicide after her father's death. The woman was unable to separate herself from her father.

Unity.   The third need is for *unity*—a sense of inner oneness with self, nature, and humanity. The person is able to say and feel "I am I." This is achieved not by regressing to animal existence but by becoming fully human (Fromm, 1973). Unity cannot be realized by trying to "forget oneself" through alcohol, drugs, sexual orgies, trances, or cultist rituals. Nor can it be realized by trying to forget one's personhood, as in overidentifying with an organization or social role, perhaps as a workaholic. Members of Western civilization have often sought a false sense of identity, security, conformity, or status by adhering to such social roles as "I am an American . . . a Protestant . . . an executive." Citizens of the 20th century also have sought to "escape from freedom" by giving up their individuality to mass totalitarian governments (Fromm, 1941). For Fromm, the only successful approach to unity that does not cripple people is the development of human reason and love.

Effectiveness.   The fourth need is for *effectiveness*—a sense of being able to do something that will "make a dent" in life. Effectiveness helps transform one's accidental and passive role of creature into that of an active and purposeful creator. It also offers some proof of one's existence and identity, based on the realization "I am, because I effect." People may experience joy by producing effects that are either positive or negative—making a noisy clatter, eliciting a smile from a loved one, creating an artistic work, doing what is forbidden, destroying property, or even causing terror in a victim. One's "ultimate choice" is whether to create and love, or destroy and hate.

Excitation and stimulation.   The fifth need is for *excitation and stimulation*, the need for the nervous system to be "exercised." The importance of this need is supported by research showing brain and dream activity during sleep and sensory deprivation, and by the abnormal reactions of infants to lack of social contact. This need can be satisfied by two kinds of stimuli: simple or activating. *Simple stimuli* are similar to reflexes in that they call for reactions more than actions, particularly surface reactions that are immediate and passive in nature. Simple stimuli are often associated with "thrill" excitements: accidents, fires, crimes, wars, arguments, sex-related movies and advertisements, and television violence. *Activating stimuli* are more complicated, in that they cause the person to become engaged in productive activity for longer periods of time. Examples include ideas, novels, landscapes, musical works, and loved ones. To Fromm, activating stimuli are healthier but require greater maturity because they do not lead as quickly to excitement. Activating stimuli require greater effort, patience, discipline, concentration, frustration tolerance, and the practice of critical thinking. Rather than reacting, the person must bring these stimuli to life, sometimes by overcoming boredom.

INDIVIDUAL AND SOCIAL CHARACTER

Individual differences among people.   Although they share common existential problems and needs, people are also different. This is seen in Fromm's definition of personality as "the totality of inherited and acquired psychic qualities which are characteristic of one individual and which make the individual unique" (1947, p. 50). Inherited, constitutional differences lead people to experience the same environment in more or less different ways. People also show uniqueness "in the specific way they solve their human problem" (1947, p. 50).

Fromm actually devotes much greater attention to the concept of character than to personality. Character develops at two levels: individual and social. It is based not on libido, as Freud believed, but on the individual's relatedness to the world.

Individual character is the pattern of behavior characteristic of a given person—"the relatively permanent system of all noninstinctual strivings through which man relates himself to the human and natural world" (Fromm, 1973, p. 226). Because character involves deeply rooted habits and opinions, it serves a decision-making function. It is a semiautomatic process of action and thought, analogous to behavioral reflexes, that saves an individual from having to make deliberate, conscious decisions every time the occasion arises. Once energy is channeled in a certain way, action takes place "true to character."

Individual differences among societies.   Thus far in this book, we have been discussing differences in persons. However, a contribution unique to Fromm is his interest in identifying differences in entire societies.

Social character represents "the core of a character structure common to most people of a given culture" (1947, p. 60). Social character is more clearly the product of one's society. In a sense, individual character becomes partly "lost" as it is subsumed by social character.

> The whole personality of the average individual is molded by the way people relate to each other, and it is determined by the socioeconomic and political structure of society to such an extent that, in principle, one can infer from the analysis of one individual the totality of the social structure in which he lives. (Fromm, 1947, p. 79)

Fromm (1947) has identified five types of social character, or forms of relatedness to others: receptive, exploitative, hoarding, marketing, and productive. These social-character types express themselves in how individuals relate to things and to people (including themselves). Fromm classifies the first four as "nonproductive" because they are distorted, incomplete, or unfulfilling. In contrast, the productive orientation is based on love, a mutual intimacy that preserves individual integrity. Although the five types are "ideals," and usually blended in people, one type is likely to be dominant depending upon cultural values. Also, because of the interaction between individual and culture, it is always possible for individuals to affect their society.

Persons of a *receptive* orientation experience the source of all good as being outside themselves. Their orientation is to receive from others, and they show their oral nature by being fond of food and drink. Receptive persons are dependent, say "yes" rather than "no," listen to others, and seek to be loved and helped. They wish for a "magic helper": "If I submit to the stronger person, he will give me all I need." The receptive orientation is found in societies in which exploitation of subgroups is firmly established through power, "expertise," or public

individual character

social character

four nonproductive orientations

opinion. This is because exploited groups, such as slave laborers, are permitted little opportunity to develop personal resources or effect change.

Persons of an *exploitative* orientation also experience the source of all good as outside themselves. However, they do not expect to receive from others but to take things away, through force or cunning. Their orientation is to grab, steal, and manipulate, while remaining suspicious, cynical, jealous, and hostile. They underrate what they have and overrate what others have. Their mottos are "I take what I need" and "Stolen fruits are sweetest." This orientation is represented in societies dominated by feudal lords and 19th-century robber barons, who exploited human and natural resources through power, wealth, ruthless competition, authoritarianism, and the right of might.

Persons of a *hoarding* orientation differ from the two preceding orientations in that they see little coming from the outside. Their security is based on an attitude of saving, of letting out as little as possible. They hold onto the past, are always ready to say "no," and are possessive in love. They set up protective walls to fortify their position. Their motto is "Mine is mine, and yours is yours." This orientation is represented by societies adopting a Puritan ethic of hard work and success, in which middle-class stability is provided through possession of property and family.

The *marketing* orientation is unique to the modern historical era, related to contemporary economic functions in society. Persons of this orientation experience themselves as a salable commodity. They seek to package and sell themselves, "to be in demand." They evaluate themselves according to their exchange value, allowing the "personality factor" to play a decisive role. Their self-esteem depends on market conditions beyond their control. Whereas the self of a productive person is based on effectiveness, meaning "I am what I do," that of marketing orientation is "I am as you desire me." Different from the preceding three, the marketing orientation does not lie within the person, who experiences emptiness. There is no specific, permanent kind of relatedness to others, except through superficial roles, pretenses, and opportunistic changes in attitudes.

productive orientation

The *productive orientation* refers to an attitude of fully developed relatedness toward the world and oneself in the process of living. It encompasses relatedness in all realms of human experience: reasoning, loving, and working. The productive orientation is not concerned with practical results or "success." Most important is the individual's use and realization of the potent powers all humans have

reason

"to do," to express one's "character." The human capacity for *productive reasoning* can be used to penetrate surface phenomena and gain understanding of their essence. The power of *productive love* can break through walls that separate people

love

from one another, allowing close understanding of another person's mental and emotional human core. It is characterized by care, responsibility, respect, and

work

knowledge. Through *productive work*, people can transform materials into other forms, using reason and imagination to visualize things not yet existing, to create, and to plan.

In essence, the productive orientation provides an answer to the basic contradictions of human existence. It suggests that a person's main task in life is to give birth to oneself, to become what one potentially is. The most important product of this effort is one's own "mature and integrated" personality or character. This is because Fromm, like Jung, believed that every person is more than "a blank sheet of paper on which culture can write its text" (1947, p. 23). *A human nature exists.* Therefore, what is ethically good in Fromm's humanistic framework is the unfolding of powers according to the laws of human nature. This led Fromm (1959) to propose a positive concept of mental health that is not just the absence of sickness but the presence of well-being: to be aware, responsive, independent, fully active, one with the world, understanding that living creatively is the only meaning of life, joyful in the act of living and expressing this throughout one's whole body, and concerned with being rather than having (Fromm, 1976). Failure to make use of one's innate, human powers results in unhappiness, psychological disturbance, and neurosis. (Fromm's concepts of culturally patterned failures and "sick societies" are discussed in Chapter 11.)

SOCIETY'S PSYCHOLOGICAL AGENT: THE FAMILY

Fromm (1973) sees the family as the psychological agency through which a child acquires the core of social character shared by most other children of the same social class and culture. Parents are the representatives of a society's atmosphere and spirit, which they transmit just by being the persons they are. An important developmental aim is for parents to help the child "desire to act" as it "has to act." This is best seen when social and individual character coincide. A person individually driven to save money, spending only for necessities, and also of the hoarding orientation, gains both psychological and social satisfactions by doing business in a society that values economic efficiency and thrift. An authoritarian person of exploitative social orientation who listens to ideological speeches about political forces so powerful that human submission is the only alternative also achieves dual satisfactions. Thus, individual psychological traits cement the social structure.

SOCIOCULTURAL REINTERPRETATIONS OF FREUD

Regarding Freud's psychosexual stages of development, Fromm (1941) suggested that Freud had reversed the causal relationship between erogenous zones and personality traits. Thus, according to Fromm, Freud's "oral" personality is not due to biologically based, erogenous sensations; rather, the "oral language of the body" reflects the person's attitude toward the world, as depicted in the concept of the receptive character. The personality originates as a *reaction* to social experiences with other people. Recognizing that parental care or affection is given only under conditions of surrender, the child becomes fearful and experiences a weakening of its strength and self-confidence. The child then gives up its natural self-initiative and learns to direct its energies toward "an outside source from which the fulfillment of all wishes will eventually come" (Fromm, 1941, p. 292).

Fromm (1947) also reinterpreted Freud's concept of the Oedipus complex. In Fromm's view, it represents the child's struggle for individual freedom and independence against the pressures of parental authority that are so much a part of patriarchal society. The child's fight is to minimize the effects of guilt or submission, which threaten to weaken the self, by seeking to become his or her type of full-fledged human being rather than a cultural robot.

Supporting Evidence

The support for social-psychoanalytic theories is largely non-empirical. Rather than formal research, it relies on personal experience and informal cultural and clinical observations. Analyses of case studies, dreams, social interactions, and cultural phenomena appear often. The social psychoanalysts also make references to independent sources of information that are historical, anthropological, sociological, philosophical, and literary in nature. However, these sources are subject to bias, through the kind of "participant observations" recognized by Sullivan.

Although the social psychoanalysts continue to influence thinking about personality and clinical practice, no social-psychoanalytic theory has undergone extensive experimental investigation. In part, some of the assumptions and concepts rise or fall on the shoulders of Freud's theory. Some of the theories are conceptually loose (Fromm, Adler), with Sullivan's being moderately systematic. Finally, the professional community has not shown any intense interest in testing the theories experimentally. When experiments have been done, they have focused on a few specific concepts, assessment methods, or therapy techniques. However, some support has come from indirect sources. Here we will review evidence that bears on a few key concepts of Sullivan, Horney, Adler, and Fromm.

SULLIVAN AND HORNEY: PHYSICAL CONTACT AND INTERPERSONAL RELATIONSHIPS

Sullivan's theory of personality development emphasizes the importance of physical contact between the infant and "a mothering one," as well as progressive involvement in peer relationships over time. The theories of Sullivan and Horney both emphasize the role of empathic, nonverbal communication in close, child-maternal relationships, which may be characterized by anxiety or security. These emphases are supported by independent lines of research.

Physical contact.   Human infants do show a need to have intimate physical contact with a parent figure, termed "primary object-clinging" by John Bowlby (1969). In a 1951 report to the World Health Organization, Bowlby concluded that mental health in infants requires the experiencing of a warm, intimate, and continuous relationship with a maternal figure, not necessarily the biological mother. He indicated that infants placed in institutional settings such as hospitals and orphanages who do not receive physical contact from a nurturing figure soon show developmental and survival difficulties attributable to interpersonal deprivation.

To illustrate, Spitz (1946) observed symptoms of depression in 45 of 123 infants who had been placed in nursery homes following separation from their parents. Symptoms included loss of appetite, trouble sleeping, crying, slow motor movements, apathy, physical withdrawal such as turning toward a wall, vulnerability to infection, and slowed development. An extreme form of this reaction is

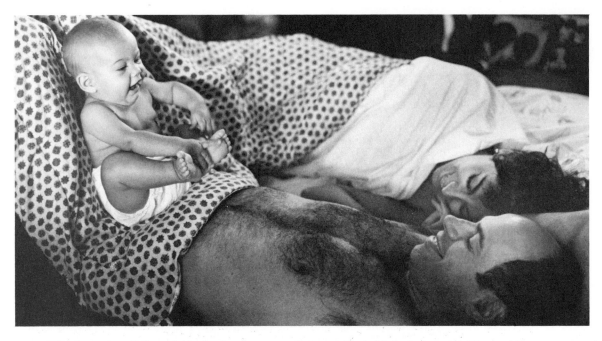

Which are more influential in the development of personality—biological or social factors? Horney, Sullivan, Adler, and Fromm emphasized social factors, especially family relationships, whereas Freud emphasized biological ones.

marasmus, a "hospitalism" syndrome in infants who self-destructively "waste away" in the absence of any demonstrable physical cause (Bosselman, 1958). Fortunately, such symptoms can be counteracted by regular, daily physical contact with a consistent nurturing person, such as a nurse or volunteer caregiver. This important finding has been translated into international prevention programs involving routine, daily "cuddling" of all babies in institutions.

Researchers have also differentiated two patterns of infant behaviors in experiments involving brief separation and reunion with mothers. On the one hand, separation may elicit "attachment" behaviors, through which infants try to find the missing caregiver and reestablish physical contact. On the other hand, infants may show "detachment" behaviors of indifference, protest, or despair (Bowlby, 1969; Suomi, Collins, Harlow, & Ruppenthal, 1976). Ainsworth (1979) has linked these two kinds of infant-mother interaction during the first year to personality adjustment at ages 4–6. In follow-up studies, infants who are "securely attached" at age 1 are not only socially more cooperative and emotionally positive in later years, but less angry, aggressive, and avoidant, compared with "anxiously attached infants." Ainsworth noted that secure attachment is fostered more by *how* the caregiver holds the infant, close to the body and face to face, rather than *how long* the infant is held.

The research of Harry Harlow (1958) and his co-workers is relevant to Sullivan's theory. Harlow (1959) placed infant rhesus monkeys in individual cages containing two substitute or surrogate mothers, one constructed of wire and the other of terry cloth. Both types of "mother" were physiologically equivalent, because they were equipped with nursing-bottle nipples through which milk was furnished. However, they proved not to be psychologically equivalent. Infant monkeys spent far more time climbing and clinging on the cloth-covered surrogates, which served as a psychological security-base of operations. When frightening stimuli were introduced into the cages, such as a toy teddy bear beating a drum, the infants immediately sought security by running to the cloth mothers. This occurred even with monkeys who otherwise obtained milk from wire surrogates. Results pointed to the "overwhelming importance" of bodily contact and the comfort it supplies to infants, more than just the libidinous "oral" sensations referred to in classical psychoanalysis.

To establish a control group, Harlow separated some infant monkeys from their mothers, thereby depriving them of physical contact altogether. After 8 months, when placed in individual cages with the two types of surrogate mothers, these "orphan" monkeys were fearful of both. Eventually, they were observed spending less than an hour with the wire surrogate but 8–10 hours with the cloth surrogate, which still was only half the time spent by monkeys who had been raised with surrogates. After another 18 months of separation, the orphans showed little evidence of reattachment during reunions with surrogates, differing once again from "raised" monkeys and providing a further indication of "psychological damage" resulting from early interpersonal deprivation.

Peer relationships.   Harlow and Harlow (1974) have stated that "the importance of peer relationships in monkeys cannot be overemphasized" (p. 199). Such social interactions provide critical opportunities for learning affection toward peers, controlled fear and aggression, grooming, sex roles through play, sexual competence, and parental behavior. (Adler often alluded to the difficulty of showing social feeling in adulthood if it had not developed during childhood.) There even may be an evolutionary advantage in having independent sources of affection, with parents and peers compensating for potential deficiencies in one another.

Suomi and Harlow(1972) reported fascinating use of younger-age peers as "therapists" in successfully rehabilitating monkeys who had been socially isolated for 6 months. Isolates were permitted to interact with socially normal monkeys who were 3 months younger. The approach reflected in the nonthreatening behaviors of the young monkey "therapists" may be analogous to the "trust" and the gradual "reeducation" dimensions characteristic of Horney and Sullivan's approaches to therapy with humans.

ADLER: BIRTH ORDER AND EARLIEST RECOLLECTIONS

Birth order.   Two aspects of Adler's individual psychology have caught the attention of researchers. First is the topic of birth order. Adler's theory addresses the impact of family size, sex of siblings, and birth order or sibling position on personality. Reviews of the literature indicate a total of 391 studies on birth order between 1963 and 1971 (Miley, 1969; Vockell, Felker, & Miley, 1973). Birth order was also the sole topic of the May 1977 issue of *Individual Psychology*.

In one study, MacDonald (1971) explored relationships between birth order and six personality variables in 1262 college students. Although mean differences among birth-order groups were slight, the following, simplified relationships were suggested: first-borns as rigid, first-borns and only-children as socially responsible, only-females as needing approval, and later-borns as controlled more externally than internally.

Contradictory findings plague this area of research, often resulting from an absence of theoretical rationale, disregard of family size and sex of siblings, and failures to separate only-children from first-borns (MacDonald, 1971; Schooler, 1972). Havassy – De Avila (1971) urged that greater attention be paid to psychological processes underlying birth-order differences, rather than looking at the simplistic fact of birth order itself. In support of this position, Jordan, Whiteside, and Manaster (1982) evaluated seven different schemas for measuring birth-order effects among 467 business majors. The only schema that predicted academic achievement was the one that included information on sex of subject and sex of siblings rather than birth position alone. Competitive desire to succeed and career strivings were highest in only-males. Personal unconcern over possible negative interpersonal consequences of achievement was highest in only-females.

Outside the framework of Adlerian theory, Zajonc and Markus (1975) have analyzed the relationship of birth order, family spacing, and family size to intellectual development, using data on nearly 400,000 Dutch 19-year-old males. Other things being equal, they found larger family size detrimental to intellectual development. The fewer the children, and the more ideal the spacing between them, the smarter each is likely to be. Older children are likely to be smarter than younger ones. However, the picture is more complicated than this, involving differences in opportunities for social contact with parents and learning experiences with siblings. Greater spacing between children is beneficial to the youngest sibling but not the oldest who already has the best possible "teachers" — mature parents.

Earliest recollections.   The second Adlerian topic that has been much studied is that of earliest recollections (ERs) (Mosak, 1969). On this topic, Olson (1979) estimates a literature base of 100 articles. Using ERs, Burnell and Solomon (1964) were able to predict success or failure in basic military training of Air Force recruits. Jackson and Sechrest (1962) reported more ER themes of fear in anxiety neurotics, abandonment in depressed clients, and illness in psychosomatic patients. In a study by Hafner, Fakouri, and Labrentz (1982), more alcoholics than non-alcoholics remembered threatening situations and showed themes of being controlled externally rather than internally. Mosak and Kopp (1973) interpreted the ERs of Adler, Freud, and Jung and concluded that Adler related to people through inadequacy, Freud through provocation, and Jung through helplessness.

FROMM: SOCIAL CHARACTER IN MEXICAN VILLAGERS

Fromm and Maccoby (1970) undertook a field study of social character in a Mexican village as a test of Fromm's (1947) theory. They wanted to demonstrate that the social character common to a group could be assessed and related to socioeconomic variables.

An open-ended "interpretative questionnaire" of about 90 items was given to 406 adults (95% of all residents) of a Mexican farming village. Social character among the villagers was found to be high in receptive orientation (44%) and low in exploitative (11%). Men were more receptive than women, who were more hoarding. Sociopolitically, villagers were most often submissive (49%) rather than democratic (7%) or rebellious (7%). Parental fixations were almost entirely toward the mother (96%). Of 14% adult male villagers identified as alcoholic, 80% were receptive in character, compared with only 37% of abstainers ($p < .01$).

The results pointed to three main types of social character: productive-hoarding, nonproductive-receptive, and productive-exploitative. These social adaptations corresponded to three distinct socioeconomic conditions: free landowner, landless day laborer, and new type of entrepreneur, respectively. The hoarding orientation was the one "best adapted" to the economic demands of peasant farming in the village, in contrast with the receptive peasant, who was seen as being "out of tune" with the world. Interestingly, even the type of crop landholders chose to plant was related to social character. Productive-hoarding landowners tended to plant rice, a crop requiring harder work but promising higher profit. Receptive landholders tended to plant sugarcane, a crop requiring less work but twice the time to grow, and promising less profit.

Overall, support was provided for the general hypothesis that "social character is the result of the adaptation of human nature to given socioeconomic conditions" (p. 230).

Applications

ADLER'S ASSESSMENT TECHNIQUE OF EARLIEST RECOLLECTIONS

In Box 4.1, you were asked to write down your earliest memory. If you haven't done this yet, you might consider doing so before proceeding.

earliest
recollection

The technique of asking people to state their earliest recollection (ER) was developed by Alfred Adler. Adler would "never" investigate a personality without asking for the first memory, which he considered one of the "most trustworthy" ways of exploring personality. In essence, ERs are summary statements about personality, closely tied to the person's style of life.

Adler's reliance on ERs reflects his special brand of determinism, which centers around the assumption that the present determines the past. This is just the opposite of Freud's determinism, which assumes that the past determines the present. According to Adler, we are necessarily "forced" to select precisely those events from our past that best represent our current personality. We have little choice in the matter. Also, it makes no difference whether or not the events appearing in our ER really occurred. It is only important that we *believe* such events happened, in the particular way we remember them.

> Among all psychological expressions, some of the most revealing are the individual's memories. His memories are the reminders he carries about with him of his own limits and of the meaning of circumstances.

There are no "chance memories": out of the incalculable number of impressions which meet an individual, he chooses to remember only those which he feels, however darkly, to have a bearing on his situation. Thus his memories represent his "Story of My Life"; a story he repeats to himself to warn him or comfort him, to keep him concentrated on his goal. . . . A depressed individual could not remain depressed if he remembered his good moments and his successes. He must say to himself, "All my life I was unfortunate," and select only those events which he can interpret as instances of his unhappy fate. Memories can never run counter to the style of life. (Adler, 1956, p. 351)

Two examples of first memories follow, accompanied by Adler's (1956) interpretations of them.

#1. When I was three years old, my father purchased for us a pair of ponies. He brought them by the halters to the house. My sister took one strap and led her pony triumphantly down the street. My own pony, hurrying after the other, went too fast for me and trailed me face downward in the dirt. It was an ignominious end to an experience which had been gloriously anticipated. The fact that I later surpassed my sister as a horsewoman has never mellowed this disappointment in the least. (pp. 354–355)

Adler offered a "blind interpretation" of this memory, which means he knew nothing about the person who gave it. He assumed the person to be a girl who was more interested in her father than her mother. There is triumph for the older sister, who may have been the mother's favorite. The girl is unable to keep up with her older sister. She believes she must be careful or her sister will always win, resulting in the girl's being left behind or in the dirt, defeated. The girl's attitude conveyed in the ER is "If anyone is ahead of me, I am endangered. I must always be first."

#2. When I was about four years old I sat at the window and watched some workmen building a house on the opposite side of the street, while my mother knitted stockings. (p. 356)

This memory was provided by a 32-year-old man, an eldest sibling whom Adler identified as the "spoiled son of a widow." His life was characterized by severe anxiety attacks, except when he was at home. Past school and professional work had proved difficult for him. While good-natured, he had found it difficult to make social contact with others. Although his ER may seem "rather insignificant," it is not. Support for his having been a pampered child is present in his recall of a situation that includes his solicitous mother. More important, his preparation for life is that of being an onlooker: "he looks on while other people work." Once his anxiety has been eliminated through therapy, planning for future work could be guided by his natural dispositions toward seeing and observing. Adler recommended a business dealing with art objects.

BOX 4.1 REVISITED	*Interpreting Your Earliest Recollection*

In Box 4.1, you were asked to write your earliest recollection. Review your ER now from the viewpoint of Adler's theory. What might it indicate about your personality? In seeking to understand the meaning of your ER, it may be helpful to respond to some Adlerian guidelines for interpretation, listed below (Manaster & Perryman, 1979).

1. *Who is present?* Mother, father, siblings, grandparents, friends?
2. *Who is not present?*
3. *How are different people portrayed?* Basic thoughts, feelings, words, actions?
4. *What is the world like?* Friendly, hostile, cooperative, not cooperative, unfamiliar?
5. *What is your role or behavior?* Active, passive, independent, dependent, sick?
6. *What is the outcome of your behavior?* Success, failure, uncertainty, good, bad, right, wrong?
7. *What is your primary social attitude?* "I" or "we"?
8. *What is your dominant emotion?* Happy, sad, fearful, worried, guilty, proud?
9. *What is your primary motive?* To gain attention, power, revenge, or to be left alone?
10. *What is the underlying "story" of your life?* Use a single sentence.

Evaluation

CONTRIBUTIONS

The major collective contribution of the social-psychoanalytic theorists has been made evident throughout this chapter. These theorists recognized the crucial role of cultural, social, family, and interpersonal influences on human behavior, not only during the childhood development of personality but through adulthood.

Anticipating social psychology.   More specifically, the social psychoanalysts anticipated later developments in *social psychology* — the study of behavior in groups and social situations. Adler made regular references to "social psychology" in his writings, and his analyses of behavior in family and school settings were based on an appreciation of group dynamics. Horney adopted a cross-cultural approach to the understanding of personality. Sullivan's theory incorporated the views of sociologists and anthropologists. Fromm's view of social character was based on a concept of personality as shaped by socioeconomic conditions.

Developing new clinical techniques.   A second area of contribution concerns the development of clinical and therapeutic techniques. The social psychoanalysts were skillful therapists, oriented toward what Horney (1939) called "new ways in psychoanalysis." Horney worked principally with neurotic adults, Sullivan with schizophrenics and obsessional neurotics, and Adler with children in families and schools.

Horney also promoted self-exploration by presenting her theoretical and clinical ideas in popular, "plain language" books. She wrote expressly for interested laypersons "who want to know themselves and have not given up struggling for their own growth" (1945, p. 8). Her purpose was not to offer clear-cut answers or cures for neurotic conflicts, which would be unrealistic as well as unprofessional, but to offer information useful for self-examination. Her books include *The Neurotic Personality of Our Time* (1937), *Self-Analysis* (1942), *Our Inner Conflicts* (1945), and *Are You Considering Psychoanalysis?* (1946). Martin (1975) has characterized Horney's therapeutic approach as one of trust, confidence, respect for each person's individual uniqueness and inner constructive resources, and adherence to the principle that exploration always precedes explanation.

Sullivan's therapeutic approach also provided patients with a "basic experience of trust," within a context of personal shyness and sensitivity (Perry, 1982). Sullivan's (1954) book on psychiatric interviewing, detailing the "remarkable intermingling" of communication and defense, is a classic.

Adler proposed group-therapy treatment for criminals, but did not pursue this direction himself. However, he did pioneer an educational form of group therapy in which an individual's psychological problems are discussed in front of a professional audience (Ansbacher & Ansbacher, 1956). Adler would first read and interpret case-history material prepared by school personnel. Then he would meet with parents. Finally, he would talk with the child. Adler also paved the way for family therapy.

Responding to social problems.   A third contribution was the social psychoanalysts' example in responding to contemporary social problems. Horney's contribution to the development of a psychology for women relates to a social issue that is still very much evident today.

Sullivan (1947) concerned himself with child-rearing practices and sexual mores. He identified the kinds of parental attitudes contributing to psychological maladjustment in children: believing the infant must be clean and dry by 15 months, becoming upset when the infant tinkers with its genitals, treating an infant as if it were being willfully troublesome, and fancying that the infant "takes after" some other person in the family. In terms of sexual attitudes, he identified Americans as "the most sex-ridden people" he knew, related to two cultural conventions: discouraging early marriage and discouraging premarital sex. The combined effect of this "lurid twilight" is to widen the gap between the awakening of adolescent lust and the proper circumstances for marriage.

Adler became something of a social reformer, turning away from direct therapeutic work with children and parents and toward the "teaching of teachers" (Stepansky, 1983). By turning to public schools, Adler placed his hope for the future of children in the hands of teachers rather than parents and therapists, whose orientation he believed was too limited by a focus on individual children.

Fromm dealt directly with sweeping societal, ethical, and political issues, including those of the great socioeconomic systems of the 20th century. Countless people have been influenced by his best-selling books, *Escape from Freedom* (1941) and *The Art of Loving* (1956). His 1973 book, *The Anatomy of Human Destructiveness*, is a cogent and provocative commentary on the forces promoting life and death in contemporary culture. His 1976 book, *To Have or to Be?*, discusses humankind's critical need to control irrational social forces and proposes guidelines for a new society.

Showing effective intellectual independence.   Finally, it should not be forgotten that the social psychoanalysts paid heavy personal and professional penalties for their intellectual independence. Along with Jung, they were harshly castigated by Freud and his followers. Tones of puzzlement, bitterness, and resentment are clearly present in references by Adler (and Jung) to Freud, and vice versa. Sullivan was an exception because Freud was probably less aware of his unorthodox ideas (Perry, 1982). Like Jung, these theorists also experienced the circumstantial misfortune of having to work in Freud's shadow (Stepansky, 1983). Nevertheless, all became influential theorists in their own right. They attracted their own adherents, published their own professional journals, and established institutes for clinical training and practice.

LIMITATIONS

Little formal experimentation.   Social-psychoanalytic theories share with classical psychoanalysis two major limitations: an absence of controlled research studies testing theoretical concepts, and an emphasis on pathology. Relatively little systematic or programmatic research activity has been reported on social-psychoanalytic theories. The scarcity of experimental literature can be traced to several factors.

First, as with classical psychoanalysis, a number of social-psychoanalytic concepts related to personality are difficult to define and measure operationally. These concepts include such broad, external influences as parents, siblings, significant others, family, society, and culture. The theories typically are loosely tied together. Fromm shows a high degree of speculation, sometimes within philosophical and ethical contexts, and Sullivan's writing style is sometimes highly opaque or subtle.

Second, a number of important social-psychoanalytic concepts related to cultural issues literally involve *generations* of human beings. The phenomena underlying Adler's and Fromm's proposals for bringing about changes in social education and cultural systems span decades. The practical limitations involved in evaluating such programs through research are very difficult, if not impossible, to overcome, and potentially unethical. How would a researcher go about the process of introducing widespread educational innovations in a society (Adler), evaluating the effects of teaching parents to interact with their children in nontraditional ways (Horney, Sullivan), influencing basic human values through mass media (Fromm), or changing a country's politically based socioeconomic system (Fromm)? Even if such interventions were possible, they would be quite long-range, require multiple teams of researchers over time, and be quite costly. Imagine what it would take simply to obtain large numbers of subjects willing and able to participate in a program of social change on a continuing basis, even assuming individual and governmental consent. Which approaches are "better" and "worse"? Would you be willing to participate? Would you want to be in the experimental or control group?

Third, formal experimentation was not a major value for these theorists, all of whom were trained as physicians and psychiatrists. Like Freud and Jung, the social psychoanalysts were clinicians and theorists much more than they were scientific researchers. As we have already noted, the social psychoanalysts placed greatest reliance on informal methods of study. Their ideas were developed in offices, hospitals, and libraries, not in experimental laboratories. Nor was experimentation considered a major priority during the first half of the century, because of the relative infancy of psychiatry both as a profession and as a science. Therapists are more apt to be guided by non-experimental but nevertheless important concerns, such as servicing the psychological and social difficulties of persons who are struggling with their lives and in need of help.

A focus on human pathology.   Social-psychoanalytic theories, like classical psychoanalysis, focus a great deal on human pathology — on what is maladaptive in human functioning and what goes wrong in human relationships. Recall Horney's concepts of "basic anxiety" and "insecurity"; Sullivan's "bad mother," defensive "security operations," and "malevolent attitude"; Adler's "inferiorities," "parental neglect," and "pampering"; and Fromm's unrelenting "existential contradictions." Fromm discusses four "nonproductive" character orientations but only one "productive" orientation.

There is also an overriding emphasis on "neurosis." This is most obviously seen in Horney's "ten neurotic needs" and popular book titles, as well as in theorists' personal references to themselves and Freud. Consider Adler's reference to classical psychoanalysts and their patients as "pampered persons" whose views are "artificially produced by the resentment of spoiled children" (1964, p. 36). Is everyone maladjusted? A review of the many factors contributing to basic anxiety and insecurity in children highlights the difficulty, sometimes the seeming impossibility, of any parent behaving as a healthy, stabilizing influence on children. Personality development becomes a fretful phenomenon. So many things can go wrong in the parenting process that it is difficult to imagine more than marginal success in raising children. It is amazing that adjustment occurs at all.

This overemphasis on the negative was undoubtedly influenced by cultural factors associated with the kinds of German militarism and anti-Semitism present during the formative years of these theorists' personal development. Other social and individual influences may have contributed as well, as glimpsed in the childhood experiences of isolation and disturbances noted in the biographies of these theorists.

On the other hand, the negative focus is partly offset by social-psychoanalytic discussions of ideal human functioning, including self-realization (Horney), creative development of one's personality in a context of social cooperation (Adler), reciprocal and loving relationships with others (Sullivan), and a productive character orientation based on reason and love (Fromm). It is also partly offset by Fromm's positive approach to defining mental health, Horney's and

Sullivan's suggestions for enhancing healthy personality development (as through nurturant and predictable interactions with significant others), Adler's guidelines for democratic social cooperation, and Fromm's proposals for world peace.

CHAPTER REVIEW

This chapter has discussed a group of psychiatrists originally trained in classical psychoanalysis who independently questioned, revised, and abandoned various Freudian concepts. They especially reacted to the one-sided importance Freud placed on sexual motivation and the Oedipus complex. These social-psychoanalytic theorists developed alternatives that were much more social and cultural than instinctual in nature.

Horney's (1950) theory of neurosis and human growth is steeped in contexts of infantile helplessness, anxiety, and insecurity in a hostile world dominated by parents. Human struggle is in the direction of self-realization. Self-confidence develops when parents show the child genuine and predictable warmth, affection, and respect. This helps the child avoid the development of excessive, rigid, neurotic social needs for affection and approval. The child is free to move toward, against, and away from people in adaptive ways. Because cultural biases overvalue masculine social roles, a psychology of women must be given consideration.

In Sullivan's (1953) interpersonal theory, personality is defined as patterns of two-person relationships. It develops through six stages, during which the individual progresses through a sequence of interactions involving mothering ones, playmates, same-sex chums, opposite-sex peers, sexual partners, and love partners. Acquisition of social habits, especially language, are essential aspects of personality development. Self-system is the direct result of social feedback, taking form as reflected appraisals of disapproval and approval from significant other people around us. We each have as many personalities as we have relationships with others.

Adler's (1964) individual psychology challenges humankind to develop social interest as it strives to meet three unavoidable tasks in life: society, work, and love. These tasks require association and cooperation with other people. Mothers and fathers work together as partners in the process of training children to value social feeling. Although every person experiences inferiority, it can be compensated for and overcome by striving for superiority. Each person is the artist of his or her own personality, as seen in the construction of a purposive style of life. Each person shows individualized movement to "Achieve! Arise! Conquer!" The past is less important than the future. Psychologically, the present and future even determine the past, as seen in an individual's early recollections.

Fromm's (1941) sociopsychoanalytic humanism carries individual differences beyond persons to entire societies, which also may be "sane" or "sick." Personality is the totality of an individual's inherited and acquired uniqueness. However, cultural influences must support human nature and its innate needs for a frame of orientation and devotion, rootedness, unity, effectiveness, and excitation and stimulation. Cultures too often produce nonproductive social characters whose orientations are overly receptive, exploitative, hoarding, or marketing. Individuals may contribute to this faulty development by failing to show their courage to be and seeking escape from their human freedom. Productive character is the ideal that engages the person in a fully developed relatedness to the world, the self, and the process of living. It is based on productive reason, love, and work, learned largely from society's psychological agent, the family.

KEY CONCEPTS

Social psychoanalysis
Horney
    Basic anxiety
    Neurotic needs
    Moving toward, against, and away from people
    Real versus idealized self
    Psychology of women
Sullivan
    Interpersonal relationships
    Significant others
    Anxiety, empathy, need for tenderness
    Six developmental epochs
    Self-system

Adler
    Social interest
    Style of life
    Creative self
    Inferiority
    Striving for superiority
    Birth order
    Earliest recollection
Fromm
    Five existential needs
    Individual character
    Social character
        Four nonproductive orientations
        Productive orientation: reason, love, work

REVIEW QUESTIONS

1. Explain how the social-psychoanalytic theories of personality departed from classical psychoanalysis. What assumptions were shared by most of the social psychoanalysts? On what major points did they disagree with Freud?

2. Compare the views of personality development and maladjustment presented by Horney, Sullivan, Adler, and Fromm.

3. What role do purposes and values play in the theories of Horney, Sullivan, Adler, and Fromm? In what way do their treatments differ from Freud's and from Jung's?

4. What limitations do the theories of social psychoanalysis share with classical psychoanalysis?

5. Review the Bowlby, Ainsworth, and Harlow research in the supporting-evidence section of the chapter. Does this research seem more supportive of social-psychoanalytic ideas than of Freud's classical psychoanalysis? Explain why or why not.

6. What guidelines do the social-psychoanalytic theorists provide for raising children? What are some do's and don'ts for you as a future parent?

5

Behaviorism: Skinner

Is there any real difference between the principles dog trainers use to teach animals and those principles that explain how human beings acquire personality?

Does environment determine behavior? language? creativity?

Is it possible to build a personality so that it turns out in some desired way?

T HE THEORISTS reviewed so far have all concerned themselves with the "insides" of personalities, with the hidden dynamics underlying observable behavior patterns. In contrast, *behaviorism* is a school of psychology for which the basic subject matter is overt (observable) behavior. In order to identify with the other sciences, behaviorists believe that the science of psychology should deal only with phenomena that can be verified by the senses, not entities that are buried away in the "mind." Behaviorists consider behavior; they do not entertain anything that is not observable (such as private thoughts, private feelings, or private motivations).

behaviorism

Because the dominant figure in behaviorism has been B. F. Skinner, most of this chapter is devoted to his point of view. However, to understand what behaviorism has become under Skinner's influence, it is helpful to know what it was before his time. Therefore, we begin by considering the thoughts of I. P. Pavlov, the first person to be identified with behaviorism. Pavlov's ideas are not just background. Some of his notions are now being related to a topic introduced in Chapter 3, introversion-extraversion. By contrast, we turn second to a psychologist whose contributions are largely of historical importance. John B. Watson's ideas are no longer being actively pursued, but his basic assumption about what psychologists should study is the backbone of behaviorism as it has become under Skinner.

The Beginnings of Behaviorism

PAVLOV

Although he was not the person who coined the term, the earliest researcher who is now popularly identified with "behaviorism" is someone whose name you are likely to know, even if this is your first psychology course. Ivan Petrovich Pavlov was the Russian scientist who trained dogs to salivate when they heard a bell. (Actually, the Russian owes much to an American who preceded him, Edward Lee Thorndike; see Boring, 1957.) As you probably recall, Pavlov's famous classical-conditioning experiment is roughly as follows. A bell is sounded, food is presented to a dog, and the animal's saliva is collected. After many repetitions of this sequence, the dog salivates to the sound of the bell, even before the food is presented. *Classical conditioning*, then, is a form of learning involving the repeated presentation of a neutral stimulus (bell) and then a primary stimulus (food) that

classical conditioning

gives rise to a physiological response (salivation) such that, in time, the neutral stimulus comes to elicit the same response as the primary stimulus.

Although classical conditioning is the main reason for Pavlov's fame, he is known for other reasons as well. Besides winning a Nobel prize for his work in physiology, Pavlov developed a theory that is addressed to classical conditioning, but goes well beyond that technique. His ideas have implications for the study of personality as it relates to the nervous system (Pavlov, 1927).

Teplov and Nebylitsyn (1969) revised and expanded the theory. The more current form revolves around four basic properties of the nervous system: strength, mobility, lability, and dynamism. *Strength* refers to the working capacity of the nervous system during continuous or intense stimulation: a strong nervous system readily adapts to such stimulation. As we shall see, "strength" relates to the well-known personality characteristics, introversion and extraversion. *Mobility* is roughly the speed with which the nervous system can shift from one process to another. This property relates to the ability of the nervous system to relearn or recondition rapidly. You can imagine that it might be related to the personality trait "flexibility." *Lability* is the speed with which responses are learned or unlearned. A labile person may be a "quick wit," able to learn very speedily which behaviors are most appropriate in a given situation. Finally, *dynamism* is the capacity of the nervous system to form new responses. A person whose nervous system is dynamic would have the potential to develop a large repertoire of behaviors. Such people might be thought of as able to do well in a great number of situations. All four of these properties are biologically based, as they are characteristics of the nervous system (Gilliland & Bullock, in press). It is possible that some or all of the properties are inherited.

While all of these properties of the nervous system are possibly associated with personality traits, only "strength" has been shown to be related to traits that have been the object of thorough research conducted over many years (Gilliland, 1985). As indicated earlier, strength of the nervous system may be related to introversion-extraversion. According to Kirby Gilliland and his colleagues, both people who have been classified as having weak nervous systems and those who are introverted have been shown to be very sensitive to sights, sounds, and other sensory inputs (Gilliland, 1985; Gilliland & Bullock, in press). By contrast, their opposites—people with strong nervous systems and extraverts—are relatively insensitive to sensory input. These individuals can tolerate strong and continuous sensory input without being overwhelmed. When sights, sounds, and other sensory inputs are quite weak, both people with weak nervous systems and introverts have fast reaction times, compared to their opposite groups. On tasks requiring that subjects remain attentive, weak-nervous-system people and introverts perform better than strong-nervous-system people and extraverts. Strong-nervous-system people and extraverts become bored with monotonous tasks more readily than do their opposites. Finally, caffeine increases arousal in weak-nervous-system people and introverts more than in strong-nervous-system people and extraverts.

The picture painted by Gilliland and colleagues is that strong-nervous-system people and extraverts are relatively insensitive to the bombardment of stimuli that assail their senses. Being able to tolerate even intense and continuous input, they can focus on the external world. Their opposites, weak-nervous-system people and introverts, are relatively sensitive to the barrage of stimuli that enter through their senses. Being relatively unable to tolerate intense and continuous stimulation, they turn inward. Although correlations between measures of nervous-system strength and typical measures of introversion-extraversion have been moderate, Gilliland (1985) is optimistic. He thinks that more attention to research on Pavlov's ideas will likely turn up relations to a number of modern personality-trait measures, in addition to introversion-extraversion.

WATSON

You may also have heard of John B. Watson, the American who gave birth to "behaviorism" (Boring, 1957). He is famous for training children to be fearful of objects, such as a rat, and then showing that their fears could be eliminated (Watson, 1930/1959). In his best-known case, he and Rayner (1920) simultaneously presented an unpleasant noise (the striking of a steel bar) and a rat to a child named Albert. Although initially unafraid of the rat, Albert soon learned to fear the rodent, even when the noise was no longer presented. Unfortunately, the child was taken from the laboratory before his conditioned fear could be eliminated.

Watson believed that genetic factors determine certain responses in humans that become the starting points for habits. A *habit* is a learned behavior that is practiced regularly with little voluntary control. Examples of inborn responses are love, rage, and fear. These responses are elaborated through conditioning until they become fully developed habits. Habits, in turn, cluster to form complex habit systems.

To illustrate, let's take one of Watson's own examples (1930/1959), the habit of shoemaking. At birth, humans are equipped with trunk and leg movements and grasping movements. These simple responses become conditioned into more and more complex activities. Although the process by which simple, inborn activities become elaborate habits and then habit systems is too complex to map (Watson, 1930/1959), we can make a rough approximation. The sight and especially the touch of a caretaker are stimuli that give rise to grasping responses. Even a newborn infant will clutch whoever picks it up. Any stimuli associated with caretakers will become conditioned. Thus, the bottle that caretakers continually carry around and hand to the infant is an object of conditioning. The infant will learn to grasp the bottle. Likewise, the grasping of other objects will be learned, as will the manipulation of objects. These learned responses, coupled with the conditioning of other simple, inborn activities such as leg and trunk movements, eventually could combine into all the behaviors needed for the habit system of shoemaking. Designing and constructing shoes once involved raising cattle, slaughtering them, tanning the hides, and only then constructing the shoes. Each of these activities constituted a habit, and together they formed the shoemaking habit system. Shoemaking was a very complex habit system.

You can see that each single habit, such as manipulating leather, is integrated with other habits to make a habit system, such as shoemaking. Following this logic, Watson defined *personality* as "the sum of activities that can be discovered by actual observation of behavior over a long enough time to give reliable information. In other words, personality is but the end product of our habit systems" (1930/1959, p. 274).

The religious habit system and the patriotic habit system are two examples of systems that, along with others, would make up a personality. The religious activity system might stem from primitive, inborn behaviors such as love and fear (God is the object of love and fear). These simple behaviors might be elaborated when a child is required to recite "Now I lay me down to sleep," is regularly taken to church, and later is required to lead the congregation in prayer. In adulthood, the fully developed habits would be manifested in a habit system that generates praying at every meal, convincing the entire family to attend church, donating a proportion of earnings to the church, and so forth. Patriotic behavior may begin out of primitive rage behavior, as well as primitive leg, trunk, and arm movements and love behavior. A form of the patriotic habit system could arise through childhood behaviors such as fighting, "playing war," and expressing love of country. In adulthood, the patriotic habit system would be manifested in volunteering for the armed forces, voting for politicians who support a strong national defense, and observing patriotic holidays. The religious habit system and the patriotic habit system would join with other systems to form the entire personality.

Watson summed up his view of personality development in a famous challenge: "Our conclusion is that we have no real evidence of inheritance of traits. I would feel perfectly confident in the ultimately favorable outcome of careful upbringing of a *healthy, well-formed baby* born of a long line of crooks, murderers and thieves, and prostitutes. Who has evidence to the contrary?" (his emphasis, 1930/1959, p. 103). Consistent with his belief that one could take any child, regardless of genetic constitution, and make of that child anything one wished, Watson saw genes as determining only those characteristics that are common to all humans — the primitive, inborn behaviors. Contrary to Watson, however, it is possible that genes can determine characteristics that eventuate in psychological *differences* among human beings — for example, differences in introversion-extraversion.

Having considered behaviorism in its infancy, you are ready for the adult version. First we describe Skinner the person, and then Skinnerian thought.

Skinner, the Person

Burrhus Frederic Skinner, born in 1904, spent his formative years in Susquehanna, Pennsylvania. In 1926, he received his undergraduate degree from a small New York school, Hamilton College. His advanced degrees were both from Harvard, an M.A. in 1930 and a Ph.D. in 1931.

Skinner was a National Research Council Fellow, 1931–1933, and Junior Fellow in the Society of Fellows, Harvard, 1933–1936. He was affiliated with the University of Minnesota from 1936–1945, during which time he conducted military research sponsored by General Mills, Inc., and served as a Guggenheim Fellow. From Minnesota he moved to the University of Indiana, where he chaired the department of psychology from 1945 until he departed for Harvard in 1947. There he was William James Lecturer until 1948, when he joined the psychology

B. F. SKINNER.
Young Skinner took up the behaviorists' cause and made it a powerful force in modern psychology.

department. At the beginning of 1958, he became Edgar Pierce Professor of Psychology, a position he continued to hold until his recent retirement.

Among Skinner's many honors is election to the National Academy of Sciences. Other awards include the Warren Medal from the Society of Experimental Psychologists, 1942, and the Gold Medal for distinguished scientific contributions from the American Psychological Association, 1958 (see "1958 Award," 1958).

Although it is probably in retrospect, Skinner (1976a) indicates that he became intrigued with psychology at a very early age. As with most people, his first interest was in the more mystical phenomena. As a third grader, he recalls, he had an "extrasensory experience." Skinner generated laughter in his class when he excitedly raised his hand to report that he had read a word just at the same moment his teacher spoke the word. As an older child, he became interested in "bronc busting," partly because he was intrigued by the notion that a horse must be tamed, but not to the point of breaking its "will." He was fascinated by performing pigeons at a country fair, and during his college years, he wrote a play on "glands that change personality" and a term paper analyzing Hamlet's madness. As a young man, Skinner recalls thinking about thinking while paddling a canoe. However, he later regretted his sojourn into "mentalism."

After graduation, Skinner drifted for a while. He very much wanted to be a writer, even receiving encouragement from Robert Frost, but he settled for an ordinary job and ordinary daydreams. Then, as if he had stumbled onto the "truth," he discovered behaviorism. The revelation was provided by Bertrand Russell, who, in a 1927 book, expressed grudging admiration for John B. Watson and his ideas. Young Skinner was even more impressed by a work of H. G. Wells. Wells pondered what to do with a single life jacket if he were standing alone on a pier, with George Bernard Shaw floundering in the water on one side and "Pav-loff" (I. P. Pavlov) slowly disappearing from sight on the other. The jacket was awarded to "Pavloff"—by implication, behaviorism—and so were Skinner's in-tellectual loyalties.

Soon thereafter, Skinner enrolled in the graduate program in psychology at Harvard. According to E. G. Boring (1957), by the time Skinner defended his dissertation, he had decided on his own brand of behaviorism and would change little in the years to come.

Even before this time, Skinner's enthusiasm for behaviorism was so great that it overwhelmed his strong need for attention from women. Aboard an ocean liner, en route to Europe for a last fling before graduate school, Skinner ap-proached an attractive young woman and was excited to learn that she was a graduate student in psychology. However, a few minutes of conversation revealed that she was not a behaviorist. Skinner politely excused himself. On the same cruise, a dinner horn blasted in his ear as he read. When he later returned to the scene of the unpleasant occurrence, he experienced anxious emotions and ex-claimed to himself, "Aha! Pavlovian conditioning."

Skinner spent some time in Greenwich Village, sampling the Bohemian lifestyle. There, in a night club, he noticed an attractive young woman, and, as was often the case when he found a woman interesting, he boldly introduced himself. When it was discovered that he was to be a psychology student, hypnotism became the topic of discussion, and she revealed a willingness to perform as a subject. Skinner readily agreed to demonstrate hypnosis and successfully placed her in a "trance." It was an important experience for him, for two reasons. It cemented his identity as a psychologist, and it was the beginning of an affair.

Skinner took up residence with the woman and thereby revealed a willing-ness to defy danger. The woman was married and often received visits from her husband, who was away on military duty. This unsettling arrangement, as well as a continuing clash with his lover's roommate, led Skinner to the decision that the lifestyle of Greenwich Village was not for him. It was his second, and apparently last, affair with a married woman, but not his last adventure.

In Europe, Skinner traveled about in airplanes of World War I vintage and, on one occasion, occupied an open cockpit during a violent thunderstorm. A side trip to Paris was highlighted by a visit to the Folies Bergère—and by a first experi-ment in psychology. In a museum, Skinner approached a neglected statue, gazed at it with great intensity, and then stepped back to watch as the figure was carefully examined by several passersby. It was his only excursion into social psychology.

It is no accident that a main character in *Walden Two* (1948), Burrhus F. Skinner's only novel, is named "Professor Burris." Burris is straightforward, a typical academic who resorts to his intellect rather than his emotions when trying to make sense of life. The public Skinner seems much like this alter ego from *Walden Two*. However, perhaps paradoxically, Skinner was capable of being frivo-lous and, on occasion, could even be the prankster. At his graduation ceremony, he delivered an oration in Latin that was designed to satirize the school adminis-tration. On the same occasion, Skinner's friends were causing such a ruckus the college president threatened not to award them diplomas. When the same school official loudly queried "Why don't they bow when given a diploma?" Skinner made a point of bowing grandly upon his turn to receive a certificate of graduation. The "cheap joke," as he put it, inspired laughter from the audience.

If one takes seriously what Skinner (1976b) says about Skinner, the most famous of the behaviorists has a personality that is difficult to pin down (Skinner, 1983). Put in terms of Chapter 1, Skinner doesn't have a lot of personality. That is, for every trait that can be inferred from his self-reports of behavior, he has also indicated behavior associated with the opposite trait. As a young man, Skinner was shy but outgoing, cautious but adventurous, intellectual yet sometimes quite silly. His personal life was rather conservative (Skinner, 1983), but he occasionally violated sexual conventions. Perhaps it is all by design. It wouldn't do for a person to have a lot of personality if he wishes to deny the existence of personality. As we shall see, Skinner openly dismisses the whole idea of personality, and yet one can read a great deal about personality between the lines of his writings. In any case, Skinner has proven that a person can be interesting, even if he doesn't clearly manifest a large number of consistent traits.

Skinner's View of the Person

ENVIRONMENTALISM: THE IMPORTANCE OF CONSEQUENCES

environmentalism

Skinner has been accused of being an "S-R," or stimulus-response, psychologist. He clearly rejects the charge (Skinner, 1972g). According to the S-R conception, a stimulus in the environment, such as the door within the door that constitutes the dog's entrance into the house, absolutely demands a response from the dog—namely, entering the house. Not so, says Skinner. The dog's door sets the occasion for the response "enter," but it does so with some probability, not absolutely. Further, to understand behavior—a dog's or a person's—one needs a concept that is missing from the S-R account: the notion that a response has a consequence. A *consequence* is an event that occurs after the response has been performed and changes the probability that the response will occur again. In our example, gaining entrance to the house is the consequence that will increase the likelihood the dog will poke its nose through its door in the future (Skinner, 1972g). This notion that stimuli have some probability of giving rise to responses is shared by other psychologists (Brunswick, 1955; Ittleson & Kilpatrick, 1951).

consequence

Skinner has also been accused of being an "environmentalist." He stands "guilty" as charged (Skinner, 1983). For Skinner (1971), the environment is everything, explains everything. Through Darwin's process of natural selection, humans and other animals have an inclination to certain consequences and tend to develop behaviors that are followed by those consequences. Natural selection can be illustrated by example. If certain birds live on an island made up of tightly packed rocks, and they must catch the bugs that constitute their food by pecking among the rocks, the island environment will select for reproduction those birds with the thinnest bills. Humans develop behaviors that are likely to be followed by the presentation of food and shelter. Also, there are individual differences among humans in the kinds of consequences that are likely to generate behavior (Skinner, 1948). Some people are genetically disposed to quantitative abilities. For them, the solution of a mathematical problem is likely to be an important consequence. Other people are inherently inclined to diagnostic skills. Such people are more likely to be found figuring out why their automobile won't run.

Genetic endowment, determined through natural selection by the environment, predisposes people to certain behaviors rather than others, but it only determines the boundaries for behavioral development. The particular environment into which each of us is born determines our own peculiar repertoire of behaviors. Individuals born with artistic skills will show artistic behaviors only if the opportunities relating to artistic behavior are available in their particular environment (Skinner, 1972c). All this is to say that the actual behaviors people develop depend upon the characteristics of the environment in which they find themselves.

"BEYOND FREEDOM AND DIGNITY"

If a stimulus has some probability of giving rise to a response; if genetic endowment, determined by environmental selection, sets the boundaries of behavioral development; and if our particular environments determine the actual behaviors we will develop, aren't we all slaves to our environments? Don't we lack freedom? Aren't we deprived of human dignity? The answer to the question about freedom is a qualified no. However, human dignity is an illusion (Skinner, 1948, 1971, 1983).

According to Skinner, *freedom* refers to our belief that we can choose from various behaviors, rather than having our actions controlled by an external force, the environment (Skinner, 1972f). Obviously, Skinner does not accept the belief that he attributes to us. To him, it is a fact that we are controlled by our environment (1983). To deny that "truth" is to risk being controlled by subtle and malignant circumstances and by malicious people. Governments and particular people sometimes control human beings for the benefit of the controller, rather than in the interest of the controlled (for example, the leaders of Nazi Germany). Often we don't detect the harm done to us by this control, because there may be immediate positive consequences, while negative consequences are deferred until a later time. For example, we may stand aside while our government is lax in regulating the level of pollutants that are allowed to escape into our waterways, because "jobs are preserved" and "the economy is stimulated"—immediate, positive benefits for us all. However, we should not lose sight of the fact that leniency in regulating pollutants has negative consequences in the long run (Skinner, 1983).

Skinner (1971) asserted, why not decide for ourselves what will determine our behaviors? The alternative is to leave the control of behavior up to chance— or, worse, leave it up to people who would control us for their own gains. When we demand freedom, what we really mean is freedom from negative or aversive consequences and access to positive consequences. We can have that freedom only by arranging our own consequences, not by leaving consequences to "government," or "fate," or "politics." Thus, Skinner does concede that we have freedom, but in a highly qualified sense. We can arrange our environment so that the consequences we desire become likely, but having done so, we are under the control of our creation (Skinner, 1983). George Kelly has proposed a similar notion about the interplay between what we arrange ourselves and what controls us (see Chapter 8).

However, *dignity* is another matter. According to Skinner, dignity is a falsehood. "We recognize a person's dignity or worth when we give him credit for what he has done" (Skinner, 1971, p. 58). When, in our everyday lives, we cannot readily identify the consequences that control an individual's behavior, we attribute the behavior to the individual, rather than to external forces. Thus, when a person makes an anonymous donation to a worthy cause, we assume she did it because of something inside her, called altruism. In so doing, we ignore the consequences in the environment of her formative years that have determined her behavior; for example, she may have been exposed to a culture that "honors" (consequence) selfless giving. To credit people when they "do good" is to ignore the consequences that gave rise to "doing good" (Skinner, 1983). Skinner (1971) suggests that we should identify those consequences and bring them under control so that more people can "do good" more often. To accept his suggestion is to give up taking credit for what we do, to give up "dignity." In return, he assures us that crediting the environment instead of ourselves will lead us to seek out the consequences that control behavior. The net result of that search will be a behavioral technology that will ensure "doing good" is a frequent occurrence and "doing bad" a rarity.

Skinner practices what he preaches. In *Walden Two* (1948), his main character, Frazier, who designed the utopia described in the book, repeatedly denies that people are to be credited with what they do. Skinner himself once ended a speech with the following:

> And now my labor is over. I have had my lecture. I have no sense of fatherhood. If my genetic and personal histories had been different, I should have come into possession of a different lecture. If I deserve any credit at all, it is simply for having served as a place in which certain processes could take place. I shall interpret your polite applause in that light. (Skinner, 1972g)

Assuming that this orientation dominates in the future, Skinner (1983) expects to be a "nonperson" in the history of psychology.

Basic Concepts: Skinner

Skinner claims not to have a theory (Skinner, 1983), and is viewed by some people as not having one ("1958 Award," 1958). We will not deal with that philosophical issue, except to indicate that Skinner's point of view has all the trappings of a theory, including numerous concepts. Here we will concern ourselves with only part of Skinner's position, the part that is most relevant to personality.

OPERANT CONDITIONING

Skinner's approach to psychology focuses on what he calls "operant conditioning." It is the same kind of conditioning that many psychologists call "instrumental" (see Kimble, 1961). In *operant conditioning,* an organism operates on its environment with consequences that influence the likelihood that the operation,

operant
conditioning

or behavior, will be repeated. Because *respondent conditioning,* Skinner's equivalent to classical conditioning, is of less importance to the study of personality, it is not covered here. (To pursue Skinner's version of classical conditioning, see Holland & Skinner, 1961.)

contingent

"Contingent" is a close second to "consequence" as the key word in Skinnerian terminology. If event B is *contingent* on event A, the occurrence of B depends upon the prior occurrence of A (Holland & Skinner, 1961). If the singing of birds is contingent on the rising of the sun, the occurrence of singing depends upon the prior appearance of the sun. In operant conditioning, consequences are contingent on the prior performance of some response, which is a very discrete and concrete behavior, such as the "handshake" of a trained dog. Three kinds of consequences can be involved in operant conditioning: positive reinforcement, negative reinforcement, and punishment.

POSITIVE REINFORCEMENT

positive
reinforcement

Reinforcement occurs when some event is contingent on the prior performance of some response, such as the meowing of a cat that alerts its master to its hunger. *Positive reinforcement* is a process whereby some event, usually a stimulus, *increases the likelihood* of a response upon which its presentation is contingent. Now you can see why the word "reinforcement" was chosen. "Reinforce" generally means "strengthen," and to positively reinforce a response means to strengthen it, in the sense of increasing its likelihood of occurrence.

With this background, we can take some examples. Skinner often placed a pigeon in a cage that bears the technical name "free-operant chamber" but has become popularly known as the "Skinner box." (True to form, Skinner rejects the credit implied by "Skinner box," 1983.) The chamber is depicted in Figure 5.1. As you can see, it looks like any other cage for housing animals, except that it has a panel that the pigeon can peck (A). Pecking the panel activates a food magazine (B) that releases grain down a tube (C) into a cup (D) inside the cage. In the simplest case, every peck of the panel is followed by the presentation of some

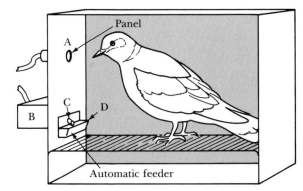

Figure 5.1
Skinner box: pigeon pecks A, which activates food magazine at B, causing food to be delivered through tube C to cup D.

grain. That is, the response "panel peck" is followed by reinforcement in the form of grain.

Some of the critical accompaniments to the example of operant conditioning of a pigeon are worth closer consideration. Notice the kind of response that occurs in operant conditioning. Unlike sweating or change of heart rate, operant responses are not automatic. The kind of response that occurs in operant conditioning is begun by the animal, rather than occurring automatically. The pigeon can peck many times, or none at all. It can peck forcefully or softly. Further, it is the pigeon that gets things going in operant conditioning. Nothing happens until the pigeon starts pecking the panel, and it must perform the response itself. You may recognize that operant responses are controlled by the somatic nervous system, which operates the somatic musculature. Responses of this kind are said to be *emitted,* because they are initiated by the organism, rather than being automatic. Don't forget what kind of response you are dealing with when you try to operantly condition your pet. Wait until it responds — offers you its paw, if you are teaching a handshake — then reinforce it with a favorite treat. Grabbing its paw and shaking, followed by stuffing food into its mouth is not ideal, although some dogs may need "prompting."

So how does operant conditioning begin? Pigeons peck quite a lot, for no apparent reason. Place one in a cage it has never entered before, and it will wander around for a while, pecking here and there, more or less at random. If it is placed in a Skinner box, eventually it will peck the panel, and grain will come down the tube into the cup. The pigeon will eat the grain and then wander around some more. Sooner or later, it will peck the panel again, with the same result as before. If one watches closely, it is evident that the time between pecks becomes less and less, until the pigeon is pecking at a fairly high rate. When the *rate of responding* becomes stable, conditioning is said to have been completed and a new response acquired. Rate of responding is also an index of strength of conditioning. In general, the higher the rate, the stronger the conditioning. *Extinction* occurs when a previously reinforced response is no longer followed by the same reinforcement and the response eventually decreases in frequency.

extinction

As you have undoubtedly already recognized, positive reinforcement occurs every day in the life of every person. As an example, imagine some of the events of a day in the life of a typical college student. These events include behaviors that have been reinforced many times in the past. After getting up in the morning, the student washes his face and brushes his teeth. The "face washing" behavior is positively reinforced by the feeling of being wide awake, clear-headed, and clean. The toothbrushing is reinforced by the sensation of a clean mouth and the assurance of fresh breath. Next, the student makes his way to the cafeteria in his dorm, where he presents his student ID, picks up a tray, and fills it with food. These behaviors are positively reinforced by the food — although, we admit, positive reinforcement may occur infrequently or rarely in some college cafeterias.

The day before these events, our student had been reinforced by winning a long and difficult campaign for Homecoming King. It was not the first time he had won a campus election. Now, as he leaves the cafeteria, several friends and acquaintances approach him with congratulations, another form of positive reinforcement. After several thank-you's, the student proceeds to class, where his "class attendance" behavior is reinforced, as usual, by the stimulating lecture emanating from one of his several outstanding professors (as we indicated, this is a typical student). Completing his classes for the day, the student retires to the library for an afternoon of study. The reinforcement for studying will be partially delayed until test day. For now, studying is followed by a rather abstract reinforcement, "the joy of learning." Leaving the library, the student reports to work, where it happens to be payday. His work on that day, and several preceding it, is reinforced with a paycheck.

NEGATIVE REINFORCEMENT AND PUNISHMENT

negative reinforcement

Positive reinforcement is not the only means by which behaviors are learned. *Negative reinforcement* is a process whereby the likelihood of a response increases when it is followed by the *termination, reduction, or absence* of a stimulus (Holland & Skinner, 1961). Negative reinforcement usually involves aversive stimuli, such as electric shock. Such stimuli are called *negative reinforcers*. Behaviors that lead to success in escaping or avoiding negative reinforcers will increase in probability of occurrence in the future.

Escape and avoidance behavior are illustrated by use of a shuttle box, as depicted in Figure 5.2. The box, actually a cage, has an electric-grid floor and a partition down the middle. The animal is placed in the box on one side of the partition, and electricity is activated on that side only. The shock is enough to be uncomfortable, but not harmful. The animal *escapes* by simply jumping to the side without shock. The jump is reinforced by the termination of the shock. *Avoidance* learning becomes possible when a light is placed at each end of the box, as in Figure 5.2. First, the animal learns to escape; then, the light on the side containing the animal is illuminated a short time before the shock is activated. At first, the

Grid floor (top view): electrified tubing

Warning light   Partition

Figure 5.2
A top view of the shuttle box.

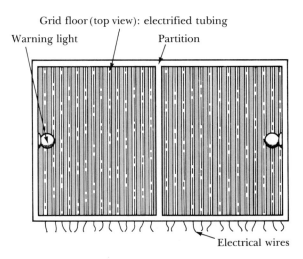

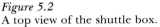
Electrical wires

light has no influence on behavior. However, after a number of presentations of the light followed by the shock, the animal will begin to jump when the light is illuminated, before the shock is delivered. In this way the animal avoids the shock, or negative reinforcer. At the same time, it also escapes the light that has become a "conditioned aversive stimulus."

Both positive and negative reinforcement involve increases in the likelihood of responses. With *punishment,* responses that are followed by the presentation of aversive stimuli *decrease* in likelihood in the future (Skinner, 1971). A moment of thought will reveal how negative reinforcement and punishment differ. In the case of negative reinforcement, responses *increase* in likelihood when followed by the *absence* (or termination or reduction) of aversive stimulation. By contrast, punishment involves a *decrease* in the likelihood of responses that are followed by the *presentation* of aversive stimuli. (This process is technically known as "positive punishment"; "negative punishment" is omission of a positive reinforcer following the performance of a certain response, resulting in a decrease in the frequency of the response.) If studying schoolwork allows a child to avoid housework, negative reinforcement is being used to increase studying. If a child's hand is spanked for getting into the cookie jar, punishment is being used to decrease pilfering of cookies.

punishment

Skinner has long maintained that punishment is not an efficient way to control behavior (for example, see Skinner, 1948). As we will see in Chapter 12, he would now admit that punishment can be very effective, although it rarely works well in practice. Nevertheless, Skinner (1971) has a point when he maintains that punishment may have only temporary effects and may be accompanied by unfortunate by-products. In some cases, punishment may lead to only temporary suppression of a behavior that is not desired by whoever administers the punishment. An organism may inhibit an undesirable behavior until the agent is no longer present. Then the behavior may be performed at a high rate, making up for responses that were suppressed when the punishing agent was present. In addition, punishment may be accompanied by fear, anxiety, aggression, failure to perform beneficial responses, and, in humans, loss of self-esteem, confidence, and initiative.

As with positive reinforcement, it is easy to recognize many everyday examples of negative reinforcement and punishment. Some students avoid class the day after a test. Their behavior is reinforced by the absence of bad news about their test performance. Sometimes students fall asleep in class. Professors occasionally punish this behavior by a rude awakening.

STIMULUS GENERALIZATION AND PHOBIAS

Because of exposure to aversive stimulation during childhood, some people may show a very strange kind of behavior, and may exhibit it for much of their lives. This unusual behavior is called a *phobia.* A *phobia* is a strong, irrational fear of an event that is not ordinarily the object of intense fear. In Chapter 6, we will consider an actual phobia and how it was eliminated. For now, let's examine how one might acquire a phobia.

Suppose that during infancy, while being pushed in a buggy through the park, a child is left alone for a few minutes. Suddenly a large bird swoops down, lands on the edge of the carriage, and lets out a loud "caaaw." The infant shows a strong startle response and appears to be in shock when its parent returns to its side. The parent thinks nothing of the episode, but later notices that the baby clutches up, pulling its arms close to its body and jerking its knees all the way to its abdomen, whenever it hears the sound of a bird or sees a bird fly over. Such responses may be considered the result of classical conditioning. Classically conditioned stimuli can become negative reinforcers that set the occasion for escape or avoidance.

When the infant grows to childhood, it shows an even stranger reaction. It will not only flee from birds, it will quickly leave an area where feathers are found. For example, when the child's aunt arrives for a visit wearing a hat adorned with plumage, the child scurries from her presence. Fleeing the stimulus "feathers" is escape behavior, and shunning areas where feathers might be found is avoidance behavior — but it is something else as well. The child's behavior illustrates *stimulus generalization.*

In *stimulus generalization,* any stimulus that is similar to the one originally conditioned will evoke the same response as the original stimulus. Any clump of feathers is likely to resemble a bird, especially to a child; thus, there is generalization from birds to feathers. Responses to birds will now be evoked by feathers. The child will escape feathers, and later will likely be able to anticipate when birds or feathers might be encountered and avoid the potential exposure (for example, a trip to the zoo). It should be noted, however, that not all or even most phobias are acquired by such simple conditioning.

SCHEDULES OF REINFORCEMENT

To this point in our account of Skinner's ideas, we have assumed that every response an organism makes is reinforced. As you may have recognized, such is often not the case in reality. You may have also recognized that reinforcing every response, or *continuous reinforcement,* is not even the most efficient way to proceed.

continuous reinforcement

Suppose you were playing a simple video game, and every time you began the game, you "won" very quickly. Would you play very rapidly? We bet you wouldn't. After a while, your response "starting the game over" would be sluggish, and you would quit easily. That is, your response rate would be low, and a short string of "losses" would be enough to put an end to your efforts.

On the other hand, imagine that you are playing a video game in which you are trying to get the little person on the screen across a battlefield of the future. Your goal is to reach headquarters to warn of an impending invasion by the Retrobrutes, beasts from another galaxy. The first time you try the game, the little person is blown up by a land mine upon first stepping onto the battlefield. On the next try, you manage to make it past the mine field, which is very reinforcing. However, your little person now enters a laser zone and is promptly "vaporized." You quickly jab the "reset button" and start over. This time, the mines get you again. You hit the reset button again. Now you make it past the mine field, through

Video games exemplify the principle of intermittent reinforcement.

the laser zone, into an artificial black hole. That was really reinforcing! But alas, your little person is immediately squashed by extraordinary pressures. On the next try, you fail even to make it across the mine field. Then you are able to get all the way through the black hole! And on and on it goes, throughout the evening. Your behavior has persisted because you have been intermittently, rather than continuously, reinforced. In the case of *intermittent reinforcement,* responses are reinforced every so often, or after some number of responses has occurred (Holland & Skinner, 1961).

    As a general rule, intermittently reinforced responses are performed at a higher rate and are more resistant to extinction than continuously reinforced responses. Thus, intermittent reinforcement generates stronger conditioning or learning. For this reason it is of more importance than continuous reinforcement. (Note, however, that a response is more easily acquired with continuous reinforcement.)

    A *schedule of reinforcement* determines whether reinforcement is to be delivered either every so often or after some number of responses has occurred (Holland & Skinner, 1961). Some schedules are based on the amount of time since the last reinforcement, while others are founded on the number of responses performed since the last reinforced response. In the case of a *temporal schedule,*

intermittent reinforcement

schedule of reinforcement

there must be a lapse of some amount of time between one reinforced response and the next. With a *ratio schedule*, some number of responses must be performed between one reinforced response and the next. Let's examine the different types of schedules of reinforcement.

Fixed schedules of reinforcement.   In a *fixed schedule*, a response is reinforced after a constant amount of time has elapsed or after a constant number of responses have been performed. In a *fixed-interval (FI) schedule*, the amount of time between one reinforced response and the next is constant (Holland & Skinner, 1961). It may be 10 minutes or 5 seconds, but it is always the same, or fixed.

fixed-interval schedule

Figure 5.3 provides a record of behavior that is reinforced on a fixed-interval schedule. The graph in this figure (and in Figures 5.4, 5.5, and 5.6) is called a *cumulative record.* In cumulative recordings, the number of responses is accumulated and plotted against time (Holland & Skinner, 1961). The cumulative records shown here all assume that learning has already occurred.

Notice that the record for the fixed-interval schedule (Figure 5.3) looks like a bunch of scallops, all interconnected. The organism begins responding slowly at the point in time labeled O. Because reinforcement does not occur until point in time P, the animal is in no hurry to produce responses. However, as the time for a response to be reinforced draws near, the rate of responding increases, as indicated by the steeper curve near the hatch mark at point P. When point P is reached, reinforcement occurs, and assuming it is food, the organism stops to eat.

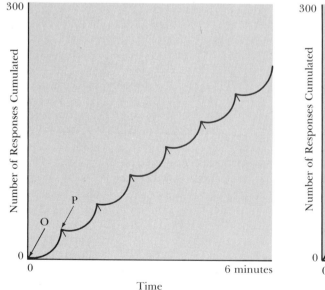

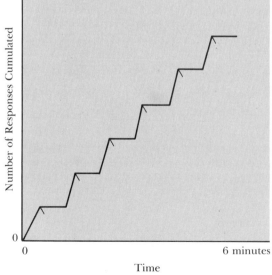

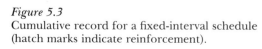

Figure 5.3
Cumulative record for a fixed-interval schedule (hatch marks indicate reinforcement).

Figure 5.4
Cumulative record for a fixed-ratio schedule (hatch marks indicate reinforcement).

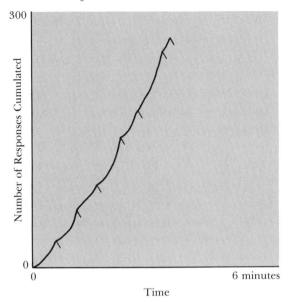

Figure 5.5
Cumulative record for a variable-interval
schedule (hatch marks indicate reinforcement).

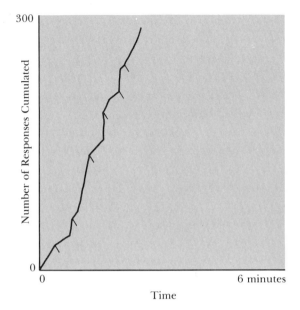

Figure 5.6
Cumulative record for a variable-ratio schedule
(hatch marks indicate reinforcement).

Then it begins responding slowly once again. This pattern of responding generates the scallops.

For some students, studying is on a fixed-interval schedule. Just after a test, the rate of studying is near zero. Then, as another test approaches, studying is performed at a higher and higher rate, until a very steep curve occurs the night before the test, which is just before students are sometimes reinforced by high grades. After the test, these students pause (often over a beer or two), savoring their reinforcement (assuming they are aware of having done well). Then the same old scallops begin again.

In a *fixed-ratio (FR) schedule,* the number of responses occurring between one reinforced response and the next is constant. For example, on an FR(5) schedule, every fifth response is reinforced. As Figure 5.4 indicates, an FR schedule generates a record that looks like stair steps, because the organism responds at a high and steady rate until reinforcement occurs, then it pauses for a moment. The pay of farm workers is sometimes on an FR schedule. Every so many bags of vegetables collected by a worker yields some predetermined amount of money. Children may also be reinforced on an FR schedule. A youngster may be told that she must perform 6 (or 2 or 10) tasks before monetary reinforcement is forthcoming.

fixed-ratio
schedule

Variable schedules of reinforcement. Variable schedules are more frequently encountered in real life. In a *variable schedule,* reinforcement is delivered after some X amount of time has lapsed, *on the average,* or after some Y number of responses have been performed, *on the average.* That is, instead of a response being reinforced after exactly X units of time have elapsed, or after exactly Y number of responses have been performed, it occurs after X units, on the average, or after Y responses, on the average.

variable-interval schedule

A *variable-interval (VI) schedule* requires that a given amount of time elapses between one reinforced response and the next, on the average. On a VI(5 sec) schedule, sometimes the organism must wait only 1 second before a response is reinforced; at other times, it must wait 9 seconds; occasionally, it waits exactly 5 seconds. Overall, the intervals average out to a 5-second wait.

Note that the record for the VI schedule, depicted in Figure 5.5, is more irregular than its fixed-interval counterpart, shown in Figure 5.3. Also, you can see that the curve is steeper than for the fixed interval. That is, the curve goes up at an angle that is closer to 90 degrees than is the curve for a fixed-interval schedule. The steeper curve is indicative of a higher rate of responding. As a general rule, variable schedules generate higher rates of responding than fixed schedules. A moment of thought will tell you why. If a pigeon can't anticipate exactly when a reinforcement is going to be delivered, it pecks away rapidly. After all, a response may be reinforced only a fraction of a second after the last reinforcement. People act the same way. Not knowing when reinforcement will be delivered, people leave little time between responses, because only moments later a response might be reinforced. Contrast this situation with that of a fixed schedule. If one knows for sure that it is going to be 1 minute until a reinforcer is delivered, why work hard responding? Why not start responding in earnest about the time a response will be reinforced?

For a similar reason, variable schedules are more resistant to extinction than fixed schedules. During extinction, reinforcement never occurs. However, organisms that have been on a variable schedule will continue to respond because past experience makes them used to long periods with no reinforcement.

Fishing seems to provide a real-life example of VI scheduling. As any person who fishes can tell you, there may be an hour between the initial cast and the one that lands the first fish, but, minutes later, a cast may land another fish. However, the next cast that lands a fish may come two hours later. It may average out so that a cast is reinforced after a forty-five minute wait. Accordingly, fishing behavior may be quite resistant to extinction despite relatively long periods without reinforcement.

variable-ratio schedule

A *variable-ratio (VR) schedule* requires that, on the average, a given number of responses be performed before a response is reinforced. As a general rule, a variable-ratio schedule will generate the highest rate of responding and the strongest resistance to extinction (see Figure 5.6). A VR(10) schedule designates a procedure by which every 10th response is reinforced, on the average. Sometimes the organism must respond 19 times before the reinforcer is delivered; sometimes, 1 response is sufficient. The schedule averages out to reinforcement after 10 responses.

There are many examples of variable-ratio schedules in real life. Shooting basketballs is on a VR schedule, as is selling merchandise. Every so many shots at the basket yields a scoring basket and every so many attempts to make a sale actually produces a sale. Perhaps the clearest example of VR scheduling is gambling. A person diligently working at a slot machine does not experience reinforcement after a fixed number of coins are placed in the slot. Nor does reinforcement occur on a per-unit-of-time basis. Rather, on the average, every so many responses of placing a coin in the slot is followed by reinforcement — the machine yielding up some of its monetary contents. Casual observation in casinos will confirm that gambling behavior is highly resistant to extinction.

To sum up, schedules of reinforcement determine delivery of reinforcement based on the amount of time that has lapsed since the last reinforced response, or on the number of responses since the last reinforced response. A fixed schedule requires that an exact amount of time must elapse or an exact number of responses must be performed before reinforcement is delivered. With variable schedules, the amount of time or the number of responses required for reinforcement to occur is not exact, but variable. On the average, X lapse of time or Y number of responses is required for reinforcement to occur. As a rule, variable schedules generate higher rates of responding and greater resistance to extinction.

PERSONALITY DEVELOPMENT

Even though Skinner rejects the concept of personality, his ideas about how behavior is acquired relates to the notion of individual differences. For example, how do people acquire their distinctive patterns of speech? Does speech develop according to an inherited script, is it acquired by mimicry, or do notions of environmental consequences to verbal responses apply? Of course, Skinner prefers the last alternative. In this section, we review Skinner's explanation of language learning, some of his notions about rearing children, and the broader implications of his ideas for the design and construction of personality.

Development of speech.   Skinner (1957, 1972e) contends that learning to use words orally is a relatively simple matter. When a child of 2 is confronted with the stimulus "red light" and utters the word "red," he is reinforced by the "verbal community" (Mom, Dad, and siblings) with everything from praise to candy. When the child puts two words together — for example, "That red" — he is reinforced by the same verbal community. Correct insertion of a verb ("That *is* red") is reinforced in a similar way, leading to the use of complete sentences that are grammatically correct. To put it more technically, use of oral language is learned by a process involving the formation of contingencies between verbal responses and reinforcements delivered by the verbal community. So-called "rules of language" are learned by the same principles as single words are learned. In fact, rules are simply statements of contingencies: If the child says "I am five years old" instead of "I are five years old," praise by Mom and Dad will follow (Skinner, 1976a). Thus, in Skinner's view, the acquisition of language in children can be explained by reference to operant conditioning.

BOX 5.1   *Baby in a Box*

Skinner has been controversial at least since his wartime attempts to use pigeons to guide missiles (Skinner, 1972d). However, nothing he has done has caused more comment than rearing his infant daughter in a box. The apparatus used to house the child has been described by Skinner (1972a), along with the behaviorist's rationale for the unusual procedure. He writes that his wife decided it was time to apply science to the nursery, in the interest of saving labor—presumably her own. The first consideration, quite properly, was the physical and psychological well-being of the child. As the picture of the child's living quarters indicates, the box is spacious, providing ample room for the child and her toys. The open area in front was normally covered by a removable pane of safety glass. Note that the floor of the compartment is covered with a sheet that can be replaced instantly by means of a roller device. Also, it is no accident that the child is depicted without clothes. In fact, she was kept quite comfortable in only her diaper, as her "home" benefited from temperature and humidity control.

Unconfined by clothes, the infant was free to move her limbs in any way she wished. Compared with some babies who are restrained by clothes, she joyously exercised with all her might. The result was the development of strong back, leg, and abdominal muscles. By-products of the exercise were unusual agility of the feet and excellent hand/foot coordination. The baby often played for hours with toys suspended from the ceiling of the box. One such toy was a music maker. Primarily with her feet, the baby was able to compose her own tunes, much to the amusement of the family.

Caring for the child—feeding, changing, and so on—took only about one and a half hours a day, excluding washing diapers and preparing formulas. Lest you get the wrong impression, this small amount of time was certainly not all that was devoted to the child. When she "signaled" that she was hungry, she was fed. If it was apparent that she needed changing, she was provided with a clean, dry diaper. If she wanted to play, she was entertained in her habitat or removed for interaction with the family. Far from being neglected, she was the center of attention. Neighborhood children were continually parading past the box for a chance to see and play with the "baby in the box."

continued

BOX 5.1
continued

Among the many advantages of the "box" were those that stemmed directly from climate control. The child never had a diaper rash, nor did her parents continually fuss with blankets and pajamas. They could confidently set the temperature control so that the child would be warm, but not uncomfortably so. As it turned out, the temperature control also provided an extra bonus. As the baby grew older, she began to awake early in the morning, too early for her parents. The problem was that she was using up the heat provided by the metabolism of her evening meal before the whole night had elapsed. The solution to the annoyance was easy. The temperature was simply raised a few degrees during the night, thus conserving the baby's natural heat.

Skinner's daughter was also protected from air pollutants. As a result, her nose and eyes were always clear. In addition, she almost completely avoided the contagious illnesses that often characterize infancy. When she was quite young, the glass screen protected her from the germs brought to her bedside when the neighborhood children trooped in to see her. Noise pollution was another problem eliminated by the "box." The child could be completely insulated from surrounding sounds. In theory, the parents could also be protected: the baby's annoying noises could be closed off from the parents' environment. However, Skinner (1972a) claims that this possibility was never tested in the case of his daughter. Her frequency of crying and fussing was negligible.

Finally, Skinner argued that instead of receiving less affection than children housed in the usual way, the baby may have received more affection of higher quality. Relieved of the usual drudgery of administering to a baby, the primary caretaker is more likely to have the time and disposition for displays of affection. Along with this improved parental attitude is likely to come better care. For example, freed from many of the more unpleasant aspects of child care, the parent may be less likely to leave the baby lying in wetness.

Skinner's attempt at control of his daughter's environment may have been his first effort to act on his belief that the environment of human beings can be designed so that beneficial behaviors result. It may also be one of the few actual attempts at long-term control of human behavior through environmental manipulation. However, Skinner's writings contain suggestions that long-term control could be exerted on a very broad scale.

Building a personality.   Skinner wastes no opportunity to dismiss personality from the realm of science. In Chapter 1 of *Beyond Freedom and Dignity* (1971), he mocks the notion of "disturbed personality" (pp. 8 and 16) and flatly states, "We do not need to try to discover what personalities, states of mind, feelings, traits of character . . . or the other perquisites of autonomous man really are in order to get on with scientific analysis of behavior" (p. 15). Yet in that book, and in *Walden Two* (1948), he subtly, and perhaps unwittingly, indicates that people do have personalities, at least in the sense of showing individual differences in behaviors that are relatively constant across time and situations.

In *Walden Two,* as we have noted, Skinner's alter ego, Professor Burris, has "little personality," an observation we made earlier. Surprisingly, however, the person one might think would be given even less personality is "blessed" with a rich and full repertoire of behaviors that distinguish him from others. Frazier, the founder and leader of Walden Two, is an impulsive individual whose temper flares on many occasions. He shows a great deal of self-confidence—to the point of thinking that he is a god—but seems rather vulnerable underneath all the bravado. At one point, Frazier bursts forth:

> You think I'm conceited, aggressive, tactless, selfish. You're convinced that I'm completely insensitive to my effect upon others, except when the effect is calculated. You can't see in me any of the personal warmth or the straightforward natural strength which are responsible for the success of Walden Two. My motives are ulterior and devious, my emotions warped. In a word—of all the people you've seen in the past four days, you're sure that I'm *one,* at least, who couldn't possibly be a genuine member of any community. (pp. 236–237)

Burris, to whom this tirade is addressed, silently agrees. Castle, the philosopher who accompanies Burris to Walden Two, also has "lots of personality." He is the "skeptic." It seems that the author who condemns personality provides excellent examples of "lots of" and "little" personality in his only novel. Elsewhere, in *Beyond Freedom and Dignity* (1971), not only is it implied that people have personality, but Skinner alludes to the possibility of developing and changing personality by design.

Table 5.1, which is adapted from that work, contains the description of a young man whose life has suddenly been dramatically transformed. As you can

TABLE 5.1   Trait versus Behavioral Description of a Disturbed Man

Trait description	Behavioral description
insecure, unsure	His behavior is weak and inappropriate.
dissatisfied, discouraged	He is seldom reinforced; therefore, his behavior undergoes extinction.
frustrated	Extinction is accompanied by emotional responses.
anxious	His behavior frequently has unavoidable aversive consequences which have emotional effects.
lack of purposefulness or sense of accomplishment	He is rarely reinforced for doing anything.
guiltiness, shamefulness	He has previously been punished for idleness or failure, which now evoke emotional responses.
disappointed, disgusted	He is no longer reinforced by the admiration of others, and the extinction that follows has emotional effects.
hypochondriacal	He concludes that he is ill.
neurotic	He engages in a variety of ineffective modes of escape.
has an identity crisis	He does not recognize the person he once called "I."

see, each standard trait that is assigned to the man is interpreted according to Skinnerian behaviorism. If the young man's behavior is weak and inappropriate and often has unavoidable consequences, rather than assuming that he is "insecure" and "anxious," Skinner sees him as a victim of transitory environmental circumstances. That is, he shows some behaviors that are performed rather consistently over time, but his actions are not the product of something that is permanently embedded within him—the traditional notion of traits. Instead, his behavior is due to something that is external to him—an environment that has changed naturally, but, by implication, could be changed through human intervention.

Whether or not one finds Skinner's attempt to dismiss internal entities (traits) convincing, it still must be granted that his notions implicitly include individual differences in behaviors that are constant across time and situations. If the relatively constant behaviors that signify "personality" can be changed through environmental intervention, it should also be possible to develop a personality by design.

Skinner became rather explicit concerning the possibility of developing a personality. In "Creating the Creative Artist" (1972c), Skinner implies that the skills of an artist may be inborn, but will not be manifested without the development of contingencies between artistic endeavor and reinforcement. But what

Can environments be designed to maximize the potential talents in a society? Would mass exposure to art produce more good artists?

exactly is reinforcing in a work of art, such as a painting? It has been argued that the content of a painting is somehow rewarding in and of itself. However, if one examines popular subjects for paintings, Skinner asserts, those objects with survival value predominate (Skinner, 1983). For example, an aspect of human anatomy in all of its strength and unique capabilities, as illustrated by the hand, is a very frequent subject, as is the entire human form. Pictures of food are also common. More abstract is the prevalence of self-portraits, and depictions of family and loved ones, themes that have been associated with survival throughout the evolutionary history of humans. Paintings are reinforcing because of their content, but it is not some intrinsic value of a picture as such. Rather, the content has value because of the evolutionary history of human beings (for example, food and the human form) and factors from the history of the particular artist.

During the lifetime of each artist, there are themes embedded in his or her works that especially appeal to people in the artist's community. When depicted on canvas, these topics result in a form of reinforcement that is familiar to us all, praise. Needless to say, the artist in question will represent in her or his works those themes that are repeatedly followed by reinforcement. Thus, the artist's own history of reinforcement, as well as the history of human beings, shapes her or his behavior when confronting the canvas.

Where in this scheme is creativity, the idea that no one has ever had before? According to Skinner (1972c), creativity, in the sense of the original idea, is an illusion. True, a successful artist does not merely copy the works of other artists, but does "copy" from her or his own experience. The resultant work of art may be unique in that no one has ever expressed the experience exactly as has our hypothetical artist. However, the work is not wholly original in that it represents an experience common to many people. Further, once an artist has arrived at a form of expression that is at least an unusual rendition of some experience, and therefore is reinforced, he or she is likely to repeat that expression throughout his or her career. To support this contention, Skinner points to Picasso. Supposedly, only the first of Picasso's paintings was not derivative. All the works that followed stemmed from the first effort.

The question still remains as to how a community might encourage the pursuit of art in general, rather than just promoting a single artist. To Skinner the answer seems simple: mass exposure to art. Widespread display of art would help to develop artists in two ways. First, there would be an increase in the number of people who would appreciate art, and thus be able to reinforce artists with praise and attention to their works. Second, Skinner seems to be suggesting that large-scale exposure to art would uncover most of those people who are genetically disposed to create works of art. You cannot produce great athletes in a society where sports are not played. If the opportunity to reinforce athletic prowess is not available, athletes will not develop, even though the genetic potential is present in members of the society. Proportional to population, East Germany has won far more Olympic medals than any other country. Skinner would explain this phenomenal success by reference to the interplay of genetics and reinforcement. Rather than simply appropriating the same material that other countries possess and doing a better job of developing it, East Germany has taken above-average material and thoroughly exploited it by constructing contingencies between athletic performance and reinforcement.

If it is possible to develop "personalities"—people who consistently behave in certain ways—what kind of society would promote such development? On the surface, it might seem to be a society in which "talent scouts" go on frequent quests for those abilities that are needed by the society as a whole. However, a look at *Walden Two* (Skinner, 1948) suggests otherwise. In Skinner's behaviorist utopia, the greatest number and variety of pursuits and accompanying reinforcements imaginable are made available to all members of the community. People receive credits for the jobs they perform daily, and, with some flexibility, they have to earn a certain number of credits per week in order to continue in the community. In contrast to real societies, Walden Two offers the most credits for tasks that are tiresome, difficult, and uninteresting (for example, collecting garbage) and the fewest credits for tasks that are enjoyable and interesting (for example, giving a lecture on a favorite topic). Under this system, medical doctors at Walden Two might receive fewer credits per unit time than laborers. Therefore, doctors would have to work longer hours than laborers to earn the same number of credits.

The net result of the credit system at Walden Two is that most people try a wide variety of pursuits, but eventually migrate to those that they are genetically disposed to perform well. "Planners," such as Frazier, presumably because of their inherited disposition to "leadership," spend much of their time planning life in the imaginary society, but sometimes they tend the garden or chop wood. Other members of the community may work at mending fences, repairing the barns, and feeding the animals on many more occasions than they are employed at teaching or serving on committees. Walden Two is an efficient society because experiences rich in number and variety are arranged, creating an environment that selects behaviors the performers are best equipped to enact. It is not necessary to search for talent. Because the society offers the opportunity for performance and reinforcement of almost any conceivable behavior, talent simply emerges.

By the way, Walden Two is not entirely hypothetical. A group of young people have built a replica of Skinner's utopia near Richmond, Virginia (Kinkade, 1973). It has been successful, but might benefit from changes that Skinner has said he would make in Walden Two, if he could do it over (see Skinner, 1983).

Research and Supporting Evidence

The number of studies that stem directly or indirectly from Skinner's research and ideas is impossible to estimate. There must be thousands of such studies. One whole journal, the *Journal of the Experimental Analysis of Behavior*, has been devoted to research in the Skinnerian tradition since its founding in 1958.

Although the great number of behavioristic research efforts guarantee a wide variety of procedures, there is a common vein running through most of the Skinnerian research. In a great number of these studies, only one subject is used, or data are analyzed for each subject separately. It is believed that behavior is readily generalized from one organism to the next, and thus observations on single animals are adequate for drawing conclusions (Holland & Skinner, 1961).

Because of this assumption, typical data analyses are rarely used. Statistics cannot be readily employed in the analysis of observations on single animals. Instead, cumulative records, as defined earlier, are the usual method of analysis and source of conclusions. In this section, we take a close-up look at a representative study, an investigation of superstitious behavior. In addition, we consider a bit of supporting evidence for Skinner's view of the relationship between experiences of reinforcement and genetic inheritance.

AN INVESTIGATION OF SUPERSTITIOUS BEHAVIOR

A study of pigeon behavior (Skinner, 1972k) illustrates Skinnerian behavioristic research and introduces an interesting form of behavior. According to Skinner, a *superstitious behavior* is a response that is accidentally reinforced, as there is no prearranged contingency between the response and reinforcement. That is, with superstitious behavior, reinforcement occurs periodically, regardless of what the organism does. However, because a given behavior and reinforcement accidentally occur together early in the learning process, the behavior is repeated and, by chance, is again followed by reinforcement.

In Skinner's (1972k) study of pigeon behavior, each animal was deprived of food and then placed in a Skinner box, where a food cup was presented to the bird for 5 seconds at regular intervals. The cup was made available to the animal no matter what it did. For six of the eight pigeons, behaviors accompanying this procedure were so distinct that two observers agreed perfectly in their count of behaviors. One bird happened to be turning counterclockwise when the cup was presented early in the experiment. After a number of accidental coincidences of counterclockwise turns and cup presentations, the bird would reliably turn two or three times in a counterclockwise direction between reinforcements. Another would thrust its head into one of the upper corners of the cage, following several accidental coincidences of head thrusting and reinforcement. Two additional pigeons learned to reliably swing their heads and upper bodies in a pendulum motion. Still another animal developed a "tossing" response, as if it were lifting up an invisible lever, and a sixth bird began to peck or brush at the floor without touching it.

Skinner found that an interval of 15 seconds between reinforcements was ideal. Longer intervals decreased the likelihood that responses performed by the pigeon would be closely followed by reinforcement. Shorter intervals limited the number and kinds of behaviors that might precede reinforcement. With short intervals, for instance, only the response "head lowered in front of the cup entrance" was likely to be reinforced. The 15-second interval produced a cumulative record that looked much like that of a FI(15 sec) schedule.

Of course, superstitious behavior is common among humans. An athlete may stick with a dirty old pair of shoes until they disintegrate, because he or she has noticed a "connection" between wearing the shoes and performing well at some sport. A former colleague of the authors', who was well schooled in Skinnerian behaviorism, once seriously refused to relinquish his seat at a poker table. He was sure his position at the table had everything to do with winning several hands and a good deal of money. It seems that few people are immune to superstitious behavior. If you doubt the assertion, examine your own behavior. For example, do you have a valueless object, such as an old hat, that you never use but refuse to relinquish?

Superstitious behaviors are quickly extinguished if it is easy to appreciate that there is no connection between the behavior and reinforcement. A former coach of the Houston Oilers football team wore the same cheap suit for each of seven victorious preseason games and through two winning regular-season games. Then the Oilers lost a contest. Into the rag bag went the suit. If each instance of a superstitious behavior is accidentally followed by the same clearly defined reinforcement, the behavior is likely to disappear the first time if it is not reinforced. Upon the first occasion that putting on the suit was not followed by reinforcement, dressing in the suit was extinguished.

However, not all superstitious behaviors are learned under the condition of reinforcement following each performance. Reinforcement is often intermittent. Take the case of astrology. A person who reads the astrological charts will only rarely experience any kind of reinforcement. However, on some occasions, reading will be followed by reinforcement not too long after the charts are consulted. For example, an individual may read "Good fortune will soon come your way." Two days later, a truck skids to a halt just before crashing into the individual's auto. The near miss may be regarded as "good fortune"—that is, a case of reinforcement. Lack of "good fortune" on the previous two days is ignored. Also, in many cases, it may be rather unclear as to what constitutes reinforcement of a superstitious behavior. The person may regard a wide variety of events as reinforcing, even some that are quite ambiguous. Under these circumstances, the superstitious behavior may last indefinitely. "Superstitious personalities" may develop in those individuals who (1) have difficulty telling the difference between actual reinforcement-behavior contingencies and cases of accidental reinforcement; (2) fail to notice instances of superstitious behavior that are not followed by reinforcement; and (3) regard an unusually wide variety of events as reinforcing, including many that are ambiguous.

THE INTERRELATIONSHIP OF GENETIC ENDOWMENT AND REINFORCEMENT

As you recall from the discussion of personality development, Skinner maintains that people are drawn to experiences that include reinforcement of behaviors to which they are genetically disposed. In a recent paper, Gromly (1982) reports an attempt to investigate the interrelationship between the genetic disposition of individuals and the history of reinforcement during their lives. He states:

> Although learning theory and biological viewpoints are sometimes presented as competing explanations for behavior, they are more likely complementary. This appears to be so in the development of personality traits. One direction this complementary process might take is that, within the limits of their particular environment, people tend to select experiences that suit their biological dispositions. In this way, the selection of preferred experiences by individuals acts as an amplifier of differences that already exist. (p. 255)

Skinner would likely agree with Gromly's statement, with one exception: people don't select experiences from their environment. To Skinner (1971), it is the environment that selects individuals' experiences, and thus their behavior. It is almost as if people, because of their genetic endowment, are drawn to experiences that are likely to include behaviors followed by reinforcements. A girl who is genetically disposed to speak well may end up on the debating team, where her ability to articulate will be amplified, provided only that a debating team is available to her.

To illustrate the possible link between genetic disposition and selection of experiences, Gromly had university fraternity men keep a log of their experiences. Essentially, logging experiences amounted to recording the situations encountered and the corresponding behaviors performed. A sample log entry would be "played basketball today." They also rated themselves on scales designed to assess the possibly inherited dispositions "energetic-physically active" and "sociable-extraverted, socially outgoing." You will note that the latter disposition is very much like the introversion-extraversion trait discussed in the previous chapter and at the beginning of the present chapter. Results showed a close relationship between the experiences that the men reported and scores on "energetic" and "sociable." Thus, measures of genetic endowment, "energetic" and "sociable," were closely related to experiences consistent with that endowment. In Skinner's terms, the environment selected energetic experiences for those people who were genetically inclined to be energetic. It is important to note that the behaviors of "energetic" people in one environment are not likely to be the same as those of energetic people in another environment. A given environment does not simply extend and refine genetic endowment. It leads to specific and concrete behaviors that go far beyond the global and abstract genetic disposition (Skinner, 1972e).

Applications

The number of potential and actual applications of behaviorism, especially the Skinnerian variety, is enormous. We will limit ourselves to two of the most beneficial kinds of applications: behavior modification and educational intervention.

BEHAVIOR MODIFICATION

behavior
modification

Behavior modification is a kind of psychotherapy in which positive and negative reinforcement and punishment are used to alter individual behavior. Almost all of the vast and indefinite number of techniques that fall under this heading were directly suggested by behavioristic research or have been validated by that research (Skinner, 1972j). Behavior modification has been successfully used for everything from treatment of obesity, heavy smoking, and alcoholism to treatment of children who do not talk or relate to adults (autistic children) and treatment of psychotic adults (people who have withdrawn from reality)(see Ullmann & Krasner, 1965).

It is beyond the scope of this book to consider even a small sample from the massive psychotherapeutic tool chest of behavior modification. However, to get a flavor of behavior modification and to see how it relates to Skinner's ideas, let's take a hypothetical example suggested by Skinner (1972l). Imagine a child of 5 who is not psychotic or autistic, but who is so shy and withdrawn that he almost never talks or relates in any way to adult strangers. You can see what a problem this child would have in attending school and relating to teachers.

How can behavior modification help this child? He is placed in a room on one of two chairs positioned side by side in front of a vending machine. It has been established that candy is a good reinforcer for the child, and the machine is capable of vending the boy's favorite confection. The machine is operated by an observer who is hidden behind a one-way mirror (the observer can see the child, but the child sees only his reflection). After a few minutes, an adult stranger enters the room and takes a seat next to the child. Nothing happens for a long while, and the adult leaves, returning shortly. Each entry is called a *trial*. Several trials occur before the child finally utters a word to the stranger. Immediately, the vending-machine operator presses a button, and out of the machine comes the child's favorite treat. Several more trials may occur before the child speaks again, but each episode of speech is reinforced by candy. Soon the child is talking regularly to the stranger, and the schedule is then changed to a VR(5). Later, the schedule is changed to deliver even fewer reinforcements per speech episode, and other strangers take the place of the original adult.

Whenever the child speaks to the stranger, the stranger replies. The replies occur at the same time as the candy reinforcement is being delivered. Thus, the stranger's replies become secondary reinforcers. *Secondary reinforcers* are stimuli that come to have all the properties of primary reinforcers (in this case, candy) through association with primary reinforcers (Kimble, 1961). Thereafter, replies can reinforce the child's utterances. Now he can go out into the real world and talk to people, with his utterances being reinforced by people's replies. This feature makes it likely that the conquest of his shyness will generalize beyond the laboratory. If "shyness" is a trait, then this boy will have undergone a "personality change."

EDUCATIONAL INTERVENTIONS

Inasmuch as Skinner's theory has been addressed primarily to processes of learning, it is not surprising that some of its applications concern education. For example, Skinner (1972i) has invented and fostered the use of teaching machines. In its simplest form, a teaching machine is a box with two windows on its front face. The student turns a knob that presents a question in the leftmost and largest window. The same turn by the student inserts a metal plate over the lower half of the right window. The student then writes in his answer above the plate and turns the knob. The plate disappears, and the correct answer is displayed just beneath the student's response. The student's response (hopefully) is reinforced by being correct (being incorrect is generally considered nonreinforcement rather than punishment). Skinner (1972i) reports that these machines are very efficient teachers. He has also extended the principle of the teaching machine to programmed textbooks (see Holland & Skinner, 1961). In these books, questions are displayed on one page and correct answers on the next page. The student reads the question, composes an answer, and turns the page to view the correct answer.

Noting the dawn of the computer age, Skinner (1983) suggests that the logic of teaching machines and programmed instruction can become more powerful than ever before if exploited by computer programmers.

Skinner's ideas have also been used to improve the efficiency of classroom techniques (1972b). One of the authors has used a Skinnerian method in his university classroom. With these techniques, students are exposed to material in small bites, with the simplest materials coming first. In the ideal situation, each student is drilled by a tutor, often an "A" student from a former class. The tutor asks questions of the student and offers praise for correct answers. After receiving help from tutors, students may be tested by paper and pencil in the usual way. However, just after each test, students get immediate feedback. They are given the answers to the questions to which they have just responded, so that reinforcement can occur. The usual method of forcing students to wait days or even weeks before knowing the degree to which they have been correct is contrary to the evidence from learning experiments (Schwartz, 1978).

In the "complete mastery" form of programmed teaching, students continue to be drilled and take tests over simpler concepts until that information is mastered. Only then do they go on to more complicated material. The process continues, sometimes beyond a single semester, until students have mastered the course to some criterion level, such as 95% correct answers on a comprehensive test. Thus, students are either awarded an "A," signifying complete mastery, or they don't complete the course.

Evaluation

Skinner's ideas—whether or not they add up to a "theory" that can be applied to personality—have certainly met the standard of "heuristic value" suggested in Chapter 2. His concepts have directed attention to specific aspects of human behavior and have inspired a formidable amount of research, commentary, and criticism.

CRITICISMS

Skinner has perhaps been most severely criticized for discounting thought, feeling, and other phenomena that exist "in the head" and thus cannot be directly observed (Skinner, 1971). Skinner admits that individuals, including himself (Skinner, 1983), do have thoughts and feelings but he argues that there is no need to consider these internal entities in order to understand people. He believes that feelings or emotions are by-products of behavior, not its determinants or predecessors (Skinner, 1971). According to this point of view, one flees (behavior), then is afraid (emotion). Assuming this sequence of events, emotions cannot be determinants of behavior. His easy adoption of the behavior-emotion sequence and rejection of its opposite (people are afraid and then flee) seems unwarranted. According to J. Jung (1978), the position that Skinner endorses is not amenable to testing by experimental procedures and has been subjected to severe criticism.

Skinnerian notions of language development and verbal ability have also come under heavy attack, beginning with Noam Chomsky's (1959) review of Skinner's book, *Verbal Behavior* (1957). If Skinner's view is correct, cognition (thinking and reasoning) is unimportant, and environment determines everything—an orientation that many people are unwilling to accept. If Skinner is incorrect, it could be argued that environmental determinism, his most basic assumption, is undermined.

As we have seen, Skinner argues that language is developed by the reinforcement of the child's utterances that is delivered by the verbal community, initially parents and siblings. Supposedly there is no such thing as Chomsky's inborn disposition to grasp the "rules" of language. To Skinner (1976a), "rules" are simply statements of contingencies. Thus, rules develop during the lifetime of the child and are not programmed into the brain at birth. But how can Skinner account for the tremendous explosion of language development between the ages of 18 months and 3 years (Mussen, Conger, & Kagan, 1979)? Language develops so rapidly during this period that a lengthy and painstaking process of primitive utterances being reinforced seems unable to account for it. Further, during this early period and later, children produce utterances that they are very unlikely to have encountered in their environment. More important, these unique utterances indicate that children do grasp the rules with no training. For example, a child might say, "Look, deers. They runned across the road." "Deers" and "runned" are incorrect usages that would rarely be employed or reinforced by adults. Yet, "deers" indicates a grasp of the rule "Plurals are formed by adding an 's.'" Similarly, "runned" represents a recognition of the rule "The past tense is formed by adding 'ed.'" Because these incorrect utterances would not have been reinforced in the past by the verbal community, the child's behavior might best be explained by reference to an innate disposition for grasping rules, rather than to environmental contingencies.

Most of us have solved a variety of mathematical problems to which we have never before been exposed. By a reasoning process, we have come up with an answer that had never occurred to us before, and thus could not have been the object of reinforcement in the past. This common experience, and others like it, constitutes evidence that thoughts unrelated to behavior are important to everyday functioning (J. Hayes, 1978). Aside from such evidence, and contrary to Skinner (1971), thoughts and feelings may be important even if they never have any observable consequences such as finding a solution to a mathematical problem. Recently, the famed British actor Sir Laurence Olivier was interviewed on TV (*60 Minutes,* January 2, 1983). He recounted that at one point in his career, he had developed severe stage fright. While portraying Shakespeare's Othello, Olivier was so overcome with fear and thoughts of inadequacy that he had difficulty catching his breath and wondered if he could go on. Yet somehow he continued. His portrayal of the troubled Moor was shown on *60 Minutes.* Nothing in his performance revealed even a trace of his internal agony. The critics had also noticed nothing unusual; as always, they had praised Olivier's performance. There were no external consequences to his stage fright. However, the solely internal terror suffered by the actor was one of the most notable experiences of his life.

Thoughts and feelings can be extremely important in the lives of people, even when unaccompanied by any external manifestations.

CONTRIBUTIONS

Even if the criticisms just noted are valid, it is still probably true that Skinner's point of view is one of the most general in all of psychology. Perhaps his theory doesn't apply to thoughts, feelings, and language; perhaps it does. In any case, it is difficult to find an introductory psychology book that does not consider Skinner in several different chapters. Likewise, social psychology, developmental psychology, personality, and psychotherapy texts typically devote considerable space to Skinnerianism. Skinner has influenced nearly every division of psychology. More important, through his contributions to teaching and behavior modification, he has had an important and positive influence on literally thousands and thousands of lives. One could certainly defend the contention that Skinner's contributions have had more positive impact on more people than those of any other psychologist.

Historically, Skinner ranks among the greatest of psychologists. A recent survey by Stephen Davis, Roger Thomas, and Melanie Weaver (1982) indicates that he is not only among the best known of living psychologists, but may be approaching recognition as one of the greatest contributors of all time. Also reported by Davis, Thomas, and Weaver is a previous version of the same survey.

Skinner may one day overtake Freud as the most influential psychologist of all time.

Both surveys were administered to chairpersons of departments with graduate programs in psychology, one during 1966 and the other during 1981.

The earlier version lists Skinner near the bottom of the top ten most important psychologists of all time, with Freud appearing in the number-one spot. Over time, however, as Table 5.2 indicates, Skinner has moved up. In 1966, Skinner had only 18% of the total points awarded to Freud by those surveyed. By 1981, he had moved up to the second position on the all-time list and had 76% of the total points awarded to Freud. At that rate, he will soon replace Freud as the most important psychologist of all time.

Obviously, the gap between Freud and Skinner during the period 1966–1981 was closed partly because Skinner moved up, but a weakening of Freud's position may have also contributed to the closure (see Table 5.2B). Although Freud was ranked number one in 1966 and again in 1981, the difference between his total points and those of the other nine psychologists on the list dropped from 422 to 267. Skinner was ranked number one among contemporary psychologists (those still living) in 1966 and again in 1981. However, instead of losing status compared to the other nine contemporary psychologists on the list, he actually gained a little between 1966 and 1981. While Freud is gradually losing importance, according to heads of training programs in psychology, Skinner is rapidly gaining in importance.

Skinner's impact on the area of personality will likely be greater in the future than it has been in the past. An examination of personality texts published over the past 20 years clearly shows that more and more pages are being devoted to Skinner's ideas. A survey of personologists' opinions taken in preparation for the writing of the present book included the following statement: "Please rate each of

TABLE 5.2   Freud Compared to Skinner on the All-Time List of Great Psychologists (A) and Skinner's ranking among living psychologists (B)

	A	
	1966	1981
All-time ranking	Freud ranked #1 Skinner ranked #9	Freud ranked #1 Skinner ranked #2
	Skinner's total: 18% of Freud's total	Skinner's total: 76% of Freud's total
	B	
	1966	1981
Ranking among living psychologists	Skinner ranked #1 Skinner vs. the other 9: 468*	Skinner ranked #1 Skinner vs. the other 9: 487*
All-time ranking	Freud ranked #1 Freud vs. the other 9: 422*	Freud ranked #1 Freud vs. the other 9: 267*

* Difference between Skinner's or Freud's points and total points of the other nine psychologists.

the following items (people or topics) according to the degree of coverage you would prefer in a textbook for your own course and using the scale below." The scale had five points, ranging from "definitely yes" to "definitely no." Out of 218 personologists who completed the survey, 189 gave "definitely yes" votes to Freud, more than any other psychologist. However, Skinner was virtually tied for second and was only 52 points behind Freud (Rogers had 144 "definitely yes" votes and Skinner 137). Skinner was far ahead of Jung (93), Adler (98), and other figures who have been traditionally identified with the area of personality. All this acclaim from personologists occurred despite the observation that Skinner has openly dismissed the whole idea of "personality" and the contention that one must "read between the lines" of his writings to discover the significance of Skinnerianism for the study of personality. Thus, we can expect that Skinner himself will never formally apply his notions to the understanding of personality, but that some of the many personologists interested in his ideas will develop them into a coherent theory of personality.

CHAPTER REVIEW

Behaviorism is a branch of psychology that has overt (observable) behavior as its basic subject matter. The first behaviorist of note was I. P. Pavlov, a Russian physiologist, famous for being the first to systematically study a kind of learning called classical conditioning. More generally, Pavlov composed a theory that suggests a relationship between personality "traits" and characteristics of the nervous system. John B. Watson, the first important American behaviorist, believed that personality is made up of many habit systems, each revolving around some theme and growing out of some inborn human capability.

While Pavlov's ideas are just recently being recirculated and Watson's are largely of historical value, B. F. Skinner's point of view has been influencing personologists for many years, and will likely have greater impact in the future. Like his alter ego in *Walden Two*, B. F. Skinner seems to have "little personality," but is very interesting nevertheless.

Rather than being a stimulus/response (S-R) psychologist, Skinner emphasizes the consequences of responses. A consequence of a response is an event that occurs after a response is performed and increases the likelihood that the

response will be repeated. Skinner is an "environmentalist" in that he thinks genetic dispositions—which are products of environmental selection—and the particular environment into which an individual is born together determine behavior. However, people do have the freedom to arrange conditions in their environment so that their surroundings determine behaviors that they desire. More controversially, Skinner believes that we must give up the notion of dignity—that we only delude ourselves in taking credit for what we do. What we do results from our genetic makeup and our peculiar environments.

Skinner emphasizes operant conditioning, in which an organism operates on its environment, producing consequences that influence the likelihood that the operation—some behavior—will be repeated. In operant conditioning, the occurrence of some stimulus (such as food or electric shock) is contingent on the occurrence of some behavior (such as foraging or stepping on an electric grid) if presentation of the stimulus is dependent on the prior performance of the behavior.

Reinforcement is a central concept in Skinnerian theory. In positive reinforcement, a stimulus increases the likelihood of a response upon which its presentation is contingent. In negative reinforcement, the termination or elimination of a stimulus increases the likelihood of a response that precedes it. Negative reinforcers are usually aversive or painful stimuli, such as electric shock. In contrast to negative reinforcement, punishment involves a decrease in the likelihood of responses that are followed by the presentation of aversive stimuli.

Surprisingly, continuous reinforcement, following each response with reinforcement, is generally not the most efficient means of conditioning. Intermittent reinforcement, in which reinforcement occurs only every so often or after every so many responses, is the more efficient means of conditioning. It generates higher rates of responding and greater resistance to extinction — the disappearance of a conditioned response that is not followed by reinforcement.

A schedule of reinforcement determines whether reinforcement is to be delivered every so often or after some number of responses has occurred. With interval schedules, there is some lapse of time between one reinforced response and the next. Ratio schedules are defined by the occurrence of some number of responses between one reinforced response and the next. With fixed schedules, the amount of time or number of responses required for reinforcement to occur is constant. In the case of variable schedules, the amount of time or number of responses required for reinforcement to occur varies from one occasion of reinforcement to the next, but averages out to some specifiable number.

According to Skinner, learning to speak a language involves uttering words and, if the utterances are correct, receiving reinforcement (often praise) from parents and peers. Vocalizing correct combinations of words is also reinforced until the individual develops the ability to communicate and converse orally.

Although Skinner rejects the concept of "personality," his writings are relevant to issues of personality development. His concepts suggest the possibility of shaping personality through environmental manipulations. His own demonstrations include rearing his daughter in an enclosed crib, complete with temperature and humidity controls. As a result, she was virtually free of the diseases that frequently characterize infancy and the frustrations that come with being bound in clothes and blankets. Freedom from the usual annoyances of infancy and good health resulted in a happy and contented baby.

On a broader scale, Skinner has suggested that societies could manipulate environmental conditions to take advantage of genetic predispositions and produce desired behaviors. Both *Walden Two* and *Beyond Freedom and Dignity* seem to indicate the possibility of "building" personalities.

Skinnerian behaviorism has inspired a multitude of experiments and practical applications. A study of superstitious behavior shows how such practices as consulting astrological charts or carrying around a rabbit's foot can be traced to accidental conditioning. Skinner's ideas have contributed to many varieties of behavior modification and techniques for improving education.

Skinner's version of how people learn language has been criticized as ignoring the observation that children pick up the rules of language without ever receiving training (the application of reinforcement). Such appears to be the case, because children make errors that could not have resulted from reinforcement but that reflect an appreciation of language rules. Also criticized are Skinner's ideas that emotion is merely a by-product of behavior and that internal phenomena (thoughts) that have no external consequences are unimportant as determinants of behavior.

The criticisms lodged against Skinner are greatly outweighed by the positive impact he has had on psychology, the discipline of personality, and the human condition. His contributions to psychotherapy, teaching, and conceptions of human beings rank him among the all-time greats in psychology. In fact, questionnaires given to influential psychologists have yielded results that suggest Skinner will one day surpass Freud as the number one psychologist of all time.

KEY CONCEPTS

Behaviorism
Classical conditioning
Environmentalism
   Consequence
Operant conditioning
   Contingent
   Positive reinforcement
   Extinction
   Negative reinforcement

Punishment
Continuous versus intermittent reinforcement
Schedule of reinforcement
   Fixed-interval
   Fixed-ratio
   Variable-interval
   Variable-ratio
Behavior modification

REVIEW QUESTIONS

1. What is behaviorism? How does it differ from the psychoanalytic tradition?
2. How did Skinner's early-life experiences contribute to his theoretical orientation and to his beliefs about personality?
3. What are some real-life examples of "schedules of reinforcement"?
4. According to Skinnerianism, how might a "personality" be created by design?
5. How has Skinner contributed to developmental, educational, and applied psychology?
6. What criticisms have been lodged against Skinner? Why does Skinner enjoy such a high status among personologists and psychologists generally?

6

Social-Learning Theory: Bandura and Rotter

Does gambling blind people to the likelihood of winning, or are some people just naturally blind to the odds?

Who are more maladjusted, people who believe they control their own destinies or those who believe they are pawns of fate?

How much of our behavior do we learn from other people?

Are people prepared by nature to learn only certain things, or are humans able to learn a broad range of behaviors, including some thought to be peculiar to other species?

What kinds of mental exercises do people carry out that allow them to be cruel to one another?

T HIS CHAPTER CONSIDERS two prominent but unique versions of social-learning theory: those of Julian Rotter and Albert Bandura. A detailed discussion of social learning comes later in the chapter (social learning will also be covered in Chapter 13). For now, we offer a broad, rather general definition. *Social learning* entails acquiring useful information through interactions with people and other elements of the environment (Phares, 1976). *Interaction,* in turn, refers to the relation of individuals to their environments— including, most especially, other people. "The unit of investigation for the study of personality," according to Rotter, "is the interaction of the individual and his meaningful environment" (1954, p. 85). In short, social learning is about people learning from other people.

Rotter, the Person

Julian B. Rotter traces his roots to Brooklyn, New York, where he was born in 1916. Noting the obligation to acknowledge the "teacher who most contributed to my intellect," Rotter (1982) cites the Avenue J Library in Brooklyn. As a high school student, he spent so much time with his "teacher" that he soon exhausted its wisdom, at least in the category of fictional works. Searching the stacks for something new, he stumbled onto books by Adler and Freud. His appetite for psychology thus stimulated, Rotter pursued psychology while an undergraduate at Brooklyn College, but only as an elective. Just as with George Kelly (Chapter 8), the background of the Great Depression caused Rotter to choose a practical major—namely, chemistry. This combination of a "hard science" and a psychology emphasis paid big dividends when Rotter later entered graduate school in psychology.

During Rotter's college years, Adler arrived in Brooklyn. The neo-Freudian's lectures further convinced young Julian that psychology was his destiny. After Brooklyn College, Rotter spent a year at the University of Iowa, where he came under the influence of social psychologist Kurt Lewin. From there he went to Worcester State Hospital, where he met his wife-to-be, Clara Barnes, and where he was irrevocably drawn to clinical psychology. The next stop was Indiana University for a Ph.D. in clinical psychology. After a clinical job in a state hospital and a brief tour as a college teacher, Rotter joined the army, serving as a psychologist and personnel consultant. There, among other contributions, he devised a method for reducing the incidence of "absence without leave."

JULIAN ROTTER.
Rotter was one of the first
personologists to consider
environmental circumstances and
internal factors in the study of
personality.

After World War II, Rotter joined the staff at Ohio State University, where he crossed paths with Kelly. It was in the army and at Ohio State that Rotter began work on his social-learning theory. In 1963, he took his current position at the University of Connecticut, where his thinking on social learning fully crystallized. Rotter has served on the Education and Training Board of the American Psychological Association (APA), on the APA Council, and on the United States Public Health Service training committee. He has been president of the APA divisions for Social and Personality and for Clinical Psychology and president of the Eastern Psychological Association.

Rotter's View of the Person

To this point we have run the theoretical gamut from a rather complete focus on external determinants of behavior (for example, Skinner, Chapter 5) to heavy reliance on explanations of behavior in terms of internal factors (for example, Freud, Chapter 3). Now we turn to a point of view that is a sort of compromise between those two extremes. Rotter (1966) does believe that people gripped by the forces of a powerful situation do show a general trend in behavior different from that shown under other circumstances. However, within such situations, persons still display individual differences in behavior.

Let's take an example. Rotter (1966) writes of several studies in which subjects were exposed to a "chance" or "skill" situation. In the "chance" situations, subjects were told that luck would determine how well they did; in "skill" situations, they were told that their own abilities would determine their performance. For example, Phares (1962) presented subjects with a list of 12 nonsense syllables (such as *ilo, pmn, rfv*). First, he determined how long each subject had to view each syllable before being able to correctly call out its letters (exposures were for fractions of a second). Then the entire list of syllables was presented ten times, with the same 6 syllables always associated with the delivery of shock to subjects and the other 6 never followed by shock. During the ten presentations, the shock that accompanied 6 of the syllables could be terminated if subjects learned which of several buttons was the one that stopped the shock. Subjects in a "chance" condition were told that sometimes a certain button would stop the shock accompanying a particular syllable and sometimes a different button would work, depending on chance. Subjects in a "skill" condition were informed that they could terminate the shock by determining which of the buttons *always* stopped the shock associated with a particular syllable. Finally, it was again determined how long each subject had to view each syllable before being able to correctly name its letters. If a subject required less viewing time to identify a shocked syllable after the ten presentations than before, it was assumed that the subject had learned the syllable during the presentations. A comparison of the exposure times before and after the ten presentations revealed that subjects in the "skill" condition *reduced* the exposure times needed to identify the nonsense syllables followed by shock more than did subjects in the "chance" condition. People do better in "skill" than in "chance" situations, because they experience a feeling of control over circumstances.

However, the behavior of individuals operating within both "chance" and "skill" situations can vary quite a bit. For example, before each attempt at the "chance" or "skill" task, subjects are usually asked to indicate how well they expect to do. Regardless of whether they have been told that chance or skill would determine their outcomes, some subjects tend to show the "gambler's fallacy," while others do not (Rotter, 1966). The *gambler's fallacy* is the expectation that failure on one attempt means a greater likelihood of success on a subsequent attempt, whereas success means greater likelihood of failure in the future. People who are prone to the gambler's fallacy think that a string of failures means they will surely soon be winners, because they believe that luck determines their outcomes, and luck is supposed to change. Other people show the opposite of the gambler's fallacy. They believe that skills determine outcomes. To them, a string of successes means that they have mastered the situation and will continue to experience success.

In sum, Rotter believes that environments can control behavior. People in the "chance" condition, as a group, behave differently from those in the "skill" condition. However, even within powerful situations, people show individual differences in behavior: some people are prone to the gambler's fallacy, and others are not, regardless of conditions. Rotter and his colleagues have demonstrated that people operating within "chance" or "skill" situations show as much difference among themselves as exists between all "chance" and all "skill" subjects (Rotter, 1966). Thus, superimposed on strictly environmental influences are individual differences, the hallmark of traits (see Chapter 1). Environments influence behavior, but so do traits.

Basic Concepts: Rotter

REINFORCEMENT VALUE, PSYCHOLOGICAL SITUATIONS, AND EXPECTANCY

For our purposes, Rotter's theory is based on three main concepts: reinforcement value, psychological situation, and expectancy (Rotter, 1975).

In Rotter's social-learning theory, *reinforcement* refers to anything that has an influence on the occurrence, direction, or kind of behavior (Phares, 1976). You may contrast this view with Skinner's narrow definition: reinforcement occurs when some event is contingent on the prior performance of some response (see Chapter 5). Also, Rotter distinguishes between reinforcements on the basis of value. *Reinforcement value* is the degree of preference for the occurrence of a certain reinforcement, given that all reinforcements possible under the circumstances are equally likely to occur. Imagine a woman named Martha who sometimes dates a man named Fred. For Martha, going out with Fred has low reinforcement value, because, given a choice among several equally likely dates, Fred would be just about the last selected.

reinforcement value

A *psychological situation* is an environmental circumstance that an individual characterizes in a way that is peculiar to her or him, allowing the person to categorize it with certain other circumstances and differentiate it from still others

psychological situation

The gambler's fallacy is the assumption that a string of "losses" is sure to be followed by a "win."

(Phares, 1976). Situations are in the "eye of the beholder." If a given situation is seen in a certain way by a particular individual, that's the way it is for her, no matter how strange the categorization might seem to others. For some individuals, an exhibition of classical music is "entertainment"; for others, it is "a scholarly endeavor"; for still others, it is a waste of time. Thus, some people see classical music as belonging in the same category as other forms of entertainment, such as baseball and movies; others would categorize it together with reading, researching library files, and other scholarly pursuits. To continue our example, let's suppose that Martha is planning to attend a rock concert, which she considers to be a "social gathering." Given this categorization, she believes that one should take a companion, but it should be a person one would not be afraid to ignore when opportunities to mingle with others arise.

expectancy

Expectancy is "the probability held by the individual that a particular reinforcement will occur as a function of a specific behavior on his part in a specific situation or situations" (Rotter, 1954, p. 107). Our hypothetical Martha has every reason to expect that should she pick up the phone and dial Fred's number, he will be right over. She knows that Fred is madly in love with her, a feeling she does not reciprocate. That is, Martha has the specific expectancy that calling Fred will be reinforced by his presence with her at the concert—an outcome of high likelihood and, in and of itself, low reinforcement value. But she has another important expectancy as well. She expects opportunities to mingle with her friends at the concert—an outcome of high reinforcement value.

generalized expectancy

In addition, Martha has a relevant generalized expectancy. A *generalized expectancy* is the assumed probability of reinforcement of a behavior that applies to a number of situations, all of which are likely to be seen as similar to some degree (Rotter, 1966). The operation of generalized expectancies becomes more likely when individuals are faced with new or ambiguous situations that they characterize as bearing some resemblance to known situations (Rotter, 1966). Martha has been to relatively few rock concerts, but she expects that these will be like other "social occasions." Her generalized expectancy for these situations is that whether she impresses her friends will be a matter of chance (whether they are "in a good mood," the concert goes well, and so on) rather than determined by her social skills. On the basis of these assumptions about Martha, we can predict that she will call Fred, who will escort her to the concert, where she will encounter friends, whom she will impress or not, depending on "what fate has in store."

LOCUS OF CONTROL: INTERNALS AND EXTERNALS

Generalized expectancy is highly relevant in the study of personality. Rotter (1966, 1967) has identified two important generalized expectancies: locus of control and interpersonal trust. Locus of control, discussed in this section, is the basis for as famous a personality measure as exists in psychology. Discussion of interpersonal trust is reserved for a later section.

locus of control

Locus of control refers to whether individuals perceive that reinforcement depends upon their own behavior or attributes, versus whether they perceive it as being controlled by forces outside of them, possibly independent of their own actions (Rotter, 1966). Persons are said to believe in *external control* of reinforcement if they perceive that reinforcement of their behaviors is due more to luck, chance, fate, powerful others, or complex and unpredictable environmental forces than to their own behaviors or characteristics (Rotter, 1966). Individuals who believe that reinforcement is dependent on their own behavior or characteristics are said to believe in *internal control* of reinforcement. People who believe in internal control are often called *internals,* while those who believe in external control are called *externals.*

internal versus external

Belief in external control or internal control might be considered traits, in the sense of individual differences. However, Rotter (1975) takes great pains to point out that externals and internals are not "types," each sharing many characteristics with others in their category and few with everyone else (see Chapter 1). Rather, similar to some notions of trait, locus of control can be thought of as a continuum, bounded on one end by *internal* and on the other by *external,* with people's beliefs distributed at all points in between, most in the middle. That is, being external or internal is a matter of degree, not all or nothing. However, locus of control is a belief based on relatively specific experience, and is thus more likely to change with a change in experience than are traits. With these cautions in mind, we can turn to a measure of locus of control, the I-E Scale.

Although there are several measures of locus of control, the one most in use has been the I-E Scale, developed by Rotter (1966). Rather than presenting it here verbatim, we have designed a measure that mimics the I-E Scale, but has items composed of everyday, "commonsense" notions. By completing our version of the I-E Scale (call it the P&A I-E Scale), you should easily get a flavor of what's involved in being an external or internal. Our measure is presented in Box 6.1. The instructions at the beginning tell you how to complete the scale, and those at the end tell you how to obtain your "score." Remember, our scale is for educational purposes (and a little fun). Don't use it in an attempt to classify yourself as an external or as an internal. We recommend that you complete the scale now, before returning to the text.

The P&A I-E Scale   **BOX 6.1**

This questionnaire is designed to give you some insight into externality and internality. Take it seriously and complete it conscientiously, but remember that it should not be used to classify you as an internal or external.

Instructions: For each item, select the alternative that you more strongly believe to be true. You must select one, and only one, alternative for each item. Be sure that the alternative you select for a given item is the one you actually believe to be most clearly true, not the one you think that you *should* choose or the one you *wish* were true. Remember that this is a measure of your personal beliefs. There are no correct or incorrect answers and no high or low, good or bad scores.

continued

BOX 6.1
continued

Don't spend much time on each item, but do make a choice for each item. In some cases, you will find that you believe both statements or neither one. Please make a decision anyway.

1. a. I often find myself saying something to the effect of "What will be will be."
    b. I believe that what happens to me is my own doing.

2. a. I deserve credit for most of my accomplishments.
    b. I've been fortunate to have done well on a number of occasions.

3. a. When your time comes, you pass away; that's just the way it is.
    b. I plan to live a long time, and I wouldn't be surprised if I made it to 100.

4. a. I'm a pretty confident person. I can make things happen.
    b. Sometimes I'm amazed at how things seem to happen to me all by themselves.

5. a. I feel like a Ping-Pong ball. Life just bounces me back and forth between happy and sad.
    b. If I want to be happy, I just choose a fun thing to do and go to it.

6. a. You get what you deserve and deserve what you get.
    b. I don't feel guilty about the good things that happen to me or moan about the bad things. It could just as well have happened to someone else.

7. a. I wish the world wasn't full of so many bullies.
    b. If people start to coerce me, I just stand up and look them in the eye.

8. a. People are good to me because I treat them right.
    b. I don't know when to expect that people are going to be nasty to me or nice.

9. a. I plan things, and they turn out as I expect.
    b. "Come what may," that's my motto. I'm a tumbleweed, caught in the wind.

10. a. I live my life one day at a time.
    b. I plan my day, my week, my month, and my year. I look ahead.

11. a. I'm not afraid to risk life and limb. What the heck, you could fall in the shower and break your back.
    b. I'm pretty careful at driving, sports, and so forth. I expect to keep this body a long, long time.

12. a. I feel pretty helpless when I'm with my friends. I usually end up doing what they want.
    b. My friends and I are democratic about deciding what we'll do together, but my voice is always heard.

13. a. My voice is heard above the crowd.
    b. People just seem to drown me out.

14. a. When it comes to making love, if my partner wants to, fine; if not, that's OK too.
    b. I tend to decide when, where, and what my partner and I do in the love category.

continued

BOX 6.1
continued

15. a. I enter many lotteries, drawings, and things like that. I keep hoping I'll strike it rich.
    b. I steer clear of everything from bingo to poker. The odds are too long.
16. a. I'm always rooting for the underdog.
    b. Me, I stick with the winners.
17. a. In this country, anyone with some talent and some sweat is going to make it.
    b. If you're lucky, you're rich; if not, join the crowd.
18. a. Minorities are doing better, because they are getting more education and working harder.
    b. Minorities are doing better, because they are finally getting a few breaks.
19. a. Some people wander around under a black cloud, while the sun shines on others.
    b. Let's face it, some people have ability and use it; some have it and waste it; and some just don't have it.
20. a. Life is a great glob of complexity. It would take an Einstein to win at it.
    b. It's really quite simple: if you're good and work hard, you succeed.
21. a. I like to compete because if I win it's great, and if I lose I can say "The gods frowned on me."
    b. I like to compete because if I win, I can say "I did it."
22. a. I think we should help each other, because misfortune could strike any of us.
    b. I think people should help themselves. If something bad happens to them, they caused it, and they can fix it.
23. a. Sometimes I feel powerful, able to do whatever I want.
    b. Sometimes I feel powerless, the victim of mysterious forces.
24. a. Things happen that puzzle me. I just can't make sense of them.
    b. Give me enough time and enough information, and I can usually make sense of anything.
25. a. We are likely to be swept up in the ebb and flow of events.
    b. If we can get to the moon, we can change the course of mighty rivers and make the weather do our bidding.

   Give yourself a point if you chose each of the following alternatives:
1. a.; 2. b.; 3. a.; 4. b.; 5. a.; 6. b.; 7. a.; 8. b.; 9. b.; 10. a.; 11. a.; 12. a.; 13. b.; 14. a.; 15. a.; 16. a.; 17. b.; 18. b.; 19. a.; 20. a.; 21. a.; 22. a.; 23. b.; 24. a.; 25. a.
   The higher the score, the more external you are.

CHARACTERISTICS OF INTERNALS AND EXTERNALS

   Internals and externals differ in many ways other than their beliefs about where control of their behavior lies. This section is devoted to the contrasts between these two kinds of people.

Because externals believe that they are hapless victims of their environments, one would expect them to be more conformist. Indeed, Phares (1976) reports that externals are more likely to conform in the standard conformity experiment (see Chapter 14). By the same token, internals react against attempts to influence them, even sometimes moving in a direction opposite to that of the influence attempt.

Rotter (1966) originally recognized a greater likelihood of maladjustment among externals. At the same time, he also hypothesized that there would be a curvilinear relationship between locus of control and psychological adjustment, with both extreme internals and extreme externals being maladjusted. However, more recently, he has indicated that such is probably not the case (Rotter, 1975). It seems that externals are much more likely than internals to be maladjusted.

Phares (1976) reports that externals are higher in anxiety and lower in self-esteem than internals. In terms of more serious maladjustment, externality may be associated with schizophrenia (withdrawal from reality, distortion of speech and thought) and possibly with depression, though the latter is preliminary and fraught with problems. Perhaps surprisingly, Phares reports that internals may be more likely to abuse substances such as alcohol and heroin. Perhaps high internality scores among substance abusers may be explained by the fact such people are continually told "Your cure is up to you." Alcoholics may therefore be using their I-E responses to reflect what they think is expected of them. In any case, much more attention should be paid to the relationship between internal or external orientation and maladjustment, as the literature does not yet allow clear conclusions.

A recent, sophisticated review of the literature on academic achievement and locus of control indicates that the higher the internality, the higher the achievement (Findley & Cooper, 1983). This same review raises another interesting question about the nature of locus of control. From the very beginning (Rotter, 1966), it has been reported that externality was greater among Blacks than Whites. This result seems to make intuitive sense, as relatively powerless persons should believe that they are at the mercy of their environments. Also, the earlier result seems to be cultural, or more generally due to factors outside the individual rather than to race in and of itself. Support for this contention comes from studies that find it is lower-socioeconomic-class Blacks who are highly external, not their middle-class counterparts (Rotter, 1966). Thus, how well one is doing in life, both practically speaking and in terms of how one is regarded by others, may determine one's level of internality-externality. The recent survey by Findley and Cooper (1983) failed to support the greater externality in Blacks reported by Rotter (1966), possibly because of the small number of studies reviewed. However, it is also possible that Blacks have changed in more recent years. This would be consistent with the hypothesis that how well one is doing in life determines one's level of internality-externality. If Blacks are in fact doing better, they should become less external.

Independent support for the notion that it is what's happening in one's life rather than something inherent in oneself that determines locus of control comes from a couple of recent studies. Baron and Byrne (1984) report that women who are physically abused by their husbands are more external than those who are not mistreated. Even more supportive is a study that found that internality-externality changes with the ebb and flow of life's fortunes. Doherty (1983) reports that women showed increases in externality following divorce, then moved back toward internality with the passage of time.

PERSONALITY DEVELOPMENT OF INTERNALS AND EXTERNALS

Researchers have also studied how the processes of personality development differ for internals and externals. After reviewing the literature on locus of control and child-rearing practices, Phares (1976) concludes that internality is linked to parental warmth, protectiveness, positivity, and nurturance. On the other side, externals tend to have cold, rejecting, and negative parents. Evidence also exists that parents may actually tutor their children to be internals or externals. Davis and Phares (1969) found that parents whose children's locus of control was similar to their own tended to be more indulgent and less disciplinarian than parents whose children's locus of control was dissimilar to their own.

Phares (1976) also reports other support for the thesis that parents may provide lessons in internality-externality. A capricious, unpredictable world, in which a given behavior is one day punished, the next positively reinforced, and the next ignored altogether, may produce a child with a belief in external control. The degree to which the outcome of a behavior is stable is the degree to which one has the possibility of claiming credit for that outcome. Following this logic, Phares (1976) reports that the literature reflects a definite connection between inconsistency of reinforcement within the family and tendency toward externality.

Whether an individual is a first or only child as opposed to a younger sibling may have an influence on internality-externality. The logic of locus of control and the evidence just reviewed would predict that the protective, demanding, but loving parents characteristic of only and first-born children should produce internal offspring. Phares (1976) reports some support for this line of reasoning, but adds that the birth-order/locus-of-control relationship is clouded by a complex of variables beyond the two of interest. For example, sex of the child and family size play a role in whether first and only children tend toward internality. In any case, the relationship between locus of control and birth order is not very strong.

Locus of Control and Interpersonal Trust: A Research Example

A great deal of what you communicate to others and what they communicate to you is done without words. Your facial expressions and posture tell other people about you, just as those factors tell you about them (Ekman & Friesen, 1974). Obviously, the better you are at "reading" others' nonverbal signals, the better able you are to ascertain whether whatever behavior you are directing to another person is working to yield reinforcement. If you are trying to fish for a compliment from someone, you're casting your line into empty waters if you can't read from the face and body of your target whether the hook is close to sinking in.

It follows from this reasoning that internals believe they control their own reinforcements partly because they have the skills to read whether they are on the right track when seeking reinforcement from others. You can expect that the behaviors you direct toward another person will yield reinforcement if you know that you can monitor that person's nonverbal signals and continually alter your course until you find the path to reinforcement. If you know that you can read the subtle signals emanating from others, you can believe that you can control the reinforcement they have to offer (Sabatelli, Buck, & Dreyer, 1983). Conversely, if you can't decipher other people's silent messages, you'll have a hard time believing you can control the availability of their reinforcements.

interpersonal trust

The ability to intercept and correctly interpret nonverbal communications may also be related to interpersonal trust. Rotter (1967) defines *interpersonal trust* as a generalized expectancy that people's verbal promises are reliable. That is, a person who possesses the generalized expectancy that he can rely on the word of other people is said to be high on interpersonal trust. Especially in view of the connection between successful detection of deception and ability to read nonverbal communications (DePaulo & Rosenthal, 1979), it seems reasonable to expect that people who trust others are people who have the ability to tell when others are being truthful. Conversely, people who are low in interpersonal trust are likely to be people who can't tell when others are being straight with them. Applying this logic leads to the prediction that people who are high in interpersonal trust will be skilled at deciphering nonverbal communications.

These hypothesized links between locus of control and ability to decode nonverbal communications and between interpersonal trust and reading silent messages were both tested in a study by Ronald Sabatelli, Ross Buck, and Albert Dreyer (1983). They recruited married couples and showed them slides of sexual scenes, landscapes, children, unpleasant scenes (people with severe burns), and unusual scenes (strange photographic effects). Unbeknown to the subjects, a hidden video camera recorded their faces and upper bodies as they talked about their reactions to the slides. Following the presentation of each slide, subjects also rated its pleasantness.

After each member of a couple had independently viewed the slides and done the ratings, spouses were ushered into separate rooms, where one completed some demographic forms while the other viewed the videotape of the first spouse reviewing the slides. With the audio portion of the tape turned off, each spouse watched the other react to the slides and, for each portion of the tape, guessed which type of slide the spouse was observing and how pleasant it had been. The result was the specific measure of decoding ability. A general measure of decoding ability, called CARAT, was also administered to each spouse. CARAT involved presenting subjects with faces of strangers who were viewing slides and was scored by the percentage of slides viewed by the strangers that subjects were able to correctly identify. All subjects also completed the I-E Scale and Rotter's Interpersonal Trust Scale.

Results showed that for the general measure of decoding ability, or CARAT, internality was associated with greater ability for females. However, contrary to expectation, externality was related to greater ability in males. With reference to the same measure of decoding, high interpersonal trust expectancies related to high deciphering ability for both males and females.

The measure of specific decoding ability—sensitivity to spouse rather than to stranger—yielded few substantive results. Highly trusting females did show greater ability than their low-trust counterparts in decoding their spouses' non-verbal messages. Such was the case both for percentage of slide-types correctly identified and the difference between that percentage and the percentage correctly identified by some students who also saw tapes of the husbands. An additional noteworthy result emerged when subjects were classified jointly according to their locus-of-control and interpersonal-trust scores. Internal/low-trust males were markedly inferior on the general measure of decoding ability to all other combinations of externality-internality and high-trust/low-trust for males.

In sum, locus of control did not relate as expected to ability to decipher nonverbal communications. For a general measure of deciphering ability, internal females were better decoders than external females, but external males were superior to internal males. To further cloud the picture, internal/low-trust males did worse than all other combinations of locus of control and interpersonal trust for male subjects. Interpersonal trust showed a better relationship with decoding ability. Using the general measure of decoding ability (CARAT), high trust was related to high ability for both males and females. High-trust females were also superior to low-trust females on the specific measure, sensitivity to spouse. It appears that locus of control relates to decoding nonverbal messages as Rotter's theory predicts only for females and only on a general measure. However, interpersonal trust predicts decoding ability for both males and females when a general deciphering measure is used, and for females when a specific measure is employed.

Applications: Changing Externals

As indicated above, compared to extreme internality, extreme externality is apparently the more serious psychological handicap. Such being the case, changing externals has occupied a number of researchers and psychotherapists. Here we discuss two examples of those applications: interventions into natural settings and psychotherapeutic interventions.

de Charms (1972) sought to change Black teachers and students from "pawns" to "origins." *Pawns,* in this terminology, are instruments of outside forces, while *origins* are the locus of their own intentions and behaviors. Obviously, pawns are essentially externals, and origins are internals. de Charms required the teachers to attend a week-long motivational training session and designed exercises for teachers to use throughout the school year. The training included (1) encouragement of self-study and evaluation; (2) becoming familar with the thought and behavior of people with affiliative, achievement, power, and other motives; (3) learning to appreciate the value of planning and setting realistic goals for the fulfillment of some motive; and (4) general training to promote origin rather than pawn behavior. The in-class exercises included attempts to improve self-concept and achievement motivation, as well as to make goals more realistic and to teach the origin-pawn concept. Results included greater professional advancement among trained compared to untrained teachers, questionnaire results suggesting that students of trained teachers saw them as encouraging the behavior of origins, and improvement of academic achievement by students of trained teachers.

Phares (1976) describes attempts to change externality in the context of psychotherapy. Among the results he reports is a greater decrease in externality among clients who seek psychotherapy because of acute problems as opposed to more chronic difficulties. He also describes the case of an adolescent who moved toward internality by adopting an active, success-oriented means of controlling his parents in place of the shrinking, meek, and submissive techniques he had been using. Finally, he reports a study in which students became more internal after four half-hour therapy sessions centering on "personal growth experiences."

One problem in bringing about any change in psychotherapeutic clients is matching the patient to the therapy. If the style and general orientation of the client and the psychotherapy don't match, the client may be resistant to attempts at change. In particular, an external may not change if the belief system he brings to therapy conflicts with the basic nature of the psychotherapy. For example, behavioristic therapy is more controlling, manipulative, and structured, while the psychotherapy of Carl Rogers (see Chapter 7) is more open, client-centered, and client-oriented. Indeed, Phares (1976) reports that college students who preferred the more directive cognitive-behavioristic approach of Albert Ellis over Rogers' nondirective method were more external than their counterparts. In a similar vein, psychotherapists who were asked to evaluate the profiles of behavioristic and psychoanalytic colleagues rated the former as more overbearing and more likely to promote externality. The psychotherapists who served as raters also took the I-E Scale and were asked to imagine that they had problems requiring psychotherapy. Those who were more internal indicated that their imagined problem would be better solved by psychoanalytic therapy, while externals chose behavioristic therapy. Phares (1976) concludes that how clients perceive a psychotherapeutic method may partly determine how they respond to it.

Evaluation: Rotter

Locus of control is the centerpiece of Rotter's point of view. Evidence for and against this crucial notion determines the validity of his theory.

CRITICISMS

Rotter himself has noted some problems with locus of control. In 1966 he presented evidence that it overlaps with social desirability. *Social desirability* refers to the need to please others by displaying the characteristics that are valued in our society (for example, goodness, honesty, sincerity). The implication of this association is obvious. In completing the I-E Scale, subjects and clients may be trying to favorably impress experimenters or psychotherapists, rather than accurately reporting their actual characteristics. One could argue that the extent to which social desirability is manifested in I-E responses is the extent to which locus-of-control scores reflect response distortion rather than an index of an actual personality characteristic. More recently, Rotter (1975) has acknowledged that the problem still exists. He complains that some researchers have persisted in regarding internals as the "good guys" and externals as the "bad guys." Perhaps such regard is at least partly justified, as respondents might actively and even consciously try to make themselves look like "good guys" by endorsing as many of the "internal" items on the I-E Scale as they can identify.

Another, perhaps even more severe, problem is the apparent existence of kinds of externals—one of which contradicts some basic assumptions about externality. *Defensive externals* are people who are highly competitive and do well on tests, but endorse external items for the apparent purpose of blaming others for their failures (Rotter, 1975). *Passive externals* (also called *congruent*) believe they are controlled by fate or chance. Whereas passive externals are consistent with Rotter's theory, defensive externals are not. According to Rotter's social-learning theory, people who indicate that they are controlled by outside forces are not supposed to be competitive.

Rotter (1975) tries to skirt the problem by claiming that the theory and the scale are still valid, but I-E scores simply identify two kinds of externals. However, this assertion does nothing to explain the puzzling nature of defensive externals. Defensive externals may well be people who are using locus of control to provide an excuse for their failures, but many other, equally plausible explanations of their behavior might also be posed. For example, defensive externals may experience alienation, with its accompanying feeling of powerlessness, but fight it by being highly competitive. *Alienation* is estrangement from others and a general loss of the feeling that one belongs. Adequately explaining how two types of externals can coexist in a theoretical domain that is constructed to account for only one remains a task for future researchers and theoreticians. Also, the I-E Scale needs to be further purged of social-desirability elements.

CONTRIBUTIONS

On the positive side, there seems to be little question that locus of control is here to stay. If anything, interest in this personality dimension is increasing. As long ago as 1975, Rotter was able to count at least 600 studies dealing with the I-E measure. Inspection of journals during the early 1980s indicates that the number has greatly increased and is going up at an accelerating rate. We predict that interest will continue to increase, because locus of control is in tune with current trends in the area of personality.

Rotter (1954, 1966) was a pioneer in recognizing that one can account for human behavior only by considering multiple determinants, including situational effects (we consider this subject in a section of Chapter 13 on Rotter's student, Walter Mischel). Rotter has always maintained that mindless use of one of a few personality measures is a fruitless approach to understanding people. In addition to expectancies, such as locus of control and situational factors, one must also consider reinforcement values (Rotter, 1975). Further, internality-externality resembles a trait dimension only in that people can be distributed along a continuum. Positions on this dimension blend one into the other, rather than being discrete points. Also, a person's position will vary at different points in time and under differing circumstances. Thus, the meaning of internality-externality must be considered in the context of many other factors and cannot be interpreted in isolation. This kind of flexibility and openness characterizes Rotter and guarantees that his ideas will contribute to psychology indefinitely.

Bandura, the Person

Our second social-learning theorist is Albert Bandura, one of the greatest of contemporary psychologists. Bandura was born on December 4, 1925, in the Canadian village of Mundare, Alberta. Not surprisingly, his early memories include the extreme cold that characterizes the area. After attending the typical small-town school, elementary through high school in one facility, he took a job patching highways in the forbidding Yukon. There he encountered a variety of individuals, ranging from parole violators and debtors to divorced men avoiding alimony payments. This experience was probably the origin of his interest in the psychological problems of everyday life.

After obtaining an undergraduate degree at the University of British Columbia, he enrolled at the University of Iowa, where he came under the influence of famed learning psychologist Kenneth Spence. Having received his doctorate, Bandura was appointed instructor at Stanford University, which was to become psychology's Mecca, partly through his own efforts. Bandura worked his way up through the ranks and now occupies an endowed chair at Stanford. In 1980, he received the American Psychological Association's award for Distinguished Scientific Contributions. He was cited "for masterful modeling as researcher, teacher, and theoretician" and for "innovative experiments on a host of topics including

ALBERT BANDURA.
Bandura has shown that modeling is among the most powerful means of changing behavior.

moral development, observational learning, fear acquisition, treatment strategies, self-control . . . self-referent processes, and cognitive regulation of behavior. . . . His vigor, warmth, and humane example have inspired his many students' own self-efficacy." (See "Awards 1980," 1981.)

Bandura's View of the Person

A major issue in the area of personality has been whether forces inside or outside of individuals control their behavior. We have seen that this issue, in its more general form, is central to Rotter's point of view. Bandura's theory relates to a more specific manifestation of the inside/outside question: behavioral consistency. Advocates of determination by factors outside of individuals emphasize the variability of behavior, due to dynamic action of the environment. Those who believe that control of behavior comes from within indicate that stable processes from inside individuals are the sources of behavior. Their point of view implies consistency of behavior. By contrast, social-learning theory focuses on both the variability and the consistency of behavior (Bandura, 1977). It is concerned with the interplay of factors inside and outside of people.

Why has the consistency of behavior been such a hot topic, a bone of contention? Those who embrace external determination, particularly behaviorists, challenge some very important values of Western society—values that are jealously defended by those who endorse internal determination. The behavioral consistency supported by the "internal" group implies the virtues of dependability, trustworthiness, and steadfastness. These characteristics are the opposites of expediency and untrustworthiness, both considered undesirable. Because it involves factors both inside and outside of people, Bandura's theory avoids these value-laden questions.

What allows people to learn? According to Bandura's social-learning theory, learning occurs because people are aware of the consequences of their responses. They can and do think about what those consequences will be. By being aware of the relationship between consequences and responses, people can be forward-looking or future-oriented rather than be controlled by past reinforcement events (Bandura, 1977). People behave in anticipation of future consequences, they do not merely observe events that have yielded reinforcement in the past, and then behave. "The eye to the future," as opposed to "eyes in the back of the head," is a philosophical position that Bandura shares with George Kelly (see Chapter 8).

Behaviorists often use animals in their research. By contrast, Bandura's social-learning theory has been oriented to human beings. Animals don't think; people do. People can record the consequences of actions as words or symbols and thereby form hypotheses concerning what will happen in the future. If one observes that smiling at waiters yields efficient and prompt service, one can store that observation in words and construct the hypothesis that smiling works with waiters. This hypothesis operates as a motivator for smiling behavior in the presence of waiters; it amounts to the anticipation of good service following smiling. That is, knowing that smiling will yield dividends in the near future motivates smiling behavior.

self-regulatory
capacities

Bandura's theory encompasses a measure of free will or self-determination, in that it emphasizes self-regulatory capacities. *Self-regulatory capacities* are abilities to arrange relationships between behaviors and consequences for oneself. People are not pawns of their environments. They shape their external circumstances by guiding their own behaviors. Self-regulation includes mentally manufacturing one's own rewards ("I'll feel good when I complete this task, no matter how it turns out") and deciding for oneself what inducements are worth pursuing.

Basic Concepts: Bandura

DEFINITION OF SOCIAL-LEARNING THEORY

social-learning
theory

According to Bandura, *social-learning theory* postulates that cognitive (mental), behavioral, and environmental factors, especially those related to human interaction, work together to determine human action. Contrary to other theories in psychology, social-learning theory emphasizes the influence of people on people and the importance of cognition. *Cognition* refers to knowing, perceiving, and thinking. Critical to social-learning notions is the assumption that, for people to be influenced by the consequences of their behavior, they must be aware of the link between the behavior and its consequences. In support of the assumption, Bandura (1977) reports considerable evidence that learning is difficult for humans if there is little or no awareness of the link between behavior and consequences. Further, it is nearly certain that learning is facilitated by awareness.

The other principal underpinning of social-learning theory is tied up in the term "social." People learn as much vicariously, through observing the behavior of others, as they learn through direct experience. Further, the terms "cognition" and "social" are close associates, because cognition is the vehicle by which people learn from people. If an individual watches another person receive a reward as a consequence of a behavioral performance, the observer will likely think (cognition) "If I behave in the same way, I'll receive the same reward." Learning can take place even if rewards are not received directly. Observing another person model some behavior that results in reward is enough for learning to occur. In fact, as we shall see, individuals may learn even if their observations in no way include rewards.

MODELS AND MODELING

model

modeling

Because learning through observation of others is unique to social-learning theory and thus distinguishes it from other psychological theories, it is emphasized here. A *model* is a person who performs some behavior for an audience, showing how it is done and what benefits accrue from it. *Modeling* refers to the act of performing a behavior before one or more observers.

When people learn from observing others, they do not simply soak up whatever models have to offer. They begin observations of others with certain predispositions and orientations that determine what they learn from what they see. People have desires for mastery over aspects of their own particular environments. Thus, they look for those behaviors, among the many displayed by available models, that will allow mastery.

When a person accepts something from a model, she does not do so passively. She "turns it over" in her mind, relating it to information she already has, rehearsing it, criticizing it, and thereby remembering it or forgetting it. In addition, a person may transform information learned from a model into symbolic form so that it can be quickly and easily turned into action in the future. For example, you might ask "Which way to the psychology building?" and hear in reply "Follow me." If you are a psychology major, and thus must go to the building several times a week, the information provided by the model might be transformed into a series of right and left turns: "right (r), left (l), r, l, l, l, r, r." In this way, information provided by the model can be represented symbolically after it has been initially accepted in concrete form.

Of course, people don't stop with accepting what is offered by models and, perhaps, transforming it into symbolic form. They attempt to turn their observations into behaviors. The extent to which they are successful depends in part on whether they have the skills to "pull off" the modeled behavior. It also depends on whether they have gleaned, from observations, all the relevant elements of the modeled behavior. If they are able to repeat the behavior they have observed, they do not simply mimic it. Observers create an internal representation of the behavior and then hone, refine, and perhaps even customize it to suit their particular needs. This "polishing" is accomplished by performing the behavior and comparing the performance to an internal prototype (a standard, like the engineer's drawing of a future auto). For example, someone who has watched an expert hitter in baseball will have a mental representation of the hitter's swing. When she practices the swing, she will match her attempt against her mental image of the expert's prototypical swing.

Characteristics of models and observers are also important in determining what is learned, or even whether anything is learned. People do not just observe anyone who happens to be present. Attractive, successful models—those who have done well, both generally and on specific tasks—are the ones whose behaviors are adopted. What a person learns from a model is determined, in part, by the observer's own, preexisting capabilities. A person totally unschooled in biochemistry is unlikely to benefit from a laboratory demonstration in that field, no matter how effective the model.

Reinforcements or rewards for the performance of modeled behaviors enter the learning sequence in three different ways. First, a person may observe a model being rewarded for performing a behavior. Such an observation would act as an incentive for performance of the model's behavior. An *incentive* is anything, concrete or abstract, that creates anticipation of a positive outcome following the performance of a behavior. Second, the model—for example, a parent trying to teach a child to pronounce a word—may reward efforts of the observer to reproduce the behaviors previously modeled. Third, and perhaps most important, the observer may reward himself for a good approximation of correct performance of a behavior. Thus, a child who is trying to learn the utterance "arithmetic" may "pat himself on the back" when he comes close to the proper pronunciation.

incentive

From very early in life, children show the ability to exactly duplicate the behavior of a model.

vicarious expectancy learning

Behavior is not all that is learned from models. Expectancies are also learned. In *vicarious expectancy learning,* people adopt other persons' expectancies concerning future events—especially expectancies of those with whom they share relevant experiences. For example, people who have lived through a hurricane but suffered little from its devastating winds still learn to anticipate future storms with much concern. They have witnessed the suffering of people like themselves and thereby adopt the victims' expectations. Their vicarious expectancy of disaster may be almost as strong as that of actual victims, as reflected in their willingness to join with others in preparing for future storms. In general, vicarious expectancy learning is most likely to be transmitted to persons from models with whom they share many experiences.

Other modeling effects include creative modeling. An individual first accepts the behaviors of a model and then branches out from there. Thus, Beethoven adopted the forms of Haydn and Mozart, later going well beyond those artistic styles into his own greater emotional expressiveness (Bandura, 1977).

response facilitation

In *response facilitation,* nothing new is learned, but some old responses may be disinhibited as a result of watching a model's performance. In this case, the model's behavior acts as a social prompt, communicating that it is "OK" to perform the behavior that was inhibited. For example, a person who is fearful of dancing because religious training has labeled it as "evil" may experience disinhibition of dancing by watching a "good" person dance with no ill effects.

diffusion of innovation

Diffusion of innovation occurs when prestigious models try something new and thereby display its benefits and advantages to others. Once people have accepted an innovative behavior, its longevity will be determined, in part, by the permanence of the inducements associated with its adoption. The more permanent the inducements for adopting something new, the longer the innovation will stay around. Fads are short-lived, because adoption results only in social recognition. New fashions have a relatively longer life, because these have more enduring benefits—for example, shelter from the elements. The automobile is an example of a novelty that has become permanent. The CB transmitter-receiver illustrates an innovation that failed to last. The automobile is obviously the more useful of the two.

There are some definite restraints on the adoption of novelties, however. These include lack of the requisite skills needed to perform behaviors associated with the novelty. Soccer is finally catching on in this country, thanks to the super model, Pele, but adoption has been limited to those with adequate athletic skills. Financial limitations also interfere with adoption of innovations. The Mercedes Benz has become so popular in this country that Detroit is copying its body lines, but alas, few can afford the genuine article.

REWARDS

While behavior is often acquired vicariously, it is primarily maintained by rewards. There has been much debate concerning the relative importance of *extrinsic rewards* (rewards originating outside the individual, such as money) and *intrinsic rewards* (rewards from within the individual, such as self-praise). From the social-learning view, both are necessary for a full account of human action. External rewards are needed to direct a person's attention to a behavior and to institute initial performance, but long-term maintenance of the behavior depends largely on development of intrinsic rewards. For instance, in order to begin the task of teaching a child to write, tangible rewards, privileges, or even money will likely be needed to generate beginning attempts. Such rewards may have to be presented even on a sentence-by-sentence basis. The child may then progress to performing for less tangible rewards, though still external, such as praise from parents for a job well done. Finally, if writing behavior is to be maintained, the child must learn what constitutes good writing behavior so that she can praise herself "under her breath" for writing a grammatically correct sentence.

rewards

intrinsic versus extrinsic rewards

Intrinsic motivation refers to the desire for intrinsic rewards, leading to the pursuit of the same. One of the problems with the notion of intrinsic motivation is that its presence is often inferred from the persistence of a behavior in the absence of any obvious external rewards. As Bandura (1977) notes, such an inference is unwarranted. To support his skepticism by example, if a person watches TV for many hours a day, one would be hard pressed to invoke intrinsic motivation. More than likely, the lack of options explains persistent glaring at the TV. To be sure that intrinsic motivation is at work, one must observe the persistence of behavior in the absence of external rewards, where other behavioral possibilities exist— including some that could lead to external reward. Further, signs of self-evaluation support the presence of intrinsic motivation. *Self-evaluation* involves assessing one's performance at various points along the way to completion of a task and issuing a vocal or "under-the-breath" judgment of its value. Thus, a clarinetist

intrinsic motivation

self-evaluation

who repeatedly sounds a note, sometimes pausing to frown and shake his head, is engaging in self-evaluation. When a smile follows an attempt at the note, observers can conclude that he has positively reinforced himself. Most forms of "practice" are likely under the control of intrinsic reward.

It has been suggested that extrinsic rewards are somehow antagonistic to intrinsic motivation (Deci, 1975). Supposedly, "being paid" for performance of behaviors implies external rather than internal control of behavior, with accompanying feelings of lost self-determination and competence. Although support for the notion that external reward destroys intrinsic motivation is mixed at best, belief in the idea persists (Bandura, 1977) — despite numerous contradictions in everyday reality. Artists, professors, athletes, and many others are more than happy to receive money for what they love to do.

Intrinsic reward is not the only way that behavior can be maintained in the absence of external, tangible rewards. Vicarious reinforcement can be very effective. *Vicarious reinforcement* involves observing reinforcement as it occurs to people other than the observer. First, let's examine the effects of observing others' rewards on the value of one's own external rewards. Then, we'll consider direct effects of observing other people being rewarded.

vicarious
reinforcement

External rewards, of course, do not have any inherent, absolute value. The value of rewards is relative, established by the process of social comparison (Festinger, 1954). Generally, *social comparison* involves determining how well one is doing in life by comparing oneself to those who share one's life situation. A factory worker doesn't determine how well she is doing in life by comparing herself with the plant manager. Instead she compares herself to people working in her same department. If, for example, she is earning as much as, or a little more than, those doing similar work, she can conclude that she is doing fine. A given dollar amount earned per month is valued or not valued, depending on its standing relative to what comparable others are earning.

social
comparison

Modeling alone works to initiate a behavior, but if models are rewarded for performances of the behavior, the impact on learning is greatly increased. Observing a model who is rewarded for performing behavior having unpleasant aspects can induce the observer to perform the behavior, even in cases where persuasion has failed. According to Bandura (1977), vicarious reward can induce people to try an undesired food, give up a valued object, and disclose personal matters. Vicarious punishment can also be effective. Bandura (1977) cites a study in which observers of models who were punished for performance of a prohibited behavior were just as unlikely to perform the behavior later as were the models.

DEFENSIVE BEHAVIORS

defensive
behaviors

Defensive behaviors are adopted in order to cope with unpleasant events that are anticipated on future occasions. If sitting in front of a room becomes associated with embarrassment because of failure to answer a question posed by a professor, the defensive behavior of sitting in the back of the room may be adopted. The adoption occurs and persists, because it allows anticipation of comfort, not because it is motivated by anxiety. If anxiety were the motivator, people would always show anxiety when they perform defensive behaviors. Instead, once they become confident that their defensive strategy is effective, they show relief. Thus, anxiety is an associate of early defensive behavior, not the cause of it (Leventhal, 1970). Initially, the unpleasant event is accompanied by both anxiety and defensive behavior. But after the defensive behavior is perceived to be a means of avoiding the unpleasant event, it is performed in the absence of anxiety. Because defensive behavior is due to anticipating the avoidance of unpleasant events in the future, rather than for the purpose of coping with present anxiety, it is very difficult to eliminate. The absence of the unpleasant event is "proof" to the performer that the defensive behavior is "working." Thus, if a child is asked "Why do you take that huge stuffed animal to bed with you?" the reply may be "Because it keeps the wolves away." To the objection "But there are no wolves around here," the rejoinder is "See how well it works!" The solution may lie in modeling. If a model in whom the defensive performer has great trust can be observed operating in the context of the unpleasant event without performing the defensive behavior, and the unpleasant event fails to occur, the defensive behavior may be discarded.

SELF-EFFICACY: AVENUE TO CORRECTION OF HARMFUL BEHAVIOR

Sometimes defensive behavior becomes so obstructive that corrective measures must be taken. From the point of view of social-learning theory, the way to eliminate inhibitions and harmful defensive behaviors is through the development of self-efficacy. *Self-efficacy* refers to beliefs concerning one's ability to perform behaviors that will yield expected outcomes. When self-efficacy is high, one has confidence in one's ability to perform those behaviors that will allow control of a difficult circumstance that might otherwise generate defensive behavior.

self-efficacy

As an illustration of the relationship between self-efficacy level and outcome expectancy, let's consider a contrast between Sarah and Sam on the subject of public speaking. Both individuals expect that making a public speech in an effective manner will be met with applause and other positive social inducements. However, Sarah has strong feelings of self-efficacy with regard to critical behaviors involved in public speaking. She is confident that she can obtain the relevant information that will go into her speech, organize it properly, memorize it, and present it in a clear and articulate way. On the other hand, Sam has a different conviction with respect to self-efficacy. He feels that he cannot adequately perform any of the behaviors that will lead to the desired outcome.

Self-efficacy not only influences whether a person will attempt a behavior or behaviors, but also determines how well the person will do when he or she makes attempts. High efficacy, entailing expectation of success, will generate persistence in the face of obstacles and frustrations. Persistence eventually leading to success will further bolster self-efficacy. Low efficacy will lower effort, thereby increasing the probability of failure and the likelihood of further decreases in efficacy. Figure 6.1 shows how feelings of personal efficacy can be increased.

The single most effective method for boosting self-efficacy is *performance accomplishment* (Bandura, 1977). Doing is believing. If a person with low self-efficacy can somehow be induced to perform the feared behavior, self-efficacy will be

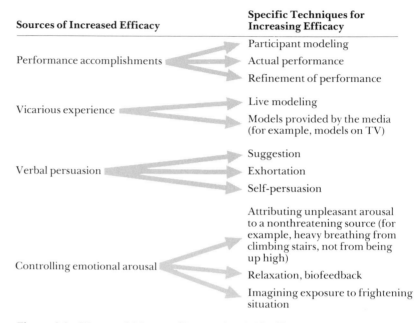

Figure 6.1   Ways and Means of Increasing Self-Efficacy

dramatically bolstered. However, vicarious experience can also be effective, especially if people with low self-efficacy can view persons who share their fears perform the inhibited behaviors. *Participant modeling*, in which the person with low self-efficacy imitates a model's efficacious behavior, is also very effective. However, verbal persuasion is not. Finally, since people read their state of efficacy by reference to their level of emotional arousal in the face of the threatening situation, any method that lowers arousal will increase feelings of efficacy. Successful actual performance or positive vicarious experience are methods of lowering arousal. False physiological feedback, in which aroused people are told that "physiological measures indicate that you are calm," seems successful only for mild fear (Valins & Nisbett, 1971). A concrete demonstration of how self-efficacy can be bolstered is presented later in this chapter.

Bandura's Theory Compared to Others

LEARNING THEORY

Bandura's social-learning theory can be contrasted with learning theories that emphasize internal drives and motives, as well as those that consider only external stimuli and responses. According to Bandura (1977), internal entities such as drives and motivations cannot account for variations in behavior across time, persons, and situations. A *drive* is a physiological tension that forces an organism to perform behaviors designed to relieve the tension. A *motive* is a reason to perform some behavior, such as "to quench a thirst." Both drives and motives push an individual toward certain goals by instituting goal-directed behavior (*motive* as in *motor,* and *drive* as in *driven*). Such internal processes imply behavioral constancy, but constancy is not the case (Mischel & Peake, 1982). Drives and motives provide ready explanations after the fact, but not predictions. In the last analysis, the worth of a theory lies in its practical applications. Bandura maintains that theories stressing motives, drives, and similar internal processes have not been highly applicable, at least not compared to social-learning theory and related methods for modifying behavior.

Bandura's social-learning theory has generated support for certain of its predictions that directly conflict with typical learning theories that ignore cognitive factors. Many learning theories postulate that one must perform a response and then, rather immediately, experience reinforcement of the response. According to social-learning theory, organisms, especially people, learn by observing. It follows that people need not perform the behavior they have witnessed at the time it is observed. Likewise, they needn't experience reinforcement, either directly or vicariously, in order to learn. They can observe a behavior—such as a method of approaching an attractive member of the opposite sex—note "That's a method that works," and then sometime much later try out the approach, with the *expectation* of reinforcement. The cognitive factor, expectation of reinforcement—not previous experience of reinforcement—is the determinant of future behavior. In summary, people learn a behavior when they view it, before they have a chance to perform it, and even if they have never been reinforced for it prior to the first performance. (Chapter 12 on aggression contains examples of how people learn a behavior before having the opportunity to perform it. It also shows that people learn even when reinforcement is absent from the sequence of events.)

Figure 6.2 graphically displays the difference between the social-learning view and that of many learning theories. As you can see, common learning theories are backward-looking: reinforcements feed back on responses, strengthening them. From the social-learning point of view, the process is forward-looking: the individual performs a response in anticipation of future reinforcement.

BIOLOGICAL PREPAREDNESS

If people can learn only what they are biologically prepared to acquire, then social-learning notions of "people learning from people" lack credibility. Why postulate that "people teach people" if humans are preprogrammed to learn? Seligman (1970) has suggested that there are severe limits to what organisms can

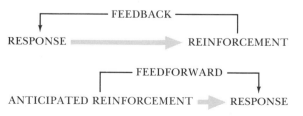

Figure 6.2
A comparison of social-learning and other learning theories.

learn, because of deficiencies associated with anatomy and physiology. His notion of *biological preparedness* is that animals, including humans, are disposed to learn easily only certain behaviors enabled by their unique physiological and anatomical constitutions. Other behaviors, not promoted by physiology and anatomy, are difficult or impossible to learn. A chimp cannot learn to talk, because it lacks the necessary vocal chords. Pigeons can learn to peck a panel for food reinforcement, but rats don't resort to their soft snouts — they employ their paws.

However, Bandura (1977) contends that humans are not so constrained by biological limitations. Humans can develop shelter and dress that enable them to survive in extreme cold almost as well as a polar bear. Humans don't have wings, but they can make wings that work pretty well — ask any hang glider. Neither do humans have webbed feet, but the fastest swimmers among them can outperform some aquatic animals.

More fundamentally, Bandura argues that the evidence for "biological preparedness" is slim. Consider, for example, taste-aversion studies that seem to support biological preparedness. Revusky and Garcia (1970) have shown that the association of taste with nausea leads readily to an aversion for the taste, but that taste aversion is not easily acquired through an association between taste and electric shock. However, the subjects were not human. With human alcoholics, the shock/alcohol association works as well as nausea/alcohol in the development of aversion to alcohol, though neither works well (Bandura, 1977). Second, the procedures used in taste-aversion studies are suspect. Apparently the time delay between the taste stimulus (sweetener) and the shock determines whether electric shock will generate a taste aversion. As a case in point, Krane and Wagner (1975) found that delayed shocks produced aversion to sweetened water, while immediate shocks did not. However, when an auditory/visual stimulus (for example, a buzzer and a light rather than sweetener) was associated with plain water, the effects of time delay were reversed. Bright, noisy stimuli associated with plain water and accompanied by immediate shock produced aversion to water, but delayed shock did not. The researchers explained their results by reference to the lingering effect of taste as opposed to the short-term effects of the bright, noisy stimuli.

Finally, biological preparedness is supposed to explain why people have predispositions to certain phobias rather than to others. A prime example is snake phobias. According to this theory, our ancestors' negative experiences with snakes have predisposed us to fear them. That is, ancient humans who survived to pass their genes along were those who had the perceptual capability to readily detect snakes, and the good sense to avoid them. Following this logic, why aren't people more frightened of and prone to develop phobias related to fire and water? Both have taken far more lives than snakes in the course of human history. The answer of social-learning theorists is that fire and water have had both positive and negative consequences during particular individuals' lifetimes, in contrast to consequences occurring throughout the ancestral past of all people. On the other hand, during their individual lifetimes, most people have been exposed to the folklore surrounding the "demon snake" but have had few if any positive experiences with the creature.

STAGE THEORIES OF DEVELOPMENT

Bandura asserts that social-learning theory is partially inconsistent with stage theories, such as Piaget's (1965) notions about cognitive development and Kohlberg's (1969) postulations concerning moral development (see Chapter 15). With moral reasoning as a case in point, stage theory hypothesizes that children at a given stage learn only what the skills available to them at the time allow them to learn. Thus, a child of age 2, whose stage of moral reasoning is primitive, thinks only of punishments in evaluating the "goodness" of an act. If he is punished for the act, it is "bad"; if not, it is "good." He cannot reason otherwise, because he lacks the necessary cognitive skills. Only later will he be able to reason at a more abstract and complex level, judging an act as "good" if other people approve of it.

Bandura (1977) argues that the evidence does not support these assumptions of stage theory. People, adults as well as children, reason at various levels or stages, depending on the circumstances (Bandura & McDonald, 1963). Bandura's theory has no trouble with variability in moral reasoning. If a 15-year-old on one occasion refuses an award from the John Birch Society because he disapproves of its lack of concern for minorities, and on another occasion cheats on a test because "everyone else is doing it," social-learning theorists are not puzzled. They will look for differing circumstances under which the judgments were made as the source of the very different moral decisions. A long-standing family concern for minorities may explain the refusal of the award, while an immediate need to perform as well as peers may explain the cheating. You may recognize that Skinner would offer a similar explanation. (We'll have more to say about moral reasoning later.)

HUMANISTIC THEORIES: UNCONDITIONAL POSITIVE REGARD AND SELF-ACTUALIZATION

Bandura's social-learning theory is also somewhat incompatible with the idea of "unconditional positive regard," as espoused by the humanists (see Chapter 7). According to Bandura, not only must there be dependency between behavioral performance and particular positive or negative outcomes for learning to occur and be maintained, but learners must be highly aware of the dependency. The very notion of "unconditional positive regard" implies a lack of any contingency between behaviors and outcomes. "Unconditional love," writes Bandura, "were it possible, would make children directionless and quite unlovable" (1977, p. 102). Young children have trouble discovering the relationship between behaviors and outcomes, which makes them almost completely dependent on immediate external reward. Such being the case, they would be doomed to total confusion if they were rewarded with affection no matter what they did.

Unconditional positive regard is often thought of as the child-rearing practice most likely to promote "self-actualization," a concept that is thoroughly discussed in the next chapter. *Self-actualization* is a person's lifelong process of realizing his or her potentialities to become a fully functioning person, or "to be that self which one truly is" (Rogers, 1961). However, according to Bandura, there is a contradiction in the connection between unconditional regard and self-actualization. If self-actualization is discovering what one's potentialities are in life and pursuing them, how is the discovery to be made if one has been told during childhood "Everything you do is wonderful"? Discrimination between worthwhile and not-worthwhile pursuits are made as a result of appreciating that certain behaviors produce worthwhile outcomes, and certain others do not — not that most behaviors result in valuable outcomes. However, the next chapter might convince you that Bandura has oversimplified unconditional positive regard.

Supporting Evidence and Application: Increasing Self-Efficacy

The studies in support of Bandura's social-learning theory are quite literally too numerous to review here. Interested readers should refer to the excellent little book by Bandura (1977). Here we have chosen to describe a recent study by Bandura, Linda Reese, and Nancy Adams (1982), which provides clear support for a critical social-learning notion, self-efficacy. It is also useful as an illustration of assessment from the social-learning point of view. There is no particular assessment technique, or techniques, associated with Bandura's social-learning theory, analogous to Freud's free association or Kelly's REP test (see Chapter 8). Assessment in the context of social-learning theory is ad hoc — that is, contrived especially for each particular situation that arises experimentally or clinically. Finally, consideration of self-efficacy brings us about as close to a "trait" as social-learning theory comes. Actually, like Mischel, Bandura and other social-learning theorists would claim not to include traits in their theories. They all emphasize cognitive factors, as opposed to the trait conceptions outlined in Chapter 1. However, self-efficacy has some characteristics in common with traits. Like traits are supposed to be, self-efficacy tends to be relatively stable over time. If no events relevant to a person's self-efficacy occur, the person is likely to maintain a constant level of the factor. On the other hand, self-efficacy is unlike a trait in that it is very specific to social or other external circumstances. Self-efficacy has reference to public speaking, handling snakes, parachuting, writing a book, swimming, and other specific circumstances. It is not the general, cross-situational phenomenon that traits are supposed to be. Nonetheless, as we're about to demonstrate, it has much practical importance.

In the Bandura/Reese/Adams study (actually the second of three studies they report), subjects were recruited through a newspaper ad for persons with severe spider phobias. The resulting 16 subjects, all female, ranged in age from 16 to 61 years. One had difficulty taking a bath, because she had once encountered a spider in the tub. Another, upon noticing a spider inside the auto she was driving, leaped from the car. One had difficulty reading or watching TV, because she was fearful that a spider would happen by and catch her unawares. At the mere sight of a spider, or even a picture of one, she would react with compulsive shivers, pounding of the heart, shortness of breath, and, on occasion, vomiting for hours. Another subject reported that whenever she even thought of a spider, she would picture herself being eaten by the creature. She had trouble sleeping at night, because she would wake up to inspect the ceiling for spiders. If she did detect one, she would stand on a stool and kill it with insect spray — then stay awake in case the spider revived and climbed back to the ceiling. Obviously, these people had an incapacitating problem. They sorely needed help.

Procedure.   Subjects first were administered a behavioral avoidance test. The test consisted of 18 items, each progressively more threatening than its predecessor. The test involved interactions with a large wolf spider, previously shown to be especially frightening to people with spider phobias (see Table 6.1). These interactions ranged from remote (approaching a plastic bowl containing the spider) to intimate (allowing the spider to crawl on one's lap). At the beginning of the experiment, the best a subject could do was to view the spider at a safe distance.

Fear arousal was measured orally, using a 10-point scale. For each of the 18 behavioral tasks, subjects rated both the amount of fear they felt in anticipation of performing the behavior and how much fear they experienced during any behavior they were able to perform.

Self-efficacy *judgments* were made quite simply. Subjects were presented with each of the 18 behavioral tasks and were asked to indicate on a 100-point scale the degree of efficacy that they felt — that is, the degree to which they felt confident that they could perform the behavior. A "1" indicated no efficacy for a given behavior, and "100" meant complete mastery of the behavior in question. A subject's efficacy score was the number of behaviors for which the efficacy rating was at least 20 on the 100-point scale.

Next, subjects were assigned, on a random basis, to a low- or medium-efficacy condition. The experimental treatment to induce either a low or a medium level of efficacy was conducted by a female experimenter using a large wolf spider, different in color and shape from the one used in the initial behavioral test.

Subjects were treated one at a time. First, they were asked just to inspect a spider that was placed in a vial. Then, the experimenter modeled several threatening behaviors, as subjects watched — first from a considerable distance, and later from close by. Initially, the experimenter placed the spider in a plastic bowl and poked it with her finger as it scurried about. Next she modeled handling the insect and controlling its movements. She removed the spider from the container and handled it as it crawled over her arms, hands, and upper body. Finally, she showed how to control a freely moving spider by placing it on a towel draped over a chair and herding it about on the piece of furniture.

TABLE 6.1   Examples of Items on Bandura et al.'s Behavioral Avoidance Test

---

Approach plastic bowl containing spider
  Look down at the spider
  Place bare hands in the bowl
Let spider crawl freely in a chair placed in front of them
Let spider crawl over gloved hands
Let spider crawl over bare hands
Let spider crawl over bare forearm
Handle spider with bare hands
Allow spider to crawl on lap

To expand on control of spiders, the experimenter then released the spider onto the floor and allowed it to run about in search of a hiding place. She pursued the creature and captured it by trapping it under a cup and sliding a thin card under the container—thereby showing how it could be confined and easily transported outside a house. Then she took the subject into a nearby lobby where a wolf spider's web was located and modeled inquisitiveness about the spider's habitat.

Periodically during the treatment, each subject took the efficacy test. These administrations of the test were repeated until each subject reached the level of efficacy corresponding to the condition to which she had been assigned (low or medium efficacy). Low efficacy was defined as being able to allow the spider to roam over a chair placed near the subject and being able to place a hand inside the bowl containing the spider. Subjects in the medium efficacy condition continued in treatment until they could endure physical contact with the spider by holding it in a gloved or a bare hand. After subjects had reached the assigned level of efficacy, the entire behavioral and fear-arousal tests, performed earlier, were repeated. At the completion of major procedures, subjects in the low-efficacy condition were raised to the medium level by further modeling, and their behavior and fear were again measured. Finally, at the end of the experiment, all subjects worked until they had achieved maximum efficacy.

Results. As Figure 6.3 indicates, there was a direct relationship between subjects' assigned level of self-efficacy and their behavioral performance after treatment. Subjects assigned to the low-efficacy condition achieved low performance on the behavior test (after treatment), while those in the medium-efficacy condition achieved medium behavioral performance (after treatment). Also, all subjects' behavioral performance was measured when they were at low efficacy and again when they were at medium efficacy (remember, the low group was raised to medium efficacy, after the main part of the experiment). As Figure 6.4 indicates, there was again a direct relationship between performance when subjects were at low efficacy and when *the same subjects* were at medium efficacy. Further, there was almost perfect correspondence between subjects' efficacy judgments and their levels of performance. If a subject indicated that she *felt* she could at most place her hands on the inverted bowl with the spider inside, she strongly tended to be unable to go beyond that performance. Self-efficacy was almost perfect in the prediction of behavioral performance. Also, level of fear arousal (accompanying performance) reported by subjects corresponded almost perfectly with level of self-efficacy. If a subject experienced high efficacy, she experienced low fear arousal. If she experienced low efficacy, she felt high fear.

Evaluation: Bandura

LIMITATIONS

A serious fault of social-learning theory appears to be that it attempts to explain too much of human behavior in too broad a sense. Many all-encompassing theories that seem to explain everything actually explain very little—mainly because they provide explanations *after* observations of behavior are made. An ideal theory explains behavior before it occurs, not after the fact (Allen, 1978). Al-

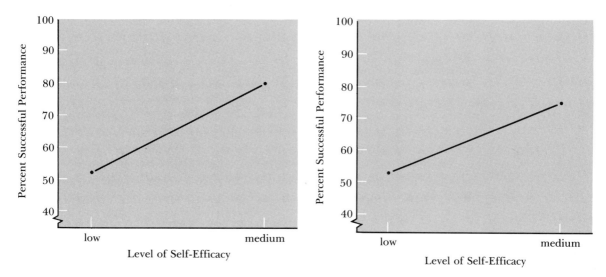

Figure 6.3
Relationship between self-efficacy and behavioral performance after treatment for the low- compared to the medium-efficacy condition.

Figure 6.4
Relationship between self-efficacy and behavioral performance for subjects when at the low-efficacy level and when at the medium-efficacy level.

though social-learning theory does make legitimate predictions, it has also been used for after-the-fact explanation (such as explaining away some of the studies on biological preparedness). As was once the case with cognitive-dissonance theory in social psychology, social-learning theory has no clear boundaries (Collins & Hoyt, 1972; Linder, Cooper, & Jones, 1967). Therefore, advocates of Bandura's theory are obligated to provide explanations of such psychological phenomena as psychosis (severe mental disorders involving withdrawal from reality) and such antisocial behaviors as prejudice, destructive obedience to authority, and deindividuation (harmful behavior that results from losing one's sense of self, as when "lost in a crowd"). Yet the theory provides no concrete explanations of these behaviors. Neither does it do any better than Kelly's cognitive theory (see Chapter 8) in accounting for human "feelings," or, more generally, emotion. Sadness and shyness, joy and jealousy are not addressed meaningfully by social-learning theory. Perhaps social-learning theorists do not intend to provide explanations for these behaviors; if so, they should say so. In the meantime the theory awaits the construction of borders about it. Like cognitive-dissonance theory, which now has definite boundaries, social-learning theory would benefit from a proclamation concerning when it does and does not apply (Wheeler, Deci, Reis, & Zuckerman, 1978). If it is known when a theory can predict and when it cannot, its percentage of accurate predictions will go up. Also, there will be no attempts to explain after the fact what the theory cannot predict.

CONTRIBUTIONS

Value of the theory.   The breadth of social-learning theory is certainly not entirely illusory. The theory makes powerful predictions and generates useful applications in many arenas of human behavior. We have already seen how the theory suggested a technique that, in a matter of hours, eliminated phobias that had plagued individuals for years. Later, in Chapter 12, we will see that social-learning theory is highly useful for understanding human aggression in general, and the influences of TV on aggressiveness in particular. Social-learning theory has also filled a void in other learning theories, by accounting for the fact humans can learn simply by observing. More generally, the theory can explain many differences between humans and lower animals, especially in the area of learning —differences that other theories have ignored or failed to explain.

Implications for humanity.   Beyond these many and varied contributions, social-learning theory has implications for the well-being and prosperity of humans in the future. Later, when we come to consider aggression (Chapter 12), we will indicate the limitations of punishment as a means of controlling undesirable behavior. For now, it should be noted that social-learning theory has important implications for the control of crime. Why do people steal despite the threat of arrest and imprisonment? A look inside the prisons suggests an answer. Poor people and minorities are greatly overrepresented in our penal institutions. Probably most are there for "stealing," in some sense of the word (larceny, burglary, robbery, criminal conversion of property, embezzlement, and so on). People will survive, and to do so they choose their methods of survival from those available to them. Two factors govern the selection of theft as a means of survival. First, it is one of the alternatives open to those relegated to the bottom of the social ladder. Second, the inducements are great, relative to other available alternatives and to the likelihood of negative outcome (being caught and imprisoned). One can work at a demeaning job, for low pay, certain humiliation, and no chance of prospering —or one can steal. In the case of theft, effort is minimal, the likelihood of being caught and imprisoned minimal, and the outcome highly positive, relative to investment. Given these perceptions, public pronouncements to the effect that "people are imprisoned for stealing" have little impact. The middle class and above may have better options, and the poor may have few more-viable options. Learning theory suggests that the value of a reward is relative—relative to the availability of other rewards and the likelihood of negative outcomes that may accompany the reward.

Bandura's theory also has implications for the understanding of more troubling behaviors. "Over the years," he observes "much cruelty has been perpetrated by decent, moral people in the name of religious principles, righteous ideology, and social order" (1977, p. 156). Bandura suggests that this behavior is best explained not by character flaws but by *self-exonerative processes*—cognitive activities that allow people to dissociate themselves from the consequences of their actions. Religion, ideology, and order in the sense of "law and order," all noble in concept, can be invoked to justify just about anything. In more technical, social-learning terms, these "noble causes" can be invoked to break the connection between behaviors and *actual* outcomes. Actual outcomes of behaviors that would otherwise be considered immoral and unforgivable are covered up, shoved aside, and thereby effectually replaced by acceptable outcomes. For example, Klansmen adopt a religious facade, including the cross symbol, to cloak their vicious behavior in an aura of purity (see *Klanwatch,* a publication of Southern

Poverty Law, 1001 South Hull Street, Montgomery, Alabama 36101). However, their behavior is sometimes so savage that it becomes difficult to justify, even "with God on our side." In order to support murder and torture, it also becomes necessary to dehumanize their victims. *Dehumanization* is a cognitive process that involves lowering the status of certain people from "human being" to "lesser being." It would be difficult to perform, much less justify, torture of a human being — but it can be done to beings that are not human.

Other cognitive activities that are helpful in setting the stage for the performance of reprehensible behavior include exaggerated comparisons, euphemistic labeling, minimization of consequences, attribution of the blame to victims, and diffusion of responsibility. When confronted with accusations that the Nazis mistreated the Jews, Hitler was in the habit of citing the subjugation of Native Americans and the oppression of Indians and other "colonials" by the British (Speer, 1970). In a more recent example of exaggerated comparison, Israel's conduct in Lebanon has been compared to Nazi atrocities.

Euphemistic labeling is the cognitive process of assigning a name to deplorable behavior that makes it seem innocuous or even laudable. The "Vietnam experience" included many such labels. Destroying crops and jungle habitats was called "defoliation." Disenfranchising and physically relocating whole villages of people was called "pacification." Killing as many people as possible and collecting their bodies as trophies was called "body count."

Blaming victims for their own fate is an all-too-common cognitive exercise (Wheeler et al., 1978). It's easy to neglect the poor if one can say "They're poor because they're lazy." Stealing from a large department-store chain can be dismissed with the comment, "They make millions a year. What's one $10 item?" Finally, one can walk right by a person who is suffering a calamity and hardly notice, so long as there are many others present onto whom one can diffuse responsibility (Latané & Darley, 1970).

While certain immoral behaviors can be predicted and explained by social-learning theory, so can some forms of self-sacrifice and altruism. Self-evaluation, the primary source of intrinsic reward, can be so dominant that it becomes more important than external rewards and punishments. Sister Teresa, winner of the 1979 Nobel Peace Prize, has such strong convictions concerning the elimination of human suffering that she worked for years in obscurity and deprivation to bring comfort to the poor, ill, and lame of Calcutta, India. Recently, a young man rushed to the aid of a woman who was being raped on a public street, thereby totally ignoring the punishments for such behavior that were implied by the inaction of many bystanders. Similarly, Lenny Skutnik stood among several people as he watched a woman flounder in the Potomac following the crash of her plane. Seeing the helpless victim slowly disappear into the icy water, Skutnik dived in and hauled her to shore. His efforts received national acclaim, including introduction to the Congress by the President of the United States (Penny Ward Moser, 1983). In January 1981, a crowd formed beneath a ninth-floor window where a man was poised to jump (Mann, 1981). It happened in Los Angeles, city of notables, one of whom was on the scene. Boxing champion Muhammad Ali talked the man from his perch. The crowd cheered. Altruism well modeled is well appreciated.

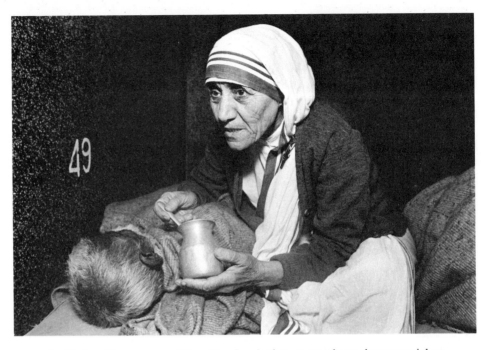

As Mother Teresa exemplifies, Bandura's theory may have the potential to explain the best in human nature.

Other models of noble behavior include Martin Luther King, Jr., and Susan B. Anthony. King "had a dream," the fulfillment of which was more important to him than life itself. Assassination haunted him wherever he went, but he refused to be silent or to cease his travels. Anthony was a respected educator whose life could be described as very comfortable and secure. She readily jeopardized these advantages, because she could not abide the absurdity and insensitivity of beliefs and practices to which the women of her day were subjected. The humane exploits of these and many other people remind us that humans are capable of compassion and kindness, attributes that can perhaps be fostered at the expense of cruelty and indifference when more is known about social-learning processes.

CHAPTER REVIEW

Social learning entails acquiring useful information through interactions with people and other elements of the environment. Julian B. Rotter has been a pioneer in the area of social learning. He believes that environments can control human action, but even within powerful situations, there are individual differences in behavior.

Rotter's concepts of reinforcement, reinforcement value, psychological situation, expectancy, and generalized expectancy allow for individual differences superimposed on situational influences. Much of Rotter's theory and research has centered on the generalized expectancies associated with locus of control. Rotter's I-E Scale is designed to assess whether the individual's locus of control is more internal or external.

There are a number of differences between "internals" and "externals." Externals are more conformist, are more often maladjusted, and display a lower level of achievement, but are less likely to be substance abusers. Blacks tend to be high in externality, as are battered wives and divorced women. In terms of personality development, parents of internals tend to be warm, protective, positive, and nurturant, while those of externals tend to be cold, rejecting, and negative. In general, inconsistency of reinforcement characterizes the family life of externals.

Sabatelli, Buck, and Dreyer (1983) investigated a possible link between locus of control, interpersonal trust, and ability to "read" nonverbal messages. Results showed that while locus of control did not relate well to decoding nonverbal messages, interpersonal trust was a strong predictor of ability to "read" other people's faces.

Applications of Rotter's theory include changing externals into internals and creating a better match between therapists and their clients. Despite problems with the I-E Scale and the observation that "externals" really constitute two categories, Rotter's contribution, characterized by flexibility, is judged to be a lasting one.

Canadian Albert Bandura is probably the best-known and most respected theorist and researcher in the area of social learning. He believes that people are oriented to the future, rather than solely shaped by their pasts. Also, Bandura assumes that while people can be controlled by powerful situational forces, self-determination is evident in self-regulatory capacities.

Bandura's social-learning theory postulates that cognitive (mental), behavioral, and environmental factors, especially those related to human interaction, work together to determine human action. Central to Bandura's theory are the notions of "models" and "modeling." The behavior of a model is often adopted because it has produced some incentive. Bandura believes that both extrinsic and intrinsic rewards influence what behaviors people adopt from models.

Behaviors are not all that people learn from other people. Through vicarious expectancy learning, individuals can adopt others' expectancies concerning future events. In response facilitation, nothing new is learned, but some old response may be disinhibited as a result of watching a model's performance. Diffusion of innovation occurs when prestigious models try something new and thereby display its benefits and advantages to others.

Desire for intrinsic rewards often leads to self-evaluation. Vicarious reinforcement is another way that behavior is maintained by intangible rewards. Social comparison provides a means of assessing rewards by contrasting one's outcomes with those of other persons sharing a similar life situation.

Defensive behaviors, which can be highly disruptive, are related to a lack of self-efficacy. Bandura, Reese, and Adams (1982) have shown how bolstering self-efficacy can eliminate one defensive behavior, fear of spiders. After a short, programmed period of observing a competent model handle spiders, even lifelong spider phobics gained in self-efficacy to the point that they were able to handle spiders without fear.

In contrast to some forms of behaviorism, Bandura maintains that people learn a behavior when they view it, before they have a chance to perform it, and even if they have never been reinforced for it prior to the first performance. Bandura also quarrels with biological preparedness. In addition, he claims that variability in level of moral judgment, a problem for theories of morality, is readily explained by his social-learning theory. Bandura is also critical of the humanistic notion of unconditional positive regard, arguing that this notion has misleading implications with regard to rearing children.

Critics have agreed that Bandura's point of view may attempt to explain too much of human behavior. On the positive side, his theory is one of the most general in psychology and has the potential to explain both the best and the worst of human behavior.

KEY CONCEPTS

Rotter
Reinforcement value
Psychological situation
Expectancy
  Generalized expectancy
Locus of control
  Internal versus external
Interpersonal trust
Bandura
Social-learning theory
Self-regulatory capacities
Models and modeling
  Incentive

Vicarious expectancy learning
Response facilitation
Diffusion of innovation
Rewards
  Intrinsic versus extrinsic rewards
  Intrinsic motivation
  Self-evaluation
  Vicarious reinforcement
  Social comparison
Defensive behaviors
Self-efficacy

REVIEW QUESTIONS

1. In Rotter's theory, how does "reinforcement value" affect reinforcement?
2. How do "expectancy" and "generalized expectancy" relate to reinforcement in Rotter's theory?
3. In what ways do "internals" and "externals" differ from each other?
4. What are the main elements of Bandura's social-learning theory? Explain the various ways in which people learn from models.

5. How do extrinsic and intrinsic rewards affect intrinsic motivation?
6. Contrast Bandura's theory with Skinnerian learning theory. What are some points of agreement and disagreement?
7. How does Bandura's theory explain the best and worst of human behavior?

7

Humanistic Psychology: Rogers and Maslow

What is the "third force" in psychology?

Do the psychoanalytic and behaviorist traditions overlook crucial aspects of personality?

Is human nature fundamentally positive, constructive, and trustworthy?

How can psychologists study the subjective, inner worlds of individual persons?

Do "super" personalities exist?

P|SYCHOLOGISTS OFTEN CLASSIFY personality theories into three major
categories: the psychoanalytic tradition begun by Freud; the behavioral tradition, represented by Skinner; and the humanistic tradition,
represented in this chapter by Carl Rogers and Abraham Maslow. In our opinion,
Rogers is the best representative of the humanistic approach because of the
unquestioned impact he has had on so many psychologists, professionals from
other disciplines, and lay persons. His ideas have also received more systematic
research study and validation than those of any other humanistic psychologist.
Accordingly, the bulk of this chapter is devoted to Rogers' ideas. We begin by first
considering the general concept of humanistic psychology.

What Is Humanistic Psychology?

humanistic
psychology

Humanistic psychology is the newest of the three theoretical orientations to
psychology just cited. It gained momentum during the 1950s and early 1960s with
the publication of several important books (Maslow, 1954, 1959, 1962; Bühler,
1962; Rogers, 1961, 1970) and the *Journal of Humanistic Psychology* founded in
1961. Proponents of humanistic psychology proclaimed their movement a "major
breakthrough" and "the third force" in psychology because of the primary importance it placed on understanding the entire person, "the functioning and
experience of a whole human being" (Bugental, 1964, p. 25). This emphasis also
characterizes psychology's holistic (Angyal, 1965), organismic (Goldstein, 1939),
and Gestalt (Perls, 1969) points of view, in which every person is understood in a
comprehensive and integrative manner as being more than the simple sum of his
or her parts (Kohler, 1947).

RELATIONSHIP TO EXISTENTIAL PSYCHOLOGY

existential
psychology

The humanistic psychology movement has been closely tied to developments
in related areas of philosophical psychology, especially existential psychology.
Existential psychology is a philosophically based approach to understanding each
person's most immediate experience and the conditions of his or her existence
(Binswanger, 1963; Boss, 1963; Kierkegaard, 1954; May, Angel, & Ellenberger,
1958; Merleau-Ponty, 1963; van Kaam, 1965, 1966, 1969). Existentialists encourage psychologists to get inside each person's world, to understand how that
person lives, moves, and experiences his or her "being-in-the-world" (Heidegger,
1949).

Concepts often are hyphenated in existentialist writings, signifying the impossibility of understanding individuals apart from their unique worlds and their relationships to them. Person-and-world is a unitary concept. No two people's worlds are alike, and no person can be defined or understood independently of the world he or she inhabits. Thus, if psychologists are to understand Pierre, a human being who lives in the Alps, their task is "first to learn the meaning of human being, and a snowy slope, then to learn what Pierre has made of these meanings as related to his own life" (Barnes, 1956, p. 24).

Existentialists also encourage psychologists to value human experiences of consciousness and personal responsibility (Frankl, 1963). Human freedom is defined not as freedom *from* responsibility but freedom *to* accept responsibility. A person's hereditary endowment, instinctual drives, and social environment may limit the scope of human freedom, but they can never totally blur human capacity to take a stand toward those conditions or choose an option. While the genetic makeup of human beings does not permit them to fly as birds do, a person can transcend this limitation by learning to hang-glide. "Conditions do not determine me but I determine whether I yield to them or brave them" (Frankl, 1961, p. 6). Some existentialists go so far as to view people as having "absolute responsibility" for making themselves (Sartre, 1943/1957). According to this view, the reality of a human life does not exist except in personal action. There is no preexisting "self" or essence that determines who we are and what we do; rather, we have the fearsome responsibility of "making" ourselves through our own choices. We cannot fall back on such excuses as our nature, parents, or upbringing. We define ourselves by the kind of life we choose to lead, for which we have total responsibility. The uniquely human experiences of conscious awareness and personal responsibility for creating meaning can be burdensome and even frightening. For this reason, existentialists often write about more negative concepts of nothingness, alienation, despair, absurdity, and anxiety.

Although humanistic psychologists have been influenced by existential concepts of subjective meaning and personal responsibility, their outlook is typically more positive, stressing the unique capacities of each individual for self-realization and personal growth. They assign greater importance than other personality theories to the study of choice, joy, love, creativity, and authenticity. In contrast to proponents of strict learning theory (Watson, 1930/1959), humanistic psychologists do not believe that human beings begin their lives as blank sheets of paper on which society writes its cultural text. Instead, similar to Fromm and Jung, they see the aim of each person's life as an unfolding of inherent powers present in human nature. They stress the uniquely human aspects of experience, including personal choice, interpersonal relationships, intentions, purposes, and transcendental or spiritual experiences (Bugental, 1964).

A PHENOMENOLOGICAL APPROACH

A major characteristic of humanistic psychology is its *phenomenological*, or subjective, approach to knowledge and understanding (Husserl, 1961; Heidegger, 1949). Phenomenology is concerned with grasping reality as *individuals* per-

phenomeno-
logical approach

The phenomenological approach emphasizes the subjective aspect of reality. Even the "same" objective event may be perceived in quite distinct and sometimes contradictory ways.

ceive it, in a "fresh" manner that is free of preconceptions. It assumes that the only "reality" anyone ever knows is subjective or personal, not objective.

> The only reality I can possibly know is the world as I perceive and experience it at this moment. The only reality you can possibly know is the world as *YOU* perceive and experience it at this moment. And the only certainty is that those perceived realities are different. There are as many "real worlds" as there are people! (Rogers, 1980, p. 102)

Consider the Santa Claus phenomenon. Compare your perceptions of "Santa" when you were younger with your current perceptions. Differences immediately become apparent, but you may find it difficult to decide which experiences are the more real. As a child, perhaps you perceived a physical Santa living at the North Pole, reading the letters you sent, talking with you at a local store about your list of presents, and eating the cookies you set out on Christmas Eve. Or you may have perceived a different Santa, of more spiritual than physical characteristics, as portrayed in the narrative "Yes, Virginia, There Is a Santa Claus." Perhaps you engaged in neither of these perspectives because you had no personal or cultural perceptions at all about Santa. Whatever your perceptions, at any age, they have undoubtedly guided your behavior, expectations, feelings, and relationships with family and friends. (Similarly, during political campaigns, voters often are unable to tell the difference between what is "image" and what is "real" about candidates for public office.)

Although a person's experiences are subjective, they are nevertheless real for that person at that particular moment in time. This is why Rogers regularly includes such qualifiers as "real for me" and "based on my experience" in his writings and conversation. It is up to each person to decide personal events for himself or herself, based on an individualized vantage point of perception and experience. A person cannot decide how other persons should behave or how they should live their lives. It follows from this that each person must assume personal responsibility for his or her own decisions. Some psychologists have been critical of Rogers' refusal to assume the role of expert therapist and answer clients' questions such as "What do you think I should do?" or "Am I right or wrong about this?"

Apart from questions of scientific truth, the phenomenological approach has particular implications for studying persons. Phenomenologically, the basis of all human experience is *interpretation*. Human beings immediately attach a unique meaning to whatever information they receive through the senses, which makes "the same" physical events different for different individuals. If we wish to understand a person, we need to get inside his or her individual world of meaning. Thus, humanistic and existential psychologists are less interested in studying behavior as a neurological event than they are in investigating the meaning that each person perceives. The stimulus-response concepts of strict behavioral psychology are believed too simplistic, because they imply that environmental events have similar psychological impacts on all persons.

As scientists and therapists, therefore, humanistic psychologists take a different approach to understanding people than do psychologists in the behavioral or psychoanalytic traditions. They value the insights they have, because they recognize that they are persons as well as professionals, and they seek to avoid "the sort of scientific detachment pretended to or achieved at great cost by other orientations" (Bugental, 1964, p. 24). Because humanistic psychologists care so deeply about the person, they wish to explore issues that have real meaning for human beings. Rather than adhering to traditional scientific procedures for their own sake, humanistic psychologists seek to validate their findings through subjective experience rather than relying solely on impersonal, objective criteria such as statistical methods and experimental tests, even if this means discovering new methods for studying human experience. Humanistic psychologists typically emphasize the *idiographic* approach described in Chapter 2, believing that meaningful discoveries will come from understanding the individual case. As Rogers writes, "What is most personal is most general" (1961, p. 26).

Rogers, the Person

Carl Ransom Rogers was born on January 8, 1902, in Oak Park, Illinois. The fourth of six children, he was "tender and easily hurt, yet feisty and even sarcastic in his own way," since this was necessary to survive in family give-and-take (Kirschenbaum, 1979, p. 5). His home atmosphere was marked by fundamentalist religious practices, little social mixing, and a firm belief in the virtue of hard work. Carl even recalled experiencing a slight feeling of "wickedness" while drinking his first bottle of soda pop.

Carl was a lonely, "solitary boy, who read incessantly, and went all through high school with only two dates" (Rogers, 1961, p. 6). An outstanding student, he was nicknamed "Mr. Absent-Minded Professor" by his practical, do-it-now family. He loved reading the Bible and adventure stories, as well as creating stories of his own. During adolescence, he became fascinated with night-flying moths, which he observed and bred year round, and he enjoyed reading advanced, scientific books on agriculture.

> There was no one to tell me that Morison's *Feeds and Feeding* was not a book for a fourteen-year-old, so I ploughed through its hundreds of pages learning how experiments were conducted — how control groups were matched with experimental groups, how conditions were held constant by randomizing procedures, so that the influence of a given food on meat production or milk production could be established. I learned how difficult it is to test an hypothesis. I acquired a knowledge of and a respect for the methods of science in a field of practical endeavor. (Rogers, 1961, p. 6)

As an undergraduate at the University of Wisconsin, Rogers majored in agriculture and history. He was one of 12 American students selected to travel to China for a World Student Christian Federation Conference, which proved "a most important experience" in stretching his thinking and teaching him that sincere and honest people could have very different beliefs. His newfound independence of thought caused "great pain and stress" in his relationship with his parents, but "looking back on it I believe that here, more than at any other one time, I became an independent person" (Rogers, 1961, p. 7).

In 1924, Rogers married Helen Elliott, a classmate of his in second grade and his first date in college. An art major, Helen was a gentle, straightforward person whose common sense and willingness to think openly about real issues appealed to Rogers. Her "steady and sustaining love and companionship during all the years since has been a most important and enriching factor in my life" (Rogers, 1961, p. 7). Carl credits their two children, David and Natalie, with "teaching me far more about individuals, their development, and their relationships than I could ever have learned professionally" (Rogers, 1961, p. 12). David later became an administrator in a medical setting, and Natalie worked with her father as a co-therapist in encounter groups.

As a graduate student, Carl studied religion at Union Theological Seminary, which had the most liberal program in the country. However, he soon eased into child psychology, "just following the activities which interested me" (Rogers, 1961, p. 9). After graduation in 1927, he worked at child-guidance centers in New York City and Rochester before accepting a clinical-psychology teaching position at Ohio State University. During these early professional years, Rogers soaked up the views of Freud and his followers. He found these ideas to be in great conflict with the rigorous, experimental aspects of his academic training, and with his work as a professional helper. Relying on his own clinical experiences with people, he began formulating a person-centered point of view. He thought it best to rely on the other person — the client — for the direction of personality change. Unlike traditional psychoanalysts, he would not adopt the role of expert in an authoritarian doctor/patient relationship, because "it is the *client* who knows what hurts, what directions to go, what problems are crucial, what experiences have been deeply buried" (Rogers, 1961, pp. 11–12).

In subsequent years, Rogers held teaching and administrative counseling positions at the University of Chicago and the University of Wisconsin. In 1947, he served as president of the American Psychological Association. He was the first psychologist in the association's history to receive both the Scientific Contribution Award and the Distinguished Professional Contribution Award, in 1972. His fellow psychologists recognize him as an innovative pioneer who has made a lasting impression on psychology. Identifications of Rogers as a "respected gadfly," a "loner," and a person willing "to stand up and be counted" reflect lifelong themes of personal independence, openness to experience, and self-trust: "I have always had a feeling that if I was given some opportunity to do the thing I was most interested in doing, everything else would somehow take care of itself (Rogers, 1961, p. 10).

Rogers (personal communication, May 9, 1985) continues to work very actively in La Jolla, California, at the Center for Studies of the Person, which he co-founded: "The days are not long enough to accomplish my purposes." Rosalind Cartwright, one of his former colleagues, has spoken of him as a living example of his own theory, "a man who has continued to grow, to discover himself, to test himself, to be genuine, to review his experiences, to learn from it, and to fight the good fight, which means to stand up and be counted, to stand for something, to live honestly, fully, in the best human sense" (Kirschenbaum, 1979, p. 394).

> So, who am I? I am a psychologist whose primary interest, for many years, has been in psychotherapy. . . . I rejoice at the privilege of being a midwife to a new personality—as I stand by with awe at the emergence of a self, a person, as I see a birth process in which I have had an important and facilitating part. (Rogers, 1961, pp. 4–5)

Rogers' View of the Person

Rogers' view of the person recognizes different influences on human behavior and personality. These sources include the biological (Freud) and environmental (Skinner), and even a vast area of experience that is not conscious (both Freud and

CARL ROGERS.
Rogers gives the "self" a central role in his theory of personality, which is derived from his experiences in person-centered therapy. He believes in an innate actualization tendency that leads everyone "to be that self which one truly is."

Skinner). However, such influences are not the whole story of personality. For Rogers, as well as other humanistic and existentialist theorists, the most important influence on personality is the person as a whole, including the individual's conscious awareness, freedom to choose, self-determination, and quality of experiences in life. In brief, it is the *person* who is placed first. This is why Rogers' theory

person-centered theory

of therapy is called the *person-centered* approach, the central hypothesis of which is that "Individuals have within themselves vast resources for self-understanding and for altering their self-concepts, basic attitudes, and self-directed behavior" (1980, p. 115). Further, these resources can be tapped by providing "a definable climate of facilitative psychological attitudes" (p. 115).

Rogers thus differs from the Freudian tradition in accenting the positive potentialities in human nature. The natural development of human beings is toward the "constructive fulfillment" of their inherent possibilities.

> I am inclined to believe that fully to be a human being is to enter into the complex process of being one of the most widely sensitive, responsive, creative, and adaptive creatures on this planet.
>
> So when a Freudian such as Karl Menninger tells me (as he has, in a discussion of this issue) that he perceives man as "innately evil" or more precisely, "innately destructive," I can only shake my head in wonderment. (quoted in Kirschenbaum, 1979, p. 250)

Although Rogers differs from learning theorists in his concept of human nature and the importance of internal, positive forces in personality, his view does emphasize general processes of learning and change. "Life, at its best, is a flowing, changing process in which nothing is fixed" (Rogers, 1961, p. 27). In particular, certain systematic kinds of supportive personal relationships are instrumental in fostering people's natural tendency toward constructive adaptation and growth. Through such relationships, individuals can come to realize their unique potentials.

Rogers recognizes that his ideas have been heavily influenced by his relationships with clients in therapy. However, he believes that these experiences are representative of all human relationships. Psychotherapy relationships are only a special instance of interpersonal relationships in general, and "the same lawfulness" governs all such relationships (Rogers, 1961, p. 39). He has supported this belief by writing a number of popular books on such topics as freedom to learn in education (1969), encounter groups (1970), becoming marriage partners (1972), and the revolutionary impact of personal power (1977).

Basic Concepts: Rogers

ACTUALIZATION

actualization

Concepts related to *actualization* are the foundation blocks of Rogers' humanistic approach. In its most general form, actualization is a biological phenomenon; in human beings, it becomes an active tendency toward self-actualization.

The general actualizing tendency.   All living things display the *general actualizing tendency,* an "inherent tendency of the organism to develop all its capacities in ways which serve to maintain or enhance the organism" (Rogers, 1959, p. 196). This constructive biological tendency is the only motive postulated by Rogers, the "one central source of energy in the human organism," giving rise to all other motivation (Rogers, 1980, p. 123).

The actualizing tendency expresses itself through a wide range of behaviors, in response to a wide variety of needs. It has four significant characteristics:

1. It is *organismic*—a natural, biological, inborn predisposition reflected in the total functioning of every living being.
2. It is an *active* process. It accounts for the organism's always being up to something, whether seeking food or sexual satisfaction, initiating, exploring, producing change in the environment, playing, or even creating.
3. It is *directional* rather than random or reactive; it inclines every form of life toward growth, self-regulation, fulfillment, reproduction, and independence from external control.
4. It is *selective*, meaning that not all of an organism's potentialities are necessarily developed, such as the ability to bear pain or to experience nausea.

Rogers illustrated the operation of the actualizing tendency using a boyhood observation. Recalling that his family stored its supply of winter potatoes in the basement, several feet below a window, he noted,

> The conditions were unfavorable, but the potatoes would begin to sprout—pale white sprouts, so unlike the healthy green shoots they sent up when planted in the soil in the spring. But these sad, spindly sprouts would grow two or three feet in length as they reached toward the distant light of the window. They were in their bizarre, futile growth, a sort of desperate expression of the directional tendency I have been describing. They would never become a plant, never mature, never fulfill their real potentiality. But under the most adverse circumstances they were striving to become. Life would not give up, even if it could not flourish. (Rogers, 1979/1983, p. 228)

Self-actualization.   In addition to the general actualizing tendency, Rogers postulates the specifically human tendency toward self-actualization. The *tendency toward self-actualization* is a person's lifelong process of realizing his or her potentialities to become a fully functioning person. What is actualized is the expression of a self-fulfillment tendency specific to human organisms—"to be that self which one truly is" (Rogers, 1961, p. 166). The direction of self-actualization is toward "the good life," defined as whatever is *organismically valued,* or selected holistically by the total person when the person is inwardly free to move in any direction.

self-actualization

fully functioning person

organismic valuing

Rogers (1961) associates the process of self-actualization with enhanced functioning in three areas. First, self-actualization involves an increased openness to experience. Rogers (1959) defines *experience* as all that is going on within the organism at any given moment that is potentially available to awareness. *Awareness* is the conscious apprehension of experience, which Rogers (1979/1983) sees as an important development in human evolution. Thus, a self-actualizing person is aware of and listens to inner feelings without being defensive. Second, the self-actualizing person lives existentially, flowing spontaneously with each moment of

Self-actualization is the lifelong process of fulfilling one's potential. For Rogers, it is associated with an increased openness to experience, spontaneity, full participation in life, self-trust, and a sense of freedom and creativity.

life and participating fully in it. The person experiences life in the "now," without rigid preconceptions about things needing to be the way they have been in the past and without needing to control how things should be in the future. Third, the self-actualizing person places greater trust in his or her organism, intuitively doing what feels right after weighing all available information, without simply relying on the past or on social conventions. In addition, the self-actualizing person shows an increased sense of free choice, creativity, a view of human nature as trustworthy, and richness of life.

The importance of these concepts is underscored by the ideas of other humanistic psychologists. Everett Shostrom (1966) has developed the concept of *time competency*— the degree to which a person lives in the present, as opposed to living excessively in the past or future. This concept is illustrated by the reaction of an existential therapist to one of her clients. Hanna Colm (1961) had been working for some time with a person who spoke excessively of his unworthiness, repeatedly confessed his sins, and dreamed of the future. Then, during one session, he stated his concern that he might be boring Colm.

> And suddenly, instinctively, spontaneously I moved my chair close and said "Yes, you do bore me. Your past sins and future poetry *do* bore me. I am interested in you as a human being *now* and in your life *now* and in what can go on between you and me *now*. But you endlessly walk around in the past or

future and it feels to me as if you ward me off. You keep yourself from your present life, keep yourself from looking at it yourself and with me. You prevent anything from happening between *us.*" (p. 39)

Fritz Perls, founder of Gestalt psychotherapy, also believed it essential for people always to be aware of their immediate life experiences, of living in "the here and now," before they could be expected to show mature personality functioning. A person who participates in the reality of the present time "can't be anxious, because the excitement flows immediately into ongoing spontaneous activity. If you are in the now, you are creative, you have your eyes and ears open, like every small child, you find a solution" (Perls, 1969, p. 3).

THE IMPORTANCE OF THE SELF

The concept of self-actualization suggests the central role played by the "self" in Rogers' theory. The existence of a self seems to be clearly implied by our everyday language: "*I* am in love. Walking in the rain makes *me* feel good. These clothes are not *me.*" However, many psychologists reject the concept of self as having any value in the scientific understanding of personality. This is particularly true of behavioral psychologists such as J. B. Watson and B. F. Skinner. Other psychologists who recognize the concept of self may assign relatively minimal importance to it, as with Freud. (See Chapter 15, Self-Concept.)

self

Belief in the importance of self is one of the distinguishing marks of humanistic psychologists. Rogers and Maslow have both answered "Yes" to the question "Is there a self?" For Rogers (1947), the person's experience of self is a basic aspect of human life, forming and determining behavior. In fact, the construct of self is such an important part of Rogerian theory that some psychologists have designated it "self theory" (Patterson, 1961). Similarly, Maslow's conception of self-actualization is the cornerstone of his theory.

Rogers did not begin his theorizing by assuming the importance of the self in human experience. Rather, he started with a notion of the self as "a vague, ambiguous, scientifically meaningless term" no longer in vogue among respected psychologists (1959, p. 200). His ideas about the self emerged from his observations of therapy clients, who regularly expressed such ideas as "I wonder *who I am,*" "I don't want anyone to know the *real me,*" "I'm not being *my real self,*" "It feels good to let myself go and *just be myself.*"

Self as self-perceptions. Although Rogers has never offered a formal definition of personality, he has come closest when discussing the self—the organizing, creative, and adapting core of personality that has the greatest influence in determining a person's behavior. In 1959, he provided the following formal definition of *self:* "the organized, consistent conceptual gestalt composed of perceptions of the characteristics of the 'I' or 'me' and the perceptions of the relationships of the 'I' or 'me' to various aspects of life, together with the values attached to these perceptions" (p. 200).

self-perception

The definition reflects Rogers' basic commitment to the phenomenological method for understanding human experience. Its emphasis is clearly on the perceptual origins of self, in which one's "self" is an abstraction—a set of perceptions, or one's "self-concept." It includes all of the individual's evaluations of his organism and relationships, "by which he tends to order and interpret his internal and external experiences" (Shlien, 1970, p. 95), along with the way in which these perceptions relate to other perceptions and objects in his whole external world (Evans, 1975). To illustrate, a person may have the self-perception "I am six feet tall." She may relate this to her perceptions of other people, as in "I am tall," and even place a value on her perception, as in "I am too tall."

How do you perceive your own "self"? The purpose of the exercise in Box 7.1 is to help you answer this question.

BOX 7.1   *Adjective Descriptions of Your Actual and Desired Self*

The following exercise introduces a major theme of Rogers' thought. To get the most out of this exercise, take a few moments to complete it before reading the rest of the chapter.

Instructions: On the left side of a sheet of paper, write down adjectives that best describe the self you are at the present time in your life (actual self). On the right side, write down adjectives that best describe the self you would like to be (ideal self).

Work quickly, and be sure to write down single words, not sentences or paragraphs. Write down at least 10–15 self-descriptive adjectives in each column. Don't worry if some of your words seem contradictory; just write whatever adjectives best describe your actual and ideal self.

Your Actual Self   *Your Ideal Self*

Interpret the results by evaluating ways in which the words you selected do or do not represent your "self." (If you think 15 words are too few, how many do you think you would need to describe yourself? Students in past research studies by Allen and Potkay, 1983a, typically write down 10–12 adjectives.) How do your descriptions compare with those of other students in the class? In what ways are your descriptions of self as you are and self as you would like to be the same or different? What do you make of words that do and do not appear on both lists?

Note that Rogers believes that the self is best understood as a continuing process, not a fixed end-point. Thus, the self is always likely to be undergoing change. This is why a person may organize self-views in different ways at different points in time. You probably do not view yourself the same today as you did five years ago, and you likely have had the experience "I used to think of myself that way, but not any longer." The words you wrote down in the exercise in Box 7.1 indicate some of the ways you are *presently* organizing your perceptions of yourself.

Even at the same point in time, a person's self is open to alternative abstractions when different people are involved. That is, other people are not likely to see you the same way you see yourself. One of our students was quite surprised to learn of this while doing a self-study term project. She had been asked to describe her true self with adjectives and then obtain adjective descriptions of her true self from mother, father, boyfriend, and girlfriend. The words she used to reflect her own self-concept were much more negative than those used by other persons in her life. They included *insecure, emotional, shy, stubborn, impulsive, negative, impatient, perfectionist,* and *nondisclosing.* Without being aware of it, she had neglected to reveal many positive attributes seen by others, such as *intelligent, friendly,* and *lovable.* Her explanation was that "I failed to update my feelings about myself to match my true self of today" (Allen & Potkay, 1983a). It is easy to see how a person's self may be comprised of different sets of perceptions reflecting many specific "selves" in each of various life contexts (Nunnally, 1955).

The ideal self.   In addition to our perceptions of how we *are,* we also have notions about how we would like to be. For Rogers, the *ideal self* is the self a person most values and desires to be. Rogerians often ask a person to describe his or her ideal self as a means of comparing descriptions of actual self and ideal self. (This is why, in Box 7.1, you were asked to write down adjectives describing the self you ideally would like to be.) The closer the correspondence between a person's actual and ideal self, the greater the person's sense of self-acceptance and adjustment.

actual self and ideal self

Congruence with experience.   Our perceptions of self may be more or less in agreement with our experience of what is really going on inside us. Rogers uses the term *extensional* to refer to accurate perceptions of self-experience. This means that the person is in a state of personal *congruence,* because experiences of "self" and "total organism" coincide in a consistent manner. The actualizing tendency is then relatively whole and unified, and the person shows mature integration and psychological adjustment.

Incongruence, by contrast, reflects an inconsistency between what people believe themselves to be like and how they actually are—between their self-perception and actual experience of self. Self-perceptions may be *intensional,* or inaccurate, because of defensive tactics such as denial of experience and beliefs that are rigid, distorted, unrealistic, or overgeneralized. *Denial* involves the inability to recognize or accept the existence of an experience that has occurred, as in the reaction "No! It can't be so!" to news that a loved one has died. *Distortion* involves a reinterpretation of an experience so as to make it consistent with how one wants things to be, as in the reaction "He's not dead, but resting. See, he's breathing."

Intensional self-perceptions can contribute to experiences of inner confusion, tension, and maladaptive behavior. Rogers cites the example of a boy who had been observed lifting girls' skirts. When questioned, the boy denied what he had done, stating that it *couldn't* have been he. The boy was in a state of incongruence. His intensional perceptions led him to maintain an artificial self-concept inconsistent with his actual experience. Because his self-concept did not include sexual feelings or desires, his picture of himself was in conflict with his organismic experiences of sexual curiosity and desire. He shut out of his awareness whatever behaviors, feelings, or attitudes might destroy a portion of his self-concept. The boy's denial reflected defensiveness, a typical response when one's self-concept is threatened, aimed at maintaining the current structure of the self in the face of contradictory information (Rogers, 1959). "In the strictly technical sense, his self-picture couldn't do it, and didn't do it" (In Evans, 1975, p. 17).

Movement toward growth and improved adjustment in this boy would require him to revise his self-concept toward congruence. The process undoubtedly would be accompanied by a subjective sense of anxiety, as the boy became aware of the incongruence between his self-concept and his total experience. The reason for the discomfort is that "each of us seeks to preserve the concept or picture that he has of himself and that a sharp change in that picture is quite threatening. Any change destroys some of the security that we feel we need" (In Evans, 1975, p. 17). If the boy were able to lower his defenses, the new information about himself then could be incorporated as part of his self-concept. If not, *maladjustment* could occur, with the boy remaining unaware of what is going on in his organism and becoming static in his growth and self-actualization.

PERSONALITY DEVELOPMENT:
THREE FAVORABLE CONDITIONS

What determines whether a person's self-structure becomes congruent or incongruent with experience? Rogers points to external circumstances, particularly of an interpersonal nature, under which personal growth is facilitated or blocked. His boyhood observation of his family's potatoes highlights the importance of environmental conditions as influences on the actualizing tendency of living things. The potatoes failed to realize their fullest potentials because of unfavorable conditions outside themselves. More favorable conditions of sunlight, soil, and moisture would have facilitated their growth, resulting in greater fulfillment of inherent potentials.

Similarly, the interactions between persons and interpersonal environments represent an important aspect of human development. The actualization tendency leads all people in the direction of becoming the persons they truly are, whether the social environment is favorable or unfavorable. However, certain interpersonal conditions facilitate actualization strivings, whereas others do not.

three conditions for personality growth and change

Rogers' work with clients in therapy led him to identify three "necessary and sufficient" conditions for growth and change in personality: unconditional positive regard, accurate empathy, and congruence. These three conditions are interrelated and may be best understood as general attitudes conveyed toward a person by other people. When these conditions are present, persons become fully functioning, showing optimal maturity and adjustment in their self-actualization.

Unconditional positive regard.   All people have needs that can be fulfilled only by other people in human relationships. Chief among these is a universally learned need for *positive regard* (Standal, 1954) — the experiencing of oneself as making a positive difference in the life of another person and as receiving warmth, liking, respect, sympathy, acceptance, caring, and trust from others (Rogers, 1959). This need is met when other people in the person's environment provide *unconditional positive regard,* allowing the person to feel accepted, valued, worthwhile, and trusted, simply by being the person that one is, with no strings attached. The person experiences the other's acceptance without feeling that it depends on his or her doing some "right" thing or having to be the way the other person thinks the person "should" be. No aspect of the person is judged "more or less worthy of positive regard than any other" (Rogers, 1959, p. 208). This applies to all the person's experiences, whether shameful, frightening, satisfying, or pleasing. There is no generalized labeling of the person as "bad" or "good." Rather, the person feels unconditionally "prized," valued, and accepted, simply for being oneself.

However, there is another, less preferred way for a person to feel valued. Under this circumstance, positive regard is received only when the person meets certain *conditions of worth* set up by significant others. The individual feels prized in some respects, but not in others. She then avoids some self-experiences judged less worthy of self-regard and seeks out others judged more worthy. This second way is "conditional" because it involves a contingent, if-then component. "If you do or say the things I like or want, then I will value you and consider you important. If you don't, then I won't." In this way, a child learns to do things consistent with the ways of others, especially parents. The child learns "If I behave in certain ways, ways that are valued by my parents who are significant to me, then I will be 'loved.' If I don't meet their values and meanings, then I will not be loved." What happens when a person's experiences differ from those of other people around her? Suppose what she considers right for her is evaluated as wrong or unacceptable by significant others? Inner conflict occurs, along with incongruence between the person's experiences of self and total organism. The person's actualizing tendency is likely to become blocked because of external conditions, thereby fostering denials or distortions of personal experiences that are natural but different from those of other people.

A common misconception about unconditional positive regard is that everything a person does or says needs to be approved of by other people, that everything must be permitted. This is not so. Rogers distinguishes between the individual as a person and the individual's freely chosen values and behaviors. For example, while parents may prize their child, it is possible for them to do this without valuing all of the child's behaviors equally. They may express pride when their child shares a candy bar with a friend, or displeasure when their child bites a friend. However, their approval and disapproval would be in relation to the child's specific acts, not in relation to the child as a person. It is the sharing that is approved and the biting that is disapproved, not the child. The child is considered neither "better than others" nor "shamefully naughty." Even though the parents might wish the child not to bite, there is no rejecting of the child as a whole. The person of the child continues to be prized.

Contrast the reactions of the father in *Fiddler on the Roof* (Stein, 1964), three of whose daughters displayed increasingly nontraditional values and behaviors. When one of Tevye's daughters went against orthodox Jewish tradition by becoming her own matchmaker, Tevye overcame his initial reluctance and planning. He actively aided her choice of the tailor as a marriage partner. When a second daughter went against tradition by not even asking her father's permission to marry, only his blessing, Tevye also was accepting of her—"What else could I do?" However, when a third daughter independently married a Russian soldier who did not hold family religious beliefs, Tevye found himself in a dilemma. He was unable to bend—"How can I accept them. . . . how can I turn my back on my own faith?" While Tevye personally disagreed with the actions and values of all three of his daughters, he was able to flow with the experiences of the first two, viewing the world as new and changing. On the other hand, his attitude toward his beloved third daughter turned to one of deep rejection of her as a person, and he sought to "forget her" as being "dead to us." He was unable to convey an attitude of unconditional positive regard toward her.

Also consider the meeting arranged by Pope John Paul II with Mehment Ali Agca, the young man who shot him during an attempted assassination. The Pope's personal value on violence as "evil" and "unworthy of man" was clear. Yet despite his having been the victim of Agca's violence, he valued and accepted Agca as a person:

> The Pope clasped Agca's hands in his own from time to time. At other times he grasped the man's arm, as if in a gesture of support. . . ."I spoke to him as a brother whom I have pardoned, and who has my complete trust". . . .The Pope forgave Agca, but Agca remains in jail, and should. (Morrow, 1984, p. 28)

Accurate empathy.   Rogers' second and third conditions of personality change and growth are more directly connected to therapy. If a person is to experience congruence with his or her real experience, others must correctly hear what the individual is experiencing and refrain from judging it. Rogers believes the ability to understand another person to be of "enormous" value. He has found it "enriching to open channels whereby others can communicate their feelings, their private perceptual worlds, to me" (1961, p. 19). This ability to accurately perceive the client's internal world in a nonevaluative way is called *accurate empathy*. Such empathic understanding goes beneath the surface of another person's words and actions, to inner feelings, attitudes, meanings, and motives.

Congruence in interpersonal relationships.   In order for a person to grow, other persons must demonstrate their willingness and ability to be themselves in relationships with that person, naturally and openly. Rogers also calls this state of genuineness or realness on the part of one person toward another *congruence*. In the context of therapy, the therapist must exhibit an openness to inner experiences in such a way that it conveys personal congruence to the client: "I am more effective when I can listen acceptantly to myself, and can be myself" without trying to act "as though I were something I am not" (Rogers, 1961, pp. 16–17). Even an experienced therapist might admit to the client, "I find myself frightened because you are touching on feelings I have never been able to resolve myself" (Rogers, 1959). A therapist uncomfortable with some aspect of the client relationship would be considered incongruent if he remained unaware of the discomfort, avoided dealing with it, or communicated opposite reactions. Incongruence is not helpful to the person in question, because the wholeness of the other person, in this case the therapist, is not present in the relationship.

Developing positive self-regard.   What happens when the favorable conditions of personality development are present? When individuals receive unconditional positive regard from others, particularly during the formative years, they will develop a favorable attitude toward themselves, termed *positive self-regard.* This, in turn, allows them to develop their own values and satisfactions in accord with their real experiences, independently of "approving" others. Although they will be aware of expectations about what they "should" do, they will trust themselves and their judgments instead of being totally bound by conventions established outside themselves. They will become fully functioning individuals. Positive self-regard unlocks the natural actualizing tendency present in all persons.

positive
self-regard

This outcome can be contrasted with what happens when others impose conditions of worth on an individual. Such conditions do not encourage personal experiences of positive self-regard, because the person's *locus of evaluation,* or source of evidence about values, does not lie within the person but outside, in others. The judgments of others are used as the criterion for valuing an experience or object, as opposed to relying on one's natural, organismic, actualizing tendency. A clear example of this appears in Box 7.2, in the form of a letter written to Carl Rogers by a young woman he had never met. The woman had not yet developed her own, inner locus of evaluation. However, she was working hard at doing so with the help of a counselor.

BOX 7.2

"Dear Dr. Rogers"

Carl Rogers has received numerous unsolicited letters from persons who have been influenced by him, either directly through therapy (Rogers, 1970) or indirectly through reading. One letter was from a young woman who had read Rogers' book *On Becoming a Person* (1961). Rogers (1980) saw the letter as illustrating a number of his ideas about personality growth and change. For example, the young woman was communicating her awareness of a discrepancy between her experience of herself and her concept of herself. She wrote of having denied her own personal experiences, even though she had found them real and good for her. She had developed a false self-concept based on an acceptance of meanings that were not her own but those of her parents, her fiancé, and society. Her false self was fine for those she was trying to please, because it was what they wanted. However, she felt uneasy within herself. She was discovering that the submissive, malleable self through which she had been living was no longer hers. Because she distrusted her own organismic experience in favor of a self desired by other people in her life, she also experienced a lowered sense of self-worth. With help, she was finding herself able to discover, accept, and value her immediate gut-level experiences, and to reconstruct a changed self more congruent with personal experiences and meanings. She was beginning to let her experience tell her what it means rather than trying to impose a meaning on it. The actualizing tendency was finally asserting itself after having been suppressed for so long.

continued

BOX 7.2
continued

Dear Dr. Rogers,

I don't know how to explain who I am or why I am writing to you except to say that I have just read your book, *On Becoming a Person,* and it left a great impression on me. I just happened to find it one day and started reading. It's kind of a coincidence because right now I need something to help me find *me.*

I think that I began to lose me when I was in high school. I always wanted to go into work that would be of help to people but my family resisted, and I thought they must be right. Things went along smoothly for everyone else for four or five years until about two years ago. I met a guy that I thought was ideal. Then nearly a year ago I took a good look at us, and realized that I was everything that *he* wanted me to be and nothing that *I* was. I have always been emotional and I have had many feelings. I could never sort them out and identify them. My fiancé would tell me that I was just mad or just happy and I would say okay and leave it at that. Then when I took this good look at us I realized that I was angry because I wasn't following my true emotions.

I backed out of the relationship gracefully and tried to find out where all the pieces were that I had lost. After a few months of searching had gone by I found that there were many more than I knew what to do with and I couldn't seem to separate them. I began seeing a psychologist and am presently seeing him. He has helped me to find parts of me that I was not aware of. Some parts are bad by our society's standards but I have found them to be very good for me. I have felt more threatened and confused since going to him but I have also felt more relief and more sure of myself.

I remember one night in particular. I had been in for my regular appointment with the psychologist that day and I had come home feeling angry. I was angry because I wanted to talk about something but I couldn't identify what it was. By eight o'clock that night I was so upset I was frightened. I called him and he told me to come to his office as soon as I could. I got there and cried for at least an hour and then the words came. I still don't know all of what I was saying. All I know is that *so much hurt and anger* came out of me that I *never really knew existed.* I went home and it seemed that an *alien* had taken over and I was hallucinating like some of the patients I have seen in a state hospital. I continued to feel this way until one night I was sitting and thinking and I realized that this alien was the *me* that I had been trying to find.

I have noticed since that night that people no longer seem so strange to me. Now it is beginning to seem that life is just starting for me. I am alone right now but I am not frightened and I don't have to be doing something. I like meeting me and making friends with my thoughts and feelings. Because of this I have learned to enjoy other people. One older man in particular — who is very ill — makes me feel very much alive. He accepts everyone. He told me the other day that I have changed very much. According to him, I have begun to open up and love. I think that I have always loved people and I told him so. He said, "Were they aware of it?" I don't suppose I have expressed my love any more than I did my anger and hurt.

continued

Among other things, I am finding out that I never had too much self-respect. And now that I am learning to really like me I am finally finding peace within myself. Thanks for your part in this.

BOX 7.2
continued

Basic Concepts: Maslow

Thus far, our focus has been on Carl Rogers and his person-centered theory of personality. We would now like to turn our attention to a second major humanistic psychologist, Abraham Maslow, and his theory of self-actualization. Although both theorists emphasize the importance of self-actualization in personality functioning and development, Maslow is more closely identified with this concept than Rogers because it is a more obvious cornerstone of his theory. Our coverage begins with a brief biographical sketch of Maslow.

MASLOW, THE PERSON

Abraham Maslow was born on April 1, 1908, in Brooklyn, New York, the son of uneducated Jewish immigrants. Maslow depicted his youth as "isolated and unhappy," growing up without friends, in libraries and among books. As "the little Jewish boy in the non-Jewish neighborhood," he likened himself to the first Black to enroll in an all-White school (1968, p. 37).

Maslow earned all of his degrees at the University of Wisconsin where, as Harry Harlow's first doctoral student, he conducted research on dominance in monkeys. Maslow was initially "sold" on behaviorism, but changed under the influence of psychoanalytic and humanistic theories, as well as important life events. He once stated that "anyone who had a baby couldn't be a behaviorist" because of the overwhelming sense of not really being in control (in M. Hall, 1968, p. 56). Maslow considered his most important educational experiences to be those

ABRAHAM MASLOW.
Humanistic psychologist Abraham Maslow sees self-actualization as the top of the hierarchy of human needs. His examples of superior personalities include Albert Einstein and Eleanor Roosevelt, persons whose lives showed clear and efficient perceptions of reality, personal autonomy, and a sense of mission.

that taught him what kind of a person he was: psychoanalysis, his marriage to Bertha, and the "thunderclap" of having a child. World War II also had a dramatic impact on him, making him want "to prove that human beings are capable of something grander than war and prejudice and hatred" (in M. Hall, 1968, p. 54). He advised his two daughters, "Learn to hate meanness."

Maslow's unique approach to understanding human experience was to find "the best" humankind has to offer — that fraction of 1% of the population representing superior self-actualization, peak experiences, and the tip of growth and progress for the whole species. He loved the sense of discovery, of being "the first runner in the relay race" (in M. Hall, 1968, p. 56). Maslow was on the faculty of Brooklyn College (1937–1951) and Brandeis University (1951–1969), where he chaired the psychology department for ten years. In 1968, he served as president of the American Psychological Association. He died of a heart attack in 1970.

NOT BY BREAD ALONE: FIVE BASIC HUMAN NEEDS

Maslow (1954, 1970) offers two answers to the question "Do people live by bread alone?" When people have no bread, the answer is "Yes." But, when bread is more plentiful, the answer is "No." Consider the example of a desperately hungry person who constantly thinks about food, dreams about food, remembers food, perceives food, and wants only food. All other interests are unimportant. Life itself is defined in terms of eating. Utopia is a place where there is plenty of food. However, the picture is quite different when bread is available and the person's belly is continuously filled. Gratification of the hunger need frees the person to pursue other needs. When these higher-order needs emerge, they begin to dominate the organism, taking the place of hunger. And when these needs are satisfied, newer and higher needs emerge.

five basic needs   What are these needs? Maslow has conceptualized five basic needs as underlying human motivation: physiological, safety and security, belongingness and love, esteem, and self-actualization.

Physiological needs encompass specific biological requirements for water, oxygen, proteins, vitamins, proper body temperature, sleep, sex, exercise, and so on. *Safety needs* include security, protection, stability, structure, law and order, and freedom from fear and chaos. They are most readily inferred from negative reactions of children to sudden unpredictability and disruption in their lives, or to any stimulus that leads them to feel psychologically endangered and threatened (similar to Horney's concept of basic anxiety, Chapter 4). *Belongingness and love needs* orient the person toward affectionate relations with people, and a sense of place in family and groups. Maslow saw the rapid acceptance of sensitivity-group participation during the 20th century as reflecting a widespread hunger for interpersonal contact, intimacy, and togetherness. He noted that most theorists have stressed the "thwarting of love needs" as a fundamental cause of human maladjustment (Maslow, 1970). *Esteem needs* are of two kinds. First, there are personal desires for adequacy, mastery, competence, achievement, confidence, independence, and freedom. Second, there are desires for respect or esteem from other people, such as attention, recognition, appreciation, status, prestige, fame, dominance, importance, and dignity. Satisfaction of esteem needs results in feelings of personal worth, self-confidence, psychological strength, capability, and a sense of being useful and necessary in the world.

The "single, ultimate value" is the overriding human *need for self-actualization,* through which every person's inherent goal is to realize his or her inner potentialities. The person's inner striving is to become everything that she or he can become—to become fully human (similar to Rogers). What a person *can* be, that person *must* be, whether athlete, parent, or community leader. Musicians must make music, artists must paint, poets must write. Every person *must* be true to his or her own nature. "At this level, individual differences are greatest" (Maslow, 1970, p. 46).

self-actualization

Maslow categorized the first four basic needs as *deficiency needs (D-needs),* because they require fulfillment by the environment in order for the person to avoid physical sickness and psychological maladjustment. Citing evidence from research studies (P. T. Young, 1941, 1948), Maslow concluded that an organism's appetites or preferred choices among different foods are a fairly efficient indication of actual physiological needs or lacks in the body. If the body is lacking a particular chemical, the organism will compensate by developing a partial hunger for that missing food element. Maslow (1970) also saw support for his concept of basic needs in Walter Cannon's (1932) theory of homeostasis, through which the body automatically attempts to maintain constant physiological balance. D-needs meet the following criteria:

deficiency needs (D-needs)

1. Persons yearn persistently for their gratification.
2. Deprivation sickens persons or stunts their growth.
3. Gratification cures the deficiency illness.
4. Steady supplies prevent these illnesses.
5. Healthy people do not demonstrate the deficiencies.

Although self-actualization does not clearly emerge until there has been some prior satisfaction of the physiological, safety, love, and esteem needs, gratification of basic needs is not sufficient to guarantee self-actualization. Self-actualizing persons certainly show sufficient gratification of their basic needs, but also demonstrate freedom from illness, positive use of their capacities, and motivation that is linked to a set of personal values. Further, while self-actualization implies the fulfillment of all four basic needs, it is different from them because its direction is positive or "growth-motivated" rather than negative or "deficiency-motivated." Self-actualization is not a D-need.

Maslow has arranged the basic needs into a hierarchy, in a first-things-first manner. Lower-order needs are *prepotent,* or stronger than higher-order needs. They occur earlier in the developmental process and require gratification prior to higher-order needs. A deficiency in a lower-order need dominates personality functioning until it is satisfied, at which time the person is freed to begin meeting the next need in the hierarchy. Safety is a "stronger, more pressing, earlier appearing, more vital need" than belongingness, and the need for food is prepotent to both (Maslow, 1959, p. 123). Figure 7.1 shows the hierarchical order of needs proposed by Maslow, with physiological needs prepotent to safety needs which, in turn, are prepotent to belongingness and love needs, and so on, up the steps.

hierarchy of needs

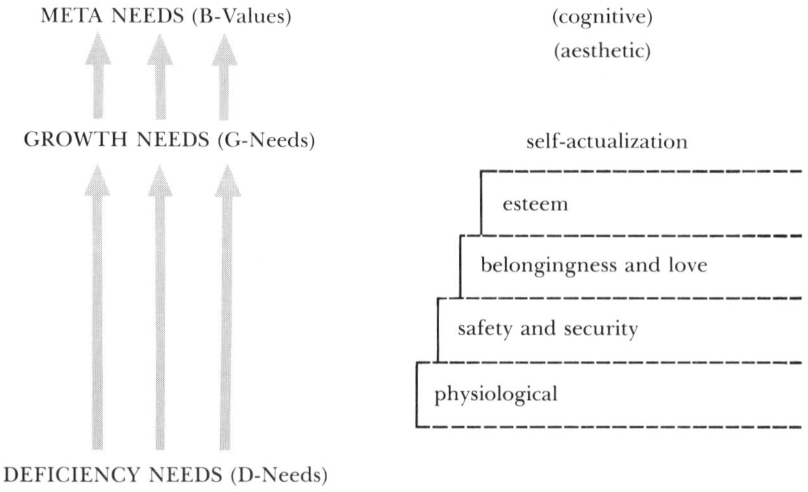

META NEEDS (B-Values)   (cognitive)
                                                   (aesthetic)

GROWTH NEEDS (G-Needs)   self-actualization

                                              esteem

                                          belongingness and love

                                      safety and security

                                  physiological

DEFICIENCY NEEDS (D-Needs)

Figure 7.1   Maslow's hierarchy of needs.

Hierarchical needs are not met in all-or-none fashion, but are overlapping. The most common pattern is for people to be both partially satisfied and not satisfied in their needs at the same time. Using arbitrary figures, Maslow (1970) speculated that the satisfactions of an average person's five needs might by 85% physiological, 70% safety, 50% love, 40% self-esteem, and 10% self-actualization. Also, hierarchical needs are not met suddenly. A person does not simply step up from one need to the next. The emergence of new needs is gradual, following satisfaction of a lower-order need. If belongingness and love needs are satisfied only 10%, esteem needs may not be visible at all; however, with 25% love satisfaction, esteem may emerge 5%. Need gratification is as important as need deprivation in influencing behavior.

There are, of course, exceptions to the order of needs appearing in the hierarchy. Romeo and Juliet were willing to die for love. India's Mahatma Gandhi was willing to deny his own safety and physiological needs for self-actualization and higher-order values, including personal dignity, social equality, and political freedom. In the most typical reversal of needs, self-esteem becomes more important than love. A person lacking in belongingness may adopt the notion that love comes to persons who are powerful, respected, feared, or aggressive. Such a person then seeks to meet this need by putting on a front of confident, self-assertive behavior, falsely believing it will elicit "love."

It is also possible to experience permanent loss of a need, as in the case of an antisocial individual whose cravings for love during infancy were never met, leading to lost desire and ability to give and receive affection. A "critical period" in this person's development was probably bypassed, similar to animals who lose their sucking or pecking reflexes when these are not exercised soon enough after birth. An individual's level of aspiration may also be permanently lowered. For example, someone who has experienced chronic poverty or unemployment may continue to seek only minimal satisfactions in life, such as just obtaining food or shelter.

HUMAN NATURE AS BORN, NOT MADE

Although Maslow recognizes that external environments may be helpful to people in actualizing their biological characteristics, he does not believe environments can teach people to be human or that environments shape humanness. Although culture, family, and parents may function as sun, food, and water to human actualization, they are not its seed. For Maslow (1970), human nature is inborn, not made. It has an essential, built-in structure comprised of potentialities and values that are intrinsic and common to all members of the species. Maslow considers all human needs and values "instinctoid," or instinct-like, because of their biological, genetic, and universal characteristics. Thus, all basic and higher-order needs are "in the strictest sense" biological needs, "related to the fundamental structure of the human organism itself," with "some genetic basis" involved, however weak (Maslow, 1969, p. 734).

Maslow's (1959, 1967, 1969) explicitness in this area is unique among psychologists, and different from most existentialists (Sartre, 1943/1957). This is because of the emphasis he places on (1) the existence of universal human values, (2) the biological rooting of these values, and (3) a firm rejection of "futile" notions about science being value-free. Like Rogers, Maslow believes that "the organism is more trustworthy, more self-protecting, self-directing, and self-governing than it is usually given credit for" (1970, p. 78). Like Rogers, he also adheres strongly to the belief in a universal, inborn *organismic valuing process,* or "bodily wisdom." Maslow (1959) refers to "hundreds" of free-choice experiments in which animals of all kinds behaved in ways that were "good" or "right" for them. Among other things, these animals were able to select beneficial diets when offered a sufficient number of alternatives (P. T. Young, 1941, 1948). With human infants, Maslow has seen psychologists learning to rely on "the internal wisdom of our babies" regarding infants' *own* choices of diet, time of weaning, amount of sleep, time of toilet training, need for activity, and so on (Maslow, 1959, pp. 120–121). This point of view contrasts with that of behaviorists seeking to maximize environmental control over infants.

Maslow has been especially critical of traditional approaches to determining norms for optimal personality functioning. Scientific approaches too readily assume that people are similar enough to animals that generalizations from animal studies can be made to studies of people. However, the essential natures of animals and people differ. Clinical approaches rely too heavily on samples of maladjusted persons, thereby offering a "lopsided view" of human nature based on negative experiences and extremes. Other approaches adopt statistical-averaging procedures in which findings from all people are treated exactly the same. Maslow considers such approaches "of little use," because they treat information from healthy persons and sick persons equally, resulting in generalized underestimates.

SELF-ACTUALIZING PERSONS: SUPERIOR PERSONALITIES

Maslow does not believe that all choices or choosers are equal. Consider animal choosers. In the studies referred to earlier (P. T. Young, 1941, 1948), chickens allowed to select their own diet showed wide variation in ability to determine what was beneficial for them. Some were "good choosers," and some were "bad choosers." Good choosers became stronger, larger, and more dominant than bad choosers, allowing them to get the best of everything. Later, when diets selected by good choosers were forced upon bad choosers, the latter did get stronger, bigger, healthier, and more dominant, although they never reached the level of good choosers. The main point is that organisms who were good choosers could choose what was good for the bad choosers better than the bad choosers actually chose for themselves.

What of human choosers? Maslow's orientation to understanding the values embedded in human nature has been to take its highest aspirations into account by focusing on positive extremes. "Only the choices and tastes and judgments of healthy human beings will tell us much about what is good for the human species in the long run" (Maslow, 1959, p. 121). Maslow has studied the "best" personalities humankind has to offer, defined as those he views as being the most psychologically healthy, mature, highly evolved, and fully human. He has designated a few of **self-actualizers** these superior persons *self-actualizers*—persons who fulfill themselves by making complete use of their potentialities, capacities, and talents, who do the best they are capable of doing, and who develop themselves to the most complete stature of which they are capable. Self-actualizers live Nietzsche's exhortation "Become what thou art!"

Who are these best personalities, and what are they like? Maslow's clearest cases of self-actualizers include Abraham Lincoln, Thomas Jefferson, Albert Einstein, Eleanor Roosevelt, Jane Addams, William James, Albert Schweitzer, Aldous Huxley, and Baruch Spinoza. A number of the common characteristics of these "super" personalities are summarized in Table 7.1.

TABLE 7.1   Characteristics of Self-Actualizing Persons

Clear, efficient perceptions of reality and comfortable relations with it

Acceptance of self, others, and nature

Spontaneity, simplicity, and naturalness

Problem centering (having something outside themselves they "must" do as a mission)

Detachment and need for privacy

Autonomy, independence of culture and environment, and will

Continued freshness of appreciation

Mystic experience, peak experience

Gemeinschaftsgefühl (feeling of kinship and identification with the human race)

Interpersonal relations (deep but limited in number)

Democratic character structure

Ethical discrimination between means and ends, between good and evil

Philosophical, unhostile sense of humor

Creativeness

Transcendence of any particular culture, resisting cultural molding

Imperfections: sometimes thoughtless, socially impolite, cold, boring, irritating, stubborn, ruthless, forgetful, humorless, silly, angered, superficially prideful, naively kind, anxious, guilty, and conflicted (without maladjustment)

Do not feel too disappointed to learn that you probably are not a self-actualizer or that self-actualizers are not likely to be present among your college classmates. Maslow's (1970) initial screening of 3,000 students yielded only one immediately usable subject, partly related to limitations of youth and experience. Even superior psychological health was defined by Maslow as applying to less than 1% of college students, those evaluated as "growing well." Any such disappointment may be tempered by learning that self-actualizers are not likely to be present among your college professors either, nor among your friends, family, or distant relatives and acquaintances. This is supported by the small number of persons Maslow has identified as meeting his criteria for self-actualization.

NOT BY BASIC NEEDS ALONE: METANEEDS

Although the basic needs are important for physical and psychological survival, they are not the only motivators or determiners of human behavior. There are, in addition, certain preconditions or immediate prerequisites for basic-need gratification, which is severely endangered or impossible without them. These conditions include a number of *personal and social freedoms*—to speak, express oneself, seek information, defend oneself, and do what one wishes so long as others are not harmed—along with a number of *ethical ideals* such as justice, fairness, honesty, and group orderliness. There are also a variety of *cognitive needs*—to know, to understand, to explain, and to satisfy curiosity—and a variety of *aesthetic needs* related to beauty, structure, and symmetry. Such needs have been

The metaneeds of self-actualizing people often reflect a type of living that reaches *beyond* everyday "motivation" toward higher values of beauty, uniqueness, order, perfection, and playfulness.

metaneeds
(B-values)

identified collectively by Maslow (1967) as *metaneeds* or *being values (B-values)*, terms used "to describe the motivations of self-actualizing people" (Maslow, 1970, p. 134).

What are the preferences, values, and motivations of superior personalities? A number of specific B-values of self-actualizers have been identified by Maslow (1967). They include truth, goodness, beauty, unity and wholeness, transcendence, aliveness, uniqueness, perfection, necessity, completion, justice, order, simplicity, richness and totality, effortlessness, playfulness, self-sufficiency, and meaningfulness. Again, all of these metaneeds or metavalues are closely enmeshed with the overriding need for self-actualization. They can be differentiated from basic needs because they represent more positive "growth" needs rather than more negative "deficiency" needs. Also, they are not, strictly speaking, "motivated" but *meta* or beyond motivation.

peak experiences

Maslow's concept of peak experiences is relevant at this point. *Peak experiences* are intense, mystical experiences associated with simultaneous feelings of limitless horizons, powerfulness and helplessness, a lost sense of time and place, and "great ecstasy, wonder and awe" (Maslow, 1970). These experiences have a high degree of personal importance, strengthening or transforming the person. They come from love and sex, bursts of creativity, moments of insight and discovery, and times of fusion with nature. Although peak experiences occur relatively infrequently for most persons, they tend to be reported by a number of self-actualizing persons. They are natural phenomena, not supernatural, and have been described by William James (1902/1958).

Supporting Evidence

Fundamental concepts in Rogers' and Maslow's theories have received some support, often of an indirect or philosophical nature. For example, the influence of an actualizing tendency has been affirmed by other theorists and some researchers, both within and outside the framework of psychology. This includes the operation of a universal formative tendency in nature, the tendency toward self-actualization, and evidence of a need hierarchy, transcendent values, and peak experiences.

ACTUALIZATION

The formative tendency.   As we have seen, Rogers distinguishes between the general biological tendency toward actualization and the specifically human tendency toward self-actualization. In recent years, he has hypothesized that the actualizing tendency may be present "at every level" of the universe, including nonliving systems:

> It is hypothesized that there is a formative directional tendency in the universe, which can be traced and observed in stellar space, in crystals, in microorganisms, in organic life, in human beings. This is an evolutionary tendency toward greater order, greater complexity, greater interrelatedness. In humankind it develops from a single cell origin to complex organic functioning,

to knowing and sensing below the level of consciousness, to a conscious awareness of the organism and the external world, to a transcendent awareness of the harmony and unity of the cosmic system including humankind. (Rogers, 1979/1983, p. 233)

Some support for "the formative tendency" has come from disciplines outside psychology (Royce & Mos, 1981). Contemporary biological concepts encompass not only *entropy,* the organismic tendency toward disorder, but *syntropy,* the ever-operating trend toward increased order and interrelated complexity that is evident at both organic and inorganic levels. Albert Szent-Gyoergyi (1974), a Nobel Prize biologist, has written of an innate drive in all living matter to perfect itself. Driesch's work (see Rogers, 1979/1983) with sea-urchin larvae has demonstrated that each of the two cells formed after a fertilized egg divides has the capacity to develop into a whole sea-urchin larva, not just portions. This is because the genetic code contains *rules* of growth, rather than specific, fixed information, leaving room for information to be generated within the organism. Another Nobel recipient, chemist Ilya Prigogine (see Rogers, 1979/1983), has developed a theoretical system of energy exchange in the environment based not on strict determinism but on relative probabilities and ever-increasing forms of complexity. Within psychology, John Lilly's (1973) research on sensory deprivation has shown that physical isolation through submersion in water tanks, without stimulation from external sources, results in new forms of self-awareness, derived from the activation of inner human experience. His work "shows how strong is the organismic tendency to amplify diversities and create new information and new forms" (in Rogers, 1979/1983, p. 229).

Self-actualization. Both Rogers and Maslow emphasize the idea of an inborn tendency toward actualization. Support for this emphasis comes from a number of other humanistic theories. Kurt Goldstein (1939), for example, saw "the drive of self-actualization" as the only human motive. Apparent displays of separate or multiple drives such as hunger, sex, and knowledge-seeking are artificial; such needs are not fundamental, but prerequisites to self-actualization. Like Maslow, Goldstein saw the organism's self-realization or "urge to perfection" as expressed through actual performance and preferred "choices" in life.

Hierarchy of needs. Graham and Balloun (1973) have reported partial support for Maslow's need-hierarchy theory, based on data from 37 San Francisco participants. First, participants responded to open-ended interview questions asking them to describe the most important things in their lives. Graduate students then rated these verbatim responses on a 5-point scale of "very high" to "little or no" desire expressed for physiological, security, social, and self-actualization needs. Results supported the hypothesis that comparisons of needs at different levels on the hierarchy would show greater satisfaction for lower-order needs than for higher-order needs. Second, participants made direct ratings of present level of satisfaction/dissatisfaction of each of the four basic needs, and their desire for "none" to "very much" improvement on each. Correlations between these ratings ranged between −.42 and −.72, with a median or middle value of $-.62$, which was statistically significant at $p < .01$. This confirmed the hypothesis that the level of satisfaction of any given need would be negatively correlated with desire for satisfaction of that need.

HIGHER-ORDER HUMAN VALUES AND PEAK EXPERIENCES

Higher, transcendent values.   Humanistic psychologists have attended to the potential in human life for meaningful values and transcendental experiences. Aspects of the new information reported by subjects in Lilly's experiments (1977) go beyond ordinary levels of consciousness toward a sense of cosmic awareness or unity. Sometimes the individual's experience of self is "dissolved in a whole area of higher values, especially beauty, harmony and love" (Rogers, 1979/1983, p. 231). Such findings support Rogers' outlook that a facilitative psychological climate could tap a level of complexity that is on the cutting edge of human ability "to transcend ourselves, to create new and more spiritual directions in human evolution" (1979/1983, p. 233).

Peak experiences.   Research findings have contributed some support to Maslow's concept of "peak experience." Ravizza (1977) interviewed 20 athletes in 12 different sports who reported expanded views of themselves as fully functioning individuals. Their "greatest moment" showed many similarities to Maslow's description of the peak experience: loss of fear (100% of sample), full attention or immersion (95%), perfect experience (95%), godlike feeling of control (95%), self-validation (95%), universe as integrated and unified (90%), and effortlessness (90%). Some aspects of Maslow's description were not met: the athletes' experiences were more narrow than broad in focus, more of the body than intellectually cognitive or spiritually reflective, and more limited in importance to immediate circumstances than pivotal in bringing about major changes in their lives.

Mathes, Zevon, Roter, and Joerger (1982) reviewed the research literature on peak experiences and then developed a 70-item scale to measure peak-experience tendencies, the Peak Scale. An "empirical picture" of individuals reporting peak experiences, consistent with Maslow's theorizing, emerged after five studies. Individuals who scored high on the Peak Scale evidenced cognitive experiences of a transcendent and mystical nature, as well as feelings of intense happiness. High scorers reported living in terms of B-values such as truth, beauty, and justice. Women, but not men, tended to show slightly higher self-actualization scores on Shostrom's (1966) Personal Orientation Inventory (discussed in the next section) compared with persons not reporting peak experiences.

Applications

ASSESSMENT TECHNIQUES

It might appear that the humanistic emphasis on subjective experience would pose problems for personality assessment. For example, to test person-centered theory experimentally, Rogers and his colleagues needed an objective method of measuring a person's self. They wanted to demonstrate differences in a client's self-concept before, during, and after psychotherapy. But how could a person's experience of *self*, so rich and complicated, be reduced to the limitations of research instruments and measured (Shlien & Zimring, 1970)? Similarly, how can an individual's degree of self-actualization, as conceptualized by Maslow, be measured? This section discusses two techniques that have shown the capability of assessing aspects of personality emphasized by humanistic psychologists.

Measuring self: Stephenson's Q-sort technique. Recall the Rogerian assumption that a person's self is a set of perceptions. A technique developed by Stephenson (1953) is designed to measure and quantify such perceptions, and is well suited to Rogerian aims. Stephenson's Q-sort technique consists of 100 statements taken from a large universe of self-descriptions made by clients in various stages of recorded therapy interviews (Butler & Haigh, 1954). The statements include such items as "I have an attractive personality," "I don't trust my emotions," "I am afraid of sex," and "Cheerful." Stephenson had each statement printed on a separate card. A person was instructed to sort each statement into one of nine piles, according to the degree to which she considered the statement "most" or "least" characteristic of herself. By using a forced-choice format, the number of cards in each pile was made to vary in such a way that their distribution took the shape of a statistical bell curve or normal distribution, with many cards placed in the middle and decreasing numbers of cards in the end categories.

Q-sort technique

Although a person is usually instructed to describe his or her actual self — one's self "as of now" — variations in target and time frames are possible. Instructions may ask for a description of one's ideal self (see Box 7.1), or of an "average" person. Also, therapists may be asked to use the Q-technique in describing their clients. Clients and therapists can make Q-sorts at specified points in time, such as at the beginning or end of therapy, or at any point in between. Different sorts can then be compared to determine consistencies and changes in client perceptions.

The value of Stephenson's Q-technique, and others like it (Block, 1961), lies in its ability to provide an operational or quantifiable definition of a concept as vague as the self (Patterson, 1961). Q-sorts obtained from a person on two or more occasions can be compared not only by content but by degree of statistical correspondence, thereby showing how much or how little the person's self-perceptions have changed over time or under different conditions. A high positive correlation in placements of self-descriptive items would signify close similarity and, consequently, little change. Low positive and low or high negative correlations would signify marked dissimilarity and, thus, much change. Consistent with person-centered theory, Q-technique lessens the emphasis on individual differences *between* people and heightens the emphasis on differences or changes occurring *within* the same person. It also focuses attention on the influence of seemingly different "personalities" in the same person, at different times and under different conditions.

The case of Mrs. Oak. As one example, Rogers (1954) detailed the case of Mrs. Oak, a woman in her late 30s who had been experiencing difficulties in relationships with her husband and adolescent daughter, and with herself. Mrs. Oak was first seen for 40 therapy sessions over 22 weeks, followed by seven months of no contact, then an additional 8 sessions over two months. Mrs. Oak completed 100-card sorts of her actual self, her ideal self, and an ordinary person at several points before, during, and after therapy. Q-sorts were also completed by Mrs. Oak's therapist, who sought to predict Mrs. Oak's responses as an index of understanding her. All of Mrs. Oak's assessment information was obtained by an independent research psychologist, not Mrs. Oak's therapist, to lessen possible biases in gathering the information. The Q-sort was only one of several assessment techniques used during the therapy, and Mrs. Oak was only one of several clients assessed.

Some of the findings from the Q-sort assessments were as follows. Mrs. Oak's descriptions of her ideal self at the beginning and end of therapy were more highly correlated (.72) than her descriptions of her actual self at the same two points (.30). This meant that her perceptions of her actual self underwent greater change than her perceptions of the self that she desired to be. Furthermore, the correlation between Mrs. Oak's descriptions of her actual self and her ideal self were much higher at the end of therapy (.79) than at the beginning (.21). This meant that her perceptions of the person she wished to be and the person she actually was corresponded more closely at the end of therapy than at the beginning. Additional support for this interpretation was provided by the higher correlation between her ideal self before therapy and her actual self at the end of therapy (.70). As expected, the correspondence between Mrs. Oak's perceptions of actual and ideal self generally became closer as therapy progressed, indexed by correlations of increasing magnitude over time: .21, .47, .45, .69, .71, and .79.

It is also possible to analyze changes in the placement of specific Q-sort items. Such an analysis illustrates how Mrs. Oak restructured her self-concept. Before therapy, Mrs. Oak perceived herself as insecure, self-centered, disorganized, responsible for her troubles, and as driven, bothered, and not relaxed. Eighteen months later, after therapy, she perceived herself as more emotionally mature, secure, confident, expressive, self-reliant, and less confused, helpless, guilty, resentful, and despising of herself. Interestingly, the Q-sort findings tallied well with the therapist's Q-sort descriptions of Mrs. Oak, other assessment results by independent interpreters, Thematic Apperception Test results, and ratings of Mrs. Oak's behaviors by two close friends.

Personal
Orientation
Inventory (POI)

Measuring self-actualization: Shostrom's POI.   Humanistic psychologist Everett Shostrom (1966) has designed an objective test, the Personal Orientation Inventory (POI), to measure the degree of an individual's self-actualization. The POI is a paper-and-pencil personality questionnaire made up of 150 pairs of items, in a forced-choice format. Persons answer by selecting one of two alternatives that best fits for them. Examples similar to POI items are "(a) I enjoy my life" or "(b) I do not enjoy my life"; and "(a) People should keep their feelings to themselves" or "(b) People should express their feelings to others."

The POI provides scores on a variety of humanistic dimensions, including "self-actualizing values," "existentiality," and "inner-directed versus other-directed." In an example cited by Shostrom (1966), the scores of two groups of therapy patients were compared. The more self-actualizing group was made up of patients averaging 27 months of therapy, and the less self-actualizing group was comprised of patients just beginning therapy. The differences between group scores were statistically significant on all dimensions. (The two groups also differed on 7 of 9 maladjustment scales of an independent measure, the Minnesota Multiphasic Personality Inventory.) Results supported the sensitivity of the POI for use in clinical settings, as well as the assumption that therapy can help persons become more self-actualizing. Robert Knapp (1976) has written a handbook for the POI, and Tosi and Hoffman (1972) have reviewed some POI limitations.

PROCEDURES FOR CHANGING PERSONALITY

Person-centered therapy.   Rogers' ideas about personality development and change have been discussed throughout this chapter as integral aspects of his theory in general. As applied to person-centered therapy, it is assumed that if certain conditions exist, then a characteristic process of personality change will occur (Rogers, 1959). These conditions include the three "necessary and sufficient" conditions of positive regard, accurate empathic understanding, and congruence. They also include the client's anxiety and internal motivation to change. The specific techniques of person-centered therapy are designed to reflect these basic premises.

Research has shown that the direction of change for clients in Rogerian therapy is from a personality that is fixed, separated, and tied to the past to one that is spontaneous, integrated, and flowing toward experiences occurring in the present. Seven characteristic stages of this process have been identified by Rogers (1961). It is impossible to capture all aspects of these complex and comprehensive stages as experienced by the client, but the following observations are representative:

Stage 1. The client's communications are mostly about externals, not about self.
Stage 2. The client describes feelings but does not recognize or "own" them personally.
Stage 3. The client talks about self as an object, often in terms of past experiences.
Stage 4. The client experiences feelings in the present, but mainly just describes them, with distrust and fear, rather than expressing them directly.
Stage 5. The client experiences and expresses feelings freely in the present; feelings "bubble up" into awareness with some desire to experience them.
Stage 6. The client accepts his or her feelings in all their immediacy and richness.
Stage 7. The client trusts new experience and relates to others openly and freely.

If this process occurs, then certain personality and behavioral changes will occur. These changes, the outcomes of therapy, lead the person toward greater self-actualization. They reflect increases in congruence, openness to experience, adjustment, correspondence between actual and ideal self, positive self-regard, acceptance of self and others, and organismic valuing.

BOX 7.1   *Rogers Describes*
REVISITED   *"Carl Rogers"*

Earlier in this chapter, you were asked to write down adjectives that described your real self and your ideal self. How do you think Carl Rogers would describe himself if he were asked to check off adjectives that best represent his "self"?

In preparing this book, we asked Rogers if he would be willing to complete a standard measure of self-description, the Adjective Check List (ACL) (Gough & Heilbrun, 1980). The ACL is a respected personality measure characterized by theoretical neutrality, a large research base, widespread use, and convenience of administration. It consists of 300 adjectives often used for purposes of individual description. The person is asked to read each word quickly and indicate "each one you would consider to be self-descriptive."

Although Rogers (personal communication, 1983) had "many reservations," he was "somewhat intrigued" by the project and filled out the ACL form. (Rogers believes that personality-assessment techniques do not convey a sense of the real person and may interfere with the development of genuine counseling relationships.) His responses appear in Figure A. Blackened circles indicate adjectives Rogers used to describe himself, and blank circles indicate adjectives he did not see as self-descriptive.

A profile of Rogers' overall scores appears in Figure B. The graph shows the pattern of Rogers' higher and lower scores on each of the 37 scales measured by the ACL. These dimensions are numbered and named in the column at the left of the figure. Using ACL guidelines to interpretation, "standard scores" of 50 are considered average, while scores of 60 or above and 40 or below are given more weight because they are one standard deviation above and below the mean, respectively. Thus, Rogers' highest score (scale #25) falls above the average, while his lowest score (scale #34) is below average. It should be noted that the meaningfulness of the profile is partially limited because the comparative norms used to plot it are derived from responses of 900 male students attending the University of California at Berkeley, not older adults or famous psychologists. However, compared with the normative sample of college students, Carl Rogers' pattern of adjective descriptions reflects the following:

High creativity, intellectual quickness, and breadth of interests (scale #25)

Low impulsiveness and a firm stance on ethical issues (scale #34)

Emotional independence and effective goal-attainment (scale #17)

A relatively cautious approach to seeking public attention (scale #13)

Gentleness and a valuing of inner feelings (scale #27)

Tolerance of the fears and weaknesses of others, and a desire to bring people together (scale #29)

A low degree of unfavorable self-descriptions (scale #3)

continued

BOX 7.1
REVISITED
continued

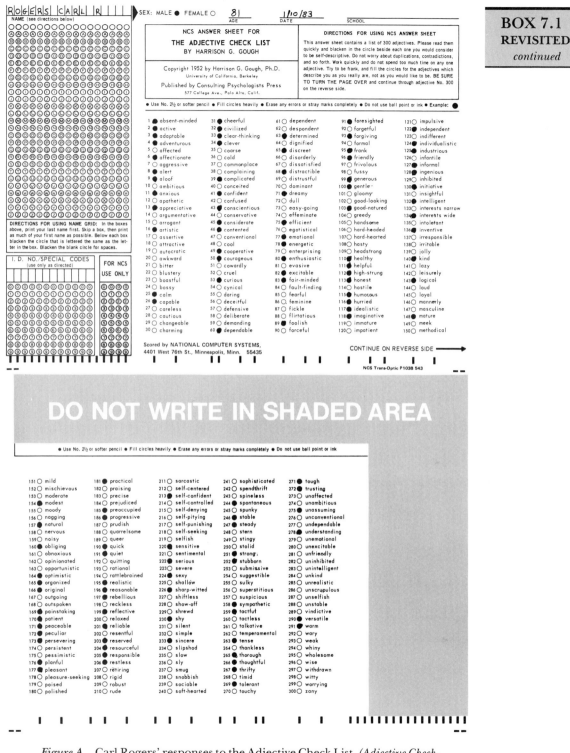

Figure A   Carl Rogers' responses to the Adjective Check List. (*Adjective Check-list reproduced by special permission of the Publisher, Consulting Psychologists Press, Inc., Palo Alto, CA 94306 from the Adjective Checklist by Harrison Gough, Ph.D. (c) 1952–1984. Further reproduction is prohibited without the Publisher's consent.*)

continued

BOX 7.1
REVISITED
continued

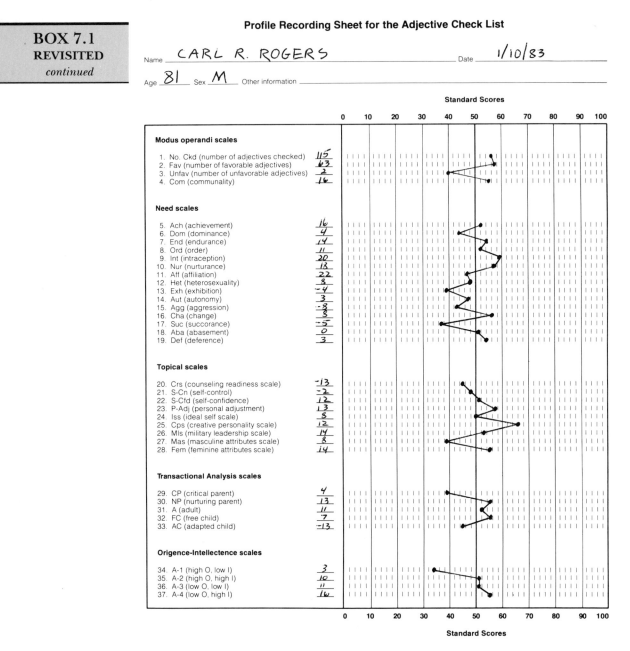

Profile Recording Sheet for the Adjective Check List

Name _CARL R. ROGERS_   Date _1/10/83_

Age _81_ Sex _M_   Other information _____

Standard Scores

Modus operandi scales

1. No. Ckd (number of adjectives checked) — 115
2. Fav (number of favorable adjectives) — 63
3. Unfav (number of unfavorable adjectives) — 2
4. Com (communality) — 16

Need scales

5. Ach (achievement) — 16
6. Dom (dominance) — 4
7. End (endurance) — 14
8. Ord (order) — 11
9. Int (intraception) — 20
10. Nur (nurturance) — 13
11. Aff (affiliation) — 22
12. Het (heterosexuality) — 8
13. Exh (exhibition) — -4
14. Aut (autonomy) — 3
15. Agg (aggression) — -8
16. Cha (change) — 8
17. Suc (succorance) — -5
18. Aba (abasement) — 0
19. Def (deference) — 3

Topical scales

20. Crs (counseling readiness scale) — -13
21. S-Cn (self-control) — -2
22. S-Cfd (self-confidence) — 12
23. P-Adj (personal adjustment) — 13
24. Iss (ideal self scale) — 8
25. Cps (creative personality scale) — 12
26. Mls (military leadership scale) — 14
27. Mas (masculine attributes scale) — 8
28. Fem (feminine attributes scale) — 14

Transactional Analysis scales

29. CP (critical parent) — 4
30. NP (nurturing parent) — 13
31. A (adult) — 11
32. FC (free child) — 7
33. AC (adapted child) — -13

Origence-Intellectence scales

34. A-1 (high O, low I) — 3
35. A-2 (high O, high I) — 10
36. A-3 (low O, low I) — 11
37. A-4 (low O, high I) — 16

Standard Scores

Figure B   Carl Rogers' Adjective Check List Profile.

Psychological utopia: Eupsychia. Maslow believed that basic human needs could be satisfied only interpersonally. Although he developed no method of psychotherapy, he often saw psychotherapy as exemplifying "good human relationships" because of the extent to which they supported human needs for security, belongingness, and self-esteem, on the way toward self-actualization (Maslow, 1970). Psychotherapy relationships dispense "psychological medicines" needed by all human beings: mutual frankness, trust, honesty, lack of defensiveness, emotional release, healthy passivity, relaxation, affection, love, and even childish silliness. Effective, democratic psychotherapists can do much to help individuals identify their inner needs and compensate for earlier deficiencies, which then transfers to relationships outside the therapy setting.

Maslow (1970) definitely believed that self-actualization could be fostered by a good environment. The characteristics of such an environment include (1) offering the organism all necessary raw materials; (2) standing aside and getting out of the way; (3) allowing the average organism to pursue its own wishes, demands, and choices; (4) accepting delays and renunciation in choices; and (5) respecting the wishes, demands, and choices of other organisms. Maslow speculated about a future *Eupsychia* (Yew-sígh-key-ah), a utopia characterized by psychological health among all its members. Its philosophical base would be anarchistic, meaning there would be no governmental imposition on individual liberty. Basic and meta needs would be respected, much more than usual. There would be more free choice than people are used to, as well as less control, violence, and contempt. It also would be Taoistic in its philosophy, valuing what is simple, loving, and unselfish. Overall, the good environment would stress spiritual and psychological forces as well as material and economic ones. (Compare Eupsychia with Skinner's Walden Two, discussed in Chapter 5.) Eupsychia would not work for all, however. "When we speak of free *choice* in human beings, we refer to sound adults or children who are not yet twisted and distorted" (Maslow, 1970, p. 278).

Evaluation

CONTRIBUTIONS OF HUMANISTIC PSYCHOLOGY

As the "third force" in psychology, the humanistic approach has been influential in enhancing the perspectives provided by behaviorism and the psychoanalytic tradition. In particular, humanistic psychologists have contributed (1) an understanding of persons, (2) an appreciation of caring interpersonal relationships as factors in personality growth and therapeutic change, and (3) demonstrations of scientific openness and theoretical flexibility.

Understanding the person. The phenomenological approach adopted by humanistic and existential psychologists has had three major influences on understanding personality. First, *it has allowed individual human beings to speak for themselves* about the nature of their own personal experiences and meanings. Phenomenologists have suspended their personal/professional views as to what a person *should* be, in order to understand how a person actually *is*. Information comes less from expert authorities with training and more from "common" persons, in more democratic, grass-roots fashion. This approach is evident in the person-centered approach of Carl Rogers, and in the existentialists' orientation of "getting into" the immediate world in which a person "lives and moves and has his being" (May, 1958). Sometimes information comes from "cream of the crop" individuals who have demonstrated maximum personality functioning (Maslow, 1970). However, even these self-actualizers are not professional experts in human behavior; they are expert human beings. As with Rogers, Maslow's method of approach to these superior personalities is observational and descriptive. Maslow did not begin with the question of what human values *should* be, but with observations of what healthy people *do* when they are permitted to choose, and live life.

Regarding scientific method, use of the phenomenological approach has questioned psychology's so-called objective frameworks for understanding human behavior. These frameworks have sought to understand people from the outside: behaviorally, mechanistically, reductionistically, and impersonally. Phenomenologists have doubted the existence of an absolute way of interpreting reality, and the desirability of even seeking such a narrow "truth" (Rogers, 1980). They have paved the way for multiple interpretations of human experience, especially at the highest, most complete levels of self-actualization where individual differences seem greatest.

Second, the humanists have contributed to the understanding of personality by *renewing interest in concepts of the self,* as a result of direct observations and experiences with a broad spectrum of normal, maladjusted, and superior people. The inclusion of concepts related to the self as central constructs in humanistic theories of personality is consistent with early philosophical traditions in American psychology. William James (1890/1950), father of American psychology, wrote of a "self of selves," a person's inner, conscious view of the sameness of his or her personality. Under the impact of behaviorism, however, psychologists avoided emphasizing concepts about the self, until the humanists revived interest in them.

Important to experimentally oriented psychologists, humanistic constructs have stimulated a large number of research investigations on various aspects of self. Ruth Wylie (1974, 1979) has provided excellent summaries of the different methods used by psychologists to assess self-concept, along with thorough reviews of many research findings and issues on topics relevant to self theory. Although Wylie has pointed out various shortcomings of self-concept measures and has evaluated research findings as inconclusive at best, the hundreds of studies available to her for review indicate an unquestioned degree of interest in concepts of self. Lynch, Norem-Hebeisen, and Gergen (1981) have spoken of a "vital rekindling of interest" in self-concept theory and research. Rychlak (1976) has judged experimental support sufficient for the concept of self "to be retained" in psychology. A more detailed discussion of self-concept appears in Chapter 15.

Third, the humanistic psychologists have tried to enhance our understanding of the person by emphasizing *trust in the organism.* Given sufficiently supportive psychological conditions, persons can be trusted to actualize their biologically based resources and move in directions that are ultimately good for them and their species. This conclusion is an outgrowth of the humanistic assumption that all organisms have inherent, natural capacities for growth, understanding, change, and purposive direction (Rank, 1945). This is not to say that positive motivations, strivings, or outcomes always occur. Histories of individuals and groups show that they do not. However, humanistic psychologists are biased in favor of the individual's making responsible use of personal consciousness and freedom. This is why most humanistic and existential psychologists are perplexed by psychoanalytic conclusions about human destructiveness and irrationality (Freud, 1930/1961) and by behavioral conclusions that human beings need to be under the control of highly structured external environments (Skinner, 1948). The humanists believe that rational solutions to human problems are possible without recourse to strict environmental controls.

A major hallmark of humanistic theories is that the self is not conceptualized as a static or permanent kind of personality "trait." Rather, it is an ongoing process that is constantly changing and in flux.

Caring about the person in human relationships.   Humanistic psychologists have reaffirmed the crucial importance of caring, interpersonal relationships in developing, maintaining, and changing personality. This has been especially true of person-centered therapy, in which the emphasis is on the therapist not as a blank screen or expert technician but as a person, "a viable human being engaged in a terribly human endeavor" (Truax & Mitchell, 1971, p. 344). Jerome Frank's (1971) analysis highlights the importance of intense relationships as one of six common denominators among all psychotherapies. Even behavioral therapists, often criticized for ignoring the contribution of interpersonal relationships in changing behavior, have modified procedures "which used to seem less than human to their critics" (Gendlin & Rychlak, 1970). It is not that specific techniques for changing personality are unimportant, but that their power pales in comparison with the "broad sweep of the therapist's personal impact" (Gurman & Razin, 1977, p. xv).

In fact, Carl Rogers has done more to revise the concepts, practices, and research methods of personality change than any single psychologist since Freud, the founder of psychotherapy. Rogers has done so, first, by demonstrating his caring as a person about persons, even when such demonstrations violated traditional psychoanalytic "rules." For instance, early in his career he showed human responsiveness by departing from routine child-guidance procedures and answering "Yes" to a despairing mother's question "Do you ever take adults for counseling here?" (Rogers, 1961). In another context, a filmed therapy interview (Shostrom, 1965), Rogers departed from traditional psychoanalytic taboos against communicating personal "countertransference" feelings to patients by saying to the client, Gloria, "I care about you right now, in this moment." He even indicated he could see himself as a father to Gloria, who would make a fine daughter. Gloria continued to keep in occasional touch with Rogers, because of the closeness achieved during this half-hour interview.

Demonstrating scientific openness and professional flexibility.   Third, Rogers has changed the field of psychotherapy through the value placed on subjecting his clinical observations to independent research investigation.

Rogers' (1942) case of Herbert Bryan was the first complete series of therapy sessions to be electronically recorded and transcribed, on 800 78-rpm record sides and 170 book pages. Never before had such a wealth of information been made available to psychologists, word for word, complete with "U-hm's" and pauses. Standard procedure, beginning with Freud, was for therapists to rely entirely on memory when summarizing sessions, often at the end of a full day's contact with six or eight patients. By exposing their practice to the scrutiny of other professionals and the public, Rogers and his students showed how psychotherapy could be demystified (Wexler & Rice, 1974). Their work "turned the field of counseling upside down" and "made possible the empirical study of highly subjective phenomena" (Rogers, 1974, p. 116). In retrospect, Rogers simply believed he had expressed an idea whose time had come.

Rogers has also changed professionals' ideas about scientific procedures and theory by adopting flexible attitudes in his work and relationships with others. His own theoretical formulation began with full recognition that every theory is a "fallible, changing attempt" to construct a network of fragile threads containing an unknown amount of error and mistaken inference (1959). Rogers believes that science may begin anywhere, even away from the laboratory and calculator. He has always been stimulated and excited by the new ideas of younger colleagues who seem "less stuffy, less defensive, more open in their criticism and more creative in their suggestions" than his older colleagues or peers (1974, p. 121). Following his example, Rogers' students and colleagues have shown a responsiveness to new ideas rather than orthodox, blind devotion (Wexler & Rice, 1974).

LIMITATIONS

Although the humanistic emphasis on subjective experience and on the self is a major contribution, this emphasis creates some difficulties for the scientific study of personality. The major limitations of the approach center on (1) the lack of an explicit definition of personality, (2) problems of operational definition of humanistic concepts, and (3) problems involved in accepting self-reports.

No explicit definition of personality.   Although references to personality appear in their writings, neither Rogers or Maslow has provided a clear definition of personality. *Personality* was not among Rogers' (1959) list of formally defined constructs. He has preferred to use the concepts *person, self,* and *self-concept* — the person's perception of his or her self at a given point in time. However, self-concept is only one aspect of personality, and provides only partial understanding of human personality and behavior (Combs, 1981, p. 11). Combs has identified seven additional variables influencing the organization of perceptions: physical status, environment, time, experience, need, goals, and change. Maslow (1970) has offered a definition of *personality syndrome* — "a structured, organized complex of apparently diverse specificities (behaviors, thoughts, impulses to action, perceptions, etc.) which, however, when studied carefully and validly are found to have a common unity that may be phrased variously as a similar dynamic meaning, expression, 'flavor,' function, or purpose" (p. 303). However, it is not clear whether "syndrome" refers solely to unity within a single individual or to similar unities across different individuals, as "types" based on different patterns of basic needs. No specific personality types have been identified by Maslow, except for references to "self-actualizers," that most accurately reflect end points of a process potentially present in all of us.

Problems of operational definition.   Scientific studies require that important concepts be *operationally defined*—that is, defined in terms of some observable and measurable phenomena that different observers can understand. However, many humanistic-psychology concepts are difficult or impossible to define. Concepts such as "truth," "joy," and "beauty" obviously are influenced by the eye of the beholder. Definitions of "peak experiences" have varied (Mathes, Zevon, Roter, & Joerger, 1982.) Maslow's identifications of "self-actualizers" (1) were based on his personal selections, (2) resulted from inferential reviews of a variety of materials not publicly available or open to replication, (3) occurred after the fact, and (4) were biased toward Western civilization and democratic values. Maslow himself recognized it was "a very shaky business to rest on just one study made by just one person" (1959, p. 125). M. Brewster Smith (1973), dismissing his own approval of Maslow's values as "beside the point" and expressing discomfort in "turning a howitzer on a butterfly," concluded that Maslow's values are too one-sided. Phillips, Watkins, and Noll (1974), contrasting Maslow's "self-actualization" with existentialist Viktor Frankl's "self-transcendence," reported differences as well as similarities between operational measures of the two concepts—the Personal Orientation Inventory (POI) (Shostrom, 1968) versus the Purpose in Life Test (PIL) (Crumbaugh & Maholick, 1969). Only one of 150 POI items was seen as referring directly to "dedication beyond the individual." Tosi and Hoffman's (1972) statistical analyses supported the POI only partially, mainly as a measure of "healthy personality" related to three factors: extraversion, open-mindedness, and existential nonconformity.

Other scales have been developed for operationally defining and measuring Rogerian concepts of "empathy," "warmth," and "genuineness." However, those developed by Truax and Carkhuff (1967) differ somewhat from those developed by Carkhuff (1969). In reappraising the therapeutic effectiveness of these dimensions, Mitchell, Bozarth, and Krauft (1977) related "inconclusive" findings to a number of issues, one of which was the relevance of the measurement scales to the constructs. Efforts have also been made to develop measures of other Rogerian concepts. Gendlin and Tomlinson's (1967) Experiencing Scale is a refinement of Rogers' (1959) earlier psychotherapy Process Scale, aimed at evaluating the degree to which a client is in touch with or avoiding personal feelings and meanings. Although this measure does not rely on client self-reports, but on therapist ratings, potential therapist biases related to personal reactions or professional expectations could influence ratings. Statistical disadvantages of Stephenson's (1953) Q-sort technique in measuring self-concept have been discussed by Kerlinger (1973). Once items have been selected, placements of new items are dependent upon preceding placements because of the forced-choice rank ordering of items. There is also a lack of information about means and standard deviations that would allow Q-sort comparisons to be made between persons or groups on level of self-concept.

Acceptance of conscious, self-reported experience.   Gordon Allport's (1937) classic text on personality alluded to the fashion of behaviorists and psychoanalysts "to distrust the evidence of immediate experience" and dismiss the self, ego, or "person" in psychology. Allport (1955) later wrote of humanistic psychologists often being at odds with behavioral and psychoanalytic psychologists, who sought to abandon ideas related to the credibility of conscious motivation, the determining influence of self-concept, and the reliability of self-reported experience. Behaviorists see no "self" and see little scientific use for self-reports; traditional psychoanalysts assign the self (ego) minimal importance; and social psychoanalysts generally give it only secondary importance, as the pawn of anxiety, defense mechanisms, and other unconscious influences.

Experimental evidence has shown that an individual's self-concept can be conceptualized as one's perceptions about oneself and operationally defined as one's self-statements. Nevertheless, there are difficulties with this approach. First, self-perceptions may be incomplete or inaccurate representations, related to inability to see oneself realistically. Second, even accurate self-perceptions may not be reflected in self-statements if the individual is unwilling to communicate them. Third, both self-perceptions and self-statements may not correspond to a person's behavior.

Despite these difficulties, moderating changes in theory have occurred among some psychologists, such as Rotter and Bandura (Chapter 6), whose approach to social learning is more "cognitive" than that espoused by traditional behaviorists. Similarly, current-day psychoanalysts (Chapter 4) assign a much more important role to ego than did Freud. In the next chapter, we consider George Kelly's cognitive theory, which makes heavy use of individuals' reported perceptions and constructions of reality.

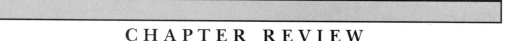

CHAPTER REVIEW

Humanistic psychology is a "third force" in psychology, different from the psychoanalytic and behavioral approaches. It has close conceptual ties with existential orientations to psychology and relies heavily on a phenomenological or subjective approach to understanding individual human beings. For humanistic psychology, personal perceptions underlie all human experience; no absolute reality exists or could even be known.

Human beings are unique in their strivings to live with purpose. Thus, knowledge of human nature is essential for establishing norms and values. Humanistic psychologists seek to understand the functioning and experience of the whole human being, in comprehensive, integrative, and holistic ways. The single most important human motivation is actualization, the unfolding of biologically inherent, preexisting capacities and potentials. This assumption characterizes the theories of both major proponents of humanistic psychology, Carl Rogers and Abraham Maslow.

Rogers' person-centered theory devotes full attention to the *person*. Every individual is seen as having vast inner resources for self-actualization, under conditions of a favorable psychological environment. Unlike psychoanalytic theorists, Rogers does not see people as innately destructive and irrational. Necessary and sufficient conditions for effective personality development and change include interpersonal attitudes of unconditional positive regard, empathic understanding, and congruence. As a psychotherapist, Rogers has come to know persons deeply. He has learned to care for them, and to trust them, as they have struggled to trust their own organismic values toward positive self-actualization, "to be that self which one truly is."

Self-actualization is fostered by congruence between inner, organismic experiences and outer, lived experiences. Central to Rogers' theory is the concept of self, the organized and consistent set of perceptions each person has of "I" or "me." Congruence between actual self and ideal self also fosters self-actualization. Degrees of congruence have been measured by Stephenson's Q-sort technique, as in the case of Mrs. Oak. Development of positive self-regard is critical for psychological health but is often blocked by other people who, instead of prizing a person, place artificial conditions of worth on that person's goodness or acceptability. Denials, distortions, and defensiveness in relation to one's natural experiences then develop, resulting in incongruence and maladjustment.

In Maslow's theory, the ultimate need for self-actualization is at the top of a need hierarchy. Four other, lower-order, deficiency needs require prior satisfaction by the environment in order for the person to avoid physical and psychological maladjustment: physiological, safety and security, belongingness and love, and es-teem. It is possible for people to live by bread alone, but only so long as this physiological need remains unsatisfied. Once a need has been fulfilled, people move on to the next-higher-order need. A select few people, such as Albert Einstein and Eleanor Roosevelt, become "self-actualizers" or superior personalities. They live their lives by metaneeds, or B-values, that go beyond "motivation." They show themselves to be good choosers, and are more likely than average persons to have mystical, peak experiences.

Degrees of self-actualization have been measured by Shostrom's Personal Orientation Inventory. Maslow's utopia, Eupsychia, is an alternative to Skinner's Walden Two. In Eupsychia, organismic valuing processes ensure wise choices within the context of a psychologically supportive environment in which respect for individual freedom is maximized.

Humanistic psychologists have contributed to the study of personality by allowing individual human beings to speak for themselves about their experiences; by renewing interest in self-concepts; by viewing the self as a continuing process rather than a static trait; by trusting in people; by changing personality through caring human relationships; and by showing scientific openness and flexibility. The tendency toward actualization may be a universal phenomenon, present in all living systems and some nonliving systems. Higher-order values also show universal qualities, as evidenced by cross-cultural reports of peak experiences and generations-old spiritual "recipes for living." Limitations of humanistic psychology include the absence of a clear and explicit definition of personality; difficulties in operationally defining such concepts as "truth" and "beauty"; endorsement of the philosophical/historical concept of self; and an overreliance on conscious, self-reported experiences that may or may not correlate with perceptions and behaviors.

KEY CONCEPTS

Humanistic psychology
  Existential psychology
  Phenomenological approach
Rogers
  Person-centered theory
  Actualization
    Self-actualization
    Fully functioning person
    Organismic valuing
  Self
    Self-perceptions
    Actual self and ideal self
    Positive self-regard

Three conditions for personality growth and
    change
Q-sort technique
Maslow
  Self-actualization
  Hierarchy of five basic needs
    Deficiency needs (D-needs)
    Metaneeds (B-values)
  Self-actualizers
    Peak experiences
  Personal Orientation Inventory (POI)
  Eupsychia

REVIEW QUESTIONS

1. State how humanistic psychology differs from psychoanalysis and behavioral psychology in its assumptions and methods of investigation.

2. What is meant by the phenomenological approach to understanding people? How can it be achieved? What limitations does this approach have as a scientific method?

3. Discuss the relative importance of inner and environmental influences in Rogers' and Maslow's theories of self-actualization.

4. In what ways are Rogers' and Maslow's views of human motivation similar? How are they different? Evaluate their views about the role of organismic valuing in personality.

5. If you have not already done so, complete the exercise in Box 7.1. In what ways are your descriptions of your real self and your desired self alike? In what ways do they differ? Do you think your responses would have been different six months ago? A year ago? How might they be different a year from now? What do your answers to these questions indicate about your "self"?

6. Assess ways in which you are, and are not, a self-actualizing person. Justify your conclusions according to the theories of Rogers and Maslow.

8

Kelly's Constructs:
A Cognitive Theory of Personality

Do personologists think of themselves as different from the people they study?

Do you tend to see the world and its people along certain dimensions, such as good-bad, intelligent-stupid, and trustworthy-untrustworthy?

Do you think it would be possible to map out your personality in detail?

O NE OF the issues that has run through the theoretical points of view covered so far has been the relative importance of factors inside and outside of people for understanding their behaviors and personality. The psychoanalysts look mainly inside, the behaviorists look mainly outside, while the social-learning theorists consider both perspectives. In this chapter, we discuss a theory of personality that emphasizes an internal aspect, cognition, while not neglecting the external world.

Kelly, the Person

George Alexander Kelly (1905–1966) was born on a farm in rural Kansas, the son of a preacher. A rugged individualist, quite literally of pioneer stock, Kelly was skeptical of psychological principles from day one of his first psychology class. Sitting in the back row of the classroom, Kelly tilted his chair against the wall and waited for something interesting to occur (Kelly, 1969). Two or three weeks elapsed, during which time he derived only one clear impression: his professor seemed nice. Then one day he was inspired to sit up and take notice. A capital *S* and a capital *R* were prominently displayed on the blackboard, connected by an

GEORGE KELLY.
Kelly was a pioneer in what has become known as the cognitive revolution in psychology.

arrow pointing from the former to the latter. Here, thought Kelly, is the meat of the matter. However, further lectures only disappointed him. Many years laters, he wrote of the experience:

> Although I listened intently for several sessions, after that the most I could make of it was that the "S" was what you had to have in order to account for the "R" and the "R" was put there so the "S" would have something to account for. I never did find out what that arrow stood for—not to this day—and I have pretty well given up trying to figure it out. (1969, p. 47)

And he pretty well gave up on psychology, for the time being, choosing instead to pursue a career in engineering. Three years later, he was out of engineering and back in school, forced by the Great Depression to start over. Being interested in sociology and labor relations, he thought it high time to have a look at Freud. "I don't remember which one of Freud's books I was trying to read," he later wrote, "but I do remember the mounting feeling of incredulity that anyone could write such nonsense, much less publish it" (Kelly, 1969, p. 47). Skepticism thus characterized his second encounter with psychology—which, ironically, may explain why he became a psychologist. Kelly needed to practice his considerable gift for healthy skepticism, and psychology provided the perfect forum: all psychological principles seemed questionable.

Skepticism is sometimes accompanied by sarcasm, and indeed, Kelly provided a case in point. Called upon to cite examples of people who had failed to benefit from experience, Kelly recalled a naval officer with "a vast and versatile ignorance" and a school administrator who "had one year of experience—repeated thirteen times" (Kelly, 1963, p. 171).

If sarcasm was a characteristic of Kelly's, it was certainly overridden by a more central feature of his personality: Kelly was a warm and accepting person. He practiced therapy to help people and to learn from them. In 30 years as a psychotherapist, he never collected a penny for his services. George Thompson, a former colleague, wrote of this preacher's son:

> At the 1963 Convention of the American Psychological Association, some 40 former students of George Kelly attended a dinner to pay tribute to their good teacher and warm friend. These professors, scientists, and therapists came from all parts of the United States. All of them knew that here was a man who had helped them find their ways to more productive lives. Many others who could not attend wrote letters of appreciation for his wise counsel and guidance. (1968, pp. 22–23)

Similarly, in the summer of 1965, Kelly's associates at Ohio State University gathered to salute their colleague and friend, who had just been granted an endowed chair at Brandeis University. Papers were read by three of Kelly's former doctoral students and by a visiting professor from England, who had spread Kelly's ideas through several British universities. At the end of these presentations, Kelly rose to invite the entire assembly to his house for dinner. Nearly 100 accepted the gracious offer. Thompson wrote of the occasion:

> There was good food for all and a characteristic abundance of warm fellowship. The dinner [was] only a token to a man who had contributed so much, but [it] did reflect in modest measure the affectionate humanity of George Alexander Kelly—scholar, teacher, and warm friend. (1968, pp. 22–23)

Above all, Kelly was open-minded. Perhaps this aspect of his personality stemmed from his extreme versatility (or perhaps the open-mindedness was the cause and the versatility the effect). That versatility is best appreciated by reference to Kelly's own words:

> I had taught soap-box oratory in a labor college for labor organizers, government in an . . . institute for prospective citizens, public speaking for the American Bankers Association, and dramatics in a junior college . . . I had taken a Master's degree with a study of worker's use of leisure time, and an advanced professional degree in education at the University of Edinburgh, and . . . I had dabbled . . . in education, sociology, economics, labor relations, biometrics, speech pathology, and cultural anthropology, and had majored in psychology . . . for a grand total of nine months. (Kelly, 1969, p. 48)

Kelly's training in psychology yielded a Ph.D. from Iowa State University in 1931. While his early career was spent at Fort Hays State College in Kansas, Ohio State University claimed him for more years than any other academic institution.

This extraordinary versatility led him to a dozen or so universities, each for an appreciable period of time, and around the globe for the purpose of applying his theory to the problems of the world. Little wonder that he embraced the assumption, adopted by many philosophers of science and dismissed by none, that in the realm of science there are no truths (Hempel & Oppenheim, 1960). In psychology, as in other sciences, there are theories that are supported by evidence to varying degrees, all of which will someday be obsolete, but no truth. For a personologist, this was an unusual assumption, but then Kelly was an unusual personologist.

Kelly's View of the Person

As you recall, Freud thought of humans as helpless particles blown about by the hidden winds of hedonic impulse. Each person's behavior was seen as the effect of inaccessible and uncontrollable causes. Even worse, from the point of view of those who endorse freedom and individuality, in part Jung saw humans as pawns of their ancestors, each much like the other because of their common heritage. Adler and Horney saw people as the products of their social environments, and Skinner went one step further, proposing a utopia called Walden Two, where external forces control human action (see Chapters 4 and 5). Refreshingly, from the point of view of humanists and libertarians, Rogers and Maslow viewed humans as capable of determining their own fates (see Chapter 7). As usual, Kelly did not adopt the orientation of any of his predecessors. With characteristic flexibility, he declared that people are controlled by internal factors called personal *constructs* (for now, think of them as concepts). Constructs are "inside the head," but they are derived from consequences of an external factor, social relations (Kelly, 1955). Thus, for Kelly, people are determined from within and from without.

Kelly also believed that people have free will, in that they can choose from many alternative constructs that emerge from their relations with others. However, once a person has made her choices, her constructs become the master and she the slave — until she desires to exercise her right of choice once again.

The classical psychoanalysts were backward-looking—a person emerges creeping from the shadows of his past—as were the social psychoanalysts, to a lesser degree. The humanists focused on the recent past as well as rather large chunks of the present, and the behaviorists attended to minute pieces of the present, stimuli. Kelly endorsed none of these views. While he did not neglect the distant past, the recent past, or the present, he dismissed "stimuli" and declared humans to be basically future-oriented (Kelly, 1963). He thought that the behavior of people was determined largely by their predictions of future events.

Why did Kelly adopt such an intellectual, anti-unconscious, and anti-emotional point of view? He was an engineer, and a person made practical by the Great Depression. It was natural for him to be oriented to thinking rather than to feeling. As a victim of the Depression, it was little wonder that he looked to the future rather than to the dismal present. As a person who was constantly changing not only physical location, but self as well, he had little inclination to the past.

Perhaps Kelly's most important departure from the precepts of traditional personality psychology was that he saw himself as no different from those he studied and attempted to help in therapy (Kelly, 1969; for more about the inconsistent views of researchers and the people they study, see Allen, 1973, and Allen & Smith, 1980). Most psychologists, he charged, viewed themselves as objective, rational scientists who determine the causes of people's actions and suggest corrections for maladaptive behavior. On the other hand, their clients in therapy and their experimental subjects are seen as incapable of objective observation, unable to sort out the causes of their behavior, and inept at developing a systematic program for positive behavioral change. By contrast, Kelly saw himself as a scientist not only in his roles as experimental psychologist and psychotherapist, but also in his everyday life. Thus, since he was no different from others, clients, experimental subjects, and people in general were also viewed as scientists.

The best way to understand Kelly's belief that all of us operate as scientists on a day-to-day basis is to consider Kelly's recollection of how he discovered "people as scientists."

> A typical afternoon might find me talking to a graduate student at one o'clock, doing all those familiar things that thesis directors have to do: encouraging the student to pinpoint the issues, to observe, to become intimate with the problem, to form hypotheses . . . to make some preliminary test runs, to relate his data to his predictions, to control his experiments so that he will know what led to what, to generalize cautiously, and to revise his thinking in the light of experience. At two o'clock I might have an appointment with a client. During this interview I would not be taking the role of the scientist, but rather helping the distressed person work out some solutions to his life's problems. So what would I do? Why, I would try to get him to pinpoint the issues, to observe, to become intimate with the problem, to form hypotheses, to make test runs, to relate outcomes to anticipations, to control his ventures so that he will know what led to what, to generalize cautiously, and to revise his dogma in the light of experience.
>
> At three o'clock I would see [the] student again. Likely as not he was either dragging his feet, hoping to design some worldshaking experiment before looking at his first subject to see firsthand what he was dealing with, or plunging into some massive illconsidered data-chasing expedition. So I would try to

> get him to [do] all the things that I had [tried to get him] to do at one o'clock. At four o'clock another client! Guess what! He would be dragging his feet, hoping to design a completely new personality before venturing his first change in behavior, or plunging into some illconsidered acting-out escapade, etc., etc. (Kelly, 1969, pp. 60–61)

Kelly had what the Freudians would call "insight." Of course, he was acting as a scientist, and so was the student, when they were discussing the student's research. However, he was also a scientist as he worked with his distressed client. And what was he doing? He was getting the client to be a better scientist. Thus, students doing research, their advisors, clients in psychotherapy, their psychotherapists, and "people on the street" behaving on a day-to-day basis all act as scientists. Each tries to pinpoint the issues relevant to his problem, make observations of the people involved in the problem, become intimate with the problem, form hypotheses, make test runs, relate outcomes of the test runs to predictions of the future, control his pursuits so he will know what led to what, generalize cautiously, and revise strongly held beliefs in the light of experience. For Kelly, people are scientists—all of them, all of the time.

Basic Concepts: Kelly

PERSONALITY AS A SYSTEM OF CONSTRUCTS

constructs

Underlying all of Kelly's thinking is the notion of personal constructs. *Constructs* are ways of construing, or "seeing," the world. The individual's personality consists of an organized system of more or less important constructs. This idea of constructs became the foundation upon which Kelly built his "fundamental postulate." A *postulate* is a basic assumption that is the starting point for a theory. It is a broad statement that is just accepted; it cannot be directly tested. Kelly's *fundamental postulate* is as follows: a person's processes are psychologically channelized by the ways in which he or she anticipates events (Kelly, 1963). The channels, or pathways, are that person's constructs. These ways of "seeing the world" provide the basis for predictions about the future. The predictions, in turn, pull the person along through life. Thus, people are not pushed by unconscious impulses and drives, or pricked into action by stimuli in the environment, but are guided by future-oriented constructs.

fundamental postulate

To set the stage for Kelly's other theoretical concepts, let's build on the notion of constructs by looking at how two individuals, Jim and Joan, go about a day in their lives. As you read, pay special attention to the words in italics.

Jim's problem.   "What's wrong now?" Joan inquired, as she approached a figure who was slumped against the wall outside a classroom. Jim's reply was inaudible, partly because his hands covered his face and partly because he was too depressed to speak up.

Undeterred by the lack of a response to her question, Joan continued, "Let me guess . . . it's Professor Martindale again."

Jim's head sprang upright. Though his hair cascaded over his eyes and nose, it failed to hide the fierce look that dominated his face. "Damn it!" he was nearly screaming. "I've tried everything. I give up."

Joan looked around self-consciously, hoping that, somehow, students passing them in the hall had not noticed the outburst. Then she eased down next to her friend. Softly she entreated, "Tell me about it."

"It's the same thing . . . same old thing," he muttered.

Joan leaned back against the wall and exclaimed with a sigh, "OK, then, tell me about your latest clash with Martindale."

"He hates me, I'm sure of it. The jerk said we could turn our papers in late, if we had a good excuse. Well, I had a good excuse. It was spring break . . . I was stuck in Florida . . . we were in somebody else's car. I mean, how could I get home?"

Joan's chin drew back and down. A familiar frown curled her lips. Martindale had looked the same when Jim had first related the "stuck in Florida" story. It was that incredulous look.

Jim's constructs. "See there, see there," rasped Jim. "You're no different. I thought I could expect some sympathy from you . . . you're supposed to be a *good friend,* someone with a little *intelligence.* Go away . . . just get lost."

Joan moved closer and slipped her arm around Jim's shoulders, but he elbowed her away. "Jim, you know you can *trust* me . . . I am your *good friend,* but gimme a break. I know you believe that your excuse is OK . . . let me just put it this way . . . try it on some other people; I'll bet you get the same reaction."

There was silence for a minute, then Joan continued. "Look, let me make a suggestion. Why don't you—"

"That's not all!" Jim broke in. This time he was shouting. Joan was looking for a place to hide. "He laughed at me! . . . said he was just kidding about the excuse. 'I don't take excuses. The other students know that . . . it was just my way of making a joke . . . a little irony, you know.' Does he ever think I'm *stupid!* He probably thinks he couldn't *trust* me farther than he could throw me. And I thought *educated* people were *good* people. Well, you live and learn. I'll know better next time."

Joan's suggestions for change. "That's what you said the last time you had it out with him." Joan could sense the taste of foot-in-the-mouth the minute she uttered the words. Jim climbed to his feet. He'd had enough of her, but before he could get away, Joan grabbed his shirt sleeve and dragged him back down. "Look, I'm sorry," she pleaded, "but it's just that . . . sometimes it seems as if you don't learn from *experience.* I mean you just stick with an old idea, no matter what. Why is it so important that Martindale like you? I don't care whether he likes me or not."

After a time, Jim settled down and began to chatter amiably with his friend, which was usual for them. They talked about Jim's relationship with Martindale. "OK, you win," asserted Joan, "so you have some kind of fixation for Martindale —father figure is what my psych teacher would say—OK, I accept that. Now let me give you a suggestion . . . try this out. I mean, you've had plenty of time to *evaluate* him. You think he's one of the '*good* guys,' right?" Jim shook his head in a vigorous "no" sign, but Joan ignored him. "What you have to do is let him know you think he belongs in select company. I mean . . . as I see it . . . you expect him to think you're a 'good guy,' but you won't put him in that same category. I know how you are. Surely you can understand that people like those who like

In her responses to Jim's statements, Joan exemplifies Kelly's notion of people-as-scientists. She tries to make sense of Jim and at the same time tries to make him a better "scientist" by challenging his construction system.

them . . . it's sort of a law. But they can't read your mind. You have to communicate your feelings to people! If I know you, you've been very stiff and formal with Martindale. Am I right?"

Jim's head was hanging down. "Yeah," he mumbled, "you do know me."

"Actually, what it amounts to," Joan was talking rapidly now, "is you think he's a 'good guy,' you *admire* him, and you want him to *admire* you. I know, because, if I like someone, I want that somebody to throw a little admiration my way."

"Admire?" You could almost see the question mark on Jim's face. "*Trust* maybe, but admire? I don't resort to hero worship."

"Well you better consider '*admiration.*' If you like someone, admiration is a way to communicate it without saying anything . . . I mean, without using words . . . the sound of your voice will do."

"All right," said Jim, almost in a whisper, "I'll try it."

Joan's construction system.   Now Jim hopped up and offered Joan a hand. They left the building and strolled along leisurely toward their dorms. Neither said anything for a while, then Jim remarked in a calm and collected voice, "You know, sometimes I wonder who I am. Who am I, anyway?" He was smiling as he posed the question.

"*Good* ole Jim, that's who you are," came the reply. "A little weird, but fun to be around."

He shoved her playfully. "OK, who are you, smarty?"

"Is that a serious question?"

"Yeah," he mocked, "who are you?"

"Well, I don't think about it all day, but I guess I'd answer in terms of who I'm *like*."

"And who is that?" asked Jim in a sober voice, adopted to match her own suddenly serious tone.

"I guess I'm an *athlete* at heart," mused Joan, who was a member of the varsity track team. "Chris Evert, that's who I'm like . . . or uh . . . who I'd like to be."

"Tough break," kidded Jim. "You haven't the legs for it."

Joan went along with the teasing and added, "Nor do I have the ability . . . but who knows, maybe I'll get better and maybe track will be as big as tennis someday."

They reached the crossing that split the paths to their dorms and paused for a moment. "Big bash at the Hillside Haven this Saturday . . . need a ride?"

"No thanks," responded Joan, as she backed down the path to her dorm. "I'm going home . . . back to God's country . . . down on the farm . . . with the *good* neighbors and the wide open spaces—"

"And the horse manure," interjected Jim in a loud voice, as they were now many yards apart.

She lobbed a rock at him. "You can have your stinking old city, full of dopers and muggers. You love it . . . I'm going back where everything is small and people are concerned . . . ," her voice trailed off.

Jim's and Joan's personalities.   Let's analyze Jim's and Joan's conversation from Kelly's point of view. A look at Figure 8.1 will allow you to examine some concrete examples of constructs (Kelly disliked the concrete, but couldn't avoid it). The figure displays Jim's and Joan's construction systems. A *construction system* is an organization of constructs having the more important constructs at the top and the less important ones at the bottom. The constructs at the top are called *superordinate,* while the ones at the bottom are called *subordinate.* The construction system is the individual's personality. construction system

Jim's most superordinate construct is represented by *trust-distrust,* while Joan's most superordinate construct is represented by *evaluative-descriptive.* To evaluate is to pass judgment on; to describe is merely to label someone or something. As Kelly (1963) readily acknowledged, constructs are like concepts. However, a construct is a special kind of concept. Constructs have two opposite poles, like a magnet. The *emergent pole* is the primary and principal end, like *good* in *good-bad* and *intelligent* in *intelligent-unintelligent* (Kelly, 1955). The *implicit pole* is the contrasting end, like *uneducated* in *educated-uneducated* and *urban* in *rural-urban.* The emergent pole is usually formed first, but as soon as it forms, the implicit pole also comes into existence. According to Kelly, people see the world in terms of contrasts: every thing or being has an opposite. The contrasts are there, even if a person adopts a construct such as *tolerant-intolerant* and has never ex-

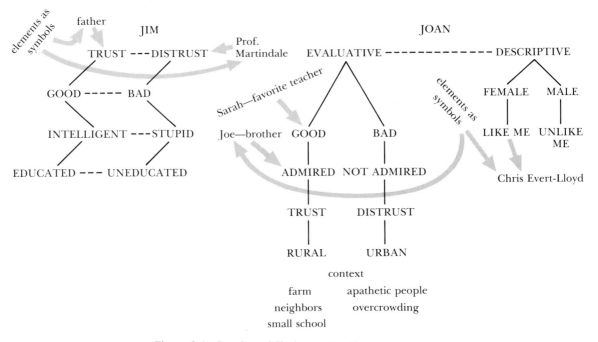

Figure 8.1 Joan's and Jim's construction systems.

pressed or is unaware of the implicit pole, *intolerant*. Adopting *tolerant* automatically carries *intolerant* with it.

It may have occurred to you that these examples of Kelly's constructs resemble the traits presented in Chapter 1. Figure 8.2 shows Jim's and Joan's constructs arranged into the behavioral dimensions corresponding to traits that were displayed in the initial chapter. You can see that Kelly's constructs are similar to behavioral dimensions. Although Kelly himself might balk at placing constructs in the trait category, it seems reasonable to so place them, as long as we don't forget

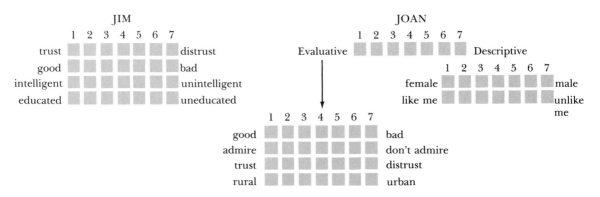

Figure 8.2 Jim's and Joan's construction systems adapted to dimensions.

that Kelly had a unique way of addressing behavioral dimensions and corresponding traits.

Armed with these concepts, it is now possible to begin the analysis of Jim and Joan. It is easy to see that Jim is highly dependent on the construct *trust-distrust,* his most superordinate construct. It has what Kelly calls a wide range of convenience. The *range of convenience* of a construct refers to the limited category of events to which it can be applied. For example, *trust-distrust* is applicable to events involving people, such as the events of Jim's conflict with Professor Martindale. It is hardly applicable to solving mathematical problems or viewing architecture. A construct's *range of focus,* on the other hand, refers to the events to which it is most readily applied. *Trust-distrust* is more readily applied to relations with people to whom Jim feels close than to relations with more casual acquaintances.

range of convenience

range of focus

Notice also that Jim's construct *trust-distrust* is relatively impermeable. *Impermeable* constructs tend not to change, in terms of range of convenience or place in the construction system. In fact, Joan noted that Jim's constructs are impermeable in general (remember, she said that he didn't learn from experience).

impermeable constructs

Trust-distrust is also part of Joan's system, but it is much more subordinate. Thus, there is commonality between the construction systems of Jim and Joan, but there is also individuality. *Commonality* refers to the sharing of constructs by two or more people whose experiences are similar. Jim and Joan are both students, and Figure 8.1 reveals that they do share constructs. *Individuality* refers to differences among construction systems, both in terms of constructs and in terms of how the constructs are organized according to differences in experiences. Joan is an athlete; Jim is not.

commonality

individuality

Jim's problem, as Joan pointed out, is that he has failed to learn from experience. *Experience* is what one learns from the events of the past. Jim continues to try the same old strategies with Professor Martindale, and they are not getting him what he wants, mutual trust. Thus, Joan suggests a change in Jim's construction system. She thinks that Jim should embrace a new construct, *admire-not admire,* and reorganize his construction system to be more like hers, with *trust-distrust* subordinated to *admire-not admire.*

Joan is trying to save Jim from his anxieties. For Kelly, *anxiety* occurs when a person's construction system does not apply to critical events, as Jim's fails to apply to his relationship with Professor Martindale. Joan should be cautious. In suggesting the new construct *admire-not admire,* she may cause her friend to become fearful. *Fear* occurs when a new construct appears to be entering the system and may become dominating. On the other hand, she needn't worry too much about threatening Jim. *Threat* refers to the possibility that a person's entire construction system will be overhauled (Kelly, 1955). Joan is suggesting a new construct and some reorganization, not a major upheaval.

Joan as scientific psychotherapist.   Joan the psychotherapist is acting like a scientist in attempting to make a better scientist of Jim. She pleads with him to make his constructs more permeable. More important, she suggests a hypothesis for Jim to test. She feels that expressing admiration will allow Jim to obtain the mutual trust that he wants in his relationship with Professor Martindale. To test the hypothesis, Jim is told to try admiration out on Martindale. He is then to observe to see how it works. If admiration has the intended effect, he is to replicate. *Replication* is repeating a test in the hope the results will be the same. Replication provides the basis for anticipating future events. If one can repeat an observation of the successful application of a construct, one can be confident that the construct will apply in the future under similar circumstances. The greater the number of replications, the greater the confidence.

constructive
alternativism

If Jim carries out Joan's suggestions, he will be acting according to one of Kelly's most basic principles: constructive alternativism. *Constructive alternativism* is the assumption that a person's present interpretations of his life situation are subject to revision and replacement (Kelly, 1963). It is assumed that a construction system cannot remain the same, but must change with changes in the person's life situation.

RELATIONS AMONG CONSTRUCTS

extension of the
cleavage line

abstraction
across the
cleavage line

Looking back at Figure 8.1, the different organizations of Jim's and Joan's construction systems can be appreciated. Jim's system is organized by extension of the cleavage line. *Extension of the cleavage line* refers to the fact that the poles of Jim's subordinate constructs fall directly under the corresponding emergent and implicit poles of his superordinate constructs—for example, *good* falls under *trust, bad* under *distrust* (Kelly, 1963). However, Joan's system begins at the top by abstracting across the cleavage line of her most superordinate construct, *evaluative-descriptive*. In *abstraction across the cleavage line,* whole constructs fall under emergent and implicit poles. The whole construct *good-bad* falls under the emergent pole *evaluative,* while the whole construct *female-male* falls under the implicit pole *descriptive*. This feature of Joan's system makes it more complex and flexible than Jim's. She can approach her life situation from an evaluative stance (there are good people and bad people) or from a purely descriptive stance (there are North Americans and Europeans).

context

The *context* of a construct is composed of all those elements to which the construct applies. *Elements* are objects, beings, or events. The context of Joan's construct *rural-urban* includes the elements farm, neighbors, apathetic people, and overcrowding. Whereas range of convenience and focus of convenience refer to rather gross and abstract circumstances, such as "relations with people" and "eating habits," context and elements refer to the actual, concrete things or people that exist in a person's life circumstance.

A *symbol* is one of the emergent elements to which a concept applies that is used as the name of the construct. Figure 8.1 indicates that, for Jim, "father" symbolizes the *trust-distrust* construct. For Joan, "Chris Evert-Lloyd" symbolizes the construct *like me-unlike me.*

Of course, the picture of Jim and Joan as indicated in their conversation and in Figure 8.1 is oversimplified. Kelly would argue that no one's personality could be neatly represented in a figure. For one thing, the figure would have to be as large as a house, and for another, many constructs are too abstract to be represented as concretely as in Figure 8.1. Also, people normally don't blurt out their constructs as cooperatively as did Joan and Jim. More sophisticated methods of getting at constructs are considered in the Applications section of this chapter.

PERSONALITY DEVELOPMENT

You may have wondered how Jim and Joan acquired their construct systems. That is, how did Jim and Joan develop their respective personalities? Kelly's comments about the transition from childhood to adulthood complements his theory nicely, as we shall see.

Predictability.   Because anticipation of future events is the foundation of Kelly's theory, it is not surprising that when Kelly discusses the development of constructs in children, a prominent consideration is predictability. *Predictability* refers to the ability to accurately anticipate the future. A construct is as useful as the degree of predictability it provides. Thus, parents, the major components of every child's environment, are well advised to provide predictability. If they fail to do so, then their child's need for predictability may be reflected in some rather extreme behavior (Kelly, 1955). If predictability is a scarce commodity in a child's life, the child may cling to instances of it, even if the resultant behavior has negative consequences.

predictability

As an illustration, assume that a child, Johnny, has parents who treat him in a consistent manner only with regard to a few issues, all involving punishment. Johnny cleans his room: sometimes it is noticed, sometimes not. Johnny helps fold clothes: sometimes he is praised, and other times he is scolded for making a mess of the laundry. However, Johnny has noticed that should he stop up the bathroom sink while playing "laundry," the consequent overflow brings a highly reliable reaction from his parents: they apply a hairbrush to his bottom, and it hurts. So, a behaviorist might say, Johnny will avoid stopping up the sink. Not so, Kelly would say. Stopping up the sink is the best way to ensure the precious predictability that Johnny so badly needs. Imagine the parents' puzzlement (not to mention the behaviorist's).

Dependency constructs.   Even with a reasonable amount of predictability in a child's social environment, early construction systems will still be characterized by impermeability of the few simple constructs that compose the systems. Children are small, weak, and vulnerable. For survival, they must depend on others. Thus, a child's early construction system often consists mainly of *dependency constructs* — special constructs that revolve around the child's survival needs. A *mother* construct would be an example. For a young child, the *mother* construct might have a context containing elements such as warmth, safety from frightening sounds, nourishment, and so forth. At first, the child might see the world in terms of *like mother/not like mother*. The construct is global, and mother is seen in a very restricted manner. The university classes she teaches and the chamber of commerce committees she chairs play no role in the child's conception of her. She is warmth, comfort, and food. However, with growth and development, the construct will become more permeable, and she will be seen less restrictively. In time, the entire construct will likely disappear altogether, and "mother" will become a symbol for some other construct or an element of several constructs. The general disposition to impermeability of constructs dissolves in the tide of ever-increasing maturation.

dependency
constructs

Role playing.   The relationship with the mother is but the beginning of a long line of relationships that will extend throughout life. The extent to which a person can appreciate the construction system of another person is the extent to which the person can play a role in the relationship with that other person (Kelly, 1963). Playing a *role* means behaving in ways that meet the expectations of important other people in one's life.

role playing

In turn, this type of behavior provides the predictability that people require. Thus, a child may assume a role, face-to-face with his or her parents, as the passive, compliant child who is "seen but not heard." If she behaves in a passive, compliant, quiet manner, she predicts that she will be fed, cuddled, provided with toys, and so on. At least during childhood, the hypothetical child's assumed role may work out fine, provided she correctly perceives that her predictions are confirmed. However, let's assume that all does not go so well. Perhaps her observations are faulty—she is seeing confirmation of her predictions where there is none. Sooner or later, she will have to stop deluding herself. Eventually, she will have to face up to the fact that her parents don't really want a passive, compliant, quiet child. Perhaps in "reality" they expect her to play the role of the assertive, active, independent child. The outcome of such a revelation would be guilt. *Guilt* results from a person's perception of being dislodged from some critical role, one that was thought to be very important in relating to important people. In more common terms, guilt comes from not measuring up, not being one's parent's child, not fitting the mold that important others have sculptured for oneself. In the last analysis, guilt results from the failure of people to accurately "read" the construction systems of other people. Perhaps Kelly would admit that people need Rogers' empathy.

Supporting Evidence

Support for Kelly's theory has been hard to come by, perhaps because of the nature of the theory: it is a tight logical system incorporating numerous abstract concepts, none of which is easy to translate into testable terms. Also, since each person's construction system is different from that of every other person, how does one use a sample of persons to make generalizations about construction systems? Nevertheless, there are some studies that seem to support Kelly's theory —in particular, the concept of poles.

POLES

Kelly (1963) indicates that a critical testable aspect of his theory is the assumption that people cast their worlds in terms of opposites. Kelly's entire theory is built on the supposition that each construct has two poles. If that supposition could be destroyed by evidence, the theory would fall. Predictions of the future would all fail if constructs took the form *all people are good,* rather than *some people are good/some people are bad.* In the former case, in fact, there would be nothing to predict. Life would be one certainty after another.

Accordingly, Kelly (1963) placed heavy emphasis on some work by William H. Lyle, a former student. Lyle first selected some words that appeared to belong to the categories *cheerful-sad, broad-minded/narrow minded, refined-vulgar,* and *sincere-insincere.* A pilot sample of subjects was then told to place the words into eight different classes represented by the eight words. This procedure provided a basis for accuracy scores in the main study. Main-study subjects were given the same words and told to place them into eight classes (plus a ninth, "don't know" class). They were given a point for "correct responses" each time they placed a word in the same class as did the pilot subjects. Thus, each main-study subject had eight accuracy scores, one for each of the eight word classes. Then, a method called *factor analysis* was used on the accuracy scores to see which word classes clustered together. (Factor analysis is discussed in Chapter 9.) Results revealed five clusters, or factors—one for "general intelligence" and four others exactly matching the original four categories. Subjects tended to lump together "cheerful" with "sad" words and "sincere" with "insincere" words. If they made classification mistakes with "refined" words, they made mistakes with "vulgar" words as well. In short, they classed or organized the words into sets of opposites, just as constructs are organized and just as Kelly would expect.

COGNITIVE COMPLEXITY

An additional source of supporting evidence was provided by another of Kelly's former students, James Bieri. Bieri (1955) defined a new dimension, cognitive complexity/cognitive simplicity. A *cognitively complex* person has a construction system containing constructs that are clearly differentiated—that is, distinguished one from the other. Complex people, having a differentiated construction system, cast other people into many categories and thus see much variety in people. *Cognitively simple* people, on the other hand, have a construction system in which the distinction among constructs is blurred—a poorly differentiated system. They cast other people into a few, or perhaps only two, categories. Thus, a very cognitively simple person would mainly use one construct, such as *good-bad,* lumping half of humanity into the *good* class and the other half into the *bad* class. Bieri (1955) showed that cognitively simple people have difficulty seeing differences between themselves and others (they tend to assume that others are pretty much like themselves), while complex people can draw sharp distinctions between themselves and others. Kelly (1955) has indicated that the more constructs one has the better one will be at predicting future events, including the behavior of other persons. Bieri (1955) confirmed this assumption. He found that complex subjects are better at predicting the behavior of others. A person who uses mainly one construct, say *good-bad,* is likely to put himself in the *good* class and, given little information about other persons (which were the conditions of Bieri's experiment) will predict "They are good, like me." Complex persons have many constructs available, some for application to themselves and some reserved for application to the many other people in their life situations. Table 8.1 summarizes the characteristics of cognitively complex and cognitively simple people.

cognitive complexity

cognitive simplicity

Over the years, other researchers have used the complex-simple dimension to provide support for Kelly's theory. For example, Signell (1966) reported that from 9 to 16 years of age, children tend to increase in cognitive complexity. Sechrest and Jackson (1961) found that social intelligence, an index of social effectiveness, was strongly related to cognitive complexity. More recently, Linville (1982) reported the following results: (1) College students showed more com-

TABLE 8.1   The Complex-Simple Dimension

Cognitively complex person	Cognitively simple person
Maintains a clear distinction among constructs	Distinction among constructs blurred
Casts others into many categories	Casts others into few categories
Can easily see differences between self and others	Has difficulty seeing differences between self and others
Skilled at predicting behaviors of others	Inept at predicting behaviors of others

plexity in their descriptions of their own age group than of an older age group. (2) People who were more simple in their representations of older males were extreme in their evaluation of older males. (3) Individuals who were induced to adopt a simple orientation toward food used in a study of taste gave more extreme evaluations than did those induced to adopt a more complex orientation. (4) Young males gave older males more extreme evaluations than they gave to members of their own age group.

Applications

REP test

Kelly's theory has implications for two important kinds of application: assessment and therapy. In this section, we review his Role Construct Repertory (REP) test (1955), an assessment device designed to reveal an individual's construction system. Then we look at how constructs might be changed through fixed-role therapy.

THE REP TEST

We had "Joan" fill out the REP test. Before going on, read the instructions to Box 8.1 and then follow the responses Joan wrote into Figures A and B. Afterward, you can test yourself.

BOX 8.1   *The Role Construct Repertory Test*
(Adapted from Kelly, 1955)

Figure A, below, lists 15 role definitions. Read each definition carefully. In each blank, write the first name of the person who best fits that role in your life. It is essential to use the role definitions as given in Figure A. If you cannot remember the name of the person, put down a word or brief phrase that will bring the person to mind. Do *not* repeat any names; if some person has already been listed, simply make a second choice. Thus, next to the word "Self" write your own name. Then next to the word "Mother" put your mother's name (or the person who has played

continued

BOX 8.1
continued

the part of a mother in your life), and so on, until all 15 roles have been designated with a specific individual.

Figure A   Definition of Roles for Demonstration

1. *Self:* Yourself _____Joan_____
2. *Mother:* Your mother or the person who has played the part of a mother in your life. _____Sandra_____
3. *Father:* Your father or the person who has played the part of a father in your life. _____Michael_____
4. *Brother:* Your brother who is nearest your own age, or if you do not have a brother, a boy near your own age who has been most like a brother to you. _____Joe_____
5. *Sister:* Your sister who is nearest your own age or, if you do not have a sister, a girl near your own age who has been the most like a sister to you. _____Sue_____
6. *Spouse:* Your wife (or husband) or, if you are not married, your closest present girl (boy) friend. _____Ed_____
7. *Pal:* Your closest present friend of the same sex as yourself. _____Ronda_____
8. *Ex-Pal:* A person of the same sex as yourself whom you once thought was a close friend of yours but in whom you were badly disappointed later. _____Sharon_____
9. *Rejecting Person:* A person with whom you have been associated, who, for some unexplained reason, appears to dislike you. _____Howard_____
10. *Pitied Person:* The person whom you would most like to help or for whom you feel most sorry. _____Ronald_____
11. *Threatening Person:* The person who threatens you the most or the person who makes you feel the most uncomfortable. _____Sally_____
12. *Attractive Person:* A person whom you have recently met whom you would like to know better. _____Paula_____
13. *Accepted Teacher:* The teacher who influenced you most. _____Sarah_____
14. *Rejected Teacher:* The teacher whose point of view you have found most objectionable. _____Donald_____
15. *Happy Person:* The happiest person whom you know personally. _____Al_____

Now look at the first row of the matrix in Figure B. Note that there are circles in the squares under columns 9, 10, and 12. These circles designate the three people whom you are to consider in Sort No. 1 (Rejecting Person, Pitied Person, and Attractive Person). Think about these three people. In particular, how are *two of them alike* in some important way that *differentiates them from the third person?* When you have decided the most important way that two of them are alike but different from the third person, put an *X* in the two circles that correspond to the two persons who are alike. Do not write anything in the third circle; leave it blank. Next, write a word or short phrase that tells how the two people are alike in the column marked "Emergent Pole." Then, in the column marked "Implicit Pole," write a word or short phrase that explains the way the third person is different

continued

BOX 8.1
continued

from the other two. Finally, consider each of the remaining 12 persons and think about which of these, in addition to the ones you have already marked with an *X*, also have the characteristic you have designated under "Emergent Pole." Place an *X* in the square corresponding to the name of each of the other persons who has this characteristic. When you have finished this procedure for the first row, go to the second row (Sort No. 2). The process should be repeated until the procedure has been carried out for each of the rows. In summary, the steps to be followed for each row (Sort) are:

1. Consider the three people who are designated by circles under their names. Decide how two of them are alike in some important way, and different from the third.
2. Put an *X* in the circles corresponding to the two people who are alike; leave the remaining circle blank.
3. In the "Emergent Pole" column, write a brief description of the way the two people are *alike*.
4. In the "Implicit Pole" column, write a brief description of the way the third person is *different* from the two who are alike.
5. Consider the remaining 12 persons, and place an *X* in the squares corresponding to those who can also be characterized by the description in the "Emergent Pole" column.
6. Repeat steps 1 through 5 for each row of the matrix.

Column headers: 1 Self, 2 Mother, 3 Father, 4 Brother, 5 Sister, 6 Spouse, 7 Pal, 8 Ex-Pal, 9 Rejecting Person, 10 Pitied Person, 11 Threatening Person, 12 Attractive Person, 13 Accepted Teacher, 14 Rejected Teacher, 15 Happy Person

Sort Number	1	2	3	4	5	6	7	8	9	10	11	12	13	14	15	EMERGENT POLE	IMPLICIT POLE
1									⊗	○		⊗				Admired	Not Admired
2		○	⊗	⊗												Trust	Distrust
3				○								⊗		⊗		Like Me	Not Like Me
4		○				⊗						⊗				Strong	Weak
5	⊗									○		⊗				Rural	Urban
6				○				⊗					⊗			Capable	Incapable
7			○			⊗			⊗							Female	Male
8					⊗					○				⊗		Cheerful	Sad
9					⊗	○					⊗					Interesting	Uninteresting
10	⊗			⊗	○											Good	Bad
11		⊗	○							⊗						Talkative	Quiet
12					⊗	○					⊗					Athletic	Unathletic
13	⊗				⊗	○										Calm	Anxious
14	⊗	○	⊗													Invulnerable	Vulnerable
15				⊗				○					⊗			Ambitious	Unambitious

Figure B

continued

BOX 8.1
continued

Let's briefly consider Joan's responses. First she completed Figure A. There Joan listed important persons in her life who fit such categories as Father, Pal, Rejecting Person, Attractive Person, and Accepting Teacher. Next, she completed the "sorts" indicated in the matrix shown in Figure B. She used the circles marked in each row to compare among different individuals. In Sort #1 Joan compared Rejecting Person, Pitied Person, and Attractive Person and indicated which two were most alike. Her *X*s show that she sees her Rejecting Person (Howard) and her Attractive Person (Paula) as more alike than other possible combinations of the three people.

For each sort, Joan was asked to write a word or phrase under "Emergent Pole" that describes how the two similar people are alike. Then she was to place a word or phrase under "Implicit Pole" to represent how the third person is different from the two similar individuals. Joan's entries for Sort #1 demonstrate that, for her, Howard and Paula are alike in being admired, while her Pitied Person (Ronald) is different from the other two in being not admired. Similarly, in Sort #4, Joan found that her Ex-Pal (Sharon) and her Accepted Teacher (Sarah) were alike in being strong, while Mother (Sandra) was seen as weak. Any additional *X*s Joan might have put in a given row would have indicated other persons who fit the label assigned to the emergent pole for that row. Taken together, Joan's responses for all the sorts reveal her construction system.

Now that you've run through Joan's responses, complete the REP test yourself. An extra form has been included for that purpose (in Box 8.2). If you follow the instructions carefully, you will master the test, and, more importantly, gain some insight. You will disclose your own construction system.

Figure A lists 15 role definitions. Read each definition carefully. In each blank, write the first name of the person who best fits that role in your life. It is essential to use the role definitions as given in Figure A. If you cannot remember the name of the person, put down a word or brief phrase that will bring the person to mind. Do *not* repeat any names; if some person has already been listed, simply make a second choice. Thus, next to the word "Self" write your own name. Then next to the word "Mother" put your mother's name (or the person who has played the part of a mother in your life), and so on, until all 15 roles have been designated with a specific individual.

Figure A   Definition of Roles for Demonstration

1. *Self:* Yourself _____
2. *Mother:* Your mother or the person who has played the part of a mother in your life. _____

continued

BOX 8.2
continued

3. *Father:* Your father or the person who has played the part of a father in your life. _____

4. *Brother:* Your brother who is nearest your own age, or if you do not have a brother, a boy near your own age who has been most like a brother to you. _____

5. *Sister:* Your sister who is nearest your own age or, if you do not have a sister, a girl near your own age who has been the most like a sister to you. _____

6. *Spouse:* Your wife (or husband) or, if you are not married, your closest present girl (boy) friend. _____

7. *Pal:* Your closest present friend of the same sex as yourself. _____

8. *Ex-Pal:* A person of the same sex as yourself whom you once thought was a close friend of yours but in whom you were badly disappointed later. _____

9. *Rejecting Person:* A person with whom you have been associated, who, for some unexplained reason, appears to dislike you. _____

10. *Pitied Person:* The person whom you would most like to help or for whom you feel most sorry. _____

11. *Threatening Person:* The person who threatens you the most or the person who makes you feel the most uncomfortable. _____

12. *Attractive Person:* A person whom you have recently met whom you would like to know better. _____

13. *Accepted Teacher:* The teacher who influenced you most. _____

14. *Rejected Teacher:* The teacher whose point of view you have found most objectionable. _____

15. *Happy Person:* The happiest person whom you know personally. _____

Now look at the first row of the matrix in Figure B. Note that there are circles in the squares under columns 9, 10, and 12. These circles designate the three people whom you are to consider in Sort No. 1 (Rejecting Person, Pitied Person, and Attractive Person). Think about these three people. In particular, how are *two of them alike* in some important way that *differentiates them from the third person?* When you have decided the most important way that two of them are alike but different from the third person, put an "X" in the two circles that correspond to the two persons who are alike. Do not write anything in the third circle; leave it blank. Next, write a word or short phrase that tells how the two people are alike, in the column marked "Emergent Pole." Then, in the column marked "Implicit Pole," write a word or short phrase that explains the way the third person is different from the other two. Finally, consider each of the remaining 12 persons and think about which of these, in addition to the ones you have already marked with an *X*, also have the characteristic you have designated under the "Emergent Pole." Place an *X* in the square corresponding to the name of each of the other persons who has this characteristic. When you have finished this procedure for the first row, go to the second row (Sort No. 2). The process should be repeated until

continued

the procedure has been carried out for each of the rows. In summary, the steps to be followed for each row (Sort) are:

1. Consider the three people who are designated by circles under their names. Decide how two of them are alike in some important way, and different from the third.
2. Put an *X* in the circles corresponding to the two people who are alike; leave the remaining circle blank.
3. In the "Emergent Pole" column, write a brief description of the way the two people are *alike*.
4. In the "Implicit Pole" column, write a brief description of the way the third person is *different* from the two who are alike.
5. Consider the remaining 12 persons, and place an *X* in the squares corresponding to those who can also be characterized by the description in the "Emergent Pole" column.
6. Repeat steps 1 through 5 for each row of the matrix.

BOX 8.2
continued

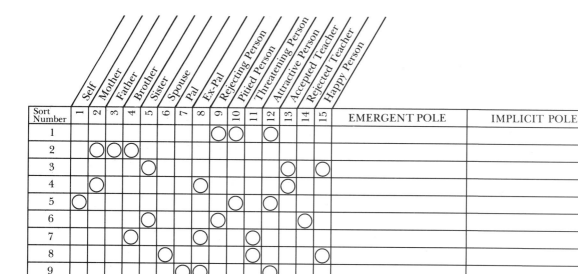

Figure B

FIXED-ROLE THERAPY

fixed-role
therapy

Now that you have gotten some idea of your own construction system, you may wonder "How could I change it for the better?" Kelly might suggest *fixed-role therapy.* In *fixed-role therapy,* a client plays the role of an imaginary character having a construction system that, if permanently adopted, would be ideally suited to the client (Kelly, 1955). The therapist uses the client's actual construction system as a basis for creating the character with the ideal construction system and then suggests that the client learn and enact the script for the character. The client should actually be involved in "writing the script." In any case, the character should be basically similar to the client, with a construction system that incorporates the client's positive aspects but includes substitutes for negative aspects. The realistic goal would not be wholesale change, but a beneficial alteration of the client's construction system after much experience with the role. Colleague James Joyce (personal communication, 1984), who used fixed-role therapy while a student of Kelly, indicates that the method is useful for enriching the social aspects of construction systems possessed by clients who are inept at relating to others.

| BOX 8.3 | *Fixed-Role Therapy* |

Try writing your own script. First, reexamine your REP test results. Next, decide what you like about your system and what you feel could stand improvement. Then, write the script for your ideal, imaginary character, incorporating your positive aspects and substituting for negative aspects. It's a good idea to give your character a fictitious name, so you'll remember that you are, after all, just acting, not transforming yourself overnight. Now, try out your new role on some friends. If the character is basically you, but with a few subtle changes in the direction you wish to move in, you might well show real improvement. If nothing else, you will have learned something about what you want to become.

Before writing your script, you might consider an example. Let's assume that Janis Jones is a real person who is thoughtful, bright, kind, and genuinely likes people, but who is shy, unassertive, and hesitant to talk in a crowd. Janis wants improvement and creates an imaginary character, Sandy Swanson. Sandy's script might be as follows:

> Sandy Swanson is known and liked by almost everyone in her small town. She has a kind word not only for those she meets, but also for anyone whose name comes up in a conversation. She also can be counted on when she is needed. Just the other day, one of her friends was being contradicted in a discussion about the economy. The friend had said that "deficit spending" hurts the economy, but couldn't come up with support for his assertion. Sandy politely but firmly interrupted the friend's adversary, saying that, with deficit spending, the government borrows so much of the money in circulation that too little is left for business to use as capital for expansion. The result is a sluggish

continued

economy. However, she went on to let her friend's opponent down easily, by pointing out that some of what he had said was reasonable. It was typical of Sandy. She is not afraid to use her considerable intellect to aid one person, even if she must oppose another, but she would never employ it to the detriment of anyone.

BOX 8.3
continued

Evaluation

CRITICISMS

Kelly's theory, our prime example of the cognitive orientation, has been criticized for being overconcerned with thought processes, to the exclusion of other aspects of people. In addition, his polar view of constructs can be questioned. Let's begin our evaluation of the theory with Kelly's basic assumption that constructs have opposite poles.

The notion of opposites.   Kelly's theory is based on the notion of constructs, and in turn, this notion is founded on the supposition of organization in terms of opposites. Undermine that foundation, and constructs along with the entire theory are in danger of toppling.

The most obvious attack on the notion of opposites is that some potential constructs do not involve opposites — at least, the opposite of the potential emergent pole is not obvious. For some constructs, the only opposite to the emergent pole is the negation of that pole. For example, *admire-not admire* was purposely used in the Jim-and-Joan illustration (see Figure 8.1). *Admire-not admire* would certainly qualify as a construct (as would just about any set of two words that are apparent opposites). However, the implicit pole is simply the negation of the emergent pole: it is not something, but the absence of something. One can admire a person, but to "not admire" a person implies no definite relationship or action.

An examination of a list of words that were all generated during the process of self-description (that is, disclosure of constructs) reveals a large number of emergent poles the opposites of which are negations (Allen & Potkay, 1983a). For example, *awful, bizarre,* and *martyred* seem to have no opposites except *not awful, not bizarre,* and *not martyred.* Kelly himself acknowledged that clients to whom he was exposed sometimes could not articulate an implicit pole for a construct. He assumed that, in such cases, the implicit pole was submerged. A *submerged* pole either has never been put into word form, perhaps because the construct is new, or is being suppressed (a client insists "all people are good" in order to escape the perception that people are bad and out to get him; Kelly, 1963). Perhaps some clients do submerge implicit poles, or it may be that they do not express an implicit pole because none exists for them.

What about Lyle's support of Kelly's notion of opposites? Examination of the word list used in that study reveals that all eight labels have extreme favorability values. For each of the four sets of words, one member of the pair refers to a characteristic that is highly valued and desired by people in our society, while the other word refers to a highly undesirable characteristic. Table 8.2 lists these words

TABLE 8.2   Lyle's Word Categories and
Associated Favorability Values*

Cheerful 475	Sad 213
Broad-minded 425	Narrow-minded 142
Refined 342	Vulgar 77
Sincere <u>504</u>	Insincere <u>107</u>
Average (mean) 437	135

* From Allen and Potkay (1983a; 550 is, for practical purposes, the upper limit of favorability and 50 the lower limit).

with their accompanying values on a scale where 550 represents highest favorability and 50 lowest favorability. All emergent poles do have rather obvious opposites that are not just negations. However, one might question whether these words are representative of construct labels used by real people. Do the emergent poles of real people's constructs all have such clear opposites? Do the constructs of real people have poles that are so extremely different in favorability? It seems intuitively obvious that some real people would have constructs with no opposites to emergent poles and constructs with poles that are not extremely different in favorability. Thus, Lyle's study should be replicated with a more representative sample of potential constructs. It remains to be seen whether his results could be repeated using words with moderate favorability values and words that can only be cast into sets of a word and its negation.

Beyond humans.   A second criticism of Kelly is that he had little to say about nonhuman elements of people's life situations. One can certainly argue that people are the most important aspects in the lives of people. However, to neglect nonhuman aspects is to suggest that these are unimportant. In fact, these aspects have such a strong presence in the lives of people that a whole school of thought, behaviorism, emphasizes nonhuman elements.

Where are the emotions?   Finally, people are not just thinkers, as is implied by the cognitive orientation of Kelly's theory; they also have emotions or feelings. While Kelly did acknowledge feelings, he had little to say about the constructs that would apply to them. He did indicate that feeling constructs would be mainly *preverbal* in nature, meaning that they had no words associated with their emergent and implicit poles. If feeling constructs are preverbal, then they are forever relegated to the unconscious, the never-never land of Freudian thought. Being in some sense unconscious, feelings or emotions are effectively dismissed from Kelly's theory, which is so clearly dominated by consciousness.

CONTRIBUTIONS

George A. Kelly is certainly one of psychology's most original thinkers. In fact, there may be relatively little research support for his theory precisely because it is so original. Kelly did not borrow from anybody. His theory is composed almost entirely of fresh, new ideas. There are no ids, archetypes, drives, or stimuli in the theory. Little wonder that researchers have found it too alien to consider. However, that state of affairs seems to be changing. Examination of current personality texts reveals that Kelly is resurgent. His theory has been around since 1955, and people have had time to get used to his very different and highly novel ideas.

If Kelly is to be criticized for neglecting nonhuman elements in people's lives and for having little to say about feelings and other noncognitive entities, he is to be congratulated for emphasizing what others have ignored—cognition, or thought, as a basis for the study of personality and of human behavior in general. Further, because Kelly was the first to successfully provide a cognitive basis for understanding personality—a heretofore neglected foundation—many of his ideas are here to stay. The notion of constructs, the dimension of complexity-simplicity, the REP test, and many other contributions will likely cement Kelly's name in the halls of psychology.

CHAPTER REVIEW

George Kelly's versatility and background in the physical sciences led to a theory based on the model of scientific thinking, rather than the mysterious internal forces of Freud or the S-R approach of early behaviorists. The theory is based on the notion of personal constructs—ways of seeing the world. Constructs are organized into construction systems—personalities. Each construct has an emergent or primary pole and an implicit or contrasting pole. The context of a construct is all the elements—objects or events—to which it applies. Each construct has a range of convenience (the category of events to which it applies) and a range of focus (the events to which it applies most readily). Any two construction systems, for reasonably similar people, are likely to reflect both commonality (overlap) and individuality (uniqueness).

In some construction systems, emergent poles lower in the system line up under those higher in the system, and the same is true of implicit poles. Such organization is called extension of the cleavage line. In abstraction across the cleavage line, whole constructs that are lower in the system fall under the emergent poles that are higher in the system, and the same is true of implicit poles.

Experience—what one learns from events—may lead to the realization that interpretations

of one's life situation are subject to change. That discovery is called constructive alternativism and can result in change in the individual's construction system.

To Kelly, personality development is a matter of evolution from primitive dependency constructs, which are based on survival needs and are relatively resistant to change (impermeable), to more flexible constructs that are addressed to social relations. Such relations become critical when individuals learn that important others in their lives have definite expectations, called roles, with regard to their behavior.

Lyle supported Kelly's theory by showing that people do organize their reality into constructs composed of opposite poles. However, the work of Bieri probably represents the most important research inspired by Kelly's theory. A cognitively complex person has a construction system that is composed of constructs that are well distinguished, one from the other. The opposite is true of a cognitively simple person.

The REP test is a valuable tool for analyzing personalities in terms of constructs. Constructs identified by the test can be changed by fixed-role therapy. Along with Kelly's cognitive approach and the notion of constructs, the REP test will likely assure Kelly's place in the history of psychology.

KEY CONCEPTS

Kelly's fundamental postulate
Constructs
    Emergent pole/implicit pole
    Range of convenience
    Range of focus
    Context
    Impermeable constructs
    Dependency constructs
Construction system
    Superordinate versus subordinate constructs

Commonality/individuality
    Extension of the cleavage line
    Abstraction across the cleavage line
Constructive alternativism
Predictability
Role playing
Cognitive complexity/cognitive simplicity
REP test
Fixed-role therapy

REVIEW QUESTIONS

1. What does Kelly mean when he says that all people are scientists?
2. Draw a construction system with extension of the cleavage line and one with abstraction across the cleavage line.
3. How does Kelly account for individual differences and commonality of individuals?
4. How do cognitively complex and cognitively simple people differ?
5. What is the link between fixed-role therapy and the REP test?
6. What behaviors or personality patterns might be hard to explain by reference to Kelly's theory?

PART THREE

Contemporary Empirical Approaches to Personality

IN RECENT YEARS personologists have shifted the focus of their efforts from constructing all-embracing theories of personality to more narrowly-based investigations of particular aspects of personality. In this part of the book, we emphasize systematic observation of specific factors related to personality and behavior.

To provide an organizing principle for presenting modern research, we examine these efforts in terms of three basic approaches. First, we discuss *how* traits are researched (Chapter 9) and *what* investigations have told us about these internal characteristics (Chapter 10). Then we apply the same procedure to situational influences on personality (Chapters 11 and 12) and to traits/situations jointly (Chapters 13 and 14).

Although the contemporary emphasis is on empirical research, theory—the interpretive side—remains relevant. There is no hard-and-fast distinction between theoretical and empirical approaches; theory and research always feed back onto each other. Finally, discussing contemporary research gives us the opportunity to explore a number of topics that you may find interesting in and of themselves, including extraversion-introversion; impulsiveness; authoritarianism; anxiety; the Jonestown incident; the college environment; aggression; rape; self-regulation; persons who are prone to heart disorders; sexual behavior; and sex differences.

9

Searching for Personality Traits and Types: Eysenck's Scientific Model

Is a scientific model of personality possible?

What is the connection between your physiological makeup and your personality?

Do scores on personality tests really predict behavior?

Are champions "born" or "made"?

Can animals have personalities?

I N CHAPTER 1, we offered a working definition of *personality*—individual differences along each of several behavioral dimensions. We also pointed out that this definition fits some approaches to personality better than others. It certainly fits the approach discussed in the present chapter, which is closely tied to other, related definitions given in Chapter 1: personality *traits*—hypothetical internal entities measured by points along a behavioral dimension; and personality *types*—subgroups of people who share patterns of related traits.

traits

types

The method of searching for personality traits and types reviewed in this chapter is of a special variety called *factor analysis*. Factor analysis is a complex-correlational method that relies on sophisticated techniques developed during the 20th century. It makes use of powerful computers to detect meaningful relationships and patterns in massive amounts of behavioral data.

factor analysis

In exploring this scientific approach to understanding personality, we will emphasize the model of Hans J. Eysenck. We recognize that we will be doing some injustice to the work of other, equally important psychologists in the area, such as Raymond B. Cattell and J. P. Guilford. However, for teaching purposes, Eysenck's approach is quite representative of the group of psychologists known as *factor analysts;* its concepts are fewer and more familiar to us; and it readily lends itself to introductory consideration as an integrative, scientific model of personality.

Before proceeding further, we would like to direct your attention to the exercise in Box 9.1 (page 296), which we will return to shortly.

Eysenck's Theory of Traits and Types

EARLY GREEK THEORISTS: TEMPERAMENTS, TRAITS, AND TYPES

"Why is it that while all Greece lies under the same sky and all the Greeks are educated alike, yet we all have characters differently constituted?" This question, asked more than 2000 years ago by the Greek writer Theophrastus, continues to be cited by Eysenck (1981). It reflects age-old observations of human behavior and is at the heart of the personality issue, individual differences. The Grecian answer focused on personality "types," assumed to be caused by physically based differences in temperament.

Can modern personality theorists do any better than the ancient Greeks? Thus far, according to Hans Eysenck, not convincingly so: "What we find is a long list of different theorists, putting forward entirely different views and hypotheses, using entirely different measures, and even types of measures; this is a far cry from the sort of *paradigm* that we are told characterizes science" (1981, p. 1).

Greek doctrine of four temperaments

Eysenck traces his own current-day theory to the ancient Greeks and their doctrine of four temperaments. *Temperament* refers to a person's natural, innate tendency to exhibit certain emotional reactions rather than others, along with greater or lesser changeability of mood. Hippocrates, the father of modern medicine, and Galen, a second-century Greek physician, thought temperaments were due to excesses in natural bodily fluids called *humors.* For them, personality was physically based. The Greeks also believed that each temperament was accompanied by certain behavioral characteristics or traits.

The classic temperaments appear in Figure 9.1, along with some corresponding trait descriptions later provided by the philosopher Immanuel Kant. Persons of *choleric* temperament are described as irritable — hotheaded and quick to become angered or take action, but without persistence. They are self-centered and want public praise and recognition. They are least happy because of the negative reactions they elicit from other people. *Sanguine* persons are

---

BOX 9.1   *Which Traits Best Describe You?*

A variety of personality traits appear below. Circle whichever individual traits you believe best describe your personality.

A	B	C	D
anxious	reasonable	quickly roused	playful
worried	high-principled	egocentric	easy-going
unhappy	controlled	exhibitionist	sociable
suspicious	persistent	hot-headed	carefree
serious	steadfast	histrionic	hopeful
thoughtful	calm	active	contented

Notice that the traits are grouped in four sets. Rank-order the sets according to the degree to which they best fit your personality. Be guided by the number of words you circled in each set, along with your personal weighting of some words more than others. Indicate your answers below, identifying each set by its corresponding letter: most = _____, second = _____, third = _____, and least = _____. Also, answer the following two statements about your personality. My personality is basically:

1. unchangeable or changeable (circle one)
2. emotional or nonemotional (circle one)

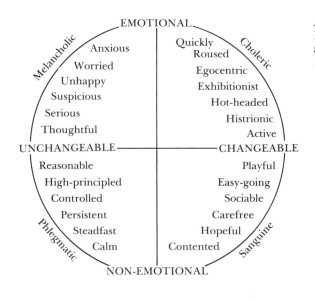

EMOTIONAL

Melancholic — Anxious, Worried, Unhappy, Suspicious, Serious, Thoughtful

Choleric — Quickly Roused, Egocentric, Exhibitionist, Hot-headed, Histrionic, Active

UNCHANGEABLE ———————— CHANGEABLE

Reasonable, High-principled, Controlled, Persistent, Steadfast, Calm — Phlegmatic

Playful, Easy-going, Sociable, Carefree, Hopeful, Contented — Sanguine

NON-EMOTIONAL

Figure 9.1
Historical schema of temperaments and traits *(adapted from Eysenck, 1981).*

enthusiastic—full of hope and optimism. They are good-natured, carefree, and contented, and have many friends. At the same time, they do not take things seriously or keep promises, and they are easily fatigued or bored by work. *Phlegmatic* persons are apathetic. They show a lack of ready emotion, although once warmed up their warmth will remain longer than it does in others. Actions are based on principle, not instinct. Dealings with people are reasonable and persist-

HANS EYSENCK.
Eysenck's search for personality traits links current-day scientific techniques with the ideas of the early Greeks. The most important of these traits is extraversion-introversion, which Eysenck believes to be an important, biologically-based influence on many human behaviors.

ent, with happiness present. Persons of *melancholic* or sad temperament are anxious and see difficulties everywhere—the opposite of sanguine. Melancholic persons worry about their interactions with others, and are suspicious. They do not make promises easily, because they insist on keeping their word.

In Figure 9.1, types and traits are arranged around the two broad personality dimensions of emotionality and changeability, based on the schema of Wilhelm Wundt (1874/1904), the father of modern psychology (see Klein, 1970). Note that the temperament types are represented as quadrants, formed by the two intersecting lines of the emotionality and changeability dimensions. Wundt, unlike Galen and Kant, did not consider the four types as totally separate categories. He saw adjacent temperaments as sharing some common characteristics. Thus, melancholics and cholerics were both predisposed to strong emotions, as opposed to the weak emotions of sanguinics and phlegmatics. Cholerics and sanguinics were predisposed to show greater changes in feelings compared with melancholics and phlegmatics.

BOX 9.1 REVISITED: YOUR "TEMPERAMENT TYPE"

At this point, you may be catching on to the meaning of the exercise in Box 9.1. Note that the adjectives listed in that exercise are the very same as those in Figure 9.1. To determine your own "historical" temperament type, simply compare your answers with the four types of temperament indicated in Figure 9.1. Which types are "most" and "least" like you? Theoretically, these two types should be in opposite quadrants of Figure 9.1, not adjacent to one another. You can also compare your judgments about how "emotional" and "changeable" you are to the position of your temperament relative to Wundt's emotional-nonemotional and changeable-unchangeable dimensions.

TRAITS AND TYPES IN EYSENCK'S THEORY

factors

The essence of Eysenck's theory (as well as Cattell's) is that personality can be described in terms of *traits*, or statistical *factors*, defined as "theoretical constructs based on observed intercorrelation between a number of different habitual responses" (Eysenck & Eysenck, 1969, p. 41). Examples of traits relevant to Eysenck's theory include physical activity, impulsiveness, risk-taking, responsibility, worrisomeness, carefreeness, and sociability.

superfactors

Traits, in turn, are often related to one another in subgroups called *types*, or statistical *superfactors*—higher-order dimensions made up of statistically intercorrelated traits. In other words, collections of personality traits (factors) often occur together, thereby contributing to personality types (superfactors). Eysenck has identified three such superfactors, reporting that they "or others remarkably similar to them" have been found repeatedly in different studies and can even be isolated in animals (1981, p. 6). (This last piece of information may surprise you, and answers a question often asked by psychology students: "Do animals have personalities?" For Eysenck, the answer is "Yes.") Eysenck's three personality superfactors or types are:

E Extraversion-introversion

N Neuroticism-stability

P Psychoticism-superego functioning

The most important and most investigated of these three dimensions is E. In fact, Eysenck believes it to be so important that he recommends that E become part of all personality research studies, even those not directly related to its consideration (1981). The least researched dimension is P.

Eysenck's belief in various personality types does *not* imply that they are categorical, or absolutely different from one another in some mutually exclusive, either/or fashion. Most people do not fall into separate and distinct compartments, showing only one clear-cut set of personality traits. Rather, personality types are *dimensional* — related to points along a continuum. This means that all people show more or less of all three superfactors. One person may show much extraversion, some neuroticism, and a little psychoticism. A second person may show little extraversion (conversely, much introversion), some neuroticism, and some psychoticism. For most people, trait values fall within the average range, placing them within the middle 16%–84% of the general population. Since very few people fall at such extreme degrees as 0% or 100%, pure types are hard to find. When it comes to extraversion-introversion, most of us are *ambiverts,* which means that we show medium degrees of this trait, with behaviors characteristic of both aspects.

Eysenck regards his dimensional approach to understanding types a modern-day reconceptualization of ancient Greek ideas. He also sees it as a corrective for popular misconceptions about Carl Jung's introvert-extravert typology (Chapter 3), especially false expectations about finding people who are *either* introverts *or* extraverts.

BIOLOGICAL ORIGINS OF TRAITS AND TYPES

Eysenck believes there is a "substantial" hereditary basis to personality. In his 1967 book, *The Biological Basis of Personality,* he lamented the fact that psychologists pay too little attention to hereditary influences on behavior. He saw this as especially true of American psychologists, whom Eysenck views as overemphasizing environmental influences and learning. Although the purpose of psychology is to study the behavior of organisms, psychologists have failed to appreciate the degree to which organisms respond differently to the same environmental stimuli, independent of learning. Differences shown by individual organisms in response to identical stimuli are not only quantitative (stronger versus weaker), but qualitative (approaching versus avoiding).

> Personality is determined to a large extent by a person's genes; he is what the accidental arrangement of his parents' genes produced, and while environment can do something to redress the balance, its influence is severely limited.

Margin notes:
extraversion-introversion

neuroticism-stability

psychoticism-superego functioning

dimensional approach

biological origins

> Personality is in the same boat as intelligence; for both, the genetic influence is overwhelmingly strong, and the role of environment in most cases is reduced to effecting slight changes and perhaps a kind of cover-up. (Eysenck, 1976, p. 20)

Eysenck definitely assumes that traits are biological in origin. The three superfactors identified previously have "a strong genetic basis" (1981, p. 6). Eysenck also indicates that E, N, and P are closely tied to psychophysiological theories (Eysenck, 1967; Eysenck & Eysenck, 1969, 1976). To illustrate, extraversion (E) has been linked with the brain's ascending reticular activating system (ARAS), which acts as an arousal mechanism. Neural messages ascend afferent or "input" sensory pathways to the reticular formation of the brain stem and areas of the cortex, arousing and alerting the organism. A loop develops when the brain, in turn, instructs the reticular formation either to continue sending arousal messages or to inhibit them, thereby controlling attention. Neuroticism (N) has been linked with the limbic system, the brain's visceral or feeling system, related to activation of "fight or flight" emotions of the autonomic nervous system, which regulates the organism's smooth muscles and glands. Psychoticism (P) has been linked with the androgen hormone system, in which chemicals from the body's endocrine glands are released to regulate the development and maintenance of male characteristics.

You have heard the expression "Champions are born, not made." Eysenck would agree with the essence of this statement, although he would generalize it to apply to all persons and characteristics, not just champions. Personality, temperament, and character are born, much more than they are made.

However, heredity is not simply a matter of a child's being "a chip off the old block." It is far more complex. Heredity can make us *unlike* as well as *like* our parents. Consider the child whose bright red hair contrasts with the brunette coloring of both parents, or whose physical coordination is noticeably above or below that of both parents. One child in a family may be quiet and shy, while its parents and siblings may be quite expressive and outgoing. Such child/parent contrasts can be understood in terms of recessive genes—hereditary factors whose influence is not dominant.

Supporting evidence for biological assumptions.   Eysenck has reviewed a number of sources of support for his belief in the genetic foundations of personality. One area of support involves research studies on twins, especially those comparing identical and fraternal twins. Identical (one-egg) twins have 100% of their heredity in common, whereas fraternal (two-egg) twins share only 50%, on the average. Thus, any differences between identical twins must be due to environmental influences, whereas differences between fraternal twins may be due to either genetic or environmental differences (Eysenck, 1967, p. 190).

Eysenck (1967) points to empirical findings that show identical twins to be much more alike in personality than fraternal twins, even when identical twins have been separated early in childhood and raised by different parents, in different families, and in different environments. Eysenck also reports that identical twins raised in separate families are slightly more alike than those raised in the same families, and that rates of concordance for criminal and neurotic behavior are considerably greater for identical twins compared with fraternal twins. *Concordance* refers to the degree to which the presence of a trait in one person predicts the presence of the same trait in a second person, typically a relative. This means that if an identical twin is identified as criminal or neurotic, it is highly likely that the second twin will also be identified as such. The pattern of all these findings "is just what would be expected on the hypothesis that heredity played a vital part in the production of individual differences in personality, criminality and neurosis"(Eysenck, 1976, p. 21).

A second important area of support for Eysenck's belief in the biological basis of personality involves research studies of adopted children. These children are more similar to their biological parents than to their adoptive parents, even when separated from the former shortly after birth. For example, Eysenck (1976) states that a child's potential for criminal behavior is related more to that of the biological parents than of the adoptive parents, even when the child has had no contact with the biological parents and constant contact with the adoptive parents. According to Eysenck, such findings "clinch the case" for heredity (p. 21).

A third area of support for Eysenck's biological emphasis has to do with the many relationships reported between individual differences in personality and bodily processes. A common assumption among psychologists is that the transmission of genetic material cannot influence human behavior directly, but that the relationship of genetic causation to this behavior is, necessarily, indirect. Genetic causation depends upon bodily structures and, thus, is mediated by physiological, neurological, and hormonal aspects of the individual. In other

Eysenck, Cattell, and other factor analysts believe personality is largely a function of biological inheritance. The similarities between identical twins support this assumption, even when the twins are reared apart in different environments.

words, hereditary causes of behavior are "predisposing": they contribute natural reaction tendencies that incline an organism to sense, perceive, and respond to environmental stimulation more readily in some ways than others (similar to the Greek doctrine of temperaments). This point of view is reflected in many of the chapter subtitles that appear in Eysenck's books, such as "Brain-Stem Arousal Systems and Personality," "The Physiological Basis of Extraversion," and "Personality and Drugs."

Implications for parenting.   Eysenck's perspective on the role of parents in developing or changing the personality of their children is quite different from that of Freudian psychoanalysts and environmental behaviorists. Freud believed that different personality types result from the kinds of experiences children have during the psychosexual stages of development (see Chapter 3). Behaviorist J. B. Watson claimed he could mold any child in any preselected direction, whether "butcher, baker or candlestick maker" (Chapter 5). For Eysenck, the greatest contribution that parents make to their child's personality occurs at the time of conception, "when they join their chromosomes and shuffle their genes into the unique pattern that will for ever after determine the looks, the behavior, the personality and the intellect of the child" (1967, p. 22). Thereafter, the influence of parents is "strictly limited." Although it is possible that the child's interaction with the environment may have some influence on the genetic endowment provided by the parents, this influence is not likely to be large. Any major change in personality is most likely to occur only under "quite unusual" circumstances, such as imprisonment in a concentration camp. Eysenck considers it unfortunate that parents do not understand this state of affairs. He finds it "tragic" that so many parents worry about raising their children, blaming themselves for whatever seems to go wrong, as if it were the parents' actions that were primarily responsible for the child's personality, character, abilities, and achievements. "How much more relaxed the parents could be if only they realized the limitations which nature has put on their later contributions!" (1967, p. 22).

ARE SOME TRAITS MORE DESIRABLE THAN OTHERS?

Is it better to have a personality that is quiet and shy or one that is expressive and outgoing? Eysenck would answer "Neither." That is, he considers personality traits and types neither good nor bad, right nor wrong. Behaving in quiet and shy ways has its strong points and its weak points, as does behaving in expressive and outgoing ways. The ways are just different. You can probably think of times when you have enjoyed simply being by yourself, and other times when you have wanted to be with other people; you probably have some outgoing friends and some shy friends. Also, some traits are independent of one another. A person high in extraversion may be low, medium, or high in neuroticism and low, medium, or high in psychoticism. Consider the question "Do persons with high sexual urges obtain greater sexual satisfaction than those whose urges are lower?" Eysenck would again answer in the negative. "It is possible to be satisfied with one's sex life regardless of the strength of one's libido; strong sexual urges, impersonal and permissive sexual behavior, do not seem to cause greater or less satisfaction than weak sexual urges'' (1976, p. 34).

Which personality traits are best? Eysenck (1976) believes society should "not press for uniformity." People have individual preferences and definitions about happiness in life, which may be reached by different routes. What is satisfactory for some people may not be so for other people, nor should it be. Even though it is possible for extreme personality characteristics to pose difficulties for people, the difficulties can be overcome. A society made up only of introverts or extraverts would be far less interesting than one made up of both. Also, such a society could be brought about only at great cost, because natural, physically based differences among people would have to be actively suppressed. People would have to go against their innate natures. Individual differences are to be valued.

TOWARD A SCIENTIFIC MODEL OF PERSONALITY

Is it possible to establish a scientific basis for constructing a model of personality? Eysenck believes so, although he notes that many psychologists have "despaired" over the difficulties involved.

Eysenck's (1981) scientific model for studying personality involves two interlocking components. The first is *description*, which seeks to answer questions about "what" personality is — for example, identifiable individual differences in traits and types. The second is *explanation*, which seeks to answer questions about "why" personality is the way it is — that is, the causes of those individual differences. In Eysenck's model, concepts are sought that will help reduce the infinite number of events observed in human behavior to a small number of variables. These variables are then tied together by rules or laws. Ideally, the concepts and laws should enable psychologists not only to understand past events after the fact, but to predict future events. Thus, Eysenck's conceptualization of personality is directed toward the scientific goal of being able to predict behavior. This is consistent with Cattell's definition of personality as "that which permits a prediction of what a person will do in a given situation" (Cattell, 1950, p. 2).

Eysenck (1981) places his model of personality in the historical context of Dutch psychologist Gerardus Heymans, whose contributions to the field were threefold: (1) *psychometrics,* the measurement of individual differences through quantitative procedures and psychological tests; (2) *experimentation,* the systematic investigation of phenomena under controlled conditions; and (3) the *hypothetico-deductive method,* or use of theoretical formulations to derive testable hypotheses for making accurate predictions about behavior and understanding its causes. Psychometrics clearly aids the descriptive component of the model, including the use of factor analysis and personality tests. Experimentation and the hypothetico-deductive method clearly aid the explanatory component, including the development and testing of hypotheses linking identified factors to generally accepted psychological and physiological concepts. All three aspects are intertwined in attempts to piece together the personality puzzle.

Eysenck's scientific model for studying personality

Cattell's definition of personality

psychometrics

Researching Traits and Types

Eysenck's model of personality is closely linked to psychometrics, a quantitative approach to psychological measurement. There have been two aspects of Eysenck's psychometric approach: first, the use of sophisticated statistical techniques, especially factor analysis; and second, the development of objective personality questionnaires. Although psychometrics may sound intimidating, it's not difficult to grasp the essentials of the idea. As an introduction to this topic, complete the questionnaire in Box 9.2. We'll return to the exercise a little later in this section.

BOX 9.2	*Maudsley Personality Inventory,* *Short Form**

Instructions: The following questions pertain to the way people behave, feel, and act. Decide whether the items represent your *usual* way of acting or feeling, and circle either a "Yes" or "No" answer for each. If you find it absolutely impossible to decide, circle the "?," but use this answer sparingly.

1. Do you sometimes feel happy, sometimes depressed, without any apparent reason?

    YES   ?   NO

2. Do you have frequent ups and downs in mood, either with or without apparent cause?

    YES   ?   NO

3. Are you inclined to be moody?

    YES   ?   NO

4. Does your mind often wander while you are trying to concentrate?

    YES   ?   NO

5. Are you frequently "lost in thought" even when supposed to be taking part in a conversation?

    YES   ?   NO

6. Are you sometimes bubbling over with energy and sometimes very sluggish?

    YES   ?   NO

7. Do you prefer action to planning for action?

    YES   ?   NO

8. Are you happiest when you get involved in some project that calls for rapid action?

    YES   ?   NO

9. Do you usually take the initiative in making new friends?

    YES   ?   NO

* Adapted from Eysenck & Eysenck, 1969

continued

10. Are you inclined to be quick and sure in your actions?

    YES   ?   NO

11. Would you rate yourself as a lively individual?

    YES   ?   NO

12. Would you be very unhappy if you were prevented from making numerous social contacts?

    YES   ?   NO

BOX 9.2
continued

FACTOR ANALYSIS

One of the ways in which Eysenck improves on the historical schema of traits and types is by seeking measurable and quantitative support for them, as patterns of statistical correlations. To uncover these patterns, Eysenck, Cattell, and others use a method called *factor analysis.*

Factor analysis is a statistical method for determining the number and nature of variables underlying larger numbers of measures (Kerlinger, 1973). Eysenck (1967) refers to it as "a correlational device for isolating the main dimensions of individual variability" (p. 26). The basic assumption is that certain types of behaviors correlate, or vary together, in such a way as to define a separate psychological dimension or factor. By determining "what goes with what" (Spearman, 1927), factor analysis is able to reduce large amounts of data from complex to simpler form.

Various kinds of items can be subjected to factor analysis, including answers to test questions, ratings made by external observers, and exact measures of behavior obtained through systematic observation. Cattell (1973) has referred to these three "comprehensive and exhaustive" sources of information about personality as Q-, L-, and T-data. In questionnaire or *Q-data,* the person is her own observer, describing her behavior and feelings through paper-and-pencil inventories, self-reports, interviews, or therapy sessions. ("I have a toothache.") In life or *L-data,* an outside observer assesses another person's behavioral traits by looking at what the person does in everyday life situations. ("Carla is studious; she has received no grade lower than a B during the past three years.") In test or *T-data,* an experimenter/observer measures a person's behavior in some standard, contrived, laboratory-test situation. ("Jesse's reaction time for pressing the green button after the red light appeared averaged .34 seconds.")

Q-, L-, and T-data

Factor analyses may include information from one or more of these three sources, or may be limited to a single type of information within a given source. Imagine that a psychological test made up of many questions is administered to a group of 100 people. If one of the test items is answered in a certain way by 40 people, it is possible that these same 40 people will answer other items in systematically related ways. Suppose that they answer "Yes" to test item #1. They might also answer "Yes" to other, related items, let's say #26, #55, and #107, and "No" to others, say #17 and #138. At the same time, another subgroup of 40 people may answer the same items in the opposite way from the first group. And, the remaining 20 people show no definite pattern. Individual differences are present because different people show different patterns of response. Yet, within subgroups, relations among the items also appear. Factor analysis is able to identify such clusters of items and determine that the items share some common denominator. At bottom, factors "are simply structures or patterns produced by covariances of measures" (Kerlinger, 1973, p. 671).

In factor analysis, "analysis" refers to the series of statistical procedures used to identify factors, involving computations of multiple intercorrelations, each item with every other item and with item clusters. Once factors have been identified statistically, they are assigned labels by the psychologist, based on his or her best professional judgment about the psychological dimension a given cluster of items seems to be measuring. Judgments are guided by the content of items making the greatest contribution to the factor, as determined by high statistical *loadings,* or correlations of particular items with a given factor, as well as a knowledge of theory and past research findings. Once defined and labeled, a factor represents a hypothetical construct or assumption about what it is that a data cluster or group of related clusters may be measuring. Some factors are *specific*— present in one test or set of data but not in others. *Group* factors are present in more than one test, while *general* factors are present in all. A general factor, such as "g" in intelligence, contributes to performance on all psychological tests.

A complicating feature of factor analysis is that not all factors are of the same order of comprehensiveness or generality. Some factors are *primary,* meaning that they are relatively pure, narrow in scope, and independent of one another. Other factors are *secondary,* or related to one other statistically. This feature partly accounts for variations in the numbers of factors obtained by different factor analysts, as in the discrepancy between Eysenck's three superfactors and Cattell's "eight or nine second-order factors" (Cattell, 1973, p. 37). How narrow or broad does the researcher expect the factors to be? Discrepancies may reflect different levels of inclusiveness.

source and surface traits

In his own work, Cattell (1965) refers to primary factors as *source traits* and secondary factors as *surface traits*. A source trait is a unitary dimension or factor that operates as an underlying "source" of observed behavior. A surface trait is a combination of dimensions or factors that go together because of several overlapping influences. Thus, Cattell considers extraversion-introversion a second-order factor, or "broad surface trait," comprised of three primary source traits labeled A, F, and H. He also considers neuroticism a surface trait because it is comprised of several elements: anxiety, indecision, inability to concentrate, irrational fears, and so on.

BOX 9.2 REVISITED:
AN ILLUSTRATION OF FACTOR ANALYSIS

Let us illustrate the procedure of factor analysis by referring to the exercise in Box 9.2, in which you were asked to answer 12 statements by circling the alternatives "Yes," "No," and "?." Review all of the statements. Assume that the

12 statements do *not* measure 12 *different* aspects of personality. Do some of the statements seem to go together? What psychological dimensions might they have in common? What traits do *you* think they are measuring? Try categorizing the items into subgroups, and assign a label to each subgroup.

This informal, commonsense approach should allow you to identify a few common denominators among the 12 statements. That is, you can probably come up with tentative answers to the questions "What is being measured?" and "How many dimensions are being measured?" However, there are many problems with such a commonsense procedure. The major problem is that the process involves a good deal of subjective judgment on your part. Even when experienced psychologists have tried to pick out seemingly related items, they have often been unable to do so. Results of their efforts have been quite arbitrary, indicating that nothing in particular was identified. This has been readily demonstrated when scores on one psychologist's test have failed to correlate significantly with scores on another psychologist's supposedly similar test (Eysenck, 1981).

What factor analysis does is to provide a more objective approach. A large number of variables, including answers to items such as those included in the exercise, are entered into a statistical program of multiple intercorrelations. Any common denominators are established empirically, with correlations providing numerical indices for determining (1) whether answers to certain items tend to "go together" to form statistical clusters; (2) which specific items contribute to each cluster; (3) each item's statistical loading, or degree of correlation, with one or more clusters; (4) how many clusters are present in the data; and (5) the degree to which clusters or groups of clusters are statistically independent of one another, thereby forming clearly definable factors.

Eysenck (1958) actually performed a factor analysis of the same 12 statements you answered in Box 9.2. (He was interested in developing a short form of a test known as the Maudsley Personality Inventory.) As he expected, two major factors became apparent, E and N. Items 1–6 showed high statistical loadings on the neuroticism factor, and items 7–12 loaded high on the extraversion factor. Actual loadings of each item on the two factors for a group of 1600 British adults are summarized in Table 9.1. The higher the correlation, the greater is the item's contribution to the factor. Thus, N is best defined by items #1 and #2, based on nearly equivalent correlation coefficients of .75 and .74, respectively. E is best defined by items #11 and #12, with coefficients of .68 and .64, respectively. Note that items loading high on one factor show minimal loading on the second factor ($r = .09$ or lower).

How closely did your judgments about what the 12 items might be measuring match those of Eysenck's more objective, statistical method?

TABLE 9.1   Factor Loadings of 12 MPI Items on N and E (Adapted from Eysenck, 1958)

	1	2	3	4	5	6	7	8	9	10	11	12
N	.75	.74	.71	.58	.58	.63	.01	.04	−.06	−.04	−.02	.09
E	.01	−.06	−.09	.02	−.06	.09	.48	.59	.59	.49	.68	.64

OBJECTIVE PERSONALITY TESTS

Eysenck's personality tests

Over the years, Eysenck has authored or coauthored a number of personality tests, each of which has been associated with the development of a different personality factor. The Maudsley Medical Questionnaire (MMQ) (Eysenck, 1952b) introduced the concept of neuroticism (N). The Maudsley Personality Inventory (MPI) (Eysenck, 1959) added the extraversion-introversion (E) factor. And the Eysenck Personality Questionnaire (EPQ) (Eysenck & Eysenck, 1968, 1976) added the psychoticism (P) factor. These questionnaires have been at the core of Eysenck's work in identifying the three major superfactors underlying the structure of personality.

Reducing observable events to a few variables: E, N, and P.   It may be helpful to visualize the process by which Eysenck reduces an infinite number of variables to a few. Consider a pyramid that has four levels (Figure 9.2). At the base of the pyramid are an individual's *specific responses (SR)* — everyday behaviors or experiences that may or may not be characteristic of the individual. Examples of SR could be saying "Hi" to a neighbor, circling "No" to a personality questionnaire item such as "I enjoy spending lots of time by myself," sneezing, and whistling while walking across campus. At the second lowest level are *habitual responses (HR),* or specific responses that recur under similar circumstances. HRs would include repetitions of any of the four SRs just given, on many occasions, as in regularly saying "Hi" to a neighbor or circling "No" to the same or similar questionnaire items. HRs represent a rough level of behavioral organization that can be measured and expressed as probabilities through *reliability coefficients* — statistical indices of the degree to which a person's responses are consistent or likely to be repeated.

At the third level, habitual responses are organized into *primary factors,* or traits. These might include such theoretical constructs as "friendly," "sociable," "allergic," and "expressive." Traits are based on observed statistical intercorrela-

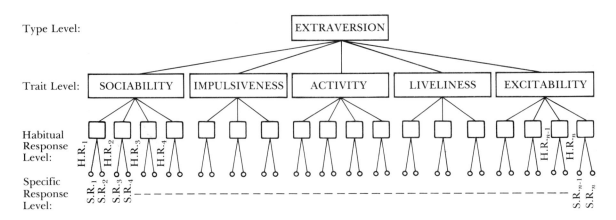

Figure 9.2   Eysenck's hierarchical model of personality description. *(From H. J. Eysenck,* The Biological Basis of Personality, *1967. Courtesy of Charles C Thomas, Publisher, Springfield, Illinois.)*

tions among a number of different HRs. At the top level of the pyramid, traits are organized into *secondary factors,* or types. Although the basis of types is, once again, statistical correlation, this time the correlations are among various traits. Thus, "sociability, impulsiveness, jocularity, carefreeness and various other traits would form a constellation of traits intercorrelating amongst themselves and giving rise to a higher order construct, the type" (Eysenck & Eysenck, 1969, p. 41).

The MMQ, MPI, and EPQ. The raw data for the analyses we have described can be obtained from personality questionnaires. A brief review of the development of some Eysenck personality questionnaires will illustrate his psychometric approach — the process of obtaining information about personality from paper-and-pencil inventories and reducing that information to a few variables through factor analysis.

Eysenck began his work by investigating neuroticism (N) as a dimension of personality. He wanted to differentiate soldiers who had been labeled "neurotic" from those considered "normal." His (1952b) Maudsley Medical Questionnaire (MMQ) met this goal successfully. On average, scores for 1000 neurotic soldiers were twice as high as those for 1000 normal soldiers — 20 points versus 10 points.

In general, N scores tend to be higher for women than for men, to be slightly higher for persons in lower socioeconomic classes, and to decrease with age. Persons with high N scores can be characterized as emotionally overresponsive and unstable, anxious, worrisome, moody, restless, touchy, having vague bodily complaints, and prone to breakdown under stress. Persons with low N scores can be characterized as emotionally stable, emotionally less arousable, calm, carefree, even-tempered, and reliable.

Eysenck then wanted a measure that would be more suitable for normal populations, not just neurotic ones. He also wanted to develop a second scale, extraversion. Although measures of both neuroticism and extraversion had already been developed (Guilford & Zimmerman, 1956), Eysenck doubted the suitability of these scales. He believed that Guilford's scales were too long and repetitious, paid too little attention to sex differences, were ambiguous in their statistical relationships with one another, and lacked unity of measurement. On this last question, it was unclear to Eysenck whether Guilford's introversion scale (R) measured an individual's true personal preference (E), or social fearfulness (N), or a dislike of people (P).

Eysenck undertook a revision of the MMQ, starting with a questionnaire containing all 40 items from his MMQ as well as 221 others from six scales developed by Guilford. This revised version was given to 400 British men and women of average education who, while "by no means representative," were mostly 20–35 years old, urban, and from middle and skilled working classes. Results were analyzed through a large number of statistical procedures. Responses to individual items were correlated with dimension scores, thus establishing the degree to which each item contributed to various psychological dimensions. Group response rates to each item were evaluated by comparing responses of women and men, and of subject groups scoring highest and lowest on various dimensions, to determine whether patterns of endorsement were the same or different. All N items had to show significant statistical correlations with Guilford's C scale but not with R, and all E items had to show significant relationships with Guilford's R scale but not with C, for both men and women. Ultimately, 24 neuroticism items (N) and 24 extraversion items (E) were selected to form two new scales. The original pool of 261 items had been reduced to 48! This new test, The Maudsley Personality Inventory (MPI) (Eysenck, 1962b), was administered to an additional 200 men. Previous results were replicated. Factor analyses supported the adequacy of items selected for the MPI by demonstrating the presence of two major factors, N and E.

In general, E scores tend to be higher for men than for women, to decrease with age, and to show no strong relationship with socioeconomic class. Persons with high E scores can be characterized as sociable, liking parties, having many friends, needing people to talk to, craving excitement, taking chances, impulsive, liking practical jokes and change, easygoing, optimistic, preferring to keep moving, tending to be aggressive, prone to lose their temper, not always controlling their feelings, and not always reliable. Persons with low E scores can be characterized as retiring, fond of books rather than people, distant except to close friends, introspective, quiet, looking before leaping, distrusting momentary impulses, serious, liking a well-ordered life, reserved, somewhat pessimistic, valuing ethical standards, seldom behaving aggressively, not losing their temper easily, keeping feelings under control, and reliable.

The third major personality factor, psychoticism (P), served as an impetus for development of the Eysenck Personality Questionnaire (EPQ) (S. Eysenck & H. Eysenck, 1968, 1975). Eysenck (1952b) was particularly interested in the theoretical question of whether psychotic and normal persons differ "in kind" or "in degree." Critical of categorical classification schemas typical of traditional psychiatric diagnosis, Hans and Sybil Eysenck (1976) saw the psychoticism concept as making sense "only within a dimensional system" of personality description, such as their own. Thus, most people would be expected to have at least a little "psychotic" or "criminalistic" tendency as part of their genetic makeup. In effect, there is no clear-cut separation between psychotic and normal states, but a continuum along which "all sorts of intermediate variations" are possible. People simply show more or less P. At the same time, "psychotic" and "neurotic" states of abnormality are not situated along the same continuum, but are independent of each other (S. Eysenck & H. Eysenck, 1976, pp. 17–18).

The EPQ is next in the Eysenck succession of related instruments involving mixtures of P, E, and N items administered to thousands of normal, adult men and women. Good P items—those consistently loading high on the hypothesized psychoticism factor—were retained for future use. Poor items—those showing little or inconsistent statistical loading on P over different samples and sexes— were discarded. Items loading high on P, but also on E and N, were rewritten. This process led to the development of improved, more internally valid versions of the questionnaire, which were tested on new groups of subjects. These new results were then factor-analyzed more than 20 times, with the final EPQ comprised of 90 items (including a subset of L, or lie, items aimed at assessing the degree to which a person's test responses are socially conventional). Checks on external validity were based on theoretical expectations of high scores for groups of psychotics and criminals. As predicted, final results indicated that scores on P are

"Extraverts" and "introverts" may seem to be distinct categories, but Eysenck presents evidence that these are dimensional traits: there is at least a *little* of the "showy" magician in all of us, and a *lot* in some of us.

independent of those on E and N. Also, the highest P scores are found among persons labeled "psychotic," especially schizophrenics, and among criminals and sociopaths who show antisocial behavior. Improvement of psychotic disorders through treatment results in lower P scores. A Junior EPQ has been developed for use with children 7–15 years old (S. Eysenck, 1965; S. Eysenck & H. Eysenck, 1973).

In general, P scores tend to be higher for men than for women, to be lower for persons in the middle socioeconomic class, and to decrease with age. Persons with high P scores can be characterized as solitary, troublesome, noncooperative, hostile, cruel, lacking in feeling and empathy, sensation-seeking, liking odd and unusual things, liking films of war and horror, undervaluing people and authority, showing social withdrawal, having impersonal sex, showing impaired thinking and memory, having attention difficulty, not valuing educational pursuits, suspicious, having mood disturbances, showing motor disturbances and suicidal tendencies, having a family history of psychosis, experiencing delusions and hallucinations, and showing originality. Since men show higher P scores than women, the Eysencks believe that P may be physiologically linked with maleness, especially the hormonal balance between androgen and estrogen.

The flavor of P is conveyed in Eysenck's (1970, p. 427) description of Don Sims, a 21-year-old young man whose high P score contrasted with his low N and E scores. When an interviewer asked Don to explain his endorsement of an EPQ item about liking to go to parties, Don answered, "Well, at parties you get free grub, free likker and a chance to screw some bird, don't you?" Then, with an angelic smile, Don added, "And sometimes you can break up the place, too."

Supporting Evidence

Eysenck has not only established the existence of personality factors empirically, through factor analysis, he has conducted experiments based on those factors using deductive, testable hypotheses. This is in keeping with his view of personality, which emphasizes the predictability of behavior. Let us look at some of the studies conducted within the framework of his theoretical expectations, focusing on Eysenck's most important personality dimension, extraversion-introversion (E).

A LEMON-JUICE TEST FOR EXTRAVERSION-INTROVERSION

How strongly do you salivate to lemon juice? Your personality type is likely to be a good predictor of your reaction (Corcoran, 1964; Eysenck & Eysenck, 1967). Recall, for example, the exercise in Box 9.2. Would it surprise you to learn that the lower your E score on that measure, the greater the likelihood you would show a strong salivation response to lemon juice?

The basis of this interesting prediction is theoretical, related to different patterns of physiological functioning in introverts and extraverts. Eysenck (1967) has hypothesized that introverts have a higher level of cortical brain arousal than extraverts (see Pavlov, Chapter 5). Thus, "under conditions of equal stimulation, effector output would be greater for introverts" (p. 1047). This hypothesis has been confirmed, and reconfirmed. Introverts, in fact, do salivate more than extraverts when pure lemon juice is placed on their tongues ($r = .70, p < .001$). N scores make no difference.

PREDICTING DIFFERENCES IN EYEBLINK CONDITIONING

Different patterns of conditioned learning also differentiate introverted and extraverted personalities in eyeblink-conditioning experiments. The unconditioned stimulus (UCS) is a puff of air to the eye. The conditioned stimulus (CS) is a tone delivered to the ear by earphone. The unconditioned response (UCR) and conditioned response (CR) are the blinking of an eyelid. Eysenck and Levey (1972) sought to make sense of a research literature "full of contradictory results" by demonstrating that it is possible to select conditions favoring either introverted or extraverted subjects. What is "interesting and important" is that the conditions can be formulated on theoretical grounds, with experimental results serving to support and verify the theory.

Eysenck's (1957a) theoretical position is that introverts condition more rapidly and more strongly than extraverts because of differences in their physiological makeup. The history of this generalization again goes back to Pavlov, who observed individual differences in the rates at which his dogs conditioned. Pavlov

(1927) explained the differences using a dimension of "strong" and "weak" nervous systems, which he related to "excitatory" and "inhibitory" brain processes, respectively.

These "strong" and "weak" personality types (Teplov, 1964) resemble Eysenck's extraverted and introverted personalities, which are closely linked, in turn, to the cortical arousal system of the brain's reticular formation (ARAS). Eysenck has shown that cortical arousal is greater in introverted than extraverted personalities, and that "cortical excitation facilitates conditioning, provided that the optimal degree of excitation has not yet been reached" (1967, p. 117).

Important to this discussion is the concept of *sensory threshold*—the lowest intensity of a stimulus to which an organism reacts. Eysenck believes that the reticular arousal threshold is lower for introverts than for extraverts. Introverts, therefore, would be expected to respond to lower levels of stimulation than extraverts, making introverts more sensitive to external stimuli. Support for this hypothesis has come from many sources. S. L. Smith's (1968) report of a link between personality and sensory threshold indicates that introverts have lower auditory thresholds than extraverts when tones are sounded through earphones. Haslam (1967; Haslam & Thomas, 1967) has repeatedly found a lower threshold for pain in introverts. When Lynn and Eysenck (1961) asked subjects to endure as much heat pain as they could, the correlation with MPI extraversion scores was .69 (and only − .36 with MPI neuroticism scores). A practical implication of these findings is that if you need to have some dental work done without benefit of a Novocaine injection, it would be better to have an extraverted personality.

However, cortical *excitation* resulting from reticular arousal is only part of the physiological pattern contributing to differences between introverted and extraverted persons. A second aspect of reticular-formation functioning that must be taken into account is cortical *inhibition,* or active interference with arousal. Eysenck has hypothesized that the "strong" nervous systems of extraverts have a low threshold of inhibiting influences on the cortex, whereas the "weak" systems of introverts have a high threshold. Therefore, even when external stimulation is sufficiently high to arouse extraverts, the arousal will be more strongly counteracted by inner sources of cortical interference in extraverts than in introverts. The overall meaning of this interaction effect is that extraverts not only will learn more slowly but will forget what they have learned more quickly, compared with introverts.

In the Eysenck and Levey (1972) eyeblink-conditioning experiment, male subjects were administered the MPI and were categorized as extraverted, introverted, or ambiverted (in-between); and as high, low, or average on neuroticism. Equal numbers of the 144 subjects were chosen from each of the nine MPI categories. Subjects were then tested under various combinations of UCS presentation (67% versus 100%), time interval between CS and UCS (400 msec versus 800 msec), and strength of UCS (3 lb/sq in. versus 6 lb/sq in. pressure). In all instances, lower values were expected to be favorable to conditioning in introverts, but not extraverts. Higher values were expected to be favorable to extraverts, but not introverts.

Results showed that conditioning over 48 trials tended to be greater for introverts than for extraverts. More important, from the standpoint of making theoretical sense of "contradictory results," were the interaction effects associated with different amounts of stimulation. Introverts were more conditionable with the weak UCS, extraverts were more conditionable with the strong UCS, and ambiverts were intermediate, as seen in Figures 9.3 and 9.4. Eysenck and Levey cited this reversal as "quite dramatic" support for their prediction. The shorter CS-UCS interval also favored conditioning in introverts. Further, correlations between introversion and conditioning under optimal and worst parameters were small but significantly different (.40 and −.30, respectively; $p < .01$).

Failure of the longer CS-UCS interval to favor conditioning in extraverts, and of the percent UCS presentation to favor either introverts or extraverts, was related to the need for a "better choice" of values for the variables used. Eysenck & Levey (1972) argued that the values selected unintentionally favored conditioning in extraverts, who are "much more at the mercy of conditions." They were further tempted to argue "that introverts form conditioned responses even under objectively unfavorable conditions, whereas extraverts only form conditioned responses when conditions are optimal" (p. 217).

BAD EXAM NEWS IS WORSE FOR INTROVERTS

College students have been found to react differently to feedback about their performance on a test of new learning, depending on their personality type. Fremont, Means, and Means (1970) administered the MPI to 200 college students. The 30 students who scored highest and lowest on E were designated extraverts (E's) and introverts (I's), respectively. Each student was then given a brief written task requiring the learning of a digit-symbol code. Equal numbers of E and I students received one of three different kinds of feedback about their performance on this task: no information, "higher than average," and "lower than average." Another test, the Multiple Affect Adjective Check List (MAACL) (Zuckerman & Lubin, 1965), was administered immediately following the feedback session, to assess each student's degree of anxiety. Results showed a signifi-

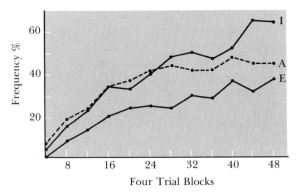

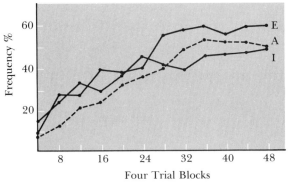

Figure 9.3
Rate of eyeblink conditioning for introverts, ambiverts, and extraverts under weak UCS conditions *(Eysenck & Levey, 1972).*

Figure 9.4
Rate of eyeblink conditioning for extraverts, ambiverts, and introverts under strong UCS conditions *(Eysenck & Levey, 1972).*

cant interaction between personality orientation and type of feedback. No significant differences in anxiety levels of I and E students were shown when feedback was positive (6.2 and 5.7, respectively) or when no feedback was provided (6.8 and 6.9, respectively). However, when feedback was negative, introverts clearly showed greater anxiety than extraverts (13.4 and 8.6, respectively; $p < .001$).

DRUGS, LIQUOR, COFFEE, AND TOBACCO

Eysenck and his followers have demonstrated that drugs affect behavior in predictable ways, depending on types of drug and personality. Eysenck's basic postulate is that "depressant drugs change behavior in an extraverted direction while stimulant drugs change behavior in an introverted direction" (1962b, p. 14). Thus, the drinking of alcohol, a depressant, should incline people toward lower task performance and more expressive behavior. The drinking of coffee or the smoking of cigarettes, both stimulants, should incline people toward higher performance and more inhibited behavior.

Powell (1981) has evaluated Eysenck's postulate as receiving "moderate but consistent support" in relation to stimulants and "more positive" support in relation to depressants. For example, B. M. Jones (1974) reported that alcohol had a detrimental effect on the performance of 40 men who had been asked to complete a paper-and-pencil measure of intellectual functioning. The men had been matched for E and intelligence, with 20 drinking alcohol at 1.32 ml/kg and 20 a placebo, or inert substance. Although the detriment applied to introverts and extraverts alike, it was significantly worse for extraverts. Results were later replicated by Jones, Hatcher, Jones, and Farris (1978), whose sample of 99 subjects also included women and whose measures included N scores. Extraverts again showed the greatest performance detriment, especially when combined with high neuroticism scores. Introverts with low N scores showed the least detriment.

In another study, Gupta and Kaur (1978) showed that a stimulant, dextroamphetamine, improved the efficiency of extraverts but not introverts on a perceptual-judgment task. This drug actually interfered with the introverts' performance. What explains this unexpected finding? It seems to be related to the *Yerkes-Dodson law,* according to which there is a predictable relationship between motivation and performance that takes graphic shape as an inverted or upside-down U. Motivation that is too low fails to promote good performance ("You're not trying hard enough"). Motivation that is too high interferes with good performance ("You're trying too hard"). Optimal performance occurs when motivation is intermediate, the peak of an upside-down U being in the middle ("Your level of effort is just right"). In Eysenck's theory, physiological "arousal" substitutes for "motivation." Thus, Powell (1981) interprets Gupta and Kaur's (1978) findings in the following way:

Yerkes-Dodson law

> They found that the drug, which increases activity in the corticoreticular loop, improved the performance of extraverts, since the cortex becomes more efficient at the judgement task when it is slightly more aroused. But the drug adversely influenced introverts' performance as Eysenck predicts—because the introvert is already quite aroused, so that the stimulant pushes the arousal level of the cortex past the point of maximal efficiency as described by the Yerkes-Dodson principle. (Powell, 1981, p. 77)

Another application of this principle pertains to the popular medical treatment of prescribing stimulant drugs, such as Ritalin, to hyperactive children. Since these children appear to be "hyper" already, what sense does it make to have them take medication, or even coffee, that is likely to stimulate them even more? The answer to the paradox requires that we not be fooled by the apparently "overaroused" behavior we see on the outside, which may be related to inefficient learning of self-control and social discipline. (Correlation is not causation, as discussed in Chapter 2.) Hyperkinetic children may be better understood from the inside, as "cortically underaroused" extraverts (Powell, 1981). Stimulants function to make them more physiologically introverted, allowing them to become more cognitively attentive, vigilant, and responsive to personal and social stimulation, as well as less impulsive or uncontrolled in their external behavior.

OTHER DIFFERENCES BETWEEN INTROVERTS AND EXTRAVERTS

We would like to conclude this section by listing some *empirically* established ways in which introverts and extraverts have been found to differ. In all cases, the behaviors or reactions are consistent with predictions based on Eysenck's theory (Blake, 1967, 1971; Eysenck, 1964, 1965, 1973, 1981; Powell, 1981). As you review Table 9.2, keep in mind that Eysenck's concept of introversion-extraversion is *dimensional*. The differences are not absolute but relative, along a continuum of more and less. Also, individual differences may be expected to occur even within groups identified as E or I. A person scoring high on E may not show all E characteristics and will likely show some I characteristics, and vice versa.

TABLE 9.2   Empirically Demonstrated Introversion-Extraversion Differences

Introversion

Higher arousal levels in the morning	More reliable, conscientious, and punctual
Better work in the morning than in the afternoon	Less absent fom work
	Quicker reaction time
Better work alone than in groups	Able to hold breath longer
Better work under quiet conditions	Higher academic achievement
Prefer slower, more accurate work approach	Emphasize virginity and fidelity
	Report more frequent masturbation
Prefer theoretical and scientific jobs, including teaching math	More masochistic
More characteristic of physics and zoology majors	Oversocialized superego
More characteristic of technical and transport managers	Abnormal behavior more likely to be obsessive-compulsive
More sustained vigilance under boring conditions	

(Continued)

TABLE 9.2   *(Continued)*

Extraversion

Greater tolerance for pain	More characteristic of housewives who smoke
Greater frequency and amplitude of alpha brain waves	More characteristic of sociology and history majors
Greater increase in arousal during the day	More characteristic of sales and marketing managers
Higher arousal levels in the evening	
Better work in the afternoon than in the morning	More charactristic of sportsmen, parachutists, and commandos
Better work in groups than alone	More characteristic of criminals
Better general adjustment	More characteristic of Americans than Britons
Prefer quicker, less accurate work approach	More tough-minded in attitudes
Prefer people-oriented jobs, including sales and social work	More subject to satiation
	More susceptible to alcohol
Less easily conditioned	Intercourse earlier in life, more often, and with more partners
Less characteristic of university students	Report having more orgasms
Less tolerance for sensory deprivation	
Lower sedation threshold	Adjust more easily to time changes
Slightly more characteristic of men	Undersocialized superego
More quickly learn how to swim during childhood	Abnormal behavior more likely to be sociopathic
More involuntary rest pauses during massed practice	
More talk and coffee breaks at work	

GRAY'S REINTERPRETATION OF EYSENCK'S THEORY

Aspects of Eysenck's theory have been given an alternative interpretation by Jeffrey Gray (1972, 1981). In some respects, Eysenck's theory has not been supported by empirical data. In other respects, his ideas simply might benefit from "better theory." One representative example pertains to Eysenck's hypotheses about criminal behavior.

Eysenck has been able to differentiate groups of criminals from controls using personality questionnaires. However, his explanations of criminal personality have been revised over time. His earlier two-dimensional schema (1962b), stemming from MPI results, linked criminality to high E and very high N. He explained that criminals were "undersocialized," largely because of lower conditionability associated with high extraversion, or lower cortical arousal. He saw them as unable to "learn" cooperative social roles and behavior. However, according to Wilson (1981), criminals and psychopaths have shown conditioning patterns "equal if not superior" to those of normal controls. The inconsistency is partly resolved by Eysenck's (1977) more current, three-dimensional schema, which adds a high P trait to criminality, based on results of the Eysenck Personality

Inventory (EPI) (Eysenck & Eysenck, 1976). He has recognized that his formula *criminal behavior* $= E \times N$ might cover some cases of psychopathy, but clearly not all. E could account for crimes committed by con artists or gangs, while P could account for aggressive crimes of unnecessary cruelty.

The issue may be more far-reaching than that of criminality. It appears that E is not a unitary factor. Rather, E seems to be made up of two components: sociability and impulsiveness. *Sociability* reflects ease in interpersonal relationships, including such descriptors as "lively," "talkative," and "not shy." *Impulsiveness* reflects such descriptors as "quick," "acting on the spur of the moment," and "nonthinking." According to Wilson (1981), it is not the sociability aspect of E that poses the main problem for criminals, but the impulsivity aspect. Thus, the main contributor to impaired learning in criminals seems to be a type of impatience, or inability to delay reinforcement.

Gray's solution to these problems involves a seemingly simple but major modification of Eysenck's two-dimensional schema. Gray would rotate the two axes of Eysenck's extraversion-introversion and neuroticism-stability factors 45 degrees, mathematically. He would then identify the two modified factors as *anxiety (Anx)*, or stable-extravert/neurotic-introvert, and *impulsivity (Imp)*, or stable-introvert/neurotic-extravert. Anx would be physiologically linked to an underlying behavioral-inhibition system, with Imp linked to some as yet unknown but independent system. Gray's (1981, p. 261) reconceptualization "has the bonus that it automatically solves the problem posed for Eysenck's theory by the discovery that Imp, rather than E-I, is the line of clearest causal influence."

Applications

The area of applied work most common to Eysenck and Cattell is that of psychometric measurement and testing. For decades, they have been test developers, devoted to the process of constructing, refining, and extending their measurement techniques. Their work has been programmatic, undertaken systematically rather than piecemeal, and tied closely to theory and research. There is no question about their beliefs that individuals differ in relative locations on traits or "semi-permanent personality dispositions," and on states or "transient internal conditions," and that these dimensions "are measurable by means of personality questionnaires" (Eysenck, 1981, p. 3). The title of Cattell's (1973) handbook on psychometrics and practical procedures summarizes these three beliefs quite succinctly: *Personality and Mood by Questionnaire.* Let us now take a look at Raymond Cattell's important 16 PF test.

ASSESSING PERSONALITY WITH THE 16 PF

Sixteen
Personality
Factor
Questionnaire
(16 PF)

The Sixteen Personality Factor Questionnaire (16 PF) (Cattell, Eber, & Tatsuoka, 1970) is a test of adult personality. Cattell (1949) developed the 16 PF as a comprehensive measure of normal "personality factors," or primary source traits, encompassing 16 scales. These factors are identified in Figure 9.5. Norms for the 16 PF are based on more than 10,000 cases, with separate tables for men,

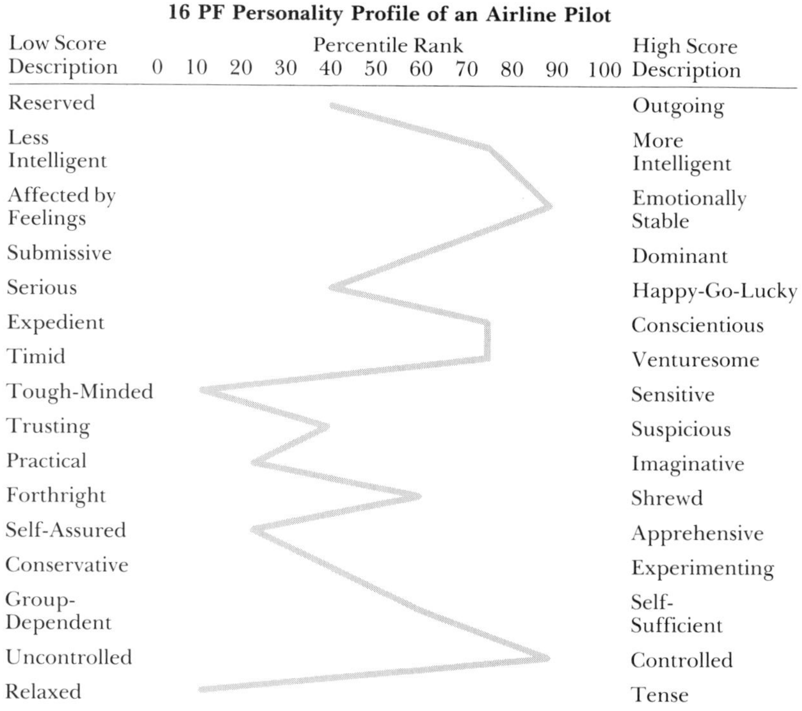

16 PF Personality Profile of an Airline Pilot

Low Score Description	Percentile Rank	High Score Description
	0 10 20 30 40 50 60 70 80 90 100	
Reserved		Outgoing
Less Intelligent		More Intelligent
Affected by Feelings		Emotionally Stable
Submissive		Dominant
Serious		Happy-Go-Lucky
Expedient		Conscientious
Timid		Venturesome
Tough-Minded		Sensitive
Trusting		Suspicious
Practical		Imaginative
Forthright		Shrewd
Self-Assured		Apprehensive
Conservative		Experimenting
Group-Dependent		Self-Sufficient
Uncontrolled		Controlled
Relaxed		Tense

Figure 9.5   16 PF profile of John Skyman *(Cattell, Eber, & Tatsuoka, 1970).*

women, the general adult population, college students, and high school seniors. The adult version has five forms, with administration times of 30–60 minutes for 105–228 items. Versions of the 16 PF have been extended downward, for use at early high school, junior high school, and elementary school levels. A 16 PF Computer Information Service offers electronic scoring of answer sheets, interpretive reports of client scores, and information on vocational and clinical patterns.

Applications of the 16 PF include business and industry, education, vocational guidance, clinical diagnosis, and research. In business and industry, the 16 PF has served as an aid to decision making about employee selection, efficiency, turnover, and promotion. In education, it has aided the planning of individualized programs for students and predicting school achievement. In vocational guidance, the 16 PF has indicated potential areas of occupational success. Cattell, Eber, and Tatsuoka's (1970) handbook for the 16 PF contains 125 occupational and clinical profiles, including job profiles for sales personnel, airline pilots, mechanics, teachers, school counselors, nurses, and electricians. In clinical settings, the 16 PF has aided the diagnosis of persons with behavior problems, anxiety, neurosis, alcoholism, drug addiction, and delinquency. It also has been used to understand similarities and differences in personalities of married couples seeking counseling.

Have you ever wanted to be an airline pilot? What personality characteristics would you need to have? Figure 9.5 presents the 16 PF profile of a hypothetical pilot, John Skyman. Note that pairs of labels are used to describe each of the 16 personality factors, thereby indicating the dimensional nature of these traits, as in *less intelligent* versus *more intelligent*. The zigzag line represents Skyman's trait profile, showing points at which his scores are average (50%), above average (85%), and below average (15%). John's profile actually conforms well with norms derived from 360 airline pilots. That is, civilian pilots typically obtain high scores on *emotionally stable* and *conscientious* and low scores on *tense, apprehensive, suspicious,* and *sensitive.* John is also high on *controlled* and *venturesome,* and about average on *self-sufficient.* This pattern is "an excellent combination for high reality contact and emotional stability under stress" (Cattell, Eber, & Tatsuoka, 1970, p. 191).

IDENTIFYING DEVELOPMENTAL TRENDS

A second application of Cattell's work involves the identification of trends in personality development, from childhood through adulthood. Knowledge of age trends permits the plotting of standardized growth curves. Comparisons can then be made between individuals within a given age group, and between groups of persons of different ages and sex. Age-related peaks and valleys on different personality traits can also be determined, evaluated, and statistically corrected for equivalence. Results are analogous to normative guidelines present in the height and weight charts used by pediatricians in evaluating patterns of physical growth in children.

For example, findings from Cattell's 16 PF measures indicate that superego strength, or conscientiousness, generally shows a moderate but decelerating increase with age. It dips during adolescence for males, but not females, "presumably because of the stronger revolt against authority" (Cattell, 1973, p. 155). Thereafter, it continues to rise slightly through age 40, then declines slightly for males around age 50. In 1973, Cattell indicated that the IPAT questionnaires were "virtually the only scales for which age trends are well established or even sketched" (p. 148). However, Sybil Eysenck (H. Eysenck & S. Eysenck, 1969) had also gathered and reported such information, as had Ames, Learned, Metraux, and Walker (1952). Findings from the Junior Eysenck Personality Inventory (S. Eysenck, 1965) indicate that extraversion scores increase between ages 7 and 13, but decline slightly thereafter, with boys showing more extraversion than girls.

CLASSIFYING TESTS AND ABNORMAL BEHAVIORS

Classifying tests.   A third area of application common to Cattell and Eysenck involves classification, although of different subject matter. In 1967, Cattell and Warburton organized a detailed compendium of 612 objective tests of personality and motivation, covering 2364 variables. The purpose was to provide an index of specific tests, along with their associated measurement factors, so that interested psychologists would be able to choose one or more tests "suitable for some practical application or for testing some theory" (p. 13). The compendium provided basic information about each test's variables, rationale, format, target population, and instructions. A broader aspect of Cattell and Warburton's schema was to support the revolutionary shift away from projective "gadgets" such as inkblots toward a measurement approach concerned with specific concepts and structures of personality, "under more ideal research conditions than clinical observation" (p. 4).

Classifying abnormalities.   Eysenck (1947, 1970) has argued for a revolutionary approach to psychiatric classification, in which his three-dimensional system of E, N, and P would replace traditional diagnostic systems (American Psychiatric Association, 1980). This new approach would be dimensional rather than categorical, and explanatory rather than merely descriptive. In essence, differences between persons considered normal and abnormal would be matters of degree, not of kind. Clinical groups would be defined according to their locations along the three major dimensions of E, N, and P. To illustrate, although groups of schizophrenics and psychopaths both show high scores on psychoticism, schizophrenics are more introverted and psychopaths more extraverted. While groups of hysterical and obsessive-compulsive neurotics show high scores on neuroticism, hysterics are more extraverted and obsessive-compulsives more introverted. Eysenck's (1964) theoretical framework and research findings about the biological substrata of personality functioning would serve as a basis for explaining and predicting differences in conditioning, learning, perception, memory, and social behavior. Eysenck (1973) has suggested that his dimensional grid could also be used as a guide to treating patients. For example, neurotics who score high on psychoticism would be expected to show low response to treatment by psychotherapy and behavior modification (Eysenck & Eysenck, 1976). Patient response patterns to different drugs could also be understood and predicted (Eysenck, 1967, 1981).

Consider the following application of Eysenck's research and theory to a case of group hysteria involving abnormal "overbreathing" among schoolgirls (Moss & McEvedy, 1966). In October 1965, an outbreak of hyperventilation occurred among girls attending a British secondary school. Typical complaints included dizziness, headache, feeling cold or hot, shivering, nausea, and fainting. The epidemic began with a preliminary fainting wave on day 0, followed by spikes on days 1, 5, and 12. Students were falling like bowling pins, with 118 of 589 hospitalized once, 32 twice, and 4 three times. Medical laboratory findings were negative.

Could the reactions have been psychological? All 25 girls who fainted on day 0 and went to school on day 1 were affected, while none of the girls absent on day 0 were affected on day 1. Some 54% of 95 affected on day 5 had also been affected on day 1, and 90% of 58 affected on day 12 had also been affected on day 1 or 5. The number of new occurrences was higher during times of school assembly than classroom lessons.

Moss and McEvedy administered the Eysenck Personality Inventory (EPI) to 535 of the students. According to Eysenck's classification of abnormal behavior, positive indicators of hysterical personality would involve a combination of high E and high N scores. Affected students consistently showed this pattern. Almost

40% of those receiving higher scores were affected, contrasted with 25% of those receiving average scores and less than 20% of those receiving lower scores. Findings were consistent with "hysterical reactivity."

An explanation was proposed. Earlier in the year, the town experienced a polio epidemic that received unfavorable press coverage. Outsiders refused to enter "polio town." On day 0, students were required to attend a lengthy church ceremony, during which time 20 girls fainted. The next day, there was much commotion over who had fainted and how many times, and new fainting began to occur during school assemblies. Fainters were asked to rest on the floor, where they remained for all to see. What became epidemic was behavior that was highly dependent on an excited emotional state. Excitement and fear led to overbreathing, accompanied by dizziness and faintness. Once learned, the behavior became "self-reinforcing," resuming spontaneously under conditions of school assembly.

Evaluation of Factor-Analytic Approaches

LIMITATIONS

It is commonly said of factor analysis that psychologists never get anything out of it they didn't put there in the first place. This is because the results of factor analysis are extremely dependent on several biasing influences.

Format of data source.   The first of these biasing influences has to do with the source or type of information obtained, whether Q-, L-, or T-data, and the representativeness of this information. Q-data alone encompasses thousands of published personality questionnaires, each of which contains a limited number of items, all preselected by the researcher. Which questionnaire is to be used? The core of Cattell's (1973) primary source traits of personality was L-data, derived from Allport and Odbert's (1936) dictionary list of 18,000 trait names. Of the 4500 personality descriptors deemed "suitable for rating," Cattell added new ones, then reduced the total to 171 by eliminating "indistinguishable synonyms." However, four of Cattell's factors (Q1, Q2, Q3, and Q4) are found only in Q-data paper-and-pencil questionnaires, not in analyses of Allport and Odbert's language terms. And three of Cattell's factors (D, J, and K) have appeared in L-data rating sources but not in Q-data sources. Anastasi (1982) believes that ratings produced by outside observers may be more revealing of the raters than of the persons being rated; that is, ratings "may reflect in part the influence of social stereotypes and other constant errors of judgment, rather than the subjects' trait organization" (pp. 513–514).

Characteristics of samples.   A second influence concerns the characteristics of persons contributing questionnaire answers or other data to the analyses. How representative are these samples of people in general? Results may vary depending on whether the research samples are comprised of American college students, middle-aged British industrial workers, male medical patients in 1943, female felons in 1986, or people of different ethnic, socioeconomic, and regional backgrounds.

No single method. Third, controversy continues over which specific method of factor analysis should be used. Eysenck has intentionally developed his factors as *orthogonal* to one another, meaning that they are statistically uncorrelated with one another and, thus, independent. Visualize this by imagining a three-dimensional sphere with three lines drawn through the center at 90 degree angles to one another: left/right, up/down, and toward/away. Now imagine that the ends of one line are labeled *extraversion* and *introversion,* those of the second are labeled *neuroticism* and *stability,* and those of the third are labeled *psychoticism* and *superego functioning.* High, medium, or low scores on E are not related to high, medium, or low scores on N which, in turn, are not related to high, medium, or low scores on P. Any combination of scores is equally likely to occur among persons in the general population. By contrast, many of Cattell's 16 primary factors are *oblique* to one another, reflecting the likelihood that factors share statistical relationships with each other. Professional opinions differ regarding the advantages and disadvantages of these methods. In Cronbach's (1970) words, "There is no one 'right' way to do a factor analysis any more than there is a 'right' way to photograph Waikiki Beach" (p. 315).

Subjective judgments remain. Finally, while factor analysis reduces the amount of subjective judgment involved in answering questions about "what" and "how many" dimensions are present in personality, it does not do so totally. Arbitrariness on the part of individual psychologists enters into the picture at three points.

First, psychologists foster certain factor-analytic solutions not only by initially preselecting sources of information likely to be "relevant" to their special interests, but by later estimating how many factors are likely to be present in the data. Cattell (1973) and the Eysencks (1969) refer to this as "the number of factors problem." Implications are that data may be underfactored or overfactored, thereby producing too few genuine or too many artificial factors. Individualized decision making among psychologists regarding the number of constructs likely to underlie personality partly explains why different factor theorists have come up with different numbers of traits to account for personality. Goldberg (1981) observes:

> The number of primary personality factors in Cattell's system is in the 20-to-30 range, of which the 16 most famous are included in his Sixteen Personality Factors questionnaire (16 PF). When his data were made available to others, however, virtually everyone who factored those data found only 5. (pp. 156–159)

Second, once factors have been identified, cutoff values are required to establish whether an item makes a meaningful contribution to a factor. Statistical loadings or correlations of .60 and .40 on a factor are likely to be judged quite acceptable, but what of .30, .20, and .10, especially when a given factor contains so few items that extra items are needed to help increase its reliability?

Third, although statistical programs are able to identify various factors present in a set of data, it is the psychologist who necessarily interprets and labels all factors. This helps explain why one psychologist's "neuroticism" and "extraversion'' (Eysenck) are another psychologist's ''anxiety'' and ''exvia'' (Cattell). It also helps explain Cattell's preference for adopting a more neutral approach to identifying factors using alphabetical symbols (A, B, C) rather than potentially misleading trait labels (''outgoing,'' ''intelligent,'' and ''emotionally stable,'' respectively).

CONTRIBUTIONS

Establishing a dimensional view of traits.   Eysenck has taken issue with popular beliefs about extraversion and introversion. He has challenged categorical notions about the existence of separate compartments for ''extraverts'' and ''introverts'' and replaced them with his own dimensional concept in which personalities show, in differing amounts, ''more'' or ''less'' extraversion, as well as neuroticism and psychoticism. He has also demonstrated the role of physiological-arousal influences underlying this important personality dimension. Eysenck has pressed psychologists to learn ''the plain historical fact'' that his brand of extraversion-introversion personality types ''owes little to Jung, and the sooner this message reaches psychological textbooks the better'' (Eysenck, 1981, p. 12).

Replicating factors.   Eysenck has also made a good case that support for his two major factors, E and N, has been ''rigorously demonstrated.'' A key criterion, for him as well as Cattell, is ''factor invariance,'' which means that the major trait dimensions hypothesized by both researchers have appeared and reappeared even ''with change in sample along such parameters as sex, age, class and education'' (Eysenck & Eysenck, 1969, p. 326). Replications of E and N have occurred ''with high accuracy'' in studies of male and female subjects; different age groups, down to age 7; citizens of European and non-European countries; and groups of subjects differing in education and intelligence. There is little question that the existence of E and N has been confirmed by ''many workers,'' from ''many countries,'' using ''many different types of tests and measures'' (Eysenck & Eysenck, 1969).

Promoting biological considerations.   Eysenck has also promoted adoption of a biological point of view toward understanding personality by pointing to its underlying physical structures. For him, the time has come for the pendulum to start swinging back to biological causes and away from social ones. It is not that Eysenck wishes to dismiss the role of environmental causes, whether physical, sociocultural, or psychological. Although biological causes are important, they are not ''all-important.'' Rather, Eysenck's (1967) primary concern is to reaffirm the balance of hereditary and environmental influences, and their mutual interaction with one another.

Defining personality as predictable behavior.   Cattell's definition of personality is, perhaps, the most direct of those we will encounter in this book: ''that which permits a prediction of what a person will do in a given situation'' (1950, p. 2). It supports his and Eysenck's adherence to psychology's scientific aim of *predicting* behavior. Cattell (1973) has even sought to develop equations for predicting behavior based on weighted scores from personality questionnaires. His attempt is similar to earlier efforts by learning theorist Clark Hull (1952) and social psychologist Kurt Lewin (1936). Cattell's definition also supports his, and Eysenck's, interest in balancing biological and environmental influences on behavior by considering what a person will do "in a given situation." This approach meshes with current developments in the personality field emphasizing interactions between traits and situations, as detailed in Chapters 13 and 14.

Integrating correlational and experimental research. Perhaps most important, Eysenck has demonstrated his commitment to a scientific model of personality. In fact, Eysenck (1967) likes to refer to two pictures hanging in his office as being symbolic of the "two faces of psychology," the nomothetic and the idiographic (Cronbach, 1957; see Chapter 2). One picture, of a Victorian aristocrat, represents Sir Francis Galton. It symbolizes psychology's concern with individual differences, genetic causes of personality development, and the statistical investigation of classification systems. The second picture, of a Russian peasant, represents Ivan Pavlov. It symbolizes psychology's concern with general laws, environmental modification of behavior, and the experimental study of functional relationships. Eysenck (1967, 1981) views the two orientations as complementary and in need of each other's support: "Experimental psychologists often seem quite unaware of the problems created by individual differences; personality theorists seem equally unconcerned with the lack of relationship between their concepts and those of the experimentalists" (Eysenck, 1967, p. 3). One of Eysenck's continuing goals has been to bring psychology's two faces together. He has met this goal well.

FIVE UNIVERSAL FACTORS

We would like to conclude with a general observation that cuts across the work of many factor analysts. Five universal factors have regularly emerged in factor analyses. Referred to as "the Norman Five" (Norman, 1963), they are *surgency* (the fusion of potency and activity), *agreeableness* (coldness versus warmth), *conscientiousness, emotional stability,* and *culture* (a mixture of intellectual or cognitive aspects) (Goldberg, 1981). These five factors may signal a universal framework for understanding individual differences in human behavior. As summarized by Goldberg (1981), people interacting with other people in everyday situations seem to be very interested in knowing the answers to at least five questions about those other people:

Norman's five universal factors

1. Is X active and dominant or passive and submissive?
   ("Can I bully X or will X try to bully me?")
2. Is X agreeable or disagreeable?
   ("Will X be warm and pleasant or cold and distant?")
3. Is X responsible and conscientious or undependable and negligent?
   ("Can I count on X?")
4. Is X crazy or sane?
   ("Will X be unpredictable or stable?")
5. Is X smart or dumb?
   ("How easy will it be for me to teach X?")

CHAPTER REVIEW

This chapter has emphasized one approach to answering questions about individual differences in personality: the search for types and traits. Special emphasis has been placed on Eysenck's scientific model. The ancient Greeks speculated that individual differences were due to four personality types, caused by physically based differences in temperament. Twentieth-century answers have been guided by the development of more empirical techniques for studying personality.

The scientific model of personality proposed by Eysenck (and Cattell) is clearly embedded in the correlational technique of factor analysis. It values an experimental-research orientation that involves hypothesis testing in controlled situations, and theoretical deduction. The model reflects interests not only in describing personality but in explaining it. It has also been applied to problems in field settings outside the laboratory.

Eysenck's (and Cattell's) search for traits and types has been associated with important psychometric developments in personality measurement. The statistical, multiple-correlation method of factor analysis has been used to identify personality traits (factors) and types (superfactors). Eysenck and Eysenck have identified three superfactors, measured by the Eysenck Personality Questionnaire: extraversion-introversion (E), neuroticism-stability (N), and psychoticism-superego (P). Cattell has identified 16 factors, measured by the Sixteen Personality Factor Questionnaire. The work of other factor analysts has resulted in a more universal framework, Norman's "big five" superfactors. Overall results are not too far removed from the fourfold Grecian schema, especially when second-order factors are taken into account. However, current concepts are dimensional (more and less) rather than categorical (either/or). Present-day variations in numbers and content of factors can be traced to limitations of factor analysis as a data-reduction technique. By definition, traits and types always remain theoretical constructs.

Beyond simply describing personality, results of factor analysis have been bolstered by the experimental testing of theoretical hypotheses aimed at *explaining* individual differences in personality. Eysenck in particular has emphasized the biological underpinnings of personality: hereditary predispositions, physical temperaments of changeability and emotionality, physiological structures in the brain, cortical arousal and inhibition, sensory thresholds, and chemical processes in the endocrine system.

Eysenck and Cattell share a common definition of personality that is quite consistent with the goal of psychology in general — that which allows a person's behavior to be *predicted*. As seen in this chapter, a number of theoretical predictions have been supported, and results often have been replicated. The next chapter identifies additional traits that psychologists have found useful in predicting human behavior.

KEY CONCEPTS

Traits
Types
   Greek doctrine of four temperaments
Eysenck's scientific model for studying personality
   Factor analysis
      Factors
      Superfactors
   Psychometrics
      Eysenck's personality tests
   Eysenck's three superfactors
      Extraversion-introversion (E)

Neuroticism-stability (N)
Psychoticism-superego (P)
Dimensional approach to personality
Biological origins of traits and types
   Yerkes-Dodson law
Cattell's definition of personality
   Q-, L-, and T-Data
   Source and surface traits
   Sixteen Personality Factor Questionnaire (16 PF)
Norman's five universal factors

REVIEW QUESTIONS

1. Explain how Eysenck's current-day ideas about personality are similar to those of the ancient Greeks. How are they different? What does it mean to say that traits and types are "dimensional"?

2. Summarize the major components of Eysenck's scientific model for studying personality. State the relationship of psychometrics, experimentation, and the hypothetico-deductive method to Eysenck's goals of description and explanation.

3. What evidence does Eysenck cite to support the biological basis of personality?

4. Differentiate the four levels of Eysenck's hierarchy of personality description shown in Figure 9.2, giving examples of each. What is the relationship of factor analysis to this hierarchy? What are the strengths and limitations of factor analysis?

5. Identify the characteristics and behaviors of extraverted and introverted persons. Do you consider yourself more extraverted or more introverted? Support your belief.

10

Traits and Behavior: Authoritarianism, Anxiety, Achievement Motivation, and Sensation Seeking

Can prejudice reflect a personality trait?

Does anxiety ever improve people's functioning?

What motivates high achievers?

What might daredevils, people who experiment with drugs, and people who like spicy foods have in common?

T HIS CHAPTER continues the theme of searching for traits, introduced in Chapter 9. Actually, we do not have to search very long to find more traits than have been discussed so far. It seems as though traits are seen everywhere. Allport and Odbert's (1936) list of dictionary terms referring to personality contains 17,953 words, about one-fourth of which are identified as "trait" labels, such as *sociable, cautious, affectionate, aggressive, thoughtful, energetic,* and *cheerful*.

Four important traits are reviewed in this chapter: authoritarianism, anxiety, achievement motivation, and sensation seeking. The selection of traits is somewhat arbitrary, but representative. That is, each is a dimension along which many psychologists believe individuals differ, and each has generated a good deal of research. As a group, they have also been derived from both the correlational technique of factor analysis and the experimental testing of theoretical hypotheses, in laboratory and field settings.

Authoritarianism and achievement motivation have been linked to important social phenomena, such as anti-Semitism and economic productivity. Anxiety is closely related to Eysenck's neuroticism (N) dimension, discussed in the previous chapter. Sensation seeking is the "newest" of the traits and, along with anxiety, has been linked to biological origins. Although traits do not absolutely control behavior, they have sometimes been found useful in predicting some human behaviors.

As an introduction to the first trait, authoritarianism, take a moment to complete the exercise in Box 10.1.

| *Modified* | **BOX 10.1** |
| *F Scale** | |

Instructions: The following items represent possible beliefs. For each item, circle the number that best indicates your degree of agreement or disagreement.

1. Obedience and respect for authority are the most important virtues children should learn.

                Disagree   1   2   3   5   6   7   Agree

* Adapted from Adorno et al., 1950.

continued

BOX 10.1
continued

2. Every person should have complete faith in some supernatural power whose decisions he obeys without question.
   Disagree   1   2   3   5   6   7   Agree

3. There is hardly anything lower than a person who does not feel a great love, gratitude, and respect for his parents.
   Disagree   1   2   3   5   6   7   Agree

4. When a person has a problem or worry, it is best for him not to think about it, but to keep busy with more cheerful things.
   Disagree   1   2   3   5   6   7   Agree

5. People can be divided into two distinct classes: the weak and the strong.
   Disagree   1   2   3   5   6   7   Agree

6. What the youth needs most is strict discipline, rugged determination, and the will to work and fight for family and country.
   Disagree   1   2   3   5   6   7   Agree

7. Human nature being what it is, there will always be war and conflict.
   Disagree   1   2   3   5   6   7   Agree

8. Nowadays when so many different kinds of people move around and mix together so much, a person has to protect himself especially carefully against catching an infection or disease from them.
   Disagree   1   2   3   5   6   7   Agree

9. Sex crimes, such as rape and attacks on children, deserve more than mere imprisonment; such criminals ought to be publicly whipped, or worse.
   Disagree   1   2   3   5   6   7   Agree

Authoritarianism

authoritarianism

During the 1940s, a group of psychologists at the University of California, Berkeley, undertook a series of studies aimed at understanding processes of prejudice and social discrimination (Adorno, Frenkel-Brunswik, Levinson, & Sanford, 1950). These psychologists were particularly interested in understanding the pervasiveness of anti-Semitism in Nazi Germany. "How could it be," they asked, "that in a culture of law, order, and reason, there should have survived the irrational remnants of ancient racial and religious hatreds" (p. v)? The focus of the Berkeley group was not on national leaders but on the followers of authoritarian regimes. Is it possible to explain "the willingness of great masses of people to tolerate the mass extermination of their fellow citizens" (p. v)? Could the phenomenon occur in the United States?

authoritarian personality

Answers to these questions centered around the concept of an *authoritarian personality* syndrome, a personality type made up of a constellation of related traits. In essence, the authoritarian personality is characterized by antidemocratic ideas and feelings that are not merely matters of surface opinion but general tendencies stemming from "unconscious forces" and "deep-lying trends" in the

How can racial and religious hatred become such an important part of an otherwise lawful and orderly culture? Research findings by Adorno et al. point to the development of prejudice as central to the authoritarian personality, a "type" fostered especially by certain kinds of parent-child relationships.

individual's personality. Authoritarian individuals typically show a broad, coherent pattern of "conservative" political, economic, and social convictions.

MEASURING AUTHORITARIAN PREJUDICE AND PERSONALITY

The aim of the Berkeley group was to measure and integrate two broad aspects of human experience: prejudice and personality. Their procedure was to identify persons high and low in *prejudice,* or ideological beliefs against minority groups, and then compare their personalities. Group findings were supplemented by case-study comparisons of two young men identified as Larry and Mack.

To assess personality, various techniques were used: interviews, open-ended questions, and stories told in response to Thematic Apperception Test (TAT) pictures. To measure prejudice, a series of questionnaires was developed. The Anti-Semitism (A-S) Scale assessed prejudice against Jews ("Most hotels should deny admittance to Jews, as a general rule"). The Ethnocentrism (E) Scale assessed an "America first" brand of chauvinistic patriotism ("America may not be perfect, but the American Way has brought us about as close as human beings can get to a perfect society"). The Politico-Economic Conservatism (PEC) Scale measured conservative ideology ("In general, full economic security is bad; most men wouldn't work if they didn't need the money for eating and living").

Fascism (F) Scale

One of the most important prejudice scales was the Fascism (F) Scale, which assessed the "potentially antidemocratic personality," or a person's readiness to show prejudice in general and anti-Semitism in particular. Items in the F scale were formulated to tap an individual's "emotional need" to submit to authority, rather than realistic respect for valid authority. The Berkeley group concluded that nine related components, or traits, contribute to the authoritarian type of personality. Persons scoring high on one component were seen as likely to score high on the others.

The exercise in Box 10.1 is an adaptation of the F Scale. Each item represents one of nine traits of authoritarianism. These traits are identified and defined in Table 10.1, numbered to correspond with their representative items in Box 10.1. (The rating interval "4" was omitted by Adorno et al. to eliminate middle-of-the-scale answers.) To estimate your own score, add the values of the ratings you gave for the nine items (maximum score = 63, minimum score = 9). For purposes of this exercise, consider scores between 26 and 40 as falling within the average range, with 25 or less below average and 41 or more above average. The higher your score, the greater the likelihood of authoritarian tendencies in your personality. The lower your score, the greater the likelihood of opposite, *equalitarian* tendencies toward nonprejudice. However, keep in mind that the abbreviated version of the F Scale in Box 10.1 offers only a rough estimate of authoritarian tendencies in personality, along a continuum of more to less. The original F Scale contains 38 items, thereby making it a more reliable indicator (test-retest $r = .90$).

TABLE 10.1   Nine Traits of the Authoritarian Personality

1. *Conventionalism:* Rigid adherence to conventional, middle-class values. Adherence is more emotional than rational, without full understanding of the principles involved. Internal superego development may be weak.
2. *Authoritarian submission:* Submissive, uncritical attitude toward idealized moral authorities of the in-group. Persons show obedience to authority.
3. *Authoritarian aggression:* Tendency to be on the lookout for people who violate conventional values, and to condemn, reject, and punish them.
4. *Anti-intraception:* Opposition to the subjective, the imaginative, and the tender-minded. Self-reflection is minimized.
5. *Superstition and stereotyping:* Belief in mystical determinants of one's fate, along with a disposition to think in rigid categories. Personal failings are seen as due to forces outside oneself. Reasoning may be simplistic or black-and-white.
6. *Power and "toughness":* Preoccupation with the dimension of dominance-submission, strong-weak, leader-follower; identification with power figures; overemphasis on conventionalized attributes of the ego; exaggerated assertion of strength and toughness. A surface appearance of power may serve to offset personal feelings of weakness.
7. *Destructiveness and cynicism:* Generalized hostility, and vilification of the human. Contempt for human nature and "deviations" may be present.
8. *Projectivity:* Disposition to believe that wild, dangerous, and evil things go on in the world; the projection outwards of unconscious emotional impulses.
9. *Preoccupation with sex:* Exaggerated concern with sexual "goings-on."

CORRELATES OF AUTHORITARIANISM

The 1000-page book by Adorno et al. (1950) details the Berkeley group's procedures and findings, with results interpreted within a general psychoanalytic framework. Adorno et al. demonstrated a number of correlations between "deep-rooted" personality traits and overt prejudice. Since then, the authoritarian-personality concept has stimulated "a continuing heavy volume of research" (Dillehay, 1978, p. 85). Some research findings are summarized in Table 10.2. Persons who score high on authoritarianism tend to show a personality pattern of social conformity, political conservatism, acceptance of authority, non-acceptance of minority groups, thinking in terms of simple categories, and aggression toward low-status groups. Persons who score low (equalitarians) show comparatively greater questioning of authority, tolerance of differences among people, and broader cultural and educational experiences.

TABLE 10.2 Behavioral Correlates of Authoritarianism

High Scorers

More politically conservative than low scorers	Less sure of assigning guilt to a person they like
More rigid and resistant to change	More punitive toward a person they dislike
More conforming to group pressure	More aggressive toward low-status individuals
More likely to believe in TV and newspaper commentators	More likely to shift their level of aspiration after a success or failure
Tend to categorize people as good or bad	Prefer lectures over classroom discussions, and objective exams
Likely to be present in Catholic and orthodox religious groups	Less supportive of the women's movement
More likely to show anti-Black attitudes	
Less sensitive toward others and more distrustful of others	

Low Scorers

More aggressive toward high-status individuals compared with high scorers	Broader psychological perspective regarding human values, customs, and differences
Less likely to sign a faculty loyalty oath	Display more positive emotions and fewer commands in groups
Higher socioeconomic status	
Higher scores on intelligence tests	
Higher education	

DEVELOPMENT OF THE AUTHORITARIAN PERSONALITY

In keeping with their general psychoanalytic framework, Adorno et al. (1950) believe the authoritarian personality develops unconsciously, through family dynamics. Consider the case of Mack, a 24-year-old college freshman. Adorno et al. (1950) saw Mack's high authoritarianism as being maintained by childhood experiences with his parents: psychological dependency on his mother, who died when he was 6; hostility toward his father, whom Mack unconsciously experienced as a powerful oppressor; submissiveness; passivity; latent homosexuality; and fear of weakness. Mack strives to conceal his weakness by adopting a tough exterior, using a leather jacket and rifle as "unmistakable" signs of masculinity. His defenses keep him from exploring his own personality with insight. He is not weak; other people are. He is not angry; other people are. He sees "only what he has seen before" and he learns "only what he already knows."

Kelman and Barclay (1963) and Dillehay (1978) have proposed alternative theories for understanding the development of authoritarianism. Dillehay's model posits two principal influences: lowered psychological capacity and lowered social opportunity. Lowered *psychological capacity* is partly defined by the nature of a person's intellectual functioning—"the disposition to think in narrow categories that are rigid and fixed," which may indicate reduced abilities to assimilate information from the environment and profit from experience (Dillehay, 1978, p. 109). The person tends to categorize complex experiences in simple ways by relying on surface appearances of reality, using social stereotypes, and adhering to superstitious thinking.

Figure 10.1 illustrates Dillehay's model. Note that the two major components of psychological capacity and social opportunity influence the development of authoritarianism, but that authoritarianism reciprocates by limiting both components. Thus, once authoritarianism develops in the personality, it further narrows the use of social opportunities for personal growth, limits psychological functioning, and increases experiences of anxiety. Anxiety-arousing "threats" to the person's inadequate understanding of the world intensify efforts to maintain simplistic categorizations of the environment, even though more complex processing is required. Dillehay's model is consistent with the Adorno et al. (1950) conclusion that a person's susceptibility to authoritarianism is partly cultural. However, it does not explicitly endorse Adorno et al.'s explanation regarding the role of unconscious family dynamics in forming the authoritarian personality.

LIMITATIONS OF THE AUTHORITARIANISM CONCEPT

A number of criticisms have been directed against the authoritarianism concept. Chief among these is that sources of bias entered into the original research, conceptually and methodologically (Christie & Jahoda, 1954; Kirscht & Dillehay, 1967; Dillehay, 1978). Conceptually, authoritarianism involves not only

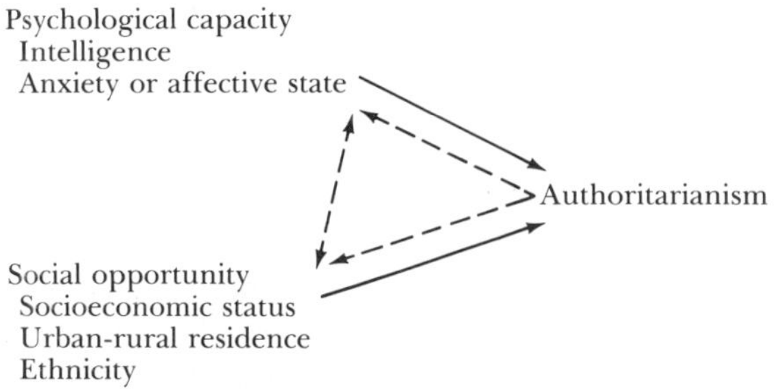

Psychological capacity
Intelligence
Anxiety or affective state

Authoritarianism

Social opportunity
Socioeconomic status
Urban-rural residence
Ethnicity

Figure 10.1
Dillehay's (1978) model of authoritarian-personality development.

"personality" but a "belief structure" embedded in ideas that have a particular political content. This content deals much more with opinions reflective of the political right ($r = .54$) than the political left ($r = .02$; Rokeach, 1967). However, critics contend that authoritarian tendencies can be shown by "liberal" as well as "conservative" people, including totalitarian-style socialists and reformers.

Further, the Berkeley research project was sponsored by a particular organization, the American Jewish Committee. International outrage over Nazi extermination programs was intense and, while clearly understandable, likely was present as an underlying influence on the researchers. Because interviewers knew ahead of time the prejudice scores of the persons they interviewed, it would have been possible for them to develop expectations about the personalities of the interviewees. Too, all research subjects who scored high in authoritarianism were interviewed by American-born Gentiles, a systematic influence that did not occur with subjects who scored low. Jahoda (1954) believes that much of the empirical evidence obtained was used "only to bear out the researchers' theoretical position assumed before they started the study and not modified after the effort" (p. 19).

In terms of method, theoretical concepts go hand in hand with the measuring instruments used to research them. If the measures show limitations, the concepts will be limited as well. The F Scale was unintentionally constructed in such a way as to have a built-in response bias: the wording of items is such that all scoring is done in a single, positive direction; that is, subjects always receive more points when they respond "Agree" than when they respond "Disagree." (Refer to the sample test in Box 10.1.) This influence is termed *acquiescence* — a response style that reflects an individual's tendency to endorse rather than question generalized test items, especially when statements are complex and reflect uncertainties (Bentler, Jackson, & Messick, 1971; Peabody, 1966). Acquiescence is a kind of measurement distortion that operates independently of the content of items. You likely are familiar with people who tend to be "yeasayers" or "naysayers" regardless of the issues involved. An "agreement" set may allow individuals to feel that they are presenting themselves in a favorable or acceptable light. Acquiescence is not typical of most psychological measures, which usually counterbalance the directions in which items are scored (Samelson, 1972). Finally, evidence regarding the separate identity of the nine F Scale components is weak (Knapp, 1976). Two of the dimensions are comprised of only three items each, thereby limiting the ability to define and measure them reliably.

RECONCEPTUALIZING AUTHORITARIANISM: DOGMATISM

Kirscht and Dillehay (1967) state that the most useful way to define authoritarianism is in terms of a cognitive style characterized by *closed-mindedness:* "The genuine authoritarian lacks ability to deal with novel cognitive material, seeks rapid closure when exposed to new situations, and ultimately depends heavily on external authority for support of his belief system" (pp. 132–133). This cognitive style also is tied to the two components identified in Figure 10.1. People who lack richness and variety in their social environments are likely to have a narrower perspective concerning human values, customs, and differences. In contrast, people with broader social experience will have the opportunity to see that "reality is, after all, largely social reality, that is, defined by people for people," (Dille-hay, 1978, p. 107). They will understand that social reality can look different, depending on one's point of view. Consequently, they will be more tolerant of those who differ from them. Persons living in a bland and homogeneous environment are likely to exhibit a narrow and limited personal perspective, developing little appreciation of the fact that there are alternative points of view about the world and the people in it.

dogmatism

These ideas can be related to those of Milton Rokeach (1954), who sought to offset some of the criticisms of the Berkeley research by reconceptualizing authoritarianism in such a way that it would not be tied to any single ideology. He developed the concept of *dogmatism*—the degree to which a person's belief system is closed or open. Rokeach's primary concern is not with the *content* of beliefs (*what* people believe), but with the *structure* of beliefs (*how* people believe). Thus, people may be closed-minded or open-minded quite apart from their particular ideas or belief systems, whether liberal, conservative, communist, Catholic, Protestant, existentialist, or Freudian. All groups are likely to have both open-minded and closed-minded members.

Dogmatism (D) Scale

Rokeach also constructed the Dogmatism (D) Scale, a questionnaire to measure individual differences on this trait. Although the content of dogmatic beliefs is less important than their structure, Ehrlich (1978) has pointed out a number of similarities between dogmatic and authoritarian beliefs: "People are unfriendly and rejecting," and "The world is fundamentally hostile." Scores on the D Scale actually are highly correlated with those on the F Scale, typically falling between .54 and .88 (Kirscht & Dillehay, 1967). This means that dogmatism content is, in fact, related to authoritarianism.

Research findings.   Rokeach's dogmatism concept has proven to be a "fruitful" formulation that has stimulated "a considerable amount of diversified research" (Vacchiano, Strauss, & Hochman, 1969), resulting in "strong empirical support" (Ehrlich, 1978, p. 130). In 1969, there were more than 1000 research reports on dogmatism in the literature (Ehrlich & Lee, 1969; Vacchiano, Strauss, & Hochman, 1969).

Rokeach (1960) and his colleagues have been able to demonstrate that important aspects of mental functioning are due not just to intellectual ability but to personality. This is because the underlying structure of a person's belief system has a common influence on many spheres of activity, including perceptions, memories, problem solving, emotions, enjoyment of music, and even artistic preferences. In dogmatism experiments, a typical procedure is to compare persons scoring high and low on the D Scale, especially on tasks requiring adoption of a new belief system that is at odds with an earlier one.

Open-minded persons are able to synthesize new beliefs more creatively into a reorganized system, compared with closed-minded persons. Closed-minded persons benefit from having all parts of a new system presented to them simultaneously, "on a silver platter," in order to effect a synthesis. In this way, old and new beliefs do not have to be reconciled internally. Closed-minded persons also benefit from having visual access to new information, as an aid to overcoming the unwillingness of "forgetful" memory in working out new belief systems.

Some interesting correlates of dogmatism have been reported. Closed-minded persons show a history of having tasted fewer foods in their lives compared with open-minded persons (Lee & Ehrlich, 1977). Closed-minded persons also show lower sensitivity to stimulation of the five senses than do open-minded persons ($r = -.61$; Kaplan & Singer, 1963).

Developmental experiences, dogmatism, and anxiety.   Rokeach and Kemp (1960) studied the relationship of dogmatism to parent/child experiences and to anxiety. They concluded that dogmatism develops partly as a function of the breadth or narrowness of a child's identification with people outside the family, which, in turn, may be connected with "the extent to which ambivalent feelings toward parents are permitted within the family atmosphere" (p. 362). They also concluded that a closed cognitive system may serve as a defense against anxiety in children. What contributed to their conclusions?

Subjects were 104 students attending a Presbyterian college, all of whom showed high religious values and were enrolled in a social-welfare training program for youth. Subjects were asked a series of questions, such as "What sort of a person was your father? . . . your mother?" Following procedures used by Adorno et al. (1950), judges categorized the answers into three types: ambivalence, mild ambivalence, and glorification of parent (90% co-rater agreement). *Ambivalence* refers to a simultaneous mixture of positive and negative feelings or attitudes toward an object, such as love *and* hate. Examples of the two most extreme categories follow (Rokeach & Kemp, 1960, p. 358):

> *Ambivalence.* "Some of the time she was a reserved autocrat in the home; other times she was different and more likeable, almost lovable. [Mother was] good to me over minor things, but didn't handle the hard things too well. She had her good and bad points."
> *Glorification.* "The best, no limit in any way." . . . "Very wonderful and understanding, kindhearted toward her children." . . . "Unselfish, loving, tireless."

Significantly greater ambivalence was expressed by the open group (66%) than the closed group (12%). Glorification was expressed more by the closed group (30%) than the open group (12%). Results replicated those of Adorno et al. (1950), who also found greater parental glorification expressed by persons high in authoritarianism, and greater ambivalence expressed by persons low in authoritarianism. Results support Frenkel-Brunswik's (1949, 1954) conclusion "that the inability to express emotional ambivalence toward parents predisposes one to form an authoritarian outlook on life" (Rokeach & Kemp, 1960, p. 359).

Second, to determine the extent of interpersonal influences outside the family, subjects were asked to answer the question "What other people (relations, guardians, friends, etc.) influenced your development?" Persons with open belief systems were expected to report more external influences than persons with closed systems. The open group differed significantly from the closed group by responding to the question in a general way, without pinpointing particular persons or groups outside the family (72% versus 8%). The closed group more often cited a clergyman or scout leader as having been influential (60% versus 8%).

Third, participants were asked to report the presence of childhood symptoms often associated with anxiety: nail biting, temper tantrums, nightmares, sleepwalking, and sleeptalking. Consistent with psychoanalytic theory, inability to express emotional ambivalence toward one's parents would be expected to increase a child's need to keep hostile feelings buried in the unconscious. The defense mechanism of repression would function to minimize anxiety, related to potential but undesired expression of negative feelings (see Chapter 3). Closed-minded persons would be expected to show more anxiety symptoms than open-minded persons, because the latter are able to express their ambivalence directly. In fact, the mean number of anxiety symptoms was significantly higher for the closed group (2.5) than the open group (.4). Also supportive were results from the question "At what age approximately did you stop wetting the bed?" The mean ages reported by the closed and open groups were 6.2 and 2.2, respectively.

In sum, with respect to personality development, Rokeach and Kemp (1960) studied the relationship of dogmatism to parent/child relationships and anxiety. Their results indicate that persons who score *low* on the D Scale express more ambivalence toward both parents, report being more widely influenced by persons outside the immediate family, and report fewer anxiety symptoms in childhood. Persons who score *high* on the D Scale show greater glorification of their parents, report a more restricted influence by persons outside the family, and report a greater number of childhood symptoms associated with anxiety. In brief, inadequate expression of ambivalence toward one's parents seems to lead to anxiety and a narrowing of possibilities for identification with persons outside the family. These characteristics, in turn, are related to the development of closed belief systems.

HOW COULD MASS PREJUDICE OCCUR?

The practical import of authoritarianism and dogmatism for personality functioning concerns individual differences in the ability to differentiate relevant and irrelevant information in a situation. In most situations, the making of appropriate responses is closely linked to the processing of relevant information in an open-minded manner. Closed-mindedness is likely to lead to relatively "unintelligent" or inappropriate responses, based on such irrelevant factors as self-protective needs to minimize anxiety or pressures from parents, peers, and authority figures; self-serving needs for approval, power, or advancement; and irrational conformity with social, institutional, and cultural norms.

Reliance on absolute authority is certainly present in dogmatic personality functioning. However, the most central, cognitive basis is a reduced ability to distinguish between substantive information and its source. What the external source says is true about the world becomes "all mixed up" with what the external source wants people to believe is true and wants people to do about it (Rokeach & Restle, 1960, p. 58). This distinction may help answer Adorno et al.'s (1950) questions about Nazi anti-Semitism. It also may be related to trait theorists' explanations of "obedient" behavior in such recent contexts as the massacre of civilians by military personnel (Auchincloss, 1971) and the maltreatment of political dissidents by law-enforcement officers ("In the Dock," 1985). Perpetrators may simply believe "I was just following orders" (see Eichmann, Chapter 2). In

brief, persons high in authoritarianism and dogmatism traits may be more predisposed than others to "just follow orders." Such persons are more apt to be
characterized by a closed-mind, uncritical acceptance of authority, rejection of
those who disagree with them, and unqualified acceptance of those who agree
with them. They may also tend toward the right of center, politically. (An alternative, situational perspective regarding obedience, proposed by Milgram, is discussed in Chapter 11.)

Concepts similar to authoritarianism have been put forth by a number of
other psychologists. They include rational versus arbitrary authority (Fromm,
1941), resistance to acculturation (Maslow, 1951), independence versus yielding
(Asch, 1952), and conformance versus nonconformance (Jahoda, 1956). Psychologists have also introduced a variety of assessment instruments related to authoritarianism, many of which have been found to measure slightly different aspects of
the authoritarian concept (R. J. Knapp, 1976). This pattern of multiple definitions and assessment techniques in relation to a single concept also characterizes
the next trait to be discussed: anxiety.

Anxiety

The study of anxiety has captured the interest of psychologists from all orienta-   anxiety
tions, researchers and clinicians alike. Anxiety has been linked to startle responses
in infants (Watson, 1930/1959), intrapsychic conflict (Freud, 1923/1936), separation of children from parents (Bowlby, 1969), classical and operant conditioning (Mowrer, 1947), drive level (Spence, 1964), emotional responsiveness (J. A.
Taylor, 1951), brain damage (Goldstein, 1939), interpersonal disapproval (Sullivan, 1953), self-creative freedom (May, 1950), failure of personal expectancies
(Kelly, 1955), self-preoccupation (Sarason, 1975), and excessive arousal (S. Epstein, 1972). May's (1950) book, *The Meaning of Anxiety,* presents 18 theories of
anxiety, 3 of which are philosophical, 4 biological, 7 psychological, 3 cultural, and
May's. Fischer (1970) discusses 9 theories and Epstein (1972) 13 theories.

At present, the anxiety construct remains many things to many psychologists
(Spielberger, 1972). The absence of an agreed-upon definition of anxiety is due
partly to the diverse orientations of theorists and partly to the complexity of the
phenomena underlying the concept. Researchers have investigated anxiety with
everything from paper-and-pencil tests to measures of physiological responses,
and there is a significant amount of disagreement among measures that supposedly measure the "same" thing. There is also controversy as to the usefulness of
conceptualizing anxiety as a personality trait, a situational state, or neither (Allen
& Potkay, 1981, 1983b). As Phares and Lamiell (1977) comment, "For a concept
that so many psychologists are convinced they cannot live without, there is very
little agreement as to its nature" (p. 131).

WHAT IS ANXIETY?

Six characteristics of anxiety.   One conclusion about anxiety is certain: it
has multiple components. Lewis (1980) lists six characteristics of anxiety. However, not all of these characteristics are likely to be present in all individuals at the

same time or in one individual across time. Furthermore, the components are likely to be weighted differently from one person to another.

First, anxiety is *an emotional experience,* involving feelings of a generalized nature.

Second, the emotional experience is highly *unpleasant.* Anxiety feelings have a quality of fear about them—alarm, fright, panic, scare, dread, terror, even impending personal "doom," disaster, collapse, or death.

Third, anxiety is *directed toward the future.* There is a sense that something terrible will happen "soon," or eventually.

Fourth, there is *no recognizable or reasonable threat.* The emotional reaction is way out of proportion to any stimulus that might elicit it. This is why anxiety is traditionally differentiated from fear. Fear takes an object, in that the person knows what she or he is afraid of. Anxiety is more "free floating," meaning that it often has no consistent target. It always seems ready to attach itself to anything in general but nothing in particular. The person reports feeling afraid of anything and everything, without knowing exactly what. Thus, fear is a realistic response, whereas anxiety is considered more unrealistic or "neurotic." Anxiety is a kind of "fear of fear," reminiscent of Franklin Roosevelt's reassurance to the American people during the Great Depression that there was "nothing to fear but fear itself." Some physiological distinctions have been made between fear and anxiety (Cattell, 1963). Fear is associated with the release of adrenaline, while anxiety is not. Fear dries the mouth more than anxiety, while anxiety increases stomach secretion.

Fifth, anxiety is accompanied by *subjectively experienced bodily discomforts,* such as tightness in the chest, difficulty breathing, butterflies in the stomach, and weakness in the legs. Restlessness and tension are typical. The person is unable to relax or sit still without feeling fidgety or jittery.

Sixth, there are *manifest bodily disturbances.* Examples include such autonomic nervous-system reactions as sweating, rapid heart rate, tremor and vomiting, and such activities as running in panic, screaming, and defecation, which ordinarily are under voluntary control.

Three sources of anxiety.   Seymour Epstein (1972) views anxiety as an unpleasant experience of "high diffuse arousal." This physiological and emotional arousal usually follows some perception of "danger," but is without direction. He identifies three sources of anxiety arousal.

three sources of
anxiety arousal

The first and most fundamental source is *primary overstimulation*—any excitation or threat that surpasses the person's biologically determined tolerance for intensity or rate of stimulation is pain. Pain motivates a person to escape from whatever is causing it and is often associated with the learning of fear—a conditioned response that leads the person to avoid previously experienced pain situations. The person experiences "frantic feelings of being overwhelmed and bombarded with stimulation," as if saying "Stop it, I can't stand it anymore" (Epstein, 1972, p. 303).

The second source of arousal is *cognitive incongruity*—the mismatch between one's expectations or cognitive understanding of the world, including oneself, and the real nature of that world. The person is unable to make necessary and accurate predictions about reality, or to integrate information consistently about what is happening, either externally or internally. When personal expectancies prove ineffective, the person feels confused and disorganized, and may experience personality disintegration. The person may think "I don't know what's going on anymore. I'm not myself."

Third, there is *response unavailability,* which refers to any condition in which an aroused response tendency cannot be expressed. The lack of expression may be due to lack of knowledge as to what is causing the arousal, a need for additional time before making a response, conflict beween opposing responses, or an inadequate repertoire of behavior for making the response. "Threat" may also prevent the person from responding (May, 1950). If the opportunity for motor discharge is blocked, the person may feel frustrated or helpless, perhaps thinking "I don't know what to do, or I can't do it. It wouldn't work anyway."

TWO ANXIETY TRAITS: CATTELL'S RESEARCH

Cattell's (1963) investigation of the nature and measurement of anxiety actually led him to identify two independent trait anxiety factors: Universal Index (U.I.) 23 and 24. (The Universal Index is a schema for coding factors by number, for reference use by researchers.) U.I. 23 is a source trait, *regression versus mobilization*—a general loss of control or interest in displaying abilities versus the ability to apply and adapt one's skills quickly. Regression is an important component of neurotic anxiety and is highly correlated with Eysenck's concept of Neuroticism (N), discussed in Chapter 9. Table 10.3 summarizes a number of behaviors characteristic of persons who score high on U.I. factor 23, *regression.* Factor loadings indicate the degree to which a given behavior correlates statistically with the trait in question (0.00 = no correlation and 1.00 = perfect correlation).

Cattell's second anxiety trait is U.I. 24, *anxiety versus relaxation.* Anxiety is a kind of "ergic tension" or frustrated drive that remains aroused but unexpressed, leading to behaviors that are tense, driven, and overactive. Representative ques-

Cattell's two anxiety traits

regression versus mobilization (U.I. 23)

anxiety versus relaxation (U.I. 24)

TABLE 10.3   Behaviors Characteristic of Persons High on Cattell's (1963) Regression Trait, U.I. 23

Variable	Factor loading
Inability to do simple addition and subtraction mentally	.57
Stuttering and upset speech with delayed auditory feedback	.57
Slow and erratic recognition of upside-down forms	.57
Aspiration level high relative to performance	.55
Poor ability to coordinate simultaneous spatial cues	.55
Low metabolic rate change in response to stimuli	.50
Low readiness to tackle unpleasant activities	.47
Numerous "indecisive" responses in questionnaires	.44
Errors in reciting alphabet with prescribed skipping	.42
Rapid increase of errors when made to hurry	.31
High motor-perceptual rigidity	.29
Greater response to color than form in artistic works	.25
High body sway under suggestible conditions	.20

tionnaire items designed to measure U.I. 24 include "Do you, when forced to remain inactive, begin to doodle, draw things on the margin of your paper, etc.?" and "Do quite small setbacks irritate you unduly?" Cattell (1963) believes that U.I. 24 offers "striking" experimental support of Freud's theory regarding the origin of neurotic anxiety. That is, the anxiety is caused partly by undischarged drive tensions, particularly of a sexual and aggressive nature, and partly by weakness of the ego, which causes internal impulses to be felt as more threatening than would be the case if ego control were strong (Cattell, 1965, p. 118). Table 10.4 summarizes a number of correlates characteristic of persons who score high on U.I. factor 24, *anxiety*. The coefficients represent average results from five factor-analytic studies, on a variety of laboratory tasks.

Cattell (1963) and his co-workers have reported several research findings related to anxiety. For example, anxiety fluctuates in childhood, rises during adolescence, and declines through adulthood "as the individual settles his problems of occupational adjustment, marriage and social setting," then rises again after age 60–65 (Cattell, 1965, pp. 120–121). Occupational groups showing high anxiety include newspaper editors, artists, and air cadets in training. Low anxiety is characteristic of police officers, clerical workers, and engineers. Among psychiatric patients, scores are highest among anxious neurotics and alcoholics. Tranquilizing drugs and psychotherapy are effective in reducing anxiety. University students show higher anxiety during weeks immediately preceding an important exam than during the exam itself. Citizens of India, France, and Italy generally report more anxiety than those of England and America.

EXPERIENCING ANXIETY

Most of us have experienced mild to moderate anxiety. It may have occurred before we participated in a sports event (locker-room jitters), performed on stage (stage fright), went on a first date, gave a speech, met some important person, or

TABLE 10.4   Behaviors Characteristic of Persons High on Cattell's (1963) Anxiety Trait, U.I. 24

Variable	Factor loading
High susceptibility to annoyance	.56
High willingness to admit common faults	.47
High tendency to agree	.38
High heart rate	.30
Slow reaction time	.28
Low writing pressure	.28
Low total physical strength	.27
High criticalness	.25
High rate of autonomic conditioning	.25
Low hand-steadiness	.22
High emotionality in verbal comments	.20
High self-criticism	.19
Less alkaline saliva	.19
Slow speed of perceptual judgment	.18

took an examination. Mild amounts of anxiety are adaptive. They sharpen the edge of human performance, alerting the individual and enhancing efficiency. Physiological monitoring of astronauts indicates that they may experience a slight increase in anxiety before lift-off.

However, intense experiences of anxiety are not adaptive. They interfere with performance, sometimes leading individuals into states of psychological emergency or paralyzing inactivity. The Yerkes-Dodson law discussed in Chapter 9 helps explain the relationship between anxiety arousal and productive functioning. Graphed as an upside-down U curve, it indicates that lesser amounts of anxiety may be helpful to effective human performance, whereas amounts greater than optimum are increasingly harmful (Martens & Landers, 1970).

Severe anxiety is at the core of many common psychological maladjustments, especially the neuroses that affect 2–4% of the general population (Freud, 1923/1936; Lopez Ibor, 1980; American Psychiatric Association, 1980). Maladjustments include *generalized anxiety disorders,* in which the person persistently experiences the kinds of difficulties illustrated in Box 10.2. Other anxiety-related maladjustments include *phobias,* or exaggerated fears of some specific object (such as snakes), activity (such as urinating in a public restroom), or situation (such as being alone outdoors). Phobias bring about excessive avoidance behavior and may be accompanied by terrifying anxiety panic attacks when avoidance cannot take place. Box 10.2 describes a college student's intense experience of generalized anxiety in relation to an upcoming examination. Should this experience be characteristic of the student over time, he would be viewed as having the maladaptive trait of excessive anxiety.

Anxiety Experienced by a College Student   **BOX 10.2**

Fischer (1970) has provided the following account of an anxiety experience in a college student who was about to take a final examination. It illustrates many of the components of anxiety discussed in this section, including cognitive ideas (worries), motor behavior (talking), and physiological reactions (nausea).

> When I think about the exam I really feel sick . . . so much depends on it. I know I'm not prepared, at least not as much as I should be, but I keep hoping that I can sort of snow my way through it. . . . I keep trying to remember some of the things he said in class, but my mind keeps wandering. God, my folks — What will they think if I don't pass and can't graduate? Will they have a fit! Boy! I can see their faces. Worse yet, I can hear their voices: "And with all the money we spent on your education." Mom's going to be hurt. She'll let me know I let her down. . . . Hell! What about me? What'll I do if I don't graduate? How about the plans I made? I had a good job lined up with that company. They really sounded like they wanted me, like I was going to be somebody. . . . And what about the car? I had it all planned out. I was going to pay seventy a month and still have enough left for fun. I've got to pass. Oh

continued

BOX 10.2
continued

hell! What about Anne? She's counting on my graduating. We had plans. What will she think? She knows I'm no brain, but . . . hell, I won't be anybody. I've got to find some way to remember those names. . . . What am I going to do? God, I can't think. You know, I may just luck out. I've done it before. He could ask just the right questions. What could he ask? Boy! I feel like I want to vomit. Do you think others are as scared as I am? They probably know it all or don't give a damn. I'll bet you most of them have parents who can set them up whether they have college degrees or not. God, it means so much to me. I've got to pass. I've just got to. Dammit, what are those names? What could he ask? I can't think . . . I can't. . . . Maybe if I had a beer I'd be able to relax a little. . . . I've got to study. . . . I can't. What's going to happen to me? . . . The whole damn world is coming apart. (pp.121–122)

ASSESSING ANXIETY

Difficulties of assessment.   Anxiety is often assessed through (1) a person's subjective self-report, (2) objective observations of overt motor behavior, and (3) sophisticated physiological techniques. However, results derived from these different measures frequently show little correlation with one another (Davison & Neale, 1982; Weinberger, Schwartz, & Davidson, 1979). From your own experience, consider the self-reports made by friends and classmates about how "terribly nervous and worried" they were while giving a talk in class. Such reports regularly elicit comments from fellow students that the anxiety "really didn't show" in their observable behavior.

McEwan and Devins (1983) compared self- and peer ratings on three traits: anxiety, friendliness, and conscientiousness. No significant discrepancies were noted for friendliness and conscientiousness. However, self-estimates of anxiety were greater than those made by peers. This was especially true of students who were high in both social anxiety and bodily signs of anxiety taking place "within the skin." These students believed they displayed a greater number of visible signs of anxiety than was actually noticed by their peers.

Janet Taylor Spence and the Manifest Anxiety Scale (MAS). One of the most important measures of trait anxiety is the Taylor Manifest Anxiety Scale (MAS), which has been used in "well over 2,000 studies" (Spielberger, 1975). The MAS was developed by J. T. Spence as part of a doctoral dissertation on eyelid conditioning at the University of Iowa (J. A. Taylor, 1951, 1953). Five clinical psychologists were asked to determine which of 200 selected MMPI items best met a definition of chronic anxiety given by Cameron (1947). High agreement was shown for 65 items at an 80% level or better. Modifications resulted in a final version consisting of 50 true/false items, such as:

Taylor Manifest
Anxiety Scale
(MAS)

"I find it hard to keep my mind on a task or job."

"I notice my heart pounding and I am often short of breath."

"I feel anxiety about something or someone almost all the time."

Differences in MAS scores are assumed to reflect individual differences in "emotional responsiveness" or motivational drive level, a dimension that is relevant to conditioned learning. That is, according to the drive theory of Clark Hull (1943) and Kenneth Spence (1956, 1958), the strength of a behavioral response (R) is a function of drive multiplied by habit strength (D × H). Persons with high MAS scores are assumed to have higher drive than those with low scores. A number of predictions derived from the Spence-Taylor drive theory have been supported (J. A. Taylor, 1956). For example, individuals with high MAS scores show significantly better performance on simple learning tasks calling for a single,

JANET TAYLOR SPENCE.
Spence has been recognized for many contributions to the personality field, including assessment. Her *Manifest Anxiety Scale* has been used in more than 2,000 studies, and her research with the *Work and Family Orientation Questionnaire* has shown that achievement motivation pertains to women as well as men.

dominant response, such as eyelid conditioning. Responses of high-MAS individuals also extinguish more slowly. However, in more complex learning situations, the performance of high-MAS individuals decreases, because high D increases the probability that *any* behavior learned in response to a given stimulus will be performed. In other words, complex tasks elicit a greater number of "interference" or competing responses, as when a person is required to learn two lists of words, one after the other. In this situation, fewer error responses are likely to be made by individuals with low MAS scores.

Anxiety as both trait and state?   Although the focus of this chapter is on traits, we would be remiss if we failed to address a major complication involved in understanding personality constructs. That is, psychologists may adopt a dual perspective toward the same personality dimension, sometimes viewing it as a permanent "trait" and sometimes as a temporary "state." Thus, in relation to anxiety, recognition is given to observations that persons with a high general level of anxiety may not experience anxiety in all situations, and those whose general level is low may experience high anxiety on some occasions.

Allen and Potkay (1981, 1983b) have argued that the trait-state distinction is arbitrary (we return to this issue in Chapter 16). However, Lamb (1978) credits the research of Cattell and his co-workers (Cattell & Scheier, 1961) as the first systematic attempt to identify and measure the dual aspects of anxiety. And Singer and Singer (1972, p. 384) have linked the "major new trend" in state-trait conceptualization to "a shift towards new instruments which attempt to differentiate anxiety as a persisting predisposition (trait) and anxiety as a momentary reaction to stress (state)." One such instrument is the State-Trait Anxiety Inventory (STAI), which measures ego-threatening anxiety (Speilberger, Gorsuch, & Lushene, 1970). Spielberger (1975) defines *state anxiety (A-state)* as "a transitory condition of the organism that varies in intensity and fluctuates over time" (pp. 136–137). He defines *trait anxiety (A-trait)* as referring to "relatively stable individual differences in anxiety proneness, i.e., to differences among people in the disposition or tendency to perceive a wide range of situations as threatening and to respond to these situations with differential elevations in state anxiety" (p. 137). Persons high in A-trait show relatively permanent and strong sympathetic arousal, fear, and emotionality. Thus, the level of their emotional arousal is generally greater than that typically experienced by the average person (Cattell, 1965). While typically showing anxiety reactions in relationships with other people or threats to self-esteem, their fearfulness of realistic physical dangers is equivalent to that of persons low in A-trait.

Another "new" instrument is the Multiple Affect Adjective Check List (MAACL) (Zuckerman & Lubin, 1965). The MAACL has two forms, both of which contain the same 132 adjectives. However, the two forms have different instructions. The General or trait form asks an individual to mark whichever adjectives best describe "how *you generally feel.*" The Today or state form asks the individual to mark off adjectives best describing "how *you feel now — today.*" The rationale is that responses about one's personality "in general" may differ from one's personality "today" because of transient personal and external influences such as fatigue, good or bad days, vulnerability to stress, and such anticipated events as examinations. Figure 10.2 illustrates changes in anxiety scores of 67

state anxiety

trait anxiety

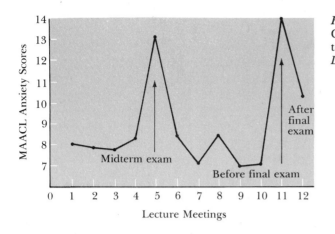

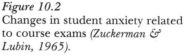

Figure 10.2
Changes in student anxiety related
to course exams *(Zuckerman &
Lubin, 1965).*

student nurses who were asked to complete the Today form of the MAACL at 12 consecutive class meetings held one week apart (C. Hayes, 1965). The influence of course examinations on anxiety is evident, including a moderate elevation in anxiety immediately following the final exam. Zuckerman and Lubin (1965) report eight replications "establishing the sensitivity of the MAACL" to these systematic changes in examination anxiety among students.

Achievement Motivation (n Ach)

Are champions "born" or "made"? Eysenck's answer to this question is that they are "born" (see Chapter 9). However, an alternative answer is possible, stemming from investigations of achievement motivation. *Achievement motivation* refers to a person's *learned* need or drive to achieve success in competition with some standard of excellence (McClelland, Atkinson, Clark, & Lowell, 1953). Within this framework, champions are "made."

achievement
motivation

Although achievement motivation is referred to as a "need," "drive," or "motive," it can be conceptualized as a trait because it is a relatively permanent characteristic of personality. Atkinson (1958) defines a need or *motive* as "a relatively enduring disposition to strive for a particular kind of goal or aim" (p. 597). The aim of any motive is identified by the particular satisfaction brought about by a person's actions, such as having a positive emotional relationship with another person (affiliation motive) or having control over the behavior of another person (power motive). The goal of achievement motivation is personal accomplishment or success, or pride in doing something well. This goal may be evidenced by (1) competition with a standard of excellence, (2) some unique accomplishment, or (3) long-term involvement with an activity performed well.

The concept of *n* Ach was introduced by Henry Murray (1938/1962), who viewed it as the desire to excel and strive to accomplish difficult things, to do things as rapidly or as well as possible, and to surpass others. He saw it reflected in ambition, aspiration, competitiveness, and the determination to win. Later, the *n* Ach concept was developed in support of a theory of motivation based on expectancies or anticipated goal responses (Atkinson, 1964; Atkinson & Feather, 1966). *N* Ach is a future-oriented drive, operating beyond immediate situations to a person's "tomorrow" (deCharms & Muir, 1978).

n Ach

Martina Navratilova, winner of numerous Wimbledon championships, illustrates many of the characteristics of high achievers: the development of personal abilities, a striving for success, self-discipline, optimism, and a positive self-concept.

MEASURING n ACH

Thematic Apperception Test (TAT)

Using the TAT. The standard procedure in n Ach research studies has been to arouse achievement motivation experimentally, through fantasy productions. For this reason, the investigation of n Ach has been closely tied to use of the Thematic Apperception Test (TAT) (Murray, 1943). The TAT is an open-ended projective technique that measures fantasy by asking people to tell or write stories in response to a set of pictures (as discussed in Chapter 2). Instructions for responding to this picture would seek to maximize achievement-related responses (Wallace, 1966), as by appealing to a person's intelligence, creative imagination, organization, and leadership. The basic instructions might read as follows:

Look at the picture, and write a short story about it. Use the questions below as a guide to writing your story.

1. What is happening? Who are the persons?
2. What has led up to this situation? That is, what has happened in the past?
3. What is being thought? What is wanted? By whom?
4. What will happen? What will be done?

Instructions similar to these were used in a study of 200 male students, largely war veterans, at three Connecticut colleges (McClelland, Clark, Roby, & Atkinson, 1949). Subjects in the experimental group were told they had "failed" to do well on a preliminary task. Under this laboratory condition, achievement-arousing instructions proved effective in increasing the number of achievement plots in TAT stories, the number of times story characters were said to want achievement, and mention of activities instrumental in dealing successfully with achievement problems. Results paralleled previous findings in which themes about food appeared in TAT stories told by naval trainees after they had been kept from eating for 1–16 hours (Atkinson & McClelland, 1948).

Scoring stories for n *Ach.* How do researchers "score" short stories for the amount of achievement motivation expressed in them? Guidelines have been provided by McClelland and Steele (1972). The first step is to determine whether a goal related to achievement, or *Achievement imagery (AI),* is present in the story: "Determine whether any of the characters in a story has an achievement goal — does he *want to perform better* or does he *care* about performing better?" (p. 34). Four criteria may be applied:

achievement imagery (AI)

1. *Outperforming someone else,* as in getting a higher grade or running faster. "Joe decided he would get first prize in the spelling contest."
2. *Meeting or surpassing some self-imposed standard of excellence,* as in doing something more efficiently or cheaply. "Edna was practicing in order to lower her golf score by three strokes."
3. *Doing something unique,* as in coming up with a new idea or inventing something. "Carol wanted to be *the first* person in the area to skydive successfully from 12,000 feet."
4. *Being involved over a long term in doing something well,* such as being successful in life, becoming a dentist, welder, professor, or businessman. "Lane has spent eight years studying ballet in preparation for his performance tonight."

If any one of these four criteria is met in a story, the story is assigned a score of +1 to indicate that AI is present. Once AI has been scored, it is possible to assign additional points, corresponding to the following categories (McClelland & Steele, 1972, p. 35):

1. *Stated need for achievement.* Someone in the story explicitly states the desire to meet an achievement goal.
2. *Activity.* Action is taken in the story toward attainment of the achievement goal.
3. *Anticipating success.* Someone in the story thinks about or anticipates reaching the achievement goal.
4. *Anticipating failure.* Someone in the story thinks about failing to reach the achievement goal, or doubts that she will reach it.
5. *Personal block.* Some characteristic of a person in the story will be a block to his achievement.
6. *World block.* Something in the environment is mentioned in the story as a block to achievement.
7. *Help.* The person with an achievement goal receives aid or encouragement from someone else in the story.
8. *Positive feelings.* The person is pleased when an achievement goal is reached.
9. *Negative feelings.* The person is discouraged when an achievement goal is not reached.
10. *Theme.* The central plot of the imaginative story contains achievement thoughts and activities.

In all, it is possible to obtain a score ranging from 0 to 11 points in a single story. Note that a story does not have to be a "success" story in order to be scored for n Ach. Failures as well as successes are scored, as well as blocks to success. The essential ingredient is the attempt to overcome difficulties related to achievement.

CORRELATES OF n ACH: THE n ACHIEVER

What are people like who have the "need for achievement"? McClelland (1961), Birney (1968), and Weiner (1978) have reviewed much of the n Ach research and have summarized a number of correlates for persons scoring high on this characteristic. Representative findings appear in Table 10.5. Overall, high "achievers" seem to be relatively realistic, task-oriented people who show optimism and positive self-concepts. In terms of developmental experiences, they have been both challenged and encouraged by their parents.

THE ACHIEVING SOCIETY

What would happen if a number of people with high n Ach were present in a given culture at a given time, all sharing the trait of achievement motivation? According to McClelland (1961), "things would start to hum."

TABLE 10.5   Behavioral Correlates of Persons High in Achievement Motivation

Characteristics

Realistic	Undertake achievement activities when opportunities arise
Prefer intermediate risk-taking	
Prefer business occupations	Perform best when achievement has significance for them
Have occupational goals that are congruent with abilities	Not ordinarily better at routine tasks
Able to delay immediate gratification for long-term goals	Choose experts over friends as working partners
Optimistic or hope-oriented in outlook	Resist social influences
Participate in college and community activities	Seek personal feedback or knowledge about themselves
Assume personal responsibility for success	Apt to volunteer for psychological experiments
Perceive themselves as high in ability	Take pride in accomplishments
Quick to notice words that are related to success	Show a positive self-concept
Remember tasks they do not finish	

Development

Achievement motivation is learned at an early age	Mothers encourage early independence
	Parents give more reward and punishment
Parents have higher expectations toward their children	Parents show more involvement in their child's performance
Parents select difficult tasks for their sons to do	
Parents value the child's doing something well	

McClelland sees *n* Ach as a key factor contributing to the effectiveness of business enterprises and, therefore, to a country's economic development. His basic hypothesis is that achievement motivation is partly responsible for a society's economic growth, because standards of excellence become socially defined and pursued in their own right. McClelland has linked this hypothesis to Max Weber's (1904/1930) concept of the Protestant Ethic, which emphasizes religious com-   **Protestant Ethic** mitment, responsibility, sacrifice, self-reliance, and inner satisfaction with "good works" that are done well. In fact, Mirels and Garrett (1971) have conceptualized the Protestant Ethic "as a personality variable," reporting that scores on their Protestant Ethic Scale (PES) correlate significantly with those on the F Scale, discussed earlier ($r = .51$). The PES includes such items as "If one works hard enough he is likely to make a good life for himself" and "Any man who is able and willing to work hard has a good chance of succeeding." McClelland's hypothesis has gained some support from Winterbottom's (1953) findings that parents of high *n* Ach children actively promote early independence and mastery training (see Table 10.5). The value of *n* Ach is further evidenced by the development of various training programs aimed at enhancing its influence in members of the business community (Heckhausen & Krug, 1982).

McClelland studied many contemporary and historical societies, ingeniously identifying a variety of sources for assessing the presence of achievement motivation in a culture: ancient literature, art appearing on vases, folktales, plays, poetry, popular ballads, speeches about war, and children's schoolbooks. He found that periods of economic growth and decline in ancient Greece were preceded by corresponding increases and decreases in achievement imagery (Berlew, cited in McClelland, 1961). The independent criterion used to determine economic growth was area of Athenian trade, in millions of square miles. In another study, deCharms and Moeller (1962) sampled pages from four American reading texts typical of 20-year periods between 1800 and 1950. Using the number of patents issued per 1 million population in the United States as an independent criterion, they observed "a characteristic wave" of achievement motivation *preceding* economic "takeoffs." Also, *n* Ach scores of stories in children's books after 1950 showed a "surprisingly high" correlation with gains in the electricity production of 39 modern societies ($r = .43$, $p < .01$).

ATKINSON'S RISK-PREFERENCE MODEL OF ACHIEVEMENT MOTIVATION

Atkinson (1957) proposes a specific explanation of the way in which achievement motivation contributes to a country's business and economic development. In brief, *n* Ach predisposes entrepreneurs to favor taking business risks that are neither extremely safe or speculative, but moderate and productive. Let us review the basis of this idea, which is supported by experimental laboratory studies.

You may have played the game of ringtoss when younger. If so, can you recall whether you liked to place the pegs far away or close to you? Peg placements by elementary school children found to be most "successful" at ringtoss support achievement-motivation theory (McClelland, 1958). That is, children high in *n* Ach placed pegs at an intermediate distance, and took more shots from middle-distance ranges, compared with children low in *n* Ach. Also, most tosses made when standing as close to the peg as possible were made by kindergarteners low in *n* Ach, as were most tosses made when standing farthest away. The higher the child's *n* Ach score, the closer the child's tendency to approximate the average distance of successful throws, not too far from a 50-50 probability of success. Results were "practically identical" with those reported by Atkinson (1958) in an earlier experiment.

Atkinson's risk-preference model

Atkinson's (1957) *risk-preference model* posits that achievement behavior results from the resolution of two conflicting tendencies, which operate simultaneously: *approaching success (s)* and *avoiding failure (f)*. The relative strengths of these two motives determine the degree of risk a person is willing to take in achievement situations.

Atkinson's model has an equation for predicting achievement behavior that is comprised of three major components: motivation *(M)*, expectancy *(P)*, and incentive *(I)*. Relationships among these components are a function of multiplying their strengths times one another *(M × P × I)*. However, the equation is a bit more complicated because each component has two aspects, *s* and *f*, both of which must be taken into consideration. Thus, *motivation* consists of simultaneous strivings for success *(Ms)* and a fear of failure *(Mf)*. *Expectancy,* a person's subjective estimate that a goal may be attained through behaviors instrumental to bringing it about, consists of the probability of both success *(Ps)* and failure *(Pf)*. *Incentive* consists of both the relative attractiveness or value of success *(Is)*, which is associated with pride in accomplishment, and failure *(If)*, which is associated with shame. Taking all aspects of the equation into account, achievement behavior then is a function of *(Ms × Ps × Is) − (Mf × Pf × If)*.

The practical value of Atkinson's equation is that it accounts for the various factors contributing to the balance between "hope of success," which encourages achievement behavior, and "fear of failure," which inhibits it. Thus, it can be used to predict the degree of "risk" persons may be willing to take regarding achievement behavior. Figure 10.3 illustrates some of these interacting relationships. The "approach" curve in Figure 10.3 shows that motivation for success is lowest in relation to tasks that are either very easy or very hard. The inverted "avoidance" curve shows that very difficult and very easy tasks arouse less fear of failure, making them less unattractive than tasks of moderate difficulty. An expectancy of .50 represents the balance point at which the motivation for success is highest and motivation to avoid failure is lowest. When probabilities depart from 50-50, the

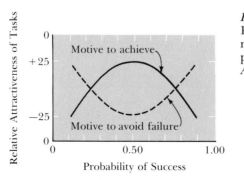

Figure 10.3
Relative attractiveness of achievement tasks differing in subjective probability of success *(adapted from Atkinson, 1957).*

motivation to avoid failure likely functions as a damper on the motivation to strive for success.

Regarding the incentive value of success, greater pride in accomplishment is likely to be experienced following success in a difficult task than in an easy one. For persons high in *n* Ach, winning at chess is less likely to elicit pride in accomplishment when the opponent is a beginner ("easy victory"), especially compared to an opponent more reasonably matched to their own level of skill. For persons highly fearful of failure, losing at chess is less likely to elicit shame when the opponent is a world champion ("impossible to win"). Thus, they tend to set either extremely low or unreasonably high goals for themselves (Atkinson, 1957).

LIMITATIONS OF THE ACHIEVEMENT-MOTIVATION CONCEPT

Low reliability of *n* Ach measures.   As you recall from Chapter 2, the reliability of a measure refers to the degree to which results can be repeated. To increase the reliability of AI measurement, McClelland and his colleagues typically ask participants to write stories to 4–6 TAT pictures. Nevertheless, *n* Ach reliability coefficients tend to be unusually low for a psychometric measure, averaging .30–.40 in research studies (Weiner, 1978). This means that persons who do or do not show AI in one TAT story may show a different outcome on other stories, or at different points in time. However, the problem of low reliability is probably less specific to the concept of *n* Ach than to the type of instrument used to measure it. Projective techniques such as the TAT are noted for having generally lower reliability coefficients compared with objective personality questionnaires, because they are so unstructured and open-ended. As you likely have learned by now, when it comes to personality, hard-and-fast rules for assessing and predicting behavior are few, even when "traits" are involved.

A male emphasis in past research.   A second limitation of the *n* Ach concept pertains to findings of a sex difference. That is, conditions of achievement arousal appear to affect men more than women. This is particularly surprising since, under neutral conditions, the scores of women are as high as, or higher than, those of men (Horner, 1971). Reasons for the sex difference are not clear. Weiner (1978) speculates that achievement may be "a more complex motivational system" for females "because of cultural inhibitions and social norms that at one time restricted females to the home" (p. 29). He also notes that the "golden age" of achievement-motivation research occurred between 1950 and 1960, prior to the impact of the women's movement. Thus, early findings of a strong sex difference in *n* Ach are less likely to be replicated today.

Matina Horner (1968) hypothesizes the influence of "a motive to avoid success" in women that functions as a counteracting psychological barrier to achievement. This hypothesis may be tied to past failures of achievement-motivation theory to predict female response patterns on the TAT (Atkinson, 1958; French & Lesser, 1964; Horner, 1968). Consistent with Atkinson's expectancy-value theory, women's motivations about success may well be equivalent to those of men (J. T. Spence, 1983); however, their expectancies or incentives may differ

sex differences in achievement arousal

fear of success

because of psychosocial factors. Horner developed a system for scoring *fear-of-success (FOS)* imagery, related to negative consequences of achievement: (1) fear of social rejection, (2) concern about one's normality or femininity, and (3) self-protective denial of achievement-related cues. Her dissertation study found that 65% of women but only 10% of men wrote stories high in fear-of-success imagery. However, later research has modified this result by showing that fear of success is an important influence on men as well as women (Condry & Dyer, 1976; Zuckerman & Wheeler, 1975), and that its influence among women may be lessening. "With greater societal acceptance of women's educational and vocational aspirations, sex differences in fear-of-success appear to be evaporating" (J. T. Spence, 1983, p. 37).

Sex roles and the TAT.   Stein and Bailey (1973) suggest that women have traditionally been socialized to make "affiliation" their primary goal, not external "achievement." Affiliation roles may take women away from independent personal achievement, or at least give rise to conflict over it. This conclusion can be linked to a sex difference present in the TAT itself. Potkay, Merrens, and Allen (1979; Allen & Potkay, 1983a) report that differential sex roles are "built in" to TAT stimuli. The pictures themselves facilitate responses in which women play loving, motherly, and concerned roles in support or care of men. Although female TAT figures are rated as showing greater mental health, greater intelligence, and equivalent achievement status compared with male figures, men simply do not identify with these female figures. Men identify primarily with male TAT figures, which are rated higher on more "important" dimensions of identification and cultural favorability (Potkay & Merrens, 1975). The structuring of sex roles in the kinds of "classic human situations" depicted in TAT stimuli took place during the late 1930s and may well impede the arousal of achievement motivation in contemporary women.

J. T. Spence's corrective.   If the failure of "achievement arousal" conditions for female subjects is due to measurement procedures and cultural influences, then different approaches to assessing women's achievement motivation are needed. In fact, Janet Taylor Spence (1983) has demonstrated the relevance of achievement motivation for women. Her research has involved development of a new assessment technique with an objective, self-report format, the Work and Family Orientation Questionnaire (WOFO). Unlike earlier workers, Spence conceptualizes achievement as multifaceted rather than unidimensional. Thus, the WOFO is comprised of three independent achievement factors:

Work and Family Orientation Questionnaire (WOFO)

1. *Mastery* is the preference for challenging tasks and for meeting internal standards of performance. "If I am not good at something, I would rather keep struggling to master it than move on to something I may be good at."
2. *Work* is the desire to work hard and do a good job. "Part of my enjoyment in doing things is improving my past performance."
3. *Competitiveness* is the enjoyment of interpersonal competition and the desire to do better than others. "I feel that winning is important in both work and games."

According to Spence, results of tests using this multifaceted measure of achievement motivation suggest that the structure of achievement motivation is similar for both sexes. However, in randomly selected groups, sex differences in the "strength" of these motives do appear, with women tending to score higher on work and men tending to score higher on both mastery and competitiveness (J. T. Spence, 1983). Thus, there is evidence that the apparent sex difference in achievement motivation results partly from *n* Ach measures and different definitions of achievement.

Sensation Seeking

Our last sample trait is called *sensation seeking*. Unlike the need for achievement, which is learned, sensation seeking appears to be biological in origin. Before learning more about it, complete the brief exercise in Box 10.3.

sensation seeking

Sensation-Seeking Exercise*   **BOX 10.3**

Two sets of designs appear below, followed by a rating scale. Look at both sets of designs. Then indicate your preference for one set of drawings compared with the other.

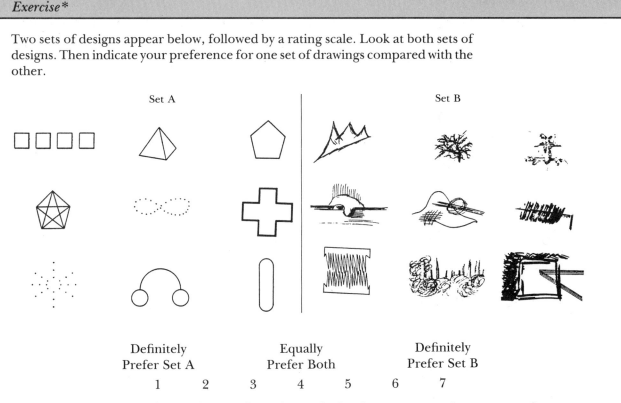

	Set A				Set B	

Definitely   Equally   Definitely
Prefer Set A   Prefer Both   Prefer Set B
    1   2   3   4   5   6   7

Draw a circle around the number on the rating scale that best corresponds to your preference.

* Adapted from Zuckerman, Bone, Neary, Mangelsdorff, & Brustman, 1972.

SENSATION SEEKING AS A TRAIT

The trait of *sensation seeking (SS)* reflects a broad need or motive to maintain an optimal level of stimulation or arousal. Initially, SS was thought of as a consistent preference for "sheer quantity and intensity" of simple, external stimulation (Zuckerman, 1979, p. 7). However, factor analyses indicate that the highest item loadings on the general factor refer to the need for *varied, novel,* and *complex* stimulation. The trait is thus defined by the need for a variety of sensations and the willingness to take physical and social risks in order to experience them. Zuckerman (1979) prefers the term *sensation* rather than stimulation because the most important aspects of SS experience are the *sensory effects* of external stimulation. Unusual sensations may be produced by emotions, drugs, and physical activities such as free-fall skydiving, scuba diving, and other behaviors that involve speed and movement outside the ordinary range. These sensations serve as primary reinforcers to persons high in SS. Zuckerman's use of the term *seeking* indicates that the trait is expressed in an active mode.

sensory-
deprivation
experiments

The SS construct received attention in relation to sensory-deprivation experiments conducted during the 1950s and 1960s. *Sensory-deprivation* experiments minimize external stimulation, as when a person is submerged in water below the neck, in a darkened, soundproof room (Lilly, 1973). Research subjects showed differences in the length of time they were willing to spend under sensory-deprivation conditions. Subjects high in sensation seeking tended to drop out of such experiments more readily than those low in SS. Evidently, persons high in SS choose external stimuli that will maximize their internal sensations.

Zuckerman (1979) hypothesizes a biological origin for sensation seeking, expressing indebtedness to Hans and Sybil Eysenck (Chapter 9) for this orientation. Research findings support the concept of sensation seeking as a trait that has both psychological and biological correlates. The psychological aspects of sensation seeking are most often measured by the Sensation-Seeking Scale (Zuckerman, Kolin, Price, & Zoob, 1964), described in the next section. The biological aspects of SS are often measured by the reflex of turning toward a source of stimulation (orienting response), the degree of electrical activity in the brain (evoked potentials), the amount of certain biochemical enzymes in the brain (monoamine oxidase), and the amount of gonadal hormones present in the body.

five criteria for a trait

According to Zuckerman, Buchsbaum, and Murphy (1980), SS meets five criteria for a trait, with psychological and biological results paralleling one another. First, psychological and biological measures of SS are both *reliable.* Differences between individuals on SS persist over time and across most situations. Second, a strong *genetic influence* appears to be present. Persons, including twins, similar on psychological measures of SS are also similar on biological measures of SS. Third, expected parallels related to the SS dimension have been observed in human and animal *behavior.* That is, animals as well as humans showing biological characteristics associated with high sensation seeking also tend to be more "adventurous," "exploratory," and "socially dominant" compared with those low in SS. Fourth, there are expected correspondences between SS and different forms of behavioral *maladjustment.* Similar biological correlates characterize overactive and nonconventional types of maladapting individuals who are at the high end of

SS (manic and sociopathic patients) and withdrawn and fearful types of maladapting individuals who are at the low end of SS (catatonic schizophrenic and phobic individuals). Fifth, findings of psychological and biological measures of sensation seeking parallel one another according to differences in *age and sex*. When biological differences are present in persons of a given age or sex, corresponding psychological differences also are present.

In sum, research findings meeting criteria such as these lend support to the validity of the sensation-seeking concept as a personality trait. From a methodological standpoint, it is also worth noting that the developmental work on sensation seeking by Zuckerman and his colleagues follows the scientific model suggested by Hans Eysenck, outlined in Chapter 9. Let us now move on to an understanding of how the psychological aspects of sensation seeking are assessed.

THE SENSATION-SEEKING SCALE (SSS)

To measure sensation seeking, Zuckerman, Kolin, Price, and Zoob (1964) developed the Sensation-Seeking Scale (SSS). In its current form, the SSS is a 40-item paper-and-pencil questionnaire comprised of four factors:

Sensation-Seeking Scale (SSS)

1. *Thrill and adventure seeking.* Engaging in physical risk-taking activities, such as riding surfboards, flying airplanes, parachuting, and climbing mountains.
2. *Experience seeking.* Pursuing new experiences of mind and senses, such as experimenting with hallucinatory drugs, meeting homosexual men and women, and liking earthy body smells.
3. *Disinhibition.* Seeking hedonistic pursuit of pleasure through extraverted activities such as wild and uninhibited parties, sexy movie scenes, and getting high in social settings using marijuana and liquor.
4. *Boredom susceptibility.* Showing an aversion to routine activities or work, and to dull or boring people, along with restlessness in an unchanging environment.

Thus, the SSS provides not only a general score for sensation seeking, but subscores on each of these four factors. Test-retest reliabilities for the General scale range between .87 and .95 for 3-week time intervals, dropping to .75 for an 8-month interval (Zuckerman, Buchsbaum, & Murphy, 1980). Refinements continue to produce updated versions of the SSS.

CORRELATES OF SENSATION SEEKING

What are sensation seekers like? More than two decades of SSS research have been summarized by Zuckerman (1979) and his co-workers (Zuckerman, Buchsbaum, & Murphy, 1980). Most of this research is correlational rather than experimental, making causation difficult to establish. Nevertheless, correlational findings suggest "where to look" in seeking to understand behavior, especially in relation to biologically based "paths of influence on brain-behavior feedback systems" (Zuckerman, Buchsbaum, & Murphy, 1980, p. 208). A number of behavioral correlates of SSS scores are listed in Table 10.6.

TABLE 10.6   Behavioral Correlates of Sensation Seeking (Zuckerman, Buchsbaum, & Murphy, 1980)

Prefer spicy, sour, and crunchy foods	Among married women, show greater sexual excitement and responsiveness, as well as more frequent masturbation, intercourse, and orgasm
Smoke cigarettes	
Report multidrug experimentation and use, particularly marijuana, amphetamines, and LSD	
	Engage in physical-risk activities such as parachuting, motorcycling, scuba diving, and fire fighting
Volunteer for unusual types of experiments such as sensory deprivation, hypnosis, and drug studies	
	Interested in gambling
Become restless in short-term isolation situations, and drop out of meditation training	More likely to show 16 PF scores reflecting an uninhibited, nonconforming, impulsive, dominant type of extraversion than a friendly type of sociability
Volunteer for unusual types of activities such as encounter groups, alpha training, and transcendental meditation	
	Among delinquents, engage in more impulsive behavior such as fighting, defiance of rules, and escape attempts
Function best in situations of social stimulation	
Participate in a greater variety of heterosexual activities, with more partners	Among psychiatric patients, more likely to show MMPI scores reflecting elevated mood and sociopathy than schizophrenia

The most important demographic or group variable affecting SSS scores is age. Sensation seeking increases with age until adolescence, then declines from the 20s on. Regarding sex differences, males generally obtain higher scores than females, especially on the SSS Disinhibition subscale. However, male and female scores are equivalent on Experience Seeking. Women tested at different college campuses showed greater differences in their levels of SSS scores compared with men at those same campuses. National/cultural patterns indicate higher SSS scores in Western than Asiatic cultures. This is especially true of American groups compared with those from Japan and Thailand. Overall SSS scores are similar among English-speaking males from different countries. Education has not yet been found to be an important influence on SSS scores, although the data are limited.

Some significant correlations have been reported between scores on the Sensation-Seeking Scale and other psychological-test measures. For example, SSS scores are related to Sybil and Hans Eysenck's (1975) traits of extraversion (E) and psychoticism (P), discussed in Chapter 9. The overall pattern is reflective of antisocial tendencies, partly explained by observations that SS is more closely tied to the "impulsive" component of extraversion than to its "sociable" component. Sensation seekers tend to be nonconformists and risk takers, guided more by their own needs than by social conventions or the needs and attitudes of others, as evidenced by their pattern of scores on Cattell's (1949) 16 PF test.

Although sensation seeking is not related to Eysenck's dimension of neurotic anxiety (N), it is related to realistic anxiety or "fearfulness." This has led Zuckerman (1979) to propose a model suggesting an interaction between sensation seeking and anxiety in risk-taking situations. As the riskiness of situations increases, realistic anxiety decreases and sensation seeking increases in persons

Are you a sensation seeker? This "Bird Man of Phoenix" is seen leaping from the top of a building onto an air bag on the ground. Persons high in sensation seeking prefer varied, novel, and complex sensory stimulation.

high in SS compared with those who are low. Thus, high-SS persons are more naturally inclined to approach "risky" or "dangerous" situations, whereas low-SS persons are more inclined to avoid them.

BOX 10.3 REVISITED: ARE YOU A SENSATION SEEKER?

Might there be a tendency toward sensation seeking in your own personality? Results reported by Neary's 1975 study (cited in Zuckerman, 1978) indicate that persons high in sensation seeking are more likely than average to describe themselves as enthusiastic, playful, pleased, adventurous, elated, imaginative, daring, zany, lucky, and mischievous. Persons low in SS are more likely than average to describe themselves as frightened, panicky, tense, nervous, shaky, fearful, afraid, worried, desperate, upset, terrified, and not calm.

Does either of Neary's two sets of adjectives describe your personality? If so, is there also a correspondence between the set of adjectives you believe best describes you and the type of designs you prefer in Box 10.3? Zuckerman, Bone, Neary, Mangelsdorff, and Brustman (1972) report that persons high in sensation seeking prefer designs that are more physically complex, sketchy, and shaded (Set B) rather than simple, geometric, and symmetrical (Set A). Consistency between corresponding adjective sets and design preferences may point toward or away from an SS tendency in your own personality.

On the other hand, consistency in seemingly SS results could also be due to chance, or to other factors not yet identified. A set of adjectives could "fit" your personality for reasons other than sensation seeking. (Recall, from Chapter 2, that correlation is not causation.) Or you may simply prefer one set of designs over the other for artistic reasons, without "psychological" reasons coming into play at all.

CHAPTER REVIEW

The four traits reviewed in this chapter are often seen as having predictable influences on behavior. All have a rich, sometimes complicated, literature background and reflect interesting combinations of theory, research, and application. Each trait has been associated with one or more assessment techniques.

Authoritarianism was conceived in an attempt to understand the characteristics and development of prejudice, especially anti-Semitism. Adorno et al. demonstrated the existence of an authoritarian type of personality characterized by anti-democratic ideas and deeply felt emotional needs to submit to external authority. However, the Fascism (F) Scale used to assess authoritarianism taps ideas more to the political right than left. This led Rokeach to develop the Dogmatism (D) Scale, which measures the trait of closed-mindedness in persons of any belief system. Persons high in authoritarianism and dogmatism are more likely to show anxiety symptoms as children, in part because of family restrictions on expressing ambivalence toward parents. Authoritarian and dogmatic personalities seem unable to separate information from its source, which may predispose them to "just follow orders."

Anxiety, the experience of unpleasant emotional arousal, is comprised of physiological, behavioral, and subjective manifestations that do not necessarily correlate with one another. Epstein traces anxiety arousal to excessive stimulation, cognitive incongruity, and unavailable responses. Cattell identifies two kinds of trait anxiety: regression, a source trait highly correlated with Eysenck's neuroticism factor; and anxiety, a kind of innate tension similar to Freud's concept of frustrated drive. Spielberger defines trait anxiety as relatively stable individual differences in a person's proneness to anxiety experiences. Trait anxiety has often been measured by Taylor's Manifest Anxiety Scale (MAS), with high scorers showing high drive and rapid eyelid conditioning.

Achievement motivation (n Ach) refers to a person's learned drive to achieve success in competition with some standard of excellence. McClelland developed a systematic method for scoring achievement imagery (AI) in fantasy productions, using the Thematic Apperception Test (TAT). AI increases in men under experimental conditions, as well as in societies prior to economic "takeoffs." Atkinson's risk-preference model predicts that persons high in n Ach are most likely to approach and least likely to avoid achievement situations when the probability of success or failure is a moderate 50-50, rather than too safe or too uncertain. The failure of n Ach to predict women's behavior has been related to cultural inhibitions, fear of success (Horner), and stereotyped sex roles portrayed in TAT stimuli. However, J. T. Spence has demonstrated the relevance of n Ach to women by reconceptualizing it as having three components, measured by the Work and Family Orientation Questionnaire (WOFO).

Sensation seeking is the need to pursue varied, novel, and complex sensations so as to maintain an optimal level of arousal. The concept developed from Zuckerman's observations of individual differences in tolerance of sensory-deprivation experiments, that minimize external stimulation. Persons scoring high on the Sensation-Seeking Scale (SSS) are likely to engage in physical risk-taking activities, such as skydiving and mountain climbing, and to avoid routine or dull environments. Although research results are largely correlational, sensation seeking meets five criteria for biologically based traits.

In closing, the past two chapters have focused primarily on relatively permanent "inner" dispositions contributing to individual differences in personality and behavior—traits. From this point of view, it's "what's inside us" that accounts for our behavior. The next two chapters offer an alternative perspective. They take us "outside" the person, to external influences contributing to behavior—situations. From this point of view, it's "what's outside us" that accounts for our behavior. Let us now explore these outside influences on our "personalities."

KEY CONCEPTS

Authoritarianism
    Authoritarian personality
        Fascism (F) Scale
    Dogmatism
        Dogmatism (D) Scale
Anxiety
    Three sources of anxiety arousal
    Cattell's two anxiety traits
        Regression versus mobilization (U.I. 23)
        Anxiety versus relaxation (U.I. 24)
    Taylor Manifest Anxiety Scale (MAS)
    Trait anxiety, state anxiety
Achievement motivation (*n* Ach)

Achievement imagery (AI)
    Thematic Apperception Test (TAT)
Achieving societies
    Protestant Ethic
    Atkinson's risk-preference model
Sex differences in achievement arousal
    Fear of success
    Work and Family Orientation Questionnaire (WOFO)
Sensation seeking
    Sensation-Seeking Scale (SSS)
    Sensory-deprivation experiments
    Five criteria for a trait

REVIEW QUESTIONS

1. Compare the behaviors of persons who are high and low on each of the four traits reviewed in the chapter—authoritarianism, anxiety, achievement motivation, and sensation seeking.
2. What social implications do you see regarding the traits of authoritarianism and dogmatism? How do these traits develop?
3. What is the experience of anxiety like? How is anxiety assessed? What are some of the issues involved in understanding anxiety?
4. Give some examples of achievement imagery. How might parents encourage development of *n* Ach in their children? Do you think it is a desirable trait for society to encourage? Why or why not?
5. What advantages and disadvantages do you see in sensation seeking as a trait?

11

Identifying Situational Influences on Behavior

Would you obey orders to administer severe electric shocks to other people?

How important were external influences on the 900 people who killed themselves at Jonestown?

Do environments have "personalities"?

What is the "bad" news about winning a $1,000,000 lottery?

Are all maladaptive behaviors due to people's personalities?

M|ANY OF the chapters you have read so far have emphasized *internal* contributors to personality and behavior. This chapter and the next take a closer look at *external* contributors.

How did you happen to end up with the set of genes that are "you"? become "best friends" with another person? or arrive at your present major? In what ways has your life been affected by such life events as loss of a parent, breakup of a love relationship, illness, personal achievement, or geographical move? or by such sociocultural events as economic recession, war, political change, and technological advancement? Answers to such questions often involve chance influences, special situations, or environmental circumstances that are beyond one individual's control. Thus, the purpose of this chapter is to stimulate greater appreciation of the view that external situations can be quite compelling influences on behavior, apart from internal personality factors (Craik & McKechnie, 1978; Moos & Brownstein, 1977; Russell & Ward, 1982; Wohlwill, 1970; Wohlwill & Carson, 1972). In a nutshell, the goal is to show how behavior can be determined by external factors rather than "personality."

Because our review will be selective, we want to caution you against drawing the conclusion that environmental conditions totally determine behavior. Most psychologists believe they do not, even those most closely associated with "environmental" points of view (Watson, Skinner, Chapter 5). In fact, extreme positions regarding inner, *dispositional* causes of behavior versus outer, *situational* causes have only served to polarize the field of personality (Alker, 1972; Endler, 1973). Recently, Funder and Ozer (1983, p. 107) evaluated both extremes as "equally lacking in empirical support (Bowers, 1973; Sarason, Smith, & Diener, 1975)." They supported their evaluation with statistical reanalyses of data from three prominent series of experiments in psychology: attitude change under conditions of forced compliance and low incentive (Festinger & Carlsmith, 1959); bystander intervention under conditions of number of onlookers present (Darley & Latané, 1968); and harmful social behavior under conditions of obedience with authority present (Milgram, 1974). In determining the effects of situations, Funder and Ozer estimated that correlations averaged "slightly less than .40," "quite comparable" to those of dispositional effects (Mischel, 1968; Nisbett, 1980).

Realistically, persons play an important role in influencing behavior, and environmental situations play an important role. Neither persons nor environments determine behavior independently of each other, as will be seen in our discussion of interactionism (Chapters 13 and 14).

Before proceeding further, we would like you to complete the exercise in Box 11.1. We will return to it later in the chapter.

BOX 11.1   *What Is Your College Like?**

Instructions: Here are some statements about college life. Decide whether each statement is probably true or probably false about *your* college.

1. Professors usually take attendance in class.
   TRUE   FALSE

2. In many classes students have an assigned seat.
   TRUE   FALSE

3. Faculty members and administration have definite and clearly posted office hours.
   TRUE   FALSE

4. Most students don't decide what courses to take until the time of registration.
   TRUE   FALSE

5. Spontaneous student rallies and demonstrations occur frequently.
   TRUE   FALSE

6. Students often start projects without trying to decide in advance how they will develop or where they may end.
   TRUE   FALSE

7. There is an extensive program of intramural sports and informal athletic activities.
   TRUE   FALSE

8. Student gathering places are typically active and noisy.
   TRUE   FALSE

9. Class discussions are typically vigorous and intense.
   TRUE   FALSE

* College Characteristics Index, adapted from Stern & Pace, 1958.

Situations as Psychological

Popular concepts of the environment often focus on physical aspects of the world that surround the organism—whatever is outside the boundary of the person's skin. Aspects of the physical environment will certainly be identified in this chapter. However, greater emphasis will be placed on the "psychological" environment. This psychological world is what Kurt Lewin (1936) referred to as the *life space* or "whole psychological situation" of the individual in relation to his or her surroundings. We are going to be particularly interested in looking at *psychological situations*—those external factors (people, social circumstances, settings) that confront a person at a given point in time and that have some determining, personal relevance or meaning for the individual who is actively engaged in perceiving, experiencing, interpreting, and responding to them.

Feshbach (1978) has defined two levels of psychological-environmental influence. The first level is *situational*—"the immediate social and physical environmental stimuli to which the organism responds and adapts" (p. 447). If you have ever seen humorous poster maps of the United States drawn from the viewpoint of a New Yorker, or a Chicagoan, or a San Franciscan, you will immediately appreciate the meaning of "psychological" environments. The details of one's hometown take up the bulk of these personal, cognitive maps, while more distant cities and geographical features are barely scrunched into the remaining few inches of paper (Gould & White, 1974). The second level defined by Feshbach is *sociocultural*—"the broader social and physical context that provides situations their meaning and their continuity" (p. 447). This is the level of John Naisbitt's (1984) new "megatrends," broad but quiet directions of social influence that are already in the process of transforming contemporary lives—for example, away from a society based on industry to one based on providing information, and away from a national to a world economy. Alvin Toffler (1970) writes of *future shock*— "the shattering stress and disorientation" individuals in contemporary society experience as a result of simply being subjected to "too much change in too short a time" (p. 4).

psychological situations

The Power of Situations

Countless psychological studies attest to the influence of predefined situational conditions on human behavior. Research psychologists regularly establish experimental conditions (independent variables) that are followed, often predictably, by particular human responses (dependent variables). Clinical psychologists regularly establish "necessary and sufficient" therapy conditions that facilitate personality changes in clients (Rogers, Chapter 7). In addition, life events periodically provide evidence of the power of situations to influence behavior, sometimes quietly, sometimes dramatically.

power of situations

LIFE'S CHANCE ENCOUNTERS

Take the case of Paul Watkins, a talented teenager who enjoyed good family and peer relationships, academic success, and a high school class presidency. One day he decided to visit a Los Angeles friend who, unknown to Watkins, had moved out of his cabin in Topanga Canyon. Watkins instead came upon new occupants of the cabin, Charles Manson and his "family." By accident, Watkins was introduced to a heady mixture of impressionable youth, communal love, group sex, drugs, religious revelations, and isolation from the outside world. Manson eventually led his followers on a rampage of senseless murders. Watkins' chance encounter launched him on a new life path of "helter-skelter" killings.

chance
encounters

Albert Bandura (1982) believes that a comprehensive theory of psychology must recognize that "chance encounters play a prominent role in shaping the course of human lives" (p. 748). *Chance encounters* are interpersonal situations involving unintended meetings of persons unfamiliar to each other. Some of these accidental encounters touch us only lightly, while others are more lasting, launching us into entirely new trajectories of life. From Bandura's (1982) point of view, unforeseen environmental events introduce elements of uncertainty into the human-behavior formula. They make the specific course of a person's life "neither easily predictable nor easily socially engineerable" (p. 749).

You can undoubtedly furnish examples of significant chance encounters from your own life—less dramatic than that of Paul Watkins, but nevertheless important to you, and long-lasting. They would include any instance in which some unexpected encounter with another person "just happened" to turn into a friendship, love relationship, traumatic experience, career direction, or personal goal.

EXTRAORDINARY SITUATIONS

Would you ever participate in a bank robbery? administer electric shocks strong enough to result in another person's death? participate in a mass suicide? Probably you would answer "No way!" to these questions. Yet there is undeniable evidence that powerful situations can lead to behaviors that seem alien to our everyday "personalities." It is more than a simple matter of the spirit being willing and the flesh weak (Fletcher, 1966; Read, 1974). Rather, situations can be quite compelling. As we will see, all the questions just mentioned have been answered "yes" by ordinary people caught up in extraordinary situations.

We would like to illustrate this idea with three psychological situations, each related to one of the three questions just raised. The first situation involves an individual, Patty Hearst, who had been kidnapped by a terrorist organization. The second involves a representative cross-section of average people who have been research subjects in Stanley Milgram's experiments on obedience to authority. The third involves a small but self-contained religious society, the Peoples Temple, that participated in a mass suicide. Thus, the direction of our coverage of extraordinary situational influences on behavior progresses from a single case to an entire social system.

Patty Hearst: "I'd be killed."   Would you participate in a bank robbery? You may have heard about the case of Patty Hearst, a newspaper heiress who was kidnapped by a terrorist group called the Symbionese Liberation Army (SLA). In 1976, Hearst was legally tried for wielding a semiautomatic rifle during an SLA robbery of a California bank—certainly unexpected behavior for a woman who had been raised in a debutante atmosphere of wealth and high society. Her defense attorney, F. Lee Bailey, argued that Patty had been influenced by circumstances of extreme duress, akin to mind control. She had been kidnapped, blindfolded, isolated, forced to live in closets, threatened with injury and death, and raped. Given a new name, Tania, she made tape recordings denying maltreatment, criticizing her parents, and supporting SLA demands. She also had to participate in gun drills during which she got kicked because she "wasn't enthusiastic enough" and was told that if she messed up in any way she would "be killed."

Although Bailey argued that Patty's sole motive for taking part in the robbery was one of survival, Mathews (1976) suggested that Patty had "no gyroscope of her own" but lived in worlds structured for her by other people. Bandura's (1982) position is that outside, chance encounters are more likely to take hold when internal personal guides are absent.

Obedience: "You have no choice."   Would you administer electric shocks strong enough to result in another person's death? Subjects in experiments conducted by Stanley Milgram (1974) were asked to help test the influence of punishment on memory and learning by becoming teachers who would administer electric shocks to learners. In actuality, the "learner" was a confederate of the experimenter. The teacher's task was to present pairs of words to the learner, who was moved to an adjacent room, out of sight but within talking range. If the learner's response to a word was correct, the teacher said "correct." If the response was incorrect, the teacher administered an electric shock to the learner using one of the switches on an impressive-looking piece of electronic equipment.

Milgram's obedience research

Teachers were told to increase the amount of shock by 15 volts each time an incorrect answer was given. The electrical switches bore labels ranging from "slight shock" (15 volts) to "danger: severe shock" and beyond to "XXX" (450 volts). At 75 volts, the learner grunted. At 120 volts, he complained verbally. At 150 volts, he demanded to be released from the experiment. At 180 volts, he shouted that he couldn't stand the pain any longer. At 300 volts, he shouted he would no longer provide answers. At 330 volts, he screamed hysterically that his heart was bothering him and that he wanted out. Of course, the "learners" never received any shocks, although the teachers believed otherwise because the teachers themselves had received a mild shock during preliminary preparations. To maintain standard conditions, the learner's "responses" were played from a tape recorder.

Milgram was not actually interested in memory and learning, but in obedience. Whenever the teacher asked the experimenter what to do, the experimenter's response was "Please continue . . . You must go on, you have no choice . . . While the shocks are painful, they are not dangerous . . . Treat the absence of a response as a wrong answer."

> The point of the experiment is to see how far a person will proceed in a concrete and measurable situation in which he is ordered to inflict increasing pain on a protesting victim. At what point will the subject refuse to obey the experimenter? (Milgram, 1974, pp. 3–4)

Milgram's results were difficult to believe. Nearly two-thirds of ordinary subjects showed substantial obedience by administering maximum shock (**XXX**). The results contrast with Milgram's additional finding that almost all subjects who received only a description of the experiment claimed they would be disobedient. Thus, most persons believing they would never administer electric shocks strong enough to result in another person's death would be quite likely to do so under the circumstances of Milgram's experiment. (What was *your* answer to the question about obedience at the start of this chapter?)

Results have been replicated over time, with a variety of adult samples from different countries. A film of Milgram's (1965) *Obedience* study is quite convincing in its depiction of the credibility of the experimental procedure. As discussed in Chapter 2, real-life facts regarding the Nazi holocaust also support the "unbelievable" involvement of many ordinary people who were "just following orders."

Milgram's (1974) search for inner, "personality" variables that might be associated with obedience proved negative. Only slight trends were observed between obedient behavior and psychological-test measures of lower moral development and higher authoritarianism (Chapter 10). Under conditions of greater physical proximity between teachers and learners, *obedience* was occasionally slightly lower for persons who had received more education, had spent fewer years in the military, had been military officers rather than enlistees, were Jewish or Protestant rather than Catholic, and were in the "moral" professions of law, medicine, and teaching rather than the technical professions of engineering and physical science. However, even these suggested trends "washed out" under different experimental conditions. Milgram's (1974) overall conclusion is quite in keeping with the main theme of this chapter:

> The disposition a person brings to the experiment is probably less important a cause of his behavior than most readers assume. For the social psychology of this century reveals a major lesson: often, it is not so much the kind of person a man is as the kind of situation in which he finds himself that determines how he will act. (p. 205)

During the course of his experiments, Milgram was able to identify several situational influences on obedience, including the five that follow (Allen, 1978):

1. *Psychological distance from the victim.* Obedience was lowered from 65% to 40% when teacher and learner were in the same room, and to 30% when the teacher had to place the learner's hand directly on a shock plate. The greater the psychological distance, the greater the obedience.

2. *Physical presence of authority.* Obedience was lowered to 23% when the experimenter left the room and gave the teacher instructions to continue by telephone. (Some teachers lied to the experimenter by saying they were administering shock levels higher than those actually given.)

3. *Prestige of institutional setting.* Changing the setting from Yale University to a nondescript office building lowered obedience from two-thirds to one-half of the subjects, although this difference did not reach statistical significance.

4. *Low personal control and responsibility.* When two collaborators playing "teachers" were asked to administer shocks, and both refused to do so, obedience among real teachers dropped to 10%. When a real teacher had direct responsibility for deciding whether the shock level was to be raised, and two collaborators urged him to increase the shock, only 18% of the real teachers obeyed to the highest level of shock. When a real teacher was asked to turn on the main power switch, but not to operate the specific shock switches (which was done instead by a fully "obedient" collaborator), obedience rose to a high of 93%. In general, the

less a real teacher felt responsible and in control, the greater the obedience, even though moral and legal responsibility remained as high as ever.

5. *Clear, unambiguous authority.* When two experimenters were present, one giving instructions to "continue" and the other to "stop" shocking, obedience was reduced to 0%. No teacher administered maximum shock under this condition. When one of two experimenters was removed from authority status to "learner" status by substituting for a "no-show" confederate, obedience reached the normative 65% rate. This occurred even though the learner who now demanded to be let out of the experiment was a former authority. However, when the experimenter stood in for the learner, while making it clear he was still in charge, no real teacher obeyed fully.

Milgram's investigations constitute a clear demonstration of the power of situations to influence behavior in surprising ways. Situational variables, not personality factors, accounted for differences in people's behaviors. In fact, Milgram was unable to demonstrate any convincing connection between personality characteristics and obedience, a finding that differs from the trait point of view discussed in Chapter 10.

Jonestown suicides: "more or less ordinary people."   Would you ever participate in a mass suicide? Consider the final actions taken by members of Reverend Jim Jones' Peoples Temple. Jones had relocated himself and his devoted followers from their church in northern California to a remote and well-fortified outpost in the jungles of Guyana, South America. A small delegation led by U.S. Representative Leo Ryan had arrived to investigate allegations that people were being held in Jonestown against their will. However, Ryan and others were shot to death before leaving Jonestown to return to the United States. Fearing retribution, Jones set in motion his final plan for the members of his congregation.

On November 18, 1978, Reverend Jones' cry went out over community loudspeakers "Alert! Alert! Alert! Everyone to the pavilion! . . . It is time to die. . . . Bring the babies first" (Mathews, 1978a, p. 38). This was the beginning of White Night, the name given the sect's frequently rehearsed suicide plan. Half-gallon jugs of cyanide poison were poured into a tub of grape-flavored ade. Within two hours, more than 900 people had succumbed, in orderly rows so thick with bodies that later investigators had difficulty counting them.

Actually, the group's behavior was not entirely voluntary. A 45-minute audio tape of Jonestown's final moments revealed that some members of the commune, including Jones' wife, Marceline, had been unwilling to accept Reverend Jones' proposition that they would not be committing suicide but performing "a revolutionary act." (Mathews, 1978b). Perhaps the greatest horror lay in the realization that "more or less ordinary people" had been so indoctrinated that "nearly anybody might be manipulated the same way" (Woodward, 1978, p. 72).

Yale psychiatrist Robert Lifton saw the Jonestown incident as a mixture of people submitting to mass suicide and submitting to murder (Woodward, 1978). No single factor could be pinpointed as *the* reason for the tragedy, although the influence of Reverend Jones and evidence of breakdown in the Jonestown system associated with Ryan's visit would have to be given high weightings. The congre-

Jonestown, November 21, 1978.

gation's passivity was brought about in part by "intensified mental manipulation of individual thought and of society's cultural environment" ("Roots of Jonestown," 1978, p. 32). At least 18 situational factors, both past and present, contributed to the series of tragic behaviors:

1. *Isolation from the outside world.* Jonestown was located in South America, in the snake-infested jungles of Guyana. Members of Jonestown were not permitted to communicate with their families, and letters from relatives and friends in the United States were never delivered. One member had been whipped with a belt three times for such "sins" as phoning her parents (Moody & Graham, 1978).

2. *Selective recruitment strategies.* Jones sought out persons from disadvantaged and oppressed social groups, including poor Blacks, prostitutes, and outcasts. The American way of life had not proved satisfying to these persons, making it more likely that they would welcome Jones' message of "egalitarianism" and his offer of a "communal home" (Lasaga, 1979).

3. *The promise of idealistic hope.* Color movies and glossy brochures painted a picture of Jonestown as a peaceful "tropical paradise," a love-filled community dedicated to good works and interracial harmony (Steele, 1978).

4. *Total commitment.* Members had to demonstrate total involvement in the Jonestown experience. They had to give their possessions, money, time, and selves. One 71-year-old member had written that her only commitment in life was to "the cause."

5. *Indoctrination.* Jonestown members were required to think and believe in ways decided by Reverend Jones. One 19-year-old former member stated, "If Father said we were homosexual, then we must have been homosexual" (Axthelm, 1978, p. 59).

6. *A sense of belonging.* An 84-year-old member felt that she finally had something to live and die for — watching the little children grow and being glad to be with older members. Leo Ryan noted "From what I've seen, there are a lot of people here who think this is the best thing that has happened to them in their whole lives" ("Nightmare in Jonestown," 1978, p. 19).

7. *Charismatic leadership.* Reverend Jones had an undeniably special appeal to his followers. A minister who knew Jones reported he had never seen anyone relate to people the way Jones could. Jones was skillful at building people up, convincing them that they were intelligent and sensitive, and that they should do whatever he wanted them to do. If others were to love him as he loved them, they must be prepared to die rather than be destroyed from the outside.

8. *General acceptance of leadership.* Jones' leadership was fully accepted by members of the Peoples Temple. One trusted member who was away from Jonestown on the fateful day stated that he would have been "honored" to have been "the first in line" to take the poison. Psychologist José Lasaga referred to "mass hypnosis at a social level," in which an entire group of people regressed to the point of total acceptance of their leader's false belief system (Greenberg, 1979).

9. *An element of abnormality.* The development of a false belief or delusional system is a serious symptom of maladaptive behavior. Jones' behavior was partly motivated by a messianic self-image through which he identified himself as "the alpha and the omega." His son, Stephan, pointed to "an insane element" in the Temple's leadership, describing his father as a very frightened man (Steele, 1978). Jones' fearfulness undoubtedly was intensified by the reality of increasing "concern" about what was happening at Jonestown by relatives and representatives of the U.S. Government.

10. *Low self-esteem.* One effect of the Jonestown system was to foster low self-esteem, inadequacy, and helplessness in its members, who often had to make public statements and confessions about their personal failings and unworthiness. A letter written by a 13-year-old member contained repeated references to being "guilty" because of "bad" behaviors — gossiping, not spending enough time with older persons, and stealing (Harper, 1978). Adults were forced to stand in front of Jones on his "throne," where they were threatened by armed security forces until they "broke down, wept and pleaded to be forgiven" (Steele, 1978).

11. *Dependency.* The system also fostered excessive dependency of members on the leadership. Obedience and respect toward "Father" Jones and "Mother" Marceline had to be demonstrated unquestioningly. Jones even tried to weaken relationships between husbands and wives by engaging in a large number of extramarital affairs, sometimes requiring one spouse — man or woman — to observe sexual acts between him and the other spouse. Jones' goal was to become the most important love object in the community (Greenberg, 1979).

12. *Physical deprivation.* The few members who escaped the mass suicide were found to be undernourished, some with half-healed sores covering their

bodies. Coleman, Butcher, and Carson (1984) point out that a lowered physical status, along with fearfulness and dependency, were common characteristics of American prisoners during the Korean war, brought about by POW camp situations.

13. *Political and economic control.* Escape from Jonestown was equated with treason and subject to severe punishment. Jones told his followers that the Guyanese government had given him authority to shoot anybody who tried to leave the area, and that the Guyanese army would torture and kill anyone found beyond the Temple area. Jones maintained possession of all passports. He had also been collecting $65,000 a month in Social Security checks being sent to older members of the commune.

14. *Ritualistic rehearsal of mass suicide.* The White Night procedures that eventually took the lives of more than 900 people had been practiced on a number of occasions prior to the final call. These rehearsals tested community obedience to Jones' commands and helped to desensitize members' fears about taking poison by forcing them to face issues of life and death ahead of time. One member wrote of feeling "afraid to die" only during the time of the first rehearsal, not thereafter.

15. *Rationalizations.* Ritual confrontations with death also led members to defend themselves against a more realistic evaluation of their behavior by encouraging the development of psychological defenses against the "threat" of death. One middle-aged member found herself relieved just by thinking "It doesn't matter if I'm dead" (Woodward, 1978).

16. *Peer pressure.* Pressure from other members proved to be a powerful source of influence on the final actions of some Temple members. When one member challenged Jones' claim that everyone had to commit suicide, the crowd shouted her down, crying "No! No! If father says to do it, you should do it"; the challenger drank the poison (Moody & Graham, 1978). Family groups were found holding hands or embracing in death.

17. *Fear.* Although the Jonestown society was supposed to be classless, it actually had "a rigid and unforgiving hierarchy" of power. All members were encouraged to inform on spouses or children who went against the rules, a policy that instilled fear (Axthelm, 1978). At the time of the mass suicide, Jones said that any survivors would be "castrated" or "tortured" by the Guyanese army. Members ultimately were told "You better do it or we're going to shoot your ass off" (Mathews, 1978a).

18. *Breakdown of the system.* The most immediate circumstance triggering the mass suicide was the fact that 14 Temple members wanted to leave with Leo Ryan. It was the straw that broke the camel's back, because it made Jones directly aware that the system had broken down. He considered it "a repudiation" of his work. Feeling defeated "by lies," Jones decided he might as well die: "I tried. I tried. I tried" (Mathews, 1978a). A tape recording of Jonestown's final moments contains the sounds of babies and children screaming, and general mass confusion.

Clearly, no one factor can account for the tragic events that took place at Jonestown. A combination of influences was responsible, especially such situational factors as geographical isolation, external controls, powerful leadership, group pressure, indoctrination, fearfulness, and the desensitizing of natural concerns about death through ritualized practice. From this point of view, everybody is vulnerable to behaving in extraordinary ways under extraordinary circumstances.

We should note, however, that our emphasis on external factors is limited by not taking inner "personality" influences into consideration, such as the unique needs and vulnerabilities of individual members. For example, cult specialist Margaret Singer suggests that although two-thirds of cult recruits are relatively average people, "one-third are very psychologically distressed people" ("Why People Join," 1978, p. 27).

Sick societies.   Erich Fromm would have considered Jonestown a "sick" society, on the "safe" assumption that a high suicide rate in a given population indicates a general lack of stability. Fromm (1955) believed that entire societies could be sick, in the sense of not allowing their citizens to meet natural human needs and goals (Chapter 4). If people live under conditions that are contrary to human nature, they cannot help reacting either by deteriorating, perishing, or bringing about conditions more in accordance with their needs. Fromm wrote of *socially patterned defects,* in which failures to attain freedom, spontaneity, and a genuine expression of self characterize the majority of a society's members. Since such defects are shared with many others in the society, individuals may never even become aware of them, because of the security and comfort that come from fitting in with the rest of society. The result is a "pathology of normalcy" in which there is insanity not of one or two persons, but a "folly of millions."

Fromm's "sick" societies

Toward a Taxonomy of Situations

As we have just seen, the power of situations as influences on human behavior is certainly worth studying. The starting point would be to understand the nature of various psychological situations, identify their similarities and differences, and classify them. Toward this end, the present section reviews efforts to establish a *taxonomy,* or classification schema, of psychological situations and physical environments relevant to human behavior.

taxonomies of situations

Until recently, psychologists have shown little interest in establishing a standard taxonomy. Frederiksen (1972) finds this surprising for two reasons. First, psychologists have obviously been interested in devising situations for use as conditions in research studies. Second, psychologists have been successful in developing classification systems for personality traits and mental abilities (Thurstone, 1938; Guilford, 1967; Cattell, 1965). In this respect, there has been a one-sided emphasis on the "response" aspect of the "stimulus-response" concept in psychology.

Why classify environments? Frederiksen (1972) suggests that a taxonomy could coordinate research and aid interpretation of personality theory. A universally accepted taxonomy of situations could be used, first, to guide the work of different investigators and, second, to facilitate the drawing of inferences from studies done by many independent investigators. Moos (1973) offers yet a third reason: taxonomies also may aid the prediction of human behavior.

> Like people, environments have unique personalities. Just as it is possible to characterize a person's "personality," environments can be similarly portrayed with a great deal of accuracy and detail. Some people are supportive; likewise, some environments are supportive. Some men feel the need to control others; similarly, some environments are extremely controlling. Order and structure are important to many people; correspondingly, many environments emphasize regularity, system, and order. (Insel & Moos, 1974, p. 179)

Because different environments show different characteristics, they are likely to elicit different reactions and require different behaviors. Cope and Hewitt (1971) made use of this observation in seeking to understand why students dropped out of college. Rather than looking at students from the inside, simply as "dropouts," Cope and Hewitt looked at students in relation to different characteristics of the college environment they had left. Questionnaire results indicated that students who had withdrawn from the arts and sciences college of a public university did so less often because of academic factors than social and religious ones. In fact, 75% of the 774 students surveyed reported attending institutions elsewhere. Social problems were reflected in questionnaire items about "feeling lost" because the psychological environment was "so big and impersonal"; not finding congenial groups; and experiencing difficulties relating to cosmopolitan students whose standards were different from their own. Recalling Moos' idea, this type of information about a college environment could aid predictions about future dropout behavior and pave the way for development of a dropout screening and prevention program.

The remainder of this section presents some of the approaches psychologists have taken in classifying environmental influences on behavior. Over time, the basis of these approaches has become more empirical. We begin with a review of Henry Murray's ideas on taxonomy.

HENRY MURRAY: ENVIRONMENTAL PRESS

Henry Murray is one of the most significant theorists in the history of personality. His theory of personality, called *personology*, is directed toward "the study of human lives," aimed especially at understanding the "totality" of a single person's development and life history.

Murray believed that the study of psychological environments could enhance understanding of differences, similarities, and consistencies in behavior, both between and within individuals. For example, different individuals may differ in their behaviors simply because they encounter different conditions. They may also show the same behavior in different situations. Or they may respond differently to the same situations. If "the child is father to the man," as Freud believed, it is because aspects of the past are always alive in the present, in the form of reaction tendencies that may be "reactivated" by the appearance of new situations that resemble earlier ones. This means that a person's current behavior is partly a product of "formerly encountered situations" that have become assimilated and integrated (Murray, 1938/1962, p. 40). Thus, within the context of this chapter, it is possible to conceptualize "personality" as the repetition of certain related behaviors called forth by certain reoccurring situations the person encounters throughout life (Chapter 6).

Murray's view of environmental influences on behavior is best represented by his concept of *press*—forces in the outside world that influence a person's behavior. The press of any object in the external environment is what it can do *to* or *for* the person. Although press are "potent evokers" of behavior—signs of things to come—they do not simply elicit some immediate, specific response, as a stimulus might do. Their impact is actually felt prior to the occurrence of an overt behavioral response, as the person anticipates what direction to take in relation to objects in the outside world (to approach or to avoid). Thus, all press have a general, directional component—the power to draw a person toward or repel a person away. Most important is the effect a given press is likely to have on the person—its power "to affect the well-being of the subject" (Murray, 1938/1962, p. 121). If the effect is expected to be "bad," the person will tend to prevent it from happening by avoiding it or defending against it. If the effect is anticipated to be "good," the person will usually approach the object and attempt to get the most out of it.

Murray conceptualized two general categories of press: alpha and beta. *Alpha press* are physical aspects of the environment—those that exist as far as objective inquiry can determine. From this perspective, a ladder would be defined as two parallel sidepieces connected by a series of perpendicular parallel bars. *Beta press* are the person's own subjective interpretations of what is perceived. From this perspective, a ladder might be defined in terms of its potentially bad effect, as "not something I want to have anything to do with because I may fall from it and get hurt." Beta press are typically more important for understanding the person's behavior, because they refer to the person's psychological environment. They are aspects of the environment that "make a difference" to the individual, in personally meaningful ways.

Press may also be positive or negative. *Positive press* are desirable, enjoyable, beneficial, and facilitating, because they hold out the promise of satisfying a need. Examples include food, a friendly companion (affiliation), and a protective ally (nurturance). *Negative press* are undesirable, obstructing, harmful, and injurious, because they threaten to frustrate a need. Examples include poison, an insulting competitor (aggression), and conditions of poverty (lack). Murray considered it possible to understand a person by listing the person's psychological attachments or "cathexes" to different positive and negative press. Such a list would summarize those aspects of the environment having the power to draw or repel the person, thereby indicating what the person is most likely to do in given situations.

Although organisms may seek out a certain press, "more frequently the press meets the organism," thereby activating a need (Murray, 1938/1962, p.42). In other words, press evoke search and avoidance activity in the organism, particularly in relation to seeking satisfaction of a particular *need,* or hypothesized inner force in the "brain-region" that organizes a person's perceptions, intellectual functions, and actions. The purpose of the organization is to reduce tension associated with a particular need. Examples of Murray's 20 needs are achievement, affiliation, aggression, autonomy, dominance, harm avoidance, nurturance, order, play, sex, and understanding.

> Murray's environmental press

press-need
themas

Environmental press often interact with a person's inner needs. Murray referred to any combination of press-and-need behavior as a *thema* — the dynamic structure of one person's interaction with the environment, often repeated throughout the person's life. To illustrate, when confronted with a press of rejection, one person might respond with a need for rejection (p rejection $\rightarrow n$ rejection). For example, in response to a teacher's statement "You never do anything well in this class," a student might tell himself "You're right, I never have and I never will." However, another person might respond with a need for achievement (p rejection $\rightarrow n$ achievement). Thus, in response to the same teacher's statement, another student might say "Well, so far I haven't, but I'm working on a project that will prove otherwise." Or, despite outcomes of past failure, a person might continue to strive for success (p failure $\rightarrow n$ achievement).

Murray and his co-workers typically assessed themas through the Thematic Apperception Test (TAT) (Murray, 1943), analyzing the stories for press, needs, and themas (Henry, 1956/1974). Murray believed that a person's biography could be reasonably abstracted in terms of themas, which would then portray the historic route of the person's life as a series of "creature-environment" (need-press) interactions.

Murray (1938/1962) classified various press in formal outlines, as guides to understanding the forces at work in a person's psychological world. One such schema, relevant to children, identified 20 press, including danger, family instability, punishment, rejection, indulgence, illness, praise, sex experiences, betrayal, and friendship. Murray also considered it important to estimate the degree of strength each press has on a person, using a 6-point rating scale (0 – 5) for this purpose.

In sum, Murray (1938/1962) was the first psychologist to offer systematic classifications of environmental influences related to behavior and personality. Although Murray devoted a great deal of attention to the internal aspects of the person (the person's inner "needs"), he also attended to external influences (the environmental "press" operating on the person). In fact, he deemed it "a serious omission" to leave out the nature of environment and represent personality only as a trait system. "We must know to what circumstances an individual has been exposed" (p. 116).

Next, we will review a classification schema that is more comprehensive than Murray's, including both psychological situations and physical environments. It is also less theoretical than Murray's, and more closely supported by research findings. The schema is one proposed by Rudolph Moos, perhaps the most prominent of contemporary taxonomists.

RUDOLPH MOOS: CATEGORIZING HUMAN ENVIRONMENTS

Moos' six
categories
of human
environments

Moos has conceptualized six general categories of human environments: (1) ecological dimensions, (2) behavior settings, (3) dimensions of organizational structure, (4) personal and behavioral characteristics of the inhabitants of a given milieu, (5) psychosocial characteristics and organizational climate, and (6) functional or reinforcement analyses of environments (Moos, 1973; Moos & Brownstein, 1977).

Ecological dimensions. *Ecological dimensions* encompass gross aspects of the physical environment, including geography, meteorology, and architecture. According to Moos (1974), environmental determinists believe there are specific connections between a region's *geographical* characteristics, such as mountains, soil conditions, and humidity, and personality traits, such as assertiveness, bravery, and laziness. To illustrate, societies whose economies revolve around preservation of food resources stress the development of personal responsibility and obedience, whereas hunting and fishing societies stress the development of achievement and self-reliance (Barry, Child, & Bacon, 1959).

Many examples can be cited of the effects on behavior of *meteorological* variables such as climate and weather. When temperatures are high, there is an increase in violent behaviors, including homicide and political uprisings. The civil riots of the 1960s in Watts, St. Louis, Chicago, and Boston occurred during hot summer months. Days of high barometric pressure have been linked to findings of better health and school performance (Moos, 1976). When arthritis sufferers lived in a *climatron,* or controlled-climate chamber, for two weeks, reports of increased pain immediately followed decreases in barometric pressure and increases in humidity, leveling off when changes ceased (Hollander & Yeostros, 1963). Tokyo residents have been found to be particularly forgetful on days of low barometric pressure, leaving more packages and umbrellas on public conveyances (Mills, 1942).

Architectural features of the environment often influence human behavior by providing a context in which physical features encourage, direct, or constrain freedom of physical movement, social interaction, and psychological experience. A fascinating look at architectural influences is provided by fast-motion films of people making use of city plazas. These morning-to-evening films show people's patterns of entering, sitting down, relocating, conversing, lunching, sunning, playing in, and exiting from particular plaza areas. Architects have linked patterns of plaza use or non-use to spatial openness, height relative to street level, benches, fountains, walls, shade trees, and the presence of other people (Nova, 1982). A review of your own experiences will quickly illustrate the importance of architectural conditions that are "just right" for personal solitude, quiet conversation, a concert, romance, and boisterous parties (size, openness, lighting, windows, noise level, and ventilation).

Behavior settings. The dimension of behavior settings, or behavioral ecology, is concerned with relatively large or "molar" units of behavior and the ecological context in which they occur. *Behavior settings* are naturally occurring situations in everyday life in which certain types of behavior can be expected to take place (basketball game, school play, supermarket). These ecological units are always made up of two components: physical environments (road, drugstore, newspaper), and behaviors related to them (walking, shopping, reading). The behavior patterns occurring in these settings are not unique to a particular person at a given time or place, but are more universal. For example, when a local radio station announces that "Ellson Drugstore will hold a sale on Friday and Saturday," any number of persons may go there. Or when the local newspaper reports that "The Midwest High School commencement was held last Tuesday," the basic

ecological dimensions

behavior settings

setting and activity are not unique to the current graduating class, since the same thing has happened in past years and will happen in future ones. Both are settings in which certain kinds of behaviors are apt to be displayed, and that have equivalents in many other communities. Research work in this area is often traced to Roger Barker (1968) and his students, who for two decades studied the everyday behaviors of people living in a small Midwestern community (Barker & Wright, 1955).

organizational structure

Organizational structure.   Social systems vary widely in their structural characteristics, and these differences affect the behavior and attitudes of organization members (Moos, 1974). Dimensions of organizational structure include an organization's overall size, nature of line and staff hierarchies, number of supervisees, degree of centralization, turnover rate, and population density. To illustrate, past NASA space missions have been centrally organized around very strict supervision by mission ground control. The low degree of crew autonomy "led to some conflicts" during the flight of Skylab 3 (Helmreich, 1983).

Gump (1974) evaluated the differential effects of big and small school organizations on young people. Although bigger schools could afford to offer more varied courses and slightly more out-of-class activities, these advantages were not always meaningful. Gump concluded that smaller schools do a better job of

What influence is this psychological situation likely to have on the students' experience and behavior? Consider your own feelings, thoughts, immediate goals, interactions with other students, and degree of relaxation or stress in similar settings. Research findings regarding size of organization do not always support the saying "The bigger, the better."

translating fewer opportunities into actual experiences for the total student body. For example, students in small schools participated in twice the number of sports, plays, concerts, and similar activities. They also reported a greater sense of responsibility to school affairs, even when their academic work was marginal. While overall size of organizational structure was certainly a dimension contributing to differences between the two types of schools, in this instance Gump found little support for the saying "The bigger, the better."

Population density has been the focus of a number of psychosocial studies. In a classic study, Calhoun (1962) confined 36 rats to a quarter-acre enclosure having abundant food, places to live, good health quality, and no predators. At the end of 27 months, the population had stabilized at 150 adults. The very high rate of infant mortality (80%–96%) was the result of social stresses associated with overcrowding and disruptions in maternal behavior. Dominant males showed *territoriality,* staking out areas of exclusive use that they would control and defend, along with their harem, thereby maintaining a type of normal "easy living." However, many more rats formed dense "behavioral sinks," or areas in which animals are collected together in unusually great numbers. These rats lived in overcrowded conditions of mass confusion, often mixing their biological, eating, and social activities in undifferentiated ways. They developed pathological patterns of fighting, passivity, "gang" formation, inappropriate sexual behavior, cannibalism, and unpredictability. Females and young pups showed the highest mortality rates, often the result of direct attacks by males, thereby increasing the likelihood of colony extinction. One obvious implication of Calhoun's work is that there is an optimum number of group members suitable for a given social organization in order for adaptive functioning to occur.

The experience of living in large cities was discussed by Milgram (1970). Three dimensions of organizational structure were readily apparent to him: (1) large numbers of people, (2) high population density, and (3) heterogeneity of population. Milgram saw these external factors as contributing to stimulus overload—the press of too many inputs for the individual to handle. He also saw adaptive responses of allocating less time to each input, and establishing selective priorities regarding what to respond to, as partially accounting for the superficial, anonymous, and transitory social encounters that sometimes typify urban living.

On the other hand, one advantage of working in a dense, centralized, highly populated city is increasing opportunities for face-to-face business contacts. This was demonstrated by Tanner (1976) through comparisons of New York City, its satellite city of Newark, New Jersey, and suburban Nassau County (Long Island). Within 10 minutes from work, by car, a Nassau County employee could meet with any of 11,000 other employees. A Newark worker, on foot, could meet any of 22,000 others. However, a midtown Manhattan employee could meet any of 220,000, on foot or by taxi, bus, or subway.

Personal and behavioral characteristics of inhabitants. The character of a given environment depends on the characteristics of its members. The underlying assumption is that much of the social and cultural environment is transmitted through other people. "If we know what kind of people make up a group, then we can infer the climate that group creates" (Moos, 1974, p. 13). Examples of group

characteristics
of inhabitants

characteristics include (1) background (age, sex, socioeconomic status); (2) external features (height, weight, physical abnormalities); (3) status (rural or urban, salary, occupation, education); (4) family and marriage factors (legal status, number of children); and (5) memberships (number and type of social memberships).

Moos considers it possible to describe a given social environment in terms of the occupations of its members. This is related to his view that differences between the climates of two professions, such as a law firm and an engineering firm, are partly related to the "personalities" of the persons engaged in them. Helmreich (1983) reported relatively few psychological problems among members of U.S. space crews. He tied this to the fact that these early astronauts, coming from the ranks of male military test pilots, were "homogeneous in background and experiences." Crew members shared common characteristics of high achievement motivation and interpersonal compatability. This pattern could change in the future because crews will be larger in number, more specialized in mission assignments, and more diverse in background.

psychosocial
climate

Psychosocial characteristics and organizational climate.   The fifth category that Moos identifies encompasses both psychological and social dimensions of the environment, within a framework of person-milieu interaction. Most of the work in this area has emphasized the importance of "insider" perceptions — the climate perceived by members actually participating in the environment. Moos (1973) and his co-workers have studied the perceived climates of nine types of social organizations: psychiatric wards; community-oriented psychiatric treatment programs, such as halfway houses; juvenile correctional institutions; military basic training units; university dormitories, fraternities, and sororities; junior high and high school classrooms; group environments; work environments; and family environments.

Three basic dimensions have been found to differentiate these various environmental subunits. First, *relationship* dimensions assess the extent to which individuals are involved in the environment and the extent to which they tend to support and help each other. Examples of scales used to measure this dimension are involvement, affiliation, peer cohesion, staff support, and expressiveness. Second, *personal-development* dimensions assess the opportunity afforded by the environment for self-enhancement and the development of self-esteem. Examples are autonomy, practical orientation, personal problem orientation, and competition. Third, *system-maintenance and system-change* dimensions pertain to "order and organization, clarity and control," with "innovation" showing up in educational and industrial environments and "student influence" in university residence halls (Moos, 1973, p. 657).

Insel and Moos (1974) reported that environments emphasizing such relationship dimensions as involvement and support are characterized by members with high morale. Psychiatric wards and correctional units emphasizing personal-development dimensions of autonomy and an orientation to personal problems are characterized by members with relatively high self-confidence and liking of staff. Further, such psychiatric wards are able to keep patients out of hospitals for comparatively longer periods of time following discharge.

Reinforcement properties.   People vary their behavior substantially from one setting to another as a function of reinforcement consequences for particular behaviors: "The importance of any stimulus of course depends in part on the specific social context in which it is embedded" (Moos, 1974, p. 23). The idea that the same people behave differently in different social and physical environments is consistent with Henry Murray's ideas, discussed earlier, and is an outgrowth of the social-learning perspective (Chapter 6). Its major implication is that behavior changes when environments change (Murray, 1938/1962).

Consider Endler and Hunt's (1968) Stimulus Response Inventories, which assess hostility and anxiety responses in relation to different categories of situations. For each of the statements listed below, would you make the same estimates of the degree to which your heart might beat faster, or the degree to which you might want to hit someone or something?

"You are talking to someone and he or she does not answer."

"Someone persistently contradicts you when you know you are right."

"Someone pushes ahead of you in a theater ticket line."

While you might exhibit hostility in all three of these situations, there would probably be differences in degree and quality. The inventories allow situations to be categorized in terms of the similarity of the reactions they elicit.

From this brief summary of Moos' taxonomy of human environments, it is easy to see that the range of environmental influences affecting behavior is very wide, and that their effects can be quite complex. At this point, let us pursue Moos' fifth category—psychosocial characteristics and organizational climate—in a little more depth, using a social organization that is quite familiar to you: the college environment. Our purpose is to show how differences in environments can be measured empirically.

ASSESSING "PERSONALITIES" OF COLLEGE ENVIRONMENTS

People differ. So do environments. And, as we have already seen, the climates of social environments have an obvious impact on many aspects of individual functioning, including attitudes, moods, morale, well-being, health, and behavior (Moos, 1976).

To develop the theme of *individual differences in environments,* we will focus on a type of setting that you are very much a part of right now: the college environment. Actually, you have already had experience understanding the "personalities" of college environments. Before coming to college, you likely thought a good deal about what you were looking for in a college. What dimensions were most and least important to you? What led you to decide on your present college or university rather than on some other one? Now that you are in a college, you have been able to gain firsthand knowledge of its unique "atmosphere" or flavor. In what ways has it turned out the way you expected? By now, you probably have learned enough about your own college to make meaningful comparisons with those of your friends or out-of-town rivals: amount of work, difficulty of tests, types of teachers, ease of grades, traditions, social life, dating, and sports.

A second theme of our discussion is apt to be less familiar to you. It has to do with how psychologists actually measure "personalities" of colleges in formal, objective ways. In Chapter 2, we discussed the use of psychological questionnaires to assess people's personalities. In this section, we are confronted with the problem of how a psychological instrument might be used to measure an *environment*. Colleges obviously cannot provide True or False responses to questionnaire items. The solution is that students can. This occurred in Box 11.1, when we asked you to describe your own college environment.

One method adopted by researchers in this area involves the idea of *consensus response,* in which the "majority rules" in determining whether group answers to items about a given campus are representative. Statements are accepted as reasonably characteristic of the environment if most persons who live in it independently answer the same way. Pace (1969), for example, considered all items endorsed by two-thirds of the students completing the College and University Environment Scale (CUES) as reflecting the "true" campus environment. Earlier, Pace and Stern (1958) relied on overall statistical indices to determine whether subgroup results for scales were "average," "above average," or "below average." Both procedures have been used to identify prevailing college "climates," accompanied by graphed "personality profiles" of individual differences on various dimensions (Chapter 1). Comparisons have been made among different colleges, among different divisions within the same college, and among different groups of students, faculty, and administrative staff within the same college.

BOX 11.1 REVISITED: THE COLLEGE CHARACTERISTICS INDEX (CCI)

Pace and Stern (1958) pioneered the development of an objective measure of environmental press for use in college settings. They did so by incorporating and modifying Henry Murray's concepts of press and needs. Their work was awarded an Honorable Mention for Outstanding Research by the American Personnel and Guidance Association. Pace and Stern saw the press of a college environment as whatever had to be faced and dealt with by the student. Their operational definition of press was "the characteristic demands or features as perceived by those who live in the particular environment" (p. 270). The working framework was grounded in the consensus-response assumption of *perceived climate*—that if a dominant press really existed in a given environment, any group of people living in the environment would be able to identify it. This framework is quite in keeping with Moos' fifth category, which refers to "insider" perceptions of human environments.

College Characteristics Index (CCI)

Pace and Stern (1958) constructed an instrument called the College Characteristics Index (CCI). The CCI consists of 300 statements about college life — curriculum, teachers, classroom activities, student organizations and interests, campus rules and regulations, administrative policies, physical features of the campus, and so on. Students are asked to respond to each statement by deciding whether it is probably true or false for their particular college. There are 10 items for each of the 30 press scales.

The items in Box 11.1, at the beginning of this chapter, are examples of those appearing in the CCI. The first three items represent *order,* the second three *impulsiveness,* and the last three *energy.* If your instructor were to poll members of the class regarding their answers to these nine statements, some preliminary estimates related to the nature of the climate at your own college or university could be made. The higher the number of your classmates answering "True" to an item, the more likely the item reflects the press of your own college environment. The more items endorsed within each of the three units, the more likely your college environment reflects the CCI dimensions of order, impulsiveness, and energy, respectively.

Comparing college climates.   Pace and Stern (1958) administered an initial draft of the CCI to students and faculty at five institutions. They found that the CCI was capable of revealing "some sharp distinctions" among colleges, reflecting "quite different environments." Also, students and faculty at the same institutions showed "tolerably good agreement" in their CCI answers, which indicated they were perceiving their college environments in relatively the same way. This confirmed the assumption that dominant press would be perceived by different groups living in the same environment.

Stern (1970) later reported results of factor analysis and norms for 11 environmental-press scales of the CCI, based on responses from 1993 students at 32 colleges. He offered a number of conclusions. Independent liberal-arts colleges were characterized by pronounced "intellectual" climates. University-affiliated liberal-arts programs and, particularly, denominational liberal-arts colleges showed low press for "academic achievement" from students. Universities stressed collegiate "play" and amusements. Denominational colleges stressed "organized" group activities and a well-ordered academic community. Engineering programs exceeded the average in "intellectual" press, with education and business-administration programs below the average. Business-administration and liberal-arts programs showed the greatest contrasts, with business "more personally constrictive" and showing "little involvement in art, music, contemporary social thought, or scholarship" (p. 78).

Table 11.1 presents summary descriptions of the "personalities" of two types of college environments, abbreviated from Stern's (1970) findings. Each summary has two parts — one pertaining to "intellectual" or academic aspects of the environment, and the other to "nonintellectual" or more general aspects. Descriptions of "high intellectual climate" were most characteristic of private, nonsectarian liberal-arts colleges known for their quality, cost, and student selectiveness (for example, Vassar, Oberlin, Antioch). Stern saw the orientation of these colleges as primarily scholarly and cultural. Descriptions of "low intellectual climate" were most characteristic of public institutions (for example, Boston University, University of Cincinnati, Northeast Louisiana State College) and nonaccredited denominational schools (for example, Fort Wayne Bible College). Stern saw the orientation of these institutions as primarily technical and noncul-

TABLE 11.1 "Personality" Descriptions of Two Types of College Environments (Adapted from Stern, 1970)

	High intellectual climate	Low intellectual climate
Intellectual dimensions	Faculty members put a lot of energy and enthusiasm into their teaching. A lecture by an outstanding literary critic would be well attended. The school has an excellent reputation for academic freedom. Working hard for high grades is not unusual. The main emphasis is on breadth of understanding, perspective, and critical judgment. Students often argue with the professor. Modern art and music get much attention here. Many students travel or look for jobs in different parts of the country during the summer. Quite a few faculty have had varied and unusual careers.	Few people know the "snap" courses to take or the tough ones to avoid. When students get together, they seldom talk about trends in art, music, or the theater. Few classes ever meet out of doors on nice days. Books dealing with psychological problems or personal values are rarely read or discussed. There are few public debates. Education here tends to make students more practical and realistic. The future goals of most students emphasize job security, family happiness, and good citizenship. There is little emphasis on preparing for graduate work.
Non-intellectual dimensions	The professors really talk with the students, not just at them. There is no period when freshmen have to take orders from upperclassmen. Student organizations are not closely supervised. Students are encouraged to be independent and individualistic. Grade lists are not publicly posted. The college offers few really practical courses such as typing or report writing. Students take no particular pride in their personal appearance. There is much studying here over the weekends, but students frequently do things on the spur of the moment. (pp. 142–145)	Students quickly learn what is done and what is not done on this campus. Professors usually take attendance in class. Classes meet only at their regularly scheduled time and place. Student papers and reports must be neat. The campus and buildings always appear well kept. Little enthusiasm or support is aroused by fund drives. Students frequently study or prepare for examinations together and help one another with lessons. There are many opportunities for students to get together in extracurricular activities. Student gathering places are typically active and noisy. (p. 145)

tural. You might find it interesting to compare these descriptions with experiences you have had at your own college, and with your answers to the exercise in Box 11.1

Stern also identified schools in his sample scoring high and low in *play.* High "play" was characteristic of large state universities, which tended to make few demands on student performance while watching their behavior closely (for example, Cornell, Florida State, San Jose State). Low "play" schools showed a somewhat stronger intellectual climate, associated with low emotional expression (for example, Ball State, Randolph Macon, Swarthmore).

Thus, the "personalities" of environments can be described in ways paralleling the "personalities" of people. Pace and Stern's research has also demonstrated the possibility of establishing differences in human perceptions of college characteristics empirically. Although our focus has been on college environments, the relevance of these procedures to other settings may be inferred. Now let us go on to explore other empirical ways of defining the "personalities" of environments.

SITUATIONAL TEMPLATES AND PROTOTYPES

Establishing situational templates.   A second empirical approach to assessing the personality of college environments has been taken by D. Bem and Funder (1978), who wanted to find a common system for describing both situations and persons. Their search led them to *criterion Q-sorts,* a method through which environments are defined according to the behavioral characteristics of *ideal* types of persons who actually function in those environments. Block's (1961) California Q-Set has been adopted for this purpose. It consists of 100 statements about personality that are sorted into a distribution of nine categories ranging from most to least like the target person (see Chapter 7).

Take a university environment such as Stanford. Criterion sorts can be established in two ways. First, trained judges can be asked to describe the characteristics of an ideal student—the sort of student "who does best" at Stanford University. Second, Q-sort items from students demonstrating the "best work" at Stanford can be correlated with the students' grade-point averages, thereby establishing an empirical rank-ordering of characteristics.

"Should Mary attend Stanford?" *Situational templates* based on Q-sorts representing various types of "ideal" students could be used to answer this question. Mary would complete the Q-sort, describing herself. Then, the order of her Q-sort statements could be correlated with that of the "ideal" student to determine the degree of similarity between the two. Perhaps Mary will fit the criterion of "students who are hard-working but somewhat shy [who] tend to get good grades but don't have much interaction with the faculty" or of "students who are bright and assertive [who] often get involved in faculty research projects but as a consequence sometimes have little social life and get lower grades than they should" (Funder & Bem, 1977, p. 2). If the situation fits for Mary, evidenced by a "match" between Mary's Q-sort behavior and an "ideal student" template, the probability of Mary's performing successfully at Stanford is increased. The model

situational
templates

predicts the degree to which Mary will display behaviors associated with the corresponding templates.

Again, while the focus of this discussion is on a college environment, the procedure could be applied more generally, to matches between a person's behavior and some ideal behavior likely to be displayed in any other given situation. The essence of Funder and Bem's contribution is that it objectifies the particulars of a specific situation, defining it in terms of an empirically established pairing of two interlocking components, template and behavior. Their framework is related to the second of Moos' taxonomic categories, behavior settings, while tapping the "insider" perceptions of Moos' fifth category. Also, the process of "matching" situations and persons implied in the question "Should Mary attend Stanford?" reflects the interactionist perspective discussed in Chapter 13.

Identifying situational prototypes.   A third approach has been adopted by Cantor, Mischel, and Schwartz (1982), who are among the growing number of personality researchers seeking to "illuminate the ways in which situations impact on the perceiver and the actor" (p. 45). Their goal was to identify people's working models or *prototypes* of situations, defined as the abstract set of features about a given situational experience that is stored in a person's long-term memory. Prototypes serve as symbolic reference points for people by structuring their knowledge and giving them something to "work with" as they behave in relation to a certain category of experience. Cantor et al. began by analyzing 36 categories of psychological situations found in everyday settings. They limited their study to four broad situation taxonomies: (1) social (for example, party, date), (2) cultural (symphony, tour), (3) psychological (interview, prison), and (4) political (demonstration, religious ceremony). They also investigated three levels of inclusiveness about situations: (a) superordinate ("social situation"), (b) middle ("party"), and (c) subordinate ("birthday party").

Cantor et al. asked students from Stanford University to describe each of four situations taken from the same level of inclusiveness. Students were instructed to list only those characteristics perceived as common to the situation, "things like physical setting and surroundings, etiquette, expectations, and rules for how to act in the situation" (p. 59). For each situation, students were free to generate any descriptors they wished within a 2-minute time period. This procedure served to establish *category prototypes*—lists of features or attributes generated by naive subjects as typical of that class of situations (Rosch, 1978).

A number of interesting observations were made about how situations are categorized. First, people *do* form images about situations. Second, these images are accessed, or brought to mind, as readily as the images that people have about persons. Third, the average number of attributes making up people's images of situations is 9. Fourth, prototypes often reflect *fuzzy feature sets,* meaning that very few attributes of situations are agreed upon by a majority of persons. Only 17% of the attributes generated were listed by two or more of the ten students asked to describe each category. This finding, that many attributes are unique to one person's list, went against classical expectations that categories would be "well defined." Fifth, attributes do not cluster randomly, but are more similar within a category than between categories. Attributes also show greater richness and dis-

situational prototypes

tinctiveness at the "middle" level of inclusiveness than at the superordinate or subordinate level. Sixth, many of the components are *psychological* in nature. They include feelings, typical reactions, and appropriate behaviors associated with being in a given situation. To illustrate, one of the situations studied was that of a college admissions interview. The consensual prototype for this situation referred not only to physical features of *desk, chairs, office,* and *application forms,* but also to social features of *nervous, firm handshake, questions, dressed up, impressive language,* and *good manners.* Further, "a substantial portion" (54%) of the features in prototype situations referred to personal and social characteristics of people commonly found in them. Thus, a situation such as "parties" is likely to be described in terms of "happy" people who "dance" and "talk." Physical features of situations account for 23% of the features, followed by nonphysical features (15%), and by physical features of people in those situations (8%).

The usefulness of these results is in clarifying the "that," "how," and "what" dimensions of people's characterizations of different situations. Cantor et al. found that persons do enter social interactions with "a vast and varied expertise about situations," a base of knowledge that can be readily tapped and translated into behavioral guidelines. The finding that many of the components present in people's mental images of situations are "psychological" in nature lends credence to the importance of psychological situations in understanding human behavior. That is, there is "a decidedly personal-social element" present in the psychology of situations (Cantor et al., 1982, p. 70).

Cantor et al. also found that some situations allow people freer, more comfortable interaction than others. That is, the situation "being on a date" is more likely to enable the display of a natural disposition toward high self-esteem, whereas the situation "being in a class" is less likely to enable the display of a high energy level. Because prototypes offer ready guidelines for social life, they are likely to influence people's choices of different life situations. A person would tend to select situations "matching" his or her natural inclinations, personal preferences, or socially desired bahaviors ("dating" versus "classroom"). People would then "contribute to their own destiny" by behaving in ways that would develop their potentialities for having access to particular social situations (Bandura, 1982).

In effect, situations may "control" behavior by stimulating the development of certain kinds of prototypes which, in turn, would have a further influence in guiding a person's selection of future situations and development of behaviors relevant to those situations. The broader theoretical significance of this observation again may be tied to the interactionist perspective discussed in Chapter 13, similar to Funder and Bem's situational template/behavior method. That is, different situations are often associated with different best-fitting behaviors or "personalities." Some kind of situation/person "match-up" is likely to be involved.

The Impact of Life's Stressors on Behavior

In this chapter, we have seen how it is possible to think about human behavior as resulting from sources other than the internal factors we call "personality." As a provocative illustration of this theme, this section examines the impact of stressful environments on behavior, where external stressors resulting in "stress" take the place of the internal concept of anxiety.

STRESSORS: A VIEW FROM THE OUTSIDE

As we saw in Chapters 9 and 10, one of the most important trait dimensions associated with inner personality is anxiety, an abstract concept that has been useful in understanding various fearful, nervous, and inefficient behaviors. However, anxiety represents only one way of looking at such behaviors. We have already noted differences in psychologists' ideas as to whether anxiety should be thought of as a trait, a state, or neither. When we use the concept of anxiety, we allow our attention to be directed toward the person who shows it. That is, we adopt "a view from within" the person.

An alternative way of looking at behaviors analogous to those associated with anxiety is to reconsider them in relation to the concept of "stress." When we use this concept, we allow our attention to be directed away from the person, toward external situations that produce certain disruptive behaviors. Adoption of this "view from the outside" suggests that the kinds of fearful and inefficient behaviors often associated with anxiety may not simply reside "in" persons, nor be due to their biological makeup or long-term learning patterns. Rather, such behaviors may stem from the environment, a result of situational pressures the person encounters in life.

stressors

All of us have experience with environmental stressors. *Stressors* are conditions of perceived imbalance between what the environment demands of us and our capacity to meet those demands, whether physical, psychological, or social (McGrath, 1970). You will immediately know what we are referring to if you recall a time when you had a week's worth of final-exam studying to do, but only a day or two left to get it done. Stressors require *adaptation*—"a concentration of effort at the site of demand" (Selye, 1978, p. 163). We tend to respond to the effects of

stress

these adjustive demands in nonspecific ways, termed *stress,* which is also an index of the rate of general "wear and tear" on the organism. Thus, stressors are the causes of stress, which is the internal condition resulting from the organism's adaptive efforts.

The relevance of stressors to understanding behavior is that, like anxiety, they often interfere with the person's routine functioning or development. They may block the person's behavioral efficiency, create new difficulties, or override more usual patterns of behavior. Rigid patterns of behavior may set in, because of the person's lessened capacity to differentiate one situation from another. Rather than showing sensitivity to differences in situations, the person may engage in the same behaviors to such an extent that they become maladaptive, inappropriately applied across different situations (Mischel, 1984; Schroeder & Pendleton, 1983). For example, a person under stress may end up studying, partying, or sleeping "all the time." If too traumatic, stressors may also result in long-range changes or deficits in personal functioning. One of the occupational hazards of being an air-traffic controller is an above-average tendency to develop ulcers.

The American Psychiatric Association (1980) has increased its appreciation of this "view from the outside." It currently suggests that all diagnoses of behavioral disorders be accompanied by a rating of the degree to which environmental stressors are involved. The association also recognizes that certain patterns of maladaptive behavior are due "primarily" to the impact of psychological and social stressors in the person's environment. For example, the essential feature of an *adjustment disorder* is "a maladaptive reaction to an identifiable psychosocial stressor" (p. 299). Perhaps you have heard about "combat exhaustion" during the Korean War, or of "delayed stress syndrome" among veterans of the Vietnam War. Or you may have read about the devastating psychological effects that tornados, earthquakes, fires, and other natural catastrophes have had on people. These examples of adjustment disorders are relatively independent of "personality," because they are not due to inner factors of irregular genes, brain tumors, or lifelong habits of faulty learning within the person. They are brought about by external, situational conditions of exaggerated, excessive, or overwhelming stress. Also, the stressors that produce adjustment reactions of tension, fatigue, and uncontrolled behavior tend to evoke symptoms of distress not just in a few people but in many people. Everyone is susceptible. Let us take a quick look at some stressors and their specific effects on behaviors.

adjustment disorders

NATURAL DISASTERS: MOUNT SAINT HELENS

The impact of a natural stressor on human behavior was detailed by Paul and Gerald Adams (1984), who studied the effects of an erupting volcano on the residents of Othello, Washington. Othello is an agricultural community of 5000 — 75% Caucasian and 25% Mexican-American. Adams and Adams' purpose was to study the community's behaviors resulting from the disaster.

A unique assumption of the study was that stress-related problems would be manifested in "observable and recorded behavior" of victims. Thus, exclusive use was made of "documented" behaviors — information drawn from official records of 12 community agencies. Past disaster studies have typically relied on subjective self-reports obtained from citizens, through interviews or questionnaires, after the fact.

The initial Mount Saint Helens disaster occurred on a Sunday morning, May 18, 1980. Postdisaster data were gathered from June 1, 1980, through December 31, 1980. Statistical comparisons were then made with the previous identical seven months. Table 11.2 summarizes the monthly averages for changes in various kinds of behavior.

Five general categories of stress-reaction behaviors were examined: illness, family problems, alcohol abuse, aggression and violence, and general adjustment. Increases in stress-related psychological and physical illnesses were clearly indicated. The average increase for three subcategories of illness was over 200%! Police reports of domestic violence increased almost 50%. Arrests for liquor-law violations increased almost 50%, although drinking-and-driving violations decreased because of difficulties in local driving conditions brought about by "ashfall," a powdery volcanic fallout that drifted down from the skies and accumulated in inches everywhere. Criminal assaults, vandalism, and police bookings all increased by about 25%. Lowered general adjustment was evidenced by increases in

TABLE 11.2   Monthly Averages Before and After the Mt. Saint Helens Eruption (Adapted from Adams & Adams, 1984)

General variables	Before	After	p
Mental-health crisis line calls	11	23	.001
Hospital emergency-room visits	287	384	.01
Community alcohol center clients	25	35	.03
District court cases	199	248	.03
Police reports of domestic violence	7	11	.04
Total number of police forms filed	297	346	.04
Mental-health clinic appointments	99	126	.05
Type-of-illness variables			
Mental illness cases	15	50	.05
Psychosomatic illness	31	100	.05
Stress-aggravated illness	45	133	.05

mental-health crisis line calls (79%), psychiatric commitment investigations (34%), and mental-health appointments (22%).

Overall results provided "substantial evidence for stress reactions" in the Othello community, resulting from the external stressor. The general trend was a sharp increase in behavioral problems for three to four months after the disaster, followed by decreases in postdisaster behavior thereafter. A definite exception to this trend was mental-health clinic appointments, which continued to increase over time.

Results such as those reported by Adams and Adams underscore the theme of this section, that maladaptive behaviors may not simply reside "in" a few maladaptive persons but may result from overwhelming stressors present in human environments. Also, as we saw in our earlier discussion of the Jonestown suicides, everyone is potentially vulnerable to these stressors. Is it really true that "everyone" is susceptible to anxious or stressful reactions? The simple answer is "Yes." However, a very important assumption needs to be made before answering the question. Where are we going to look for the answer — "inside" the person or "outside," at the environment? From the point of view of this chapter and the next, our potential vulnerability for showing maladaptive behaviors is going to be related to the kinds of situations we find ourselves in (Milgram, 1974). Most of us are fortunate because our "person" resources are never fully tested by our environments. But some people aren't so lucky; they are forced to deal with the situational horrors of wars, prison camps, terrorist captivity, nuclear radiation leakage and potential "meltdown" episodes, the presence of hazardous environmental toxins in the neighborhood, multiple losses of loved ones, major failures, and so on.

CHANGE AS A STRESSOR

change

All of us are affected to varying degrees by the phenomenon of change. Although change is not a situation, but a process, the amount of change in our lives at any given time can be quite stressful (Toffler, 1970). That is, apart from any specific situation, the sheer number of situations we have to adapt to may serve as a stressor that results in maladaptive behavior and physical illness.

Measuring change-related stress.   To measure the cumulative amount of stress to which a person has been exposed over a given time period, typically one year, Holmes and his colleagues developed a Social Readjustment Rating Scale (SRRS) (Holmes & Rahe, 1967; Ruch & Holmes, 1971; Pasley, 1969). They asked 394 adults to rate 43 life events according to the average degree of "necessary readjustment" demanded by the events. "Marriage" was arbitrarily selected as the reference point, and given an impact weighting of 50. Death of a spouse (100) and divorce (73) were rated at the top of the list. Christmas (12) and minor law violations (11) were rated at the bottom. Table 11.3 lists the SRRS items and their readjustment values.

Social Readjustment Rating Scale (SRRS)

Holmes and Masuda (1973) reported a highly significant linear relationship between scores on the SRRS and the occurrence of serious physical illness during the next year or two among independent samples of subjects, including physicians (*rho* = .65). In one study, 88 physicians were asked to report their life events and

TABLE 11.3   Social Readjustment Rating Scale (Holmes & Rahe, 1967)

Events	Impact	Events	Impact
Death of spouse	100	Son or daughter leaving home	29
Divorce	73	Trouble with in-laws	29
Marital separation	65	Outstanding personal achievement	28
Jail term	63	Wife begins or stops work	26
Death of close family member	63	Begin or end school	26
Personal injury or illness	53	Change in living conditions	25
Marriage	50	Revision of personal habits	24
Fired at work	47	Trouble with boss	23
Marital reconciliation	45	Change in work hours or conditions	20
Retirement	45	Change in residence	20
Change in health of family member	44	Change in schools	20
Pregnancy	40	Change in recreation	19
Sex difficulties	39	Change in church activities	19
Gain of new family member	39	Change in social activities	18
Business readjustment	39	Mortgage or loan less than $10,000	17
Change in financial state	38	Change in sleeping habits	16
Death of close friend	37	Change in number of family get-	
Change to different line of work	36	togethers	15
Change in number of arguments with		Change in eating habits	15
spouse	35	Vacation	13
Mortgage over $10,000	31	Christmas	12
Foreclosure of mortgage or loan	30	Minor violations of the law	11
Change in responsibilities at work	29		

all major health changes during each of ten years. Three levels of annual "life change" crisis were defined, using SRRS scores: mild (150–199), moderate (200–299), and major (300+). As the magnitude of change in a physician's life increased, so did the risk of serious physical illness (37% of those in the mild, 51% of those in the moderate, and 79% of those in the major crisis category). Some 93% of all major health changes occurred within two years after the physicians' SRRS scores showed "life crisis" clusters of at least 150 points. The researchers concluded that life-change events "enhance the probability of disease occurrence," probably by evoking adaptive efforts and by lowering bodily resistance (Holmes & Masuda, 1973, p. 182).

In taking the SRRS, a person checks off all the events that have occurred during the past year and then sums the rated values for those events to obtain an overall life-change score. You can estimate the amount of change occurring in your own life during the past year by following the guidelines in Box 11.2.

BOX 11.2   *Identifying Stressors*
in Your Own Life

What is the cumulative impact of external stressors in your own life for the past year? You may find it interesting to assess this by calculating your own score on the Social Readjustment Rating Scale (SRRS).

Read each item in Table 11.3. If the item applies to you during the past 12 months, circle the value. Then add all of the circled values to obtain a total score. Evaluate your score in relation to the three levels of "life change" crisis: mild (150–199), moderate (200–299), and major (300+). You may wish to compare your score with those of other students, or with the score you would obtain by retaking the SRRS using a different 12-month time period in your life. Computation of the mean and standard deviation of SRRS scores for the class as a whole would enable you to determine whether your life stress score is average, above average, or below average in relation to the "local norms" of your own college peer group. Rahe's (1975) four-part taxonomy of family, personal, work, and financial items may also be helpful in interpreting areas of relatively greater and lesser impact. Finally, if you were a physician in Rahe and Holmes' study, what implications would there be regarding your health status during the next year or two?

Be careful not to take the results at face value, but as tendencies or estimated trends. As we learned in Chapter 2, all measurement techniques are characterized by a certain degree of unreliability, and need to be validated against many criteria.

The stress of "good" changes. In Toffler's (1970) concept of future shock, introduced earlier, the direction of change, negative or positive, is less important in understanding stress than the *rate* or amount of change. This is consistent with Selye's (1978) position that the body undergoes "virtually the same" nonspecific responses whether stimuli are those of harmful *distress* or pleasant *eustress,* although the effects of eustress admittedly are less damaging (p. 74). Examples of eustress are vacations, holidays, joyous social occasions, promotions, and personal successes. In this regard, your textbook authors were somewhat surprised to document a significant drop in subjects' generally favorable adjective descriptions of "Christmas" over a seven-week period. The dip occurred a few days before Christmas Day and was associated with being "rushed, harried, exhausted, busy and a drag" (Potkay, Allen, & Merrens, 1975). Christmas holidays are fun, but the preparations they require are nonetheless demanding.

What is the "bad" news about winning a multimillion-dollar lottery? Consider the eustress of the 1984 winner of a $40-million lottery in Illinois. Michael Wittkowski "jumped up and screamed" for joy when he found he had beaten the 3.5 million-to-1 odds ("Lotto Winner Will Stay on Job," 1984). He would receive $2 million a year for each of the next 20 years, compared with his annual salary of $20,000. During newspaper and national television interviews, which were entirely new to him, he repeatedly stated "This will not change me. I will continue to be the same person. I will continue to go to work." Almost immediately, however, this convincingly sincere, family-oriented young man and his employer agreed that it might be best for Michael to take the next week off from work. He needed refuge from two days of talk shows and a steady stream of visitors. Even a surface newspaper look at Michael's life events would show a "mild crisis" SRRS score of 152 change units for the coming year: change in financial state (38), outstanding personal achievement (28), upcoming marriage (50), revision of personal habits (24), and Christmas (12). Other possible events, if they occurred during the year, would bring Michael's total number of SRRS points over 300: business readjustment (39), wife-to-be begins or stops work (26), change in living conditions (25), change in residence (20), change in recreation (19), vacation (13), and change in number of family get-togethers (15). From this perspective, it may not be too surprising that Michael made an out-of-state telephone call to a lottery official to say he'd "had enough" for one week — "I gotta go find a beer" ("Newest Millionaire's Wish," 1984, p. 34). (A few months later, Wittkowski did quit his job and began looking into buying his own business, a bowling alley.)

One week later, machinist Ronald Holaway won $9 million in the same Illinois lottery. He immediately quit his job, which he had begun only two months earlier, and his wife said she would probably quit hers ("Lotto Winner: Working Days . . . ," 1984). A total of 164 SRRS points is reflected in this information: outstanding achievement (28), financial change (38), change in work (36), second change in work (36), wife's change in work (26).

During the same week, a television news program presented follow-ups of some past lottery winners whose eustress had turned to distress. One man had experienced envy and strained relationships with fellow workers and had turned toward self-imposed isolation. Another had been jailed for writing checks without sufficient bank funds, which he said was based on factual expectations that guaranteed money would be coming to him annually. Another expressed deep disappointment over social relationships she experienced as depending upon her willingness to provide "loans" that were never repaid. Finally, one man reported he had given every penny of his winnings to a friend, simply because he "just didn't want the hassle." In brief, even positive events may lead to unexpected or undesired outcomes much larger than one person's ability to foresee or handle.

CHAPTER REVIEW

External, situational influences can profoundly affect human behavior, somewhat independently of inner personality dispositions. Many behaviors may be related less to the kinds of persons we are than to the kinds of situations we find ourselves in. Although physical environments are important, psychologists are becoming increasingly interested in psychological environments — the external factors that confront a person at a given point in time and that have meaning for that person in his or her individualized life space. Some situational influences may be relatively quiet, as in the unplanned chance encounters we sometimes have with people who are unfamiliar to us. However, the power of situations may be quite dramatic, as evidenced by the extraordinary behaviors shown by relatively ordinary people under Milgram's conditions of obedience to authority, and the role of external influences in contributing to the mass suicides of 900 people at Jonestown. Under extraordinary circumstances, everyone is vulnerable to behaving in extraordinary ways.

Efforts to establish suitable taxonomies of situations are gaining some momentum. These efforts can be traced to Henry Murray's concepts of external press — including alpha (objective) and beta (subjective), positive and negative — and the appearance of press-need themes in fantasy as recurring patterns of behavior throughout a person's life. Current classification efforts are most prominently associated with the work of Rudolph Moos, who has proposed a six-category schema. However, efforts to establish a universally accepted taxonomy remain at a beginning stage, with no approach showing general acceptance. Taxonomies are useful in guiding research, interpreting results obtained by independent workers, and aiding the prediction of human behavior.

Environments, like people, show individual differences and can be described in terms of their unique "personalities." Various empirical approaches to measuring these characteristics have been devised. Assessment methods include reliance on group consensus in perceiving psychological, social, and physical climates; behavior-based templates of situations; and category prototypes or working images of psychological situations. It is also possible to evaluate the impact of environmental influences by making use of factually documentable behaviors, as occurred in the study of Mount Saint Helens as a stressor, and rating scales that provide scores reflecting cumulative stress during a given period of time in a person's life. Even positive experiences of eustress (such as winning a lottery) are identified as stressors, because of their contribution to the amount of change taking place in a person's life.

The next chapter continues our emphasis on situational influences on behavior. It complements some of the more general, background, and theoretical flavor of this chapter by taking an in-depth look at how researchers have studied situational effects on aggressive behaviors in more controlled laboratory and field settings.

KEY CONCEPTS

Psychological situations
Power of situations
   Chance encounters
   Milgram's obedience research
   Fromm's "sick" societies
Taxonomies of situations
   Murray's environmental press
     Press-need themas
   Moos' six categories of human environments
     Ecological dimensions
     Behavior settings

Organizational structure
Characteristics of inhabitants
Psychosocial climate
Reinforcement properties
Assessing "personalities" of environments
   College Characteristics Index (CCI)
   Situational templates
   Situational prototypes
Stressors, stress, change
   Adjustment disorders
   Social Readjustment Rating Scale (SRRS)

REVIEW QUESTIONS

1. Explain the theoretical and research implications of seeking to understand human behavior by looking at the person, "inside," versus looking at the environment, "outside."

2. Give an example that is not mentioned in the text of how situational influences may produce surprising or extraordinary behavior.

3. What is your own evaluation of Milgram's conclusion that "it is not so much the kind of person a man is as the kind of situation in which he finds himself that determines how he will act"? Justify your answer.

4. What are the advantages of a taxonomy of situa-

tions? Give examples of each of Moos' six categories of human environments.

5. Contrast various approaches to assessing "personalities" of environments and the "stresses" environments may produce. What are some strengths and limitations of each method?

6. Compare the physical, psychological, and social climate of your college with that of another you know. Or compare two classrooms you are now taking courses in. How might individual differences in the "personalities" of these environments influence your behavior?

12

Situations and Behavior: Aggression

What outside influences might predispose people to aggression?

Does violent television programming really make children more aggressive?

Is punishment an effective way to deal with aggression?

How prevalent is a tendency to rape among "normal" men?

O N OUR WAY to considering the relationship between traits and situations, we have shown how some behaviors can be understood by reference to traits — influences inside individuals. Continuing in this direction, Chapter 11 reviewed how psychologists have studied situations — influences outside individuals. In this chapter, we take the final step toward considering traits and situations together by examining aggression, a kind of behavior that is heavily influenced by situations.

Many studies of aggression have been designed to detect situational influences. Thus, it is not surprising that there is much evidence pointing to situational control of aggression. Nevertheless, just as the behaviors considered in our discussion of traits may be thought of as influenced by situations, the behaviors considered in this chapter may be considered subject to trait influences. Olweus (1979) discusses that possibility.

We begin by looking at how aggression is defined and studied experimentally. We then consider the major sources of aggression in human beings, some of which have influences that are not quite what people think them to be. These include frustration, racism, erotic stimulation (pornography), heat, and noise. Then we cover a source commonly known as "imitation" but technically called *observational learning*. It is shown that observational learning is even more powerful in generating aggression than is usually assumed. Related to this source is one of the most heavily investigated questions in psychology, "Do children and adults learn aggression by observing the behavior of television characters?" (Before reading this chapter, what would your answer be?) Because we think the evidence bearing on this question is unusually clear, we provide a definite answer.

Most people would agree that aggression is generally undesirable behavior. Given the research into the sources of aggression, it is only natural to ask how aggression can be controlled. Does punishment prevent or stop this kind of behavior? Is aggression lessened if people have the chance to "get it off their chests" by attacking someone (catharsis)? Does witnessing the non-aggressive behavior of models lower the probability of violence? Would exposure to sexual materials or humor lessen the likelihood of subsequent aggression? Can development of empathy, improvement of child-rearing practices, and exposure to anti-aggression therapy help? First, we focus on methods of lowering aggression that don't work as well as is generally believed. Then, we turn to ways of controlling aggression that may be more effective than traditional procedures, but are less well known to the public.

We close with a consideration of rape, a form of aggression that has received much recent attention in the media and about which there is a great deal of new knowledge. The discussion of rape will provide a bridge to some of the remaining chapters by raising the issue of how the masculine and feminine sex roles influence behavior. Sex roles are especially emphasized when examples of interactions are presented (Chapter 14).

Box 12.1 begins an account of an actual rape that came to the public's attention a few years back. It sets the stage for a second box that introduces a section on rape, a form of aggression. A third box, found at the end of the chapter, provides some more optimistic thoughts about rape: the efforts of many activists are changing orientations toward rape for the better. These boxes constitute a needed supplement to the text. Discussions of research about rape are of primary importance in creating understanding of that phenomenon, but cannot reveal the complexity and emotional impact of real sexual assault. Thus, we suggest you pay close attention to the boxes.

BOX 12.1	*Woman Raped*
	*While Bar Patrons Cheer**

New Bedford, Mass. — Big Dan's Tavern is gutted now. Workmen applied a chain saw to the bar, then carted off the infamous pool table, the Pac Man game, and everything else in the place. But last Sunday night, the hole-in-the-wall on New Bedford's waterfront was the scene of an event that will likely be recounted for some time to come. A 21-year-old mother of two entered the dismal gin mill to buy a pack of cigarettes and lingered to chat with a friend. On the way out, a man seized her, stripped away all but a pink sweater, and raped her on the barroom floor. Before she was dragged to a pool table, two other men made her perform oral sex. As the attack was renewed on the tabletop, her screams for help went unheeded. Someone did say "Knock it off, this is getting out of hand," but others cheered and applauded.

Later, an investigating officer exclaimed "In ten years of working on the force, I've never seen anything like this." "According to our information," said the officer "some of the men in the place were watching and cheering, 'Go for it, go for it.'" Later it was discovered that there were at least ten customers in Dan's during the rape. Not one lifted a finger to rescue the victim, though a patron supposedly phoned the police, but dialed incorrectly. "They were scared," reported the investigator, "afraid of being beaten up."

Finally, the young woman escaped the clutches of her assailants and ran into the street, naked below the waist. Frantically she waved down a motorist, who helped her contact the police. She was treated at the local hospital and released.

* Adapted from the *Peoria Journal Star,* March 10, 1983; the *Peoria Journal Star,* March 18, 1983; and *Newsweek,* March 21, 1983.

continued

Four men, aged 22 to 26, were indicted in the Bristol County Court on charges of aggravated rape. Charges were also filed against two men who allegedly held the woman down during the assault. All pleaded innocent. Bail was initially set at a modest $1000, but was raised to $200,000 for one defendant who attempted to skip the country.

BOX 12.1
continued

What Is Aggression?

Because there are many, many definitions of aggression available in the literature of psychology, we cannot point to a single "correct" definition—one that would be accepted by almost all psychologists who study human aggression (we will not be concerned with aggression in nonhuman animals). However, it is possible to adopt a widely accepted definition that has proven fruitful as the guiding principle for one of the most active and respected investigators of aggression, Robert A. Baron (1977).

According to Baron, *aggression* is any form of *behavior* performed with the *intention* or goal of *harming* another *living* being who is motivated to *avoid harm* (Baron & Byrne, 1982). This definition is very handy because it allows those who adopt it to eliminate some of the "gray" behaviors that don't seem to fit into either the aggression or the non-aggression category. Also, it allows them to focus on those behaviors that most clearly threaten the survival and prosperity of human beings. Let's briefly consider the major components of the definition.

aggression: components of definition

Behavior.   First, aggression is behavior. As you will recall from Chapter 1, *behaviors* are actions that involve the musculature of the body, including the muscles used in speech, as well as other actions, such as thinking and feeling. It may seem obvious to you that aggression is behavior, rather than some other form of human capacity. However, consider an example of a human capability with which aggression can be confused. *Aggression* and *anger* are sometimes used as if the terms referred to the same thing, but anger is best considered to be a kind of motivation. Anger is what usually occurs prior to aggression; it is the motor that drives a person to aggression. The difference between anger and aggression can be easily appreciated if it is recognized that anger is something inside of us that only sometimes leads to aggression (for example, the notion of pent-up anger). We may be angry from time to time, but fortunately, most of us rarely resort to aggression.

Intention.   Perhaps the most important concept in Baron's definition is intention. *Intention* refers to the conscious planning and execution of a behavior. If harming someone else is not a person's goal, whatever behavior that person performs cannot be called aggression, no matter how damaging it might be. Let's take a few examples. Suppose you are racing to class one day and, rounding the corner at full stride, you collide with an unsuspecting fellow student. There lies your victim, books scattered all over the place, while you look on with much concern and embarrassment. You've harmed someone, but you didn't mean to do it. Thus, your sincere apology for the accident is very likely to be accepted. Without the notion of intention, all accidents in which one person harms another would have to be called aggression. If we didn't recognize intention, many useful members of our society would be labeled aggressors. Examples would be dentists (think of how much that drill hurts) and surgeons (each cuts thousands of people during a career), not to mention boxers, soldiers, and people who engage in a variety of sports.

Harm.   Obviously, aggression is harmful or injurious action. *Harm* is considered to have occurred as a consequence of a behavior if there is physical injury or damage that outweighs any benefits resulting from the act. One can commit acts that are directly harmful, such as striking another person. However, harm can also be indirect. Destroying a person's property can be very harmful.

Acts that are intended but not harmful cannot be called "aggression." As Baron (1977) points out, intention must be inferred from the act itself and the circumstances surrounding it. In our example where you hypothetically harmed someone while racing to class, we can infer that you did not intend to do so, because the offended person was a stranger whose presence you obviously did not detect. Had you exclaimed "Ha ha, Joe, that'll teach you," our inference about your behavior would have been different. But suppose you did slam into Joe intentionally. If, in doing so, you knocked him from the path of an oncoming vehicle, it would be difficult to build a case that aggression had occurred. No jury would convict you of assault, even though you were known to dislike Joe and had injured him when you hit him. Acts that do more good than harm cannot reasonably be labeled aggression. How would you label the behavior of a person who approached you saying "I'm going to wreck your life . . . by giving you a million dollars"?

Living being.   Have you ever been engrossed in a gripping TV show, only to have the set suddenly cease to function right in the middle of the best part? Join the crowd. Maybe you've been known to give the obstinate appliance a good, stiff kick. If so, have you aggressed? The answer would be yes only if the TV set said "ouch." A *living being* has a nervous system that allows it to experience pain and suffering. Only targets that feel can be said to have been harmed by an attack. Remember, among living beings, we are restricting ourselves to humans.

Studying Human Aggression: The Buss-Shock Method

Now that you know what we mean by aggression, the next step is to consider how it is studied. In order to understand something, it is helpful to appreciate how the evidence bearing on it has been obtained. In this section, we will consider how the evidence has been collected pertaining to the determination, prevention, and control of aggression.

THE STIMULATOR-RESPONDER PROCEDURE

As you can imagine, there are many ways to study human aggression. Fortunately for our purposes, one general technique has dominated the field. It is called the *Buss-shock method* (see Buss, 1961). An outline of Buss' technique will give you a good idea of how psychologists have approached the understanding of aggression. It will also provide helpful background, because most of the studies described in this chapter have involved the technique.

Buss-shock
method

With the Buss-shock method, each subject is convinced that he has been recruited to administer painful electric shocks to another person, described as a subject, but who is actually a confederate of the experimenter. The method is illustrated by reference to one of Baron's recent studies (1978). Baron and Ball (1974) had shown that the presentation of humorous material has an influence on the subsequent performance of aggression, but they had considered only humor without hostile content. Baron (1978) sought to determine whether the effects of hostile humor differed from the effects of nonhostile humor. In the first part of the experiment, 41 male University of Texas students were either angered by a confederate, who gave them a decidedly negative written evaluation, or were not angered. Then, all subjects were told that the second part of the experiment would involve investigating "the impact of unpleasant stimuli upon physiological responses." In a rigged selection process, each subject was "chosen" to be a "stimulator" who would deliver unpleasant electric shock to the confederate, designated the "responder." The alleged purpose was to stimulate the responder so that his physiological reactions could be measured. Of course, the actual reason for the shocks was to give the subject an opportunity to aggress.

Before subjects had the opportunity to aggress against the confederate, some of them examined several nonhumorous pictures (scenery, furniture). Others were given cartoons depicting nonhostile humor (an example, not included in Baron's study, would be Garfield the cat parading about the house with the family dog strapped to his back like a blanket; the caption reads "Maybe this will convince him to turn up the heat"). Finally, still other subjects viewed cartoons depicting hostile humor (a woman is shown talking on the phone; in the background a body is seen dangling from a rope; the woman exclaims "It all turned out just like you said it would, Mother"). All subjects were told that the pictures and cartoons were to be used in a separate study and that subjects might as well rate them while they waited for the confederate's physiological reactions to stabilize. In almost all such studies, materials expected to influence aggression are examined before subjects have the opportunity to aggress. Each picture and cartoon was rated on amusement and hostility scales. These ratings showed that the cartoons were indeed viewed by subjects as being nonhostile and hostile, respectively, although the cartoons were seen as equally humorous. Finally, subjects "stimulated" the confederate with 20 electric shocks, the intensity and duration of which was of their own choosing.

The apparatus used by Baron is depicted in Figure 12.1. It is typical of equipment employed in conjunction with the Buss-shock method. Note how shock level and duration are recorded.

It was expected that the experimental conditions would differ in terms of the average intensity and duration of the shocks delivered by subjects. Just what were

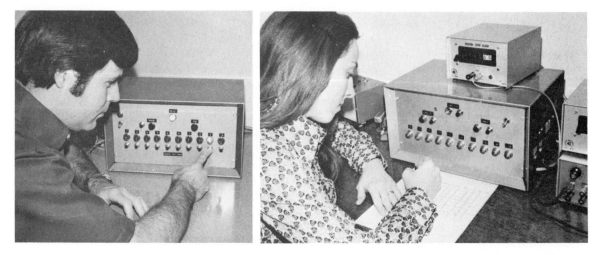

Figure 12.1   The Buss-shock machine and recording apparatus. (Left) The subject can select one of ten levels of shock, the leftmost switch "delivering" the lowest level possible and the rightmost "delivering" the most shock possible. Note that the subject is behaving in an aggressive manner. (Right) The experimenter records shock level from the ten lights on her panel, corresponding to the subject's ten switches. From the smaller box, she records the duration of each shock, which is determined by how long a switch is depressed.

the specific expectations and the actual results for the intensity and duration dependent variables is left for a later portion of this chapter.

First, as we are sure you guessed, confederates don't really receive electric shocks. However, the evidence is clear that participants in aggression studies believe they are delivering shock to another human being (Berkowitz & Donnerstein, 1982; Milgram, 1974). Such being the case, one might wonder whether subjects suffer ill effects from the perception that they may have harmed another person. Several lines of evidence indicate that subjects are not harmed (Baron, 1977; Milgram, 1974). Debriefing, which occurs after aggression experiments, provides relief from any anxieties and concerns that subjects may have developed during the course of experimentation. During debriefing, subjects are assured that the confederate was not shocked, and they are convinced that they behaved reasonably (Allen, 1978).

TEACHER-LEARNER PROCEDURE AND THE BUSS-SHOCK METHOD

The experimental design used by Baron is actually a variation of a more common procedure, the one used by Milgram (see Chapter 11). With this method, subjects are told to shock a confederate playing the role of learner as "punishment" for failure to learn some words. The reason that Baron altered this more typical procedure is the complaint by some critics that subjects in aggression experiments of the "punishment" type may shock confederates to help them learn rather than to aggress against them (Baron, 1977). Changing to the stimulator-responder design eliminates any reason for this criticism. Subjects clearly cannot help responders by giving them severe shocks of long duration. Nor can they believe that they can help the experimenter by delivering intense shocks, because they have been led to believe that "any shock will do" to produce a physiological reaction in the confederate.

Other critics say that, regardless of whether the teacher-learner or stimulator-responder procedures are used, the Buss-shock method gives subjects no choice: they must shock the confederate. The point of this criticism is that "forced shocking" in the laboratory provides little information about *real-world aggression*. Baron (1977) countered this criticism in various ways. For example, he pointed to a study by Wolfe and Baron (1971) in which it was shown that men imprisoned for violent crimes delivered more intense shocks than men enrolled at a university.

Berkowitz and Donnerstein (1982) make an additional point in support of the contention that the Buss method produces valid evidence concerning aggression. They contend that the validity of a psychological study designed to investigate aggression does not depend on the degree to which the context of the study resembles real-life settings in which aggression is likely to occur (for example, the real-life situation "men vying for a place in an employment line"). Rather, validity depends on whether behavior displayed by subjects during the course of the study is interpreted by them as aggression. If subjects see themselves as having displayed aggressive behavior during the study, measures of that behavior can be considered indexes of aggression. Berkowitz and Donnerstein report impressive evidence that subjects do see themselves as hurting the confederate in the typical aggression experiment. For example, they cite a study done in Belgium by Leyens in which child subjects actually were informed that their responses would harm other children. Under these conditions, the children who were rated as most aggressive by their peers were most intense in their harmful behavior during the laboratory portion of the study.

Table 12.1 shows the general experimental procedure that has been associated with the Buss-shock method. As you can see, the procedure is the same whether the "stimulator-responder" or the "teacher-learner" cover story is used. Learning the contents of the table will be a great help to you in reading the pages that follow.

TABLE 12.1   Procedure of the Buss-Shock Method

	Procedures	Conditions created
Phase One	Confederate writes evaluation of subject Subject chosen as "stimulator" (or "teacher"), confederate as "responder" (or "learner")	anger/no anger
Phase Two	Stimulator (or teacher) examines stimulus materials (such as cartoons) under guise of allowing responder's (or learner's) physiological responses to "settle down"	variations of materials
Phase Three	Subjects "shock" responder (or learner) to "create physiological responses" (or to "teach")	results

Sources of Aggression in Human Beings

situational
influences on
aggression

There are, of course, several situational sources of aggression in humans. We will concentrate on those that have been the focus of research. First, we will consider some possible situational determinants that may not influence aggression in quite the way or to the degree that is usually assumed.

FRUSTRATION

frustration

Perhaps frustration is the source that has been around psychology the longest. *Frustration* results from a situation that blocks a particular goal the individual is trying to achieve. A sample situation would be failure on a test. The original psychological theory of the link between frustration and aggression was posed by Dollard and his colleagues (Dollard, Doob, Miller, Mowrer, & Sears, 1939). Simply put, the frustration-aggression theory states that frustration always leads to aggression and aggression is always preceded by frustration. Although the theory was later qualified to indicate that aggression is only one kind of response to frustration (Miller, 1941), Baron has argued that aggression is not even the usual response (Baron & Byrne, 1982).

When it occurs frequently, frustration can create depression. Although he has used frustration to generate aggression in some of his studies, Albert Bandura (1973) has indicated that depression may be a more usual response to frustration than is aggression. Numerous studies by Martin Seligman and his colleagues suggest that frustration can lead to a condition called *learned helplessness,* which is

Brussels, May 29, 1985. The occasion is a championship soccer match, but the situation builds rapidly toward mass aggression. Belgian riot police were helpless to prevent a bloody encounter between fans of the British and Italian teams. The ensuing riot left 28 people dead and provoked a period of national soul-searching in England. What situational factors could account for the fans' behavior?

related to depression. In the case of learned helplessness, people learn to be helpless if they experience no connection between their behaviors and the rewards and punishments that they encounter (see Abramson, Seligman, & Teasdale, 1978, and Seligman, 1975).

Although frustration may not always, or even usually, result in aggression, most people have seen cases where it was followed by aggression. One of us witnessed the frustration-aggression sequence following a test in a psychology class. After having discovered his score on the test, an enormous male student rose up out of his seat, slammed his test booklet down on his desk, mumbled something about "unfair tests," and stomped out of the classroom. By attacking the test, he was indirectly aggressing against the professor. Later the professor feared direct aggression, when he looked up to find the student towering over him. Fortunately, the young man had returned to apologize for his outburst, which he readily attributed to feelings of frustration at not doing as well as he had hoped.

RACE AND AGGRESSION

Race is another factor for which the relationship to aggression is not quite what we have assumed it to be. It is not possible to predict simply that members of the majority race in this society will aggress against members of the minority race. As we shall see, the relationship between race and aggression, as indicated by research, is not straightforward. Racial aggression shows up in relatively few situations.

Racism is defined as widespread negative sentiment directed toward people solely on the basis of their race. In this section, we will focus on a particular form of racism: anti-Black sentiment. It is our assumption that anti-Black sentiment is primarily a cultural rather than a psychological factor. Therefore, it is not the same thing as racial prejudice, a psychological phenomenon that is covered in Chapter 10. To be sure, there are highly prejudiced White people who publicly proclaim their hatred for Blacks. However, fortunately for us all, they are few in number. Their problem is unique to each of them and, therefore, is psychological in nature. Most Whites would find such a proclamation of racial hatred to be highly offensive and impossible for them to make, but they do adopt a culture with built-in bias against Blacks (Allen, 1978). Of course, the culture that White Americans carry around in their heads determines many of their behaviors, including reactions to Blacks.

racism

Recently, anti-Black sentiment has become something of an underground phenomenon (Allen, 1975). Most White people do not readily display the behaviors that would be expected, given the anti-Black sentiment that exists in North America. Researchers have had to use subtle methods to uncover a relatively few situations in which anti-Black sentiment influences people (see Dutton & Lennox, 1974, and Gaertner & Dovidio, 1977). Our goal is to illustrate these situations for you.

Edward Donnerstein and his colleagues investigated subtle reactions to clearly show the effects of anti-Black sentiment on human aggression (Donnerstein & Donnerstein, 1976). They used the Buss-shock method, teacher-learner version, and the same shock machine employed by Baron (1977) and others. Since their experiments all fall into the same general pattern, we will present a composite of their work.

Donnerstein and his colleagues generally lead their White, male subjects to believe that they are shocking either a Black or a White confederate. First, subjects think they are being shown a videotape of a learner in an adjoining room performing on a just-completed learning task. Actually, they are viewing a tape of a Black or a White confederate who is not really present in the experimental area. Second, subjects are all told that they are not to deliver shocks to the learner when he is correct, but they are to punish him by using one of the shock-intensity buttons when he makes an error. Finally, subjects are divided into two conditions. In one, the experimenter makes it clear that subjects are going to be held accountable for their behavior—that their names will be associated with their shock responses, or that the confederate may learn their identities or even be able to shock them. In this condition, subjects face social disapproval or possible retaliation. In the other condition, subjects are not held accountable for their responses. The situations of interest here are those in which White people are held accountable for aggression against Blacks and those in which they are not held accountable. After assigning subjects to one of the conditions and informing them about it, the experimenter goes to an adjoining room and activates an audio tape that plays a program of correct and incorrect responses supposedly made by the learner. In sum, each subject performs in one of four combinations of conditions: Black learner, accountable; White learner, accountable; Black learner, not accountable; White learner, not accountable (see Donnerstein & Donnerstein, 1973; Donnerstein & Donnerstein, 1972; Donnerstein, Donnerstein, Simon, & Ditrichs, 1972).

Results of Donnerstein's experiments are always reported in terms of both intensity and duration of shock (see Figure 12.1). Shock intensity is called *direct aggression,* because subjects have to be aware of the intensities they are using, and they know that anyone who can associate their names with their responses will also know the intensity. Shock duration—how long a subject depresses an intensity button—is called *indirect aggression,* because variation in duration is not apparent to the naked eye of the subject or anyone else involved in the experiment. It constitutes the more subtle measure of the effects of racism.

In terms of the very visible direct-aggression measure, subjects aggressed less against the Black than the White learner when they were accountable—in situations where social disapproval or retaliation was possible. However, they aggressed more against the Black than the White learner when they were not accountable—when they would not face social disapproval or retaliation.

The more subtle measure of indirect aggression produced different results. When subjects were accountable, they actually used shocks of longer duration on the Black than on the White confederate. When they were not accountable, race of the confederate made no difference: duration of shocks delivered to the Black and White confederate didn't differ significantly.

Donnerstein and his colleagues demonstrated that aggression by Whites against Black depends on whether the situations in which Whites have the opportunity to aggress entail accountability for their actions. Results of their experiments show that when White subjects were accountable, they were more lenient toward the Black than the White learner in terms of the highly visible direct measure of aggression. At the same time, they were harsher toward the Black than the White learner in terms of the subtle, nonvisible, indirect measure of aggression. Only when they were not accountable were they harsher toward the Black than the White learner in terms of direct aggression. That is, in situations where Whites discriminated in favor of Blacks directly, they compensated by discriminating against them indirectly. By contrast, in situations where they discriminated against Blacks directly, they had no need for the indirect compensation.

Ronald Rogers and Steven Prentice-Dunn (1981) report similar results. These researchers used the same Buss-shock method as Donnerstein, as well as a Black and a White confederate playing responders. In addition, they created a condition in which some subjects were angered and one in which others were not angered. White subjects who were not angered were more lenient toward the Black than White confederate. However, angered White subjects were harsher toward the Black than the White confederate. Rogers and Prentice-Dunn concluded that White subjects were racially liberal when not angry, but regressed to racism when angered.

Baron (1979a) reports the subtle effects of racism on aggressive responses directed by Whites toward Blacks. Previously, he had shown that an attacker who realizes that his aggression has resulted in pain tends to be relatively non-aggressive thereafter (Baron, 1971). In the later study, Baron (1979a) set up a situation in which White stimulators received pain feedback from Black and White victims. Using the Buss-shock method, he found results consistent with his previous findings when the responder was White, but not when he was Black. Expressions of pain by the Black responder had no influence on White subjects. Racism can show up in a lack of sensitivity to the suffering of Blacks.

EROTIC STIMULATION

Situations involving *erotic stimuli*—materials having definite sexual meaning—can also generate aggression. The more negative term for such materials is *pornography*. Stimuli of this sort have strong and complex influences on aggression—influences that some readers may find surprising. In this section, we will deal with facilitation of aggression by erotic stimulation, but we will have occasion to consider such stimulation twice more.

strong erotica

Using Baron's version of the Buss-shock method, Baron and Bell (1977) had male subjects view either the scenery used in Baron's humor study, pictures of seminude women (attractive women in skimpy garments such as bathing suits and negligees), pictures of nude women taken from the pages of *Playboy* magazine, pictures of sexual acts (men and women engaging in mutual masturbation and intercourse), or written passages containing highly explicit descriptions of sexual activity. As in the humor study, presentation of the neutral scenery or erotic stimulation was interposed between the opening evaluation by the male confederate and the opportunity to shock the confederate. Table 12.2 summarizes the procedure for the Baron and Bell study.

Evidence from this study, and from previous work, indicated that the written passages were the most arousing, followed in order by the sexual acts, nudes,

TABLE 12.2   Procedure and Results of Baron and Bell's (1977) Erotic-Stimulation Study

Conditions	Neutral scenery	Mild erotica	Nude Women	Sexual acts	Passages
	Furniture, abstract art	Seminude pinups of females	*Playboy* centerfolds	Pictures of men and women performing a variety of sexual acts	Highly explicit written descriptions of sexual behaviors
Procedure	Standard Baron "stimulator-responder" method, with presentation of the materials described above sandwiched between the evaluation of the subject by the confederate and the opportunity for the subject to shock the confederate.				
Results	The passages condition generated as high a level of aggression as the neutral scenery condition, which generated a standard high level of aggression.				

seminudes, and neutral stimuli. Results indicated that the most arousing material, the passages, generated electric shocks as strong as those associated with the condition most like the one generating strong shock in previous studies, the neutral condition. That is, highly arousing erotic stimulation is associated with high levels of aggression. Because coverage of results for the other conditions will be more relevant later, we will not consider them here.

ENVIRONMENTAL INFLUENCES: HEAT AND NOISE

heat and noise

Simple intuition tells each of us the environment contains situations that influence aggression (see Chapter 11). Among these are heat and noise.

Heat.   We have all heard about the "long hot summer." Supposedly, as the temperature goes up, so do our irritability indexes. However, a moment's thought will tell you that aggression is hard work and can really heat up a person. If you were already burning up, would you be more or less inclined to avoid aggression than is usual for you? The answer seems obvious: when the temperature is very high, the last thing you would want to do is aggress. Based on experimental evidence, Baron (1977) came to the same conclusion. More specifically, he argues that the more heated or otherwise unpleasant the surroundings, the more the aggression—up to a point. If circumstances, including high temperatures, become unpleasant enough, however, one thinks only of getting out of the situation, not making it worse by aggressing. This position leads to the prediction that moderately high temperatures will be associated with high levels of aggression, but that very high temperatures will be associated with low levels of aggression. The theory is depicted in Figure 12.2. You will see that this theory has much in common with the classic Yerkes-Dodson law, discussed in Chapter 10. Baron has supported his position both in the laboratory and under real-life circumstances (Baron, 1977; Baron & Bell, 1976; Baron & Ransberger, 1978; note that Carlsmith and Anderson, 1979, disagree with the interpretation of the last study). The simple, straight-line relationship between heat and aggression may exist mainly in our commonsense notions, rather than in reality. However, more recently, Baron

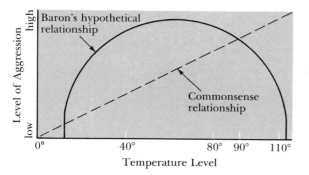

Figure 12.2
Comparison of the commonsense notion of the relationship between heat and aggression and Baron's hypothetical relationship.

has acknowledged that when it comes to violent crime, as opposed to simple aggression, the hotter it is, the greater the aggression (Baron & Byrne, 1984).

Noise.   Noise bears a simpler relationship to aggression. Have you ever been waiting for a stoplight to change when, one millisecond after it becomes green, the motorist behind you directs a long blast of his horn at you? Haven't we all. The impatience of people is irritating enough, but the loud noise produced by the horn may even bring on thoughts of shifting one's auto into reverse. Baron (1977) has reported several studies showing that loud noise, at about the level of a subway train as it goes by the platform, creates high aggression, relative to low noise or no noise. However, one qualification is needed. Noise raises aggression only if irritating or annoying events have already disposed potential aggressors to violence.

OBSERVATIONAL LEARNING AND MODELS

In Chapter 6, you learned that among the more powerful situations determining behavior are those in which significant persons in your life—models—   modeling
display behaviors for you to learn. In fact, the young of many species can observe the actions of a model, such as a mother, and learn the behavior performed by her. *Observational learning* is the label given to acquiring new behaviors by watching intently while someone acts (Bandura, 1973). More relevant to our discussion, children readily learn novel aggressive behaviors in situations where models perform new aggressive responses. Such is the case even when reinforcements and punishments never enter the learning sequence and observers have no opportunity to practice the behaviors.

One of Bandura's most famous studies is an example of how children learn new aggressive behaviors by observing a model (Bandura, Ross, & Ross, 1963). Children whose average age was 4 years, 4 months served as subjects in the study. In a "live-model" condition, an experimenter led subjects into a playroom, where they witnessed an adult model being escorted into an area of the room containing a 5-foot inflated Bobo doll. After the experimenter left the playroom, the model began to aggress against the doll using novel responses, unlikely to have been previously experienced by children. Subjects in a "film-aggression" condition were treated similarly, but watched aggression against the doll performed on film by the same person who played the model in the live-model condition. In a "cartoon-TV" condition, subjects were treated the same as in the other conditions, except that the experimenter remarked upon leaving, "I guess I'll turn on the TV." A film depicting an adult dressed up like "Herman the Cat" was rear-projected onto the screen of the TV. In a fantasy-land surrounding, Herman the Cat aggressed against the Bobo doll. Even though aggression in this study was against a nonliving being, we'll assume for now, and later support the contention, that such aggression is closely related to aggression against humans. A control condition involved no modeling of aggression.

After these conditions were instituted, subjects were led to an adjoining room, where they were allowed to play with some attractive toys. However, once they had become involved with the toys, the experimenter interrupted them, saying that the toys were her best, and were reserved for other children. This mild frustration predisposed the children to aggress after they were led into still another room, where they encountered a Bobo doll. Procedures and results are summarized in Table 12.3. Note that the experimental conditions differ only slightly, and that each differs from the control by including modeled aggression.

Results showed that all experimental conditions gave rise to significantly more aggression than did the control condition. Overall, experimental subjects showed nearly twice as much aggression as control subjects. Surprisingly, there was evidence that filmed violence was slightly more effective in initiating aggression than were the other two experimental conditions. Also, unrealistic cartoon aggression seen on TV, which was expected to be ineffective relative to the other two conditions, in fact was quite comparable. As is apparent in Figure 12.3, many of the children's aggressive behaviors were carbon copies of the model's behaviors. Thus, children learned new aggressive behaviors by observing a model perform.

Baron (1977) reports several studies in which subjects observed a model aggress within the context of the Buss-shock method. When subjects later took over control of the electric-shock machine, they showed significantly more ag-

TABLE 12.3   Procedure and Results of Bobo Doll Study

Conditions	**Live model**	**Film**	**Cartoon-TV**	**Control**
	Adult model beats up Bobo	Same model beats up Bobo on film	"Herman the Cat" beats up Bobo on mock TV	No modeling
Procedure	Each child-subject is frustrated by being prohibited from playing with attractive toy. Then each subject is taken to a room and allowed to aggress against the Bobo doll.			
	The dependent variable is the aggressive acts copied from the model and novel acts improvised by subjects.			
Results	The above conditions are ranked below, with "1" indicating greatest aggression and "4" the least:			
	2	1	3	4

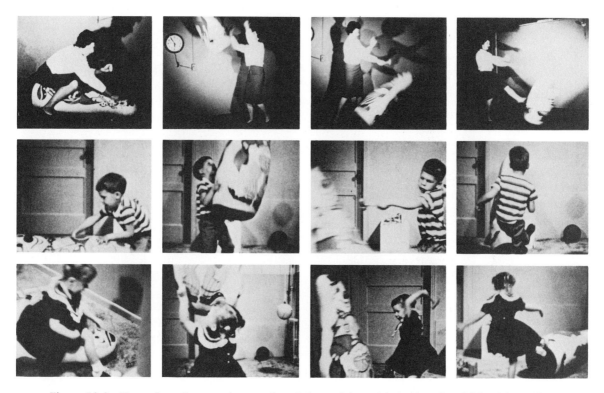

Figure 12.3 Examples of aggressive acts by adult models and imitations by child subjects *(from Bandura, Ross, & Ross, 1963).*

gression against an insulting confederate than did subjects in the control condition. Situations in which models aggress are universally powerful means of teaching aggression.

TELEVISION AND AGGRESSION

So far in our discussion of observational learning, we have been fairly general in references to situations in which models teach aggression. In this section, we become more specific. Television is one of the most powerful situational factors that intrude upon your life. Its characters have been particularly potent models of aggressiveness. Accordingly, we now turn to violence on television as a source of aggressiveness.

television

For several years, there has been much discussion in the media and many tax dollars spent in attempts to determine whether viewing violent TV shows is associated with a tendency toward aggression. Let's take a look at what researchers have found.

Stage 1 research.   Baron (Baron & Byrne, 1982) traces three stages of psychological research pointing to the existence of a link between violent TV programming and aggression. The earliest studies were those of Bandura and

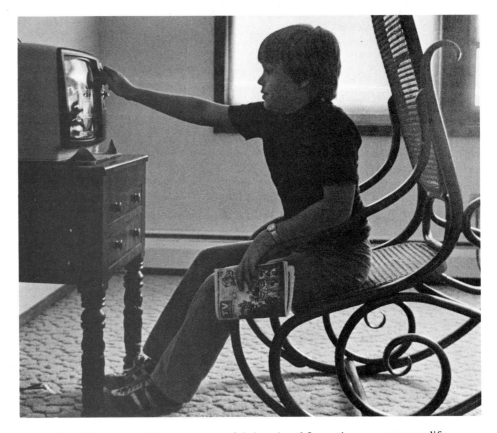

Television is one of the most powerful situational forces in contemporary life. Considerable evidence suggests that its influence on children's aggression can be long-lasting.

colleagues (Bandura, Ross, & Ross, 1963; Bandura, 1973). As you recall, the Bobo-doll study included a TV condition that generated considerable novel aggression in children via the mechanism of observational learning. Even though these studies did not involve human targets of aggression, it is possible to generalize to the case of humans because, as we shall see, Bandura's results are entirely consistent with those of later studies.

Stage 2 research.   The second stage of research involved laboratory studies using human targets. A good example is provided by Liebert and Baron (1972). Children aged 5 to 9 first viewed either some excerpts from a rather violent TV show, "The Untouchables," or an equally exciting but non-aggressive track-and-field sequence. Then they were told that a child in another room was trying to win a prize and that they could decide to either help or hurt the child by pressing a help or hurt button. The help button presumably contributed to winning the prize, while the hurt button heated up the handle that the child was supposedly manipulating. A signal light provided 20 opportunities to help or hurt. Subjects who had watched the violent TV program inflicted more "burns" on the "child who was trying to win the prize" than did their counterparts who had watched the nonviolent TV program.

Stage 3 research.   The third wave of studies took a further step toward demonstrating the link between TV viewing and aggression. This research involved follow-ups of aggression performed by children who were exposed to TV violence and who behaved in their usual, everyday circumstances. One of the best of the studies in this category was conducted by Leyens, Camino, Parke, and Berkowitz (1975), using delinquent schoolboys from Belgium as subjects. Two groups of the boys saw five violent movies, such as those that now appear regularly on TV, while two other groups saw five nonviolent movies. The movies were shown one each day for five days. Results indicated that in the week of the film presentations, boys who viewed the violent movies displayed more aggression against their peers during everyday activities than they had shown prior to watching the media violence. One of the groups that had been exposed to the neutral movies showed no change, but the other neutral group actually showed a slight decline in aggressiveness. Most striking was the observation that aggression of the boys who watched violent movies was obviously enhanced just after the films were presented, and many of the boys duplicated the aggressive acts of film characters. As you recall, Bandura, Ross, and Ross (1963) found similar results for movie- and TV-viewing conditions.

Ten-year follow-ups.   If a five-day diet of vicarious violence can make children more aggressive, you might guess that exposure to violence for an indefinitely large number of consecutive days would have rather profound and possibly permanent influences on the level of aggression displayed by children. Indeed, research by Leonard Eron and his colleagues clearly shows the adverse effects of early exposure to TV violence. Eron, Huesmann, Lefkowitz, and Walder (1972) did a follow-up study of 425 teenagers who, ten years earlier, had been rated on aggression by peers and scored as to amount of violent TV watched. These children had been third-graders in the earlier study. At the time of the ten-year follow-up, they were one year out of high school and were called "13th-graders." The teenagers were again rated on aggression by peers and scored on amount of violent TV watched. Results showed a significant correlation between preference for violent TV at the third grade and aggressiveness ten years later. Alternative sources of the late aggressiveness were ruled out. For example, being aggressive at the 13th grade was not determined by watching violent TV at that time, because the amount of violent TV viewed at the 13th grade was unrelated to aggressiveness at that age. Also, special correlational methods indicated that aggressiveness at the third grade did not determine both early violent TV viewing and late aggressiveness. Apparently, early exposure to violent TV was an important determinant of aggressiveness during the late teens.

Twenty-year follow-ups.   More than 20 years after the original study, Eron followed up the same sample once more (Eron & Huesmann, 1984). Even though subjects were now about 30 years old, the link between early violent-TV viewing and later aggressiveness still held.

An international follow-up.   Eron and his group did not stop with their impressive ten-year follow-up. Because they suspected that there was a sensitive period between 8 and 12 years of age during which violent TV makes its indelible mark on children, they did another study encompassing the age range 6 to 10 years (Eron, 1982). Using measures similar to those employed earlier, they found significant relationships between exposure to TV violence and aggressiveness for each of the first five school grades. Further, the same study was repeated in Finland, Poland, and Australia, producing similar results. Eron (1982) suggested that low popularity, low intelligence, a tendency toward aggressive fantasy, as well as rejecting, physically punishing parents, all contributed to aggression. A tendency for parents to endorse attitudes and behaviors often seen in people with little conscience was an additional factor contributing to aggressiveness in children. Later we'll return to Eron and his colleagues' method for reducing aggressiveness in children.

A massive British study.   Finally, even the TV people themselves are getting into the act. CBS granted British researcher William Belson nearly $300,000 to study the possible link between viewing violence on TV and aggressiveness (Muson, 1978) — and they didn't like what their money bought them. A sample of 1565 teenage boys from London were interviewed extensively to determine what TV episodes they had seen between 1959 and 1971. Visual aids and various probing methods were used to ensure that the boys actually had seen what they claimed to have viewed. Based on this interview, they were divided into those who had been heavy consumers of TV violence and those who had not. Subjects then looked at 50 cards, each indicating a violent act, and reported which acts they had performed. Visions of the book and movie *A Clockwork Orange* come to mind when one reads the items on the cards: "I deliberately dropped a lighted match into a grocery bag." "I kicked a guy in the crotch, as hard as I could." "I took a hammer and bashed a car." Results showed that boys who had viewed much violence on TV committed significantly more aggressive acts than those who had not. Using correlational methods similar to those employed by Eron's group, Belson attempted to eliminate alternative ways to explain his findings. Although his efforts seemed clearly successful, CBS rejected his results.

We think that the evidence for a possible link between viewing violence on TV and aggressiveness is convincing. Nevertheless, the connection will likely remain controversial. For cautions concerning assumption of the link, as conceived by Eron and his colleagues, see Kaplan (1982) and Coughlin (1985).

A NOTE ON INSTIGATION

One source of aggression is so obvious that it might be taken for granted. It is instigation. To *instigate* is to incite, goad, or spur someone into aggressive action. To put it simply, people don't tend to aggress unless someone or something has made them upset or angry. Investigators of human aggression rather routinely include anger and no-anger conditions in their experiments, because differences among experimental conditions usually occur only within the anger condition (Baron, 1977). Anger brings out aggression and highlights its determinants, such as presence versus absence of an aggressive model.

Applications: Preventing and Controlling Aggression

With so many sources of aggression, it is little wonder that we see so much of it. In fact, the situations that determine aggression may seem so numerous and powerful, it may appear that we are all doomed to be perpetrators or victims of aggressive acts. While, at least to some degree, such a view may be realistic, there is cause for optimism. It is possible to devise situations that prevent and control aggression.

manipulation of situations to control aggression

In examining means of controlling and preventing aggression, we will begin with those procedures that have seemed to work well, but may not be highly effective after all. Then, progressively, we will consider methods that have been shown to be quite efficient in reducing or eliminating aggression.

PUNISHMENT AND CATHARSIS

Punishment. Does punishment—for example, the administration of physical punishment to children—deter aggression? *Punishment* occurs in any situation where unpleasant stimulation follows the performance of a response. (See Chapter 5 for a more complete and technical definition.) The use of unpleasant stimulation to deter or control behavior is seen by some theorists as only appearing to be effective. B. F. Skinner (1948, 1971) has suggested that punishment may appear to control behavior, but its effects are only temporary. The behavior that draws punishment is suppressed while the punishing agent (for example, a parent) is present. However, when the punisher leaves the area where the prohibited acts are likely to occur, the punishee performs more such acts than usual to make up for those suppressed earlier. Kids whose hands are slapped as these appendages emerge from the cookie jar will stay out of the jar, but only until the source of the punishment turns her back. Then the children will eat more cookies than before, in order to make up for those not consumed while the punishing agent was present. Punishment may lead to only temporary suppression of a response, such as an aggressive act. W. K. Estes (1944), a student of Skinner, provided apparently impressive support for his mentor's position.

punishment

However, research that is not quite so old leads to opposite conclusions. Solomon and Wynne's (1953) classic laboratory experiment showed it is possible to set up conditions that make the application of unpleasant stimulation the most effective available means of controlling behavior. Under some circumstances, the application of unpleasant stimulation may, for practical purposes, permanently eliminate a behavior. This notion is widely accepted in psychology and fits nicely with the commonsense belief that punishment will allow for the prevention or control of any behavior, including aggression.

Thus, Skinner was not entirely correct. Experimental studies imply that punishment can occasionally have strong and permanent effects. Nevertheless, we cannot dismiss Skinner's contention that punishment is a rather poor way to deal with aggression. After all, what works in the laboratory and what works in real life are sometimes two different things. Let's first see how punishment may fail in practice. That way we can look at some conditions that must be met if punishment is to be effective. Since these conditions are somewhat different for *actual* and *threatened* punishment, the two approaches to use of aversive stimulation are separated below. Finally, we'll examine why punishment, even if it works, may carry with it costs that outweigh its benefits.

Although Baron acknowledges that actual punishment may sometimes be an effective means of deterring aggression, he lists three reasons why it may often fail (Baron & Byrne, 1982). First, a person may interpret punishment for aggression as an attack by the punisher. Thus, an attempt to deter further aggression may actually increase the likelihood of more aggression. Second, imagine a situation in which a child has aggressed against a parent and the parent immediately administers physical punishment to the child. The parent hopes to make the child less likely to aggress in the future, but he may serve as a model and thereby teach the child to aggress (Mussen, Conger, & Kagan, 1979). Third, despite the parent's explicit behavior, implicitly she may communicate to the child, "It's all right to aggress — if you are more powerful than your potential victim."

Consistent with results of the classic study by Solomon and Wynne (1953), there is no question that threat of punishment can work to control behavior, including aggression. But under exactly what circumstances does it work?

Let's take perhaps the most practical example, the one that may weigh heaviest on our minds: under what circumstances will the threat of punishment deter violent crime? Both older (Kimble, 1961) and newer sources (Schwartz, 1978) of information about learning agree. First, if there is a long delay between when a response is performed and the time at which some stimulus is introduced, it doesn't matter whether the stimulus is pleasant (for example, food) or unpleasant (for example, electric shock). The availability of the stimulus is unlikely to influence future performances of the response. Thus, if a person is contemplating a violent crime and is considering the possibility of punishment for the act, he is likely to know that, if caught, punishment could be years down the road.

Second, the studies on race and aggression by Donnerstein and colleagues indicate that the probability of punishment influences the likelihood of performing an aggressive act. If the threat of punishment for the act is great, because retaliation is probable, aggression is less likely to occur. Needless to say, our hypothetical contemplator of violence is likely to be aware that, if he is caught, the probability of being punished for an aggressive act is not very great, given the present circumstances of our overcrowded courts.

Third, the threatened punishment must be very severe, if aggression is to be deterred (Baron, 1977). Let's assume that our would-be aggressor is consciously or unconsciously considering violence. The person may be aware that should he be arrested and convicted even for the ultimately violent act of murder, the punishment may be only a few years in jail. If so, he is not likely to be deterred. Incidentally, violent acts are often committed "in the heat of passion" when there is no conscious or unconscious consideration of consequences (Zimbardo, 1970).

Fourth, only if our would-be aggressor is not very angry and has little to gain from violence will he refrain from aggression (Baron & Byrne, 1982). Aggressors who are very angry and who have much to gain are probably going to aggress, even when conscious of a threat that punishment will result.

In sum, threat of punishment can control aggression if the threatened punishment is severe, will very likely occur, will occur soon after the aggressive act, and if the potential aggressor is not very angry and has little to gain from aggression. You can see that these conditions rarely hold in real life. Thus, in practice, threat of punishment may work only infrequently to deter aggression. Further, physical punishment that actually follows an aggressive act may be seen as an attack calling for retaliation, may serve to teach punishees how to be better aggressors, and may convince them that aggression is the right of the powerful.

Finally, when the application of unpleasant stimulation does work to control aggression and other behavior, it can have tragic side effects (Skinner, 1971). The behavior of abused children, including aggressive behavior, may be rather perfectly controlled by their brutish parents, but it may also make the children passive, compliant, and emotionally disturbed as children and violent themselves, once they become adults (Mussen, Conger, & Kagan, 1979).

Catharsis.   It has been thought that any situation that provides the opportunity for catharsis lowers the likelihood of subsequent aggression. *Catharsis* generally means verbally or behaviorally expressing a deep-seated need or emotion. More specific to our present purposes, catharsis is expressing anger by displaying aggression in some way or another. The very act of expression is supposed to lower the likelihood of future aggression. Let's see if it works.

catharsis

You can well imagine that when, in the mid-1950s, Hugh Hefner began *Playboy* magazine, there were "a few" objections. Some thought the sight of naked females might twist the minds of young males and make them sexual deviates. In rebuttal, Hefner resorted to the Freudian notion of catharsis. According to this theory, there is an internal psychic energy that drives us to perform certain behaviors, such as sexual or aggressive acts. If we perform those acts, even indirectly, as in watching and identifying with an aggressive character in a movie, we release some of the pressure and make the acts less likely to occur in the future. Thus, argued Hefner, viewing naked women provides men with a "harmless" way to release sexual energy, and thereby lowers the likelihood of harmful sexual behaviors in the future. We will consider the correctness of Hefner's statement later. For now, let's turn to catharsis and aggression.

If you are beginning to recall the discussion of TV and violence and are doubting that catharsis effectively reduces aggression, you're on the right track. Indeed, catharsis—directly or indirectly expressing aggression—may increase as often as decrease the likelihood of aggression on subsequent occasions. Let's take a research example.

Ebbe Ebbesen, Burt Duncan, and Vladimir Konečni (1975) conducted an elegant study that took advantage of a natural source of aggression: being fired from a well-paying, highly prestigious job. Aerospace engineers and technicians had been hired by a Southern California firm to complete what they were told would be a long-term national-defense project. Instead, after less than a year, 200 of them were released because the government abruptly canceled the contract. To make matters worse, the company had kept the impending layoff secret.

The researchers capitalized on the fact that the firm provided "exit interviews" with all employees who were leaving. When 100 of the employees who were fired showed up for the interview, they encountered an experimenter posing as an employee. He assigned them to one of several conditions. In the "no-verbal-aggression'' condition, the interviewer asked employees questions, the answers to which allowed no opportunity to aggress against anyone (for example, "What do you think about your insurance?"). Employees in one verbal-aggression condition were asked questions that provided them with an opportunity to aggress against the company (for example, "How has the company been unfair to you?"). Others were asked questions that gave them the chance to aggress against their supervisors (for example, "How has your supervisor been unfair to you?").

Employees were then directed to a secretary who "had some final forms" for them to complete. Actually, the secretary randomly assigned employees to alternative questionnaires, each providing a different target for aggression. Sample questions were "Would you recommend the *company* to a friend?" and "If your *supervisor* invited you to a party, would you go?"

Those who had been able to aggress against the company during the interview showed high aggression against the company on the company questionnaire, relative to the level of aggression shown on the company questionnaire by employees in the other interview conditions. Likewise, those in the "aggress-against-the-supervisor" interview condition showed high aggression against the supervisor on the supervisor questionnaire, relative to the level of aggression shown on the supervisor questionnaire by employees in the other conditions. Table 12.4 summarizes the procedures and results of the aerospace-workers study. Note the match between conditions encompassed in the procedure and results for the different types of questionnaires.

In sum, these results indicate that aggression leads to more aggression—exactly the opposite of what would be expected on the basis of the catharsis notion. The same outcome has been found in a laboratory study (Geen, Stonner, & Shope, 1975). Even in the case of vicarious or indirect expression of aggression, such as identifying with a movie character, there appears to be little support for the claim that catharsis occurs (Baron & Byrne, 1981). More generally, catharsis may reduce emotional arousal, but there are only limited circumstances under

TABLE 12.4 Procedure and Results of the Aerospace-Worker-Layoff Study

Conditions	No verbal aggression (A)	Aggress against company (B)	Aggress against supervisor (C)
	No opportunity to aggress against anyone during the exit interview	Questions during the exit interview allowed aggression against the company	Questions during the exit interview allowed aggression against the supervisor
Procedure	After the exit interview, subjects were directed to a secretary who administered an "aggression against company," or "aggression against supervisor" questionnaire.		
Results	Questionnaires		
	"Aggress against company"		"Aggress against supervisor"
	Subjects (B) who had had a prior opportunity to aggress against the company showed the highest aggression on this questionnaire		Subjects (C) who had a prior opportunity to aggress against the supervisor showed the highest aggression on this questionnaire

which it can lower aggression (Baron, 1977). Nevertheless, in other realms, expressing an underlying need or emotion can be very beneficial (see Chapters 3 and 7).

NON-AGGRESSIVE MODELS, HUMOR, EMPATHY, AND MILD EROTICA

After our discussion of punishment and catharsis, you may be somewhat pessimistic about the possibility of controlling aggression. Research does not seem to support the effectiveness of these two factors. However, there are efficient means of dealing with aggression. Let's consider them.

Non-aggressive models.   Baron (1977) reports several studies, using the Buss-shock method, that clearly indicate the presence of non-aggressive models lowers the aggression of subjects. In these studies, a non-aggressive model displays low aggression for observers in a situation where aggression might seem appropriate. Having subjects observe a model who delivers shocks of low intensity lowers the intensity of shocks subsequently delivered by subjects. The Bandura (1973) work showed similar results with children. It follows that if parents become non-aggressive models for their children, their progeny will become less aggressive people, as children and as adults.

models

Humor.   Recall the study in which Baron devised a humorous situation by presenting cartoons to subjects. Now we can consider the results of that investigation. Baron (1978) expected that non-hostile humor would lower aggression below that shown in the neutral condition (scenery), and he was correct. However, hostile humor actually raised aggression, relative to the neutral condition. Thus, humor works well to reduce aggression, but only if it's non-hostile.

humor

Empathy.   The ability to perceive and understand the feelings of another person, without those emotions being communicated by words, is called *empathy*. It is standing in someone else's "emotional shoes." Empathy is, of course, the same concept that we considered in Chapters 4 and 7. As you might guess, any situation that promotes empathy will lower aggression. If subjects "feel" the pain "suffered" by a learner or responder in psychological experiments, they will subsequently show less aggression against the person playing those roles. In fact, Baron (1977) reports several studies showing a reduction of aggression upon reception of feedback indicating that the learner or responder is in pain. However, you have already seen from the Baron race and pain-feedback study (1979a), such is not always the case. We would add that, if subjects are very angry, feedback indicating pain might even increase shock levels, relative to no pain feedback (Baron, 1974, 1977).

empathy

Mild erotica.   As we saw earlier, highly explicit sexual stimuli that are highly arousing (passages describing all sorts of sexual acts) will bring aggression up to the level of the most representative condition in experiments using the mild erotica

Buss-shock method. What about mild erotica (inexplicit sexual stimuli such as seminudes)? Both the Baron and Bell (1977) study mentioned above and a study by Donnerstein and his colleagues (Donnerstein, Donnerstein, & Evans, 1975) showed that mild sexual stimuli *reduced* aggression in the Buss-shock experiment below that found in other conditions.

How can mildly erotic stimuli lower aggression if strongly erotic stimuli raise it? Donnerstein, Donnerstein, & Evans (1975) offer a resolution to this apparent contradiction by arguing that erotica not only arouses subjects, but also may distract them so that their thoughts are drawn away from aggression. Mild erotica may reduce aggression because it produces more distraction than arousal. Dolf Zillmann and his colleagues have shown that general arousal can be listed as a source of aggression (see Zillmann, Katcher, & Milavsy, 1972; Zillmann, Bryant, & Carveth, 1981; Zillmann, Bryant, Comisky, & Medoff, 1981). Strong erotica, such as explicit sexual passages, may increase aggression, because it produces more arousal than distraction. In a complementary explanation, Baron (1977) has suggested that erotica produces both positive and negative feelings. Mild erotica may reduce aggression because it produces more positive than negative feelings, while strong erotica increases aggression because it produces more negative than positive feelings. Table 12.5 indicates how the interplay of distraction and arousal, as well as that of positive and negative feelings, can determine level of aggression.

Most aggression studies have used males as subjects, including the ones on erotica and aggression (we'll get to sex differences on aggression in Chapter 14). Would females show the same effects of exposure to erotica? Baron (1979b), using pictures of seminude males, showed that mild erotica reduces aggression in women. He also found that strong erotica increased aggression in women. A similar effect was reported by Cantor, Zillmann, and Einsiedel (1978). Female subjects who had viewed an erotic film delivered unpleasant noise to an "opponent" more frequently than those who were exposed to non-erotic films.

TABLE 12.5   The Donnerstein and Baron Explanations of the Erotic-Aggression Relationship

	Donnerstein			
	Relationship			Outcome
Mild erotica	distraction	outweighs	arousal	low aggression
Strong erotica	arousal	outweighs	distraction	high aggression
	Baron			
	Relationship			Outcome
Mild erotica	positive feelings	outweigh	negative feelings	low aggression
Strong erotica	negative feelings	outweigh	positive feelings	high aggression

Hugh Hefner would not be surprised at the results of aggression studies involving the display of mild erotica. Indeed, it now seems clear that single, brief exposures to mild erotica may reduce aggression just after materials are presented. But an important question remains. What influence does repeated exposure to mild erotica have on the orientation of men toward women? Does it promote "women as passive objects"? We return to this question in the last section of the chapter.

CHILD-REARING PRACTICES AND ANTI-AGGRESSION THERAPY

Prevention and control of aggression, like charity, may begin at home, but may at times extend to the psychologist's office. Researchers have offered several suggestions for preventing and controlling aggressive behavior in children.

Parents.   As has already been indicated in the discussion on modeling, parents have a profound influence on the level of aggression shown by their children. At the same time, parents also teach sex-appropriate behavior, called *sex-role training* (Eron, 1980, 1982; also see Chapter 14). The result is that boys and girls receive somewhat different lessons about aggression. Eron (1980) noted that results of his earlier studies investigating the TV-aggressiveness link showed significant effects mainly for boys. Although he is now finding similar results for girls, his advice to parents still holds. Apply to boys some of the techniques traditionally used for girls only: teach them tenderness, cooperativeness, nurturance, and sensitivity, and boys will show less aggression (Eron, 1980). The possible favorable change that might result would have little to do with biological maleness or femaleness. In 1982, Eron reported that both boys and girls who were neutral with regard to their sex-role behaviors showed less aggressiveness than did those who were masculine.

parents

Therapy.   Eron (1980, 1982) and Huesmann, Eron, Klein, Brice, and Fisher (1983) report two methods that show promise as means of reducing aggression. The first method involved showing children that TV violence is not "real." They were shown excerpts from violent programs and told how the sound and visual effects were designed to mimic reality. This procedure had a possible sleeper effect. In a *sleeper effect,* the results of applying some procedure are weak immediately after application, but become stronger after a lapse of time. The therapy seemed to have no effect initially, but effects showed up later. Second, Eron (1982) and his colleagues Huesmann et al. (1983) took a page from social-psychology textbooks and had children write an essay on "why TV violence is unrealistic and why it is bad for viewers." Writing an essay against one's point of view moves one's beliefs in the direction of the essay (Baron & Byrne, 1981). The subjects were then videotaped reading their essays and told that the tape would be shown to schoolchildren in their city. Relative to their peers in a control group, subjects showed lowered aggression. Baron (1977) similarly reports that the presence of disapproving adults during violent TV shows lowers aggression in children.

therapy

Although popular methods, especially punishment and catharsis, may not work so well in controlling aggression, other ways of dealing with violent behavior are available. It is particularly encouraging that some of these more effective procedures are relatively easily manipulated by important people in children's lives, such as parents and educators. Parents can avoid using aggression on their children, and they can model non-aggressive solutions to problems. They and other people who work with children can also use humor, develop empathy in their charges, and learn therapeutic methods. Lowering the likelihood of aggression is genuinely possible.

Rape, Rapists, and Erotica

As indicated in the introduction to the present chapter, this last section will be partly devoted to laying the groundwork for the consideration of sex roles that is to occur in some of the chapters that follow. At this point, we will learn how the masculine sex role, in relation to its feminine counterpart, disposes some men to a violent sexual orientation toward women. Situations are considered at two different levels of generality. We focus on certain concrete and specific situations that incite males to violence against females — for example, viewing violent erotica. At other points in this section, we also discuss more abstract situational forces that cause males to regard females as adversaries — for example, being trained to dominate women. As an introduction to this section, read the material in Box 12.2.

BOX 12.2   *Rape in the Media:*
Blaming the Victim and Excusing the Rapists

Fall River, Mass. (AP)[*]— Her voice was soft and devoid of emotion as she related how six men attacked her in a rundown waterfront bar. "When I tried to leave, one guy grabbed the back of my coat and another took hold of my ankles." Allegedly, they dragged her to the pool table and took turns raping her. Others joined in. She escaped when her captors were distracted in conversation.

Not so, contended one of the defense attorneys, Judith Lindhal. The woman who fled Big Dan's bar had come there looking for a sexual liaison. One of the defendants testified, "She enjoyed it; she was smiling." It was an old story. The victim of rape found herself on trial. While a television audience of many thousands hung on every word, her real name was mentioned in the same breath as "liar" and "slut." But the jurists believed her. In separate trials, four of the six defendants were convicted and sentenced to prison. The two who supposedly watched, cheered, and assisted were acquitted. Her reputation ruined, her life threatened by members of her own ethnic group, the victim chose seclusion.

[*] Adapted from the *Peoria Journal Star,* March 20, 1983; the *Chicago Tribune,* April 10, 1983, article by Peter Gorner; Associated Press articles dated February 26, 1984, to March 18, 1984; and the "David Brinkley Show," NBC, March 25, 1984.

continued

BOX 12.2
continued

"It's better than the soaps," exclaimed a TV addict from New Bedford, Massachusetts, former home of Big Dan's. A talk-show host said that nobody wanted to discuss anything else. "As soon as I hang up the phone, another call comes in." Trials on TV are apparently also good for business. The proprietor of a discount bakery located in the building that was Big Dan's seemed to be prospering. "People don't really come in for bread. They look around and ask, 'Where was the pool table?'" Meanwhile, as experts debated whether justice was possible in televised trials, a boy was arrested for raping a girl while his friends watched. "I got the idea from the TV trial," he claimed.

After learning the surnames of the accused—Silvia, Cordeiro, Raposo, Vieira, Medeiros, and Medeiros—the Portuguese community of New Bedford has been on the defensive. Although they constitute half the city's population, they do not possess half the political and economic power. Portuguese leaders have good reason to feel that the incident has brought bigotry to the surface. The local talk show received phone calls suggesting that the town would be better off if the Portuguese were sent back to their homeland.

Ms. Alda Mello led a group of Portuguese protesters in condemning the verdict against four men who share their ethnic heritage. The ironies are many. Earlier, thousands had marched in support of the victim. Now, seemingly, Ms. Mello and her companions were standing squarely behind the accused rapists. Even stranger, the victim is Portuguese, as is Prosecutor Ronald Pina and half of the jurists.

What was at first an outpouring of sympathy for the victim is turning into something ugly. The young mother, known for a while as Jane Doe, became an instant martyr for the movement to end violence against women. A deluge of letters offering understanding and money arrived from all over the United States shortly after the attack. A week after the incident, 4000 paraded by candlelight to show solidarity with Jane Doe and those she symbolized, rape victims everywhere.

However, over the past month, the original story of Jane's plight is being revised. Now, thanks largely to comments phoned to the local talk show, it is rumored that Jane is a prostitute "who got what she deserved." Psychologist Melvin Lerner would invoke his "just world" hypothesis to explain the turn of events. In a "just world," you "get what you deserve and deserve what you get." Having had time to consider the threat of rape, some citizens of New Bedford may have reasoned that if a bad thing happened to Jane, it must be because she is a "bad person." Being "good people," they or the women in their lives needn't worry. New Bedford activist Darlene Wheeler suggests, "By blaming the victim, women don't have to deal with the fact that they, too, might be raped." This is the dilemma of the victim: the more the victim suffers, and the greater the perceived likelihood that others will meet with a similar fate, the greater the probability of blaming the victim.

Belief in the "just world" is not the only reason rape is blamed on the victim. Activist Wheeler acknowledges that a common misconception also promotes condemnation of victims. People who believe that rape is a sexual act are likely to think

continued

BOX 12.2
continued

victims got what they unconsciously wanted all along. Provocative dress, flirtatious behavior, and presence in a dangerous situation all are taken as evidence of
seeking sexual contact. But, like other feminists, Wheeler asserts ''Rape is a crime
of violence, not a sex act.'' If the activists' view becomes widely accepted, blaming
rape on the victim will become less likely. Given that acceptance, to believe that
some women want to be raped is to believe that they actively seek violence in the
form of humiliation, injury, and dehumanization.

rape

A consideration of rape has obvious importance in its own right. As a topic in
personality, questions about rape bear on several key issues. Are rapists abnormal? Is there such a thing as a ''rapist personality''? We'll cover these issues as well
as continue our concern for situational influences on aggression.

Is rape a sexual or an aggressive act? Are rapists ''rare birds'' or, as some
feminists claim, do many men harbor a tendency to rape (French, 1977)? Does
erotica, even the sadomasochistic variety, have little effect on aggression toward
women and men, as the Presidential Commission on Obscenity and Pornography
(1970) indicated, or does it promote aggression, as some feminists (for example,
Brownmiller, 1975) and even the ''Moral Majority'' contend? Recent research has
confronted these emotionally charged questions.

UNMASKING AGGRESSION AGAINST WOMEN

You may wonder why such important questions haven't been definitely
answered a long time ago. The reason is subtlety. Just as with aggression against
Blacks, only when the ''right'' questions and the ''right'' procedures are used is it
revealed that erotica increases aggression by men against women. Donnerstein
and his colleagues discovered this fact rather dramatically.

Inhibition of aggression against women. Donnerstein and Barrett
(1978) used the standard Buss-shock teacher/learner method, but included a
blood-pressure measure and female as well as male learners. Male subjects, who
were either angered or not, viewed either a neutral film (wildlife) or an erotic film
(various forms of sexual behavior). Relative to the neutral condition, the erotic
film increased aggression for angered but not for unangered subjects. However, it
had no influence on shocks delivered to female as opposed to male learners. True
to the notion that ''gentlemen do not hurt ladies,'' male subjects shocked the
female learner less. However, the blood-pressure measure indicated these male
subjects may have been inhibiting aggression against the female learner.

To consider the latter possibility, Donnerstein and Hallam (1978) repeated
the study by Donnerstein and Barrett, but added new wrinkles. Male subjects saw
an erotic, neutral, or aggressive film (excerpts from *The Wild Bunch*); had a chance
to shock a male or female learner; and then, after a 10-minute rest, again had an
opportunity to shock the male or female learner. On the first occasion, the
aggressive and erotic films produced more aggression than the neutral film, but

sex of the learner did not influence results. However, on the second occasion, the film effect was reproduced, and the female learner was shocked more than the male learner in the erotic-film condition. In fact, the aggression by male subjects against the female in the erotic-film condition was the highest found in the study. Time and prior opportunity to shock a female eliminated the males' inhibition of aggression against females. Here we have an example in which a situational factor —presentation of filmed erotica—was not sufficiently potent until another factor—a lapse of time between a first and a second opportunity to shock—was added.

Viewing a rape. Donnerstein (1980) knew that aggression can be increased by the situational factor, aggressive content in pictorial or written presentations. Therefore, he reasoned that erotica with aggressive content would have an even more profound affect on males' aggression against females than erotica alone. Armed with this logic, he essentially repeated his studies with Barrett and Hallam, adding a rape-scene condition. Via videotape recorder, male subjects were shown either a neutral, an erotic, or an aggressive-erotic film (a man forces a woman to have sexual intercourse at gunpoint). This time, the female learner was shocked more than the male learner, but only in the aggressive-erotic condition. Further, even unangered subjects shocked the female more in the aggressive-erotic condition than in the other conditions. Since instigation is usually necessary to show the effects of various conditions on aggression, this last finding is especially important. Obviously, most males who go to see a violent-erotic film are not angry when they enter the theater. Nevertheless, the film may influence their orientation toward females.

violent erotica

Donnerstein and Berkowitz (1981) repeated and qualified the results of Donnerstein (1980). They reported that angered males were uniformly more aggressive against a female in an aggressive-erotic condition, compared to the other two conditions. However, unangered subjects in the aggressive-erotic condition showed more aggression against a female than in other conditions only when the ending of the film was "positive." What was the "positive" ending? The female victim was depicted as "enjoying" being raped.

Males' reactions to feedback from a rape victim. Neil Malamuth, Seymour Feshbach, and their colleagues have produced equally unsettling results, using different methods than those employed by Donnerstein and colleagues. Their primary concern was the situational factor "feedback from a rape victim." Malamuth, Heim, and Feshbach (1980) presented male and female subjects with a rape story that varied. For some subjects, the victim expressed pain, while for others she indicated no pain. For some subjects, the rape was premeditated, and for others it was unplanned. Finally, for some, the victim expressed nausea, and for others she was depicted as having an orgasm. Each subject read only one of the eight possible stories. The most important dependent-variable measure was a paper-and-pencil index of sexual-arousal response. Females were more sexually aroused after reading the no-pain/orgasm passage, but males were most aroused by the pain/orgasm passage. In effect, some males were indicating "If it hurt her and she liked it, it turned me on." Believing that women like being raped, or are masochistic, is a major rape myth (Burt, 1980).

Carolyn Sherif (1980) commented on studies in which females had to read about victimization of females and males were exposed to the very thing that may promote rape and aggression against women. The details are beyond the scope of this book, but Sherif saw the effects of such exposure to be quite negative, especially for females. She also wondered what people will think of psychologists once the media get wind of such studies. Malamuth and colleagues replied to Sherif in a convincing manner (Malamuth, Feshbach, & Heim, 1980). They argued for and later supported the contention that the potential benefits for subjects and society at large of research like their own outweigh the minimal risk of some possible damage to a few subjects. In fact, such research indicates that the overall effect of participating in studies concerning rape is a significant reduction of beliefs in rape myths, thanks to the inclusion of educational material during debriefing (Malamuth & Check, 1984; Check & Malamuth, 1984).

RAPE TENDENCY IN NORMAL MEN

You may have noticed that the studies reviewed so far make no mention of special or abnormal personalities. "Ordinary" male subjects showed increased aggressiveness toward females when faced with several different situational influences. This observation raises the question "How prevalent is rape tendency among normal men?" Studies by Malamuth and colleagues suggest an answer.

rape tendency among normal men

In one of their studies, male and female subjects were first exposed to situational influences — either a nonviolent sexual passage taken from *Penthouse* magazine or a violent version of the same passage (Malamuth, Haber, & Feshbach, 1980). The violent version was sadomasochistic: pain was inflicted on a female, and she found it sexually arousing. Then, all subjects read a passage depicting rape: a woman politely refuses a man's attentions, but he reacts to the rejection by pulling a knife and forcing sexual interaction. Results showed that the correlation between sexual arousal and subjects' perceptions that the victim suffered pain, both measured by paper and pencil, were negative for female subjects in both the violent and the nonviolent condition, and for males in the nonviolent condition. However, the correlation was positive and significant for males in the violent condition. Males who had read the violent passage before the rape story were sexually aroused by the perception that the victim suffered pain.

Probably you have wondered about the validity of the paper-and-pencil measures of sexual arousal. First, these measures correlate well with physiological measures of genital sexual arousal. Second, if anything, subjects are inclined to inhibit reports of arousal following exposure to sexual violence, because it implies a socially unacceptable positive reaction to rape. If they do report sexual arousal, it is probable that they really experienced it (Malamuth, Heim, & Feshbach, 1980). Finally, virtually all of the central findings reported by Malamuth and colleagues have been replicated with the use of physiological measures (for example, see Malamuth & Check, 1980; Malamuth & Check, 1984).

Malamuth, Haber, and Feshbach (1980) also found that females clearly indicated that they would not enjoy being victimized. Nevertheless, for males, there was a clear relationship between reported willingness to engage in rape and callous attitudes toward women coupled with acceptance of myths about rape. Finally, when there was no mention of punishment, 17% of the male college-student subjects indicated some likelihood that they would engage in rape. If they were assured of not being punished, fully 51% indicated that there was some possibility they would engage in rape. Further, male subjects must have had in mind the violent-sexual aspects of the passages, rather than the sexual aspects alone, when they reported their willingness to rape: there was a significant, positive correlation between sexual arousal and willingness to participate in a rape for the violent-sexual condition, but not for the nonviolent-sexual condition.

Over all the studies done by Malamuth and colleagues, 35% of male subjects have reported willingness to participate in a rape if they would not be punished (Malamuth, 1981b). However, some caution must be exercised in interpreting this result. The statistic was obtained with the use of a 5-point scale where any response above 1, indicating "would not rape," was accepted as evidence of willingness to rape.

Table 12.6 (page 428) summarizes the studies performed by Donnerstein's group and by Malamuth and colleagues. Note how earlier studies set the stage for later investigations.

CULTURAL SUPPORTS FOR RAPE

During World War II, Soviet troops approaching Berlin were given the unofficial word that they could rape German women at will (Ryan, 1966). Many rapes resulted. Did official sanction produce unusual behavior in the men, or did knowing that they wouldn't be punished bring out a tendency to rape? Did the subjects of Malamuth and colleagues' studies indicate they would rape because the experimenter implicitly said it was OK, or is fear of punishment the only thing that keeps some men from raping? These are difficult questions, but there is at least tentative evidence that many men harbor some disposition to sexually attack women. Preliminary statements to explain this tendency can also be made.

Acceptance of rape myths and violent orientation to women.   Martha Burt (1980) investigated the possible relationship between acceptance of rape myths and several other variables. She found that three factors relating to the abstract situational influence "sex-role training" were associated with acceptance of rape myths. (An example of a rape myth is "In a majority of rapes, the victim is promiscuous or has a bad reputation.") These factors are (1) sex-role stereotyping (for example, agreement with "It is worse for a woman to get drunk than for a man"); (2) adversarial sexual beliefs (for example, "A woman will only respect a man who will 'lay down the law to her'"); and (3) acceptance of interpersonal violence (for example, disagreement with "A wife should move out if her husband strikes her").

Following this lead, Briere, Malamuth, and Ceniti (1981) had college males indicate whether they would use force in a sexual encounter, would use force as well as rape, or would use neither force nor rape (the provision that no punish-

TABLE 12.6   Summaries of the Donnerstein and Malamuth Studies of Rape

1. Donnerstein and Barrett (1978)

   Erotica and aggression against women: Males were shown a neutral or erotic film. They showed less aggression against a female than a male learner, but blood pressure indicated that they were inhibiting aggression against females.

2. Donnerstein and Hallam (1978)

   Disinhibition of aggression against women: Males saw a neutral, erotic, or aggressive film. Sex of the learner did not influence results during a first opportunity to shock, but males shocked the female more than the male learner in the erotic condition, upon a second opportunity to shock the learner.

3. Donnerstein (1980)

   Erotic-aggressive film and aggression against women: Males saw a neutral, erotic, or erotic-aggressive (rape) film. They shocked the female learner more than the male learner only in the rape condition. Even non-angered subjects shocked the female learner more in the rape condition than in other conditions.

4. Malamuth, Heim, and Feshbach (1980)

   Males' reactions to feedback from a victim: Males and females read a rape story. In it, the victim expressed pain or no pain, and nausea or orgasm. Females found the no-pain/orgasm version most sexually arousing, but for males, the pain/orgasm version was most arousing.

5. Malamuth, Haber, and Feshbach (1980)

   Violent erotica and males' willingness to rape: Males and females first read either a sexual or violent-sexual passage. Then all subjects read a rape passage. The correlation between sexual arousal and perceptions of the victim's pain were positive for only one combination of conditions: males in the violent-sexual condition. For males, there was a significant relationship between willingness to engage in a rape and callous attitudes toward women. With no mention of punishment, 17% of the males indicated willingness to engage in rape. Assured that they wouldn't be caught and punished, 51% expressed willingness to engage in rape.

6. Briere, Malamuth, and Ceniti (1981)

   A continuum of tendency to rape: Males were asked whether they would use force in a sexual encounter, use force and also rape, or reject both force and rape. A violent orientation toward women was found to be on a continuum, with a few males showing no tendency to the orientation, most showing some tendency, and a few showing strong tendency.

ment would result was used throughout). Their responses to a questionnaire containing Burt's rape-supportive attitudes items were also collected. A violent orientation toward women was found to be on a continuum. A few males showed absolutely no disposition to violence; most males showed some disposition; and a few males showed a strong disposition. (More than 50% showed some likelihood of resorting to force or rape; but see the caution, above.) The findings suggest that a tendency to violence toward women in a sexual context is not all or none, but a matter of degree.

Sex roles and sexual violence.   Putting together two facts suggests that   sex roles
rape is not confined to a "few twisted individuals" (Koss, Leonard, Beezley, & Oros, 1981). First, there is little evidence that personality factors play a role in males' tendency to violence toward women. One can find no compelling support for the existence of a relatively few men with "rape personalities." Second, acceptance of rape-supportive attitudes that are part of our culture is strongly related to violence-proneness. Thus, the culture that influences most men, rather than warped minds that are confined to a few, may determine a rather widespread tendency to violence toward women. In short, it is not biological maleness that disposes some men to rape. Rather, it is the male sex role that encompasses a dominant, adversarial orientation to women. This is not to say that masculinity is "bad." In fact, there is much that is beneficial about it. Recent studies show that people generally favor masculine characteristics, regardless of who shows them (Taylor & Hall, 1982).

As a result of these insights, Briere et al. advise that eliminating rape and other forms of sexual assault will come from "reprogramming" to equalize male/female relationships, to redefine sexual interaction as noncoercive and nonadversarial, and to strengthen cautions against viewing media displays that imply acceptance of violence against women. Submitting convicted rapists to therapy is apparently not a sufficient answer.

Briere et al. also provide support for another important contention (Brownmiller, 1975): rape appears to be mainly an aggressive rather that a sexual act (Weidner & Griffitt, 1983). Questionnaire items relating to purely sexual matters were, for the most part, unrelated to willingness to use force or rape. However, other work by Malamuth and colleagues indicates sexual inhibition—a tendency to sexual guilt and sexual conservatism—relates to willingness to engage in sexual violence (Briere, Malamuth, & Check, in press). Since the traditional male sex role demands that males seek dominance over and sexual interaction with females, many men may confuse sex with violence (Pogrebin, 1980). This possible confusion would not be surprising to Freud, who viewed sex and aggression as linked and thought children would interpret the sexual act as an aggressive interaction (see Chapter 3).

Sex roles and erotic/aggressive situational influences.   If it's the male sex role, not biological maleness, that disposes some men to violence toward women, a film that is devoid of erotic content, but displays a man attacking a woman, should increase subsequent aggression toward women. Results supporting this speculation were reported by Donnerstein (1983). In a study very similar to those considered earlier, male subjects were exposed to a neutral, erotic, aggressive, or erotic-aggressive film. The aggressive film displayed a man beating up a woman, but had no erotic content. When the confederate was female, subjects in the aggressive-film condition delivered more intense shocks to her than subjects in either the neutral or the erotic condition. The female confederate received the most intense shocks in the erotic-aggressive condition.

Given that it is the male sex role, not biological maleness, that determines the tendency of some men to rape, men who are highly involved in the male sex role, called "high sex-typed," should act like rapists in some respects. More specifically, high-sex-typed males should react to erotic and erotic-aggressive stories much like convicted rapists. Indeed, Check and Malamuth (1983) found that rank-and-file male college students who were highly sex-typed displayed the same level of arousal to a story of intercourse between consenting individuals as to a story of rape committed by a stranger of the victim. Equal arousal to intercourse between consenting people and to rape by a stranger is typical of convicted rapists.

Interesting results that may be related to the link between masculinity and disposition to violence toward women are provided by Dolf Zillmann and Jennings Bryant (1982). Some of their male and female subjects experienced massive exposure to erotica. Spread over a six-week period, they saw 36 erotic films, for a total of 4 hours and 48 minutes of exposure. An intermediate exposure group saw 18 films (2 hours and 24 minutes) over the six-week period. A no-exposure group saw 36 non-erotic films. The erotic films were very explicit, but contained no violence in any form.

Responses to a rape story and a questionnaire, both administered after the exposures were completed, were submitted to analysis. Results showed that the greater the exposure to erotica, the more lenient were subjects' recommendations for punishment of rapists. The exposure effect was the same for male and female subjects, but females recommended stronger punishment, regardless of conditions. Other results suggested that lack of compassion for victims of rapists generalized to lack of compassion for women. The greater the exposure, the less the support for the women's movement. Again, the effect of exposure was similar for male and female subjects, but females showed stronger support for the movement. Finally, the greater the exposure to erotica, the more callous were men in their sexual attitudes toward women (an example of callousness was endorsement of the statement, "Pickups should expect to put out").

Why did exposure to explicit, but non-aggressive, erotica generally lower compassion for women? Erotic displays, whether aggressive or not, often depict women as passive objects, to be used by dominant men (Malamuth & Donnerstein, 1982). Such erotica may promote that aspect of masculinity that dictates men should dominate women. If so, exposure to even non-aggressive erotica may strengthen the link between the male sex role and disposition to violence toward women, by promoting the dominance of males over females.

Other work by Malamuth and colleagues indicates that while sexual violence in the media is increasing (Malamuth & Spinner, 1980), actual Hollywood films containing violence toward women—as opposed to contrived laboratory episodes—generate increases in men's acceptance of violence toward women (Malamuth & Check, 1981). Malamuth (1983) reported that questionnaire measures of tendency to direct aggression toward women, similar to those used in his previous studies, provided valid predictions of behavior in the Buss-shock experiment. Malamuth (1981a) found that sexually violent men were more aroused by a rape depiction than relatively nonviolent men, and that, regardless of violence orientation, exposure to a rape depiction increased rape fantasies. Finally, Mala-muth and Check (1980) showed that penile tumescence (increase in blood volume of the penis) was greater when a rape victim was depicted as indicating sexual arousal than when she indicated abhorrence.

In sum, the "battle of the sexes" is not a laughing matter. All those cultural forces that depict women as passive sexual objects who defy dominant aggressive men by withholding sexual favors, and who enjoy being forced to engage in sex, come together to make men predators and women their victims. Equalizing the sex roles seems to be an important step toward ending the "battle" once and for all.

Activists Are on the Move: **BOX 12.3**
Attitudes toward Rape Are Changing*

New Bedford, Mass., and New York — Big Dan's Tavern is no more. Gone is the Pac-Man game, the oval bar, and the notorious pool table. In its place, a new institution has arisen: the Coalition Against Sexist Violence. Only a week ago, 2500 marched to proclaim their abhorrence of violence against women. The rally drew many activists. Gloria Steinem could not attend, but sent a telegram stating "What happened to the woman in New Bedford happens to every woman." The coalition is establishing a rape crisis center and will begin sensitivity training for police officers.

One coalition member, a professor of political science at Southwestern Massachusetts University, saw good coming from the event that had so stunned this fishermen's haven. Commenting on the numerous offers to help her group, Rita Moniz indicated "The way to end violence against women is to change how women are treated in our society. As long as women are regarded as inferior people, they will be victims of violence."

Meanwhile, ordinary citizens gathered in angry clumps, debating how such a thing could happen in their quiet community. During the two hours of rape and humiliation, from 9 to 15 men cheered on the attackers. Many of them, including some of the assailants, were still at Big Dan's when the police arrived. They were bellied up to the bar, swilling beer. It appeared that the rape had been of no more significance to them than a game of Pac-Man. The professor offered, "They must have felt safety in numbers. No one was going to take the word of a woman over that of 20 men." Maybe, but such a point of view could become a thing of the past. Susan Brownmiller, author of *Against Our Will,* thinks that progress has been made. "Twenty years ago, it would not have gotten to the police station." Now she believes that men will think twice before they assume that their word will be taken over their victim's.

There's a rape every six minutes. Victims range from 70-year-old grand-

* Adapted from the *Peoria Journal Star,* March 20, 1983, article by AP's Dolores Barclay; the *Peoria Journal Star,* March 20, 1983, article by AP's Fred Bayles; and the "David Brinkley Show," NBC, March 25, 1984.

continued

BOX 12.3
continued

mothers to 16-year-old cheerleaders. Like cancer, it can strike anyone, rich or poor, educated or not. And strike it did, 82,088 times in 1980 and 81,536 times in 1981. But those are only the ones that were reported.

With statistics like these, one would hope for change. In fact, events like the gang rape in New Bedford are raising consciousness, the first step toward meaningful shifts in public opinions. Alterations in attitudes are already showing up in the form of self-defense courses and rape-prevention lectures. Some victims have even successfully sued assailants, seizing their property and garnishing their wages. But the biggest change may be in the way rape victims are being treated by authorities.

No more is it common for policemen to grill victims about their sex lives and react with suspicion because they were "out late" or dressed "provocatively" on the occasion of the attack. The case of "Karen" provides an illustration of a growing trend in methods for dealing with rape and its victims. The 28-year-old mother of two and resident of the nation's capital was awakened by an assailant brandishing a knife. While the rapist was engrossed in the attack, she wrested the weapon from him and managed to exact a measure of revenge. He fled but was soon captured. What happened next might serve as a model for treatment of rape victims. "Karen" called a special number contacting a policewoman who "told me to stay on the phone until the police arrived." She was taken to a hospital, accompanied by two police sex-crime specialists. "They didn't question me. They just wanted to know how I was doing." At the hospital, "Karen" was greeted as a heroine. When the questioning finally began, a male officer treated her with sensitivity. "They made it known that they are human beings, not pigs. The police are more concerned about rape than ever."

CHAPTER REVIEW

Situational influences on aggression have been found in a large number of studies. Aggression is any form of behavior performed with the intention of harming another human being who is motivated to avoid harm. It is not the same thing as anger or hostility, nor can unintended harm, attack that helps more than hurts, attack on a non-living thing or, more controversially, attack on an animal be considered aggression.

The Buss-shock method is the most widely used technique for studying aggression in the laboratory. It involves having a confederate of the experimenter insult or not insult a subject; exposing the subject to some materials or experi-

ences that may influence aggressiveness; and then providing the subject with an opportunity to shock the confederate. Using this and other methods, it has been found that frustration is at best an uncertain source of aggression. However, learning to aggress merely by watching an aggressive model is a common phenomenon, well established by research.

Racism exerts a subtle influence on aggressiveness. Aggression against Blacks can be detected if situational factors that hold Whites accountable for their violent acts are investigated. While Whites may readily attack Blacks when aggression cannot be detected, open aggression against Blacks is rarely encountered in laboratory experiments, and, probably, in real life as well. Erotica, heat, and lack of empathy are additional situational sources of aggression. Numerous approaches to studying the possible link between viewing television violence and behaving aggressively have led to the conclusion that TV is one of several ways children learn to be aggressive.

Among relatively ineffective methods for controlling or preventing aggression are punishment and catharsis. More useful means of prevention and control include exposure to non-aggressive models; humor; empathy; mild erotica; and some forms of therapy. Altering child-rearing practices is one of the best hopes of preventing aggression in the future.

Detecting a tendency for males to aggress against females is difficult, because of the rule that "gentlemen don't hurt ladies." However, subtle experimental manipulations of situational influences reveal that sometimes men will aggress more against women than against other men. Exposure to strong erotica (sexual acts), especially of a violent sort, is one way to instigate aggression against women on the part of men. Apparently, a tendency to aggress in the context of sexual interaction—rape being the extreme example—is not confined to a few "twisted individuals." Even normal men may harbor some disposition to mix violence with sex in a sexual exchange. The masculine sex role may be the source of this disposition.

KEY CONCEPTS

Aggression: components of definition
Buss-shock method
Situational influences on aggression
    Frustration
    Racism
    Strong erotica
    Heat and noise
    Modeling
    Television
Manipulation of situations to control aggression
    Punishment

Catharsis
Models
Humor
Empathy
Mild erotica
Parents
Therapy
Rape
    Violent erotica
    Rape tendency among normal men
    Sex roles

REVIEW QUESTIONS

1. How is aggression defined, and how is it studied?
2. What are the situational determinants of aggression?
3. Describe the circumstances under which punishment may effectively control aggression. How do these conditions compare to the reality of criminal deterrence?
4. How does exposure to erotica influence aggression? What difference does it make if the erotic stimuli are mild or strong, with or without violent content?
5. What evidence is there for a general rape tendency among normal men? What situational factors of a cultural nature contribute to this tendency?

13

Searching for a Reconciliation of the Trait and Situational Approaches: Interactionism

Which of these statements makes the most sense? "People behave according to their individual traits, regardless of situations." "In a given situation, all people behave in much the same way." "A given person behaves according to a particular trait in some situations, but not in others."

How many situations can you name that might cause everyone in them to behave alike?

If all traits don't correspond well with behavior, can you name a few that do?

H ISTORICALLY, THE TRAIT approach has dominated the study of personality. As you recall from Chapter 1, a given trait supposedly determines much the same behavior in class, at work, or at a party. However, it could be the other way around. As you saw in Chapter 12, situations can determine behaviors. People could *all* act much the same at work, but all behave in a different way at a party.

Having considered both the trait and the situational orientations, the next obvious step is to entertain how traits and situations might act in concert, or interact. *Interactionism* is the point of view that traits and situations combine to determine behavior, such that a given person will manifest behavior corresponding to a given trait in some situations, but not in others.

interactionism

In the back of your mind, you probably have an intuitive feel for interactionism, and may use it in your everyday life. By completing the exercise in Box 13.1, you can become more aware of interactions. We suggest that you do the exercise at this time.

A Mental Exercise
in Interactionism

BOX 13.1

First, think of a person that you have known well for a long time. Then, think of a trait that you believe this person possesses. Next, make a list of situations in which the person often finds herself or himself. Examples would be church, work, meeting, dinnertime, athletic event, dance, party, class, and talking with friends. Now, taking the situations in the order that you've listed them, imagine the person operating in the first situation. On a 7-point scale, where "7" is the maximum and "1" the minimum degree, estimate the extent to which the person, when in that situation, displays the behavior that corresponds to the trait you have assigned. For example, if you assigned the trait "helpful" to the person, and the situation is "work," you might select "5" to show that the person demonstrates a moderately high degree of helpfulness at work. Next to the label for the situation you have imagined, write down a number representing the degree you have chosen. Now go to the second situation on your list, and carry out the same procedure. After

continued

BOX 13.1
continued

you've finished your list of situations, you may wish to think of another person and complete the process once again. Then look at your list or lists. For any given person, did you assign the same number in each situation? Probably not. Like subjects in a recent study, you likely assigned different numbers for different situations, showing that a person with a given trait displays it to a different degree in different situations (Allen & Smith, 1980). If so, you have demonstrated that you can be an interactionist.

In the first portion of this chapter, we reconsider traits and situations and their limitations, so you can see why it might be beneficial to combine the two and how it might be done. Next, we present Norman Endler's classification of methods for supporting the interaction position and his description of different conceptions, or models, of interactionism. Then, we turn to perhaps the most popular theory of interactionism in the field of personality, Walter Mischel's social-learning position. Finally, because we criticize traits in the course of this chapter and suggest that interactionism might be a superior approach, we end by defining limited circumstances in which traits, by themselves, might be useful predictors of behavior.

A Comparison of the Trait, Situation, and Interaction Approaches

To help with the comparison, let's return to the example employed in Chapter 1. The behaviors of Jane, John, and Julie that relate to three traits are plotted for three different situations in Tables 13.1, 13.2, and 13.3. Please remember that these figures and the next two depict highly idealized circumstances that are useful for illustrative purposes, but are not to be taken as a general reflection of reality.

TRAITS

The trait position is illustrated in Table 13.1 You can see that Jane is unaffiliative in class, at work, and at a party. By contrast, both John and Julie are highly affiliative in all three situations. On the other hand, Jane is high in assertiveness, John is low, and Julie is moderate, regardless of situation. Individual differences also exist for being conscientious, whether the situation is work, class, or party.

SITUATIONS

As you can see upon examination of Table 13.2, exactly the opposite outcome is expected from the situational point of view. In one situation, everyone behaves in a particular way, but in a second situation, they all behave in a different way. At work, the circumstances demand concentration on the task at hand. There, all three people are unaffiliative. The same holds true for the classroom

TABLE 13.1 Behavioral Dimensions (Trait Point of View)

	Assertiveness (1 = assertive)					Affiliativeness (1 = affiliative)			
	Classroom	Work	Party	Mean		Classroom	Work	Party	Mean
Jane	1	2	1	1.33	Jane	5	5	5	5.00
John	6	6	6	6.00	John	1	1	1	1.00
Julie	4	3	4	3.67	Julie	1	1	1	1.00

	Conscientiousness (1 = conscientious)			
	Classroom	Work	Party	Mean
Jane	6	7	7	6.33
John	2	1	2	1.67
Julie	5	6	5	5.33

situation. By contrast, the party situation demands affiliative behavior, and all three people respond accordingly. Likewise, assertiveness is appropriate at work, but less so at a party or in the classroom. Finally, conscientious behavior is demanded in class as well as at work, and all three people respond appropriately. Notice that, under situational assumptions, the names of the people need not be mentioned. Distinctions among people are not necessary, because situational demands are assumed to make everyone behave much like everyone else. There are few if any individual differences in behavioral scores.

TABLE 13.2 Behavioral Dimensions (Situation Point of View)

	Assertiveness (1 = assertive)					Affiliativeness (1 = affiliative)			
	Classroom	Work	Party	Mean		Classroom	Work	Party	Mean
Jane	6	1	5	4.00	Jane	5	6	1	4.00
John	5	1	6	4.00	John	6	5	1	4.00
Julie	6	1	5	4.00	Julie	5	6	1	4.00

	Conscientiousness (1 = conscientious)			
	Classroom	Work	Party	Mean
Jane	2	1	5	2.67
John	1	2	5	2.67
Julie	2	1	5	2.67

INTERACTION

Table 13.3 depicts the state of affairs from the interaction point of view. Observe that Jane is highly affiliative at work, moderately so at a party, and hardly at all in the classroom situation. John, by contrast, reserves affiliative behavior for

According to interactionism, people's behaviors at a party reflect the interaction of trait and situational variables.

parties, while class is the only place where Julie is even moderately affiliative. The trend is the same for conscientious and assertive behaviors. Each person shows a particular pattern of behaviors across situations that is different from the pattern of other persons. None of the people displays the behavioral consistency across situations that is predicted by the trait approach. Neither does any situation evoke the same behavior from all persons as would be expected by the situational approach.

TABLE 13.3   Behavioral Dimensions (Interaction Point of View)

	Assertiveness (1 = assertive)					Affiliativeness (1 = affiliative)			
	Classroom	Work	Party	Mean		Classroom	Work	Party	Mean
Jane	7	6	3	5.33	Jane	6	1	3	3.33
John	1	7	7	5.00	John	6	6	2	4.67
Julie	6	1	4	3.67	Julie	3	5	6	4.67

	Conscientiousness (1 = conscientious)			
	Classroom	Work	Party	Mean
Jane	2	6	7	5.00
John	7	1	3	3.67
Julie	4	7	2	4.33

Notice that the interaction point of view requires mention of both names of people and labels for situations. With the trait position, only the name of the person is necessary for prediction; from the situational position, only the label for the situation need be known. Interactionists reason that one can't predict behavior without specifying both persons and situations. They affirm that people may have traits, in the sense of often performing a given behavior, but their traits are tied to situations. A person may be assertive, but only at work. From the interaction perspective, a person's behavior is predictable, given identification of the person and the situation, because the person will tend to behave the same each time she or he encounters a given situation. However, the same person will tend to behave differently in different situations and, in a specific situation, differently from others.

TRAITS, SITUATIONS, OR THEIR INTERACTION: WHICH IS CORRECT?

As you probably guessed, it is not the case that one of the three positions is "right" and the others "wrong." Some traits do provide a reasonable degree of prediction, and taking the trait position may be very helpful to clinical psychologists and others who try to solve the real psychological problems of real people. Likewise, there are powerful situations that can dominate human behavior, sometimes with tragic consequences. Interactionism, however, appears to be the general position that offers the most power for understanding whole, complex human beings — and that, after all, is the goal of the psychology of personality.

Even though the trait approach, as we have broadly defined it in this book, has dominated personality research and theory, relatively recent investigations have shown that its underlying assumption is not strongly supported. The underlying assumption is that on a given behavioral dimension, a person will behave consistently from one situation to another, even when the situations are quite different. If a person has the trait "friendly," for example, he will behave in a friendly manner in each of a wide variety of situations.

In 1968, Walter Mischel published a book in which he argued that the tendency for a person to behave the same from one situation to another is quite weak. Mischel showed that the correlation between behavior performed in one situation and behavior along the same dimension performed in a different situation is small. The average cross-situational correlation coefficient that he estimated was only .30 (1.00 is perfect). Such a small coefficient implies that behavior performed in one situation accounts for behavior displayed in another to only the 9 percent degree ($.3 * .3 = .09 = 9$ percent). (This is a crude statement of the "variance controlled" notion. We will elaborate later.) If Mischel is correct, there is precious little cross-situational consistency in the performance of behaviors, such as those in the "assertiveness" category.

Several psychologists have strongly disagreed with Mischel over the years since 1968 (for example, Alker, 1972), and others have asserted that he is correct only in cases where inadequate techniques have been used to study personality. Nevertheless, Mischel has not backed down (Mischel & Peake, 1982, 1983). Further, his assumption about consistency has become more and more widely accepted (Byrne & Kelly, 1981; Lamiell, 1981).

Another problem with traits is how to tell them from their opposites—moods or states (Allen & Potkay, 1981). Whereas "trait" implies consistency, a mood is something that is supposed to happen only now and again, not often enough to imply consistency from situation to situation. But where is the dividing line? If you are "happy," are you in a mood? Most individuals would probably say "Yes." But what if you are happy most of the time? Should you be described as having the "happy" trait? The trouble is, no one is able to specify how often you have to be happy in order to qualify for the "happy" trait, rather than just a "happy" mood. Let's suppose that you are "conscientious." Is that a trait? It is likely that most people would reply in the affirmative. But, again, how often and in how many different situations do you have to show "conscientiousness" in order to claim a trait, rather than simply a mood?

Most researchers and clinicians try to solve the problem of discriminating between trait and state or mood in three ways: (1) by indicating that whether a label such as "happy" or "conscientious" is a state or a trait depends on whether it is found on a mood or personality trait test; (2) by arguing that if assessment involving a label occurs at short intervals (every day), mood is being measured, and if long intervals are used, trait is being measured; and (3) by arguing that traits and moods are tied up together, so that averaging over mood measures ("happy" test responses) will provide an index of trait ("happy" trait). Unfortunately, these three agruments are merely assertions, unsupported by either evidence or sound logic (also see Allen & Potkay, 1983b, and Zuckerman, 1983).

The case of situationism is even more confusing. First, situationism in the area of personality is sort of a straw person. We are unable to find a single personality theorist who can be described as a situationist. Mischel has been accused of supporting situationism, but the charge is incorrect, as we'll see. Situationists do exist, but they are all social psychologists (for example, Milgram, 1974; Ross, 1977). Almost by definition, social psychology is an attempt to understand the influence of social situations.

Second, situationism in personality has been severely and convincingly criticized (Bowers, 1973). It has been claimed that situationism is no more powerful for explaining outcomes in personality studies than is the trait approach. We will demonstrate this contention shortly, when considering the work of Norman Endler and J. McVicker Hunt (1969). There are situations that can control the behavior of almost all who perform in them (Baron & Byrne, 1981), and it is important to investigate each of them. However, such situations represent only a small portion of all the situations that a typical person encounters in everyday life. For example, Milgram (1974) and Zimbardo (1970) describe situations that determine unethical or even immoral behaviors in most people. Likewise, Latané and Darley (1970), Gergen, Gergen, and Barton (1973), and Johnson and Downing (1979) describe situations that determine highly prosocial behaviors in most individuals. Examination of this research indicates that situations generating highly positive or highly negative behavior in most people are very unusual and may occur rarely, if at all, in the lifetime of a given individual. Further, a recent analysis has gone so far as to suggest that even these extreme and rare situations may not exert as powerful an influence on behavior as has generally been assumed (Funder & Ozer, 1983).

It is even more difficult to find situations that lead to less extreme behavior in most individuals. Under real-life rather than laboratory circumstances, the authors (Allen & Potkay, 1983a, Chapter 5 of that book) failed in attempts to create situations that would determine the same behaviors in most of their subjects. We did locate some natural rather than contrived situations that influenced most subjects in much the same unextraordinary way: preparation for a forthcoming holiday, and preparation for a test in a university class. However, these situations were a distinct minority of all those faced by subjects. In general, we found that the influence of situations on people was unique to particular persons. That is, a given situation, such as a party, would have a strong influence on some individuals and not on others. If you think that this sounds like interactionism at work, you are entirely correct. Each subject tended to display a unique pattern of behavior, represented by behavioral labels recorded during self-description. Although subjects were exposed to many of the same situations, each tended to respond to the common situations differently. Finally, while it is possible to argue that situations select the behaviors that people perform, it is also possible to show that personality traits play a role in selecting the situations in which people behave (see Chapter 5).

In sum, social situations can be powerful determinants of behavior, but situations that determine the same behavior in most individuals are rare. Likewise, traits can have important influences on behavior, but generally, the effects of traits are not strong. Thus, interactionism seems to provide a more general and flexible way to explain behavior than the other two approaches. Let's turn now to means of supporting interactionism.

Methods of Supporting the Interaction Position

THE VARIANCE-COMPONENTS METHOD

Endler (1983) identifies two basic methods for supporting the interaction position. One of these, the *variance-components method*, involves partitioning the variation in some behavior — such as that corresponding to anxiety — into components controlled by situations, by persons, and by the interaction of the two factors. *Persons* represent individual differences on any *traits* that have been identified and on other psychological factors that reside within individuals — in our example, the trait *anxiety*. In a study of anxiety, assume that the person factor controls more variance than its two rivals, situations and interaction. In that case, it would be true that the strongest tendency was for each person to consistently maintain his or her own peculiar level of anxiety, relative to other people, when performing in each of the different situations included in the study.

With Endler's use of the variance-components method, rather than researchers' creating situations that may generate anxiety, subjects respond to naturally occurring situations, usually through the medium of imagination, and then certain physiological signs of anxiety, such as palpitations of the heart and muscle tension, are assessed. Next, it is determined whether individual differences in anxiety (persons), situations, or their interaction controls the most variation in the physiological manifestations, which we will call *anxious reactions*.

variance-components method

NORMAN ENDLER.
Endler's careful research has clearly demonstrated the relative strength of interactionism compared to the trait and situation approaches.

Some studies by Endler and Hunt (1969) provide excellent examples of the variance-components method. These investigators developed six different questionnaire forms to investigate the relative contribution of several variance components to explaining anxious reactions. Each form contained a separate page for each situation to be considered. At the top of the page, the situation was described. Below the situational description were listed several reactions that might result from being in the situation. Subjects were asked to indicate the degree to which each reaction would be characteristic of them when performing in the situation described at the top of the page. For each reaction, one of five degrees could be reported, with a value of "1" assigned to the lowest degree, representing virtual absence of the reaction, and a value of "5" assigned to the degree representing intense reaction. All but one of the six forms used in the research contained 10 reactions listed beneath each situational description. The lone exception included 14 reactions. The number of situations described in the forms ranged from 11 to 18, with 14 being the most usual number. Table 13.4 contains some examples of situations and reactions.

One of the six forms was given to 43 different samples of subjects, 22 composed of males and 21 of females. Forms were administered at sites varying from major universities to small colleges, and from junior-high to high schools. Age categories included adults (attending night school), college age, high-school age, and junior-high-school age. Social classes ranged from upper-lower class (families whose head of household was a skilled laborer) to lower-upper class (families whose head of household was in one of the professions). Sample sizes ranged from 31 to 206, with the total number of subjects close to 3000. Obviously this large overall sample of subjects contained a wide variety of people, making it possible to generalize results to a broad cross-section of the U.S. population.

TABLE 13.4 Some Examples of Situations and Reactions in the Endler and Hunt (1969) Study

Situations	Reactions
"You are sitting down to dinner."	"hands trembling"
"You are undressing for bed."	"get fluttering feeling in stomach"
"You are starting on a long auto trip."	"have sweaty palms"
"You are getting up to give a speech before a large group."	"need to urinate" "have loose bowels"
"You are about to take an examination in a course in which your status is doubtful."	
"You receive a summons from the police."	
"You are on a high ledge upon a mountain."	
"You are driving down the road when you meet two racing cars approaching you abreast."	

The most extensive breakdown of results was by sex of subject and form used. In eight out of ten possible comparisons (five forms by the two sexes), the person-by-situation interaction controlled more variance in anxious reactions than did either persons alone or situations alone (one form was not included because it was given to only one male and one female sample). This outcome is very similar to Bowers' (1973) report of more variance controlled by interactions in 14 of 18 comparisons of the three rival components. In the Endler and Hunt study, persons accounted for about 4 percent of the total variance in anxious reactions for all administrations of the forms, situations controlled 4 percent for males and 8 percent for females, and interaction controlled about 10 percent. It is risky to say much about the absolute as opposed to relative size of percentages of variance controlled. The number of factors in the experiment and other considerations influence absolute size (see Allen & Potkay, 1977a, and Allen, 1976). One must even be cautious about overemphasizing percent size, in and of itself (Diener, 1983). However, the absolute size of the percentages for the components listed above were probably underestimated because of the nature of the reactions included in the study. Reaction types, called *modes of response,* varied over a wide range and "ate up a lot of variance," leaving little for the other components. Variation in reactions ranged from the innocuous ("feeling uneasy") to the socially undesirable ("loose bowels"). Nevertheless, the relative size of percentages can be taken seriously. For the extremely large and varied overall sample of Endler and Hunt, interaction consistently controlled more variance in anxious reactions than either situations or persons.

What explains the Endler-Hunt results? Apparently a given individual may be anxious in some types or classes of situations, but not in others. Another individual may be anxious in a different set of situational types, but not necessarily the same ones as the first person. Figure 13.1 illustrates this possibility. You can see that hypothetical person Robert is anxious in that class of situations in which

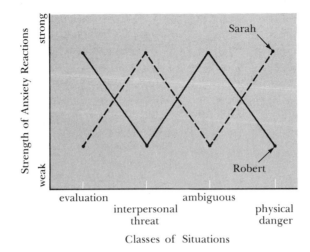

Figure 13.1
Strength of anxiety reactions for two hypothetical persons as a function of class of situation *(adapted from Endler, 1983).*

others may evaluate him as a person, called *social-evaluation situations* (for example, "giving a speech in class"). He is also anxious in situations that are *ambiguous* (for example, "trying out a new sport"). On the other hand, Sarah is anxious in *interpersonal-threat situations* (for example, "two good friends are having an argument in your presence") and in *physical-danger situations* ("you are on a ledge high upon a mountainside"). She shows little anxiety in the kinds of situations that trouble Robert. Actually, the classification of situations used in Figure 13.1 was developed by Endler (1983) and colleagues by examining aspects in common among the several situations included in their questionnaire forms. Endler (1983) reports experimental results using the classification system that are quite similar to those illustrated in the figure. As you read on, you may wish to refer back to Figure 13.1 as a prime example of person-by-situation interaction.

THE EXPERIMENTAL METHOD

experimental
method

As you will recall from Chapter 2, the experimental method involves assignment of values to independent variables by the experimenter in order to determine possible influences on dependent variables. Applying this method to the investigation of the interaction between persons and situations, the experimenter would "assign values" to the situational variables by selecting degrees of some situations, and then expose subjects to those varying degrees. For example, an experimenter could select, for presentation to subjects, a high and a low degree of physical danger, a high and a low degree of interpersonal threat, and so forth, thereby assigning values to independent variables. By contrast, the variance-component method, as we have described it, is a correlational method. The experimenter merely induces subjects to think of situations that they have directly or indirectly encountered.

Phillip Kendall (1978) reported an elegant demonstration of the experimental method for studying the interaction of persons and situations. First, he had 96 male college students complete some questionnaires that assessed anxious reactions and tendency to be anxious in physical-danger situations and in social-evaluation situations. As you recognize, these latter two measures were developed by Endler and colleagues. Second, subjects were invited to the psychological laboratory in small groups. Some groups first saw a physical-danger situation depicted on film and then, for the social-evaluation situation, completed an extremely difficult arithmetic-decoding task, which no subject could master in the allotted time. The film showed a horrible automobile crash. Subjects were told that the arithmetic task "will give me [the experimenter] some information about your abilities so I can evaluate you." Other subjects did the task first and then saw the film. Finally, subjects completed the anxious-reactions questionnaire again.

Subjects who performed in the study had been selected based on their responses to the questionnaires administered earlier. Those in a "high physical-danger trait group" had been among the 40 percent of the entire original sample who were highest on physical-danger anxiety. Likewise, those in the "low physical-danger trait group" were the 40 percent who had scored lowest on physical-danger anxiety. The same 40 percent criterion was used to create high and low social-evaluation trait groups.

Results showed that, as expected, subjects high on physical-danger trait were made to display much more anxious reactions to the film than their counterparts in the low physical-danger group. However, high and low physical-danger trait groups did not differ in anxious reactions to the social-evaluation situation created by the difficult arithmetic task. In the same vein, high social-evaluation trait subjects showed much higher anxious reactions to the social-evaluation situation generated by the arithmetic task than did their counterparts in the low group, but the two groups did not differ in anxious reactions to the physical-danger situation created by the film.

As Kendall predicted, there was an interaction between persons and situations such that those high and low on physical-danger trait and social-evaluation trait differed in anxious reactions when exposed to a situation that was relevant to their situation-specific trait. However, when exposed to a situation that was not related to the trait on which they were high or low, they did not differ in anxious reactions. There was an interaction between the person factors physical-danger trait and social-evaluation trait, and the physical-danger and social-evaluation situations corresponding to the traits.

Having discussed ways to support interactionism, we now turn to the question "What is the best analogy, or model, for conceptualizing interactionism?"

The Mechanistic and Dynamic Models of Interaction

Endler (1983) refers to two different conceptions of the interaction between persons and situations. The model illustrated by the two studies just considered is called the *mechanistic model*. In the mechanistic model, persons simply combine in some way with situations to determine behavior, but persons and situations are not influenced by behavior or by one another. Figure 13.2 depicts this model. As in previous examples, a person factor (such as anxiousness about physical danger) combines with a situation (such as "an automobile wreck") to determine anxious reactions. According to Endler (1983), there is plenty of evidence for this model.

mechanistic model

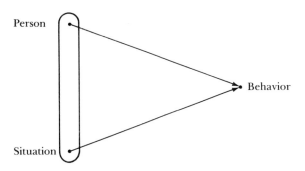

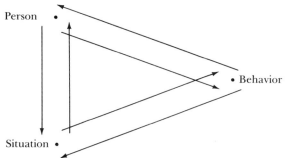

Figure 13.2
The mechanistic model of interaction *(adapted from Endler, 1983).*

Figure 13.3
The dynamic model of interaction *(adapted from Endler, 1983).*

dynamic model   Alternatively, Endler (1983) offers the *dynamic model,* illustrated in Figure 13.3. Here, person factors and situations also combine to determine behavior, but each reflects back on the other. For example, let's suppose that a person who possesses the tendency to react with anxiety when exposed to physical danger is exposed to such danger. Imagine that the person is asked, under safe conditions, to peer out over a ledge atop a tall building, and complies. Suppose, further, that none of the horrible experiences, such as nausea, trembling, weak knees, and the like, occurs as a result of looking over the ledge. According to the dynamic model, the behavior, once performed, has consequences of its own. Once the person has successfully looked over the ledge without horrible experiences, the person factor, tendency to show anxious reactions to physical danger, is lowered. That is, the behavior will feed back on the person factor, changing it. The person factor may now feed back on the situation, so that looking over a ledge high above the ground no longer is seen as involving such high physical danger.

The two models clearly lead to different expectations. The mechanistic model is a "one-way street," with the person/situation combination affecting behavior, but not the other way around. In the dynamic model, each of the components in the interaction, person/situation/behavior, feeds back on the others, potentially changing them. Although Endler endorses the dynamic model as potentially more valuable than the mechanistic model, he sees few attempts to support that model and, thus, little evidence to confirm it. Perhaps the theory that we will cover next and its supporting data will eventually change his mind.

Mischel's Social-Learning Theory

As you recall from Chapter 6, social-learning theory emphasizes how people learn from other people. It is addressed to personality and, in some of its forms, amounts to an interaction point of view. In fact, Mischel's (1973) thesis is such an excellent example of interactionism that we have chosen to present it here, rather than in Chapter 6.

WALTER MISCHEL.
Mischel started a revolution when he declared traits to be weak predictors of behavior. Now his theory is providing personologists with an alternative to the trait approach.

For Mischel, certain person factors interact with situations to produce behavior. However, his point of view, called *cognitive social-learning theory,* posits that important person factors are cognitive rather than traitlike. (*Cognitive* refers to thought processes.) Specifically, Mischel's person factors are memories of previous experiences, from the past history of an individual, that determine strategies the person employs for producing behavior at the present time. In interaction terms, Mischel's theory predicts that the history of rewards and punishments experienced in a given situation and observations of others made in that situation will determine present behaviors.

Mischel's cognitive social-learning theory

As you can now see, person factors are not limited to traits. Memories, experiences, and intellectual factors also interact with situations to produce behavior. For Mischel, it is not the "set-in-stone" traits of people that determine behavior. Nor is behavior somehow determined by those traits combined in some way with situational forces. Rather, past reinforcements and thought processes based on past experience in a situation determine present behavior in the situation.

THE MISCHELIAN PRINCIPLES

Mischel's concepts dovetail neatly into concrete predictions. We'll examine the concepts and then pursue some predictions.

Competencies. Just what does a person acquire from his past history of operating in a situation that allows him to perform effectively in that situation at

the present time? For one thing, a person gains the perception that he is competent to perform effectively in the situation; or operation in the situation teaches
him how to behave effectively. A *competency* is either a cognitive ability to size up a
situation so that one can operate effectively in it, or a behavior that one can
perform that will lead to success in the situation. Competencies involve "knowing
what to do" in a situation and being able to do it, rather than just knee-jerk
repetitions of previous behaviors in the situation. Some people may not know that
the ability to engage in "small talk" is critical for success at a party, defined as
repeatedly receiving invitations. Others may know the importance of small talk,
but just can't do it. Still others may know the importance of small talk and also do
well at it. Only this last set of people would have the competency leading to success
at parties.

competencies

Of course, people vary in how many competencies they possess. Some people have a large "bag of tricks" they can use in a wide variety of situations. Others,
unfortunately, have rather few competencies and can operate efficiently in a
relatively small number of situations. However, it is important to remember that
success does not depend so much on the number of competencies that a person
possesses as on the suitability of these competencies for the specific situations that
she is likely to encounter in her life. A generally effective person can size up the
specific situation in which she finds herself, determine what behaviors are appropriate at each instance during the situation, and effectively perform those behaviors. She can do so because she has profited from the experience of having
previously operated in the situation.

Characterizing events.   Now we can be more specific about what constitutes "sizing up a situation." No situation encountered in real life is likely to be
simple. In fact, situations tend to be complex, each composed of many components. A *component* of a situation is some part or aspect of the total situation,
such as physical characteristics or, more important, people who are present when
the situation is in progress. Components generate events. *Events* are simply occurrences that are produced by components of a situation. "Stuffiness" is an example
of an event produced by a component of a possible college-class situation—a
small, poorly ventilated room. More potent events are the behaviors that are
performed by persons who operate in a situation. Placing events associated with a
situation into categories is the first step in sizing up a situation. Such placement is
called *characterizing events*. Once events are characterized, one can begin to see
what behaviors might lead to success.

characterizing
events

A person may characterize events associated with an entire situation, or with
individual components of it. For example, one student may place events associated with the college-class situation into the "silence is golden" category, signifying that speaking out is inappropriate. Another student may decide that the
college class is an appropriate place for voicing any opinion that is relevant to the
topic at hand. Obviously, these two people will behave quite differently in class. In
addition to, or instead of, such global characterization, a person is likely to place
specific events associated with a situation into separate categories. These specific
events are often behaviors of critical persons who are found in the situation. For
example, a particular student may characterize his professor's rapid and enthusi-

astic speech as "imparting important information"—that is, the stuff tests are made of. Such a characterization could lead to some frantic note taking. Another student may interpret the professor's dramatic pause following presentation of a "main point" as a signal that she should ask a question reflecting her vital interest in the topic.

One of the most usual ways that people characterize the behaviors of other individuals operating in a situation is to apply trait labels to the individuals. The process involves placing people in such categories as "introverted," "dishonest," "sincere," "humorous," and so forth, based on their behaviors. Such placement then allows individuals to decide what behaviors to perform in a situation when interacting with people who are categorized. In discussing characterization of behaviors by application of trait labels, Mischel (1973) makes reference to Kelly's personal constructs, a topic covered in Chapter 8. As you recall, a personal construct is a way of seeing the world. Each construct can be seen as a trait category into which one's own and other people's behavior is fitted. Thus, a person's construction system—all the constructs that he or she possesses— guides the person's own behavior, but is also used to assess others' behaviors. While Mischel continues to believe that placing people in trait categories is not the best strategy for understanding them, he has acknowledged that people do use traits to characterize themselves and others, a fact that psychologists must consider (Mischel & Peake, 1982, 1983).

Special note should be taken of the observation, made from the point of view of a given individual, that others' actions are not the only important behavioral events in a situation (Mischel, 1973). The person who is trying to size up a situation is also one of its components. That person's own behaviors are important events associated with the situation as well. In fact, for a given situation, one of the most valuable cognitive competencies that a person can possess is the realization there are certain behaviors he can perform that will change the situation, making it one in which he can operate more easily. If you think that our discussion is beginning to have the flavor of Endler's dynamic interactive model, you are correct. According to Mischel, people do not just passively respond to situations; they actively shape them. For example, Sue finds herself at a business meeting during which the participants are all talking loudly and in unison. She is not able to "do her thing," which is to apply precise logic to practical problems. Being somewhat soft-spoken, she feels the need to change the situation to better suit her capabilities. Thus, she makes her way to the front row, waves her hand so that the chairperson can't miss it, and raises a "point of information." This action causes the chairperson to pound her gavel until there is silence in the room and then to turn the floor over to Sue. Now Sue has transformed the situation into one in which she has a long past history of effective operation.

Expectancies. An extensive past history in a situation is likely to give a person a good grasp of what to expect when certain stimuli are present and when certain behaviors are performed. For Mischel, a *stimulus* is a very definite, well-defined component or event associated with a situation that can be either physical or behavioral. Anybody who has spent years as a lawyer will likely believe that certain stimuli lead to predictable outcomes in the courtroom. When the person

expectancies

dressed in black robes emerges from an adjoining room and steps behind the bench, lawyers have the expectancy that everyone will rise. An *expectancy* is a belief based on past experience that provides a prediction of future outcomes. In our courtroom example, the stimulus may be a component of the situation—the judge—or a behavior—the bailiff's verbalization "All rise." In either case, the stimulus gives rise to the expectancy of certain outcomes, often behaviors.

People also have beliefs with regard to what will occur should they or others behave in a certain way in a given situation. That is, people have expectancies concerning the outcome of particular behavioral performances. Knowing the rules of the court, a lawyer can easily predict what will happen if she or her client continually interrupt the proceedings by shouting at the judge.

In sum, to know a situation is to know what will happen when a certain stimulus is present. It is also to know what will result from the performance of a given behavior.

Values of outcomes.   In sizing up a situation so that successful behaviors can be performed, it is not enough to know what to do and be capable of doing it. If one fails to accurately characterize the situation—its components and its events—one will not know when to do whatever will lead to success. However, accurate characterization is still not enough. One must know what to expect when specific stimuli emerge from the situation and when specific behaviors are performed in the situation. Additionally, the definition of success itself may depend on values one attaches to outcomes associated with the situation.

values of outcomes

To take an example from Mischel (1973), people familiar with a particular form of psychotherapy will know that clients who make favorable references to themselves experience a definite outcome — approval from the therapist. Among those people are some who, when acting as clients, will greatly value the approval that results from favorable self-reference. However, other clients will not value approval. It is a good bet that the frequency of favorable self-reference will be very different for the two groups of knowledgeable clients. The value of an outcome, be it a behavioral outcome or the outcome of some stimulus, is a powerful part of "sizing up" a situation. Knowing the outcomes that are typical of a situation, a person will adopt strategies and perform behaviors that will increase the likelihood of valued outcomes. In fact, *success* may be defined as effectively performing the behaviors that yield the outcomes that are valued by the performer.

self-regulatory plans

Self-regulatory plans.   A final aspect of sizing up a situation is one's own self-regulatory plans. *Self-regulatory plans* are rules, established in advance of the opportunity for behavioral performance, that act as guides for determining what behavior would be appropriate under particular conditions.

Self-regulatory plans involve more than rules covering a kind of situation, such as being at a party. People are aware that situations don't stay the same from one point in time to the next. A given situation will tend to vary even on a single occasion during which it is in effect. Have you ever attended a party where everyone engaged in the same activities throughout the entire duration of the affair? Neither have we. Parties generally start with "feeling each other out," figuratively speaking, until people are thoroughly acquainted or reacquainted with one another and, thus, feel comfortable with one another. Then the merry-makers loosen up, and the fun really begins. Although one may have plans for parties in general—such as how to dress, whether to approach others or wait for them to approach you, and so forth—one must also have plans concerning what to do at different phases of the party. What happens if somebody has a little too much to drink? What do you do when "things are dragging a little"? People generally have answers to these and other questions worked out in advance, in the form of plans.

Self-regulatory plans tend to be different for different people, because each person has a unique past history. Furthermore, plans are flexible. They may change permanently because of experience, or may be altered temporarily because of the demands of the situation in which a person finds herself. To demonstrate this point, Mischel, Ebbe Ebbesen, and Antoinette Zeiss (1972) investigated self-regulatory plans designed to delay gratification. *Delay of gratification* refers to postponing some pleasure so that it can be enjoyed to the maximum degree or in its most optimal form. In the present case, some male and female children, 3½ to 5½ years of age, were given a choice between a marshmallow and a pretzel, whichever they preferred—but there was a catch. If a child wanted the preferred object, he would have to wait until the experimenter returned to him—a 15-minute delay. If he couldn't wait, he could ring a bell to call the experimenter and consume the less preferred food when the experimenter arrived. Other children were instructed in the same way, but also were given a Slinky to play with. A third group of children were told to "think a fun thought" while waiting. These two groups were distracted from thinking about the preferred food by the toy or by the "fun thoughts."

Results showed that none of the children in the "no-distraction" condition was able to wait the entire 15 minutes. Six of the ten children in the "fun-thoughts" condition were able to wait. They demonstrated a self-regulatory plan that some children, and adults, typically employ to delay gratification. If a child can spend her allowance "now" for some less preferred candy, or wait until a parent can take her to get a preferred "goodie," ice cream, and she chooses to wait, she may pass the time thinking about distracting, fun things, other than ice cream.

Four of the ten children in the "toy" condition were able to wait. Their behavior provides an illustration of how situational demands may alter plans or even create new plans. We can assume that at least some of the children in the "toy" condition did not have self-regulatory plans that would allow them to successfully wait the required 15 minutes. Nevertheless, four of those children were able to wait the required time, because a component of the situation, the toy, provided them with a plan that worked to allow successful delay.

Summarizing the principles.   To tie together Mischel's principles "in one small, easy-to-handle package," let's take an example that involves all of them. The example will also show how the principles are manifested differently in different people.

Let's assume that Diane and Don are participating in a sandlot softball game (from Allen & Potkay, 1983a). Their competencies are quite different. Whereas

Diane is an excellent ballplayer, Don is just average. Their characterizations of events associated with the game situation are also different. Don sees softball on the sandlot as an occasion for "having fun and cutting up," while Diane is dead serious. Their views of stimulus and behavioral outcomes are both similar and different. Both might recognize that a solid hit is an exciting event, but only Don sees the behavior "hitting the ball" as an occasion for back slapping and cheering. Further, the values they assign to outcomes are different. Diane finds the praise that follows a long hit to be better than "money in the bank," while Don couldn't care less. Finally, their self-regulatory plans are different. Don plays with abandon, trying to turn every hit into a home run, whereas Diane is careful not to stretch a hit too far and risk being thrown out.

With this general introduction to social-learning theory in mind, let's now turn to an experimental demonstration of the Mischelian thesis.

INTERACTIONISM IN A MISCHELIAN STUDY

Procedure.   Mischel, Ebbesen, and Zeiss (1973) recruited male and female university students to investigate the relationship between repression-sensitization, a person factor, and situations. *Repression-sensitization* refers to a scale anchored on the left by a tendency to deny and avoid threatening stimuli (repression) and on the right by a tendency to approach and to understand as well as control threatening stimuli (sensitization). Repression and sensitization can be thought of as cognitive strategies that are alternate self-regulatory plans. Subjects took the repression-sensitization test before the experiment and, based on their scores, were split into two equal groups: those scoring toward the repression end of the scale, and those scoring toward the sensitization end.

Upon arriving at the laboratory for the experiment, subjects were confronted by a fancy "concept-learning" apparatus and by an experimenter whose dress and manner were designed to convey "professionalism." All subjects were informed that the experiment concerned a new intelligence test that was designed to discriminate among college students. The test was supposedly based only on concept learning.

Some subjects were then asked to take the concept-learning test, while others, control subjects, were merely to help "check the apparatus" by running through the test procedure. Subjects taking the test were divided into two groups. After completing the task, one group was told that they had done better than at least 90 percent of college students. They constituted the success condition. Subjects in the failure condition were told that they had done better than only 20 percent of college students.

The three groups—labeled success, failure, and control—were further divided to create expectancy and no-expectancy conditions. In the expectancy condition, subjects were told that after a 10-minute delay, during which the apparatus "was to be adjusted," they would again complete the concept-learning test. Subjects in the no-expectancy condition were not led to believe that they would repeat the test.

Dependent-variable measurement took place during the 10-minute delay. Subjects were told that they could either examine "computer strategies" for

TABLE 13.5 Summary of Procedures of Mischel, Ebbesen, and Zeiss (1973)

1. Subjects took the repression-sensitization test and were split into those scoring near the repression end and those scoring near the sensitization end.
2. Upon arriving at the lab, subjects were informed about a new intelligence test.
3. Control subjects merely helped "check the apparatus," while "success" subjects performed the task supposedly better than 90 percent of college students, and "failure" subjects supposedly did better than only 20 percent of students.
4. The three groups were further subdivided into those who expected to perform the task again after a 10-minute period, and those who had no such expectation.
5. All subjects could then examine for 10 minutes some "computer strategies for mastering" the intelligence test or their personality liabilities or personality assets — the latter two supposedly taken from a previous personality assessment.
6. The dependent variables were the amount of time spent examining liabilities and amount of time spent examining assets, as determined by observations made through a one-way mirror.

mastery of concept learning, examine personality-test results for questionnaires completed at the time the repression-sensitization scale was administered, or do anything else they wished during the 10-minute period. Three kinds of information were placed at conspicuously different locations in the waiting room. These were the computer strategies, information based on the tests of personality that indicated their assets, and information indicating their liabilities. The experimenter then retired so that subjects could examine the information. From an adjoining room, an observer watched subjects through a one-way mirror (a silvered mirror on the subjects' side and a window on the observer's side). Two dependent-variable measures were taken by simply recording the amount of time that subjects spent examining their personality liabilities and the amount of time spent examining their assets. After the 10-minute period, subjects were thoroughly debriefed concerning reasons for the procedures and informed that the concept-learning task was not a real test.

Table 13.5 summarizes the procedures used in this study. Table 13.6 provides examples of personality assets and liabilities.

TABLE 13.6 Personality Assets and Liabilities (Mischel, Ebbesen, and Zeiss, 1973)

Assets		
Affiliation: capable of cooperating and reciprocating deeply in relations with others	Surgency: interested, knowledgeable, and genuinely engaged	Autonomous: desires independence and freedom to act according to own fundamental ideals

Liabilities		
Dominance: manipulative persuasion or self-seeking commands	Nonperserverative: procrastination and distractability	Ego weakness: indecisiveness, brittle defenses, flat emotional affect

Results.   Figures 13.4, 13.5, and 13.6 show results of the study. Figure 13.4 shows that there was an interaction between persons and situations, with repressers and sensitizers reacting differently to the failure, success, and no-experience (control) situations. In the failure and control situations, sensitizers and repressers differed in that the latter spent more time examining assets. However, the difference between the two groups was small and nonsignificant in the success situation.

When liabilities were considered, repressors and sensitizers again differed, but only in the failure and control situations (see Figure 13.5), again reflecting an interaction. Expectancy and repression-sensitization interacted only for amount of time spent examining assets. As depicted in Figure 13.6, repressors and sensitizers did not differ at all in the expectancy situation, but repressors spent more time on assets in the no-expectancy situation. Overall, after failure or in a neutral context (control, no expectancy), repressors emphasized assets and ignored liabilities, while sensitizers did the opposite. With success or expectation of a "replay," they did not differ. In sum, cognitive strategies, which could be considered self-regulatory plans, interacted with situations to determine how much time individuals spent examining personality liabilities and assets.

Traits Revisited

Just because interaction theory seems to be the wave of the future in the area of personality does not mean that personologists have abandoned traits. They have not, nor should they. The complexity of human behavior is such that many points of view are needed to understand it. The error of personologists who have relied

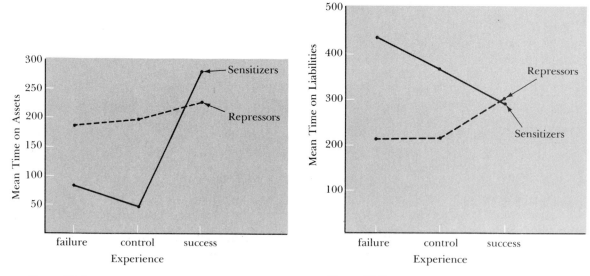

Figure 13.4
Mean amount of time (in seconds) spent on assets by sensitizers and by repressers in each experience condition *(adapted from Mischel et al., 1973)*.

Figure 13.5
Mean amount of time (in seconds) spent on liabilities by sensitizers and by repressers in each experience condition *(adapted from Mischel et al., 1973)*.

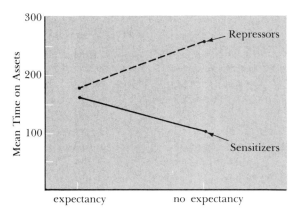

Figure 13.6
Mean amount of time (in seconds) spent on assets by sensitizers and by repressors in each expectancy condition *(adapted from Mischel et al., 1973).*

heavily on traits to explain behavior is not that they have chosen a fruitless orientation. Rather, it is probably that they have expected too much of traits. Each and every trait simply does not determine the behavior of each and every person, all the time. Campus (1974), Bem and Allen (1974), and Snyder (1974) simultaneously published papers suggesting that *some traits* may determine behavior, but only for *some of the people.* Douglas Kenrick and David Stringfield (1980) followed up the Bem and Allen work and, in so doing, added another suggestion. A *few traits* may be reasonably strong determinants of *many people's behavior.* Their research is worth a close look.

THE KENRICK/STRINGFIELD STUDY

Procedure.   Kenrick and Stringfield had 72 university students rate themselves on 16 traits. Ratings were made on scales having seven degrees. These ratings were the focus of the predictions described below.

Next, subjects rated the degree to which their behaviors varied from situation to situation for each of the 16 traits. Subjects also indicated the degree to which they felt that their behaviors related to traits that were easy for others to observe, as opposed to being difficult to observe. An easily observed behavior is one that is public, concrete, and definite, such as a "hello" wave. A behavior that is difficult to observe lacks these three characteristics; an example would be a facial expression indicating self-assurance. Like the personality-trait ratings, the variability and observability ratings were completed on seven-point scales. Finally, subjects placed a mark by the single trait among the 16 on which they were most consistent from one situation to another — that is, the trait on which they were least variable. A mark was also placed by the trait for which they were least consistent (that is, most variable). Thus, if a subject put a mark by a trait relating to "friendliness" in response to the "most consistent" instruction, he viewed himself as displaying about the same degree of friendliness in each of the various situations he encounters. Likewise, a mark by a trait corresponding to "shyness" in response to the "least consistent" instruction indicated that the respondent viewed himself as displaying different degrees of shyness in different situations.

Kenrick/String-
field study

A parent and a peer, usually the subject's roommate, completed exactly the same questionnaire rating their friend/offspring on each of the 16 traits, as well as on consistency, observability, and most/least consistent trait. In other words, parents and peers responded to the same questionnaire in the same way as did subjects, except that their ratings were of their friend/offspring rather than of themselves.

Results.   To determine whether traits were useful in making predictions about people, ratings by each of the three raters—self (subject), parent, and peer—were intercorrelated. The combinations of the three kinds of ratings yielded three sets of correlations: (1) self (subject) trait ratings with parent trait ratings, (2) self-ratings with peer ratings, and (3) parent ratings with peer ratings. When all subjects and all traits were considered, the ratings by one group did a rather poor job of predicting the ratings by another group. The overall self/parent correlation yielded a coefficient of only .26. Those for self/peer and parent/ peer were only .27 and .21, respectively, for an overall average of only .25. Thus, for the traits taken as whole, there was very little ability to predict from one kind of rating to another.

However, when guided by the notion that, for each subject, some traits allow prediction and others do not, results became more impressive. Considering only the trait that each subject marked in response to the "most consistent" instruction, the self/parent, self/peer, and parent/peer ratings correlated $r = .62$, $r = .61$, and $r = .61$, respectively. On the other hand, for the trait that each subject marked in response to the "least consistent" instruction, the three kinds of ratings correlated $r = .16$, $r = .12$, and $r = .39$, respectively. Averaging over the three correlations, the coefficient for "most consistent" traits was .61, and for "least consistent" traits it was .23. Thus, when the trait on which subjects felt "most consistent" was used, prediction was improved (average $r = .61$), compared to that obtained using all traits (average $r = .25$).

Results were similar for the traits marked by peers in response to the "most consistent" and "least consistent" instructions. Again, averaging over the three types of correlations (self/parent, self/peer, parent/peer) yielded a coefficient of .60 for the "most consistent" trait and .27 for the "least consistent" trait. Parents did a little better. Their average coefficients across the three correlations were .73 and .18 for the traits they selected in response to the "most consistent" and "least consistent" instructions, respectively. These results are presented in the second column of Table 13.7.

For the next analysis, two groups were created based on subjects' responses to the "most consistent" instructions. One group consisted of those whose observability ratings of their "most consistent" trait fell in the top half of the observability ratings made by all subjects. For example, if a subject marked "friendly" when asked on which trait he or she was most consistent and then gave "friendly" such a high observability rating that it fell among the top 36 such ratings, the person was included in this group. (Assuming there were 72 subjects available in all cases, there were 72 observability ratings overall and 36 in the top half of the ratings.) The other group was composed of subjects who gave such a low observability rating to the trait they had rated as "most consistent" that it fell among the lowest 50 percent of the observability ratings. Two corresponding

TABLE 13.7 Mean Intercorrelations for Most and Least Consistent Traits, and for Subanalyses of Most Consistent Traits Based on Median Splits

Assessed by	Most/least consistent traits	Subgroupings of most consistent traits	
	All subjects	High/low observa-bility	"Best" "worst"[a]
Self	.61/.23	.68/.49	.74/.47
n[b]	71	36	25
Parent	.73/.18	.74/.72	.75/.57
n	61	32	15
Peer	.60/.27	.72/.46	.84/.31
n	63	32	16

Note. Data on all subjects based on mean of self/parent, self/peer, and parent/peer correlations. Other figures based on same computation for various subgroupings.

[a] Traits chosen as "most consistent," which were above the median on both the observability and consistency indices = "best"; those below the median on both = "worst."

[b] n = number of subjects.

groups were formed based on parents' observability ratings for subjects' "most consistent" traits. Likewise, two more groups were formed based on peer observability ratings.

Results for this analysis are shown in the third column of Table 13.7. Averaging across self/peer, self/parent, and parent/peer correlations, the correlation between the ratings of one rater and another generated a coefficient of .68 for "most consistent" traits chosen by subjects that were also among the highest 50 percent on the observability ratings by subjects. That is, on the traits on which subjects had indicated that they were most consistent and to which they had assigned observability ratings in the top 50 percent, the coefficient of correlation between ratings was a high .68. Knowing the observability level subjects assigned to their "most consistent" traits improved prediction over that obtained when observability was not considered. By contrast, on traits on which subjects saw themselves as being consistent, but to which they had assigned observability ratings falling in the lowest 50 percent, the coefficient of correlation between ratings averaged only .49.

Correlations taking "observability" into account were also computed, in the same way, based on parent and peer observability ratings of traits selected by subjects in response to the "most consistent" instruction. The coefficients for these correlations are found in rows two and three of column three, Table 13.7.

To summarize, prediction from the trait ratings of one rater to those of another was accurate when only those traits were used for which subjects saw themselves as being behaviorally consistent. Prediction improved somewhat when behaviors corresponding to "most consistent" traits were also rated as being among the most observable. However, these rather small increments in prediction were realized at the cost of cutting the sample about in half. Only an average of 34 subjects remained in the sample when only "most consistent" traits that were also rated as most or least observable were considered.

One final qualification was adopted. One group each was formed based on subject, peer, and parent ratings of traits upon which subjects saw themselves as most consistent, and for which observability ratings *as well as* consistency ratings were among the top 50 percent. For three more groups of subjects, peer, parent, or subject ratings of "most consistent" traits were among the bottom 50 percent of *both* the observability *and* the consistency ratings. "Most consistent" traits isolated in this manner were called "best" and "worst," respectively. The case of ratings by subjects themselves is presented in column four, row one, of Table 13.7. The correlation among personality ratings produced an average coefficient of .74 for the "best" traits and .47 for the "worst" traits. Results for ratings by parents and peers are presented in column four, rows two and three, of Table 13.7.

Knowing that "most consistent" traits were also "most observable" and had been rated among the highest in consistency further improved prediction between one personality rating and the next, compared to knowing only observability of "most consistent" traits. However, once more, the improvement was obtained at the cost of further reduction in the number of people to whom the prediction applied. On the average, only 19 subjects had "most consistent" traits that were among the most observable and most consistent, or among the least observable and least consistent. As more and more qualifications were made, prediction improved progressively, but applied to fewer and fewer people. For "best" and "worst" traits, predictions applied to only about 26 percent of the entire sample (19 out of 72).

Kenrick and Stringfield (1980) also provide evidence that a few traits may allow a reasonable level of prediction for many, if not most, people. Without any qualifications at all, the average coefficient for correlations of subject/parent, subject/peer, and parent/peer trait ratings was of moderate size for 4 of the 16 traits considered in the study. The traits in questions were related to friendliness ($r = .36$), assertiveness ($r = .35$), shyness ($r = .40$), and practicality ($r = .43$). These coefficients average to about .39. Thus, it is implied that ratings of one kind account for ratings of another kind to the 15 percent degree ($.39 * .39 = .15 = 15$ percent). Sticking our necks out a little, we would go so far as to speculate that some such traits may be inborn to a degree. For example, developmental psychologists write of inborn temperament (Mussen et al., 1979). Some infants seem to be very active, alert, and responsive to adults from day one. They may grow up to be among those we tend to call "friendly." That is, what we refer to as "friendliness" behavior may begin at birth and, thus, may be at least partly inborn (see Scarr, Webber, Weinberg, & Wittig, 1981, for a consideration of this possibility as well as its limitations).

Thomas Monson and his colleagues, John Hesley and Linda Chernick (1982), have pointed out another intriguing possibility for improving the usefulness of traits in making predictions of behavior. A trait, even if it is not qualified in any way, may form the basis for reasonably strong predictions in some situations, but not in others. If situational pressures are quite strong, as when people were ordered to obey in the Milgram (1974) experiments, traits may not predict well (see the next chapter and Cox, 1971, in Allen, 1978). But when pressures are not strong, given traits may provide useful predictions in given situations.

SUMMARY AND DISCUSSION

Kenrick and Stringfield's (1980) follow-up of the Bem and Allen (1974) theory and research produced some useful and hopeful results. On the average, the 16 traits allowed rather poor prediction from one personality rating to the next, as represented by an average coefficient of only .25. However, when prediction was limited to the single trait for which subjects' behavior was seen as most consistent, one situation to the next, prediction was greatly enhanced (average $r = .65$). Prediction was improved further by using only those "most consistent" traits corresponding to behaviors that were among the most observable (average $r = .71$). Finally, there was an additional improvement in prediction when consideration was limited to only those "most consistent" traits that fell among the top 50 percent of both the observability and consistency ratings (average $r = .78$). However, the improvement in prediction achieved by the addition of observability and consistency information came at the cost of greatly reducing the number of subjects to whom predictions applied. The more one bolsters the usefulness of traits for prediction by qualifying them, the fewer the number of people to whom predictions will apply.

There is a second important conclusion that can be drawn from the results of Kenrick and Stringfield. These researchers also produced data suggesting that at least a few traits may allow useful predictions for many people, even without the qualifications. To put it another way, there may be a few traits that can be used to make reasonably strong predictions for many, if not most, people. This interpretation may be the salvation of those who wish to ignore interactions with situations and continue basing predictions on unqualified traits.

It should be noted that as time goes by, the Kenrick and Stringfield (1980) follow-up of Bem and Allen (1974) has been subjected to more and more criticism (Mischel & Peake, 1982, 1983; Rushton, Jackson, & Paunonen, 1981; Schneiderman, 1983; also see reply to Rushton et al. by Kendrick & Braver, 1982). The most serious objection has been that nowhere did they measure actual behavior. The personality ratings of Kenrick and Stringfield amounted to global impressions of how subjects behaved in general, not ratings of behaviors as these were actually performed. Mischel and Peake (1982, 1983) have shown that studies using the Bem and Allen method employed by Kenrick and Stringfield yield reasonably high levels of prediction only when the global ratings are used, not when actual behavior is considered.

CHAPTER   REVIEW

Historically, the field of personality has been dominated by the trait position. This approach implies that people display much the same behavior across situations. Thus, the person, not the situation, is the most important factor in the de-termination of behavior. Alternatively, situationism suggests that people operating in a given situation all behave in much the same manner. Here, the situation dominates behavior; factors related to persons are unimportant. Interactionism provides another possibility: a person's behavior may correspond to a particular trait in one situation, but not in another. Both persons and situations contribute to the determination of behavior.

Endler (1983) has convincingly argued that the interaction between person factors and situations allows a more complete understanding of people, in the form of better prediction of behavior, than considering only traits (or only situations). If a person factor that is specific to a situation, as "anxiousness over physical danger" is specific to situations in which physical danger is possible, strong predictions of behavior can be made. General measures of traits such as anxiety don't take into account the specific situations in which behavior is to be performed — a deficiency that greatly reduces the usefulness of these measures.

The evidence indicates that traits have not been as strong a determinant of behavior as was once assumed. Similarly, situations do exist that determine the behavior of most persons performing in them, but such powerful situations are quite rare. However, interactions between traits and situations may provide a potent and general explanation of behavior.

Two avenues have been taken in the exploration of interactions: the variance-components method and the experimental method. These two approaches to understanding interactions have been labeled "mechanistic" and may eventually be replaced by "dynamic" conceptions.

Mischel (1973) has offered really the only reasonably well-developed theory of interactionism available in the area of personality. He claims that when cognitive person factors are considered as these interact with situations, strong predictions of behavior can be made. The person factors considered by Mischel are competencies, characterizations of situational factors, perceived outcomes of behaviors and stimuli, values of outcomes, and self-regulatory plans. A study with Ebbesen and Ziess (Mischel et al., 1973) showed how one of these person factors interacted with situations to determine behavior.

Interactionism may become the dominant force in the area of personality. However, traits are "alive and well," as Seymour Epstein (1977) has indicated, even though not as hale and hearty as was once the case. Kenrick and Stringfield (1980) showed that prediction based on traits is enhanced if the only trait used in prediction is the one selected by each subject as "most consistent." Further, small improvements in ability to predict are realized if "most consistent" traits are also associated with behaviors that are rated as highly observable. "Most consistent" traits that are highly observable and also receive high consistency ratings allow an even greater level of prediction. For each person, there are a few traits that allow for a reasonable level of prediction.

Traits may be "alive and well" in another sense, one that has been strangely neglected. There may be a few traits that allow for at least fair prediction for many people. Some of these may even be inborn, to some degree.

One final point seems worth some thought. In Chapter 1, we asked how well personologists' ideas agreed with those of ordinary people. With the revelation by Mischel (1968) that the trait approach has serious shortcomings, there has been the observation that people in general are "guilty" of overreliance on traits in attempts at predicting and understanding the behavior of their fellows (see Ross, 1977). Supposedly, since ancient times, people have been naive trait theorists and, as a result, have neglected situations as determinants of behavior (Bem & Allen, 1974). While this position is defensible, and indeed each of us may catch ourselves sticking a trait label on others with little thought of situational influences, people are probably not all that naive. Recent evidence provided by Allen and Smith (1980), Cantor and Mischel (1977), and Zuroff (1982) suggests that people are at least capable of appreciating the interaction between person factors and situations. If the "right" questions are asked, people will say, in effect, "Why yes, I am assertive (or friendly, or shy), but not always. It depends on the situation."

KEY CONCEPTS

Interactionism
    Variance-components method
    Experimental method
    Mechanistic model
    Dynamic model
Mischel's cognitive social-learning theory

Competencies
Characterizing events
Expectancies
Values of outcomes
Self-regulatory plans
Kenrick-Stringfield study

REVIEW QUESTIONS

1. What are the differences between the trait, situation, and interaction positions? What prediction does each position entail?

2. In what ways does available evidence fail to support the trait approach? the situational approach?

3. How does the variance-components method differ from the experimental method? How does the mechanistic model differ from the dynamic model?

4. How would you explain the behavior of two different people at a party using Mischel's theory? Use the "softball" example as a model.

5. If interactionism is the "wave of the future" in personality, should personologists abandon traits? Answer in terms of Kenrick and Stringfield's results.

6. To what extent does interactionism agree with commonsense ideas about personality?

14

Interactions and Behavior: Examples

Can your personality affect your physical health?

Do differences between the sexes in their sexual behaviors and beliefs occur only under certain circumstances?

Are there situations in which males are more easily influenced than females?

Are females really less aggressive than males?

T HIS CHAPTER illustrates interactions between situations and four classes of person factors: traits, personality types, social styles, and gender. As you recall from the last chapter, person factors are embedded within the individual, whereas situations are the specific external circumstances that confront the individual at any given time. How interactions between person factors and situations are defined and studied was the topic of the preceding chapter. Here we are concerned with demonstrating how interactions explain behavior, as broadly defined in earlier chapters.

classes of person factors

Traits have been emphasized so far in this book, but they represent only one class of person factors, albeit perhaps the most important one. Other non-trait person factors already mentioned include Mischel's "competencies" and "self-regulatory plans." In this chapter, the first class of person factors examined is traits. Specifically, we reconsider authoritarianism as it interacts with situations.

Second, we discuss interactions in which the person factor is a personality type. As you recall from Chapter 9, a type consists of a category of people who share several traits in common. Our sample person factor of the "type" class is Type A versus Type B personalities. Individuals at these two extremes show differences in behavior related to different susceptibilities to heart disorders. However, does how they differ in behavior depend on the situation in which they are operating?

Third, the focus is on self-monitoring, a "class by itself." Self-monitoring may be thought of as a "social style," rather than a trait or type. People who do a lot of self-monitoring pay considerable attention to the social circumstances that surround them. Their counterparts are relatively unconcerned about the social events into which they are submerged. How these two kinds of people differ shows up in some situations and not in others.

Finally, we explore an often researched person variable, gender. *Gender* refers to "male" and "female" categories, but focuses on the cultural rather than the biological aspects of those two classes of people. Readers interested in a biological contrast between the sexes are referred to Beach (1969), Goleman (1978), and Begley and Cary (1979) for "plain English" treatment of the topic and to A. Arnold (1980) and Greenough, Carter, Steerman, and DeVoogd (1977) for more technical discussions. Our emphasis on interactions between person factors and situations limits us to the cultural side of male/female similarities and differences (we will use "sex" and "gender" interchangeably). You are going to discover that whether males and females are similar or different often depends on what situation you are talking about.

For each of the four person-factor classes considered in this chapter, interactions between person factors and situations will be presented in a figure, a table, or in the text. When there is a graph, the behavior, such as sexual arousal, is displayed on the vertical axis. Either the person factor or the situation is depicted on the horizontal axis, with the remaining factor presented in the main body of the graph. In the case of tables, the behavior is represented by the numbers in the main body of the table. The person and situational factors are indicated by the columns and rows of the table. Simple interactions are described in words. For example, it is sometimes pointed out that a person factor influences behavior in one way for a given situation and in another way for a different situation.

The Trait Class: Authoritarianism

The trait *authoritarianism* was thoroughly described in Chapter 10. Briefly, people who are high in authoritarianism show unusually strong fear of and high respect for authority figures. By contrast, low authoritarians tend to question and defy authority. Given these orientations toward authority, Ralph Epstein (1965) reasoned that people differing in authoritarianism would react differently to target persons who are high in social status, compared to those low in status, because high-status persons have more authority. Thus, a person factor was expected to interact with a situational determinant to produce behavior.

authoritarianism and social status

Epstein noted that harsh and punitive parental discipline characterized the childhood of high authoritarians. Such parental practices sensitize high authoritarians to the uses of power. Having been treated in a punitive fashion by people more powerful than themselves, authoritarians have come to assume that it is the right of the powerful to suppress the powerless. Thus, high authoritarians expect to exercise power over those lower in status than themselves and to submit to those high in status. Just as people with ''parental status'' were free to aggress against them when their status was that of a powerless child, as adults high authoritarians would feel free to attack persons lower in status than they. On the other hand, they would fear attacking a high status person. By contrast, low authoritarians, coming from democratic homes, have some disdain for authority. They would be more likely to attack high- than low-status persons.

To support his thesis, Epstein (1965) recruited the 40 students who scored highest and the 40 lowest scorers on a test of authoritarianism from a pool of 240 students in introductory psychology classes. These subjects were run through the Buss-shock procedure, teacher/learner version, that is detailed in Chapter 12. For half of the high and half of the low authoritarians, the learner was dressed in old, worn-out clothes and indicated orally that his parents were uneducated as well as unemployed and that he was planning to drop out of school. In the high-status condition, the remaining high and low authoritarian subjects were introduced to a well-dressed learner whose parents were college-educated professional people. He indicated plans to pursue a master's degree in business. As shown in Figure 14.1, Epstein's hypothesis was confirmed. Low authoritarians aggressed more against the high- than the low-status learner, and high authoritarians shocked the low-status learner more than the high-status counterpart. Con-

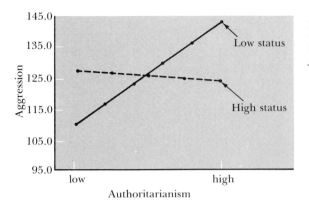

Figure 14.1
Effects of authoritarianism and status upon aggression *(adapted from Epstein, 1965).*

trary to the trait position, knowing whether people were high or low in authoritarianism did not allow accurate predictions of their behavior. Correctly anticipating the behavioral outcome depended on also knowing whether they would be operating in a high- or low-status situation.

The Type Class: Type A/Type B

In recent years, a great deal of attention has been paid to Type A and Type B personality types, because behaviors associated with these categories influence the likelihood of contracting heart disease (Dembroski & MacDougall, 1985). Type A individuals share a constellation of traits that distinguishes them from

Hard-driving "Type A" individuals seem to share a number of traits, but their difference from "Type B" persons may reflect an interaction between person factors and situations of stress.

Type B persons, and from many others as well (Brigham, 1986; Dembroski & MacDougall, 1985; Friedman, 1977; Jenkins, Zyzanski, Ryan, Flessas, & Tannenbaum, 1977). They are hard-driving workaholics who are impatient, concerned about efficient use of time, competitive, and hostile. As you might expect, these individuals show a strong desire to achieve and may meet with success under some circumstances (Baron & Byrne, 1984). As indicated above, they are also prone to disorders of the heart (Dembroski & MacDougall, 1978). By contrast, Type Bs are relaxed, easygoing, and sociable (Friedman, 1977).

Type A/Type B personalities and stress

After reviewing the literature, Theodore Dembroski and James MacDougall (1978) concluded that Type As and Type Bs don't always differ. Rather, they are most likely to behave in contrasting ways when they are acting under stress. Put together all the traits that Type As display, and you get a picture of individuals who are strongly motivated to exercise control over their environment. When not under stress, they reasoned, Type As are not threatened with loss of control and would behave much like Type Bs. However, when stressed, Type As would fear loss of control. They would do whatever was necessary to ensure that control was maintained. Should they have to complete a job under stress, Type As would want to "take charge" and would find others a hindrance to task completion, especially if one of those others was a leader who might tell them what to do. In this situation, their desire to work alone would be greater than that of Type Bs. By contrast, if they were not under stress, whether they would perform some task alone or with others would not matter. They would be no more likely than Type Bs to desire solitude on the job.

To see if their expectations were met, Dembroski and MacDougall (1978) gave a Type A/Type B scale to a number of students. Then they selected as subjects those 25 students whose scores were closest to the Type A end of the scale and the 25 whose scores reflected the most Type B orientation. Some subjects in each group were threatened. They were told to expect electric shock and a blood test during participation in a study of how sensory stimulation influences various kinds of mental tasks. Other Type As and Type Bs served in a no-threat condition. Next, subjects were all asked to indicate the degree to which they would prefer to work alone, with others, or in a group with a leader who was a "member of the research team." Responses were on 11-point scales.

Results showed, first, that Type A subjects in the high-threat condition yielded higher scores on desire to work alone than did any other group of subjects. These same subjects scored lower than any other category of subjects on preference to work in the leader-directed group. Second, each subject's score on desire to work with others was added to the corresponding score on preference for working in a group headed by a leader and an average calculated. This average preference for working in a group was subtracted from the score on preference for working alone. The result was a number that reflected preference for working alone as opposed to in a group. As you can see in Figure 14.2, unthreatened Type A and Type B subjects did not differ in preference for working alone. However, under the great stress of the high-threat condition, Type As showed a much stronger preference for working alone than Type Bs. As expected, there was an interaction between the situational variable "threat" and the person factor, Type A/Type B. Other studies have also found interactions between situations and

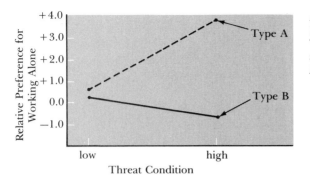

Figure 14.2
Preference for working alone for Type As and Type Bs under high and low threat *(adapted from Dembroski & MacDougall, 1978).*

Type A/Type B (Baron, Russell, & Arms, 1985; Musante, MacDougall, & Dembroski, 1984; Strube, Turner, Cerro, Stevens, and Hinchey, 1984).

The Social-Style Class: Self-Monitoring

Before beginning this section please complete the exercise in Box 14.1. When you have finished, calculate your score according to the instruction at the end of the scale.

Self-Monitoring   **BOX 14.1**
Scale*

Instructions: The statements that follow concern your personal reactions to a number of different situations. No two statements are exactly alike, so consider each statement carefully before answering. If a statement is *TRUE* or *MOSTLY TRUE* as applied to you, put a "T" for true to the left of the statement. If a statement is *FALSE* or *NOT USUALLY TRUE* as applied to you, put an "F" for false to the left of the statement. It is important that you answer as frankly and as honestly as you can.

_____   1. I find it hard to imitate the behavior of other people.

_____   2. My behavior is usually an expression of my true inner feelings, attitudes, and beliefs.

_____   3. At parties and social gatherings, I do not attempt to do or say things that others will like.

_____   4. I can only argue for ideas which I already believe.

_____   5. I can make impromptu speeches even on topics about which I have almost no information.

_____   6. I guess I put on a show to impress or entertain people.

* Used by permission of Mark Snyder.

continued

BOX 14.1
continued

_____ 7. When I am uncertain how to act in a social situation, I look to the behavior of the others for cues.

_____ 8. I would probably make a good actor.

_____ 9. I rarely seek the advice of my friends to choose movies, books, or music.

_____ 10. I sometimes appear to others to be experiencing deeper emotions than I actually am.

_____ 11. I laugh more when I watch a comedy with others than when alone.

_____ 12. In a group of people, I am rarely the center of attention.

_____ 13. In different situations and with different people, I often act like very different persons.

_____ 14. I am not particularly good at making other people like me.

_____ 15. Even if I am not enjoying myself, I often pretend to be having a good time.

_____ 16. I'm not always the person I appear to be.

_____ 17. I would not change my opinions (or the way I do things) in order to please someone else or win their favor.

_____ 18. I have considered being an entertainer.

_____ 19. In order to get along and be liked, I tend to be what people expect me to be rather than anything else.

_____ 20. I have never been good at games like charades or improvisational acting.

_____ 21. I have trouble changing my behavior to suit different people and different situations.

_____ 22. At a party, I let others keep the jokes and stories going.

_____ 23. I feel a bit awkward in company and do not show up quite so well as I should.

_____ 24. I can look anyone in the eye and tell a lie with a straight face (if for a right end).

_____ 25. I may deceive people by being friendly when I really dislike them.

Give yourself one point for each response that matches the following: 1-f; 2-f; 3-f; 4-f; 5-t; 6-t; 7-t; 8-t; 9-f; 10-t; 11-t; 12-f; 13-t; 14-f; 15-t; 16-t; 17-f; 18-t; 19-t; 20-f; 21-f; 22-f; 23-f; 24-t; 25-t. The higher your score, the more you are a self-monitorer.

Mark Snyder and his colleagues have developed the idea that people can be categorized according to how much attention they pay to their behavior in social settings, or the degree to which they are *self-monitoring* (Snyder, 1974; Snyder & Monson, 1975). High self-monitoring persons strive to display the kind of behavior that is ideal for the situation in which they are operating at any given time. They look at how other people behave in a situation and at their own actions, in order to match their behavior to that of the others. Their goal is to be the right person, in the right place, at the right time (Snyder & DeBono, 1984). The projection of a favorable social image is their greatest concern. Needless to say, they tend to change their behavior from situation to situation, because each different situation demands somewhat different behavior (Snyder, 1974). On the other hand, low self-monitoring individuals tend not to mold their behavior to fit the demands of the situation in which they happen to be operating. Instead, their behavior tends to be guided by the dictates of internal dispositions, such as traits. If low self-monitoring persons are aware of possessing the trait "conscientious," they will strive to behave conscientiously in each and every situation they encounter. These people don't care so much what other people think. They are concerned about living up to their own internal standards. As you might guess, low self-monitoring individuals tend to be consistent from situation to situation, relative to high self-monitoring people (Allen & Potkay, 1983a).

Snyder and DeBono (1984) believe that the realm of advertising contains situations to which high and low self-monitoring individuals may react differently. They suggest that there are two kinds of advertisers: those who believe in the "soft sell," and those who advocate the "hard sell." "Soft sellers" create ads that appeal to the *image* associated with the use of a product. They might have made the "Marlboro man" ad that emphasizes a rugged, masculine smoker and ignores the quality of the cigarettes. "Soft sellers'" ads ought to attract high self-monitoring individuals, whose primary concern is projecting the best possible image to others. "Hard sellers," on the other hand, construct ads that stress the *quality* of the product. An example would be the Pepsi-Cola ad that challenges Coca-Cola to a "taste test." Here, image is ignored in favor of "proof" that Pepsi is the highest-quality cola. Such ads should appeal to low self-monitoring individuals. These people would want to know the quality of a product so they could see if it meets their internal standards.

self-monitoring and advertisements

To determine whether situations, in the form of "image ads" and "quality ads," interact with level of self-monitoring, Snyder and DeBono (1984) gave the Self-Monitoring Scale that you just completed to 40 male and female undergraduates. Based on their scores, the 20 highest self-monitoring individuals were separated from the 20 who scored lowest. Subjects from both of these groups then examined "image ads" or "quality ads" for three different products. One ad pictured a bottle of Canadian Club whiskey resting on a blueprint. It was accompanied either by the inscription "You're not just moving in, you're moving up" (image) or the words "When it comes to great taste, everyone draws the same conclusion" (quality). The second ad showed a handsome gentleman about to light up a Barclay cigarette. In the background, an equally attractive lady rests her hand on his shoulder. The accompanying image message read "Barclay . . . you can see the difference." The quality counterpart was "Barclay . . . you can taste the difference." Finally, an ad for Irish Mocha Mint coffee pictured a man and a woman smiling at each other in a dimly lit room. The image pitch was "Make a chilly night become a cozy evening with Irish Mocha Mint." The "quality" message read "Irish Mocha Mint: A delicious blend of three great flavors—coffee, chocolate, and mint."

Subjects were exposed to either the image ads or the quality ads in groups of three to four persons. After seeing one of the two versions of each ad, subjects indicated how much they would pay for the product. They could choose anywhere from $5 to $15 for the Canadian Club, 50¢ to $1.50 for the cigarettes, and $2 to $5 for the coffee.

The results indicated that high self-monitoring persons were generally willing to pay more for a product if they had been exposed to the image ad than if they had been exposed to the quality ad. For low self-monitoring people, it was the other way around. They were willing to pay more for a product if they had been exposed to the quality ad rather than the image ad. Thus, ad situations interacted with the person factor, self-monitoring. Perhaps advertisers should decide whether their products are better suited for high or low self-monitoring persons and design their ads accordingly.

Now you can interpret your self-monitoring score. If your score is higher than 11, you might consider yourself a high self-monitoring individual (Allen & Potkay, 1983a). A score of 11 or below might be regarded as indicating low self-monitoring tendency. If you scored high, you might regard yourself as an adaptable individual who can adjust to the different demands of different situations. By contrast, if you scored low, you could think of yourself as a reliable person, one who is able to maintain the same standards of behavior in many different situations. As with any person-factor scale score, the more extreme your score, the more confidence you can have that it categorizes you meaningfully. If your score was not extreme, self-monitoring does not characterize you very well.

Gender and Situations

gender and situations

As you recall, *gender* refers to the sexes, but focuses on the cultural aspects of being male or female. In previous chapters, we have referred to those cultural aspects under the label *sex roles*. The masculine and feminine sex roles are the cultural prescriptions for behaviors deemed "appropriate" to biologically male and biologically female persons, respectively (see Chapter 12). In this section, when we discuss sex or gender, we will be primarily considering how sex roles interact with situations to determine behavior and attitudes. Because our purpose is to explore interactions, you should look elsewhere for a comprehensive comparison of the sexes (see Hoyenga & Hoyenga, 1979, Maccoby & Jacklin, 1974). We consider five broad areas in which the sexes are often thought to differ: sexual behavior and beliefs, conformity, obedience to authority, aggression, and anxiety.

SEXUAL BEHAVIOR AND BELIEFS

sexual behavior and attitudes

Oral/genital contact and religion.   Many people tend to believe that "unusual heterosexual behavior" such as oral/genital contact is the province of men. In fact, oral sex is neither unusual nor mainly practiced by men. Only 21% of the males and 17% of the females in a survey conducted by Robert Athanasious, Phillip Shaver, and Carol Tavris (1970) had not orally stimulated the genitals of members of the opposite sex. Only 23% of the male respondents and 17% of the female respondents had not experienced oral stimulation of their genitals. Finally, more females than males reported frequent active (41% versus 38%) and frequent passive (37% versus 34%) oral/genital participation. Athanasious (1972) did another survey involving males and females in America and in France. His second sample mimicked the first in terms of oral/genital activity. Similar results have been reported more recently by Herold and Way (1980).

However, not all people are like the magazine readers surveyed by Athanasious et al. These individuals were rather normally distributed as to amount of exposure to religious principles. Some attended church frequently, others did not go at all, but most were somewhere between those extremes. You might guess that highly religious people would engage in oral/genital contact less frequently than other individuals, and that religious females might be less prone to oral sex than religious males. Michael Young (1980) investigated the behaviors of Southern Baptist college students, where the student body was concerned with religious principles on a daily basis. Overall, females reported less oral/genital activity than males (36% versus 55%), and the activity level for males and females combined was low, compared to that of the Athanasious et al.'s sample. Thus, there was an interaction between gender and the situational factor, level of continuing exposure to religious principles, in the determination of oral/genital behavior. There seems to be no sex difference in oral/genital activity for persons who, on the average, receive little exposure to religious principles. However, for people who are heavily exposed, males are more active than females. This interaction is displayed in Figure 14.3.

Incidentally, highly favorable attitudes toward oral/genital contact predicted participation in that activity. Also, women more than men *reported* that romance was a prerequisite to oral/genital activity. Whether they actually *reacted* differently is another matter. There are important differences between reports of feelings, orientations, and preferences, on the one hand, and actual reactions on the other. We consider these discrepancies thoroughly in the next section.

Pornography.   As far back as Kinsey et al. (Kinsey, Pomeroy, Martin, & Gebhard, 1953), females have reported little interest in erotic pictures, books, and films. That males are more inclined to pornography—or more neutrally, "erotica"—may seem as obvious as the make-up of porno-shop clientele.

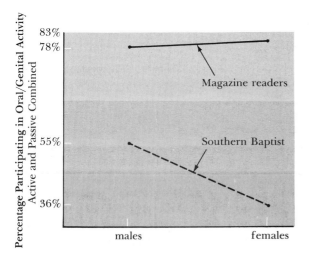

Figure 14.3
Oral/genital activity levels for highly religious persons and persons who are not highly religious *(Athanasious, Shaver, & Tavris, 1970; M. Young, 1980).*

Do men and women differ in their preferences for and reactions to erotica?

If you are among those who think that the sexes are in all respects different in their orientations to erotica, you will likely find the outcomes of recent studies rather surprising. Several studies have shown that the sexes do not differ in actual reactions to erotica, once they have been exposed to it (for example, Fisher & Byrne, 1978, and Heiman, 1975). Underscoring the paradox, Fisher and Byrne reported that females were more likely to rate the erotic materials to which they were exposed as pornographic (negative reaction), to favor restrictions on availability of such materials, to report being less aroused in the past by erotica, and to indicate less contact with erotica.

The relevant situational factor here seems to be pressure on individuals to adopt the role deemed "appropriate" for their biological sex. The more pressure on a female to be feminine, the more she is led to believe that erotica is inappropriate for her, and the more she avoids it. Thus, there may be an interaction between gender and sex typing for the determination of interest in erotic materials. *Sex-typed* persons are heavily invested in the sex role that society assigns to them.

Douglas Kenrick and his colleagues provide support for this interaction (Kenrick, Stringfield, Wagenhals, Dahl, & Ransdell, 1980). Under the guise of setting up an experiment, these researchers had male and female subjects indicate a choice between a "hard-core" erotic film (explicit sex) and a "soft-core" erotic film (only suggestive of sexual interaction). Subjects were free to refuse exposure to any kind of erotic film in favor of a non-erotic movie. Females were significantly more likely to prefer the soft-core film than were males. Almost half of them declined to view an erotic film, while only about a quarter of the male subjects refused.

More important for our purposes, Kenrick et al.'s subjects were divided into those who were sex-typed and those who were androgynous. *Androgynous persons* display behaviors associated with both roles and, thus, are not so bound by what is considered appropriate for people of their biological sex. Females among these individuals may be less inhibited about sexual matters than their sex-typed counterparts and, thus, may be less inclined to think that erotica is not for them. Table 14.1 breaks down the results for sex-typed versus androgynous subjects. As you can see, for sex-typed subjects, males were much more likely to volunteer for the erotic film than were females, but for androgynous subjects, females were actually more likely to volunteer for the erotic film than were males. Pressure to adopt the "sex-appropriate" role, as reflected in sex typing, interacted with gender to determine level of interest in erotica. If, in the future, females become less sex-typed, they may no longer consider erotica inappropriate for them and may become equally as attracted to it as males.

sex-typed persons

androgynous persons

Satisfaction with sex.   Athanasious and colleagues (1970) found that although men reported more interest in sex and more sexual partners, women reported greater satisfaction with their sex lives and more frequent participation in sexual intercourse. It seems that men may simply be more prone to boasting (for example, two high school boys sharing tales of sexual exploits). If verbal responses uttered in a social context and actual physical performance of sexual behavior can be considered different situations, it seems reasonable to hypothesize an interaction between gender and situations for the determination of satisfaction with sex. Men may verbalize more enjoyment of sex, but when it comes to actually performing sexually, women may enjoy sex more. This possibility is depicted in Figure 14.4. Of course, this hypothesis would have to be examined in future research.

Alcohol and sexual behavior.   Another interesting hypothesis that might be profitably investigated is the possible interaction between consumption of alcohol and gender for the determination of sexual enjoyment. Females may enjoy sex more once it is experienced, but one might point to their claimed lack of interest in erotica and argue that they are more sexually inhibited. If that assertion is correct, females may need a source of disinhibition, such as alcohol. Contrary to popular belief, alcohol is a depressant (Baron & Byrne, 1981). Many people tend to think of alcohol as enhancing sexual interest and performance, because it does

TABLE 14.1   Volunteering for an Experiment Involving Erotica: Sex-Typed versus Androgynous Males and Females (Adapted from Kenrick et al., 1980)

	Percentage of males volunteering	Percentage of females volunteering
Sex-typed	85	35
Androgynous	83	100

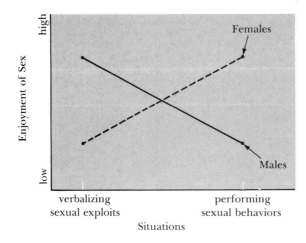

Figure 14.4
Hypothetical interaction between gender (male/female) and sexual behavior (verbal versus physical performance).

lower inhibitions. A few drinks may get rid of sexual guilt, but a few more will likely make it difficult to act according to the whims of the newly liberated conscience. Nevertheless, the fact that alcohol removes sexual inhibitions leads to an interesting prediction. If alcohol gets rid of sexual inhibitions, females should be more likely to report that liquor increases enjoyment of sexual behavior. Athanasious et al. (1970) report that 68% of the women, but only 45% of the men, indicated that alcohol greatly enhanced sexual pleasure. These statistics suggest the hypothesized interaction. The situational factor "type of social gathering (alcohol served versus not served)" may interact with gender for the determination of sexual pleasure. Men will likely enjoy sexual interchanges — kissing, dancing, and later more intimate behavior — associated with a party where the punch is "spiked" about the same as at a gathering where the liquid refreshment is "straight." For women, there may be a difference. Figure 14.5 illustrates this speculation. Experimental support for our hypothesis would help in understanding why females seem to experience as much as or more sexual pleasure than men, but report relatively little interest in sexual matters. They may be just as capable of performing and enjoying sex as men, but may be inhibited by cultural prescriptions.

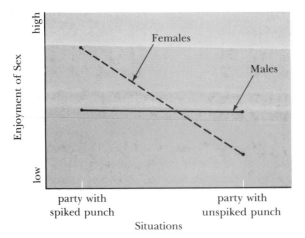

Figure 14.5
Hypothesized interaction between party type (spiked punch/unspiked punch) and gender (male/female) in determining sexual pleasure.

Birth control.   One of the most powerful situational factors to enter the sexual arena in recent years is technologically advanced birth control. It has changed the face of sexuality. Some parents worry that, should they offer birth control to their daughters, they will be providing a license to engage in sexual behavior (S. Gordon, 1976). According to this view, contraception is thought to breed promiscuity (tendency to engage in sexual behavior indiscriminately) in females. Intuitively, contraception provided by parents or made readily available by society might seem to furnish both the approval of and the means by which young women can participate in sexual activity without fear of pregnancy or censure. Such reasoning would lead to the expectation that, for women, the more effective the birth-control method, the greater the likelihood that the user would be promiscuous.

The results of Athanasious et al. (1970) indicate otherwise. The effectiveness of birth-control methods and the number of premarital partners were *unrelated* for female participants in the survey, but positively related for male respondents. A literal interpretation of these results is that the use of effective contraception promotes promiscuity in men, not women. In interaction terms, the more effective were the birth-control methods used by men, the more they were promiscuous, but birth-control effectiveness made no difference for women. More generally, others have noted that contraceptive use does not lead to promiscuity and, in fact, may have the opposite effect (Byrne & Kelly, 1981; S. Gordon, 1976).

How do men and women view people who use contraception? Jazwinski and Byrne (1978) posed this question to male and female subjects after they watched a couple engage in intercourse on film. There were three experimental conditions (situations): the couple was said to have used contraception, not to have used it, or there was no information about contraception. Results revealed an interaction between gender and the situational variable, use of contraception, for determining the degree to which the sexual partners were seen as caring for one another. Males saw the couple as caring more if no contraceptive device had been used than if contraception had been employed. For female subjects, it was the other way around: contraception enhanced the perception that the couple cared for one another. From the man's point of view, she cares for him if she will risk pregnancy. For the woman, he cares for her if he protects her from pregnancy. This interaction is illustrated in Figure 14.6.

Summary.   While the sexes are quite similar in sexual beliefs and behaviors, they do show some differences. Men and women may be equally capable of participating in and enjoying sexual exchanges, but the masculine and feminine sex roles that they adopt may cause them to show different sexual reactions in some situations.

CONFORMITY

To continue with consideration of the person class "gender," as it interacts with situations, we turn now to some topics in the area of social influence. Who influences whom under what circumstances can dictate the relative quality of life for men and women.

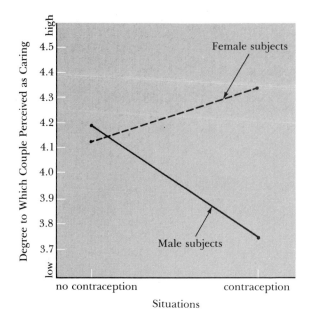

Figure 14.6
Interaction between contraception (present or absent) and gender (male/female), on perceived caring *(adapted from Jazwinski & Byrne, 1978).*

conformity

Throughout most of the history of psychology, it has been assumed that females are more conforming than males (Krech, Crutchfield, & Ballachey, 1962; Worchel & Cooper, 1976). To *conform* is to give up one's own opinion on a given issue for that of other people. Thus, if an individual hears other people express the opinion "the federal government spends too much," and thereafter adopts the same opinion or changes his opinion in the direction of the expression, he has conformed. The feminine sex role, almost universally played by women, is commonly seen as the reason that women presumably conform more. It is assumed that females are taught to be more pliable, more dependent, and more passive — characteristics that would lead to more conformity (Worchel & Cooper, 1976).

Is there a sex difference to explain?   Alice Eagly (1978) became suspicious of the widespread assumption about a sex difference in conformity when she noticed that very few and very old studies were being cited in support of the supposed difference. It seemed almost as though the earlier writers were citing the earliest writers and the more current writers were citing each other. Thus, she did what had somehow not occurred to other psychologists: she looked up all the available studies on conformity. The result was quite a surprise — probably to herself, and certainly to her colleagues. There was, in fact, little evidence in published studies that females conformed more than males. Only when the influencing agent was present during influence attempts did females show even a slight tendency to conform more than males. An *influencing agent* is simply a person who influences others. When the influencing agent was absent or did not exercise surveillance over subjects (see examples to follow), or when persuasive communication was considered, most studies showed no statistically significant sex difference. Table 14.2 displays a summary of Eagly's (1978) findings. Eagly

ALICE EAGLY.
Eagly has contributed to the understanding of attitude-behavior relationships, conformity, and the expectations that arise from observations of the roles women and men typically play.

and Carli (1981) later confirmed these results, but qualified them somewhat. Obviously, the sexes sometimes differ in response to social pressure and sometimes don't. What are the situational factors that interact with gender to determine level of conformity or persuasion?

Materials used in conformity studies. In an already classic study, Frank Sistrunk and John McDavid (1971) investigated an intriguing possibility. They were aware of the well-known fact that people are most likely to show conformity on issues they find uninteresting or irrelevant (Krech, Crutchfield, & Ballachey, 1962). They also recognized that conformity had been studied mainly by male

TABLE 14.2 Sex Differences in Conformity and Persuasibility
(Adapted from Eagly, 1978)

	Percentage females yielding more	Percentage no difference	Percentage males yielding more
Conformity: influencing agent present (60 studies)	33	63	4
Conformity: influencing agent absent (18 studies)	11	83	6
Persuasive communication (54 studies)	19	80	1

experimenters, who probably chose issues primarily of more interest to their own sex. Therefore, Sistrunk and McDavid hypothesized that any tendency for females to conform more than males in typical conformity experiments may be due to the routine use of issues of more interest to males than to females. "Interest value of issues" is the relevant situational factor here. To make their case, Sistrunk and McDavid (1971) selected items involving issues of primary relevance and interest to females, other items involving issues of primary relevance and interest to males, and some issues of no greater relevance or interest to males than to females. All three kinds of items were then formed into a questionnaire, and subjects were asked to indicate whether they agreed with each item.

BOX 14.2	*Conformity Questionnaire**

Majority Response

disagree	23.	Columbus discovered America in 1492.
disagree	24.	It's relatively safe to have babies up to the age of 35, after which birth defects become increasingly likely.
agree	25.	Elton John is strange.
disagree	26.	Prior to Hank Aaron, Roger Maris was the home-run king.
agree	27.	The book is always better than the movie based on it.
disagree	28.	Dr. Spock has more important advice to give than Dr. Ginott.
disagree	29.	Oral-contraceptive use over a long period of time has been linked to cancer.
agree	30.	Basketball is a much more exciting game than football.
disagree	31.	Breast-fed babies are happier babies.
agree	32.	Sex before marriage has been linked to insanity.
disagree	33.	Every U.S. citizen has the right to vote.
disagree	34.	The way a house is constructed can influence the psychological well-being of its inhabitants.
disagree	35.	A football field is 100 yards long and 50 yards wide.
disagree	36.	Something like 90% of all Americans marry for at least a while.
agree	37.	People who masturbate risk going blind.
agree	38.	Women tolerate pain more readily than do men.
agree	39.	To be successful in business, a sense of "teamwork" is required.
disagree	40.	There is a life after death.

* Based on Sistrunk and McDavid, 1971.

Box 14.2 shows a model questionnaire of this type, containing sample items that we devised. Notice that the left-hand column is headed *Majority Response,* and under that heading, the word *agree* or *disagree* is typed beside each item. Subjects were informed that *agree* next to an item meant that at least 51% of a sample of people like themselves had previously endorsed that statement. *Disagree* meant that at least 51% had not approved of the statement. Finally, subjects were told that they could pay attention to or ignore the "majority response," as they pleased. Of course, the "majority-response" method was used to induce conformity of the nonsurveillance variety (subjects completed the questionnaire in private). Pressure to conform was applied by writing "agree" next to a statement that ran counter to some fact, and by writing "disagree" next to a correct statement. For statements that were matters of opinion, "agree" and "disagree" were randomly alternated in the *Majority Response* column.

Across four different experiments, results were exceedingly consistent. There was an interaction between gender and the situational factor, interest value of issues associated with items, in determining level of conformity. Males tended to conform more on items of greater relevance and interest to females; females tended to conform on items of greater relevance and interest to males; and neither conformed more than the other on items of no greater relevance or interest to one sex than to the other.

Currency of reports and sex of authors.   Eagly and Carli (1981) found some support for Sistrunk and McDavid's contention that a bias toward use of items of greater relevance and interest to males exists and partly determines the tendency for females to show conformity. However, they concentrated on other matters. First, as in Eagly (1978), they found that the more recent the study, the less likely were results to show that females conform more. Perhaps sex roles are changing (see Allen, 1978, for a caution related to this possibility). Second, they found that fully 79% of papers reporting research on influence attempts had male authors. Further, compared to female writers, male authors found a stronger tendency for female subjects to be influenced more than their male counterparts (conformity and persuasion studies both were included). Until recently, conformity research has been dominated by males. Perhaps predominantly male experimenters, almost all of whom have adopted the masculine sex role, unwittingly have leaked masculine bias into their experimental procedures. Considering the situational factors "era during which the research was done" and "gender of the researcher," the following interactional statement can be made: in early studies and in those reported by males, females were more likely to yield to social pressure, but in recent studies and those with female researchers, the sexes are less likely to differ.

Additional evidence for interactions is provided by Eagly and her colleagues (Eagly, Wood, & Fishbaugh, 1981). They reasoned that if part of the feminine sex role is greater concern for the maintenance of smooth and conflict-free interpersonal relations, females should conform to a high degree, and to a greater degree than males, when influencing agents can exercise surveillance over them. To not

Are women really more conforming and passive than men? Examples of contemporary leaders such as British Prime Minister Margaret Thatcher lend support to the contention that situational variables have played a role in the definition of many supposed "sex differences."

conform would be to risk disharmony in interpersonal relations. In other words, surveillance should interact with gender to determine level of conformity.

A test of this possibility was devised by first having some male and female psychology students indicate their opinions on some issues during class. Later, subjects were invited to the psychology laboratory, where they faced attempts to change their opinions on 4 of the 20 issues considered in class. Subjects reported in groups of four, two males and two females. Individual subjects were placed in separate cubicles and told that during the experiment, they would form impressions of fellow participants based only on their written opinions. Subjects were to receive and read an opinion on an issue expressed by each of the other three group members, and then form an impression of each member. Next, they were to indicate their own opinion on the issue in question. The task, "forming impressions," was designed to distract subjects from the real purpose of the study. The expression of opinions was repeated four times, once for each of the four issues.

Subjects who were to be under surveillance were told that the other group members would see their opinions. They received opinion forms that included the names of the group members who supposedly had completed the forms, and blank opinion forms having their own names printed on the face. For each issue, a given subject examined each of the opinion forms of the others and provided his or her own impressions and opinion. Then each subject witnessed the experimenter pick up her or his form with the comment "I'll take your opinion form to the other group members." For subjects who were not to be under surveillance, the procedure was the same, except that no names were used on any of the forms, the forms were left on the subjects' desks, and subjects were told that "other members will not see your opinions, because you're last in the sequence." The experimenter added, "Please complete the forms for the purpose of 'experimental control.'"

As shown in Table 14.3, in the surveillance condition, males conformed less than females. In the condition without surveillance, there was no sex difference in conformity. The person factor "gender" interacted with the situational variable "level of surveillance." However, a measure of "concern for the quality of inter-personal relations among group members" failed to yield any effects. Thus, predictions were confirmed, but the assumption that females show greater "concern for interpersonal relations" could not explain results. Because of this outcome, Eagly and her colleagues focused on the male sex role. One reason that males conform less only under surveillance of influencing agents may be that being "independent" and "not easily influenced" is a requirement of the masculine sex role. Males may feel the need to continually put on a show of independence and nonconformity in order to meet that requirement. Ironically, this hypothesis suggests that males may conform less than females under surveillance conditions in order to conform more to their "sex-appropriate" role.

Alternatively, males may conform less under surveillance because they have, on the average, higher status than females in the eyes of members constituting groups to which they belong (Eagly, 1983). This advantage for males benefits them in two important ways. First, because of their relatively high status, males may have more license to defy other members by refusing to accept their opinions. Second, their relatively high status may make males more potent influencing agents. High status may cause their defiant opinions to have more impact on other members, relative to the influence of nonconformity among low-status members. In other words, possession of high status may make males' nonconformity pay off in more successful influence on other group members. Recently, Eagly and Wood (1982) have confirmed the importance of sex differences in status for understanding sex differences in conformity.

In summary, females appear to conform more than males, although the difference is small. Research indicates that the slight sex difference in conformity might be explained by masculine bias built into conformity (and persuasion) experiments, or by the masculine sex role that dictates being "independent" and "not easy to influence." The feminine sex role, encompassing passivity, compliance, and need for smooth interpersonal relations, may be less important in

TABLE 14.3   Results of the Sex and Conformity Study by Eagly et al.[a]

	Male subjects	Female subjects
Surveillance	6.92[b]	8.51
No surveillance	8.12	8.55

[a] A 15-point scale was used, with 15 the greatest possible conformity or agreement with others.

[b] Adapted from Eagly, Wood, & Fishbaugh (1981).

understanding the sex difference in conformity than researchers have traditionally thought it to be.

OBEDIENCE TO AUTHORITY

obedience to
authority

Unlike conformity, *obedience to authority* involves a single influencing agent. Conveying orders is a form of social influence about which there has been considerable controversy. Stanley Milgram conducted a series of studies during the early 1960s that have been among the most important experiments ever done in psychology. Before considering the interaction between gender and situations in determining level of obedience to authority, you may want to review the section on Milgram's work in Chapter 11.

In some 22 studies involving about 1000 subjects, Milgram used only 40 women. In a single experiment, those women obeyed at the same level as men: 65% went all the way to the end to the series of switches. Based on this one experiment, Milgram (1974) has confidently asserted that there is no gender difference in tendency to obey. Allen (1978) notes that Milgram was aware of other studies relevant to the possible gender difference, but appeared to ignore them. A review of those studies has led to a qualification of Milgram's contention (Allen, 1978).

There were three studies considered in Allen's review. Sheridan and King (1972) had male and female college students actually shock a "cute" puppy. Their procedures were much like Milgram's, except that the puppy had to "learn" to respond to signal lights at either end of a cage with an electrified floor. If the puppy was pointed toward the left light when the subject's score sheet indicated that orientation to the right was the correct response, he received a shock. Of course, the problem was impossible for the puppy to solve, and the score sheet allowed for many incorrect responses.

Sheridan and King reported that 100% of female subjects obeyed fully, whereas only 54% of the males showed complete obedience. They implied that their female subjects suffered more — protesting, cringing, and even crying — but that observed sex difference in reactions to the experience of shocking the puppy was not statistically significant.

Kilham and Mann (1974) repeated the Milgram experiment almost exactly, except that their male and female subjects served in a chain of command. When males were subjects, a male experimenter commanded a male subject to administer the learning task and inform another male when to shock a male learner and how much shock to apply. The male experimenter also started the chain involving female administrators, female "shockers," and female learners. Overall, 54% of the males obeyed fully, but only 28% of the females were completely obedient. The researchers speculated that lower obedience by females may have been partly the result of having a member of the opposite sex order females "to do in" a member of their own sex — a circumstance that didn't hold for males.

Being aware that results pertaining to possible sex differences in obedience had been mixed, and suspecting that gender of the authority figure might be important, Greg Smith (1973) had males and females perform a trivial task at the behest of either a male or a female authority figure. Subjects arrived for an experiment only to find a note, signed by a male or a female, containing the message "The experiment for which you are to receive credit will start later. In the meantime, staple these questionnaires." Also present were items obviously belonging to a male or a female (for example, a man's or a woman's coat was draped over a chair). Obedience was measured by the number of questionnaires stapled in a 15-minute period. The experimenter, stationed in the adjoining hallway, started the timing upon hearing the first click of the stapler. Results disclosed that females obeyed more than males *regardless* of whether a male or a female experimenter had left the written order.

The review ended with the comment that Milgram had been hasty in concluding "no sex difference" (Allen, 1978). In view of the small number of studies and the mixed results, no conclusion seemed the best conclusion. However, since Allen (1978) went to press (in 1976), two additional studies have been published by Jordanian psychologists Mitri Shanab and Khawla Yahya (1977, 1978). Taken together, these new experiments are noteworthy in that male and female subjects were employed, a female served as the experimenter, and subjects varied in age from 6 years to adulthood. No sex difference was found in either study for any age range. Thus, we suggest an amendment to Allen's (1978) conclusion. We predict that future experiments will reveal no *overall* sex difference in obedience. Table 14.4 summarizes the studies that contrast the sexes on obedience.

TABLE 14.4 Summaries of Procedures and Results of Studies of Sex Differences in Obedience

Researcher(s)	Procedure	Results
Milgram (1974)	40 women perform in the teacher/learner experiment.	As in comparable studies with males, 65% obey fully.
Sheridan and King (1972)	At the behest of an authority figure, male and female college students shock a "cute" puppy.	100% of the females and 54% of the males obey fully.
Kilham and Mann (1974)	Milgram's experiment repeated using both males and females, who are ordered by a male experimenter to administer shocks.	54% of the males and 28% of females comply fully.
G. Smith (1973)	Male and female subjects perform a trivial task at the behest of a male or a female experimenter.	Females show more obedience, regardless of sex of the experimenter.
Shanab and Yahya (1977, 1978)	Milgram's experiment repeated using child to adult subjects of both sexes and a female experimenter.	Sex and age make no difference in level of obedience displayed by subjects.

The existence of some studies finding males more obedient, others showing more obedience in females, and still others reporting no difference makes it almost certain that level of obedience is influenced by interactions between gender and situations. However, these same studies do not reveal which situations generate a difference between the sexes in obedience and which yield no difference. Perhaps identification of those situations should be the focus of research in the future.

AGGRESSION

aggression

It is widely believed that females are less aggressive than males. The examples of "sex differences" already discussed suggest that this bit of "common knowledge" may deserve another look. Could it be that sex differences in aggression depend on the situation?

As Baron (1977) points out, many more males than females have served as subjects in aggression experiments. However, there are a sufficient number of studies available that involved female subjects to allow for a statement about an overall difference between the sexes. Over time, studies of aggression have probably found females less aggressive than males more often than not (Baron, 1977). Perhaps females do actually, openly express aggression less often than do males. However, change in many situations may have accompanied evolution of the culture. Baron (1977) notes that sexual equality with regard to aggression is a more likely result, the more recent the study. This possibility is consistent with the observation that, as time goes by, the restraints placed on females have lessened (Baron & Byrne, 1982). As you recall, Eagly and Carli (1981) came to a similar conclusion with regard to conformity.

The evidence for interactions comes from a couple of experimental observations. First, there appears to be an interaction between the situational factor "amount of provocation" and gender for the determination of aggression. Baron (1977) reports that females are likely to aggress less than males only when provocation is weak (for example, a mild insult; see Chapter 12). With strong provocation, the sex difference disappears. Second, a recent study showed that whether aggression is public (thereby strongly invoking the "sex-appropriate" role) or private interacts with sex of subject to determine level of aggression. In fact, whether there is present any stimulus to invoke the "appropriate" sex role — such as another person of the same sex — apparently interacts with gender to determine level of aggression.

Deborah Richardson, Sandy Berstein, and Stuart Taylor (1979) investigated this interaction using a method devised by Taylor. Figure 14.7 gives a clear idea of how their procedure works. Please turn to it before proceeding.

Each of the subjects was told that she would engage in a reaction-time contest against a male who was supposedly in an adjoining room. There were three conditions. In the "public" condition, a female collaborator passed herself off as a student whose advisor had requested that she observe an experiment. In the "private" condition, the observer was absent. In the "supportive-other" condition, the observer urged the subject to retaliate. The experiment consisted of four blocks of opportunities for the reaction-time competition. With successive blocks,

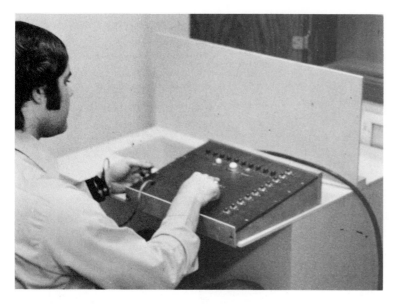

Figure 14.7
Apparatus for the Stuart Taylor procedure. The subject has his finger on the "reaction-time button." Above, a light is illuminated to signal positioning of finger on button. At the top, a series of lights tells the subject, before the signal, what level of shock the "other subject" will deliver if the real subject "loses" the trial. Down the right-hand side is a bank of switches for indicating shock level to be delivered by the real subject should the "other" subject "lose." Note the cuff for delivery of shocks to the subject's left wrist.

there was an increase in the intensity of the shocks delivered to the subject when she lost a trial of the reaction-time contest.

With Taylor's method, aggression is shown if the subject increases shock level with each increase by the competitor. As shown in Figure 14.8, in the public condition, increases in the intensity of shocks delivered to the subject with each successive block of contest opportunities were *not* accompanied by increases in the intensity of the shocks subjects delivered to the male contestant. However, in the private condition, the "sex-appropriate" role, gentleness aspect, was not likely to be invoked, since there was no observer. Here, shock intensity increased with each successive block until a high level was reached. Similarly, when the sex role was suspended because a person of the same sex was urging the subject to shock the competitor, the intensity of the shocks delivered by subjects increased with each successive block.

The study by Richardson and her colleagues only partially confirms the gender-by-situation interaction, because of the lack of male subjects. Had male subjects been competing with other males, it would be expected that the "macho" aspect of the masculine role would dictate increases across blocks in the shock intensities delivered by males performing in public (as you recall from Chapter 12, males shocking females is a complicated matter). Figure 14.9 shows this hypothetical result. Males in private would be expected to perform like females in public, since in private the expectation that males should be aggressive would not be invoked. A comparison of Figures 14.8 and 14.9 indicates that *no* sex difference is expected in the supportive-other condition. Support from the same-sex "observer" would invoke the masculine role for males and would release females from the feminine role, thus forcing males to aggress and allowing aggression in females.

Looking across Figures 14.8 and 14.9, you can appreciate the interaction between situations (public, private, and "supportive other") and gender. (This

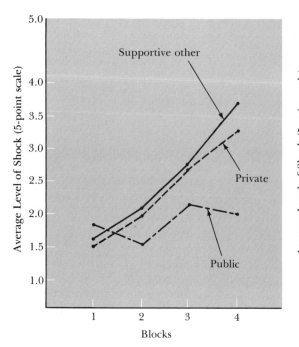

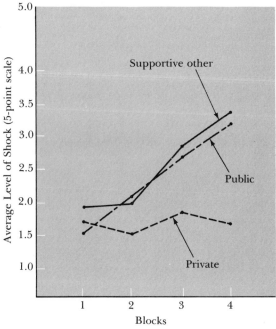

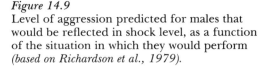

Figure 14.8
Level of aggression reflected in shock level, as a function of the situation in which female subjects performed *(adapted from Richardson et al., 1979).*

Figure 14.9
Level of aggression predicted for males that would be reflected in shock level, as a function of the situation in which they would perform *(based on Richardson et al., 1979).*

technically more complicated interaction has been simplified for these purposes.) Aggression may be the same for the sexes when a supportive person of the same sex is present, but different under public and private conditions.

Additional research indicates that the social/physical context in which aggressiveness is displayed may be an important determinant of whether a gender difference is observed. Towson and Zanna (1982) had males and females imagine that they had been provoked either in a "woman's situation" (dance-exercise room) or a "man's situation" (weight-lifting room). Then they were asked to state how typical persons like themselves would react to the provocation. Males indicated more aggression in the "weight room" than did females, but there was no sex difference for the "dance room."

The possible interaction between gender and situation can be summarized by suggesting that, while females may display less aggression on a day-to-day basis (Maccoby & Jacklin, 1974), they are capable of showing equally as high a level of aggression as exhibited by males (Deaux, 1984). This may be particularly true if males and females are asked to imagine themselves in an extreme situation. One of the authors asked introductory social-psychology students to indicate whether, in time of war, they would kill women and children, as Lieutenant Calley and his men allegedly did during the My Lai incident in Viet Nam. A total of 8 females and 7 males, or 36% of the sample, answered in the affirmative; 12 females and 11 males, or 55% of the sample, answered negatively. The remaining 4 males, 9%, were undecided. These results were replicated about a year later. Although the outcome was not as extreme as in an earlier survey (Kelman & Lawrence, 1972), one could certainly argue that the results of the survey are alarming. However, no one could contend that a sex difference is clearly indicated by the findings. Admiral Elmo Zumwalt, former head of the U. S. Navy, offers an authoritative opinion that females are as capable of aggression as are males. His observations of female Viet Cong have convinced him that women can serve in combat alongside men (1980 interview by *Peoria Journal Star* columnist Art Andrews). Women may aggress less than men on a day-to-day basis, but "combat" is an extreme situation in which the gender difference may disappear.

In their classic text on sex differences, Maccoby and Jacklin (1974) reported few established sex differences, but confidently stated that studies show males to be more aggressive than females. Along with the evidence just presented, recent examinations of the strength of sex effects on aggression indicate that Maccoby and Jacklin were guilty of overstatement. Janet Hyde (1983) reported that sex of subjects controlled only about 6% of the variance in aggressiveness (see Chapter 13). That is, 94% of the variation in aggressiveness is controlled by factors other than sex.

Incidentally, Maccoby and Jacklin also indicated that while females have greater verbal abilities, males are superior in mathematical and visual/spatial abilities (being able to perceive in depth and distance and to conceive in multiple dimensions). Again, they appear to have been incorrect by way of overstatement. Hyde (1981) found that sex controlled only 1% of the variation in verbal ability, 1% of the variation in mathematical ability, and 4.5% of the variation in visual/spatial ability. Additionally, Eagly, Renner, and Carli (1983) found little difference between the sexes in giving and receiving help. Like Unger (1979), Hyde (1983) concludes that similarities between the sexes are the rule, not differences.

ANXIETY

Two comprehensive reviews by Maccoby and Jacklin (1974) and Hoyenga and Hoyenga (1979) conclude that females generally score higher on tests of anxiety (see Chapter 10 for a more general discussion of anxiety). The possible   anxiety
gender difference has been investigated using two different methods. *Longitudinal studies* follow single individuals over several days, weeks, months, or even years. Multiple measures are taken on each individual at several points in time. *Cross-sectional studies* involve multiple measures of two or more groups taken at a single point in time. In cross-sectional studies, any difference between groups may exist only on the single measurement occasion that was chosen. Thus, longitudinal studies have an important advantage. Should a researcher find that one group studied longitudinally differs, on the average, from another group studied in the same way, the result cannot be explained as a chance difference that could occur when groups are compared on a single occasion.

Stephany Joy and Paula Wise (1983) provide an example of a cross-sectional study of anxiety using the Adjective Generation Technique (AGT) (Allen & Potkay, 1983a). The AGT entails instructing subjects to record (usually) five adjectives that are descriptive of themselves. The adjectives are then scored for anxiety by reference to a list of 2200 adjectives whose values vary over seven degrees of anxiety (0 – 6; the list also contains values on two other dimensions; see Allen & Potkay, 1983a). Each of the adjectives generated by a subject is given a value from the list (the value for a given adjective is the sum over 100 ratings, or 0-600). The average (mean) of the five values assigned to the adjectives becomes the subject's anxiety score. Female and male undergraduates completed the AGT for Joy and Wise as a part of an investigation concerning how maternal employment during childhood might affect offspring after they have grown to college age. Results indicated that females showed significantly higher scores on anxiety as measured by the AGT. Earlier, Maccoby and Jacklin (1974) had speculated that females' higher scores are due to their greater honesty in reporting reactions to the anxiety-provoking stimuli constituting typical measures of anxiety. Joy and Wise disagreed. The AGT involves few if any effective stimuli, and none that would provoke anxiety. Therefore, females' alleged greater honesty could not account for their higher anxiety scores.

An example of a longitudinal study is one conducted by Charles Potkay (Allen & Potkay, 1983a). Nine female and seven male students described themselves for 28 consecutive days during an AGT self-study project. For the entire period of the study, females showed greater average anxiety than males. Although the difference was slight, it can be taken seriously, because it is entirely consistent with other male/female comparisons on anxiety as measured by the AGT. It is also in tune with the literature reviews mentioned above.

There seems to be widespread agreement that females show more anxiety than males. However, it is implausible to assert that this would be the case in every situation. Just as the interaction between public/private and male/female helps to explain the possible sex difference in expressing aggression, interactions between sex and situations may shed some light on the difference between the sexes in anxiety. Although females show more anxiety overall, they may display less anxiety than males in certain situations, and the same level of anxiety under other circumstances. For example, females may show more anxiety than males in a situation where "looking good" is important, such as a formal dance. After all, the burden of being attractive falls more heavily on females (Allen, 1978). On the other hand, males may be more anxious in a situation involving "evaluation of skills," because they are pressured to be highly skilled (Deaux & Wrightsman, 1984).

Finally, it may in time be found that the gender difference in anxiety exists mainly at the level of expression rather than in terms of actual experience. It may be found that *capabilities* for experiencing anxiety are equal for the sexes, just as seems to be true for aggression. Further, in time, two important observations may be made concerning the overall sex difference in anxiety. First, variance-components methods like those discussed in the previous chapter may reveal that the sex difference is small, similar to differences between the sexes in mathematical ability, verbal ability, and conformity. Second, the difference may fade as the culture and associated sex roles change.

Interactionism: A Summary

Interactions between situations and the person factors authoritarianism, self-monitoring, and Type A/Type B have helped to explain a variety of behaviors. Also, interactionism has been useful in understanding gender similarities and differences in sexual attitudes and behaviors, conformity, obedience, aggression, and anxiety. While there may be no overall difference between two person categories, considering interactions will often lead to the conclusion that differences do exist for at least some situations. Taking interactions into account may also lead to the discovery that an assumed difference between person categories is actually due to a big difference in only one or two situations (for example, Type A/Type B differences in performance depend on the kind of task). Finally, even in the more usual case where there is no overall difference between person categories, the consideration of interactions may allow for the specification of exceptions to the "rule" (for example, exposure to religious principles and gender for determination of oral/genital contact).

In short, things aren't as simple as they seem. Human behavior is terribly complicated. Rather than being able to say that some category of a person factor is always or even usually different from another category, both professional and lay students of human behavior may be better off looking for the *situations* in which one category of persons differs from another, and the *situations* in which the difference is reversed or is non-existent. Considerations such as these indicate that interactionism may be a more fruitful approach to the study of personality than one that concentrates on person factors alone.

CHAPTER REVIEW

This chapter examines interactions between different classes of person factors and situations. A member of the trait class, authoritarianism, was seen to interact with a situational factor, social status, in the determination of level of aggression. The type class was represented by Type A/Type B. Classification into these two categories interacted with type of task in determining preference for working alone as opposed to working with others. In the social-style class, self-monitoring interacted with kind of advertisement in determining how much subjects were willing to pay for products.

The fourth person class is gender, or cultural aspects of being male and female. Contrasting the sexes is so complex that it may be more fruitfully conceived in terms of interactions rather than simple distinctions. This may be particularly true in the realm of sexual behavior and beliefs. For example, females are not necessarily less disposed to oral/genital contact or less satisfied with their sex lives. The differences exist for some situations and not for others. To put it differently, the person factor, gender, interacts with social situations to determine sexual behaviors and beliefs. Also, differences exist in how the sexes react to birth control and alcohol, but only in some situations. For reactions to erotica, gender differences may be displayed by sex-typed individuals but not by androgynous persons.

It seems that females are a bit more inclined to conform and to be persuaded. However, the differences are small and can probably be explained by interactions of gender with situational factors such as experimental bias, cultural conditions, and the fact that males have produced most of the conformity research.

The evidence relevant to a possible gender difference in obedience to authority is meager at present, but suggests no difference. As was the case with conformity, the answer to the question of possible gender differences will hinge on the identification of situations in which the sexes differ and ones in which they don't differ.

Females probably display less aggression than males under everyday circumstances, but the difference may be explained by gender/situation interactions and by sex roles. Sex roles are changing over time, and so is the tendency for females to display less aggression in psychological experiments. Also, it is possible to eliminate the gender difference experimentally, by making both male and female subjects very angry. Finally, public versus private situations were shown to interact with gender in determining level of aggression.

The evidence seems to indicate that females are more anxious, as indicated by scores on standard anxiety tests. Undoubtedly, future research will demonstrate that this difference is true only for some situations.

Someday, additional research may reveal that differences in person factors are not general. Rather, differences exist for some situations and similarities for others. For these reasons, interactionism may be the "wave of the future" in the field of personality.

KEY CONCEPTS

Classes of person factors
Authoritarianism and social status
Type A/Type B personalities and stress
Self-monitoring and advertisements
Gender and situations
   Sexual behavior and attitudes

Sex-typed persons
   Androgynous persons
Conformity
Obedience to authority
Aggression
Anxiety

REVIEW QUESTIONS

1. If person factors were the essential determinants of behavior, what general expectation would you have about individuals' behavior in different situations? How does this expectation differ from the research results reviewed in this chapter?
2. With what situational factors did authoritarianism, Type A/Type B, and self-monitoring interact? Draw a graph of each interaction.
3. List and describe factors that interact with gender to determine sexual behavior and beliefs.

4. What factors interact with gender to determine level of conformity and of aggression?
5. Speculate about the factors that may interact with gender for the determination of level of obedience and of anxiety.
6. How does the evidence presented in this chapter support the contention that interactionism may lead to discoveries that would not be found using a pure trait approach to personality?

PART FOUR

Integrating Perspectives

THIS CONCLUDING PORTION of the book integrates much of the material presented in preceding chapters. First, we are concerned with "self-concept," or personality as seen from the "inside" (Chapter 15). That consideration allows us to explore the development of personality in detail. Self-concept is also significant in its own right. You will learn that it has great practical importance to you in your everyday life. Our last chapter pulls together the various issues and themes we have discussed throughout the book. Here you will be able to review your own orientation to personality. We end with a look into the future of personality theory and research.

15

Self-Concept and Personality Development

How do we develop a sense of self?

Is an identity crisis a good thing?

Do people go through identifiable stages in developing a conscience?

How can an inadequate self-concept be corrected?

I N THIS CHAPTER, we focus on *self-concept,* a variation of personality. In effect, self-concept is the individual's own perception of his or her personality. As aspects of self-concept are threaded through several theories, you will gain insights into how personality develops and how self-concept links theories. After looking at self-concept and related ideas from several theoretical perspectives, you will also have a better understanding of your own self-concept and how it came to be.

Notions of "self" are many in number and varied in content. We have already considered some ideas about "self" in a broad, general sense — for example, those of Jung and Rogers. In addition, there are more specific notions, such as *self-identity, self-image, self-esteem,* and of course, *self-concept.* It is this last idea with which we are concerned here — but what about the others? We need a way to account for the several words that begin with *self.* Gordon W. Allport provides what we need. Thus, we will begin with his account of the more specific notions of self, especially self-concept.

Allport's contributions suggest the central importance of "identity." Accordingly, we turn second to probably the strongest contributor to the understanding of identity, Erik H. Erikson. Another issue raised by Allport is "conscience and morality." A sense of morality is very important to the self-concept. Because the work of Lawrence Kohlberg has probably created the greatest interest in morality in recent years, his theory is considered next.

Having covered the needed theoretical background, we turn to implications of our contention that self-concepts are individuals' own perceptions of their personalities. We focus on the thorny problem of how one can have a meaningful conception of oneself in view of the behavioral inconsistency documented in the immediately preceding chapters. Some new ideas about criteria for traits help us with our problem.

Ideas about self-concept have direct application to real-life issues, as you will see when we consider the problem of inadequate self-concept. How can an inadequate self-concept be corrected? In the final section of the chapter, we present suggestions that emerge from the theories of the personologists discussed in earlier portions of this book.

Gordon Allport: The Sense of Self

In possibly his most important written work, Allport (1961) devotes a chapter to what he calls "sense of self." Because of the confusions revolving around notions of "self," he invented his own label for the sense of self—*proprium.* The pro-

sense of self

proprium

GORDON ALLPORT.
A psychologist for all seasons,
Allport has done respected work in
a number of areas, including social
psychology, experimental psychology, and personality.

prium is "me as felt and known . . . the self as 'object' of knowledge and feeling"
(p. 127). An examination of several books in personality and general psychology,
including those that deal specifically with self-concept, reveals that Allport's sense
of self, or proprium, is essentially the same as self-concept. For example, Ruth
Wylie (1974) begins her book on self-concept with the following definition: the
"actual self or real self, that is, his concept of himself as he actually is" (p. 8).
Literal translations of *sense of self* and *self-concept* are "one's perception of oneself"
and "one's conception of oneself," respectively. Thus, we will consider *sense of self,*
proprium, and *self-concept* to be one and the same, and no further distinctions will
be made among the three terms. Now we can turn to the question of how Allport's
idea of self-concept encompasses those other, more specific, notions of self.

PERSONALITY DEVELOPMENT: THE EVOLVING SELF-CONCEPT

Allport's seven
stages of
self-concept
development

Allport (1961) sees the self-concept as evolving over the childhood years. He
organizes the development of self-concept around seven stages.

Early infancy.   The first stage, *early infancy,* is characterized as involving no
sense of self. Infants initially are unable to separate themselves from their environment. They are conscious, but not self-conscious. If an infant picks up an
object, the fingers and the object are one and the same. If she hurts her own foot,
she has no idea that it is *she* who inflicted the pain. She sort of melts into Mother,
and they become fused. Later, as motor skills help the infant work out of this early
phase, she crawls about and bumps into objects. In this way, the infant learns that

there are "things" that are apart from her body. The vague perception that there are objects "out there" in another world comes with this new awareness. However, the infant doesn't yet know that she is apart and distinct from that other world.

Bodily self.   The most primitive predecessor of self-concept is *bodily self.* During the second part of the first year, infants become aware of sensations that emanate from the muscles, joints, tendons, eyes, ears, and so on. These sensations constitute the bodily self. Frustrations relating to the body, such as a stubbed toe or an unsatisfied hunger, also contribute to appreciation of the bodily self. The bodily self becomes the foundation of the self-concept and remains with us forever. However, the bodily self is rarely noticed. Only under unusual conditions, such as the sensory deprivation associated with driving at night on an unlighted road, is the bodily self apparent. People undergoing sensory deprivation report loss of a sense of self (Bexton, Heron, & Scott, 1954). Allport (1961) suggests a way of appreciating how all your bodily parts and elements are "you": contrast swallowing your own saliva with spitting it into a cup and drinking it. Your saliva is a part of you that you take for granted, until it becomes physically separated from your body—then it's alien.

bodily self

Self-identity.   The bodily self is only the first chapter, not the whole story of the self. During the second year of life, Allport's third stage, a more advanced sense of self emerges, called *self-identity.* Self-identity is the continuity of self over past, present, and future that results from the operation of memory. "Today I remember some of my thoughts of yesterday, and tomorrow I shall remember some of my thoughts of both yesterday and today; and I am certain that they are the thoughts of the same person—of myself" (Allport, 1961, p. 114). Because we all are changing over time, even as adults, this feeling of continuity is essential to a self-concept. Of course, the learning of language underlies the ability to appreciate continuity. The thoughts that one remembers that assure him he is the same person today as yesterday are in the form of words. The most important of those verbal thoughts is the child's name. A child named Johnny will remember "Johnny went to the store yesterday." The child's name is a sort of anchor to which the ship of self-identity is tied. Each time our hypothetical child hears "Johnny"—as in "Where's Johnny's nose?" "Good, Johnny!" "Johnny, stop that!"—his feeling of self-identity is strengthened.

self-identity

Self-esteem.   If bodily self is the cornerstone of self-concept, and self-identity its framework, we still have only the beginnings of a structure. Some walls and a roof must yet go up. One of the needed parts involves self-evaluation. *Self-esteem* can be translated literally as "the esteem in which one holds oneself." Allport was a bit more restrictive in his definition of self-esteem. For him, self-esteem is pride in one's pursuits and accomplishments. During the third year, Allport's fourth stage, one of the child's favorite exclamations is "Let me!" "Me" has evolved beyond just a body and a sense of continuity to a feeling of instrumentality—the capability to successfully manipulate the environment. Part and parcel of this prideful insistence on doing for oneself is a refusal to let others

self-esteem

do for one. "I can do it" implies "You mustn't do it for me, or it will look as though I can't do it." Born with self-esteem is its fraternal twin, negativism. Allport relates the case of a child whose greeting upon arrival at his grandmother's house was "Grandmother, I won't." If pride results from successful operation in one's environment, shame follows the failure implied by permitting others to do for oneself. In a sense, a child learns to say "I am what I am able to do; don't diminish me by doing for me."

Extension of self.   A sense of body, of continuity, and of pride is a great part of our self-concept structure, but not nearly the whole. Yet to be taken into account is the most important part of the environment—other people. During Allport's fifth stage, bounded by the years 4 to 6, the child develops a fourth aspect of the self-concept and begins a fifth. Especially in the early part of the fifth stage, children are egocentric. They think that God, Santa Claus, Mom, and Dad are there to serve them. However, this self-focus contains an advancement. "He" becomes not merely himself, but is extended to include all that he "possesses." It is "his dog, his house, his sister." According to Allport, the *extension of self* involves expanding oneself to include all those significant aspects of one's environment, including people. Now, the family is united with the self. They are like an external conscience that may turn on the child should he fail.

extension of self

Self-image.   Related to this emergent relationship to others is the fugitive *self-image* that begins to develop also during the fifth stage, ages 4 to 6. The self-image is composed of the hopes and aspirations that develop from the perceptions and expectations that others have of oneself. Parents say of the child that she is "good" or "naughty." Peers say that she is "smart" or "fat." She learns that

self-image

The development of identity is a central concept for both Allport and Erikson.

she must talk "dirty" when with friends, but "nice" when home with her parents. She must do this, do that, be this, be that — whatever others expect. To discover whether she is living up to her developing self-image, she will compare others' expectations of how she should behave with her actual behavior.

Rational coper.   During the sixth stage, covering ages 6 to 12, the self-image continues to develop, and the child begins to develop the self as a *rational coper*. The self as a rational coper is not merely able to solve problems, but can reason them through "in the head" and come up with logical solutions. Allport indicates that the rational coper is much like Freud's ego (see Chapter 3). Like the ego, the rational self tries to efficiently satisfy the demands of the body (id), the external environment, and society (superego). As the rational coper develops, children become able to think about thinking.

rational coper

Propriate striving.   During the seventh stage, adolescence, the individual continues to develop the self-image and experiences a renewed search for self-identity. The self-identity problem becomes tying together the teenager and the would-be adult. A teen may ask "How can I be an adult and still be me?" Continuity must be maintained in the face of a major transition from one phase of life to the next. Society does little to solve the teenager's dilemma. Some states grant permission to drive during early adolescence; others do not. A teenager can join the army, but can't buy a drink. Teens must pay full price to get into a movie, but they can't see an R-rated film unless their parents accompany them. So they experiment in the form of rebellion. They stay out late, drink, and become sexually active — all the while hoping that their parents' restrictions on these activities will help define them. They want to become adults, but at the same time be faithful to themselves as they were. Finally, the rebirth of their search for identity evolves to the selection of a career and life goals. At this point, yet another component of self-concept comes into play —*propriate striving*.

propriate striving

Propriate striving is planning for the future by setting long-range goals toward which one wishes to work. During adolescence, the individual comes to realize that success in life will depend on planning ahead. To involve legitimate propriate striving, goals must be reasonably narrowly focused and in tune with the individual's capabilities. Earlier, there may have been thoughts of being a movie star, a famous athlete, or some less glamorous but equally heroic figure, such as a fire fighter or a crusading lawyer. Now, to be mature and thus fit the notion of propriate striving, goals must be realistic and married to a step-by-step plan for accomplishment.

PATTERNS

Allport also sees certain patterns emerge from the evolution of the self-concept. These patterns are subjective conditions that influence the functioning as well as the structuring of personality and involve, in varying degrees, aspects of the self-concept such as self-esteem, self-image, rational coping, and propriate striving. Allport defines two patterns: feelings of inferiority, and conscience. Both lead into important matters of self-concept that are covered later in this chapter.

patterns

feelings of
inferiority

Feelings of inferiority.   The first pattern, *feelings of inferiority,* involves perceptions of deficiency because of physical weakness, unpleasant appearance, sexual impotence, or social inadequacy (for example, poverty). Here, Allport follows Adler rather closely (see Chapter 4). He writes of college women who, by virtue of their selection to outstanding universities, are the intellectual equal of their male counterparts, but who feel inferior to the men who share their classes because society has defined them as lesser. Inferiority, then, is a problem of self-image—living up to, or down to, others' expectations. Men are expected to be "better," and thus women see themselves as "worse," even in the face of contrary evidence (we must remember that Allport was writing on this issue more than two decades ago). Allport also anticipates Rotter's internal locus of control (Chapter 6) when he reports that people with feelings of inferiority believe that the average citizen has little or no influence on the course of events in a democracy.

Like Adler, Allport indicates that compensation is a method for dealing with inferiority. He writes of *compensation*—the unathletic boy who turns to his studies—and *overcompensation*—the frail child who becomes the mighty big-game hunter (Theodore Roosevelt). *Defense mechanisms* can also be used to handle inferiority. The all-too-firm handshake to hide insecurity, the bullying manner to hide inner weakness, beards to hide imperfect facial features, thick-soled shoes to bolster a small stature, and overuse of flattery are examples of defense mechanisms at work. *Rationalization* is a technique for curing the "wound to self-esteem" that Allport believes accompanies inferiority. Seeing fine athletes as "dumb jocks," intellectuals as impractical "eggheads," and a pretty face as "lacking character" are cases of rationalization. Finally, *autistic thinking* can be an extreme mode of dealing with feelings of inferiority. The autistic thinker dwells in a world of fantasy in which all sorts of improbable but powerful roles are filled at will (recall Sullivan's theory, Chapter 4). One can be a queen, an avenging judge, a world leader—whatever it takes to rise above the squalor of inferiority.

conscience

Conscience.   The second pattern, *conscience,* is an indicator, like a thermometer, that tells people some activity on their part is disrupting, or has disrupted, an important aspect of their self-image. A "good" conscience seems to be almost "not there." Those who have such a conscience go about their business without the internal censor making itself known. Those who are not so fortunate cower in the face of a "bad" or "outraged" conscience that nags them without end.

Allport writes that early conscience is the "must" sayer and late conscience is the "ought" sayer. The child of the first few stages learns that she must do that and must not do this, or she will be punished. Children are "moral realists," learning the rules and adhering to them lest something bad happen. Young children do as they must, mainly when the punishing agent is present, but backslide in his or her absence (recall the discussion in Chapters 5 and 12). Older children internalize the rules and correct themselves (as well as everyone else) when they go astray. By adolescence, individuals are in an identity crisis, manifested by ridicule and defiance of parental rules. They try to cast off the conscience that parents, peers, and society have forced upon them and build their own. At this point, conscience shifts from outside the self-concept to within. Now, self-esteem is bolstered by doing what is "right." The self-image includes aspiring to do what *ought* to be done, and propriate striving encompasses plans to be a fair, kind, altruistic, and otherwise worthwhile person. As the adolescent passes into adulthood, he no longer performs good deeds to avoid a vengeful conscience, but to strive actively for worthy goals that will support a mature self-image.

TABLE 15.1 Allport's Evolving Sense of Self

	Proprium (the self as felt and known)	
Stage	Aspect of self-concept	Definition
1	Early infancy	No sense of self
2	Bodily self	Awareness of bodily sensations
3	Self-identity	Continuity of self
4	Self-esteem	Pride in one's pursuits
5	Extension of self	Self includes significant aspects of environment
	Self-image	Hopes and aspirations based on others' expectations
6	Rational coper	Reasoning and solving problems "in the head"
7	Propriate striving	Planning for the future

	Patterns
Feelings of inferiority	Wounded self-esteem; inadequate self-image
Conscience	A self-image including what *ought* to be done; propriate striving encompassing plans to be fair

Table 15.1 summarizes Allport's theory regarding the various aspects of self-concept and the stages at which they come into play, as well as the two crucial patterns, feelings of inferiority and conscience. The section that comes next describes another "stage theory" — one that expands on one of Allport's central concepts, *identity*.

Erik Erikson: Identity Crises

Erik H. Erikson was a person with a long-standing identity problem, reflected in his name and apparently solved by application of his theory to himself. Erik Homburger Erikson — literally, Erik son of Erik, stepson of Jewish physician Theodor Homburger — never knew his real father and never was quite sure what role to assign his stepfather ("Erik Erikson," 1970). He was born in 1902, the son of a German mother and a Danish father, who abandoned his mother before his birth (E. Hall, 1983). Apparently, all he has of his biological father is the name Erik. As a child, Erikson was well treated by his stepfather. Earlier in his career, he used the physician's surname as his own, but his ambivalence showed later when he relegated Homburger to a middle initial. However, the confusion about his stepfather was only a rare outward sign of the identity crises that occurred repeatedly. An ideal Aryan in appearance — he was tall and blond — Erikson faced taunts served up by the children at his father's synagogue; at the same time, he was shunned by some of his German schoolmates because of his stepfather's religion. Later, he toyed with the idea of following in his stepfather's professional foot-

ERIK ERIKSON.
Erikson's own struggle with
defining his identity led him to
construct a theory that has influenced millions of people. His
writings made him a hero to young
people in the 1960s; today, he has
also become a champion of the
elderly.

steps, but then threw it aside, turning his back on formal education after achieving only a high school diploma. The lack of advanced degrees would haunt Erikson when he later joined the faculty at Harvard (Keniston, 1983). How did this vacillation between one kind of identity and another affect the young Erikson? " 'I was,' he recalls, 'morbidly sensitive' " ("Erik Erikson," 1970, p. 87). Nevertheless, Erikson did not succumb to the crises that fate had forced on him. Rather, he used them to construct a theory that would be a great help to many of the millions of people in search of identity.

ERIKSON'S VIEW OF IDENTITY

Like Allport, Erikson believes that identity is a reoccurring theme. Also like Allport, Erikson writes of crises, in which identity expands and changes its focus or regresses back toward immaturity. However, Erikson's point of view is much more elaborate than Allport's. Unlike Allport, Erikson believes that identity crises don't just occur during childhood and adolescence. Conflicts involving identity are a lifetime concern.

Apparently, Erikson was strongly influenced by German philosopher Georg Hegel, who advocated a reality in which thesis and antithesis—the conflict of opposites—yielded synthesis, the resolution of conflict. According to Erikson, the identity struggle occurs eight times throughout life, with each crisis involving a clash of opposites. Maturity and contentment result from synthesis; stagnation and maladjustment follow failure to resolve conflicts. However, lest the reader think that Erikson is a pessimist, let us hasten to indicate that resolution of conflicts is normal and expected, and "crises" are welcomed turning points, not threats of catastrophe (Erikson, 1968a). Each resolution of a crisis results in a new strength. Now let's turn to Erikson's eight crises.

THE EIGHT CRISES OF IDENTITY

The logic of Erikson's eight stages is very much akin to that of Allport and other stage theorists. Each stage is characterized by a psychosocial crisis. *Psychosocial* apparently refers to a union of Freud's physical yearnings (id) and the cultural forces that act on the individual ("Erik Erikson," 1970). Each crisis involves a dilemma that goads the individual toward its resolution before moving on to the next stage.

Erikson's eight crises of identity

Infancy.   Infants arrive with basic physiological needs that parents must be willing and able to meet. Nearly always, parents satisfy those needs, at least to some degree. The opposite condition — the one that generates the first crisis — is the inevitable delay or neglect of satisfaction and the occurrence of weaning. Basic trust results from the infant's sense that it can count on satisfaction of its needs (Erikson, 1968a); the world takes on the aura of a "trustworthy realm." Its opposite is *basic mistrust* — the feeling of abandonment and helpless rage that accompanies uncertainty of satisfaction.

infancy: basic trust versus basic distrust

Basic trust lays the foundation for *hope* — the enduring belief in the attainability of basic satisfactions. Hope is the strength that results from resolution of the first crisis. It is the foundation of faith (E. Hall, 1983), often manifested in adult religious practices. In fact, religion may be regarded as an institutional safeguard of faith. An *institutional safeguard* is a cultural unit that protects and promotes products of crisis resolution. Failure to develop basic trust yields mistrust and hopelessness — conditions that can lead in adulthood to severe addiction or psychotic states.

Early childhood.   During this stage, the child develops motor skills that open up the first possibilities of independence (Erikson, 1968a). Children can now move to desired objects and thereby possess them without the aid of parents. Also, the dawning of grasping ability allows children to experience the power of imprisoning an object within fingers, hands, and arms. Power comes from letting go — but so does conflict. To hold can be destructive, as in restraining, or it can be positive, as in to "have and hold." Letting go can also have two meanings: giving up something desirable, or casually "letting it be." If all this "holding and letting go" sounds a bit Freudian, you are quite right: Erikson acknowledges a heavy debt to Freud (Evans, 1967). Also, there is a hint of Fromm's dilemma of freedom: to let go of something is to be free of it, but it is also to be without it.

The poles of the crisis of early childhood are *autonomy,* or independence, versus *shame and doubt*. With the newly acquired muscular skills, the child experiences doing for himself. Unfortunately, he also knows the frustration generated by needing the help of others who can do more for him than he can do for himself. For Erikson as well as Allport, self-esteem derives from doing for oneself. *Autonomy* is independence stemming from the reasonable self-control that allows chil-

early childhood: autonomy versus shame and doubt

dren to hold rather than restrain, to let be rather than lose. *Shame and doubt* is the estrangement that results from the feeling of being controlled and of losing self-control. It is the precursor of neurosis and paranoia — the former a desperate struggle for control of one's environment, and the latter a manifestation of feeling controlled by others.

The strength that emerges from resolution during early childhood is *will power*. *Will power* "is the unbroken determination to exercise free choice as well as self-restraint in spite of the unavoidable experience of shame, doubt, and a certain rage over being controlled by others" (Erikson, 1968a, p. 288). The exercise of free choice has its institutional safeguard — the principles of law and order and of justice. However, Erikson argues that "law and order" gone awry can rob people of the very choice it is supposed to protect.

Play age.   In the third or fourth year, children become aware of the differences between the sexes. Sex-role playing and sexual feelings occur at this point for the boy-child, but Erikson sees the girl-child as playing the feminine role, dwelling on attractiveness as well as motherliness, rather than sexuality. Conscience appears at this stage and forever places a restraint on actions, thoughts,

play age:
initiative versus
guilt

and fantasies. *Initiative* is one side of the coin at this stage, and *guilt* is the other. *Initiative* is acting on one's desires, urges, and potentials. *Guilt* is the harness that restrains pursuit of desires, urges, and potentials — the exercise of an overzealous conscience. The boy-child learns that competition for a favored position with his mother leads to the inevitable fear of damage to his genitals, and the resultant guilt at having taken the initiative well beyond that which is permissible (Evans, 1967; recall the discussion of the Oedipal situation in Chapter 3). Presumably, the girl-child has analogous problems associated with pursuit of her father's attentions. For both sexes, guilt can arise from a failure to demonstrate competency when the initiative is taken (Evans, 1967).

At first, children's play does not involve real purpose, but wish fulfillment and fantasy. Gradually, this begins to change. "The child begins to envisage goals for which his locomotion and cognition have prepared him. The child also begins to think of being big and to identify with people whose work or whose personality he can understand and appreciate" (Evans, 1967, p. 25). That is, children begin to display realistic, practical *purpose* — "the courage to envisage and pursue valued and tangible goals guided by conscience but not paralyzed by guilt and by fear of punishment" (Erikson, 1968a, p. 289). It is the strength that comes from resolution of the play-age crisis. Failure at resolution leads to general repression or inhibition and to adult pathology such as sexual impotence, overcompensatory exhibitionism, and sociopathic acting out. All of these are attempts to regain the lost initiative.

School age.   During the school years, children begin to lay the groundwork for becoming a parent. For the first time, they relate to the larger society and one of its core elements, work. The crisis for this period involves *industry* versus

school age:
industry versus
inferiority

inferiority. *Industry* entails children's becoming absorbed in the "tool world" of their culture — the workaday world — thereby preparing them "for a hierarchy of learning experiences which [they] will undergo with the help of cooperative peers and instructive adults" (Erikson, 1968a, p. 289). Of course, school is the first productive situation that provides an inkling of the "tool culture." *Inferiority* occurs if children perceive their skills or status among peers to be inadequate. Race or ethnic background may become barriers that prevent children from a successful apprenticeship and the accompanying actualization of the will to learn. Inferiority can yield regression to the hopelessness of Oedipal rivalry. There is also the danger that work will become the only criterion for worthwhileness. People who become overinvolved with work may find that it becomes the sole source of their identity.

Resolution of the crisis at the school age gives children critical experiences, including working beside and with others and "division of labor." From this resolution emerges the strength of *competence* — "the free exercise (unimpaired by an infantile sense of inferiority) of dexterity and intelligence in the completion of serious tasks" (Erikson, 1968a, pp. 289–290). With competence, children are ready to become cooperative participants in some segment of the culture.

Adolescence.   As Allport indicated and most theorists agree, the adolescent search for self represents the fulcrum upon which the lifelong struggle for identity is balanced. For Erikson, the period allows a synthesis of previous stages, but it is more than the mere sum of what developed earlier. It is also an extension into the future. Adolescent *identity* is accumulated confidence that the sameness and continuity one has previously cultivated are now appreciated by others — allowing, in turn, the promise of careers and lifestyles to come. The opposite of

adolescence: identity versus identity confusion

In Erikson's theory, resolution of the crisis of identity is the major task of the adolescent years.

identity is *identity confusion*—the failure of previous identity developments to coalesce in such a way that it is clear what roles one is expected to play in the future. The victory of confusion predicts acute maladjustments due to a feeling of meaninglessness. These symptoms can lapse into psychotic episodes.

In their struggle to answer the question "Who am I?" teenagers often form cliques. These clans bolster self-images and provide a mutual defense against "enemies" whose different characteristics challenge the "truth" of their own developing identity (E. Hall, 1983). If teens turn this condemnation of the "different" against society, delinquency can result. However, adolescent rebellion is not seen by Erikson as a negative force, at least when the larger culture is considered (Erikson, 1968a). Societies must be flexible, and Erikson sees adolescent challenges as a source of cultural rejuvenation. Youth, in their quest for identity, question the norms of their society, vigorously supporting those that meet the challenge and contributing to the demise of rules that cannot bear close scrutiny. Times of unrest among the young attest to the sickness of a society failing to meet the promise of youth—that the best will rule and the rulers will bring out the best in people. During periods of upheaval, the mind of youth and that of society become one in the pursuit of ideological unification and return to coherent purpose.

The strength that comes from the adolescent period is *fidelity*. Fidelity "is the opportunity to fulfill personal potentialities . . . in a context which permits the young person to be true to himself and true to significant others . . . [and to] sustain loyalties . . . in spite of inevitable contradictions of value systems" (Erikson, 1968a, p. 290). For Erikson, fidelity is the cornerstone of identity.

Young adulthood.   During previous stages, strengths allowed the sexes to merge in cooperation and fruitful communication. When "falling in love," teenagers attach themselves to another in an attempt to arrive at self-definition. Teens "in love" see themselves reflected in an "idealized other," but do not actively attempt to differentiate themselves from the other. Now, the biological differences come to the fore, so that the sexes, similar in consciousness and language,

young adulthood: intimacy versus isolation

become different in the mature quest for love and procreation. *Intimacy* "is really the ability to fuse your identity with somebody else's without fear that you're going to lose something yourself" (Evans, 1967, p. 48). It is more than the mere physical intimacy that occurs in sexual exchanges (E. Hall, 1983). The other pole in the crisis for this stage is *isolation*—the failure to secure close and cooperative relationships with the same and especially the opposite sex such that partners' identities are important to, but distinct from, one's own. The triumph of isolation dooms the individual to infantile fixations and lasting immaturities that interfere with love and work. On the other hand, intimacy brings the strength of this period—love. *Love* is the force that promotes the power of cultural and personal facets of the self-concept, which, in turn, bind competition/cooperation and procreation/production into a "way of life" (see Chapter 4). Love is also the shared devotion that overcomes antagonisms caused by differences in functions assigned to partners in a relationship.

Adulthood.   Humans are not only "learning animals" — they are teachers as well. It is at maturity that the need to be needed and the accumulation of wisdom lead to assumption of the "teacher" role. Thus, during the seventh stage, people strive for *generativity* — "the concern with establishing and guiding the next generation" (Erikson, 1968a, p. 291). Its failure leads to *stagnation* — the arrest of the ripening process that comes with inability to funnel previous development into the formation of the next generation. Boredom is the constant companion of stagnation, as is false intimacy and adult self-indulgence. Inevitably, the failure of generativity shows up in the next generation as the aggravation of estrangements in childhood, adolescence, and early adulthood.

Care, the strength of maturity, is "the broadening concern for what has been generated by love, necessity, or accident — a concern which must consistently overcome the ambivalence adhering to irreversible obligation and the narrowness of self-concern" (Erikson, 1968a, p. 291). Care is a major force behind utilization of "proven methods with which each generation meets the needs of the next" (Erikson, 1968a, 291).

Old age.   Strength in old age is wit in full bloom — a storehouse of knowledge, an inclusive understanding, and a maturity of judgment. These intellectual contributions provide a bridge to the next generation by reminding all that the

adulthood:
generativity
versus stagnation

According to Erikson, achieving generativity — an active concern for the coming generations — is a critical part of personality development for mature adults.

old age: integrity versus despair

knowledge of a given generation is not "truth," but a cog in the infinitely large and ever-turning wheel of human experience. Crisis at this time involves contributing to the continuity of the human condition versus distraction from that noble purpose by an obsession with death. Successful resolution brings *integrity*—"an emotional integration faithful to the image bearers of the past and ready to take (and eventually renounce) leadership in the present" (Erikson, 1968a, p. 291). Lack of resolution leads to *despair*—a feeling that time is too short for the achievement of integrity and the accompanying contribution to the connection between generations. Despair can result in bitterness at not being able to extend oneself into the future—a losing battle with death, rather than a calm acceptance of it. Despair yields psychological death before the physical counterpart. The symptoms of despair often include depression, hypochondria, and paranoia.

The strength that comes from resolution of the eighth crisis is *wisdom*—a "detached and yet active concern with life in the face of death" (Erikson, 1968a, p. 292), not magical access to "higher knowledge" (E. Hall, 1983). With wisdom, death is accepted, and one's role in the human drama is assured.

Table 15.2 summarizes Erikson's eight stages and the crisis of identity associated with each.

TABLE 15.2   Erikson's Identity Crises

Stage	Crisis	Resolution	Failure to resolve	Strength that results from resolution
Infancy	Basic trust versus basic mistrust	Confidence in satisfaction of needs	Rage due to uncertainty of satisfaction	Hope
Early childhoood	Autonomy versus shame and doubt	Independence stemming from self-control	Estrangement due to being controlled	Will power
Play age	Initiative versus guilt	Acting on desires, urges, potentials	Conscience restrains pursuits	Purpose
School age	Industry versus inferiority	Absorbed in the "tool world"	Skills and status inadequate	Competence
Adolescence	Identity versus identity confusion	Confident that sameness seen by others	Previous identity developments fail	Fidelity
Young adulthood	Intimacy versus isolation	Fusing identity with another	No close relationships	Love
Adulthood	Generativity versus stagnation	Guiding the next generation	Arrest of ripening process	Care
Old age	Integrity versus despair	Emotional integration	"Time is too short"	Wisdom

If Allport has indicated the importance of "identity" for a sense of self, Erikson has shown it to be the backbone of the self-concept. Identity is the thread that ties together the "you" of yesterday with the "you" of tomorrow. However, conscience—the pattern involving the self-conceptual aspects self-image and propriate striving—must be considered in more detail before the whole "you" is understood. Accordingly, we now turn to Kohlberg's theory of how conscience develops from a primitive level of moral functioning to a high level where a concern for human well-being is all-important.

Lawrence Kohlberg: Six Stages of Moral Development

Building on the ideas of famed developmental psychologist Jean Piaget, Lawrence Kohlberg (1981) has posed a theory of how moral functioning changes as the conscience develops. Piaget believed that children pass through three stages. First, they accept adults' pronouncements as to what's "right"; second, they cooperate in developing rules of fair play; and finally, they promote fair and equal treatment of everyone (Piaget, 1932/1965). Kohlberg's major assumption is that conscience does not develop in a vacuum. Rather, developments in the cognitive realm shape the conscience's role in moral judgment. In fact, he believes that cognitive development underlies moral reasoning and resultant moral judgments. "Since moral reasoning clearly is reasoning, advanced moral reasoning depends upon advanced logical reasoning" (Kohlberg, 1976, p. 32). Before reading further, take a moment to complete the exercise in Box 15.1.

LAWRENCE KOHLBERG.
Kohlberg's controversial but well-respected theory raises the question of whether morality can be taught in the schools.

BOX 15.1	*A Moral Dilemma*

In addition to the section on Lawrence Kohlberg's stages of moral development, you might enjoy reacting to one of his better-known "moral dilemmas" (Kohlberg, 1976, 1981). As in most of the dilemmas, one moral rule conflicts with another. The dilemma involves Heinz, a European who needs a certain drug for his dying wife, but finds that the greedy druggist who invented the drug demands ten times what it is worth, and much more than the husband can afford. Heinz borrows half the inflated price, but the druggist refuses to allow the distraught husband to pay the rest later. Heinz breaks into the drugstore and steals the drug. The question is "Should Heinz have done that?" Answer the question in a paragraph or two, telling what Heinz should have done and, more important, why he should have done it. Later we'll tell you how to score your answer.

THREE LEVELS OF MORAL DEVELOPMENT

Kohlberg's three levels of moral development

preconventional

Kohlberg's theory involves three levels, each of which has two stages. The *preconventional* level applies to people for whom society's rules are external to the self-concept (Kohlberg, 1976). At this level, individuals don't really understand and uphold society's rules; rather, they refrain from disapproved behavior to avoid punishment or to receive their share of positive outcomes. Generally, children under 9 function at the preconventional level — but so do some adolescents, and many adolescent and adult criminal offenders.

conventional

The *conventional* level involves reasoning and judgments by persons who have internalized society's rules and the expectations of others, especially those of authority figures (Kohlberg, 1976). People operating at the conventional level refrain from disapproved behavior and perform approved behavior in order to avoid censure by others and to obtain praise from others, especially those in authority. Most adolescents and adults in our society and other societies function at the conventional level.

postconventional

The *postconventional* level is reserved for the relatively few individuals who have differentiated their self-concept from the rules of society and the expectations of others and define their values in terms of self-chosen principles. Individuals making judgments at this level perform or don't perform behaviors according to their own principles, following society's rules and honoring the expectations of others when these coincide with self-chosen moral tenets. A minority of adults reach this level of moral functioning, and those who do generally have attained at least the age of 20.

sociomoral perspective

Individuals operating at the three different levels show different sociomoral perspectives. A person's *sociomoral perspective* "refers to the point of view the individual takes in defining both social facts and sociomoral values, or oughts" (Kohlberg, 1976, p. 33). The concrete-individual perspective is adopted by preconventional people. They are only concerned with "what's in it for me," including avoidance of punishment. Conventional people show a "member-of-society" perspective. Here, defense of society's rules and the prerogatives of authority figures are paramount. The "prior-to-society" perspective is embraced by people who make judgments at the postconventional level. They place their own principles, which they view as universal in nature, before the rules of society and the expectations of others.

THE SIX STAGES OF MORAL DEVELOPMENT

Stage 1 (preconventional). At the first stage, the emphasis is on avoidance of punishment. Children do "right" so that they will not be physically harmed. The interests of others are not considered, nor is anything "psychological" (for example, "If I do wrong, you won't like me"). When children operating at this stage are presented with Heinz's "moral dilemma," which is contained in the moral-judgment test developed by Kohlberg and his colleagues (Kohlberg, 1976, 1981), their reactions reflect a lack of value for life when it conflicts with property and law. When asked "Should Heinz have done that?" (see Box 15.1), a typical reply is "He shouldn't do it . . . Because then he'd be a thief if they caught him and put him in jail" (Kohlberg, 1976, p. 42). Stage 1 children project their own feelings onto Heinz: one should consider one's own welfare, not that of others.

six stages of moral development

The rather complicated and somewhat arbitrary method of scoring reactions to dilemmas on the test involves classifying responses, such as the one above, at one of the stages. If, for example, most of a child's responses to the various dilemmas are classified at Stage 1, the child would be thought to function mostly at that stage.

Stage 2 (preconventional). "Let's make a deal" might be considered the motto for Stage 2. Here, children recognize that obtaining what they want depends on trading off with others. "Right" is represented by an equal exchange. A child operating at this stage recognizes the needs of others in that she will let them do what they want, if she can do what she wants without interference from them. At Stage 2, the peer group "is like a 'bank.' Members meet to exchange favors but you cannot take more than you give" (Kohlberg, 1981, p. 47). You don't "rat" on a peer, because if people tell on each other, then everybody gets into trouble. You don't bother others; you live and let live (Kohlberg, 1981). When confronted with another dilemma—brother misbehaves, should Father be told?—at 10 years of age, Stage 1 children center on punishment. They worry that Father will "beat them up" if they don't tell and later the deed is discovered, or the brother will get them if they do tell. By Stage 2, the same children at 13 might say "You shouldn't tell or you'll get your brother in trouble. If you want your brother to keep quiet for you sometime, you'd better not squeal now" (adapted from Kohlberg, 1976, p. 39). At this point in conscience development, the "trade-off" mentality has taken over.

Stage 3 (conventional). The orientation of Stage 3 is meeting the expectations of important people in one's life—friends, family, and authority figures. It is not yet adhering to the more abstract "rules of society." Showing trust and loyalty and following the "golden rule" are valued at this stage. Shared feelings, agreements, and expectations take precedence over individual interests. At Stage 3, it becomes important for members of a group to trust each other and respect each other's possessions (Kohlberg, 1981). Members of the group should care about each other and take care of one another. When asked what to do about a brother who misbehaves, a Stage 3 individual responded that the sibling of the offending brother "should think of his brother, but it's more important to be a good son. Your father has done so much for you. I'd have a conscience if I didn't tell, more than to my brother, because my father couldn't trust me. My brother would understand; our father has done so much for him, too" (Kohlberg, 1976, p. 38). Here, children show concern with meeting the expectations of authority, and also express the feeling that others share the belief in displaying loyalty to those who have provided for them.

Stage 4 (conventional).   At Stage 4, the "member-of-society" perspective is fully developed. Now of prime importance are fulfilling the duties that one has agreed to accept and upholding the laws, except in rare cases where society's edicts conflict with higher social values. Contributing to society, primary groups and institutions also becomes important. To keep society running smoothly and its institutions healthy is an important goal for the individual operating at Stage 4. In short, the Stage 4 individual might be thought of as the "establishment person." The point of view of the system is adopted, and individual relations are considered in terms of where each fits in the system. Persons are responsible for themselves, but also share responsibility for others. Stealing becomes wrong because it harms the community, rather than primarily the individual (Kohlberg, 1981). A 17-year-old functioning at Stage 4 was asked "Why should a promise be kept, anyway?" He replied, "Friendship is based on trust. If you can't trust a person, there's little grounds to deal with him. You should try to be as reliable as possible because people remember you by this, you're more respected if you can be depended upon" (Kohlberg, 1976, p. 37). Mutual trust is of great importance to individuals operating at Stage 4, as is dependability.

Stage 5 (postconventional).   A sense of democracy pervades the Stage 5 conscience. People at Stage 5 recognize that rules are mostly "relative." That is, instead of absolute rules, each group may have its own, and the rules of each group should be respected. "Life, liberty, and the pursuit of happiness" are exceptions to the belief in the relativity of rules. In general, protecting the rights and welfare of all people and "providing the greatest good for the greatest number" are the major pursuits at Stage 5. Stage 5 individuals have a "prior-to-society" perspective, in that they recognize individual rights and values as taking precedence over social contracts and agreements. Such people can integrate the workings of agreement and contract with those of impartiality and due process. However, they have nearly equal reverence for the moral and legal points of view and may fail to integrate the two. This confusion is reflected in the response of a Stage 5 individual to Heinz's dilemma (Box 15.1): "Usually the moral and the legal standpoints coincide. Here they conflict. The judge should weigh the moral standpoint more"

(Kohlberg, 1976, p. 39). The "way out" for such a person might be to advise stealing and then suggest that a mild punishment is in order. At Stage 5, moral principles are important, but not yet dominant.

Stage 6 (postconventional).   At Stage 6, the highest attainment of conscience, moral principles supersede laws, rules, and agreements. Individuals select principles for themselves, as opposed to simply accepting them from an outside source in knee-jerk fashion, but view these "moral edicts" as universal. The principles in question include equality of human rights, respect for the dignity of humans, and the belief that each person should be treated as a unique individual. When laws and rules conflict with such principles, the principles should be followed. In fact, laws and rules have value only insofar as they support universal moral principles, each of which is assumed to be "self-evident" to any rational person. In short, it is people who are important, not rules, laws, or agreements. People are ends in themselves. The following is a Stage 6 response to Heinz's dilemma:

> It [stealing the drug] is wrong legally but right morally. Systems of law are valid only insofar as they reflect the sort of moral law all rational people can accept. One must consider the personal justice involved, which is the root of the social contract. The ground of creating a society is individual justice, the right of every person to an equal consideration of his claims in every situation, not just those which can be codified in law. Personal justice means, "Treat each person as a end, not a means." (Kohlberg, 1976, p. 39)

For the rare individual operating at Stage 6, the well-being and rights of people are all that is really important.

Kohlberg's stages of moral development are summarized in Table 15.3.

TABLE 15.3   Kohlberg's Theory of Morality

Level	Stage	Focus	Orientation to others
I Preconventional	1	Avoiding punishment	No appreciation of others
	2	Getting what you want by trade-off	Recognizes that others have interests to pursue
II Conventional	3	Meeting expectations of important people	Shared feelings, agreements, expectations over individual interests
	4	Fulfilling duties, upholding laws	Individuals responsible for self and shared responsibility for others
III Postconventional	5	Sense of democracy and relativity of rules	Individual rights over rules and agreements
	6	Self-selection of universal principles	Dignity, uniqueness, and well-being of humans above all else

Your score on "Heinz's dilemma."   Now look back at your response to Heinz's dilemma (Box 15.1). In scoring your response, remember that the response to one dilemma is insufficient to determine your overall level of moral functioning. Also, understand that to decide what level of moral functioning is "good" or "correct" is to make a value judgment. With that in mind, you should score your response as Level I (preconventional) if you thought that Heinz should not do it because he would be punished. If you thought he should not do it because his parents or other authority figure might disapprove, or because "it's against the law," the response belongs at Level II (conventional). Finally, if you tried to mediate between the law and the wife's well-being, or if you ignored the law in favor of the wife, your response belongs at Level III (postconventional). Scoring at stages would be trickier.

KOHLBERG'S THEORY: EVALUATION AND ALTERNATIVES

Kohlberg's theory may be the most popular of several attempts to explain the moral-functioning aspect of conscience. It has even found its way into the mass media. Also, his stages of moral development may be the most heavily investigated theoretical orientation of its kind. However, the theory remains controversial — in part because Kohlberg assumes that moral judgment is based on cognitive development and implies that there are such things as "universal moral principles" (White, Flatley, & Janson, 1982; Krebs, 1982).

What has research shown about Kohlberg's theory? Dennis Krebs (1982) indicates that evidence for a link between functioning at one of Kohlberg's stages and corresponding moral behavior has been somewhat mixed. Also, he notes that some researchers question the applicability of the theory to "real-life" moral reasoning and to prosocial issues (issues concerning helping or otherwise benefiting other people). Nevertheless, Krebs believes that meaningful support for Kohlberg's theory will be forthcoming when researchers consider more than just the correspondence between moral stage and moral behavior. Researchers too frequently give subjects Kohlberg's test, determine each subject's stage of moral functioning, and then determine whether each displays the moral behavior expected of people at that level. Such experimental practice ignores Kohlberg's belief that the reasoning behind a moral decision is more important in understanding subsequent moral behavior than is the decision itself. Thus, a study does no damage to Kohlberg's theory if it shows that students at Stage 2 and Stage 6 both "sat in" to protest the behavior of local authorities, when "sitting in" would seem to be expected only of Stage 6 individuals. Stage 2 individuals may have "sat in" in order to "get even" with authorities, while people at Stage 6 may have protested for the sake of preserving free speech. Knowing a person's stage of moral operation and whether she performed a certain moral behavior is not sufficient to test the correspondence between moral stage and moral behavior. One must also know the reasoning behind the decision to perform the behavior. It is also noteworthy that Krebs identifies a number of researchers who ignore the importance of the reasoning behind decisions to behave, but still find a positive relationship between stage and behavior. Kohlberg's theory seems hale and hearty, though possibly not strong enough to justify actual programs to teach moral reasoning (Kohlberg, 1976).

Peter Lifton (1982) reviews two other prominent theories of moral functioning: those of Haan (1978) and Hogan (1973; Hogan, Johnson, & Emler, 1978).

Haan, like Kohlberg, follows Piaget, but she sees morality in terms of social rather than cognitive skills. In contrast to the principle of "justice," which Lifton believes underlies Kohlberg's theory, Haan relies on universal "equality." According to Lifton, Haan sees equality as guiding interacting people toward a balanced solution among the competing needs of all parties. Morality in Haan's view progresses over five stages, from self-concern, to concern for others, to concern for all parties.

Hogan views humans as social animals. To survive, they band together in groups, and to preserve the groups they develop moral codes. Although the morality of the human species is born of evolutionary necessity, its development within a given person is a function of three personality characteristics. The first, *socialization,* is concern for society and develops during childhood as a result of interactions with parents, teachers, and authority figures. The second, *empathy,* is concern for others and develops during adolescence as a consequence of interacting with peers. *Autonomy,* the third characteristic, is concern for self and develops during adulthood, after soul-searching, contemplation of one's uniqueness, and maturation of the self-concept.

Lifton (1982) examines the views of Kohlberg, Haan, and Hogan and finds that each paints a different picture of what the "truly moral" person is like. We are left with the conclusion that the ideal for morality depends somewhat on the theoretical orientation from which it is derived. He also suggests that the sophistication of a person's moral reasoning may be partially a function of her personality, not just her intellectual functioning, as Kohlberg contends.

Theories like Kohlberg's seem to imply that the development of moral reasoning stops at young adulthood. To the contrary, a recent interest in older people, one of the most rapidly growing segments of our total population, indicates that moral reasoning may vary over the life span. More specifically, research is beginning to show that as people get older, there is an increased tendency toward "contextual relativism" (White, Flatley, & Janson, 1982; Roodin & Hoyer, 1982). As the name implies, *contextual relativism* involves varying moral judgments according to the context in which judgments have to be made. On the surface, contextual relativism looks like the "situationism" we have considered in previous chapters. However, closer examination indicates that unique attributes of older people may *interact* with context or situation to produce moral decisions (Roodin & Hoyer, 1982; see Chapters 13 and 14). In any case, older people, especially the elderly, may have a greater tendency than younger people to take the context of judgment into account when they make moral decisions. So doing violates Kohlberg's notion that moral judgment is relatively consistent across situations (White et al., 1982).

contextual relativism

One other recent development in the study of conscience seems worth brief mention. You may have wondered about the excuses that people make for their behavior. Can a good excuse actually make a harmful behavior seem legitimate? Perhaps so, according to John M. Darley and Mark Zanna (1982), psychologists who are constructing a theory of rules for making acceptable excuses. Based partly on analogies to court cases, Darley and Zanna are beginning to show that certain excuses can absolve perpetrators of harmful acts from blame. They are also working on just how children are taught the rules for deriving legitimate excuses. Perhaps someday we will have a method for judging the morality of a harmful act based on the excuse by which it is justified. Then we can make more reasonable and useful judgments about whether a person has "a good excuse."

Self-Concept and Personality

The notion of self-concept brings together a number of ideas associated with personality. In fact, we will go so far as to say that self-concept is an individual's view of her or his own personality. It is the perception of personality from the "inside."

The notion that self-concept is a variation of personality raises two important questions. First, as we have seen in previous chapters, "personality" is something we infer from behavior, and yet behavior is often inconsistent. How do people form a relatively clear picture of their personalities if their behavior is inconsistent? Second, from their own point of view and from that of other people, how do individuals acquire "traits"?

SELF-CONCEPT AS THE PERCEPTION OF ONE'S OWN PERSONALITY

Allport's definition of *proprium,* you recall, is "me as felt and known . . . the self as 'object' of knowledge and feeling" (Allport, 1961, p. 127). In effect, your proprium or self-concept is your perception of you—that is, your perception of your personality. To put it another way, your concept of your self is the way you feel and know your own personality.

How does this idea about self-concept fit with typical notions of personality? Implicitly or explicitly, psychologists, psychiatrists, and others interested in human behavior assume that personality is something that practicing professionals in the psychological sciences perceive in you, via personality assessment or clinical interview. That is, personality seems to be thought of as something that professionals see in laypeople. Which is the "best" view of personality—yours or that of the professionals?

The underlying, and generally unexpressed, assumption has been that professionals' assessment of your personality is more meaningful and accurate than your own. However, that has not been a universal opinion. Some writers (for example, Mischel, 1973) assert that if professionals want to know about your personality, the best thing they can do is ask you about it—which is equivalent to asking you to state your self-concept. In support of the contention that your report of your self-concept is your perception of your personality, many self-concept tests amount to a list of trait labels that respondents are asked to check off

(Allen & Potkay, 1983a). On these tests, in a sense, all the trait labels that a respondent checks are added up to provide an index of self-concept. If "personality" is made up of traits, and on self-concept tests you indicate the traits that you see yourself as possessing, then a self-concept test measures your perception of your personality.

Indeed, isn't stating your self-concept—your own perception of your personality—an everyday exercise? People are forever remarking "I'm gentle, but tough-minded," or "I'm a thoughtful person who is something of a loner," or "I'm optimistic, but not gullible." We all have perceptions of our own personalities, and we are in the habit of expressing them.

As is usually the case, one perspective is not necessarily better than another. Both your view of your personality and that of professionals are important. Self-perceptions of personality cannot be entirely objective, and professionals' perceptions will miss some information to which only you are privy. Thus, each perspective complements the other. However, even though both perspectives are valid, the idea of self-concept as the perception of one's own personality is perhaps a more concrete and practically useful notion.

SELF-CONCEPT AND BEHAVIORAL INCONSISTENCY

Now that you are equipped with a more practical notion of self-concept, we can consider the thorny question "How can I have a self-concept if my behavior is inconsistent?" Of course, the question assumes that behavior *is* inconsistent, although several personologists would disagree. Nevertheless, as discussed in Chapter 13, there is a growing tendency to question the existence of behavioral consistency, and it seems reasonable to assume for present purposes that consistency is not great. Given that assumption, are notions of self-concept meaningful?

Your self-concept implies something unique to you—something substantial, anchored to a solid foundation. From your point of view, personality is the traits that you have. According to Chapter 1, each trait is inferred by the observation of consistency in behavioral performance along a dimension corresponding to a trait (for example, "aggressive" is inferred by observations of aggressiveness consistently performed in many different situations). If your self-concept is your perception of your personality—of the traits that you possess—you can see that your self-concept is founded on behavioral consistency and appears to be undermined if our assumption of little consistency is correct. To put it in more common terms, it would seem difficult for you to state your self-concept—that you have this trait or that—if you don't rather consistently perform behaviors corresponding to traits.

Does all this mean that you don't have a self-concept after all? We think not. Perhaps there is a need to rely less on behavioral consistency as a "test" of personality, or self-concept. Even in the absence of behavioral consistency, if it can be shown that you have a set of traits that are different from those of other people, then you have a personality and a self-concept to report. We think we can accomplish that goal by offering some new criteria for establishing the existence of traits—criteria that don't depend so heavily on behavioral consistency. Robert Hogan's theory of personality suggests the needed criteria.

DRAMATURGICAL QUALITY AND VALUE

Hogan's theory

Just how do you arrive at your self-concept — that is, your rendition of your personality? The answer holds the key to the new criteria for traits. A theory of personality by Robert Hogan (1983) can help direct us to the answer. Hogan's (1983) answer can be summarized in the admittedly oversimplified statement "You are your perceptions of how other people view you." In the language of attribution theory (Baron & Byrne, 1984), people observe your behavior and attribute traits to you. In turn, Hogan suggests, you pick up those traits that others see in you and form them into your own view of your personality.

But what do people look for to determine the traits that you have? Obviously, people may attend to behavioral consistency as a sign of traits. If you consistently display "kind" behaviors, others are likely to attribute the trait "kind" to you, and you may well ascribe "kind" to yourself. However, behavioral consistency needn't be the only sign of traits that others tune in, and it may not even be the most important. People may focus on other factors as well.

dramaturgical
quality

We might build on Hogan's theory as follows. Let's suppose that you perform a behavior in excellent fashion. Perhaps you don't display the behavior consistently or very often, but when you do, you do it so well that others sit up and take notice. We can say that the *dramaturgical quality* of your performance is high. (Theodore Sarbin and William Coe are to be credited for suggesting this and related concepts; see Coe & Sarbin, 1977, and Sarbin, 1982.) *Dramaturgy* has to do with the scripts from which actors' performances are derived. *Dramaturgical quality* refers to the precision, clarity, and effectiveness with which a behavior is performed. If the dramaturgical quality of your behavioral performance is high, others will not only notice, they may also attribute the corresponding trait to you. If they do make an attribution, you may pick it up for use in your self-concept.

Let's take an example. Suppose that Ralph is at the local PTA picnic and notices that a crowd has gathered in a tight circle. Being taller than most of the others, he peers over the heads of the throng and sees the reason for the commotion. A child is crying and kicking, in the midst of a full-blown tantrum. Singly or in combination, members of the crowd step forward in an attempt to comfort the child, but his thrashing drives them back. If anything, efforts directed toward the child only make matters worse. The youngster seems to be close to a seizure. Gently, Ralph threads his way past the onlookers. When he reaches the center of the circle, he kneels slowly a couple of feet from the distressed child, but he does not try to reach out. Instead, he begins to whisper to the little boy, in a soft and soothing voice, so low that bystanders cannot hear what he is saying. This approach causes the child to momentarily slow his flailing arms and legs, and as Ralph talks, his violent cries become sobs and his limbs become motionless. Finally, the child is still, and Ralph extends his hands, inviting the child to seek the comfort of his arms. With the little boy resting against his chest, Ralph rises and walks through the parting crowd, all the time talking softly to the child. They search for and find the boy's parents, whose absence was the source of the problem all along. Onlookers have never seen Ralph behave this way before, and most will never see him do it again. However, almost all attribute "nurturance" to Ralph, and later they communicate the ascription to him. Nurturance becomes a part of Ralph's self-concept.

Dramaturgical value is another sign that may tell people about the traits of a given individual. A behavior has *dramaturgical value* to the extent that it is an uncommon behavior directed toward several different targets or performed under several different circumstances (see Kelley, 1973). Dramaturgical value is a double-barreled notion. To be high in dramaturgical value, a behavior must be *both* uncommon *and* directed to different targets or performed under different circumstances. A behavior directed to only one target or performed under just one circumstance might be seen as stemming from the target or circumstance, not the performer. However, if a person performs an uncommon behavior and directs it to several targets, observers are likely to attribute the corresponding trait to the performer. If they do, the performer may perceive that attribution and make that trait a part of her self-concept. Again, an example will help make the point.

dramaturgical value

Pat ambles into the company assembly hall. The atmosphere is electric. For the first time, employees have been talking "union." They've been bullied by company officials long enough. The hierarchy of ABCO is arrogant and arbitrary. If they don't like your attitude, they lay you off. There are no recreational facilities, and fringe benefits are just about non-existent. But still people are afraid. After all, a job, any job, is better than no job. They are like a group of citizens cowed by a knife-wielding thug: if they acted as a group, they could easily overwhelm the villain, but nobody will be the first to step forward. Pat has been to meetings like this before. It's always the same. Company officials take turns making patronizing statements, and no one has the intestinal fortitude to challenge them. Nothing ever gets done.

Pat makes her way to the front row and slouches in a folding chair. The meeting begins. The president tells them "how proud he is of them," and a vice-president follows with an announcement concerning the annual company picnic. Another vice-president takes the podium and is interrupted by a question about insurance. He waffles in his answer and cuts short a second question on the topic. Nobody does anything. Next, the personnel manager takes the microphone and generalizes about "company spirit."

Finally, Pat can stand it no more. She rises up out of the audience, strides up to the stage, and addresses the president in a firm voice. The personnel manager stops spewing out platitudes and stares. The president is embarrassed. No employee has ever spoken to him this way before. Pat comments about their low pay increase and the broken promise to rehire workers who had been laid off. The president begins to promise "to look into the matter," but is interrupted in midsentence. Pat has turned her attention to the first vice-president. "Why are you talking 'picnic' when we don't even have decent vacation time?" She doesn't stop there. As a crowd gathers at the stage, she begins to lecture the personnel manager and, one by one, all the other officials present. She has never done this before, and she doesn't do a particularly good job. Pat is not very articulate. Had she addressed just the personnel manager, fellow workers would probably see her behavior as due to him. Who wouldn't tell off that wimp? But employees leave the assembly hall saying "I've never seen anything like that. . . . It's about time." They are also saying that Pat is a courageous person. She overhears some of them.

If you are good at performing a behavior, or if you perform an uncommon behavior, and you direct it at a number of targets, people will notice. It won't matter so much that you don't perform the behavior consistently. They will likely attribute a trait to you corresponding to the behavior, and will probably communicate their ascription to you. In this way, you will pick up another trait to expand your perception of your personality — your self-concept.

The ideas of dramaturgical quality and value are not part of Hogan's theory, but the theory suggests something of this kind. Hogan's theory (1983) is much richer and broader than indicated in the brief description at the start of this discussion (also see Johnson, 1983). Besides attributional processes, Hogan's theory also relates biology and early experience to personality.

In addition, the theory suggests that people often present themselves to others in a way that determines the attributions they will receive. Thus, dramaturgical quality and value may be consciously manipulated by individuals in order to reinforce already existing components of personality, rather than just playing a role in the acquisition of new components.

Applications: Changing an Inadequate Self-Concept

If self-concept is essentially the perception of one's own personality, then it would seem to matter a great deal whether one's self-concept is positive and healthy or inadequate and constricting. As you recall from Chapter 7, this point of view has been emphasized by the humanistic psychologists. Looking at how an inadequate self-concept can be changed will illustrate the importance of self-concept in personality study and also suggest some highly practical applications of personologists' thinking.

WHAT IS AN INADEQUATE SELF-CONCEPT?

We suggested earlier that you often report your self-concept as a matter of course, during conversation. In talking to others, you describe yourself using various trait labels. By accepting such self-descriptions as statements of self-concept, you can see what is an adequate and what is an inadequate self-concept.

Recall the discussion of "social desirability" in Chapter 6. *Social desirability* is the need to display the characteristics that are valued in our society. Probably everyone shows social-desirability motivation to some degree, which accounts for at least some highly desirable trait labels included in reports of self-concept. A preponderance of desirable labels in self-descriptions would seem to indicate a healthy self-concept. However, excessively glowing self-descriptions indicate a person who "doth protest too much." Such a person may be trying to deny the undesirable traits that are included in the self-concept (Allen & Potkay, 1983a). Therefore, so long as self-descriptions are not *too* radiant, reports composed mainly of desirable labels indicate a person to whom others are directing favorable attributions and who is accepting those ascriptions as components of the self-concept.

If a predominance of desirable trait labels indicates an adequate self-concept, a consistent majority of undesirable labels in self-descriptions suggests an inadequate self-concept. Again, a caution is in order. We have found in our work that, given enough opportunity for self-description, everybody is likely to include some undesirable labels (Allen & Potkay, 1983a). It seems that people include themselves when they endorse the belief that "nobody is perfect." Thus, an inadequate self-concept, like an adequate one, is a matter of degree. Generally speaking, a self-concept can be considered inadequate if the majority of the labels used in self-description are undesirable. How do you decide whether a label is desirable or not? The most important criterion is how the individual feels about the label. If the person thinks it is desirable or undesirable, so it is.

CORRECTING AN INADEQUATE SELF-CONCEPT: SUGGESTIONS FROM THE MAJOR THEORISTS

Given Hogan's notion that a self-concept arises from perception of others' attributions, an adequate self-concept requires reception of desirable attributions from others (Sullivan seems to share this idea). In turn, such reception will depend in part on generating positive feelings in others (Hogan, 1983). With this in mind, it is possible to derive suggestions for changes in self-concept from the theories discussed in Part 2 of this book. Do remember, however, that perceptions of one's own personality are complicated. Changing a self-concept is difficult and can require considerable concentration, effort, and work. Even with an all-out effort, change is likely to be less than complete and regressions probable.

Freud. Freud believed that defenses cover up material in the unconscious that one cannot accept. People tend to have an intuitive grasp of this Freudian notion, though they may not understand that the cover-up is thought to be an unconscious process. Frequent rationalizing, projecting, and so on, will indicate to others that an individual has something to hide. Overuse of defenses creates an unfavorable impression in two ways. First, employing defenses may be seen as "hiding something," which, in turn, may be regarded as using deception. People don't like those who deceive. Individuals who are not liked are not going to receive many desirable attributions. Second, "hiding something" implies that an individual is not presenting the "real person." If attributers think they are not seeing the "real person," they're going to be reluctant to make attributions, especially positive ones. People who depend too heavily on their defenses should probably seek help. Others' self-concepts may benefit from dropping some defenses.

Jung. Some would argue that Jung's outstanding contributions are the notions of extraversion and introversion. As seen in Chapters 4, 5, and 9, extraversion-introversion is once again creating excitement among researchers.

Extraverts are outgoing individuals. Such individuals are always providing others with a great deal of information upon which to base attributions. Conversely, introverts are, by definition, people who are not directing information about themselves to the external world where it can be used for forming attributions. In short, to be the subject of attributions, an individual may wish to become something of an extravert. However, some words of caution are in order. Extraverts tend to "tell all," including that which could lead to undesirable attributions.

Also, Jung did not believe that it is necessarily better to be an extravert than to be an introvert.

Adler.   Adler may be best known for his ideas about inferiority. As we saw in Chapter 4, he believed that we are all "afflicted" with feelings of inferiority. However, Adler would agree that there are degrees of feeling inferior. If a person feels inferior, she will likely communicate that feeling to others and receive the undesirable attribution she wishes to avoid. But a paradox materializes when we consider how to eliminate inferior feelings. As Allport (1961) argues, feelings of inferiority are associates of the self-concept. As long as the self-concept is inadequate, the inferior feelings will remain. Hence the paradox: a person cannot develop a fully adequate self-concept until he eliminates inferior feelings, but he cannot do that until he corrects the inadequate self-concept. The resolution of the dilemma is that if an individual has inferior feelings, he should concentrate on the larger problem—correction of an inadequate self-concept. Elimination of inferior feelings will follow correction of the self-concept. Methods of correcting self-concept are offered by other theorists reviewed in this section. Later, we will have some suggestions of our own. For now, it is sufficient to indicate that avoiding expressions of inferiority will lessen the probability of making matters worse. Communicating to others that one feels inferior will only elicit undesirable attributions and increase the inadequacy of one's self-concept.

Horney and Sullivan.   Horney wrote of movement toward others and away from others. It should be obvious that positive movement toward others will be critical in the reception of desirable attributions. Moving toward people will give them the opportunity to know one well enough to make positive attributions. Furthermore, a positive orientation toward people will create a favorable impression, increasing the likelihood of desirable attributions (Hogan, 1983). However, openly approaching people will inevitably lead to occasional disapproval. No one can please all the people all the time. As Sullivan indicated, occasional disapproval is something one should expect and learn to accept. If one reacts badly when other people show disapproval, the negative impression that others have formed will only worsen, and so will the associated disapproval. An effective way to minimize disapproval is to accept it as inevitable and go about one's business.

Maslow.   To become a self-actualizer is to finesse the issue of self-conceptual adequacy. As indicated in Chapter 7, self-actualizers have achieved solutions to lower-level problems of motivation. They can turn to self-understanding, creativity, and appreciation of beauty, because the basic physiological needs as well as the need to be loved and esteemed are satisfied. In other words, not only is self-concept adequacy not a problem for self-actualizers, it is not even relevant anymore.

Of course, most people are not yet fully self-actualized, nor do they have wholly adequate self-concepts. Nevertheless, they can eventually expect to achieve self-conceptual adequacy. Once this is done, Maslow's theory suggests continuing on to attempts at self-actualization. In so doing, individuals may pass beyond self-conceptual problems, and if actualization is achieved, not have to look back. Further study of Maslow's theory will provide means to the end, self-actualization.

Rotter and Bandura.   In Chapter 6, it was shown that, generally speaking, internal locus of control provides the most effective adaptation to one's environment. That alone is enough to generate admiration for internals. However, there is something about being an internal, in and of itself, that attracts admiration (Rotter, 1966, 1975). In fact, this is so much the case that social-desirability motivation distorts I-E scale responses. It seems that many respondents want to indicate they are internals, because it is socially desirable to do so. Internals manifest the rugged individualism that is embraced by many Americans. Thus, to be an internal is not only adaptive, it increases the likelihood of receiving desirable attributions.

Everyone needs a little help in selecting and learning to perform the behaviors that are likely to yield desirable attributions from others. The most obvious suggestion from Bandura's theory is to choose excellent models. People who get along well with other people are socially successful individuals (Hogan, 1983) and should be the most effective models. Adopting some of their behaviors will increase the probability of receiving desirable attributions.

Skinner.   The most obvious suggestion from Skinner's theory with regard to collecting desirable attributions is to positively reinforce others (Chapter 5). People tend to reciprocate reinforcement, and the return could be in the form of desirable attributions. Less obvious is a suggestion that others have derived from behaviorism (Hatfield & Walster, 1982). If an individual arranges to interact with important others under conditions where positive reinforcements predominate, the favorability of the person's relationships will increase. For example, heterosexual couples who are together mostly under positively reinforcing conditions, such as at an elegant restaurant, are likely to have lasting, happy relationships (Hatfield & Walster, 1982). The more favorable one's relationships with others, the more likely one is to receive desirable attributions from them.

Kelly and Rogers.   We have saved Kelly and Rogers for last, because they allow us a bridge to the next section. Kelly believes that part of the responsibility for effective psychological functioning falls directly on the individual. One must be willing and able to change with changes in the circumstances that one shares with others (see Chapter 8). A change in jobs will likely dictate changes in some behaviors. If a person changes with variations in his situations, he will be an effective model for others and will facilitate their adjustment to change. Helping others in this way will feed back on the self-concept via desirable attributions. Of course, efficient adjustment to change will help a person directly by increasing the effectiveness of her daily functioning.

As you discovered in Chapter 7, Rogers' most basic assumption is that people must assume responsibility for themselves. They are the best agents for correcting their own psychological problems. His entire theory and therapy rest on that assumption. Only by restructuring one's own thoughts and emotions can one become "that self one truly is." In that spirit, we can now turn to some of our own suggestions concerning self-correction of the self-concept.

MONITORING THE SELF-CONCEPT

The suggestions gleaned from the major theorists of personality can be supplemented with some observations based on ideas about self-concept derived from Hogan's theory. According to the theory of self-concept that we have founded on Hogan's point of view, a self-concept is determined by one's perception of how others view oneself. In turn, attributions directed toward people may be based on the dramaturgical quality and value of their behaviors as much as or more than on the behavioral consistency they show. Therefore, the first step in correcting an inadequate self-concept, or improving an adequate one, is to consider which behaviors an individual performs well (dramaturgical quality) and which behaviors are rather distinctive or uncommon (dramaturgical value). In the latter case, the individual will need to select uncommon behaviors that she is willing to perform under a number of circumstances or direct to a number of targets. The next problem is how to make those selections.

One way to get to know your self-concept is to monitor it. By monitoring your self-concept, you can see what you're doing "right" and what you're doing "wrong." If you are performing behaviors that are feeding back on self-concept, generating aspects you don't favor, these will show up in statements of self-concept. Also, whatever you are doing that is contributing to a favored self-concept will be reflected in your self-descriptions. Of course, monitoring your self-concept will reveal what is missing from your behavioral performances that could be making a positive contribution to your self-concept. After getting to know your self-concept through monitoring, you can decide what you want to continue to do and perfect, what to stop doing altogether, and what to begin doing.

BOX 15.2   *Monitoring Your*
Own Self-Concept

How can you monitor your self-concept? Perhaps the easiest and least disruptive way to do it on a continuing basis is to periodically sit down, think about yourself, and list the traits that you see yourself as possessing. You can write them down if you want, or you can take mental note of them. You will discover that on different occasions, you will likely list different traits (Allen & Potkay, 1983a). That is one reason why you must monitor on a number of occasions. Another is that you will be looking for change and will be able to detect it only by frequent monitoring over time. There is a reasonably good chance that the change over time will be in the direction of increasing conformity to the ideal self-concept you have in mind (Mummendey, Wilk, & Sturm, 1979).

continued

To make the connection between your statement of your self-concept (the traits you listed in your self-description) and your behaviors, you will need to think of the behaviors that correspond to each trait that you list. For example, if you list "kind," think of what you have done to give rise to your choice of that trait label: helped someone? been a good listener? comforted someone? Bearing this procedure in mind, you can look for traits that tend to show up on your list more often than others. These traits probably correspond to behaviors that you do well or behaviors that are uncommon. From this sublist of repeated trait labels, you can decide what you want to "keep," what you want to "throw out," and what you want to "add."

For example, suppose that "assertive" appears on your list more often than other traits. Suppose, further, that you find being assertive a good thing to be. You may be able to assume that you are pretty good at being assertive (high dramaturgical quality). If so, try to do even better. Further monitoring will tell you whether you are succeeding. Should you succeed, "assertive" will probably show up even more often on your list.

BOX 15.2
continued

The attribution of a trait characteristic, such as "daring," is strengthened by uncommon behaviors performed in a variety of settings.

continued

BOX 15.2
continued

Continuing the example, suppose that you find "critical" on your list fairly often and you don't look favorably on being critical of others. Think about the behaviors that correspond to "critical" — behaviors that others may be using as a basis for their attributions. If you can discover those behaviors, you can begin to eliminate them. Again, further monitoring will tell you whether you are succeeding.

Now let's suppose that you notice "daring" appearing relatively often on your list. It is reasonable to assume that "daring" corresponds to fairly uncommon behaviors. If you like being "daring," think about the behaviors that have led to that attribution. If you can discover what "daring" behaviors you have been performing, you may be able to bolster that aspect of your self-concept. One avenue to enhancing a component of self-concept corresponding to an uncommon behavior is to be sure that you perform the behavior under many different circumstances (for example, skiing? skydiving? public speaking?) or direct it toward different targets (confront a person who likes to bully others? confront your legislative representative?).

What if something is missing from your list? You aspire to be "cool-headed," but apparently are not getting feedback to support that goal. What can you do? Obviously, you can be "cool-headed" only if you know what to do and how to do it. The easiest solution to the problem is probably to locate a "cool-headed" model (Bandura, Chapter 6). Watching that person can allow you to increase dramaturgical quality to the point where others will begin to notice.

To monitor your own self-concept, try using the accompanying log sheet. Make several copies, and use one sheet per day of self-observation. As you do so, keep the following points in mind. First, don't try to create monitoring occasions artificially by attempting to think what list you might have generated had you thought about yourself a day ago, a week ago, or what have you. For one thing, recollected self-concept statements are difficult to interpret, because memory is sometimes faulty and events that have occurred since the remembered occasion may color recall (Hans Dieter Mummendey, personal communication, 1983). Make your self-concept statements apply only to the point in time at which you actually sit down to contemplate yourself. Second, take note of what has happened to you during the time frame to which your self-concept statement applies. If you make a self-description applicable to a given day, think about what happened to you on that day. As you learned in Chapters 11 and 12, situational factors can strongly influence behaviors. You don't want to take behaviors solely "due to circumstances" too seriously. Of course, such behaviors may be the ones you wish to cultivate. If so, you can learn what situations to seek out because they yield desirable behaviors. Perhaps, in time, you can transfer the locus of such behaviors from the situation to you. Monitoring what happens to you can also help you learn when to expect stressful or anxiety-provoking situations, so that you can avoid them. Additionally, you may be able to locate situations that mesh particularly well with components of the self-concept that you favor. If you want more information concerning monitoring self-concept and "what happens to you," see Allen and Potkay (1983a).

continued

Self-Concept Record Sheet

BOX 15.2
continued

DAY# _____.   DESCRIBE YOURSELF AS YOU ARE TODAY.

Think of yourself as you have been today, and write down five adjectives that best describe you.

1. _____

2. _____

3. _____

4. _____

5. _____

Write down the most important thing that happened to you today.

_____

_____

_____

_____

_____

_____

CHAPTER REVIEW

Following self-concept through the developmental process sheds much light on the development of personality and indicates the importance of self-concept in its own right. Allport's self-concept, called *proprium,* is the "me as felt and known . . . the self as 'object' of knowledge and feeling." He details seven developmental stages, from infancy when the self-concept doesn't really exist, through adolescence when the individual learns to plan for the future by setting long-range goals. Patterns—subjective conditions that influence the functioning and structuring of personality—emerge from the aspects of self-concept that are associated with the stages. Important patterns include feelings of inferiority and conscience.

The notion of identity, so central to Allport's theory, is considerably expanded in the hands of Danish-German psychologist Erik H. Erikson. Erikson has written of eight crises, each involving a conflict of orientations and the opportunity for constructive resolution. Unlike Allport's stages, Erikson's extend into adulthood and old age.

Allport's notion of conscience leads into a consideration of Kohlberg's theory of moral functioning. Kohlberg posits three levels of moral development: preconventional, conventional, and postconventional. From his point of view, the direction of development is from fear of punishment, toward increasing concern with society's rules, to possible adoption of universal moral principles that emphasize the dignity, uniqueness, and well-being of humans. Although Kohlberg's theory has been criticized, the six stages have held up relatively well under scrutiny. One shortcoming of the theory is that continuing development during the adult years is neglected. Other researchers have suggested that adults move progressively toward a position of contextual relativism.

Self-concept can be thought of as the perception of one's own personality. However, can self-concept exist in the face of behavioral inconsistency? The answer is that there may be criteria other than behavioral consistency by which personality can be established. Building on Hogan's suggestion that "you are your perceptions of how other people view you," we have looked at two features of behavior that may confirm "personality" without dependence on consistency. *Dramaturgical quality* refers to the precision, clarity, and effectiveness with which a behavior is performed. The performance of behaviors that are high in dramaturgical quality will likely yield attributions of traits to the performer that the person will then incorporate into her or his self-concept. A behavior has *dramaturgical value* to the extent that it is uncommon and is directed toward several different targets. If a person performs a behavior that is rarely seen, a corresponding trait is likely to be attributed to the performer and incorporated into his or her self-concept.

An inadequate self-concept is indicated by a consistent majority of undesirable labels included in statements of self-concept. Several suggestions for improving an inadequate self-concept can be distilled from the writings of the major personality theorists. Based on Rogers' belief that "you are your own best therapist," monitoring self-descriptions is suggested as a first step toward increasing the adequacy of self-concept.

KEY CONCEPTS

Allport
  Proprium/sense of self
  Seven stages of self-concept development
    Bodily self
    Self-identity
    Self-esteem
    Extension of self
    Self-image
    Rational coper
    Propriate striving
  Patterns
    Feelings of inferiority
    Conscience
Erikson
  Eight crises of identity
    Infancy: basic trust versus basic mistrust
    Early childhood: autonomy versus shame and
      doubt

Play age: initiative versus guilt
School age: industry versus inferiority
Adolescence: identity versus identity confusion
Young adulthood: intimacy versus isolation
Adulthood: generativity versus stagnation
Old age: integrity versus despair
Kohlberg
  Three levels of moral development
    Preconventional
    Conventional
    Postconventional
  Sociomoral perspective
  Six stages of moral development
  Contextual relativism
Hogan's theory
Dramaturgical quality
Dramaturgical value
Inadequate self-concept

REVIEW QUESTIONS

1. Outline Allport's seven stages of evolving self. What two patterns emerge from this developmental sequence?
2. Describe Erikson's eight stages of personality development and the crises associated with them. What does "identity crisis" mean in the context of Erikson's theory?
3. For each of Kohlberg's levels of moral functioning, what distinguishes between the two stages?
4. Is Kohlberg's theory convincing? Comment in light of (a) the assumption of universal moral principles and (b) the omission of adulthood from the theory.
5. How do Hogan's ideas relating to acquisition of self-concept lead around the problem of behavioral consistency?
6. Which of the suggestions for improving self-concept drawn from the major personality theorists seem most workable and persuasive to you? Would you adopt any of them, or would you choose the monitoring approach? Why?

16

Theories and Research in Review

What are some of the major similarities and differences among personality theorists?

To which psychologists are your own ideas about human behavior closest?

Why does the "interactionism" perspective seem to offer the greatest promise for future personality research?

Which of your initial assumptions and beliefs about personality have changed the most during the course?

Why are there so many personality theories and research concepts?

T HIS CHAPTER is a comprehensive, integrative review of the field of personality as it has been presented in this book. We review both theories and research, as an aid in making end-of-course comparisons (and preparing for final-exam taking). At the end of the chapter, we identify some immediate needs and future directions for the personality field. Where they exist, formal *definitions of personality* are identified, along with each theorist's view of *individual differences.*

As we review personality theory and research, we will be linking and contrasting many of the ideas previously discussed. Although similarities and areas of overlap are important, you should keep in mind that personality issues are complex and that significant differences divide even closely related theorists and approaches. (That's why there are separate chapters representing different points of view.) Nevertheless, we believe it is important for you to recognize points of overlap, even among different theoretical and research approaches to understanding personality. Recognizing general connections will be a great help to you as you endeavor to understand the complex and fascinating field of personality, and its future.

Personality Theories in Review

SIGMUND FREUD: CLASSICAL PSYCHOANALYSIS

Freud conceptualizes personality as *a closed energy system* comprised of three internal psychological subsystems (id, ego, superego) whose characteristic pattern of dynamic, conflicting interactions is formed during five childhood stages of development (oral, anal, phallic, latency, genital). The id is biological, seeks immediate gratification, and operates according to the pleasure principle of seeking pleasure and avoiding pain. The ego is psychological, seeks safety and compromise, and operates according to the reality principle of knowing what is true and false. The superego is sociocultural, seeks perfection, and operates according to the morality principle, representing what is right and wrong. Personality has instinctual origins and operates at a largely unconscious level.

Individual differences are reflected in different personality types associated with the five psychosexual stages, so-called because of their linkage to erogenous pleasure zones of the body. Pregenital types of personality include oral-receptive, oral-aggressive, anal-retentive, anal-expulsive, and narcissistic. These personality types represent unconscious fixations or regressions resulting from overuse of particular ego defense mechanisms. Mature personality results only after psychological issues of boyhood castration anxiety and girlhood penis envy are resolved through childhood identification with the same-sex parent. Such introjection resolves a boy's Oedipus complex or girl's Electra complex, thereby fostering successful development of a superego. The mature, genital personality type channels energy through sublimation in the directions "to love and to work."

CARL JUNG: ANALYTICAL PSYCHOLOGY

Jung views personality as a lifelong process of *self-realization*—the highest realization of the inborn distinctiveness of the individual. Personality is the expression of dynamic, psychic forces that preexist in an unconscious that is not just personal, as Freud believed, but collective. The collective unconscious contains archaic patterns of instinctual behavior called archetypes (self, persona, shadow, anima/animus) that are transmitted genetically. Individual differences result when these universal forms, forces, and potentials are translated through a person's symbols and behavior. Each person separates from the collective through the developmental process of individuation, which leads the person to become a psychological individual that is a separate, indivisible unity, or whole. The fullest expression of a person's individuality is the self (central archetype), which is purposive.

The four stages of life-span development are childhood, youth, middle age, and old age; life comes full-circle when the individual dies and returns to the collective. Jung's concept of personality type refers to a person's habitual attitude or "characteristic way." He considers all persons one of two psychological types according to their innate readiness to turn psychic energy either outward toward the world (extravert) or inward toward subjective experience (introvert). These types combine with four psychological functions of sensing, thinking, feeling, and intuiting. Archetypes in the collective unconscious, as well as emotional complexes in the personal unconscious, may become so powerful as to constitute a separate personality system. As with Freud, personality is largely unconscious. "Man is not master in his own house." Unlike Freud, Jung questions the universality of the Oedipus complex.

KAREN HORNEY: BASIC ANXIETY

Horney's theory is more a theory of neurosis than normal personality. However, similar to Jung, the goal of personality development in Horney's theory is *self-realization*—the development of one's potentialities. All of us experience feelings of basic anxiety or insecurity during childhood, of isolation and helplessness in a world that is potentially hostile. This basic anxiety gives rise to additional feelings of self-hatred and alienation, stemming from a sense of personal vulnerability and weakness. However, the anxiety is related to an absence of social safety and security, not to inhibited instinctual gratification, as Freud believed. Attempts to cope with anxiety encompass four strategies: avoidance, denial, rationalization, and narcotization.

Basic anxiety is systematically influenced by the quality of parent/child relationships. It increases when parents transmit their incapacity to love the child, along with excessive personal needs for reassurance: "The basic evil is invariably a lack of genuine warmth and affection." The outcome is "a disturbance in human relationships," which is then perpetuated as a cycle in which one generation of neurotic parents produces a new generation of neurotic parents-to-be, and so on. The child develops exaggerated, rigid needs for social affection and approval, revolving around ten neurotic needs. Self-realization becomes blocked as these needs crystallize into enduring motivational patterns in the personality. Genuine self-realization is sacrificed to an idealized self — an artificial pride system created to provide the personality with a sense of unity that does not in fact exist. Basic anxiety decreases when parents show their children genuine and predictable warmth, affection, and respect. Self-confidence develops, which enhances self-realization. The child then is able to be flexible and adaptable in showing individual differences in attitudes toward others and self as he moves toward, against, and away from people. Like Adler, Horney reinterprets Freud's concept of penis envy in sociocultural terms. Like Jung, Horney sees Freud's emphasis on sexuality as excessive.

HARRY STACK SULLIVAN: INTERPERSONAL THEORY

Sullivan formally defines personality as "the relatively enduring pattern of recurrent interpersonal situations which characterize a human life" (1953, pp. 110–111). Each of us has as many personalities as we have relationships with other people, whether real or fantasied. Personality does not exist in the absence of other people. It is the pattern of regularities or repetitions in these relationships that constitutes our personality.

Individual differences are reflected in Sullivan's tentative identification of at least 50 patterns of friendly and sexual human relationships. Similar to Horney, Sullivan views anxiety-security experiences in child/parent interactions as critical to personality development. This is because of the infant's absolute dependency (Horney) and powerlessness (Adler) in relationships requiring interaction with a cooperative adult.

Instead of Freud's instinctual needs, Sullivan sees infants as eliciting a reciprocal, *interpersonal* need for tenderness in nurturant adults, who then engage in activities that bring about satisfying relief from various tensions in themselves as well as the child. All social experiences are fraught with anxiety, which is sensed empathically. Anxiety gives rise to the self-system (analogous to Freud's ego) — a security system aimed at preserving feelings of well-being by defending against anxiety related to anticipated social disapproval. The self-system is a major part of personality that develops out of reflected appraisals received from significant other people. The self-system, and lust, are dynamisms — relatively enduring patterns of energy transformation. Dynamisms have the power to dominate personality, analogous to Horney's neurotic needs and Jung's archetypes and emotional complexes. Subpersonalities are also present in supervisory patterns — psychological representations of significant others, such as our parents, that we carry around with us throughout life (analogous to Freud's superego).

Sullivan's six developmental epochs revolve around the learning of major social tasks, such as acquiring language that is consensually valid, forming friendships, and establishing a preferred pattern of sexual intimacy. Like Freud, Sullivan sees personality as an energy system whose chief work is to reduce tension. Unlike Freud, Sullivan sees tensions as interpersonal as well as physical.

ALFRED ADLER: INDIVIDUAL PSYCHOLOGY

In Adler's social-interest theory, the appreciation of individual differences is unquestioned. "Every single case represents something unique, something that will never occur again" (1964, p. 188). Individual differences are present in each person's relatively permanent law of movement, as reflected in his or her unique style of life, which is different in tempo, rhythm, and direction from all others. The *style of life* is the whole of personality that integrates the parts. It consists of "certain automatised attitudes" derived from personal interpretations of one's innate capacities, defects, and first impressions of the environment. Every person is the self-creative artist of his or her own personality, constructed between the ages of 3 and 5.

All personality development stems from inferiority, especially from defects in physical organs, parental neglect, or overindulgence. To be human is to feel a constant sense of inferiority. To be human is also to compensate for inferiority by striving for superiority or perfection: "Achieve! Arise! Conquer!" The popularized concept of "inferiority complex" refers to a more exaggerated form of personal weakness than average. Similarly, "superiority complex" is an exaggerated form of overcompensation. Both are related to a deficiency in social feeling — the ultimate norm of civilized society. The foundation for social interest is provided during childhood by both parents, who encourage it by working cooperatively together. Without adequate preparation of social interest, persons will be unable to successfully meet the three unavoidable tasks of life: society, work, and love. However, educational programs and psychotherapy may be helpful in overcoming deficiencies in social feeling.

Adler's appreciation of individual differences led him to approach the question of types very cautiously. Sometimes he talked of children as being passive or active, unwanted, pampered, and influenced by their birth-order position in a family. Personal fictions are adopted "as if" true, and when they clash with reality, psychological shock or neurosis may occur. Rejecting Freud's emphasis on the past, Adler views personality as being intentionally directed toward future expectations in the form of finalistic goals.

ERICH FROMM: SOCIOPSYCHOANALYTIC HUMANISM

Fromm formally defines personality as "the totality of inherited and acquired psychic qualities which are characteristic of one individual and which make the individual unique" (1947, p. 50). People show both similarities and differences. Similarities are present in the human sharing of five common existential needs: a frame of orientation and devotion, rootedness, unity, effectiveness, and excitation and stimulation. Differences are shown in the specific ways people solve the contradictions of human existence that are built into human nature (conscious but powerless, part of but alone, living but dying, free but responsible). Human reason is both blessing and curse, with people sometimes seeking to escape from freedom. Like Jung, Fromm believes that *a* human nature exists.

Similarities and differences are also apparent in people's character, a concept Fromm discusses even more than personality. Individual differences are reflected in individual character — "the pattern of behavior characteristic for a given individual"(1947, p. 54), "the (relatively permanent) form in which human energy is canalized in the process of assimilation and socialization" (1947, p. 59). Assimilation and socialization involve relatedness to things and to people, respectively. Submission and domination are symbiotic or destructive forms of relationship, different from love.

Individual differences also exist among entire societies, some of which may be "sick." Group similarities or social character types represent "the core of a character structure common to most people of a given culture" (1947, p. 60). There are four nonproductive types of social character, or forms of relatedness to others: receiving, exploiting, hoarding, and marketing. There is also a productive type of social character that reflects fully developed relatedness toward the world and oneself in the process of living, working and loving (Freud, Adler), and reasoning.

Like Adler, Fromm sees the family as the psychological agency through which a child acquires the core of social character shared by most other children of the same social class and culture. Role modeling likely comes into play, a concept developed further by social-learning theorists. Similar to Horney, Fromm reinterprets Freud's concept of "oral character" as a psychological reaction to social experiences with people, rather than a product of psychosexual, erogenous sensations. He is like Adler in reinterpreting the Oedipus complex in terms of a child's struggle for individual freedom and independence, against the pressures of parental authority.

J. B. WATSON: BEHAVIORISM

Watson formally defines personality as "the end product of our habit systems. . . . the sum of activities that can be discovered by actual observation of behavior over a long enough time to give reliable information" (1930/1959, p. 274). Habits are learned behaviors that are practiced regularly and require little voluntary control. They originate from a few inborn reflexes (leg and trunk movements, grasping) and three primitive emotional responses (love, rage, fear).

For Watson, nearly everything is learned. Simple behaviors are elaborated through conditioning. Smaller habits develop into larger habit systems, such as a religious or patriotic-activity system. Individual differences in personality consist of the most dominant habit systems, of which there are hundreds by the time a person is 24 years old. Watson "guaranteed" he could turn a healthy infant into "any type of specialist I might select," whether doctor, lawyer, artist, beggar, or thief.

Whatever individual differences exist at birth are due to relatively minor structural and chemical variations. Although genes determine only a few primitive, inborn behaviors, these human commonalities are much more obvious and important than individual differences. Unlike Eysenck, Watson saw "no real evidence of inheritance of traits," whether capacities, talents, temperament, mental constitution, or other characteristics. Unlike Freud and Jung, Watson contended that there are no instincts but only unlearned behaviors, the natural consequences of bodily structure and functioning. Nor is there a built-in human nature, as there is for Fromm and Jung. For Watson, as for Skinner, social-learning theorists, and social psychoanalysts, environmental influences are very important.

B. F. SKINNER: ENVIRONMENTAL DETERMINISM

Skinner offers neither a definition of personality nor even a theory of personality. In fact, he believes that personality simply does not exist. "We do not need to try to discover what personalities, states of mind, feelings, traits of character . . . or the other perquisites of autonomous man really are in order to get on with scientific analysis of behavior" (1971, p. 15). Only *behaviors* exist, and all behaviors are controlled largely by one's environment, which offers certain possibilities for behavior to occur. For example, athletic champions are made more than they are born, especially in environments that promote mass exposure to athletic programs.

According to Skinner, environmental stimuli have some probability of giving rise to a behavioral response. Behavior is shaped and maintained through operant conditioning, reinforced by consequences that result when an organism operates on its environment. These reinforcing consequences, or contingencies, influence the likelihood of a behavioral operation being repeated.

Individual differences, not necessarily permanent, are reflected in the kinds of consequences likely to generate behavior. The organism's spontaneously emitted responses may be reinforced, either to occur (positive and negative reinforcement) or not to occur (punishment). Skinner differs from Watson in emphasizing positive reinforcement rather than punishment. Reinforcement schedules vary; they may be continuous or intermittent, fixed or variable. Stimulus generalization results when stimuli similar to those originally conditioned evoke the same response as the original. Extinction results when a response previously reinforced is no longer followed by the same reinforcement.

Genetic predispositions are influential in setting natural tendencies and boundaries of behavioral development, but these also are partly determined by the environment, through the process of natural selection. Skinner shares with Freud, Jung, and Watson the belief that all behavior is determined. Human freedom, as we usually think of it, is an illusion. The only freedom is freedom from aversive consequences and access to positive consequences. People are neither "good" nor "bad," except insofar as their environmental histories make them so. Nor do people "choose" their own environments. Environments select people, through consequences that are reinforcing; and environments can be designed to elicit behaviors deemed valuable, as in *Walden Two*. Behaviors can be changed through systematic behavior-modification programs that rearrange contingencies. Consequences can even be self-arranged to control behavior—a view similar to Bandura's and analogous to Kelly's. Unlike Freud and Rogers, Skinner maintains that insight and self-understanding are unnecessary for changes in behavior to occur.

JULIAN ROTTER: SOCIAL LEARNING

Rotter also offers no formal definition of personality, noting that such concepts are simply unnecessary abstractions of reality. Although Rotter agrees with Skinner that environments can control behavior, he sees preexisting individual differences as superimposed on strictly environmental influences. People will show individual differences in *behavior* even within powerful situations.

Rotter's theory is based on three main concepts relevant to individual differences: reinforcement value, psychological situation, and expectancy. Reinforcement value is the individual's degree of preference for one reinforcement over equally likely possibilities. A psychological situation is the individual's peculiar characterization of an environmental circumstance, as in the "eye of the beholder." Expectancy is the individual's subjective probability that a particular reinforcement will occur in a situation as a function of some specific behavior. Thus, generalized expectancies, such as internal or external locus of control and interpersonal trust, apply to a number of similar situations. Expectancies are learned, especially in interactions with parents—a view shared by the social psychoanalysts. Internality is linked to parental warmth, protectiveness, and nurturance (Horney), whereas externality is linked to parental coldness, rejection, and inconsistency (Rogers).

Rotter recognizes individual differences—the hallmark of "traits"—but only insofar as people can be distributed along a continuum, a conceptualization similar to Eysenck's. However, unlike Eysenck, Rotter contends that such dimensions as internal-external are not necessarily stable but vary at different points in time and under different circumstances (Cattell's "states"). This is because behavior results from multiple determinants, external as well as internal.

ALBERT BANDURA: SOCIAL LEARNING

For Bandura, individual differences are related to cognitive, behavioral, and environmental factors that work together to determine individual action, especially in social situations. Contrary to such stimulus-response (S-R) approaches as Watson's, Bandura believes that people can learn a *behavior* through observation before actually performing it themselves, even without prior reinforcement. This is because people are aware of consequences, able to anticipate future outcomes, and motivated by internal incentives as well as external ones. An incentive is anything that creates an anticipation of positive outcome following performance of a behavior. Social learning entails acquiring useful information through interactions with people and other elements of the environment. Observational learning through modeling is central to this process, since observers are apt to adopt the behaviors or expectancies of those who serve as models. Models show how a behavior is done, and the benefits that accrue from it, by performing it.

Human awareness is important for Bandura, as it is for Fromm, Rogers, Maslow, and Kelly. It plays a role in ongoing processes of self-evaluation, vicarious reinforcement, and social comparison. People are not pawns but shapers of circumstances (Kelly). Individual freedom is reflected in self-regulatory capacities to rearrange relationships between behaviors and their consequences (Skinner). Bandura's concept of self-efficacy, or beliefs about one's ability to perform behaviors that will yield expected outcomes, is similar to Rotter's internal locus of control. As with Freud, Jung, and the social psychoanalysts, defensive behaviors may be adopted to cope with anticipated events that are unpleasant.

Bandura's emphasis on the social aspects of experience is reminiscent of a parallel emphasis among the social-psychoanalytic theorists. However, social-learning theory is partially inconsistent with stage theories of development, such as those of Piaget, Kohlberg, Freud, Erikson, Jung, Sullivan, and Maslow. Bandura believes that there is little support for such theories. He is also critical of such humanistic concepts as unconditional positive regard and self-actualization (Rogers, Maslow). Finally, he disagrees with the concept of biological preparedness suggested by Seligman and Jung, which focuses on innate predispositions and limitations based on anatomical or physiological characteristics.

CARL ROGERS: PERSON-CENTERED THEORY

Rogers comes closest to defining personality with his concept of the self— "the organized, consistent conceptual gestalt composed of perceptions of the characteristics of the 'I' or 'me' and the perceptions of the relationships of the 'I' or 'me' to various aspects of life, together with the values attached to these perceptions" (1959, p. 200). Rogers' emphasis on self is similar to that of Maslow, Allport, and Jung, but quite different from Skinner and Eysenck. Skinner and Watson flatly deny the existence of, or need for, a concept of self. Rogers differs from Freud, Jung, and Sullivan in assigning much greater importance to the conscious, rational, integrative, responsible, and self-deterministic aspects of the self.

As Sullivan believes that personality does not exist in the absence of interpersonal relationships, Rogers believes that self does not exist in the absence of personal perceptions. As with Adler, the self is not an end point but a creative process. Rogers' phenomenological framework is grounded in an appreciation of subjectively meaningful perceptions and evaluations. The idea that subjective, individualized experiences are "really true" is also affirmed by the existentialists, and parallels Jung's concept of "personal myths," Adler's "as-if" fictions, Kelly's "personal constructs," and the "psychological situations" discussed by Rotter, Bandura, and Lewin. Like Kelly, Rogers believes that the self is influenced by constructions, which also change and reorganize in different ways over time.

For Rogers, biological influences (Freud, Jung, Eysenck) and environmental influences (Skinner, social-learning theorists) both play important roles in personality development. Biology contributes the actualizing tendency—an innate formative tendency characteristic of all living organisms. The actualizing tendency is the human organism's one central source of energy or motivation. Individual differences are reflected in the tendency toward self-actualization, a concept also emphasized by Maslow. Rogers sees self-actualization as every person's lifelong process of "realizing" his or her potentialities (Horney, Jung), to become a fully functioning person and "to be that self which one truly is."

The person is placed first in Rogers' person-centered theory: the most important influence on personality is the person as a whole (Allport, Jung, Murray, existentialists). The fully functioning person is consciously aware, free to choose, valuing from within, self-regulating, and self-directing. This concept is similar to those of Maslow, Kelly, Fromm, Bandura, and Rotter, but not Skinner, Freud, or Jung.

For Rogers, behavior is "the goal-directed attempt of the organism to satisfy the experienced needs for *actualization* in the reality as *perceived*" (1959, p. 222). This future-oriented perspective is consistent with Adler, Jung, Kelly, Rotter, and Bandura, who see behavior as goal-directed rather than "pushed" by the past and by inner forces. Like Maslow, Rogers disagrees with Freud's view of people as innately irrational, destructive, and aggressive.

Rogers believes that the person's vast inner resources for self-actualization can be utilized only under conditions of a favorable psychological environment, which is often interpersonal (social psychoanalysts, Erikson, social-learning theorists). Positive self-regard is essential for psychological health but is often blocked by others in the social environment, who place artificial conditions of worth on the individual's goodness or acceptability, especially during childhood.

Rogers' three necessary and sufficient conditions for effective personality development, as well as therapeutic change, are interpersonal attitudes of unconditional positive regard, empathic understanding, and congruence (Bandura would disagree). Psychological maladjustment is closely associated with discrepancies between the person's internal and external experiences. Like Horney, Rogers stresses that one's ideal self may be discrepant with one's actual self. Another form of incongruence is between one's inner, organismic experiences and one's outer, lived experiences—similar to Freud's "unacceptable impulses," Jung's "projections," and Kelly's "incompatible constructs." Defensiveness and anxiety occur when the self-concept is threatened and the person seeks to maintain his or her current structure of self in the face of contradictory information (Sullivan's "self-system," Kelly's "threat").

Obviously missing in Rogers' theory are concepts of traits, types, and developmental stages, because of the value that Rogers places on the person as a whole, whose development follows a single, directional process of self-actualization.

ABRAHAM MASLOW: SELF-ACTUALIZATION

Maslow proposed a preliminary definition of a "personality syndrome" as "a structured, organized complex of apparently diverse specificities (behaviors, thoughts, impulses to action, perceptions, etc.) [having] a common unity that may be expressed variously as a similar dynamic meaning, expression, 'flavor,' function, or purpose" (1954, p. 32). Maslow's theory combines an ultimate need for self-actualization with prior levels of needs in a sequential hierarchy. Once a lower-order need is fulfilled, people move on to the next need in the hierarchy. There are four lower-order, or deficiency, needs (D-needs) requiring satisfaction:

physiological, safety and security, belongingness and love, and esteem. A deficiency in a lower-order need dominates personality functioning until it is satisfied, thereby freeing the person to move on. Self-actualization, the fifth basic need, is at the top of the hierarchy. Higher-level needs emerge gradually and may overlap with earlier needs.

As with Rogers, individual differences are greatest in relation to self-actualization—the overriding need of every person to meet an inherent goal to realize his or her inner potentialities. All people *must* be true to their own nature. What a person *can* be, he or she *must* be. Self-actualizers are people who become superior personalities. These select few fulfill themselves by making complete use of their potentialities, capacities, and talents. They go beyond deficiency motivations, living their lives according to growth motivation—high-level cognitive and esthetic metaneeds (B-values). They are good choosers who are likely to have mystical, peak experiences. Similar to Jung, Maslow takes strong issue with the scientific use of statistical averages to represent individual personality.

Maslow believes human nature is born rather than made, a view shared by Fromm, Rogers, Freud, Jung, Eysenck, and Cattell. Unlike Skinner, he does not believe that environments shape humanness. Human values are rooted in biology (Rogers, Fromm); their assumed genetic basis and universal characteristics make them instinct-like (Freud, Jung). Maslow's utopia, Eupsychia, is an alternative to Skinner's Walden Two. In Eupsychia, external controls are minimized, and respect for individual freedoms and choices is maximized (Rogers, Fromm). Organismic valuing ensures that human beings will make wise choices, within the context of a psychologically supportive environment (Rogers).

GEORGE KELLY: A COGNITIVE THEORY OF CONSTRUCTS

Kelly views personality as *a system of personal constructs*—individual ways of construing or interpreting the world. Human behavior is controlled not by instincts, needs, or environments, but by constructs arrived at consciously through the use of cognitive or mental functions. People behave as scientists. They determine their own behavior by making personal predictions about future events. Their focus is not on the past (Freud, Skinner) but toward the future (Adler, Rogers, Rotter, Bandura).

The fundamental postulate of Kelly's theory is that individuals' processes are psychologically channelized by the ways in which they anticipate events. Anticipations are analogous to the "expectations" discussed by social-learning theorists. The channels are personal constructs. Every construct has two poles, one of which is emergent or primary and the other implicit or contrasting, as in tolerant-intolerant. Constructs have varied ranges of application and may be changeable or impermeable. When constructs fail to predict experience, the accompanying realization that one's personal hypotheses require changing begins to set constructive alternativism into motion. However, people experience threat when their construction systems do not apply to important events in life, and anxiety when their construction systems are in need of reorganization. This account of anxiety is similar to those of Rogers and Sullivan.

Individual differences are reflected by variations in the number, content, and organization of constructs. Kelly recognizes that two or more people whose experiences are similar may share some constructs (Fromm's "social character"). Personality development is a matter of evolution, from primitive dependency constructs based on survival needs to more flexible constructs addressed in social relations (trust-distrust). Like Rogers and Maslow, Kelly sees human behavior as determined largely from within. However, he is similar to Sullivan, Rotter, and Bandura in maintaining that internal constructs result from the consequences of an external factor, social relations. Roles involve understanding the construction systems of others and behaving in ways that meet the expectations of important other people in one's life (social learning, Sullivan).

What Is Your View of Personality?	**BOX 2.1** **REVISITED**

In Chapter 2, we asked you to explore your own assumptions about personality (Box 2.1). We now invite you to compare your initial assumptions with those you have read about in this book. (The results may also serve to guide your future reading about personality.) In what ways are your ideas similar to or different from those of Freud, Horney, Skinner, Rogers, and others? It is unlikely that you will show total agreement with any one theorist, but you may be able to determine which theorists you are most in sympathy with and would like to know more about. Have any of your earlier assumptions changed during the course?

The list below shows how various theorists stand on the questions covered in Box 2.1. Not all theorists and researchers are covered on every dimension; instead, we have tried to include those theorists whose positions offer the clearest or most representative examples on the various dimensions.

Theorists' Assumptions about Personality

1. Human behavior results primarily from *heredity,* what has been genetically transmitted by parents, or from *environment,* the external circumstances and experiences that shape a person after conception has occurred.

                 1   2   3   4   5   6   7
   heredity   –   –   –   –   –   –   –   environment
             EYSENCK, CATTELL,   SOCIAL PSYCHOANA-
             PAVLOV, SHELDON,   LYSTS, SKINNER,
             FREUD, JUNG   WATSON, ROTTER,
                                        BANDURA, ROGERS

2. An important part of every person is a *self,* some central aspect of personality referred to as "I" or "me," or there really is *no self* in personality.

                 1   2   3   4   5   6   7
   self   –   –   –   –   –   –   –   no self
             ALLPORT, ROGERS,   WATSON, SKINNER,
             MASLOW, ERIKSON,   ROTTER, MISCHEL
             HORNEY, JUNG

continued

3. Personality is relatively *unchanging,* with each person showing the same behavior throughout a lifetime, or personality is relatively *changing,* with each
person showing different behavior throughout a lifetime.

	1	2	3	4	5	6	7	
unchanging	–	–	–	–	–	–	–	changing

FREUD, SOCIAL   ROGERS, SOCIAL
PSYCHOANALYSTS,   LEARNING, MISCHEL
EYSENCK, CATTELL

4. The most important influences on behavior are *past* events, what has previously occurred to a person, or *future* events, what a person seeks to bring
about by striving to meet certain goals.

	1	2	3	4	5	6	7	
past	–	–	–	–	–	–	–	future

FREUD, JUNG,   ADLER, KELLY,
FROMM, EYSENCK   ROGERS, MASLOW,
                                    BANDURA,
                                    MCCLELLAND

5. The most important characteristics about people are *general* ones, those
commonly shared by many people, or *unique* ones, those that make each
person different from every other person.

	1	2	3	4	5	6	7	
general	–	–	–	–	–	–	–	unique

WATSON, SKINNER,   ALLPORT, ADLER,
EYSENCK, FROMM   ROGERS, KELLY,
                                    BANDURA, ROTTER

6. People are motivated to cooperate with others mainly because they are *self-
centered,* expecting to receive some personal gain, or mainly because they are
altruistic, seeking to work with others only for the benefit of doing things with
and for others.

	1	2	3	4	5	6	7	
self-centered	–	–	–	–	–	–	–	altruistic

FREUD, JUNG,   ADLER, FROMM,
KOHLBERG   MASLOW, ROGERS,
                                    BANDURA

7. People learn best when they are motivated by *reward,* involving pleasure, or by
punishment, involving pain.

	1	2	3	4	5	6	7	
reward	–	–	–	–	–	–	–	punishment

SKINNER, BANDURA,   WATSON
PAVLOV, FREUD,
MASLOW

8. The main reason you behave as you do (for example, attend college) is because of conscious *personal* decisions to do so, or because *social* factors outside
your control leave you little real choice in the matter.

continued

BOX 2.1
REVISITED
continued

```
              1     2     3     4     5     6     7
personal      –     –     –     –     –     –     –     social
         ROGERS, MASLOW,         SKINNER, SULLIVAN,
         ALLPORT, FROMM          BANDURA, MISCHEL
```

9. Human nature is essentially *constructive,* with people showing positive personal growth and a desire to help others fulfill their potentials, or *destructive,* with people showing behavior that is ultimately self-defeating and a desire to keep others from improving themselves.

```
                 1     2     3     4     5     6     7
constructive     –     –     –     –     –     –     –     destructive
         ADLER, ROGERS,                FREUD
         MASLOW
```

10. Human beings have *no purpose* or reason for their existence other than what they experience on a day-to-day basis, or human beings have some *purpose* for living that is outside themselves.

```
                1     2     3     4     5     6     7
no purpose      –     –     –     –     –     –     –     purpose
         SKINNER, WATSON,         ADLER, FROMM,
         BANDURA, MISCHEL        HORNEY, ROGERS,
                                 MASLOW, JUNG,
                                 EXISTENTIALISTS
```

11. An additional characteristic about people that I have found helpful for understanding or predicting their behavior is _____.
(Add any new characteristics you may have learned to value since Chapter 2, along with a corresponding theorist or researcher.)

Contemporary Empirical Approaches to Personality in Review

SEARCHING FOR PERSONALITY TRAITS AND TYPES: EYSENCK'S MODEL

To review the working definition introduced in Chapter 1, *personality* reflects *individual differences along each of several behavioral dimensions.* Each behavioral dimension corresponds to a *trait,* or hypothetical construct, believed to be more or less of some internal influence. A trait can be measured according to the degree to which it characterizes a person's behaviors along a behavioral dimension. Persons can then be compared and contrasted by the degrees to which they are characterized by different traits, as when a series of traits is graphed in a *profile* to show individual differences in personality. *Types* are commonalities in trait profiles of subgroups of individuals who share patterns of related traits. This orientation is the essence of Rorer and Widiger's definition of personality as "a collection of traits" (1983, p. 444).

The definitions just reviewed are most clearly represented by Eysenck's *dimensional* concept of traits. That is, individuals differ along a continuum in the degree to which they show a trait, as with more-to-less extraversion, rather than being either introverted *or* extraverted, as Jung suggested. This orientation is also reflected in the use of Cattell's 16 PF profile sheet, which allows an overall pattern of 16 traits to be graphed using connecting lines to indicate different degrees of each trait within a standard scoring framework.

Although Allport believes the number of individual traits to be countless, most researchers report a limited number of traits. Traits often operate relatively independently of one another. Hans and Sybil Eysenck identify three independent traits; extraversion-introversion, neuroticism-stability, and psychoticism-superego functioning. Although Cattell identifies 16 traits, subgroups of these are intercorrelated. The two largest of Cattell's six higher-order factors pertain to extraversion and anxiety, similar to Eysenck's dimensions of extraversion and neuroticism. Norman's "big five" universal traits are activity/dominance, agreeableness, conscientiousness, emotional stability, and culture/smartness.

Correlational and experimental methods.   Factor analysis is a correlational method that aids *description* (the "what") of traits, reducing massive quantities of data about habitual behavior into summary form by identifying their statistical interrelationships. However, the *explanation* (the "why") of individual differences comes from other methods, especially hypothetico-deductive theory and experimentation. Theoretical explanations for traits are most often grounded in biological terms: genetic predispositions, biological temperaments, physiological structures in the brain, physicochemical processes of arousal and inhibition, and hormonal processes in the endocrine system (Pavlov, Eysenck, Cattell, Zuckerman). Factor theorists believe that personality is born, not made, a view opposite to that of more environmental theorists such as Skinner and McClelland. Eysenck sees the role of environment as generally effecting only "slight changes" in personality. He believes that American psychologists fail to appreciate the degree to which organisms respond differently to the same environmental stimuli, independent of learning. In marked contrast to Watson's view of child rearing, he contends that parents have little real influence on the behavior of their offspring and would be better off not assuming excessive "responsibility." Eysenck would also minimize the ideas of social psychoanalysts and social-learning theorists, who place parent/child, family, interpersonal, social, and cultural relationships at the forefront of personality development. Accidental combinations of genes are much more powerful in determining behavior than environments. At bottom, individual differences can be traced to hereditary predispositions that incline an organism to sense, perceive, and respond to environmental stimulation more readily in some ways than in others.

Regarding experimentation, many predictions about traits have been confirmed and replicated by hypothesis testing under systematically controlled conditions. Research findings offer evidence of trait-related "strong" and "weak" nervous-system arousal, related to individual differences in several areas: cortex excitability and inhibition; sensory thresholds; responses to drugs, alcohol, caffeine, and tobacco; conditioning, learning, perception, memory, social behavior, and therapeutic treatment; and reactions to college exam results. A reliable laboratory test even shows that introverts salivate more than extraverts in response to lemon juice. Sybil Eysenck and Cattell report developmental trait profiles characteristic of children, adults, and elderly persons. Both Eysencks and Cattell also report psychological test profiles for hundreds of occupational, social, prison, and clinical groups. Experimental findings derived from thousands of samples of human subjects, and sometimes lower animals, have supported and verified many predictions formulated and stated on theoretical grounds. The pattern of these research procedures and results is consistent with Cattell's definition of personality as "that which permits a prediction of what a person will do in a given situation" (1950, p. 2).

OTHER TRAITS THAT INFLUENCE BEHAVIOR

The extensive factor-analytic work of H. Eysenck and Cattell does not encompass the vast number of trait labels reported in the psychological literature. Even within the framework of Eysenck's theory, Gray reinterprets extraversion away from "sociability" toward "impulsiveness." The term *trait labels* is used intentionally: although the words theorists use to describe a trait may differ, the underlying behavioral dimension represented by these word-labels can often be inferred from the high correlations among them. For example, Eysenck's "neuroticism," Cattell's "anxiety," and Norman's "lack of emotional stability" are three such labels. The reason is that personality concepts such as *trait* and *self* do not exist in any real, physical sense. They are hypothetical constructs or abstractions of reality.

Four major trait dimensions serve to illustrate the relationship of traits to behavior: authoritarianism and dogmatism, anxiety, achievement motivation, and sensation seeking.

Authoritarianism and dogmatism. *Authoritarianism* refers to antidemocratic or prejudiced ideas, feelings, and overall tendencies that are more than surface opinion, having sources deep within the structure of the person. The theoretical framework employed by Adorno, Frenkel-Brunswik, Levinson, and Sanford to understand this personality syndrome is loosely psychoanalytic, with references to unconscious forces, defense mechanisms, sadomasochism, and deep-lying trends within the personality (Freud, Fromm). However, indications of middle-class susceptibility to development of an authoritarian personality tie this trait to parental and cultural influences (social psychoanalysts), to the kind of exaggerated "emotional need to submit" to authority present in situational obedience (Milgram), and to observational or social learning of aggressive behavior (Bandura).

The ideological beliefs of authoritarianism are adhered to more often by persons of the political right than left and are directly linked to anti-Semitism, ethnocentrism, politico-economic conservatism, and fascism. For these reasons, Rokeach explored development of an alternative construct, dogmatism, that might be content-free. *Dogmatism* is the degree to which the structure of a person's belief system is closed or open, independent of content. However, correlations between measures of authoritarianism (belief content) and dogmatism (belief structure) are high. Research findings that dogmatic persons lack the ability to deal with new, contradictory information, and seek rapid closure when exposed to new situations, seem related to Kelly's cognitive concepts of range of convenience, impermeability, and fear. Closed-minded persons utilize fewer personal constructs, and do so more rigidly, than open-minded persons, supported by Bieri's findings about cognitive simplicity and cognitive complexity. Rogers' "openness to experience" is also relevant to open-mindedness.

Regarding Adorno et al.'s question of how great masses of people in a society could tolerate mass extermination of their fellow citizens, authoritarianism and dogmatism concepts answer that some persons may be more predisposed than others to "just follow orders." Thus, important aspects of mental functioning are tied not just to intellectual ability, but to personality. The inability of dogmatic persons to separate relevant information from irrelevant sources is related to such personality influences as self-protection from anxiety (Sullivan, Rogers, Kelly), self-serving needs for social approval and power (Horney, Adler, Fromm), and the valuing of certain social rewards (Rotter, Bandura).

Anxiety.   Anxiety constructs appear everywhere. They are represented in theories, research, clinical concepts, personality development, dynamics, traits, states, factors, drives, behaviors, self and cognitive processes, interpersonal relationships, situations (stressors), and hundreds of assessment techniques. Anxiety of some kind is discussed by nearly all personality psychologists. In addition to the factor-analytic labels referred to previously, there are Taylor's manifest anxiety, Spielberger's trait-state anxiety, Horney's basic anxiety, Freud's neurotic anxiety, and the American Psychiatric Association's anxiety disorders, among others.

Additional traits are related to anxiety. Dillehay's model of development indicates that authoritarianism is fostered by anxiety-arousing threats to cognitive understanding. Rokeach and Kemp find dogmatism developmentally linked to anxiety in parent/child relationships. Zuckerman reports an inverse correlation between realistic anxiety (Freud) and sensation seeking in risk-taking situations. Only the behaviorists (Skinner) avoid using an anxiety concept, because they want to infer nothing about traits or self or personality within the organism. Their orientation is to see only what is external and observable, especially environmental conditions. At that, Watson writes of innate startle and fear responses.

The absence of an agreed-upon definition of anxiety is due partly to the diverse orientations of psychologists, and partly to the complexity of the phenomena underlying it. Too, the multiple components of anxiety (self-report, motor behavior, physiological responses) may or may not correlate with one another, leading to assessment difficulties. *Anxiety* is an unpleasant experience of high, diffuse arousal, in the absence of an identifiable, fear-producing object. Epstein identifies three sources of anxiety: primary overstimulation (Freud), cognitive incongruity (Rogers, Kelly), and response unavailability (social learning). The Yerkes-Dodson law helps explain the relationship between anxiety arousal and productive functioning, graphed as an inverse U curve (Eysenck).

Achievement motivation (*n* Ach).   *Achievement motivation* (n *Ach*) refers to a person's learned need or drive to achieve success in competition with some standard of excellence. Atkinson defines a need or motive as "a relatively enduring disposition" to strive toward a particular goal-state or aim. Other aims include power and affiliation (social psychoanalysts, Maslow). Atkinson's risk-preference model predicts achievement behavior according to a formula of motivation $\times$ expectancy $\times$ incentive (social learning), complicated by conflicting motives to approach success and avoid failure.

McClelland's system of scoring *n* Ach in TAT stories predicts achievement behaviors of men but not women. This is partly due to social norms and cultural inhibitions that restrict women's roles, a subject addressed by Horner, Horney, and Adler. Predictions for women are more successful using J. T. Spence's reconceptualization of achievement as multifaceted, including the dimensions of mastery, work, and competitiveness. An increase in *n* Ach among a society's business entrepreneurs, associated with the adoption of values consistent with Weber's Protestant Ethic and a productive risk-taking ratio of 50-50, often precedes a country's economic growth. Concepts related to *n* Ach include productive character orientation (Fromm), striving for superiority (Adler), self-realization (Horney, Jung), self-actualization (Maslow, Rogers), and sublimation (Freud).

Sensation seeking.   *Sensation seeking* is a trait defined by the need for varied, novel, and complex sensations and experiences, along with a willingness to take physical and social risks to obtain them. It reflects a broad motive to maintain an optimal level of stimulation or arousal (Fromm). Its origins are genetic (Eysenck, Cattell), and it shows reliable biological and behavioral correlates.

Traits versus states.   Constructs such as anxiety have been conceptualized in dual ways — sometimes as a relatively consistent and permanent predisposition (trait), and sometimes as a momentary reaction to a stressful situation (state). Persons generally high on a given trait may not show it in all situations, and those generally low may show it on some occasions. Also, a person's experience of anxiety, hostility, dependency, or sensation seeking "in general" may differ from the experience of it "today" (Zuckerman & Lubin). Cattell, Epstein, Spielberger, and Zuckerman address the merits of the trait-state distinction. However, the distinction remains somewhat arbitrary (Allen & Potkay, 1981, 1983b).

First, the same labels or variables are often used to refer to both the state and the trait. Allen and Potkay's analysis of four assessment techniques, using Allport and Odbert's list of 18,000 words for describing personality, showed 4%–5% "state" words appearing on two trait measures and 48%–48% "trait" words appearing on two state measures. Thus, one psychologist's *trait* is sometimes another psychologist's *state*. Cattell uses some of the same variables, such as annoyability and emotionality, when defining anxiety as a trait and as a state. Zuckerman and Lubin's Multiple Affect Adjective Check List (MAACL) employs the same 132 adjectives to measure trait and state dimensions of anxiety, hostility, and depression, respectively.

Zuckerman (1983) replies that measurement scales are more reliable than individual words in differentiating traits and states. Referring to anxiety scales, he indicates that (1) state scores vary more than trait scores from occasion to occasion, (2) state scores have low correlations with trait scores on single occasions, (3) state scores correlate more highly with other state scores than with trait scores on single occasions, and (4) trait scores show little sensitivity to immediate state-arousal conditions. However, Kendall, Finch, Auerbach, Hooke, and Mikulka reported "a surprising finding" that "A-Trait scores varied significantly across administrations" (1976, p. 411).

Second, whether an assessment instrument measures a trait or a state may depend only on the instructions used. The only change on the two MAACL forms is in instructions asking for self-descriptions either "in general" or "now—today."

Third, trait and state constructs are so closely tied together that a measure of state is often used to derive an index of the trait. To quote from Spielberger, "Individual differences in A-Trait are inferred from the frequency and the intensity of A-State reactions over time" (1972, p. 490). What frequency or intensity of behavior establishes the presence of a trait, especially in advance of gathering data? At what point does a state end and a trait begin? Zuckerman indicates that mood ratings over one week's time "may be a period of time that begins to sample what is typical for a person's general reactions (a trait)" (1983, p. 1085). However, there are no clear-cut answers to these questions (Alston, Murray). Arbitrary judgments partly enter into the distinction.

Concluding generalizations about traits.   Three concluding generalizations may be added about traits. First, no traits are "best," generally speaking. Traits are neither good nor bad, right nor wrong, better nor worse. However, be aware that complicated issues of personal and social values may be raised regarding authoritarianism, dogmatism, and sensation seeking. Most psychologists believe that society should not press for behavioral uniformity (Eysenck, Fromm, Rogers, Maslow, Skinner). Traits essentially reflect individual differences.

Second, many psychologists give greater recognition to the importance of social environments in trait development contrasted with Eysenck, Cattell, and Zuckerman. Support for this generalization is clearer in relation to authoritarianism, dogmatism, and achievement motivation compared with extraversion, psychoticism, and perhaps anxiety. Adorno et al., Rokeach, McClelland, and Winterbottom pay particular attention to early parent/child interactions (Horney, Sullivan, Adler), along with broad cultural influences (Fromm, existentialists' "Age of Anxiety").

Third, a difficulty with trait and type concepts is that they show no necessary correspondence with a specific behavior on any one-to-one basis. The same trait may reveal itself in different behaviors, as with extraversion (developing many friendships, having fun at parties, liking changes). Thus, in a 50-item test of extraversion, two people could receive the same score by referring to different behaviors and experiences. Person A could answer all the even-numbered items and person B all the odd-numbered items. Also, different traits may evoke the same behaviors, as with extraversion and sensation seeking (developing many friendships, having fun at parties, liking changes).

IDENTIFYING SITUATIONAL INFLUENCES ON BEHAVIOR

Whereas traits refer to *internal,* predisposing personality influences, situations refer to *external* influences on behavior, such as those discussed by Skinner and the social-learning theorists. These environmental influences can be physical, psychological, social, or sociocultural. Most important is the *psychological* environment—the perceptions, experiences, and relationships having greatest personal meaning for the individual in his or her own life space (Lewin, Rogers, Kelly). This emphasis affirms the existential embeddedness of creature-and-environment noted by Fromm and the existentialists, as well as the view of person-and-situation as a single integrated unit (Murray, social-learning theorists, interactionists). Personality and behavior can be seen as "a product of formerly encountered situations" that have become assimilated and integrated (Murray).

The power of situations is unquestioned, although sometimes it is quiet rather than dramatic. The quiet power of situations is seen in life's chance encounters, such as beginning a friendship or career (Bandura); going on vacation or celebrating holidays (Holmes & Rahe); experiencing the wear and tear of everyday stressors, physically and emotionally (Selye); and living during times of sociocultural megatrends and "future shock" (Naisbitt, Toffler). The power of situations is more dramatic during experiences of death or divorce in one's family, the sudden appearance of a delayed-stress syndrome in Vietnam veterans, or a natural disaster such as the volcanic eruption at Mount Saint Helens. The compelling power of psychological situations to elicit surprising behavior is also evident in the case of Patty Hearst, subjects in Milgram's obedience experiments, and members of Reverend Jim Jones' Peoples Temple. Even desirable "eustress" can be dramatic in its power to change human lives, as state lottery winners quickly learn. Thus, people's behavior may be determined less by the kind of persons they are and more by the kind of situations they find themselves in.

Since all change is stressful, maladaptive reactions to psychosocial stressors may occur. *Stressors* are conditions of perceived imbalance between environmental demands and a person's capacity to meet those demands. Mischel points to fixed patterns of behavior, in which people respond rigidly and indiscriminately across situations, perhaps in ways labeled "neurotic" by Horney, Kelly, and Pavlov. However, the ability of human beings to adapt to the demands of environmental influences is remarkable, as Skinner and Rogers have noted.

The "personalities" of environments. Environments have unique "personalities" of their own (Insel & Moos). These can be measured through group consensus about the humanlike attributes of environments (Pace & Stern), and by factually documented behaviors of the kind seen in the study of Mount Saint Helens (Adams & Adams). The psychosocial climates of college environments is evidenced by higher or lower degrees of intellectualism and play. Funder and Bem developed templates of college situations using group Q-sorts that defined the behavioral characteristics of several ideal types of students. Cantor, Mischel, and Schwartz established category prototypes of social, cultural, psychological, and political situations on college campuses. "Fuzzy features" about situations often reflect human characteristics. Different characteristics of environments are likely to elicit and select different reactions and behaviors (Skinner, social learning). These differences have yet to be classified in a workable, predictive taxonomy, although some beginning efforts have been made, including Murray's environmental press and Moos' six categories of human environments.

About humanlike descriptions of environments.   The degree to which psychologists and lay people find it useful to conceptualize environments in "human" terms deserves special mention. For example, Pace and Stern's development of the College Characteristics Index is not derived from Murray's schema of environmental *press,* but from his schema of personality *needs.* Cantor, Mischel, and Schwartz find that "a substantial portion" of the features in prototype situations refer to personal and social characteristics of people commonly found in them (happy, dancing, talking, nervous, impressive language, good manners). And Fromm believes entire societies may be "sane" or "sick." These observations are consistent with the discussion in Chapter 1, which indicated that people tend to be implicit trait theorists, laypersons and psychologists alike (Bem & Allen; Lamiell). Perhaps we are unaccustomed to thinking of objects and events in other than "human" terms or a "personal" perspective, paralleled historically by people's tendency (until Galileo) to think of the sun as circling the earth.

SITUATIONS AND AGGRESSIVE BEHAVIOR

Aggression is sometimes thought of as a biologically based instinct; certainly Freud adopted this view. However, it often is dominated by psychosocial situations. Baron defines *aggression* as any form of behavior performed with the intention or goal of harming another living being who is motivated to avoid harm. In experimental settings, the most widely used technique for studying aggression is the Buss-shock method.

A number of external sources of aggression have been identified, including frustration, racial prejudice, modeling, observational learning, certain kinds of erotic stimulation, heat, noise, television violence, and instigation. Dollard's original frustration-aggression hypothesis — that frustration always leads to aggression and aggression always follows frustration (Freud) — has an uncertain status. The hypothesis has been modified to allow for other reactions to frustration, including depression (Bandura) and learned helplessness (Seligman). Baron argues that aggression is not even the usual response to frustration. Learning to aggress merely by watching an aggressive model in films, cartoons, television, and real-life acts (hitting a Bobo doll) is a common phenomenon, well established by research; this finding is consistent with the view of social-learning theorists.

Racism exerts a subtle influence on aggressiveness. Direct aggression toward Blacks is shown more when Whites remain anonymous and face no censure or retaliation (Allen; Donnerstein & Donnerstein). Rape, too, is associated with subtle influences on aggressiveness that are difficult to detect. Immediate circumstances may lower male inhibitions about aggressing toward women, including stong exposure to aggressive or erotic stimulation, viewing a filmed rape, and adopting false cultural beliefs that women enjoy rape, pain, and suffering. Although women clearly indicate that they do not wish to be victimized, Malamuth, Haber, and Feshbach found that 51% of male college students reported they would engage in rape if assured they would not be punished. These men may be confusing sex with violence, an idea proposed by Freud. External sociocultural influences regarding sex roles of "masculine" dominance and the inferior status of women are general contributors to these aggressive patterns (Brownmiller, Horney, Adler).

Various external methods of preventing and controlling aggression have been suggested, including punishment, catharsis, exposure to non-aggressive models, mild erotic stimulation that serves as a distractor, humor, empathy, child-rearing practices, sex-role training, and anti-aggression therapy. The relative ineffectiveness of punishment is linked to harmful side effects and temporary influences (Skinner, Estes). Also, aggression begets aggression, as seen in popular observations that physical, sexual, and emotional abuse of children is likely perpetuated through parent/child interactions (Sullivan's "malevolent attitude"). Threats of punishment are most likely to control aggression *if* the threatened punishment is severe, is very likely to occur, occurs soon after the aggressive response, the aggressor is not angry, and the aggressor has little to gain from the aggression. Catharsis has also been found to be relatively ineffective in controlling aggression, contrary to psychoanalytic expectations.

In sum, although aggressive behaviors are not confined to "a few twisted individuals," there is little evidence that personality traits or instincts play the predominant role in human aggression. The evidence is convincing that situations may dominate aggressive behavior, whether general, racial, or sexual.

SEARCHING FOR A RECONCILIATION: INTERACTIONISM

Interactionism is the point of view that traits and situations combine to determine behavior. A person will manifest behavior corresponding to a given trait in some situations but not others. Interactionism also implies a continuous interrelationship between persons and the situations they encounter (a dynamic rather than mechanistic model). Situations affect persons who, in turn, affect situations (Bandura, Rotter, Mischel, Endler, Magnusson).

From the trait point of view, persons who possess a certain trait will express it in a wide variety of situations. People show individual differences regardless of the situations they are in. This approach is represented not only by Eysenck and Cattell, but by Freud and the social psychoanalysts. From the situational point of view, traits are unimportant. Situational demands make everyone behave much like everyone else. Situations tend to elicit similar behaviors, regardless of people's "internal" characteristics. From the interaction point of view, different people behave differently in different situations.

Traits? Situations?   Rorer and Widiger claim they have never met anyone who, from a behavioral view, was not a trait theorist. Otherwise, human activities such as selecting a mate, interviewing job applicants, and evaluating students according to the degree to which they work up to their abilities would be relatively meaningless. If one really believes that situations determine behavior, one could simply rely on situations to elicit desired behaviors, as in Milgram's obedience experiments and Skinner's *Walden Two*. Situations would make the person.

Rorer and Widiger do not question the impact of some situations on some behaviors. People do not typically go to a restaurant for a haircut, read books in movie theaters, make love during church services, or sleep during football games. These situations clearly dominate behavior. However, a person's traits "may determine whether one goes to a movie or to a football game, or if one stays home and sleeps or reads a book" (1983, p. 446). Rorer and Widiger further indicate that such facts about the role of traits is not likely to be discovered by psychologists conducting experiments in which people are placed into situations ahead of time, because the subjects have minimal opportunity to select their own situations.

Jackson and Paunonen note that few theorists can be found who believe in the "extreme position that variables associated with the person play no role in behavior" (1980, p. 523). Funder and Ozer add that trait and situational extremes are equally lacking in empirical support. Where does this leave us? Right in the middle of things, which is exactly where we wish to be! That is, neither persons nor environments determine behavior independently of each other. Persons play an important role in influencing behavior, and environmental situations play an important role. There is . . . an interaction!

Interactionism endorsed as a future direction. Our belief is that the interaction position offers the greatest power not only for understanding but for *predicting* the whole, complex human being, which is the goal of the psychology of personality. Interactionism is likely to become the dominant force in personality research.

This belief is supported by three considerations. First, nearly all personality psychologists recognize the role of *both* person and situation influences on human behavior. Murray cites need-press themas; Lewin sees behavior as a function of person $\times$ environment; social psychoanalysts and social-learning theorists give credence to both internal and external determinants of behavior; existentialists conceptualize the person-in-a-situation; Rogers and Maslow see environmental conditions as facilitating or blocking organismic development; and Kelly's personal constructs are derived from life experiences. Current-day trait theorists such as Eysenck and Cattell do not dismiss the "slight" influence of environment, and environmentally oriented psychologists such as Skinner admit to differences in the effectiveness of reinforcements among different individuals that can be traced to their biological endowments and past histories.

Second, as Mischel argues, statistical relationships indexing a person's trait behavior across different situations and over time, as well as the influence of situations considered independently, are weak and inconsistent. "Diverse data challenge and undermine the central assumptions of the traditional trait approach to personality" (1973, p. 252). Mischel's historically important estimate of the correlation for trait effects is low, about .30, and he continues to affirm its representativeness. At the same time, Funder and Ozer's estimate of the correlation for situation effects is a "quite comparable" .40.

Third, relatively greater variance in human behavior is accounted for by interaction effects rather than by traits or situations alone. Endler and Hunt have made this case for behavioral variance in anxiety reactions. Kendall has demonstrated strong interaction effects using a controlled experimental method.

Leading the way toward integration: Mischel.   Mischel offers an integrative, comprehensive personality model for conceptualizing interactionism. Drawing from cognitive orientations such as Kelly's, and from social-learning theory, his *cognitive social-learning theory* substitutes thought processes for traits as person factors. It emphasizes "the interdependence of behavior and conditions, mediated by the constructions and cognitive activities of the person who generates them" (1973, p. 279). Present human behavior is determined by a person's memory of his or her history of reward and punishment experiences in a situation, along with observations of others in similar situations. Individual differences are reflected in combinations of five variables:

1. Displaying cognitive competencies in sizing up and performing effectively in a situation—"knowing what to do and doing it"
2. Characterizing events or categorizing them (Cantor and Mischel's prototypes) —"determining what's what," sometimes using trait labels as personal constructs (Kelly)
3. Utilizing expectancies or beliefs about the outcomes of behaviors in relation to stimuli, based on past experience—"predicting future events" (Kelly, social learning)
4. Attaching personal values to behavioral and stimulus outcomes—"knowing what you want" (Rogers, Maslow, existentialists, social learning)
5. Making self-regulatory plans—"developing advance guidelines" regarding appropriate behavior in a situation (Bandura, Skinner), as in delaying gratification

RESEARCH EXAMPLES OF INTERACTIONS AND BEHAVIORS

Interactions between person factors and social situations have helped explain a variety of behaviors. Thus, the trait of authoritarianism interacts with the situational factor of social status in determining the level of aggressive behavior: individuals high in authoritarianism have shown more aggression toward persons who are lower than higher in social status, whereas the pattern is reversed for individuals low in authoritarianism. Person factors also include types (Type A and Type B) and social styles (self-monitoring), as well as traits. Interactionism has also been useful in understanding gender similarities and differences in sexual behavior, conformity, obedience, aggression, and anxiety. Men and women show differences in some situations, but not others; or a given difference may reverse itself from one situation to the next. Consider conformity. Sistrunk and McDavid report that males and females conform on items of greater interest to the opposite sex, but not on items of equivalent interest for both sexes. Eagly, Wood, and Fishbaugh report no sex difference in conformity, except under a surveillance condition resulting in less conformity for males. Regarding aggression, although women aggress less than men when provocation is weak, there is no sex difference when provocation is strong (Richardson, Berstein, & Taylor). Many assumed sex differences probably exist only at the level of expression, not at the level of capability. Where sex differences exist, some may be traced to broad social-psychological situations, especially sex-role learning (Horney, social learning, Skinner). Others may be due to biological influences (Eysenck, chromosomes). However, there certainly are many more sex similarities than differences. Rather than stereotyping members of a group, it is best to look for situations in which one category of persons may be similar to or different from another category of persons.

SELF-CONCEPT AND PERSONALITY DEVELOPMENT

One of the most important considerations in understanding personality development is *self-concept*. Allport refers to this personal sense of self as the *proprium*—"me as felt and known . . . the self as 'object' of knowledge and feeling" (1961, p. 127). Thus, our *self-concept* is our own view of our personality (Rogers). For Allport, self-concept evolves over seven stages of development. His subjective pattern *feelings of inferiority* recalls Adler, while the pattern *conscience* is reminiscent of Freud and Kohlberg. *Propriate striving,* which involves planning for the future by setting and working toward long-range goals, is philosophically similar to the views of Adler, Maslow, Kelly, and the social-learning theorists.

Erikson elaborates on *self-identity* (Allport, Fromm, Maslow), the thread that ties together the "you" of yesterday with the "you" of tomorrow. (The interest in identity is also seen in the theories of Jung and Sullivan.) Healthy resolution of each of eight crises is associated with a particular developmental outcome.

Kohlberg's theory of *moral development* enlarges on Allport's notion of conscience, while following Jean Piaget's assumption that *cognitive* stages of development underlie moral reasoning and judgment (Fromm, Kelly, Mischel). Kohlberg posits six stages of moral development, related to three levels: preconventional ("what's in it for me"), conventional ("member of society"), and postconventional ("prior to society"). Two alternatives to Kohlberg's "justice" principle are Haan's equality principle and Hogan's socialization-empathy-autonomy orientation. Also, the observation that people tend toward greater contextual relativism as they get older raises questions about the universal, transsituational consistency referred to in Kohlberg's schema.

Is it possible for self-concept to exist in the face of behavioral inconsistency (Eysenck, Freud, social psychoanalysts)? The answer is "Yes," because behavioral consistency may develop in ways other than by showing consistent behavioral repetition, as discussed by Mischel and other interactionists. One way is through feedback received from others about the consistency of our behavior, as in Hogan's idea that we may become our perceptions of how other people view us (Sullivan, Rogers). We may also show behavior that has "dramaturgical" quality or value, as in performing an uncommon behavior in relation to different targets or circumstances (Coe & Sarbin). Even an infrequent behavior, performed effectively, may stand out dramatically in the minds of observers, leading them to attribute a corresponding trait to the performer, as if generalizing from the

People are both alike and different. However, it is their differences that fascinate personality theorists and researchers. In what ways do individuals differ? What makes them different? Is it possible to predict a person's behavior? How can we improve upon our past understanding and prediction of behavior? Questions such as these continue to stimulate psychologists' efforts in the changing field of personality.

behavior. Guidelines for improving one's self-concept can be found in the ideas of many theorists covered in this book, especially linked to conscious self-monitoring of personal behavior, interpersonal relationships, social desirability, and personal values.

Concluding Themes and Observations

This book began by asking two questions: "What is personality?" and "How is personality studied?" By now, you have received answers to both questions. Perhaps you are surprised at how many answers there have been. If so, consider that such variation is quite in keeping with the overall theme of the book, individual differences. Personality is obviously different things to different theorists and researchers, all of whom are different persons in pursuit of understanding of phenomena that are complex and elusive. The study of personality is also approached in different ways, including controlled experiments, correlational studies, group comparisons, individual lives, clinical settings, and research settings.

WHY SO MANY THEORIES AND RESEARCH CONCEPTS?

Personality is an abstraction.   Why are there so many theories and research concepts? One answer is that personality is an abstraction, not something tangible. The less tangible a phenomenon is, the more room there is for theorizing about it. If you have had a course in physics or chemistry, you will recall that there are relatively few theories about a given concept. However, what we study in psychology in general, and personality in particular, is different. Psychologists cannot focus their eyes directly on personality, much less lay their hands on it. You can easily understand the fact that anything that cannot be appreciated by the senses is wide open to various interpretations. Some psychologists do not even believe that personality exists (Skinner), or that it is necessary to study behavior in terms of personality (Rotter, Bandura).

This is not to say that personality falls in the same category as soul or mind. Although psychologists cannot get at personality directly, they can study it indirectly. In Chapter 2, *personality theory* was defined as a related, internally consistent set of ideas and assumptions as to why people show individual differences. Individual differences *are* obscure, so the solution is to draw conclusions about the personalities of people by observing their behaviors. Also, don't be too hasty to conclude that indirect methods make personality less important than what is studied in the physical sciences. Although nuclear physicists have given us awesome nuclear weapons and useful sources of nuclear power, they cannot tell us how to control the applications of their inventions. Psychologists considering such phenomena as personality and behavior can allow us to understand people who have their fingers on the buttons that launch nuclear missiles. Without such understanding, human beings may not survive. What could be more important to the human species?

Breadth and complexity.   A second answer to our question has to do with the breadth and complexity of phenomena falling under the umbrella of personality. Personality potentially encompasses "everything" about a person. Recall your first textbook in psychology. All the chapter titles of that introductory textbook represent areas of human experience that can be brought to bear on "personality": biological foundations, physiological processes, perception, learning, development, memory, cognition, emotion, motivation, social behavior, adjustment, and so on. It is no wonder that agreement about single theories, and attempts to integrate multiple theories of personality, occur so infrequently (Thorne, 1967). The task is simply overwhelming. This point is underscored by Sundberg, Tyler, and Taplin's hierarchy of systems (see Figure 16.1). Not all levels of a complex system can be addressed simultaneously and comprehensively. In Figure 16.1, the most immediate focus of personality is the organismic system of the individual person, which obviously is embedded in other systems at lower and higher levels.

Vast literature.   A third answer has to do with the vastness of the psychological literature related to personality, which is simply "enormous" (Pervin). Expert psychologists writing in the *Annual Review of Psychology* regularly allude to the impossibility of covering all of it. Personality-assessment techniques number in the thousands, and there may be several measures of such concepts as anxiety, extraversion-introversion, aggression, and authoritarianism. Each measure has its own literature base, with research reports sometimes numbering in the thou-

SupraNational System
e.g., Common Market, United Nations, satellite communications network

Societal System
e.g., one nation, a large part of a nation

Organizational System
e.g., industrial concern, social agency, professional association

Group System
e.g., family, work team, recreational group, animal group

Organismic System
e.g., individual person, animal, or plant

Organ System
e.g., nervous system, alimentary system

Cell System
e.g., individual cells within a body

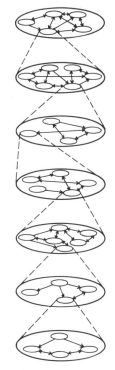

Figure 16.1
Hierarchy of systems *(Sundberg, Tyler, & Taplin, 1973)*.

sands, as we saw with the Taylor Manifest Anxiety Scale, Maudsley Personality Inventory, Rorschach inkblot technique, and MMPI.

Personal beginnings. Fourth, as you now are in a better position to appreciate, concepts and entire theories of personality often have their start in individual, personal experiences of the psychologists doing the investigating. Some of these biographical influences include maternal attachment (Freud), childhood loneliness (Jung, Sullivan, Rogers), a sense of inner fragmentation (Jung), anxiety (Horney), physical illness (Adler), transient personality breakdown (Sullivan), fascination with contradictory human experience (Fromm), nurturant caring (Rogers), independence (Kelly), identity problem (Erikson), and little "personality" (Skinner). Some broader, social and cultural influences can also be identified: World War II (Horney, Fromm, Adler), anti-Semitism (Freud, Adorno et al., Rokeach), Great Depression (Kelly), death-camp experiences (Frankl), and life's chance encounters (Bandura). Living life under certain conditions, at a certain span of time, colors the psychologist-as-person's perceptions, interpretations, and values. As Sullivan noted, psychologists are always participants as well as observers in their efforts to understand human beings.

Professionals' fascination with individual differences. Fifth, the personal individualism of psychologists is likely to carry over to their professional behavior. Perhaps it is their personal and professional curiosity in wanting to understand uniqueness that leads many personality psychologists to maximize individual differences. Personologists seem always "set and ready" to understand the uniqueness of particular individuals (Korchin). This attitude is reflected in the 2000-year-old question of how the Greeks, even though educated alike, "all have characters differently constituted." Psychologists living in Western, democratic societies may also be led to deemphasize similarities in human behavior because of strong sociocultural values placed on individualism. This influence could operate even though psychologists as scientists are interested in establishing general principles applicable to all people (Skinnerian reinforcement, actualizing tendency, Yerkes-Dodson law). It also could operate despite initial recognition of commonalities in human nature (Jung, Fromm, Maslow)—that individual differences among human beings may be less important than their commonalities (Watson), or that people are much more alike in their humanness than otherwise (Sullivan).

Lack of active appreciation for alternative viewpoints.   A sixth factor contributing to the development of so many theories and research concepts is an apparent lack of active appreciation of alternative viewpoints, even within a single framework—an attitude certainly manifested by Freud in relation to the social psychoanalysts. Although theorists and their followers obviously are aware of one another's ideas, they sometimes seem more interested in highlighting differences than commonalities. Debate is far more frequent than synthesis: classical *versus* social psychoanalysis, humanism *versus* behaviorism, persons *versus* situations, traits *versus* states. Psychologists as persons may be prone to encourage questioning, criticism, dissatisfaction, change, and independence, especially in ambiguous areas of philosophical assumptions and human values. Personality psychologists may also be taken with the idea of making some unique contribution to the field, perhaps by introducing a "new" concept or developing an "alternative" assessment technique. As discussed in Chapter 2, strict adherence to one's own theoretical framework leads to a narrowness of perspective, decreased appreciation of the ideas of others, and limited range of applicability to a richer spectrum of personalities.

Absence of research-mindedness by some theorists.   Seventh, an absence of research-mindedness by adherents of some theories has probably worked against acceptance of their ideas. Psychoanalytic theorists are one clear case in point. Very little experimental research is currently being undertaken within social-psychoanalytic frameworks (except the Adlerian), despite the existence of institutes, associations, and journals supportive of these theories. Also, while most psychoanalytic theorists value talking about personality, many never formally define it (Freud, Jung, Horney, Adler).

At the same time, general sources of support for selected concepts and emphases related to these theories exist and could be cited with relatively minimal effort (anxiety, defenses, parent/child relationships). These potential sources of support seem unimportant to followers of social-psychoanalytic theory, who do not appear to be exploring, valuing, or linking them to their theoretical ideas. Support for a theory may come from unlikely sources. For example, Harlow's research on the effects of maternal deprivation in monkeys is relevant to Horney's and Sullivan's assumptions about the critical importance of nurturant social contact early in life. Suomi and Harlow's social rehabilitation of isolate monkeys using peer "therapists" relates to Sullivan's preadolescent therapy treatment approach to schizophrenic males. Cattell's factor of "ergic tension" is similar to Freud's concept of frustrated drive. Interestingly, psychoanalytic theory continues to guide important aspects of present-day research in what Carlson describes as "an implicit, diffuse fashion" (1975, p. 397). Also, there are previously underemphasized connections between Murray's need-press assumptions and current-day interactionism (Rabin, Aronoff, Barclay, & Zucker).

Social-psychoanalytic theorists might respond to this discussion by pointing out the greater relevance of unreported or unsystematic clinical observations to the client populations they serve as therapists. Pervin, in fact, concludes that much of the research being published in personality journals is not relevant to real people. He believes there is too little correspondence between the people and behaviors he sees in his office as a practicing psychotherapist and what psychologists report in the experimental literature.

Lack of professional support for integration. Finally, many of the recurring issues in personality have now been around for two or three generations of psychologists. This suggests that the field may need to convey stronger support for efforts aimed at integrating research findings and theories. Such support would encourage psychologists to think about points of conceptual overlap among different theories, identify more common denominators in research, link ongoing research findings with a greater variety of existing theories, and reconcile theoretical differences. One criterion proposed by Hall and Lindzey involves the *heuristic value* of a conceptualization—its capacity to stimulate the thinking of other psychologists and generate research. Professional recognition could be given to integrative theoretical or research investigations, perhaps in special editions of personality journals or annual awards sponsored by the American Psychological Association. Greater professional attention needs to be given to ideas and findings of most help in moving the personality field forward. Greater selectivity is also needed to help filter out "poor research" (Pervin). Continued professional and academic acceptance of the chaotic, mixed-up state of the personality field has outlived some of its usefulness.

SOME RECOMMENDATIONS TO STUDENTS

Before closing, we would like to offer a few recommendations to those of you who will be taking more advanced courses in personality, or psychology more generally, whether as majors, minors, or students in search of electives.

1. Be on the lookout for similarities. Although you may be surprised by so many differences in the field of personality, differences are not the whole story. It is valuable to consider differences in ideas, but not at the expense of commonalities. There are broad areas of overlap in personality, including subgroups of general similarities and common assumptions. Look for similarities among theories and research findings. Explore ways in which various theories and research concepts are the same. Identify potential points of integration and synthesis, even among ideas that seem contradictory. Here are a few such general themes.

a. Internal influences. What's inside the person is important for understanding personality and behavior. The origin of these internal influences may be biological, psychological, or sociocultural. Examples of internal constructs include:

traits	Eysenck, Cattell, Adorno, Spielberger, J. Taylor, Zuckerman
types	Jung, Sheldon
energy systems	Freud
dynamisms	Sullivan
needs	Horney, Murray, Maslow, Atkinson
habits	Watson
personal fictions	Adler
expectancies	Kelly, Rotter, Bandura, Mischel
character structures	Fromm
self-actualization	Maslow
process of becoming a person	Rogers

b. External influences. What's outside the person is also important. Environmental perspectives redirect attention away from the inner person, toward specific situations and behavioral responses to them. Some situations may be understood sufficiently well to predict the behaviors of groups of people (obedience, aggression, racism, sex roles). It can even be useful to think about human behavior entirely from an external perspective, without making any references to internal aspects of "personality," "traits," or "self" (Watson, Skinner, social learning). External influences include:

physical environment	Skinner, Moos, Mount Saint Helens
press	Murray
psychological situations	Lewin, Kelly, Rogers, existentialists, social-learning theorists, Mischel
chance encounters	Bandura
life stressors	Holmes and Rahe, Selye, Jonestown
prototypes of situations	Funder and Bem, Cantor, Mischel
environmental climates	Pace and Stern
entire societies	Fromm, McClelland

c. Personality development. The importance of personality development is appreciated by almost all personality theorists and researchers. It is traditionally envisaged as a series of stages (Freud, Jung, Sullivan, Erikson, Allport, Kohlberg). Sometimes it is seen as a continuing process (Rogers, Maslow), and sometimes as a function of learning in similarly reoccurring situations (Rotter, Bandura, Mischel,

Murray). Many developmental patterns of early parent/child and family interactions influence personality and behavior:

physical contact	Horney, Sullivan, Harlow
anxious-secure relationships	Horney, Sullivan, Suomi
interpersonal trust	Rotter, Erikson, Kelly
belongingness	Fromm, Maslow
social interest	Adler, Bandura
interpersonal feedback	Sullivan, Hogan
identification	Freud, Erikson
observational learning	Bandura
parental modeling	Bandura, Fromm, Adler
parental reinforcement	social learning, Skinner
attitudes toward love and work	Freud, Adler, Fromm, Maslow, May
sex roles	Horney, Adler, Horner
authoritarian attitudes	Adorno, Fromm, Frenkel-Brunswik
openness to experience	Rogers, Rokeach and Kemp
valuing achievement	McClelland, Winterbottom
adjustment-maladjustment	social psychoanalysis, social learning, Rogers

d. Cognitive functioning. Concepts related to cognitive factors are present in most theories and research areas in some form. They include:

personal myths	Jung
personal fictions	Adler
personal constructs	Kelly
subjective meanings	Rogers, Fromm, existentialists
thinking and reasoning	Jung, Fromm
cognitive belief and structure	Adorno, Rokeach
parataxic distortions	Sullivan
self-statements	Watson
psychological situations	Rotter, Bandura
expectancies	social learning, Mischel
goal seeking	Maslow, Jung, Atkinson
fuzzy feature sets	Cantor
prototypes	Mischel
cortical activity	Eysenck

e. Anxiety. Constructs related to anxiety appear almost everywhere, including theories, correlational studies, and controlled research studies. There also are hundreds of assessment techniques that measure anxiety. The Yerkes-Dodson law, represented by an inverse U curve, is often used to understand human behavior, not only in relation to anxiety (Eysenck) but to aggression (Baron) and achievement motivation as well (Atkinson).

2. Keep an open mind.   Be open to alternative ideas about personality. No one approach captures everything about personality. Human experience is varied and complex, subject to a myriad of influences from past, present, and future. Nearly all theories contribute important concepts, methods, and perspectives to our understanding of human experience and behavior.

3. Think eclectically.   Consider adopting an orientation that is eclectic — one in which you are free to select assumptions, concepts, and methods from various sources rather than only from one. Overreliance on a single point of view is often too limiting, because once you commit yourself to a particular concept, model, or theory, you are likely to become partially blind to alternative possibilities. Avoid simplistic conclusions such as "Psychoanalysis is dead!" and "Long live the behaviorists!" Evaluate your ideas against the frameworks of others, even those whose ideas and assumptions may differ notably from your own. Seek a balance among different points of view, in methods as well as ideas. Also, appreciate the value of additions and changes within theories, as an index of continuing growth and responsiveness to new information. We saw this in Gray's modification of Eysenck's theory of extraversion, and in the expansion of social-learning to cognitive social-learning theory.

4. Strive to integrate ideas.   Now that you are on the lookout for similarities, keeping an open mind, and thinking eclectically, take the next step: begin to put different ideas and conclusions together, even at the beginning level. Recall the comprehensiveness of Freud's psychoanalytic theory. Follow the lead of Mischel's reconceptualization of social-learning theory along cognitive lines. Also remember Eysenck's model of personality, which places a premium on integrating theoretical ideas and research findings. It makes use of both correlational techniques and formal, experimental testing of predictive hypotheses arrived at in a hypothetico-deductive manner. Although the comprehensiveness of Eysenck's model is limited by an overemphasis on inner traits, individuals identified as high or low on a given trait dimension are understood from multiple viewpoints simultaneously: biological, psychological, and behavioral. The model is also linked to 2000 years of history, and it shows ongoing revision and expansion.

5. Value what predicts behavior.   From the point of view of scientific psychology, a critical question concerns the extent to which behavior can be predicted. One of psychology's continuing goals is to predict human behavior more often and more accurately than it has been able to do in the past. Pay close attention to what predicts behavior. Predictions may be based on factors related to persons (Eysenck, Cattell), situations (Milgram, Baron), or interactions between the two (Mischel, Endler, Magnusson). Note whatever characteristics of the person-in-the-environment (Murray, May) actually allow predictions to be made. Recognize that some psychologists who talk least about personality do the most in the way of predicting or controlling behavior (Skinner). The ability to predict human behavior is a major index of the degree to which human experience is understood. It is also a hallmark of scientific progress.

6. Do not lose sight of the person. At the same time, value what enables you to make sense of "personality" as a totality and to understand the unique *person* (Allport, Rogers). Consider the comprehensive study of lives important (Murray, R. W. White).

In Conclusion

We would like to leave you with a brief classroom exchange about personality that took place during our own university experience. A graduate student once offered the conclusion that "It really doesn't matter what a person's specific preferences in food really are. When you get right down to it, food is food." The instructor (M. B. Arnold) reacted with intense dismay. She exclaimed sharply, "It makes all the difference in the world for understanding individual differences in personality!"

Glossary

abstraction across the cleavage line In Kelly's cognitive theory, a pattern of constructs within a construction system in which both poles of a subordinate construct fall under a higher emergent pole *or* a higher implicit pole.

accurate empathy The ability to perceive, nonjudgmentally, the internal world of another person as it really appears to that person (essential to person-centered therapy). See *empathy*.

achievement imagery (AI) In assessing achievement motivation, the expression of a goal related to performing well, meeting standards, or overcoming obstacles, especially in stories told in response to ambiguous stimuli.

achievement motivation A learned need or drive to succeed in competition with some standard of excellence.

acquiescence A tendency of subjects to answer test items positively ("yes"), irrespective of content.

actualization In humanistic psychology, the process characteristic of every organism that impels it toward growth, development of its capacities, and fulfillment of its inherent potential.

adaptation Change in response to environmental demands.

adjustment disorder Psychological dysfunction characterized by a temporary maladaptive behavioral reaction to some identifiable external stressor.

aggression Any form of behavior performed with the intention of harming another living being who is motivated to avoid harm.

AI See *achievement imagery*.

alpha press Objective, physical aspects of the environment that influence a person's behavior (Murray).

ambivalance A mixture of simultaneous positive and negative attitudes or feelings, such as love and hate.

androgynous Term used to characterize persons who display behaviors associated with both sex roles, rather than being bound by social definitions of "sex-appropriate" behavior. Compare *sex-typed*.

anima In Jungian theory of archetypes, the feminine aspect present in all men.

animus In Jungian theory of archetypes, the masculine aspect present in all women.

antisocial personality A pattern of behavior in which an individual is unable or unwilling to honor social rules or maintain normal social relationships.

anxiety An experience of intense emotional arousal and discomfort, often accompanied by physical symptoms, and often unrelated or disproportionate to any specific external stimulus.

apperception A unique personal interpretation of an ambiguous stimulus, as in the Thematic Apperception Test.

archetypes In Jungian theory, innate psychic dispositions that lead all human beings to experience and respond to the world in certain common ways; the contents of the collective unconscious.

assessment The measurement and evaluation of personality, using psychological tests, for clinical or scientific purposes.

authoritarianism A personality type, or group of traits, that includes uncritical submission to authority, rigid adherence to convention, stereotyping, and generalized hostility; also may be seen as a trait.

authoritarian personality See *authoritarianism*.

avoidance Means of escaping anxiety by physically or psychologically steering clear of all situations, thoughts, or feelings that might arouse anxiety.

Barnum effect The willingness of most people to accept generalized descriptions of personality as being accurate, individualized descriptions of themselves.

battery A combination of personality-assessment techniques used to gather information about an individual from several different perspectives.

behavioral dimension A continuum anchored at either end by the two extremes of a given behavior.

behaviorism A school of psychology, associated with B. F. Skinner, for which the basic subject matter is overt, observable behavior.

behavioral measure Assessment technique in which subjects or trained observers record actual behaviors in specific situations.

behavior modification An approach to behavioral change using principles of positive and negative reinforcement and punishment.

behavior setting A naturally occurring situation in everyday life in which certain types of behavior can be expected to take place.

beta press Subjective interpretations of the environment that influence a person's behavior (Murray).

between-subject variance Difference in values on any given variable from one person to another.

biofeedback A method for learning to control physiological responses, such as heart rate, using information from electronic instruments.

biological preparedness A theory that animals, including humans, are disposed to learn easily only certain behaviors that stem from their unique physiological and anatomical constitutions.

bodily self Aspect of self-concept defined by physical sensations (Allport).

Buss-shock method Experimental technique used in studying aggression, in which the subject, as "stimulator" or "teacher," is asked to administer electric shocks to a "responder" or "learner" (actually a confederate of the experimenter), and the intensity and duration of the "shocks" administered under various experimental conditions are recorded.

B-values See *metaneeds*.

castration anxiety In Freudian theory, a generalized fear among boys at the phallic stage of losing their own sex organs, initiated by the realization that girls don't have penises.

catharsis Outward expression, verbal or behavioral, of a deep-seated need or emotion; in psychoanalytic theory, such expression is thought to reduce the likelihood that certain impulses will be expressed in behavior.

classical conditioning A form of learning whereby an initially neutral stimulus (such as a bell), after repeated association with a primary stimulus (such as food), is sufficient to trigger a physiological response (such as salivation).

clinical Related to the professional assessment and treatment of psychological problems.

coefficient of correlation (r) A number, ranging from -1.00 to $+1.00$, representing the degree and direction of linear relationship between two variables; 0.00 indicates there is no linear relationship present.

cognition Internal mental processes, including knowing, thinking, perceiving, and imagining.

cognitively complex person An individual whose construction system (Kelly) contains many constructs that are clearly differentiated—that is, distinguished one from the other.

cognitively simple person An individual who has a limited and poorly differentiated construction system (Kelly) in which the distinction among constructs is blurred.

collective unconscious In Jungian theory, basic experiences that have existed since ancient times and that are common to all human beings.

complexes In Jungian theory, clusters of emotionally related ideas, feelings, and memories.

concordance The degree to which the presence of a trait in one person predicts the presence of the same trait in a second person, typically a relative.

congruence In Rogers' person-centered theory, the degree of consistency between self-perception (how one sees oneself) and actual experience of self (how one is); also, the degree of genuineness shown by a person, especially by a therapist relating to a client.

conscience In Freudian theory, the representation within the superego of parental or other authoritative norms, standards, and taboos; source of guilt.

consensus response Method of assessing the characteristics of an environment through "group answers"—the mutual agreement of independent reports by a majority of those living within the environment.

consequence In behaviorism, an event that follows a response, thereby changing the probability that the response will occur again.

construct In Kelly's cognitive theory, a way of constructing, or "seeing," the world.

construction system In Kelly's cognitive theory, an organization of constructs having the more important constructs at the top and the less important ones at the bottom.

constructive alternativism In Kelly's cognitive theory, the assumption that a person's present interpretations of his or her life situation are subject to revision and replacement.

contingent Used to describe an event whose occurrence depends on the prior occurrence of some other event.

continuous reinforcement Reinforcement of a response every time it occurs.

continuum   A continuous scale or series of values indicating amount or degree.

conventional   Kohlberg's second level of moral development, based on upholding the rules of society and the expectations of others.

correlational research   A type of formal research involving the systematic collection and analysis of data in order to measure the relationship between two or more unmanipulated variables.

criterion Q-sorts   A method for defining a psychological environment using the Q-sort technique. See *Q-sort.*

cross-sectional study   A research design that compares different individuals at the same point in time.

cumulative record   A graph showing an accumulation of responses plotted against time.

defense mechanisms   In Freudian theory, internal, unconscious strategies used by the ego to cope with the anxiety generated by threatening id demands.

defensive behaviors   In Bandura's social-learning theory, behaviors adopted in order to cope with unpleasant events that are anticipated on future occasions.

dehumanization   A cognitive process that involves lowering the status of certain people from "human being" to "lesser being."

deficiency needs (D-needs)   In Maslow's humanistic theory, the first four (of five) basic needs: physiological, safety, love, and esteem.

denial   Means of escaping anxiety by ignoring its stimulus, thereby excluding anxiety from awareness.

dependency construct   In Kelly's cognitive theory, special constructs that revolve around the child's survival needs.

dependent variable   In experimental research, a factor whose values may change following changes in one or more independent, or deliberately manipulated, variables. See *independent variable.*

diffusion of innovation   In Bandura's social-learning theory, a process that occurs when prestigious models try something new and thereby display its benefits and advantages to others.

displacement   In Freudian theory, a defense mechanism whereby anxiety is redirected from its true source in "forbidden" urges onto some less threatening, external object.

D-needs   See *deficiency needs.*

dogmatism   A trait or cognitive style characterized by a closed belief system and a lowered ability to deal with new input; may be associated with authoritarianism.

Dogmatism (D) Scale   A pencil-and-paper questionnaire designed to assess dogmatism, or closed-mindedness.

dramaturgical quality   The precision, clarity, and effectiveness with which a behavior is performed.

dramaturgical value   The extent to which a behavior is (a) uncommon and (b) directed toward several different targets or performed under several different circumstances.

D Scale   See *Dogmatism (D) Scale.*

E   Extraversion-introversion; one of Eysenck's three superfactors, or basic dimensions of personality. See also *N* and *P.*

ego   In Freudian theory, the psychological aspect of the personality, partly conscious, that enables the personality to relate realistically to the outside world.

ego defense mechanisms   See *defense mechanisms.*

ego ideal   In Freudian theory, the positive normative standards, incorporated within the superego, with which the individual seeks to identify; source of pride and self-esteem.

Electra complex   In psychoanalytic theory, a universal aspect of personality development among girls at the phallic stage of psychosexual development, involving hostility toward the mother and love for the father.

emergent pole   In Kelly's cognitive theory, the primary or principal end of a bipolar construct. Compare *implicit pole.*

empathy   Sensing and participating in the emotions of another person. See *accurate empathy.*

EPQ   See *Eysenck Personality Questionnaire.*

erogenous zones   Freudian term for sensitive areas of the body from which instinctual satisfactions can be obtained.

Eros   In Freudian theory, the instinct for life, including love of self and love of others. Compare *Thanatos.*

euphemistic labeling   A cognitive process that involves assigning a name to undesirable behavior that makes it seem innocuous or even laudable.

Eupsychia   Maslow's humanistic utopia characterized by free choice, mutual respect, and psychological health.

eustress   Source of stress that is "positive" in content, such as a job promotion or sudden good fortune.

expectancy   A belief based on past experience that provides a prediction of future outcomes. In Rotter's social-learning theory, the probability held by the individual that a particular reinforcement will occur as a function of a specific behavior in a specific situation or situations.

experimental research   A type of formal research in which an experimenter manipulates the environment of subjects and observes subsequent changes in their behavior.

extension of the cleavage line   In Kelly's cognitive theory, a pattern of constructs within a construction system in which emergent poles line up under emergent poles and implicit poles under implicit poles.

external   In Rotter's social-learning theory, an individual who believes that reinforcement depends mainly on outside forces over which one has little control. Compare *internal*.

externalization   Means of escaping anxiety by experiencing internal processes as if they occurred outside oneself.

existential   The condition of self awareness, and resulting contradictions of psychological experience, rooted in the very existence of humankind.

existential psychology   Philosophical approach to understanding each person's immediate experience within his or her own unique world and personal responsibility for making choices in life.

extinction   In behaviorism, the process whereby a previously reinforced response that is no longer reinforced decreases in frequency.

extraversion   An "outward-turning" of psychic energy, characterized by a primary interest in and focus on external objects, events, and people; one of two major personality types in Jungian theory. Compare *introversion*.

extrinsic rewards   Rewards originating outside the individual (such as money or praise).

Eysenck Personality Questionnaire (EPQ)   Pencil-and-paper inventory developed by Eysenck and Eysenck to measure psychoticism-superego functioning (P), along with E and N.

factor   Trait or characteristic that is statistically defined based on intercorrelations among a number of different responses or behaviors.

factor analysis   A method of statistical intercorrelation, involving numerous correlations, used to determine the number and nature of the main variables or dimensions underlying a large number of observations.

Fascism (F) Scale   A pencil-and-paper questionnaire designed to assess authoritarianism.

finalism   In Adler's personality theory, a fictional goal toward which psychological energy is directed, unifying the personality.

fixation   In Freudian theory, a state of arrested development at a particular psychosexual stage because of excessive satisfaction, frustration, or anxiety experienced at that stage.

fixed-interval schedule   Pattern of intermittent reinforcement characterized by a constant time interval between one reinforced response and the next.

fixed-ratio schedule   Pattern of intermittent reinforcement characterized by the occurrence of a constant number of responses between one reinforced response and the next.

fixed-role therapy   Clinical methodology based on Kelly's cognitive theory in which a client plays the role of an imaginary character having a construction system that, if permanently adopted, would be ideally suited to the client.

frame of orientation   In Fromm's theory of sociopsychoanalytic humanism, a cognitive map (whether true or false) of the natural and social world that enables people to organize data and place themselves in a context of intellectual understanding.

free association   Freud's primary assessment technique for getting at the unconscious by permitting ideas, images, memories, and feelings to flow spontaneously without conscious guidance or control.

F Scale   See *Fascism (F) Scale*.

future shock   Stress and disorientation experienced as a result of being subjected to too much change in too short a time (Toffler).

gambler's fallacy   The expectation that failure on one attempt means a greater likelihood of success on a subsequent attempt, and vice versa.

generalized expectancy   In Rotter's social-learning theory, the assumed probability of reinforcement of a behavior that applies to a number of situations, all of which are likely to be seen as similar to some degree.

habitual response (HR)   A specific behavior that recurs under similar circumstances.

humanistic psychology   Theoretical approach, advocated by Carl Rogers and Abraham Maslow, that focuses on the whole person and stresses the unique capacities of each individual for conscious self-determination, personal growth, and self-actualization; the "third force" in psychology.

hypothetico-deductive method   Use of theoretical formulations to derive testable hypotheses for making predictions about behavior and understanding its causes.

hysterical neurosis   Physical symptom, such as paralysis, resulting (according to Freud) from exaggerated overcontrol of instincts.

id   In Freudian theory, the biological aspect of personality, including reflexes and instincts, governed by the pleasure principle.

ideal self   The self that a person most values and desires to be.

idiographic   Approach to studying human behavior that seeks to identify the unique characteristics of individuals and to understand their behavior in terms of these characteristics. Compare *nomothetic.*

impermeable construct   In Kelly's cognitive theory, constructs that tend not to change in terms of range of convenience or place in the construction system.

implicit pole   In Kelly's cognitive theory, the secondary or opposite end of a bipolar construct. Compare *emergent pole.*

incentive   Anything that creates anticipation of a positive outcome following the performance of a behavior.

independent variable   In experimental research, a factor whose value is varied by deliberate experimenter manipulation. Compare *dependent variable.*

individual psychology   Term used to describe the social-psychoanalytic theory of Alfred Adler.

individuation   In Jungian theory, the process by which a person becomes differentiated from the collective and develops into a separate whole, or self.

interactionism   Approach to personality that sees behavior as determined by a combination of traits and situations; that is, a given trait will manifest itself in some situations but not in others.

intermittent reinforcement   Reinforcement of a response every so often, or after some number of responses has occurred.

internal   In Rotter's social-learning theory, an individual who believes that reinforcement depends mainly on one's own behavior or attributes. Compare *external.*

interpersonal trust   In Rotter's social-learning theory, a generalized expectancy that people's verbal promises are reliable.

intrinsic motivation   The desire for intrinsic rewards, leading to the pursuit of same.

intrinsic rewards   Rewards originating inside the individual (such as self-praise).

introjection   In Freudian theory, the process by which the superego incorporates the values of external authority figures and the culture at large, especially through identification with the same-sex parent.

introspection   The process of examining and exploring one's own experiences, thoughts, and reactions.

introversion   An "inward-turning" of psychic energy, characterized by a primary interest in and focus on internal thoughts, feelings, and experiences; one of two major personality types in Jungian theory. Compare *extraversion.*

inverse correlation   See *negative correlation.*

L-data   Information about a person's behavior that comes from an outside observer. Compare *Q-data* and *T-data.*

libido   In Freudian theory, a generalized pleasure drive, or psychosexual urge, central to Eros (the instinct for life).

linear relationship   A correlation between two variables in which their values show consistent, mutual, systematic change.

loading   The correlation of a particular test item or variable with a given factor.

locus of control   In Rotter's social-learning theory, refers to whether individuals perceive that reinforcement depends upon their own behavior and attributes or whether they perceive reinforcement as controlled by forces outside of them and as occurring independently of their own actions. See *internal* and *external.*

longitudinal study   A research design that follows the same individuals over a period of time.

mandala   In Jungian theory of archetypes, the "magic circle" that represents wholeness, unity, self.

Manifest Anxiety Scale (MAS)   A paper-and-pencil questionnaire designed to assess a person's tendency to experience emotional responsiveness (anxiety) or motivational drive (J. Taylor).

manipulation   A deliberately created change in the environment of an experimental subject.

marasmus   A syndrome found in institutionalized infants, characterized by self-destructive wasting away with no demonstrable physical cause; effectively counteracted by regular close physical contact with a consistently nurturing caregiver.

Maudsley Medical Questionnaire (MMQ)   Pencil-and-paper inventory developed by Eysenck to measure neuroticism-stability (N).

Maudsley Personality Inventory (MPI)   Pencil-and-paper questionnaire developed by Eysenck to measure both neuroticism-stability (N) and extraversion-introversion (E).

metaneeds (B-values)   In Maslow's humanistic theory, the highest level of self-actualizing needs or "being values," including ethical, cognitive, and aesthetic ideals.

Minnesota Multiphasic Personality Inventory (MMPI)   The most popular objective test used in personality assessment, providing scores on nine scales of abnormality.

MMQ   See *Maudsley Medical Questionnaire.*

MMPI　See *Minnesota Multiphasic Personality Inventory.*

model　An analogy, using one way of viewing reality (such as a computer program) to represent another (such as a psychological process); (noun) In Bandura's social-learning theory, a person who performs some behavior for an audience, showing how it is done and what benefits accrue from it; (verb) To perform a behavior before one or more observers.

morality principle　In Freudian theory, the guiding force of the superego, representing cultural values of right and wrong.

MPI　See *Maudsley Personality Inventory.*

N　Neuroticism-stability; one of Eysenck's three superfactors or basic dimensions of personality. See also *E* and *P.*

n Ach　Need for achievement. See *achievement motivation.*

narcotization　Means of escaping anxiety by overusing alcohol, drugs, sex, sleep, work, or other distractors.

need　An inner disposition to seek a particular goal or satisfaction that will reduce tension. See *thema.*

negative correlation　A linear relationship in which the values of two variables move in opposite directions; that is, as one increases, the other decreases. Compare *positive correlation.*

negative reinforcement　A process whereby the likelihood of a response increases when it is followed by the termination, reduction, or absence of some aversive event or stimulus (such as electric shock or spanking).

neurosis　A pattern of abnormal behavior resulting from exaggerated use of defense mechanisms to control id urges or instincts (according to Freud), or from faulty learning (according to behaviorists).

nomothetic　Approach to studying human behavior that seeks to identify universal characteristics of people and broad principles governing their behavior. Compare *idiographic.*

objective test　Personality-assessment technique in which a subject answers a highly structured pencil-and-paper questionnaire, usually in a true/false or multiple-choice format; for example, the Minnesota Multiphasic Personality Inventory (MMPI).

observational learning　Acquisition of new behaviors by watching intently while someone acts.

Oedipus complex　In Freudian theory, a universal aspect of personality development among boys at the phallic stage of psychosexual development, involving envy and hostility toward the father and love and lust for the mother.

operant conditioning　A form of learning in which an organism operates on its environment with consequences that influence the likelihood that the operation, or behavior, will be repeated. Central concept of behaviorism.

operational definition　Representation of a concept in terms of observable procedures that different observers can agree upon to measure it.

organismic　Inherent in the organism; biologically based. Central to Rogers' and Maslow's theories.

parataxic　In Sullivan's interpersonal theory, the mode of experience characteristic of childhood, involving primitive symbolic speech but little logical understanding (an ongoing feature of rote habits). Compare *prototaxic* and *syntaxic.*

peak experience　In Maslow's humanistic theory, a type of extraordinary, intense, mystical event of great personal significance.

penis envy　In Freudian theory, a generalized feeling among girls at the phallic stage, initiated by the realization that boys have penises, of their own inferiority and desire to obtain a male sex organ.

personality development　The process whereby individuals are shaped by their social and physical environment, as well as their genetic makeup, to emerge as unique personalities.

personality profile　A line connecting the degrees on various behavioral dimensions associated with personality traits; graphic summary of an individual's personality.

personality type　A category of individuals who share a number of traits in common.

Personal Orientation Inventory (POI)　A paper-and-pencil assessment technique designed to measure a person's degree of self-actualization on a variety of humanistic/existential dimensions.

person factors　Influences on behavior that are embedded within the individual, including personality traits, types, social style, and gender.

personologist　A psychologist who specializes in the study of personality.

personology　(1) The study of personality. (2) Henry Murray's theory of personality.

phenomenological　Reality as perceived and defined subjectively by a person's individual experience.

phobia　A strong, irrational fear of some stimulus or activity that is not ordinarily the object of intense fear.

pleasure principle　In Freudian theory, the guiding force of the id, preoccupied with the immediate reduction of tension (pain), whether physical or psychological.

POI See *Personal Orientation Inventory.*

positive correlation A linear relationship in which the values of two variables increase together and decrease together. Compare *negative correlation.*

positive reinforcement A process whereby some event or stimulus (such as food or praise), contingent on a response, increases the likelihood that the response will be repeated.

positive self-regard A favorable attitude toward oneself.

postconventional Kohlberg's third level of moral development, based on pursuit of one's own self-chosen moral principles.

postulate A basic assumption that cannot be tested directly but is simply accepted as the starting point for a theory.

preconventional Kohlberg's first level of moral development, based on avoidance of punishment or pursuit of rewards.

press Forces in the outside world that influence a person's behavior (Murray). See *thema.*

primary factor Eysenck's term for a trait that is relatively pure and independent of others and is based on statistical correlations among habitual responses or recurrent behaviors; called a *source trait* by Cattell.

projective technique A personality-assessment method that provides an unstructured, ambiguous, or open-ended stimulus on which a subject can "project" personal perceptions, fantasies, and attitudes; for example, Rorschach inkblots, Thematic Apperception Test (TAT).

propriate striving Aspect of self-concept defined by realistic planning for the future and setting of long-term goals (Allport).

proprium Allport's term for sense of self, or self-concept.

prototaxic In Sullivan's interpersonal theory, the mode of experience characteristic of infancy, involving sensation rather than thought, with no awareness of self as separate from the world. Compare *parataxic* and *syntaxic.*

prototype A working model.

psychoanalysis The systematic "talking-out" procedure developed by Freud whereby personally and socially unacceptable id experiences buried in the unconscious are made conscious to the ego, thereby ridding the personality of neurotic conflicts.

psychohistory A type of personality evaluation that combines psychological and historical techniques, applied in retrospect to some important public figure.

psychological determinism A philosophical belief that nothing in human behavior occurs by chance and that all behavior is determined by psychological forces.

psychological situation (1) A set of external factors (people, settings, circumstances) that confront a person at any given time and that have some personal, determining relevance for that person. (2) In Rotter's social-learning theory, the personal, often idiosyncratic characterization of an environmental circumstance that enables one to categorize it, together with certain types of circumstances, and differentiate it from others.

psychometrics The measurement of individual differences through quantitative procedures and psychological tests.

P Psychoticism-superego functioning; one of Eysenck's three superfactors, or basic dimensions of personality. See also *E* and *N.*

punishment In behaviorism, a process whereby responses that are followed by the presentation of aversive stimuli (such as electric shock or spanking) decrease in frequency.

Q-data Information about a person's behavior or feelings that comes from the person in question, through paper-and-pencil questionnaires, self-reports, interviews, or therapy sessions. Compare *L-data* and *T-data.*

Q-sort A self-report assessment technique involving the sorting of statements into categories that is designed to measure and quantify a person's self-perceptions, permitting comparisons over time.

r See *coefficient of correlation.*

racism Widespread, culturally embedded negative sentiment directed toward people on the basis of their race.

range of convenience In Kelly's cognitive theory, the limited category of events to which a construct can be applied.

range of focus In Kelly's cognitive theory, the category of events to which a construct is most readily applied.

rationalization Means of escaping anxiety by justifying unacceptable behavior or explaining it away.

rational coper Aspect of self-concept defined by the ability to satisfy the demands of the body, the external environment, and society, through the application of reasoned thought (Allport).

reality principle In Freudian theory, the guiding force of the ego, enabling it to mediate between id's subjective demands for immediate gratification and the objective resources and dangers of the outside world.

reinforcement A process that occurs when some event is contingent on the prior performance of some response. See *positive reinforcement, negative reinforcement,* and *punishment.*

reinforcement value In Rotter's social-learning theory, the degree of preference for the occurrence of a certain reinforcement, given that all reinforcements possible under the circumstances are equally likely to occur.

reliability The quality of consistency in a test or other assessment measure; that is, repetition of the same test on the same individual should produce the same results.

reliability coefficient Statistical correlation indexing the degree to which a person's responses are stable or likely to be repeated.

repression In Freudian theory, a defense mechanism that allows the ego to be conscious only of those thoughts and urges that it finds acceptable, pushing "unacceptable" thoughts and urges deep into the unconscious.

REP test See *Role Construct Repertory.*

response facilitation In Bandura's social-learning theory, a process whereby previously learned but suppressed behavior is disinhibited as a result of watching a model perform the behavior without negative consequences.

risk-preference model Atkinson's theory that achievement behavior is a function of motivation, expectancy, and incentive, each of which has two dimensions: seeking success and avoiding failure.

Role Construct Repertory (REP) A pencil-and-paper assessment technique designed to reveal an individual's construction system.

role playing In Kelly's cognitive theory, behaving in ways that meet the expectations of significant others.

rootedness In Fromm's theory of socio-psychoanalytic humanism, a deep craving to maintain ties with people and places, and to avoid separation and isolation.

Rorschach A projective technique of personality assessment using inkblots, with scoring of responses based on content and other dimensions.

schedule of reinforcement Plan by which a response is reinforced, some time after the last reinforced response, or some number of responses after the last reinforced response.

secondary factor Eysenck's term for a type, or superfactor, based on statistical intercorrelations among any primary factors or traits that are related to one another; called a *surface trait* by Cattell. See *superfactor.*

secondary reinforcement The process whereby a neutral event or stimulus, through association with a primary (positive or negative) reinforcer,

comes to have the reinforcing properties of the primary stimulus.

self-actualization In humanistic psychology, a person's lifelong process of realizing his or her inherent potentialities.

self-actualizers In Maslow's humanistic theory, those rare individuals who actually achieve full use of their potentialities.

self-concept An individual's own perception of his or her personality.

self-efficacy In Bandura's social-learning theory, beliefs concerning one's ability to perform behaviors that will yield expected outcomes.

self-esteem Aspect of self-concept defined by pride in one's pursuits and accomplishments (Allport).

self-exonerative processes Cognitive activities that allow people to dissociate themselves from the consequences of their actions (as by invoking religion or ideology).

self-identity Aspect of self-concept defined by a sense of continuity over past, present, and future (Allport).

self-image Aspect of self-concept composed of hopes and aspirations that develop from others' perceptions and expectations of oneself (Allport).

self-monitoring A "social style" that, in the extreme, is characterized by high attention to discerning and displaying "appropriate," socially-approved behaviors in any given situation (rather than relying on internal standards).

self-regulatory capacity The ability of humans to arrange relationships between behaviors and consequences for themselves.

self-regulatory plans Rules established in advance of the opportunity for behavioral performance that act as guides for determining what behavior would be appropriate under particular conditions (Mischel).

self-system In Sullivan's interpersonal theory, one's core personality, which incorporates the do's and don'ts of significant others and seeks to minimize anxiety; partly analogous to Freud's concepts of ego and superego.

sensation seeking A generalized need to pursue varied, novel, and complex stimulation.

Sensation-Seeking Scale (SSS) A pencil-and-paper questionnaire designed to assess a person's need for novel and varied stimulation.

sensory deprivation Experimental condition minimizing external stimulation, as by immersing the subject in water from the neck down in a darkened, soundproof room.

sensory threshold The lowest intensity of a stimulus to which an organism reacts.

sex role Behaviors deemed socially and culturally appropriate for individuals of one gender as opposed to the other.

sex-typed   Term used to characterize persons who are heavily invested in the particular sex role that society assigns to them. Compare *androgynous*.

significant others   Those people who are most central to one's life and personality development.

situational template   Pattern of behavioral characteristics of the "ideal" person optimally suited to a particular environment (Bem, Funder).

Sixteen Personality Factor Questionnaire (16 PF)   Widely used personality-assessment test, developed by Cattell, that produces a profile of scores on 16 trait dimensions.

social comparison   A method of determining how well one is doing in life by comparing oneself to those who share one's life situation.

social character   In Fromm's theory of social-psychoanalytic humanism, a core of personality characteristics that are common to most people within a given culture.

social desirability   The motivation to please others by displaying the characteristics that are valued in society.

social interest   Feelings related to association and cooperation with other people. Central concept of Adler's personality theory.

social learning   Acquiring useful information through interactions with people and other elements of the environment.

social psychology   The study of how individuals both influence others and are influenced by them.

sociopath   See *antisocial personality*.

sociopsychoanalytic humanism   Term used to describe the social-psychoanalytic theory of Erich Fromm.

specific response (SR)   An individual instance of behavior that may or may not be typical of the person in question.

SSS   See *Sensation-Seeking Scale*.

standard deviation   A statistic that indexes the average degree of variability of values around the mean in a given distribution of values.

state anxiety   Transitory experience of unpleasant emotional arousal, often situation-specific. Compare *trait anxiety*.

statistical significance   The degree to which the change in a dependent variable or the strength of a relationship between variables is greater than would be expected on the basis of pure chance.

stimulus generalization   A process whereby any stimulus that is similar to the originally conditioned stimulus comes to evoke the same response as the original stimulus.

straight-line relationship   See *linear relationship*.

stress   The internal condition, similar to anxiety, that results from an organism's efforts to adapt to environmental demands.

stressor   A condition of perceived imbalance between the demands of the environment and one's capacity to meet those demands.

subject   A person being studied in a psychological experiment or clinical assessment.

sublimation   In Freudian theory, the transformation and redirection of repressed urges into personally and culturally accepted forms of expression, including intellectual and artistic pursuits.

subordinate constructs   In Kelly's cognitive theory, the less important constructs located at the bottom of a construction system.

superego   In Freudian theory, the social aspect of personality, including conscience and ego ideal, that internalizes the norms and standards of the surrounding culture.

superfactor   Statistically defined group of traits, or personality type, based on consistently found correlations among certain traits. See *secondary factor*.

superordinate constructs   In Kelly's cognitive theory, the more important constructs located at the top of a construction system.

surface trait   See *secondary factor*.

synchronicity   Jungian principle of acausality; the simultaneous occurrence of two events (such as archetypes and behaviors) that have a close and important, but not direct cause-and-effect, relationship.

syndrome   A cluster or pattern of traits characteristic of a particular personality type or personality disorder.

syntaxic   In Sullivan's interpersonal theory, the mode of experience that emerges during the juvenile era, characterized by fully developed interpersonal communication based on conventionally understood symbols. Compare *prototaxic* and *parataxic*.

TAT   See *Thematic Apperception Test*.

taxonomy   A classification system, or list of categories.

Taylor Manifest Anxiety Scale   See *Manifest Anxiety Scale (MAS)*.

T-data   Information about a person's behavior that comes from objective measurement, such as reaction time. Compare *Q-data* and *L-data*.

teleology   The intentional directedness of human behavior toward a goal or purpose of its own making.

template   An ideal or normative pattern against which actual cases can be compared.

Thanatos   In Freudian theory, the instinct for death and destructiveness, directed toward oneself and others. Compare *Eros*.

thema   A particular interaction between press and need that characterizes a person's life (Murray). See *need* and *press*.

Thematic Apperception Test (TAT)   A projective technique of personality assessment in which a subject is asked to look at a series of ambiguous pictures and make up stories about them.

theory   An interrelated, internally consistent set of ideas and assumptions used to explain certain observations of reality.

trait   An internal characteristic that corresponds to an extreme position on a behavioral dimension.

trait anxiety   A generalized tendency to experience unpleasant emotional arousal and to perceive situations as threatening. Compare *state anxiety*.

transference   In psychoanalysis, the process whereby patients project onto the analyst the personality of some person from the past (such as a parent) with whom they have experienced psychological conflict.

Type A   A personality type, or group of traits, characteristic of the hard-driving, highly competitive, efficiency-oriented workaholic.

Type B   A personality type, or group of traits, characteristic of people who are relaxed, easygoing, and sociable.

unconditional positive regard   An attitude of valuing and accepting an individual as a person, rather than making acceptance contingent upon specific behaviors.

validity   The degree to which a test or other assessment technique actually measures what it is designed to measure and can predict behavior.

variable   Anything measurable that can assume different values.

variable-interval schedule   Pattern of intermittent reinforcement based on an average amount of time elapsed between one reinforced response and the next.

variable-ratio schedule   Pattern of intermittent reinforcement in which, on the average, a given number of responses must be performed before a response is reinforced.

variance-components method   Technique for testing the interactionist position by partitioning the variation in some behavior into components controlled by persons (including traits), situations, and the interaction between the two.

vicarious expectancy learning   In Bandura's social-learning theory, a process whereby people adopt other persons' expectancies concerning future events—especially expectancies of those with whom they share relevant experiences.

vicarious reinforcement   In Bandura's social-learning theory, a process that involves observing reinforcement as it occurs to other people.

waking-dream fantasy   Jungian technique in which patients are encouraged to simulate dream experiences by actively engaging in imagination while fully awake.

within-subject variance   Difference in values on any given variable from time to time in the same person. Compare *between-subject variance*.

Word Association Test   Assessment technique developed by Jung calling for rapid and spontaneous associative responses to a standardized list of words.

working image   A tentative descriptive model of an individual's personality, based on professional assessment.

Yerkes-Dodson law   The generalization that the relationship between motivation, or anxiety, and performance can be represented by an inverted U curve; that is, both too little and too much motivation can be detrimental to performance.

References

Abramson, L., Seligman, M., & Teasdale, J. (1978). Learned helplessness in humans: Critique and reformulation. *Journal of Abnormal Psychology, 87*, 49–74.

Abt, L. E., & Bellak, L. (Eds.). (1950). *Projective psychology: Clinical approaches to the total personality.* New York: Grove Press.

Achterberg, J., & Lawlis, G. F. (1978). *Imagery of Cancer.* Champaign, IL: Institute for Personality and Ability Testing.

Adams, P. R., & Adams, G. R. (1984). Mount Saint Helen's ashfall. *American Psychologist, 39*, 252–260.

Adler, A. (1898). *Gesundheitsbuch für das Schneidergewerbe.* Berlin: Heymanns.

Adler, A. (1917). *Study of organ inferiority and its psychical compensation: A contribution to clinical medicine.* New York: Nervous and Mental Diseases Publishing Company. (Original work published 1907)

Adler, A. (1930). Individual psychology. In C. Murchison (Ed.), *Psychologies of 1930* (pp. 395–405). Worcester, MA: Clark University Press.

Adler, A. (1956). In H. L. Ansbacher & R. R. Ansbacher (Eds.), *The individual psychology of Alfred Adler.* New York: Basic Books.

Adler, A. (1964). *Social interest: A challenge to mankind* (J. Linton & R. Vaughn, Trans.). New York: Capricorn Books. (Original work published 1939)

Adler, A. (1982). *Co-operation between the sexes* (H. L. Ansbacher & R. R. Ansbacher, Eds). New York: Norton.

Adorno, T. W., Frenkel-Brunswik, E., Levinson, D. J., & Sanford, R. N. (1950). *The authoritarian personality.* New York: Harper & Brothers.

Ainsworth, M. D. S. (1979). Infant-mother attachment. *American Psychologist, 34*, 932–937.

Alexander, F. G. (1950). *Psychosomatic medicine: Its principles and applications.* New York: Norton.

Alexander, F. G., & Selesnick, S. T. (1966). *The history of psychiatry.* New York: Harper & Row.

Alker, H. (1972). Is personality situationally specific or intrapsychically consistent? *Journal of Personality, 40*, 1–16.

Allen, B. P. (1973). Perceived trustworthiness of attitudinal and behavioral expressions. *Journal of Social Psychology, 89*, 211–218.

Allen, B. P. (1975). Social distance and admiration reactions of "unprejudiced" whites. *Journal of Personality, 43*, 709–726.

Allen, B. P. (1976). Race and physical attractiveness as criteria for white subjects' dating choices. *Social Behavior and Personality, 4*, 289–296.

Allen, B. P. (1978). *Social behavior: Fact and falsehood.* Chicago: Nelson-Hall.

Allen, B. P. (1984). Harrower's and Miale-Selzer's use of Hjalmar Schacht in their characterizations of the Nazi leaders. *Journal of Personality Assessment, 48*, 257–258.

Allen, B. P. (1985). After the missiles: Sociopsychological effects of nuclear war. *American Psychologist, 40*, 927–937.

Allen, B. P., & Potkay, C. R. (1973). Variability of self-description on a day-to-day basis: Longitudinal use of the adjective generation technique. *Journal of Personality, 41*, 638–652.

Allen, B. P., & Potkay, C. R. (1977a). The relationship between AGT self-description and significant life events: A longitudinal study. *Journal of Personality, 45*, 207–219.

Allen, B. P., & Potkay, C. R. (1977b). Misunderstanding the Adjective Generation Technique (AGT): Comments on Bem's rejoinder. *Journal of Personality, 45*, 334–342.

Allen, B. P., & Potkay, C. R. (1981). On the arbitrary distinction between states and traits. *Journal of Personality and Social Psychology, 41*, 916–928.

Allen, B. P., & Potkay, C. R. (1983a). *Adjective Generation Technique: Research and applications.* New York: Irvington.

Allen, B. P., & Potkay, C. R. (1983b). Just as arbitrary as ever: Comments on Zuckerman's rejoinder. *Journal of Personality and Social Psychology, 44*, 1087–1089.

Allen, B. P., & Smith, G. (1980). Traits, situations and their interaction as alternative "causes" of behavior. *Journal of Social Psychology, 111,* 99–104.

Allport, G. W. (1937). *Personality: A psychological interpretation.* New York: Henry Holt.

Allport, G. W. (1942). *The use of personal documents in psychological science.* New York: Social Science Research Council.

Allport, G. W. (1955). *Becoming: Basic considerations for a psychology of personality.* New Haven, CT: Yale University Press.

Allport, G. W. (1961). *Pattern and growth in personality.* New York: Holt, Rinehart & Winston.

Allport, G. W. (1968). *The person in psychology: Selected essays.* Boston: Beacon Press.

Allport, G. W. & Odbert, H. (1936). Trait-names: A psycho-lexical study. *Psychological Monographs, 47* (Whole No. 211), 1–171.

Alston, W. P. (1975). Traits, consistency, and conceptual alternatives for personality theory. *Journal for the Theory of Social Behavior, 5,* 17–48.

American Psychiatric Association. (1980). *Diagnostic and statistical manual of mental disorders* (3rd ed.). Washington, DC: Author.

American Psychological Association, (1974). *Standards for educational and psychological tests.* Washington, DC: Author.

American Psychological Association. (1980). *A career in psychology.* Washington, DC: Author.

Ames, L. B., Learned, J., Metraux, R. W., & Walker, R. N. (1952). *Child Rorschach responses: Developmental trends from two to ten years.* New York: Harper & Row.

Anastasi, A. (1982). *Psychological testing* (5th ed.). New York: Macmillan.

Angyal, A. (1941). *Foundations for a science of personality.* Cambridge, MA: Harvard University Press.

Angyal, A. (1965). *Neurosis and treatment: A holistic theory.* New York: Wiley.

Ansbacher, H. L. (1964). Introduction. In A. Adler, *Problems of Neurosis: A book of case histories* (P. Mairet, Ed.) (pp. ix–xxvi). New York: Harper & Row/Torchbooks.

Ansbacher, H. L., & Ansbacher, R. R. (1956). *The individual psychology of Alfred Adler.* New York: Basic Books.

Arendt, H. (1964). *Eichmann in Jerusalem: A report on the banality of evil* (rev. ed). New York: McGraw-Hill.

Arnold, A. (1980). Sexual differences in the brain. *American Scientist, 68,* 165–173.

Arnold, M. B. (1962). *Story sequence analysis: A new method of measuring motivation and predicting achievement.* New York: Columbia University Press.

Arnold, M. B., & Gasson, J. A. (1954). *The human person: An approach to an integral theory of personality.* New York: Ronald Press.

Asch, S. E. (1952). *Social psychology.* New York: Prentice-Hall.

Astin, A. W. (1962). Productivity of undergraduate institutions. *Science, 136,* 129–135.

Astin, A. W. (1968). *The college environment.* Washington, DC: American Council on Education.

Astin, A. W., & Holland, J. (1961). The Environmental Assessment Technique: A way to measure college environments. *Journal of Educational Psychology, 52,* 308–316.

Athanasious, R. (1972, July). French and American sexuality. *Psychology Today,* pp. 54–56, 86–87.

Athanasious, R., Shaver, P., & Tavris, C. (1970, July). Sex. *Psychology Today,* pp. 37–42.

Atkinson, J. W. (1957). Motivational determinants of risk-taking behavior. *Psychological Review, 64,* 359–372.

Atkinson, J. W. (Ed.). (1958). *Motives in fantasy, action, and society: A method of assessment and study.* New York: Van Nostrand.

Atkinson, J. W. (1964). *An introduction to motivation.* Princeton, NJ: Van Nostrand.

Atkinson, J. W., & Feather, N. T. (Eds.). (1966). *A theory of achievement motivation.* New York: Wiley.

Atkinson, J. W., & McClelland, D. C. (1948). The effect of different intensities of the hunger drive on thematic apperception. *Journal of Experimental Psychology, 38,* 643–658.

Auchincloss, K. (1971, April 12). The Calley verdict: Who else is guilty? *Newsweek,* pp. 27–45.

Awards for Distinguished Scientific Contributions: 1980–Albert Bandura. (1981). *American Psychologist, 36,* 27–34.

Axthelm, P. (1978, December 4). The emperor Jones. *Newsweek,* pp. 54–60.

Backteman, G., & Magnusson, D. (1981). Longitudinal stability of personality characteristics. *Journal of Personality, 49,* 148–160.

Baillargeon, J., & Danis, C. (1984). Barnum meets the computer: A critical test. *Journal of Personality Assessment, 48,* 415–419.

Bandura, A. (1973). *Aggression: A social learning analysis.* Englewood Cliffs, NJ: Prentice-Hall.

Bandura, A. (1977). *Social learning theory.* Englewood Cliffs, NJ: Prentice-Hall.

Bandura, A. (1982). The psychology of chance encounters and life paths. *American Psychologist, 37,* 747–755.

Bandura, A., & McDonald, F. (1963). The influence of social reinforcement and the behavior of models in shaping children's moral judgments. *Journal of Abnormal and Social Psychology, 67,* 274–281.

Bandura, A., Reese, L., & Adams, N. (1982). Microanalysis of action and fear arousal as a function of differential levels of perceived self-efficacy. *Journal of Personality and Social Psychology, 43,* 5–21.

Bandura, A., Ross, D., & Ross, S. (1963). Imitation of film-mediated aggressive models. *Journal of Abnormal and Social Psychology, 66,* 3–11.

Barber, T. X. (1978). "Hypnosis," suggestions, and psychosomatic phenomena: New look from the standpoint of recent experimental studies. In J. Fosshage & P. Olsen (Eds.), *Healing: Implications for psychotherapy* (pp. 269–297). New York: Human Sciences Press.

Barker, R. G. (1968). *Ecological psychology: Concepts and methods for studying the environment of human behavior.* Stanford, CA: Stanford University Press.

Barker, R. G., & Wright, H. F. (1955). *Midwest and its children: The psychological ecology of an American town.* New York: Row, Peterson.

Barnes, H. E. (1956). Translator's introduction. In J-P. Sartre, *Being and nothingness* (pp. viii–xliii). New York: Philosophical Library.

Baron, R. (1971). Aggression as a function of magnitude of victim's pain cues, level of prior anger arousal, and aggressor-victim similarity. *Journal of Personality and Social Psychology, 18,* 48–54.

Baron, R. (1974). Aggression as a function of victim's pain cues, level of prior anger arousal, and exposure to an aggressive model. *Journal of Personality and Social Psychology, 29,* 117–124.

Baron, R. (1977). *Human aggression.* New York: Plenum.

Baron, R. (1978). The influence of hostile and nonhostile humor upon physical aggression. *Personality and Social Psychology Bulletin, 4,* 77–80.

Baron, R. (1979a). Effects of victim's pain cues, victim's race, and level of prior instigation upon physical aggression. *Journal of Applied Social Psychology, 9,* 103–114.

Baron, R. (1979b). Heightened sexual arousal and physical aggression: An extension to females. *Journal of Research in Personality, 13,* 91–102.

Baron, R., & Ball, R. (1974). The aggression-inhibiting influence of nonhostile humor. *Journal of Experimental Social Psychology, 10,* 23–33.

Baron, R., & Bell, P. (1976). Aggression and heat: The influence of ambient temperature, negative affect, and a cooling drink on physical aggression. *Journal of Personality and Social Psychology, 33,* 245–255.

Baron, R., & Bell, P. A. (1977). Sexual arousal and aggression by males: Effects of type of erotic stimuli and prior provocation. *Journal of Personality and Social Psychology, 35,* 79–87.

Baron, R., & Byrne, D. (1981). *Social psychology: Understanding human interaction* (3rd ed.). Boston: Allyn & Bacon.

Baron, R., & Byrne, D. (1982). *Exploring social psychology.* Boston: Allyn & Bacon.

Baron, R., & Byrne, D. (1984). *Social psychology: Understanding human interaction* (4th ed.). Newton, MA: Allyn & Bacon.

Baron, R., Byrne, D., & Kantowitz, B. (1980). *Psychology.* New York: Holt, Rinehart & Winston.

Baron, R., & Ransberger, V. (1978). Ambient temperature and the occurrence of collective violence: The "long, hot summer" revisited. *Journal of Personality and Social Psychology, 36,* 351–356.

Baron, R. A., Russell, G. W., & Arms, R. L. (1985). Negative ions and behavior: Impact on mood, memory, and aggression among type A and type B persons. *Journal of Personality and Social Psychology, 48,* 746–754.

Barry, H., Child, I., & Bacon, M. (1959). Relation of child rearing to subsistence economy. *American Anthropologist, 61,* 51–64.

Beach, F. (1969, July). It's all in your head. *Psychology Today,* pp. 33–38.

Bechtal, R. (1967). Hodometer research in architecture. *Milieu, 2,* 1–9.

Beck, S. J. (1952). *Rorschach's test: Vol. 3. Advances in interpretation.* New York: Grune & Stratton.

Beck, S. J. (1960). *The Rorschach experiment: Ventures in blind diagnosis.* New York: Grune & Stratton.

Begley, S., & Cary, J. (1979, November 26). The sexual brain. *Newsweek,* pp. 100–105.

Bell, P. A., & Byrne, D. (1978). Repression-sensitization. In H. London & J. E. Exner, Jr. (Eds.), *Dimensions of personality* (pp. 449–485). New York: Wiley.

Bem, D. J. (1977). Predicting more of the people more of the time: Some thoughts on the Allen-Potkay studies of intraindividual variability. *Journal of Personality, 45,* 327–332.

Bem, D. J., & Allen, A. (1974). On predicting some of the people some of the time: The search for cross-situational consistencies in behavior. *Psychological Review, 81,* 506–520.

Bem, D. J., & Funder, D. C. (1978). Predicting more of the people more of the time: Assessing the personality of situations. *Psychological Review, 85,* 485–501.

Bem, S. L. (1974). The measurement of psychological androgyny. *Journal of Consulting and Clinical Psychology, 42,* 155–162.

Bender, L. (1938). *A Visual Motor Gestalt Test and its clinical use.* New York: American Orthopsychiatric Association.

Bentler, P. M., Jackson, D. N., & Messick, S. (1971). Identification of content and style: A two-dimensional interpretation of acquiescence. *Psychological Bulletin, 76,* 186–204.

Bergin, A. E. (1971). The evaluation of therapeutic outcomes. In A. E. Bergin & S. L. Garfield (Eds.), *Handbook of psychotherapy and behavior change: An empirical analysis* (pp. 217–220). New York: Wiley.

Bergin, A. E., & Suinn, R. (1975). Individual psychotherapy and behavior therapy. *Annual Review of Psychology, 26,* 509–556.

Berkowitz, L. (1969). *Roots of aggression.* New York: Atherton.

Berkowitz, L., & Donnerstein, E. (1982). External validity is more than skin deep: Some answers to criticisms of laboratory experiments. *American Psychologist, 37,* 245–257.

Bernstein, D. A., & Nietzel, M. T. (1980). *Introduction to clinical psychology.* New York: McGraw-Hill.

Berscheid, E., & Walster, E. (1972, March). Beauty and the best. *Psychology Today,* pp. 32–36.

Bexton, W., Heron, W., & Scott, T. (1954). The effects of decreased variation in the sensory environment. *Canadian Journal of Psychology, 8,* 70–76.

Bickman, L., & Zarantonello, M. (1978). The effects of deception and level of obedience on subjects' ratings of the Milgram study. *Personality and Social Psychology Bulletin, 4,* 81–85.

Bieri, J. (1955). Cognitive complexity-simplicity and predictive behavior. *Journal of Abnormal and Social Psychology, 51,* 61–66.

Binswanger, L. (1958). The case of Ellen West: An anthropological-clinical study. In R. May, E. Angel, & H. F. Ellenberger (Eds.), *Existence: A new dimension in psychiatry and psychology* (pp. 237–364). New York: Basic Books.

Binswanger, L. (1963). *Being-in-the-world: Selected papers of Ludwig Binswanger* (J. Needleman, Trans.). New York: Harper & Row.

Birney, R. C. (1968). Research on the achievement motive. In E. F. Borgatta & W. W. Lambert (Eds.), *Handbook of personality theory and research* (pp. 857–889). Chicago: Rand McNally.

Blake, M. J. F. (1967). Relationship between circadian rhythm of body temperature and introversion-extraversion. *Nature, 215,* 896–897.

Blake, M. J. F. (1971). Temperament and time of day. In W. P. Colquhoun (Ed.), *Biological rhythms and human performance* (pp. 109–148). New York: Academic Press.

Block, J. (1961). *The Q-sort method in personality assessment and psychiatric research.* Springfield, IL: Charles C Thomas.

Block, J., & Ozer, D. (1982). Two types of psychologists: Remarks on the Mendelsohn, Weiss, and Feimer contribution. *Journal of Personality and Social Psychology, 42,* 1171–1181.

Blum, G. (1949). The Blacky Test. *Genetic Psychology Monograph, 39,* 13–22+.

Blum, G. (1950). *The Blacky pictures: A technique for the exploration of personality dynamics.* New York: Psychological Corporation.

Blum, G. (1962). The Blacky Test—Sections II, IV, and VII. In R. Birney & R. Teevan (Eds.), *Mea-suring human motivation* (pp. 119–144). New York: Van Nostrand.

Blum, G. (1964). *Psychoanalytic theories of personality.* New York: McGraw-Hill.

Boring, E. (1957). *A history of experimental psychology* (2nd ed.). New York: Appleton-Century-Crofts.

Boss, M. (1963). *Psychoanalysis and daseinsanalysis* (L. B. LeFebre, Trans.). New York: Basic Books.

Bosselman, B. C. (1958). *Self-destruction: A study of the suicidal impulse.* Springfield, IL: Charles C Thomas.

Bottome, P. (1939). *Alfred Adler: Apostle of freedom.* London: Faber & Faber.

Bowers, K. (1973). Situationalism in psychology: An analysis and a critique. *Psychological Review, 80,* 307–336.

Bowlby, J. (1969). *Maternal care and mental health.* New York: Schocken Books.

Breuer, J., & Freud, S. (1950) *Studies in hysteria.* Boston: Beacon Press. (Original work published 1895)

Briere, J., Malamuth, N., & Ceniti, J. (1981, August). *Self-assessed rape proclivity: Attitudinal and sexual correlates.* Paper presented at the meeting of the American Psychological Association, Los Angeles.

Briere, J., Malamuth, N., & Check, V. (in press). Sexuality and rape-supportive beliefs. In P. Caplan, C. Larsen, & L. Cammaert (Eds.), *Psychology changing for women.* Montreal: Eden Press.

Brigham, J. (in press). *Social psychology.* Boston: Little, Brown.

Brody, B. (1970). Freud's case-load. *Psychotherapy: Theory, research and practice, 7,* 8–12.

Brownmiller, S. (1975). *Against our will: Men, women and rape.* New York: Simon & Schuster.

Brunswick, E. (1955). Representative design and probabilistic theory in a functional psychology. *Psychological Review, 62,* 193–217.

Bryant, J., & Zillmann, D. (1979). Effect of intensification of annoyance through unrelated residual excitation on substantially delayed hostile behavior. *Journal of Experimental Social Psychology, 15,* 470–480.

Buber, M. (1958). *I and thou* (2nd. ed.). New York: Scribners.

Bugental, J. F. T. (1964). The third force in psychology. *Journal of Humanistic Psychology, 4,* 19–25.

Buhler, C. (1962). *Values in psychotherapy.* New York: Free Press.

Buhler, C. (1965). Some observations on the psychology of the third force. *Journal of Humanistic Psychology, 5,* 54–55.

Burks, H. F. (1971). *Manual for Burks' Behavior Rating Scales.* Huntington Beach, CA: Arden Press.

Burnell, G. M., & Solomon, G. F. (1964). Early memories and ego function. *Archives of General Psychiatry, 11,* 556–567.

Burt, M. (1980). Cultural myths and supports for rape. *Journal of Personality and Social Psychology, 38,* 217–230.

Buss, A. (1961). *The psychology of aggression.* New York: Wiley.

Butcher, J. N. (Ed.). (1972). *Objective personality assessment.* New York: Academic Press.

Butler, J. M., & Haigh, G. V. (1954). Changes in the relation between self-concepts and ideal concepts consequent upon client-centered counseling. In C. R. Rogers & R. F. Dymond (Eds.), *Psychotherapy and personality change* (pp. 55–75). Chicago: University of Chicago Press.

Byrne, D. (1961). The Repression-Sensitization Scale: Rationale, reliability, and validity. *Journal of Personality, 29,* 334–349.

Byrne, D., & Kelly, K. (1981). *An introduction to personality.* Englewood Cliffs, NJ: Prentice-Hall.

Calhoun, J. B. (1962, February). Population density and social pathology. *Scientific American,* pp. 139–148.

Cameron, N. (1947). *The psychology of the behavior disorders.* Boston: Houghton Mifflin.

Campbell, D. P. (1977). *Manual for the Strong-Campbell Interest Inventory* (rev. ed.). Stanford, CA: Stanford University Press.

Campbell, D. T. (1975). On the conflicts between biological and social evolution and between psychology and moral tradition. *American Psychologist, 30,* 1103–1126.

Campbell, D. T., & Fiske, D. W. (1959). Convergent and discriminant validation by the multitrait-multimethod matrix. *Psychological Bulletin, 56,* 81–105.

Campus, N. (1974). Transsituational consistency as a dimension of personality. *Journal of Personality and Social Psychology, 29,* 593–600.

Cannon, W. G. (1932). *Wisdom of the body.* New York: Norton.

Cantor, J., Zillmann, D., & Einsiedel, E. (1978). Female responses to provocation after exposure to aggressive and erotic films. *Communication Research, 5,* 395–412.

Cantor, N., & Mischel, W. (1977). Traits as prototypes: Effects on recognition memory. *Journal of Personality and Social Psychology, 35,* 38–48.

Cantor, N., & Mischel, W. (1979). Prototypes in person perception. In L. Berkowitz (Ed.), *Advances in experimental social psychology* (Vol. 12, pp. 3–52). New York: Academic Press.

Cantor, N., Mischel, W., & Schwartz, J. C. (1982). A prototype analysis of psychological situations. *Cognitive Psychology, 14,* 45–77.

Carkhuff, R. R. (1969). *Helping and human relations: A primer for lay and professional helpers* (Vols. 1–2). New York: Holt, Rinehart & Winston.

Carlsmith, J., & Anderson, C. (1979). Ambient temperature and the occurrence of violence: A new analysis. *Journal of Personality and Social Psychology, 37,* 337–344.

Carlson, R. (1975). Personality. *Annual Review of Psychology, 26,* 393–414.

Carlyn, M. (1977). An assessment of the Myers-Briggs Type Indicator. *Journal of Personality Assessment, 41,* 461–473.

Carskadon, T. G. (1978). Use of the Myers-Briggs Type Indicator in psychology courses and discussion groups. *Teaching of Psychology, 5,* 140–142.

Carson, R. C. (1969). *Interaction concepts of personality.* Chicago: Aldine.

Cattell, R. B. (1946). *The description and measurement of personality.* New York: World Book.

Cattell, R. B. (1949). *The Sixteen Personality Factor Questionnaire.* Champaign, IL: Institute for Personality and Ability Testing.

Cattell, R. B. (1950). *Personality: A systematic, theoretical and factual study.* New York: McGraw-Hill.

Cattell, R. B. (1963, March). The nature and measurement of anxiety. *Scientific American,* pp. 96–104.

Cattell, R. B. (1965). *The scientific analysis of personality.* Baltimore, MD: Penguin.

Cattell, R. B. (1973). *Personality and mood by questionnaire.* San Francisco: Jossey-Bass.

Cattell, R. B., Eber, H. W., & Tatsuoka, M. M. (1970). *Handbook for the Sixteen Personality Factor Questionnaire.* Champaign, IL: Institute for Personality and Ability Testing.

Cattell, R. B., & Scheier, I. H. (1961). *The meaning and measurement of neuroticism and anxiety.* New York: Ronald Press.

Cattell, R. B., & Warburton, F. W. (1967). *Objective personality and motivation tests: A theoretical introduction and practical compendium.* Urbana: University of Illinois Press.

Cautela, J. R., & Upper, D. (1976). The Behavioral Inventory Battery: The use of self-report measures in behavioral analysis and therapy. In M. Hersen & A. S. Bellack (Eds.), *Behavioral assessment: A practical handbook* (pp. 77–109). New York: Pergamon Press.

Check, J., & Malamuth, N. (1983). Sex-role stereotyping and reactions to depictions of stranger versus acquaintance rape. *Journal of Personality and Social Psychology, 45,* 344–356.

Check, J., & Malamuth, N. (1984). Can there be positive effects of participation in pornography experiments? *The Journal of Sex Research, 20,* 14–31.

Chomsky, N. (1959). A review of *Verbal Behavior* by B. F. Skinner. *Language, 35,* 26–58.

Christie, R., & Jahoda, M., (Eds.). (1954). *"The Authoritarian Personality."* Glencoe, IL: Free Press.

Ciminero, A. R., Calhoun, K. S., & Adams, H. E. (Eds.). (1977). *Handbook of behavioral assessment.* New York: Wiley.

Coe, W., & Sarbin, T. (1977). Hypnosis from the standpoint of a contextualist. *Annals of the New York Academy of Sciences, 296,* 2–13.

Coleman, J. C., Butcher, J. N., & Carson, R. C. (1984). *Abnormal psychology and modern life* (7th ed.). Glenview, IL: Scott, Foresman.

Collins, B., & Hoyt, M. (1972). Personal responsibility for consequences: An integration and extension of the "forced" compliance literature. *Journal of Experimental Social Psychology, 8,* 558–593.

Colm, H. N. (1961). The affirmation of distance and closeness in psychotherapy. *Review of Existential Psychology and Psychiatry, 1,* 33–43.

Combs, A. W. (1981). Some observations on self-concept research and theory. In M. D. Lynch, A. A. Norem-Hebeisen, & K. J. Gergen (Eds.), *Self-concept: Advances in theory and research* (pp. 5–16). Cambridge, MA: Ballinger.

Condry, J., & Dyer, S. (1976). Fear of success: Attribution of cause to the victim. *Journal of Social Issues, 32,* 63–83.

Conn, J. H., & Kanner, L. (1947). Children's awareness of sex differences. *Journal of Child Psychiatry, 1,* 3–57.

Conway, F., & Siegelman, J. (1978). *Snapping: America's epidemic of sudden personality change.* New York: Lippincott.

Cooper, H. (1979). Statistically combining independent studies: A meta-analysis of sex differences in conformity research. *Journal of Personality and Social Psychology, 37,* 131–146.

Cooper, H. (1981). On the significance of effects and the effect of significance. *Journal of Personality and Social Psychology, 41,* 1013–1018.

Cope, R. C., & Hewitt, R. G. (1971). Types of college dropouts: An environmental press approach. *College Student Journal, 5,* 46–51.

Corcoran, D. W. J. (1964). The relation between introversion and salivation. *American Journal of Psychology, 77,* 298–300.

Corsini, R. J. (1984). *Current psychotherapies* (3rd. ed.). Itasca, IL: F. E. Peacock.

Coughlin, E. (1985, March 13). Is violence on TV harmful to our health? Some scholars, a vocal minority, say no. *The Chronicle of Higher Education,* pp. 5, 8, 9.

Cousins, N. (1979). *Anatomy of an illness as perceived by the patient.* New York: Norton.

Craik, K. H., & McKechnie, G. E. (Eds.). (1978). *Personality and the environment.* Beverly Hills, CA: Sage.

Cramer, P. (1968). *Word association.* New York: Academic Press.

Cronbach, L. J. (1957). The two disciplines of scientific psychology. *American Psychologist, 12,* 671–684.

Cronbach, L. J. (1970). *Essentials of psychological testing* (3rd ed.). New York: Harper & Row.

Crow, L., & Crow, A. (Eds). (1954). *Readings in general psychology.* New York: Barnes & Noble.

Crumbaugh, J., & Maholick, L. (1969). *Manual of instructions for the Purpose in Life Test.* Munster, IN: Psychometric Affiliates.

Curran, C. A. (1945). *Personality factors in counseling.* New York: Grune & Stratton.

Danto, A., & Morgenbesser, S. (1960). *Philosophy of science.* Cleveland, OH: Meridan.

Darley, J. M., & Latané, B. (1968). Bystander intervention in emergencies: Diffusion of responsibility. *Journal of Personality and Social Psychology, 8,* 377–383.

Darley, J. M., & Latané, B. (1974). When will people help in a crisis? In J. B. Maas (Ed.), *Readings in psychology today* (3rd ed., pp. 353–357). Del Mar, CA: CRM Books.

Darley, J. M., & Zanna, M. (1982). Making moral judgments. *American Scientist, 70,* 515–521.

Davidson, P. O., & Costello, C. G. (Eds.). (1969). *N = 1: Experimental studies of single cases.* New York: Van Nostrand Reinhold.

Davis, S., Thomas, R., & Weaver, M. (1982). Psychology's contemporary and all-time notables: Student, faculty, and chairperson viewpoints. *Bulletin of the Psychonomic Society, 20,* 3–6.

Davis, W., & Phares, E. (1969). Parental antecedents of internal-external control of reinforcement. *Psychological Reports, 24,* 427–436.

Davison, G. C., & Neale, J. M. (1982). *Abnormal psychology: An experimental clinical approach* (3rd ed.). New York: Wiley.

Deaux, K. (1984). From individual differences to social categories: Analysis of a decade's research on gender. *American Psychologist, 39,* 105–116.

Deaux, K., & Wrightsman, L. (1984). *Social psychology in the 80s* (4th ed.). Monterey, CA: Brooks/Cole.

de Bonis, M., & Delgrange, C. (1977). A psycholinguistic approach to the measurement of anxiety. In C. D. Spielberger & I. G. Sarason (Eds.), *Stress and anxiety* (Vol. 4, pp. 67–76). New York: Wiley.

de Charms, R. (1972). Personal causation training in the schools. *Journal of Applied Social Psychology, 2,* 95–113.

de Charms, R., & Moeller, G. H. (1962). Values expressed in American children's readers: 1800–1950. *Journal of Abnormal Psychology, 64,* 136–142.

de Charms, R., & Muir, M. S. (1978). Motivation: Social approaches. *Annual Review of Psychology, 29,* 91–113.

Deci, E. (1975). *Intrinsic motivation.* New York: Plenum.

Dembroski, T., & MacDougall, J. (1978). Stress effects on affiliation preferences among subjects possessing the Type A coronary-prone behavior pattern. *Journal of Personality and Social Psychology, 36,* 23–33.

Dembroski, T., & MacDougall, J. (1985). Beyond global Type A: Relationships of paralinguistic attributes, hostility, and anger-in to coronary heart disease. In T. Field, P. McAbe, & S. N. Schneiderman (Eds.), *Stress and coping* (pp. 223–242). Hillsdale, NJ: Erlbaum.

DePaulo, B., & Rosenthal, R. (1979). Telling lies. *Journal of Personality and Social Psychology, 37,* 1713–1722.

Deutsch, H. (1945). *The psychology of women* (Vol. 2). New York: Grune & Stratton.

Diener, E. (1983). *The phenomenon of person consistency.* Unpublished paper, Department of Psychology, University of Illinois, Champaign, IL.

Diener, E., & Larsen, R. (1984). Temporal stability and cross-situational consistency of affective, behavioral, and cognitive responses. *Journal of Personality and Social Psychology, 47,* 871–883.

Diener, E., Larsen, R., & Emmons, R. (1984). Person X situation interactions: Choice of situations and congruence response models. *Journal of Personality and Social Psychology, 47,* 580–592.

Diener, E., & Wallbom, M. (1976). Effects of self-awareness on antinormative behavior. *Journal of Research in Personality, 10,* 107–111.

Dillehay, R. C. (1978). Authoritarianism. In H. London & J. E. Exner, Jr. (Eds.), *Dimensions of personality* (pp. 85–127). New York: Wiley.

Dixon, N. (1971). *Subliminal perception: The nature of a controversy.* London: McGraw-Hill.

Doherty, W. (1983). Impact of divorce on locus of control orientation in adult women: A longitudinal study. *Journal of Personality and Social Psychology, 44,* 834–840.

Dollard, J., Doob, L., Miller, N., Mowrer, O., & Sears, R. (1939). *Frustration and aggression.* New Haven, CT: Yale University Press.

Dollard, J., & Miller, N. (1950). *Personality and psychotherapy.* New York: McGraw-Hill.

Donnerstein, E. (1980). Aggressive erotica and violence against women. *Journal of Personality and Social Psychology, 39,* 269–277.

Donnerstein, E. (1983). Erotica and human aggression. In R. Geen & E. Donnerstein (Eds.), *Aggression: Theoretical and empirical reviews* (Vol. 2, pp. 127–154). New York: Academic Press.

Donnerstein, E., & Barrett, G. (1978). The effects of erotic stimuli on male aggression toward females. *Journal of Personality and Social Psychology, 36,* 180–188.

Donnerstein, E., & Berkowitz, L. (1981). Victim reactions in aggressive erotic films as a factor in violence against women. *Journal of Personality and Social Psychology, 41,* 710–724.

Donnerstein, E., & Donnerstein, M. (1972). White rewarding behavior as a function of potential for black retaliation. *Journal of Personality and Social Psychology, 24,* 327–333.

Donnerstein, E., & Donnerstein, M. (1973). Variables in interracial aggression: Potential ingroup censure. *Journal of Personality and Social Psychology, 27,* 143–150.

Donnerstein, E., & Donnerstein, M. (1976). Research in the control of interracial aggression. In R. Geen & E. O'Neal (Eds.), *Perspectives on aggression* (pp. 133–168). New York: Academic Press.

Donnerstein, E., Donnerstein, M., & Evans, R. (1975). Erotic stimuli and aggression: Facilitation or inhibition. *Journal of Personality and Social Psychology, 32,* 237–244.

Donnerstein, E., Donnerstein, M., Simon, S., & Ditrichs, R. (1972). Variables in interracial aggression: Anonymity, expected retaliation, and a riot. *Journal of Personality and Social Psychology, 22,* 236–245.

Donnerstein, E., & Hallam, J. (1978). The facilitating effects of erotica on aggression against women. *Journal of Personality and Social Psychology, 36,* 1270–1277.

Dreikurs, R. (1972a). Family counseling: A demonstration. *Journal of Individual Psychology, 28,* 207–222.

Dreikurs, R. (1972b). Technology of conflict resolution. *Journal of Individual Psychology, 28,* 203–206.

Dry, A. (1961). *The psychology of Jung: A critical interpretation.* New York: Wiley.

Dutton, D., & Lennox, V. (1974). Effect of prior "token" compliance on subsequent interracial behavior. *Journal of Personality and Social Psychology, 29,* 65–71.

Duval, S., & Wicklund, R. A. (1972). *A theory of objective self awareness.* New York: Academic Press.

Duval, S., & Wicklund, R. A. (1973). Effects of objective self awareness on attribution of causality. *Journal of Experimental Social Psychology, 9,* 17–31.

Eagly, A. (1978). Sex differences in influenceability. *Psychological Bulletin, 85,* 86–166.

Eagly, A. (1983). Gender and social influence: A social psychological analysis. *American Psychologist, 38,* 971–981.

Eagly, A., & Carli, L. (1981). Sex of researchers and sex-typed communications as determinants of sex differences in influenceability: A meta-analysis of social influence studies. *Psychological Bulletin, 90,* 1–20.

Eagly, A., Renner, P., & Carli, L. (1983, August). *Using meta-analysis to examine biases in gender-difference research.* Paper presented at the meeting of the American Psychological Association, Anaheim, CA.

Eagly, A., & Wood, W. (1982). Inferred sex differences in status as a determinant of gender stereotypes about social influence. *Journal of Personality and Social Psychology, 43,* 915–928.

Eagly, A., Wood, W., & Fishbaugh, L. (1981). Sex differences in conformity: Surveillance by the group as a determinant of male nonconformity. *Journal of Personality and Social Psychology, 40,* 384–389.

Eaves, L. J., & Eysenck, H. J. (1975). The nature of extraversion: A genetical analysis. *Journal of Personality and Social Psychology, 32,* 102–112.

Ebbesen, E., Duncan, B., & Konečni, V. (1975). Effects of content of verbal aggression on future verbal aggression: A field experiment. *Journal of Experimental Social Psychology, 11,* 192–204.

Eckardt, M. H. (Ed.). (1980). Foreword. In K. Horney, *The adolescent diaries of Karen Horney* (pp. vii–ix). New York: Basic Books.

Ehrlich, H. J. (1978). Dogmatism. In H. London & J. E. Exner, Jr. (Eds.). *Dimensions of personality* (pp. 129–164). New York: Wiley.

Ehrlich, H. J., & Lee, D. (1969). Dogmatism, learning, and resistance to change: A review and a new paradigm. *Psychological Bulletin, 71,* 249–260.

Ekman, P., & Friesen, W. (1974). Detecting deception from the body or face. *Journal of Personality and Social Psychology, 29,* 288–298.

Ellenberger, H. (1970). *The discovery of the unconscious: The history and evolution of dynamic psychiatry.* New York: Basic Books.

Ellis, A. (1974a). Experience and rationality: The making of a rational-emotive therapist. *Psychotherapy: Theory, Research and Practice, 11,* 194–198.

Ellis, A. (1974b). *Rational-emotive theory.* In A. Burton (Ed.), *Operational theories of personality* (pp. 308–344). New York: Brunner/Mazel.

Elms, A. C. (1976). *Personality in politics.* New York: Harcourt Brace Jovanovich.

Endler, N. S. (1973). The person versus the situation—A pseudo issue? A response to Alker. *Journal of Personality, 41,* 287–303.

Endler, N. S. (1981). Persons, situations, and their interactions. In A. I. Rabin, J. Aronoff, A. M. Barclay, & R. A. Zucker (Eds.), *Further explorations in personality* (pp. 114–151). New York: Wiley-Interscience.

Endler, N. S. (1983). Interactionism: A personality model, but not yet a theory. In M. M. Page & R. Dienstbier (Eds.), *Personality—Current theory and research, 1982 Nebraska symposium on motivation* (pp. 155–200). Lincoln: University of Nebraska Press.

Endler, N. S., & Hunt, J. McV. (1968). S-R inventories of hostility and comparisons of the proportions of variance from persons, responses, and situations for hostility and anxiousness. *Journal of Personality and Social Psychology, 9,* 309–315.

Endler, N. S., & Hunt, J. McV. (1969). Generalizability of contributions from sources of variance in the S-R Inventory of Anxiousness. *Journal of Personality, 37,* 1–24.

Endler, N. S., and Magnusson, D. (Eds.). (1976). *Interactional psychology and personality.* New York: Wiley.

Endler, N. S., & Okada, M. (1975). A multidimensional measure of trait anxiety: The S-R Inventory of General Trait Anxiousness. *Journal of Consulting and Clinical Psychology, 43,* 319–329.

Engleman, E. (1976). *Berggasse 19: Sigmund Freud's home and offices, Vienna 1938.* New York: Basic Books.

English, H. B., & English, A. C. (1958). *A comprehensive dictionary of psychological and psychoanalytical terms.* New York: Longmans, Green.

Epstein, L. H. (1976). Psychophysiological measurement in assessment. In M. Hersen & A. S. Bellack (Eds.), *Behavioral assessment: A practical handbook* (pp. 207–232). New York: Pergamon Press.

Epstein, R. (1965). Authoritarianism, displaced aggression, and social status of the target. *Journal of Personality and Social Psychology, 2,* 585–588.

Epstein, S. (1972). The nature of anxiety with emphasis upon its relationship to expectancy. In C. D. Spielberger (Ed.), *Anxiety: Current trends in theory and research* (Vol. 2, pp. 291–337). New York: Academic Press.

Epstein, S. (1977). Traits are alive and well. In D. Magnusson & N. Endler (Eds.), *Personality at the crossroads: Current issues in interactional psychology.* (pp. 83–98). Hillsdale, NJ: Erlbaum.

Erik Erickson: The quest for identity. (1970, December 21). *Newsweek,* pp. 84–89.

Erikson, E. H. (1968a). Life cycle. In D. Sills (Ed.), *International encyclopedia of the social sciences* (Vol. 9, pp. 286–292). New York: Macmillan & Free Press.

Erikson, E. H. (1968b). Womanhood and the inner space. In E. H. Erikson, *Identity, youth, and crisis* (pp. 261–294). New York: Norton.

Erikson, E. H. (1975). *Life history and the historical moment: Diverse presentations.* New York: Norton.

Eron, L. (1980). Prescription for reduction of aggression. *American Psychologist, 35,* 244–252.

Eron, L. (1982). Parent-child interaction, television violence, and aggression of children. *American Psychologist, 37,* 197–211.

Eron, L. & Huesmann, L. (1984). The control of aggressive behavior by changes in attitudes, values, and the conditions of learning. In R. J. Blanchard & D. C. Blanchard (Eds.), *Advances in the Study of Aggression* (Vol. 1, pp. 130–171). New York: Academic Press.

Eron, L., Huesmann, L., Lefkowitz, M., & Walder, L. (1972). Does television violence cause aggression? *American Psychologist, 27,* 253–263.

Estes, K. (1944). An experimental study of punishment. *Psychological Monographs, 47* (No. 263).

Evans, R. I. (1964). *Conversations with Carl Jung, and reactions from Ernest Jones.* Princeton, NJ: Van Nostrand.

Evans, R. I. (1967). *Dialogue with Erik Erikson.* New York: Harper & Row.

Evans, R. I. (1975). *Carl Rogers: The man and his ideas.* New York: Dutton.

Exner, Jr. J. E. (1978). *The Rorschach: A comprehensive system: Vol. 2. Current research and advanced interpretations.* New York: Wiley-Interscience.

Eysenck, H. J. (1939). Primary mental abilities. *British Journal of Educational Psychology, 9,* 270–275.

Eysenck, H. J. (1947). *Dimensions of personality.* London: Routledge & Kegan Paul.

Eysenck, H. J. (1952a). The effects of psychotherapy: An evaluation. *Journal of Consulting Psychology, 16,* 319–324.

Eysenck, H. J. (1952b). *The scientific study of personality.* New York: Macmillan.

Eysenck, H. J. (1953). *The structure of human personaity.* London: Methuen.

Eysenck, H. J. (1957a). *The dynamics of anxiety and hysteria.* New York: Praeger.

Eysenck, H. J. (1957b). *Sense and nonsense in psychology.* Baltimore, MD: Penguin.

Eysenck, H. J. (1958). A short questionnaire for the measurement of two dimensions of personality. *Journal of Applied Psychology, 42,* 14–17.

Eysenck, H. J. (1959). *Manual of the Maudsley Personality Inventory.* London: University of London Press.

Eysenck, H. J. (Ed.). (1960). *Experiments in personality* (Vols. 1–2). London: Routledge & Kegan Paul.

Eysenck, H. J. (1962a). *Know your own IQ.* Baltimore, MD: Penguin.

Eysenck, H. J. (1962b). *The Maudsley Personality Inventory manual.* San Diego, CA: Educational and Industrial Testing Service.

Eysenck, H. J. (Ed.). (1964). *Experiments in motivation.* New York: Pergamon Press.

Eysenck, H. J. (1965). *Fact and fiction in psychology.* Baltimore, MD: Penguin.

Eysenck, H. J. (1967). *The biological basis of personality.* Springfield, IL: Charles C Thomas.

Eysenck, H. J. (1970). *The structure of human personality.* London: Methuen.

Eysenck, H. J. (1971). *Race, intelligence and education.* London: Temple Smith.

Eysenck, H. J. (1973). *Eysenck on extraversion.* New York: Halsted.

Eysenck, H. J. (1975, August). The ethics of science and the duties of scientists. *British Association for the Advancement of Science,* New Issue, *1,* 23–25.

Eysenck, H. J. (Ed.). (1976). *The measurement of personality.* Baltimore, MD: University Park Press.

Eysenck, H. J. (1977). *Crime and personality.* London: Routledge & Kegan Paul.

Eysenck, H. J. (1980). Hans Jurgen Eysenck. In G. Lindzey (Ed.), *A history of psychology in autobiography* (Vol. 7, pp. 153–187). San Francisco: W. H. Freeman.

Eysenck, H. J. (Ed.). (1981). *A model for personality.* New York: Springer-Verlag.

Eysenck, H. J., & Eysenck, S. B. G. (1969). *Personality structure and measurement.* San Diego, CA: Knapp.

Eysenck, H. J., & Eysenck, S. B. G. (1976). *Psychoticism as a dimension of personality.* New York: Crane, Russak.

Eysenck, H. J., & Levey, A. (1972). Conditioning, introversion-extraversion and the strength of the nervous system. In V. D. Nebylitsyn & J. A. Gray (Eds.), *Biological bases of individual behavior* (pp. 206–220). New York: Academic Press.

Eysenck, H. J., & Wilson, G. (1976). *Know your own personality.* New York: Harper & Row.

Eysenck, M. W. (1977). *Human memory: Theory, research and individual differences.* New York: Pergamon Press.

Eysenck, S. B. G. (1965). *Manual of the Junior Eysenck Personality Inventory.* San Diego, CA: Educational and Industrial Testing Service.

Eysenck, S. B. G., & Eysenck, H. J. (1967). Salivary response to lemon juice as a measure of introversion. *Perceptual and Motor Skills, 24,* 1047–1053.

Eysenck, S. B. G., & Eysenck, H. J. (1968). The measurement of psychoticism: A study of factor analytic stability and reliability. *British Journal of Social and Clinical Psychology, 7,* 286–294.

Eysenck, S. B. G., & Eysenck, H. J. (1973). Test-retest reliabilities of a new personality questionnaire for children. *British Journal of Educational Psy-*

chology, 43, 126–130.

Eysenck, S. B. G., & Eysenck, H. J. (1975). *Manual of the Eysenck Personality Questionnaire.* San Diego, CA: Educational and Industrial Testing Service.

Fairbairn, W. R. D. (1954). *An object-relations theory of personality.* New York: Basic Books.

Farber, A. (1978). Freud's love letters: Intimations of psychoanalytic theory. *The Psychoanalytic Review, 65,* 167–189.

Farberow, N. L. (1970). A society by any other name. *Journal of Projective Techniques and Personality Assessment, 34,* 3–5.

Fear of criminals drives couple to suicide. (1978, October 8). *Peoria Journal Star,* p. 2.

Fein, G. G., Schwartz, P. M., Jacobson, S. W., & Jacobson, J. L. (1983). Environmental toxins and behavioral development: A new role for psychological research. *American Psychologist, 38,* 1188–1197.

Fenichel, O. (1945). *The psychoanalytic theory of neurosis.* New York: Norton.

Ferenczi, S. (1916). *Contributions to psychoanalysis.* Boston: Badger.

Feshbach, S. (1978). The environment of personality. *American Psychologist, 33,* 447–455.

Festinger, L. (1954). A theory of social comparison processes. *Human Relations, 2,* 117–140.

Festinger, L., & Carlsmith, J. M. (1959). Cognitive consequences of forced compliance. *Journal of Abnormal and Social Psychology, 58,* 203–210.

Findley, M., & Cooper, H. (1983). Locus of control and academic achievement: A literature review. *Journal of Personality and Social Psychology, 44,* 419–427.

Fischer, W. F. (1970). *Theories of anxiety.* New York: Harper & Row.

Fisher, W., & Byrne, D. (1978). Sex differences in reponse to erotica? Love or lust. *Journal of Personality and Social Psychology, 36,* 117–125.

Fiske, D. W. (1971). *Measuring the concepts of personality.* Chicago: Aldine.

Fletcher, J. (1966). *Situation ethics: The new morality.* Philadelphia: Westminster Press.

Fliegel, Z. (1982). Half a century later: Current status of Freud's controversial view on women. *The Psychoanalytic Review, 69,* 7–28.

Frank, J. D. (1961). *Persuasion and healing: A comparative study of psychotherapy.* New York: Schocken Books.

Frank, J. D. (1971) Therapeutic factors in psychotherapy. *American Journal of Psychotherapy, 25,* 350–361.

Frank, L. K. (1939). Projective methods for the study of personality. *Journal of Psychology, 8,* 389–413.

Frankl, V. E. (1960). *The doctor and the soul: An introduction to logotherapy.* New York: Knopf.

Frankl, V. E. (1961). Dynamics, existence and values. *Journal of Existential Psychiatry, 2,* 5–16.

Frankl, V. E. (1963). *Man's search for meaning: An introduction to logotherapy.* New York: Washington Square Press.

Frankl, V. E. (1968). *Psychotherapy and existentialism: Selected papers on logotherapy.* New York: Simon & Schuster/Clarion Books.

Frederiksen, N. (1972). Toward a taxonomy of situations. *American Psychologist, 27,* 114–123.

Fremont, T., Means, G. H., & Means, R. S. (1970). Anxiety as a function of task performance feedback and extraversion-introversion. *Psychological Reports, 27,* 455–458.

French, E. G., & Lesser, G. S. (1964). Some characteristics of the achievement motive in women. *Journal of Abnormal and Social Psychology, 68,* 119–128.

French, M. (1977). The women's room. New York: Jove.

Frenkel-Brunswik, E. (1949). Intolerance of ambiguity as an emotional and perceptual personality variable. *Journal of Personality, 18,* 108–143.

Frenkel-Brunswik, E. (1954). Further explorations by a contributor to "The Authoritarian Personality." In R. Christie & M. Jahoda (Eds.), *"The Authoritarian Personality"* (pp. 226–275). Glencoe, IL: Free Press.

Freud, A. (1967). *The ego and the mechanisms of defense* (rev. ed.). New York: International Universities Press. (Original work published 1936)

Freud, A. (1976). Changes in psychoanalytic practice and experience. *International Journal of Psychoanalysis, 57,* 257–260.

Freud, E. (Ed.). (1961). *Letters of Sigmund Freud.* New York: Basic Books.

Freud, S. (1936). *The problem of anxiety.* New York: Norton. (Original work published 1923)

Freud S. (1949). *An outline of psychoanalysis.* New York: Norton. (Original work published 1940)

Freud, S. (1952). *An autobiographical study* (James Strachey, Trans.). New York: Norton. (Original work published 1925).

Freud, S. (1957). Leonardo da Vinci and a memory of his childhood. In J. Strachey (Ed. and Trans.), *The standard edition of the complete psychological works of Sigmund Freud* (Vol. 11, pp. 59–138). London: Hogarth. (Original work published 1910)

Freud, S. (1958). *The interpretation of dreams.* New York: Basic Books. (Original work published 1900)

Freud, S. (1959). Some psychological consequences of

the anatomical distinction between the sexes. In J. Strachey (Ed.), *The collected papers of Sigmund Freud* (Vol. 5, pp. 186–197). New York: Basic Books. (Original work published 1925)

Freud, S. (1961a). Civilization and its discontents. In J. Strachey (Ed. and Trans.), *The standard edition of the complete psychological works of Sigmund Freud* (Vol. 21, pp. 59–148). London: Hogarth. (Original work published 1930)

Freud, S. (1961b). *The ego and the id.* London: Hogarth. (Original work published 1923)

Freud, S. (1961c). *The ego and the id* (James Strachey, Trans.). New York: Norton. (Original work published 1923)

Freud, S. (1963a). Analysis of a phobia in a five-year-old boy. In S. Freud, *The sexual enlightenment of children* (pp. 47–183). New York: Collier. (Original work published 1909)

Freud, S. (1963b). In P. Rieff (Ed.), *Three case histories.* New York: Collier.

Freud, S. (1964). *Moses and monotheism* (K. Jones, Trans.). New York: Knopf. (Original work published 1939)

Freud, S. (1965). *New introductory lectures on psychoanalysis.* New York: Norton. (Original work published 1933)

Freud, S. (1965). *Psychopathology of everyday life.* New York: Mentor (New American Library). (Original work published 1901)

Freud, S. (1970). Why war? In E. I. Megargee & J. E. Hokanson (Eds.), *The dynamics of aggression* (pp. 10–21). New York: Harper & Row. (Original work published 1932)

Freud, S. (1977). *Introductory lectures on psychoanalysis.* New York: Norton. (Original work published 1920)

Freud, S., & Bullit, W. C. (1966). *Thomas Woodrow Wilson: A Psychological Study.* New York: Avon.

Friedman, M. (1977). Type A behavior pattern: Some of its pathophysiological components. *Bulletin of the New York Academy of Medicine, 53,* 593–604.

Fromm, E. (1941). *Escape from freedom.* New York: Holt, Rinehart & Winston.

Fromm, E. (1947). *Man for himself: An inquiry into the psychology of ethics.* New York: Holt, Rinehart & Winston.

Fromm, E. (1955). *The sane society.* New York: Rinehart.

Fromm, E. (1956). *The art of loving.* New York: Harper & Brothers.

Fromm, E. (1959). Values, psychology and human existence. In A. H. Maslow (Ed.), *New knowledge in human values* (pp. 151–164). New York: Harper & Brothers.

Fromm, E. (1961). *May man prevail?* Garden City, NY: Doubleday/Anchor Books.

Fromm, E. (1962). *Beyond the chains of illusion: My encounter with Marx and Freud.* New York: Pocketbooks.

Fromm, E. (1964). *The heart of man: Its genius for good and evil.* New York: Harper & Row.

Fromm, E. (1968). On the sources of human destructiveness. In L. Ng (Ed.), *Alternatives to violence* (pp. 11–17). New York: Time-Life.

Fromm, E. (1973). *The anatomy of human destructiveness.* New York: Holt, Rinehart & Winston.

Fromm, E. (1976). *To have or to be?* New York: Harper & Row.

Fromm, E., & Maccoby, M. (1970). *Social character in a Mexican village: A sociopsychoanalytic study.* Englewood Cliffs, NJ: Prentice-Hall.

Funder, D. C., & Bem, D. J. (1977, August). *A proposal for assessing the personality of situations.* Paper presented at the meeting of the American Psychological Association, San Francisco.

Funder, D. C., & Ozer, D. (1983). Behavior as a function of the situation. *Journal of Personality and Social Psychology, 44,* 107–112.

Funk, R. (1982). *Erich Fromm: The courage to be human.* New York: Continuum.

Gaertner, S., & Dovidio, J. (1977). The subtlety of white racism, arousal, and helping behavior. *Journal of Personality and Social Psychology, 35,* 691–707.

Garfield, E. (1978). The hundred most cited authors. *Current Contents, 45,* 5–15.

Garrison, M. (1978). A new look at Little Hans. *The Psychoanalytic Review, 65,* 523–532.

Geen, R., Stonner, D., & Shope, G. (1975). The facilitation of aggression by aggression: Evidence against the catharsis hypothesis. *Journal of Personality and Social Psychology, 31,* 721–726.

Gelman, D., & Hager, M. (1981, November 30). Finding the hidden Freud. *Newsweek,* pp. 64–70.

Gendlin, E. T. (1961). Experiencing: A variable in the process of therapeutic change. *American Journal of Psychotherapy, 15,* 2.

Gendlin, E. T. (1962). *Experiencing and the creation of meaning.* New York: Free Press.

Gendlin, E. T., & Rychlak, J. F. (1970). Psychotherapeutic processes. *Annual Review of Psychology, 21,* 155–190.

Gendlin, E. T., & Tomlinson, T. M. (1967). The process conception and its measurement. In C. R. Rogers (Ed.), *The therapeutic relationship and its impact: A study of psychotherapy with schizophrenics* (pp. 109–131). Madison: University of Wisconsin Press.

Gerard L. (1962). *Sigmund Freud: The man and his theories.* New York: Fawcett.

Gergen, K., Gergen, M., & Barton, W. (1973, October). Deviance in the dark. *Psychology Today,* pp. 129–130.

Gibson, H. B. (1981). *Hans Eysenck: The man and his work.* London: Peter Owen.

Gilberstadt, H., & Duker, J. (1965). *A handbook for clinical and actuarial MMPI interpretation.* Philadelphia: Saunders.

Gill, M. (1981). Special book review: A new perspective on Freud and psychoanalysis. *The Psychoanalytic Review, 68,* 343–347.

Gilliland, K. (1985). The temperament inventory: Relationship to theoretically similar Western personality dimensions and construct validity. In J. Strelau, A. Gale, & F. Farley (Eds.), *Biological foundations of personality and activity* (pp. 59–82). New York: Hemisphere.

Gilliland, K., & Bullock, W. (in press). The relationship and integration of Soviet nervous system strength with biologically-based personality research. In G. L. Mangan & T. Paisey (Eds.), *Temperament and personality: An East-West dialogue.* London: Pergamon Press.

Goh, D. S., Teslow, C. J., & Fuller, G. B. (1981). The practice of psychological assessment among school psychologists. *Professional Psychology, 12,* 696–706.

Goldberg, L. R. (1981). Language and individual differences: The search for universals in personality lexicons. In L. Wheeler (Ed.), *Review of personality and social psychology* (pp. 141–165). Beverly Hills, CA: Sage.

Goldstein, K. (1939). *The organism.* New York: American Book Company.

Goleman, D. (1978, November). Special abilities of the sexes: Do they begin with the brain? *Psychology Today,* pp. 48–59, 120.

Golub, S. (1981). Coping with cancer: Freud's experiences. *The Psychoanalytic Review, 68,* 191–200.

Gordon, J. E. (1957). Interpersonal prediction of repressors and sensitizers. *Journal of Personality, 25,* 686–698.

Gordon, S. (1976). *Myth of human sexuality* [Audio tape]. National Public Radio, 2025 M St., NW, Washington, DC 20036.

Gorlow, L., Simonson, N. R., & Krauss, H. (1966). An empirical investigation of the Jungian typology. *British Journal of Social and Clinical Psychology, 5,* 108–117.

Gough, H. G., & Heilbrun, A. B., Jr. (1980). *The Adjective Check List manual* (rev. ed.). Palo Alto, CA: Consulting Psychologists Press.

Gould, P., & White, R. (1974). *Mental maps.* Baltimore, MD: Penguin.

Graham, W. K., & Balloun, J. (1973). An empirical test of Maslow's need hierarchy theory. *Journal of Humanistic Psychology, 13,* 97–108.

Gray, J. A. (1972). The psychophysiological basis of introversion-extraversion: A modification of Eysenck's theory. In V. D. Nebylitsyn & J. A. Gray (Eds.), *The biological bases of individual behavior* (pp. 182–205). New York: Academic Press.

Gray, J. A. (1979). *Ivan Pavlov.* New York: Penguin.

Gray, J. A. (1981). A critique of Eysenck's theory of personality. In H. J. Eysenck (Ed.), *A model for personality* (pp. 246–276). New York: Springer-Verlag.

Green, H. (1964). *I never promised you a rose garden.* New York: Signet.

Greenberg, J. (1979, December 1). Jim Jones: The deadly hypnotist. *Science News,* pp. 378–379+.

Greenough, W., Carter, C., Steerman, C., & DeVoogd, T. (1977). Sex differences in dendrite patterns in hamster preoptic area. *Brain Research, 126,* 63–72.

Griffith, W. (1979, May). *Sex and sexual attraction.* Paper presented at the meeting of the Midwestern Psychological Association, Chicago.

Gromly, J. (1982). Behaviorism and the biological viewpoint of personality. *Bulletin of the Psychonomic Society, 20,* 255–256.

Gross, O. (1981). Die zerebrale Sekundarfunktion. Leipzig, Germany: 1902. Cited in H. J. Eysenck (Ed.), *A model for personality.* New York: Springer-Verlag.

Groth, A. N., & Birnbaum, H. J. (1979). *Men who rape: The psychology of the offender.* New York: Plenum.

Guilford, J. P. (1959). *Personality.* New York: McGraw-Hill.

Guilford, J. P. (1967). *The nature of human intelligence.* New York: McGraw-Hill.

Guilford, J. P., & Zimmerman, W. S. (1956). Fourteen dimensions of temperament. *Psychological Monographs, 70* (Whole No. 417).

Gump, P. V. (1974). Big schools—small schools. In R. H. Moos & P. M. Insel (Eds.), *Issues in social ecology: Human milieus* (pp. 276–285). Palo Alto, CA: National Press Books.

Gupta, B. S., & Kaur, S. (1978). The effects of dextroamphetamine on kinesthetic figural aftereffects. *Psychopharmacology, 56,* 199–204.

Gurman, A. S., & Razin, A. M. (Eds.). (1977). *Effective psychotherapy: A handbook of research.* New York: Pergamon Press.

Haan, N. (1978). Two moralities in action contexts. *Journal of Personality and Social Psychology, 36,* 286–305.

Hafner, J. L., Fakouri, M. E., & Labrentz, H. L. (1982). First memories of "normal" and alcoholic individuals. *Individual Psychology, 38,* 238–244.

Hall, C. S., & Lindzey, G. (1978). *Theories of personality* (3rd ed.). New York: Wiley.

Hall, C. S., & Nordby, V. J. (1973). *A primer of Jungian psychology.* New York: Mentor Books.

Hall, C. S., & Van de Castle, R. L. (1965). An empirical investigation of the castration complex in dreams. *Journal of Personality, 33,* 20–29.

Hall, E. (1983, June). A conversation with Erik Erikson. *Psychology Today,* pp. 35–42.

Hall, M. H. (1968). The psychology of universality. [A conversation with the president of the American Psychological Association.] *Psychology Today, 2,* 34–37, 54–57.

Harel, I. (1975). *The house on Garbaldi Street.* New York: Viking Press.

Harlow, H. F. (1958). The nature of love. *American Psychologist, 13,* 673–685.

Harlow, H. F. (1959, June). Love in monkeys. *Scientific American,* pp. 68–74.

Harlow, H. F., & Harlow, M. K. (1974). The young monkeys. In J. B. Maas (Ed.), *Readings in psychology today* (3rd ed, pp. 198–203). Del Mar, CA: CRM Books.

Harper, C. J. (1978, December 4). What I saw. *Newsweek,* pp. 42–43.

Harris, M. E., & Greene, R. L. (1984). Students' perception of actual, trivial, and inaccurate personality feedback. *Journal of Personality Assessment, 48,* 179–184.

Harrower, M. (1976). Rorschach records of the Nazi war criminals: An experimental study after thirty years. *Journal of Personality Assessment, 40,* 341–351.

Hart, J. T., & Tomlinson, T. M. (1970). *New directions in client-centered therapy.* Boston: Houghton Mifflin.

Hartl, E., Monnelly, E., & Elderkin, R. (1982). *Physique and delinqent behavior.* New York: Academic Press.

Hartmann, H. (1958). *Ego psychology and the problem of adaptation.* New York: International Universities Press.

Haslam, D. R. (1967). Individual differences in pain threshold and level of arousal. *British Journal of Psychology, 58,* 139–142.

Haslam, D. R., & Thomas, E. A. C. (1967). An optimum interval in the assessment of pain threshold. *Quarterly Journal of Experimental Psychology, 19,* 54–58.

Hastorf, A. H., Schneider, D. J., & Polefka, J. (1970). *Person perception.* Menlo Park, CA: Addison-Wesley.

Hatfield, E., Sprecher, S., & Traupmann, J. (1978). Men's and women's reactions to sexually explicit films: A serendipitous finding. *Archives of Sexual Behavior, 7,* 583–592.

Hatfield, E., & Walster, W. (1982). What is this thing called love? In J. Brigham & L. Wrightsman (Eds.), *Contemporary issues in social psychology* (pp. 65–75). Monterey, CA: Brooks/Cole.

Hathaway, S. R., & McKinley, J. C. (1943). *Manual for the Minnesota Multiphasic Personality Inventory.* New York: Psychological Corporation.

Hathaway, S. R., & McKinley, J. C. (1967). *The Minnesota Multiphasic Personality Inventory manual* (rev. ed.). New York: Psychological Corporation.

Havassy–De Avila, B. (1971). A critical review of the approach to birth order research. *The Canadian Psychologist, 12,* 282–305.

Hayes, C. (1965). Changes in MAACL Anxiety scale scores during 11 class meetings. Cited in M. Zuckerman & B. Lubin, *Manual for the Multiple Affect Adjective Check List* (pp. 7–9). San Diego, CA: Educational and Industrial Testing Service.

Hayes, J. (1978). *Cognitive psychology: Thinking and creating.* Homewood, IL: Dorsey Press.

Heckhausen, H., & Krug, S. (1982). Motive modification. In A. J. Stewart (Ed.), *Motivation and society* (pp. 274–318). San Francisco: Jossey-Bass.

Heidegger, M. (1949). *Existence and being* (W. Brock, Trans.). Chicago: Henry Regnery.

Heidegger, M. (1959). *An introduction to metaphysics* (R. Manheim, Trans.). New Haven, CT: Yale University Press.

Heider, F. (1958). *The psychology of interpersonal relations.* New York: Wiley.

Heiman, J. (1975, April). Women's sexual arousal. *Psychology Today,* pp. 91–94.

Helmreich, R. L. (1983). Applying psychology in outer space. *American Psychologist, 38,* 445–450.

Hempel, C., & Oppenheim, P. (1960). Problems of the concept of general law. In A. Danto & S. Morgenbesser (Eds.), *Philosophy of Science* (pp. 198–204). New York: World.

Henry, W. E. (1974). *The analysis of fantasy.* New York: Wiley. (Original work published 1956)

Herold, E., & Way, L. (1980). Oral-genital behavior in a sample of university females. *The Journal of Sex Research, 19,* 327–338.

Hersen, M., & Barlow, D. H. (1976). *Single case experimental designs, strategies for studying behavior change.* New York: Pergamon Press.

Hersen, M., & Bellack, A. S. (1976). *Behavioral assessment: A practical handbook.* New York: Pergamon Press.

Hirsch, J. (1981). To "unfrock the charlatans." *Sage Race Relations Abstracts, 6* (May), 1–67.

Hochreich, D. J. (1979). Personality series: Some new texts. *Contemporary Psychology, 24,* 752–754.

Hogan, R. (1973). Moral conduct and moral character. *Psychological Bulletin, 79,* 217–232.

Hogan, R. (1976). *Personality theory: The personological tradition.* Englewood Cliffs, NJ: Prentice-Hall.

Hogan, R. (1983). A socioanalytic theory of personality. In M. M. Page and R. Dienstbier (Eds.), *Personality — Current theory and research, 1982 Nebraska symposium on motivation* (pp. 55–89). Lincoln: University of Nebraska Press.

Hogan, R., Johnson, J. A., & Emler, N. P. (1978). A socioanalytic theory of moral development. In W. Damon (Ed.), *New directions for child development* (Vol. 2, pp. 1–18). San Francisco: Jossey-Bass.

Holland, J. (1973). *Making vocational choices: A theory of careers.* Englewood Cliffs, NJ: Prentice-Hall.

Holland, J., & Skinner, B. (1961). *The analysis of behavior.* New York: McGraw-Hill.

Hollander, J., & Yeostros, S. (1963). The effect of simultaneous variations of humidity and barometric pressure on arthritis. *Bulletin of the American Meteorological Society, 44,* 489–494.

Holmes, T. H., & Rahe, R. H. (1967). The Social Readjustment Rating Scale. *Journal of Psychosomatic Research, 11,* 213–218.

Holmes, T. H., & Masuda, M. (1973). Life change and illness susceptibility. In American Association for the Advancement of Science, *Separation and Depression* (Publication No. 94, pp. 161–186). Washington, DC: Author.

Holtzman, W., Thorpe, J., Swartz, J., & Herron, E. (1961). *Inkblot perception and personality: Holtzman inkblot technique.* Austin: University of Texas Press.

Horner, M. S. (1968). *Sex differences in achievement motivation and performance in competitive and noncompetitive situations.* Unpublished doctoral dissertation, University of Michigan, Ann Arbor.

Horner, M. S. (1971). Femininity and successful achievement: A basic inconsistency. In M. H. Garskof (Ed.), *Roles women play: Readings toward women's liberation* (pp. 97–122). Belmont, CA: Brooks/Cole.

Horney, K., (1926). The flight from womanhood: The masculinity complex in women as viewed by men and by women. *International Journal of Psychoanalysis, 7,* 324–329.

Horney, K. (1937). *The neurotic personality of our time.* New York: Norton.

Horney, K. (1939). *New ways in psychoanalysis.* New York: Norton.

Horney, K. (1942). *Self-analysis.* New York: Norton.

Horney, K. (1945). *Our inner conflicts: A constructive theory of neurosis.* New York: Norton.

Horney, K. (1946). *Are you considering psychoanalysis?* New York: Norton.

Horney, K. (1950). *Neurosis and human growth: The struggle toward self-realization.* New York: Norton.

Horney, K. (1967). In H. Kelman (Ed.), *Feminine psychology.* New York: Norton.

Horney, K. (1980). In M. H. Eckardt (Ed.), *The adolescent diaries of Karen Horney.* New York: Basic Books.

Hoyenga, K. I., & Hoyenga, K. T. (1979). *The question of sex differences.* Boston: Little, Brown.

Huesmann, L., Eron, L., Klein, R., Brice, P., & Fisher, P. (1983). Mitigating the imitation of aggressive behaviors by changing children's attitudes about media violence. *Journal of Personality and Social Psychology, 44,* 899–910.

Hull, C. L. (1943). *Principles of behavior.* New York: Appleton-Century-Crofts.

Hull, C. L. (1952). *A behavior system.* New Haven, CT: Yale University Press.

Hunt, J. M. (1979). Psychological development: Early experience. *Annual Review of Psychology, 30,* 103–144.

Husserl, E. (1961). *Ideas* (W. R. Boyce Gibson, Trans.). New York: Collier Books.

Hyde, J. (1981). How large are cognitive gender differences? A meta-analysis using ω^2 and d. *American Psychologist, 36,* 892–901.

Hyde, J. (1983, August). *A developmental meta-analysis of gender differences in aggression.* Paper presented at the meeting of the American Psychological Association, Anaheim, CA.

Inkeles, A., & Levinson, D. (1969). National character: The study of modal personality and sociocultural systems. In G. Lindzey & E. Aronson (Eds.), *The handbook of social psychology* (2nd ed., pp. 418–506). Reading, MA: Addison-Wesley.

Insel, P. M., & Moos, R. H. (1974). Psychological environments: Expanding the scope of human ecology. *American Psychologist, 29,* 179–188.

In the dock. The Popieluszko trial begins. (1985, January 7). *Time,* p. 72.

Ittelson, W., & Kilpatrick, F. (1951, August). Experiments in perception. *Scientific American,* pp. 50–55.

Jackson, D. B., & Paunonen, S. V. (1980). Personality structure and assessment. *Annual Review of Psychology, 31,* 503–551.

Jackson, D. N. (1967). *Personality Research Form manual.* Goshen, NY: Research Psychologists Press.

Jackson, M., & Sechrest, L. (1962). Early recollections in four neurotic diagnostic categories. *Journal of Individual Psychology, 18,* 52–56.

Jacobi, J. (1962). *The psychology of C. G. Jung* (rev. ed.). New Haven, CT: Yale University Press.

Jahoda, M. (1954). Introduction. In R. Christie & M.

Jahoda (Eds.), *"The Authoritarian Personality"* (pp. 11–23). Glencoe, IL: Free Press.

Jahoda, M. (1956). Psychological issues in civil liberties. *American Psychologist, 11,* 234–240.

James, W. (1950). *The principles of psychology* (Vols. 1–2). New York: Dover. (Original work published 1890)

James, W. (1958). *The varieties of religious experience.* New York: Mentor Books. (Original work published 1902)

Jarman, T. L. (1961). *The rise and fall of Nazi Germany.* New York: Signet.

Jarvik, L., Klodin, V., & Matsuyama, S. (1973). Human aggression and the extra Y chromosome: Fact or fantasy? *American Psychologist, 28,* 674–682.

Jazwinski, C., & Byrne, D. (1978). The effect of a contraceptive theme on response to erotica. *Motivation and Emotion, 2,* 287–297.

Jenkins, C., Zyzanski, S., Ryan, T., Flessas, A., & Tannenbaum, S. (1977). Social insecurity and coronary-prone Type A responses as identifiers of severe atherosclerosis. *Journal of Consulting and Clinical Psychology, 45,* 1060–1067.

Jensen, A. R. (1969). How much can we boost IQ and scholastic achievement? *Harvard Educational Review, 39,* 1–123.

Jensen, A. R. (1978). Sir Cyril Burt in perspective. *American Psychologist, 33,* 499–503.

Johnson, J. A. (1983). Criminality, creativity, and craziness: Structural similarities in three types of nonconformity. In W. S. Laufer & J. M. Day (Eds.), *Personality theory, moral development, and criminal behavior* (pp. 81–105). Lexington, MA: D.C. Heath.

Johnson, R., & Downing, L. (1979). Deindividuation and valence of cues: Effects on prosocial and antisocial behavior. *Journal of Personality and Social Psychology, 37,* 1532–1538.

Jones, B. M. (1974). Cognition performance of introverts and extraverts following acute alcohol ingestion. *British Journal of Psychology, 65,* 35–42.

Jones, B. M., Hatcher, E., Jones, M. K., & Farris, J. J. (1978). The relationship of extraversion and neuroticism to the effects of alcohol on cognitive performance in male and female social drinkers. In F. A. Seixas (Ed.), *Currents in alcoholism* (pp. 243–264). New York: Grune & Stratton.

Jones, E. (1953). *The life and work of Sigmund Freud* (Vol. 1, p. 97). New York: Basic Books.

Jones E. (1955). *The life and work of Sigmund Freud* (Vol. 2). New York: Basic Books.

Jordan, E. W., Whiteside, M. M., & Manaster, G. J. (1982). A practical and effective research measure of birth order. *Individual Psychology, 38,* 253–260.

Joseph, E. (1980). Presidential address: Clinical issues in psychoanalysis. *International Journal of Psychoanalysis, 61,* 1–9.

Joy, S., & Wise, P. (1983). Maternal employment, anxiety, and sex differences in college students' self-descriptions. *Sex Roles, 9,* 519–525.

Jung, C. G. (1910). The association method. *American Journal of Psychology, 21,* 219–269.

Jung, C. G. (1959). The archetypes and the collective unconscious. In R. F. C. Hull (Trans.), *Collected works* (Vol. 9, Part 1). Princeton, NJ: Princeton University Press. (Original work published 1934)

Jung, C. G. (1963). *Memories, dreams, reflections* (A. Jaffe, Ed.). New York: Pantheon.

Jung, C. G. (Ed.). (1964). *Man and his symbols.* New York: Dell.

Jung, C. G. (1971). Psychological types. In R. F. C. Hull (Trans.), *Collected Works* (Vol. 6). Princeton, NJ: Princeton University Press. (Original work published 1921)

Jung, C. G. (1978). *Flying saucers: A modern myth of things seen in the skies* (R. F. C. Hull, Trans.). Princeton, NJ: Princeton University Press. (Original work published 1958)

Jung, J. (1978). *Understanding human motivation.* New York: Macmillan.

Kal, E. F. (1972). Survey of contemporary Adlerian clinical practice. *Individual Psychology, 28,* 261–266.

Kanfer, F. H., & Goldstein, A. P. (Eds.). (1980). *Helping people change: A textbook of methods* (2nd ed.). New York: Pergamon Press.

Kaplan, M. F., & Singer, E. (1963). Dogmatism and sensory alienation: An empirical investigation. *Journal of Consulting Psychology, 27,* 486–491.

Kaplan, R. (1982). TV violence and aggression revisited again. *American Psychologist, 37,* 589.

Katcher, A. (1955). The discrimination of sex differences by young children. *Journal of Genetic Psychology, 87,* 131–143.

Kelley, H. H. (1967). Attribution theory in social psychology. In D. Levine (Ed.), *Nebraska symposium on motivation* (Vol. 15, pp. 52–81). Lincoln: University of Nebraska Press.

Kelley, H. H. (1973). The process of causal attribution. *American Psychologist, 28,* 107–128.

Kelly, G. A. (1955). *The psychology of personal constructs* (2 vols.). New York: Norton.

Kelly, G. A. (1963). *A theory of personality: The psychology of personal constructs.* New York: Norton.

Kelly, G. A. (1969). The autobiography of a theory. In B. Maher (Ed.), Clinical psychology and personality: The selected papers of George Kelly (pp. 40–65). New York: Wiley.

Kelman, H. (1967). Introduction. In K. Horney, *Feminine Psychology*. New York: Norton.

Kelman, H., & Lawrence, L. (1972, June). American response to the trial of Lt. William O. Calley. *Psychology Today*, pp. 41–45.

Kelman, H. C., & Barclay, J. (1963). The F scale as a measure of breadth of perspective. *Journal of Abnormal and Social Psychology, 67,* 608–615.

Kendall, P. C. (1978). Anxiety: States, traits—situations? *Journal of Consulting and Clinical Psychology, 46,* 280–287.

Kendall, P. C., Finch, A., Auerbach, S., Hooke, J., & Mikulka, P. (1976). The state-trait anxiety inventory: A systematic evaluation. *Journal of Consulting and Clinical Psychology, 44,* 406–412.

Keniston, K. (1983, June). Remembering Erikson at Harvard. *Psychology Today*, p. 29.

Kenrick, D., & Braver, S. (1982). Personality: Idiographic *and* Nomothetic! A rejoinder. *Psychological Review, 89,* 182–186.

Kenrick, D., & Stringfield, D. (1980). Personality traits and the eye of the beholder: Crossing some traditional philosophical boundaries in the search for consistency in all of the people. *Psychological Review, 87,* 88–104.

Kenrick, D., Stringfield, D., Wagenhals, W., Dahl, R., & Ransdell, H. (1980). Sex, androgyny, and approach responses to erotica: A new variation on the old volunteer problem. *Journal of Personality and Social Psychology, 38,* 517–524.

Kerlinger, F. N. (1973). *Foundations of behavioral research* (2nd ed.). New York: Holt, Rinehart & Winston.

Kierkegaard, S. (1950). *Fear and trembling, and sickness unto death* (W. Lowrie, Trans.). Garden City, NY: Doubleday/Anchor Books.

Kilham, W., & Mann, L. (1974). Level of destructive obedience as a function of transmitter and executant roles in the Milgram obedience paradigm. *Journal of Personality and Social Psychology, 29,* 696–702.

Kimble, G. (1961). *Hilgard and Marquis' conditioning and learning*. New York: Appleton-Century-Crofts.

Kinkade, K. (1973, January). Commune: A Walden-Two experiment. *Psychology Today*, p. 35.

Kinsey, A., Pomeroy, W., Martin, C., & Gebhard, P. (1953). *Sexual behavior in the human female*. Philadelphia: Saunders.

Kirschenbaum, H. (1979). *On becoming Carl Rogers*. New York: Delacorte.

Kirscht, J. P., & Dillehay, R. C. (1967). *Dimensions of authoritarianism: A review of research and theory*. Lexington: University of Kentucky Press.

Klein, D. B. (1970). *A history of scientific psychology, its origins and philosophical backgrounds*. New York: Basic Books.

Klein, G. (1970). *Perceptions, motives and personality*. New York: Knopf.

Klein, M. (1932). *The psychoanalysis of children*. London: Hogarth.

Klein, M. (1961). *Narrative of a child analysis*. New York: Delta.

Kleinmuntz, B. (1982). *Personality and psychological assessment*. New York: St. Martin's Press.

Kline, P. (1972). *Fact and fantasy in Freudian theory*. London: Methuen.

Klopfer, B., Meyer, M. M., & Brawer, F. B. (Eds.). (1970). *Developments in the Rorschach technique* (Vol. 3). New York: Harcourt Brace Jovanovich.

Knapp, R. J. (1976). Authoritarianism, alienation, and related variables: A correlational and factor-analytic study. *Psychological Bulletin, 83,* 194–212.

Knapp, R. R. (1976). *Handbook for the Personal Orientation Inventory*. San Diego, CA: EdITS Publishers.

Koestler, A. (1972). *The roots of coincidence*. New York: Vintage.

Koffka, K. (1935). *Principles of Gestalt psychology*. New York: Harcourt.

Kohlberg, L. (1966). A cognitive-developmental analysis of children's sex-role concepts and attitudes. In E. E. Maccoby (Ed.), *The development of sex differences* (pp. 82–173). Stanford, CA: Stanford University Press.

Kohlberg. L. (1969). Stage and sequence: The cognitive-developmental approach to socialization. In D. Goslin (Ed.), *Handbook of socialization theory and research* (pp. 347–480). Chicago: Rand McNally.

Kohlberg, L. (1976). Moral stages and moralization. In T. Lickona (Ed.), *Moral development and behavior-theory, research, and social issues* (pp. 31–53). New York: Holt, Rinehart & Winston.

Kohlberg, L. (1981). *The meaning and measurement of moral development*. Worcester, MA: Clark University Press.

Kohler, W. (1947). *Gestalt psychology: An introduction to new concepts in psychology*. New York: Liveright.

Kohut, H. (1971). *The analysis of the self*. New York: International Universities Press.

Koppitz, E. M. (1975). *The Bender Gestalt Test for young children: Vol. 2. Research and application, 1963–1973*. New York: Grune & Stratton.

Korchin, S. J. (1976). *Modern clinical psychology: Principles of intervention in the clinic and community*. New York: Basic Books.

Korchin, S. J., & Schuldberg, D. (1981). The future of clinical assessment. *American Psychologist, 36,* 1147–1158.

Koss, M., Leonard, K., Beezley, D., & Oros, C. (1981, August). *Personality and attitudinal characteristics of sexually aggressive men*. Paper presented at the meeting of the American Psychological Association, Los Angeles.

Krane, R., & Wagner, A. (1975). Taste aversion learning with a delayed shock US: Implications for the "generality of the laws of learning." *Journal of Comparative and Physiological Psychology, 88,* 882–889.

Kratochwill, T. R. (Ed.). (1978). *Single subject research: Strategies for evaluating change.* New York: Academic Press.

Krebs, D. (1982, August). *Moral knowledge and moral conduct.* Paper presented at the meeting of the American Psychological Association, Washington, DC.

Krech, D., Crutchfield, R., & Ballachey, R. (1962). *Individual in society: A textbook of social psychology.* New York: McGraw-Hill.

Kretschmer, E. (1925). *Physique and character* (W. J. H. Spratt, Trans.). New York: Harcourt. (Original work published 1921)

Kuhn, T. S. (1962). *The structure of scientific revolutions.* Chicago: University of Chicago Press.

Lamb, D. H. (1978). Anxiety. In H. London & J. E. Exner, Jr. (Eds.), *Dimensions of personality* (pp. 37–83). New York: Wiley.

Lamiell, J. (1981). Toward an idiothetic psychology of personality. *American Psychologist, 36,* 276–289.

Langer, W. C. (1972). *The mind of Adolf Hitler: The secret wartime report.* New York: Signet.

Lasaga, J. I. (1979, December 1). Quoted in J. Greenberg. Jim Jones: The deadly hypnotist. *Science News,* pp. 378–379+.

Latané, B., & Darley, J. (1970). *The unresponsive bystander: Why doesn't he help?* New York: Appleton-Century-Crofts.

Lauzun, G. (1962). *Sigmund Freud, the man and his theories.* Greenwich, CT: Fawcett.

Lawrence, A. (1938). The voice of Sigmund Freud: An audio tape. *Psychoanalytic Review.*

Lee, D. E., & Ehrlich, H. J. (1977). Sensory alienation and interpersonal constraints as correlates of cognitive structure, *Psychological Reports, 40,* 840–842.

Leventhal, H. (1970). Findings and theory in the study of fear communications. In L. Berkowitz (Ed.), *Advances in experimental social psychology* (Vol. 5, pp. 119–186). New York: Academic Press.

Levine, D. (1981). Why and when to test: The social context of psychological testing. In A. I. Rabin (Ed.), *Assessment with projective techniques* (pp. 265–295). New York: Springer.

Levy, M. R., & Fox, H. M. (1975). Psychological testing is alive and well. *Professional Psychology, 6,* 420–424.

Lewin, K. (1936). *Principles of topological psychology.* New York: McGraw-Hill.

Lewis, A. (1980). Problems presented by the ambiguous word "anxiety" as used in psychopathology. In G. D. Burrows & B. Davies (Eds.), *Handbook of studies on anxiety* (pp. 1–15). New York: Elsevier/North-Holand Biomedical Press.

Leyens, J., Camino, L., Parke, R., & Berkowitz, L. (1975). Effects of movie violence on aggression in a field setting as a function of group dominance and cohesion. *Journal of Personality and Social Psychology, 32,* 346–360.

Liddell, H. S. (1964). The role of vigilance in the development of animal neurosis. In P. H. Hoch & J. Zubin (Eds.), *Anxiety* (pp. 183–196). New York: Hafner.

Liebert, R., & Baron, R. (1972). Some immediate effects of television violence on children. *Developmental Psychology, 6,* 469–475.

Lifton, P. (1982, August). *Personality correlates of moral reasoning: A preliminary report.* Paper presented at the meeting of the American Psychological Association, Washington, DC.

Lifton, R. J. (Ed.). (1974). *Explorations in psychohistory: The Wellfleet papers.* New York: Simon & Schuster.

Lilly, J. C. (1973). *The center of the cyclone.* New York: Bantam Books.

Lilly, J. C. (1977). *The deep self.* New York: Warner Books.

Linder, D., Cooper, J., & Jones, E. E. (1967). Decision freedom as a determinant of the role of incentive magnitude in attitude change. *Journal of Personality and Social Psychology, 6,* 245–254.

Lindzey, G., & Hall, C. S. (Eds.) (1965). *Theories of personality: Primary sources and research.* New York: Wiley.

Linville, P. (1982). The complexity-extremity effect and age-based stereotyping. *Journal of Personality and Social Psychology, 42,* 293–311.

Loehlin, J. C. (1968). *Computer models of personality.* New York: Random House.

Lopez Ibor, J. J. (1980). Basic anxiety as the core of neuroses. In G. D. Burrows & B. Davies (Eds.), *Handbook of studies on anxiety* (pp. 17–20). New York: Elsevier/North-Holand Biomedical Press.

Lorenz, K. (1966). *On aggression.* New York: Harcourt, Brace & World.

Lothane, Z. (1981). Special book review: A new perspective on Freud and psychoanalysis. *The Psychoanalytic Review, 68,* 348–361.

Lotto winner will stay on job. (1984a, September 4). *Macomb Daily Journal,* p. 1.

Lotto winner: Working days are over now. (1984b, September 11). *Macomb Daily Journal,* p. 12.

Louttit, C. M., & Browne, C. G. (1947). Psychometric instruments in psychological clinics. *Journal of Consulting Psychology, 11,* 49–54.

Lubin, B., Wallis, R. R., & Paine, C. (1971). Patterns of psychological test usage in the United States: 1935–1969. *Professional Psychology, 2,* 70–74.

Lynch, M. D., Norem-Hebeisen, A. A., & Gergen, K. J. (1981). *Self-concept: Advances in theory and research.* Cambridge, MA: Ballinger.

Lynn, R., & Eysenck, H. J. (1961). Tolerance for pain, extraversion and neuroticism. *Perceptual and Motor Skills, 12,* 161–162.

Maccoby, E., & Jacklin, C. (1974). *The psychology of sex differences.* Stanford, CA: Stanford University Press.

MacDonald, A. P., Jr. (1971). Birth order and personality. *Journal of Consulting and Clinical Psychology, 36,* 171–176.

Maddi, S. (1968). *Personality theories: A comparative analysis.* Homewood, IL: Dorsey Press.

Magnusson, D., and Endler, N. S. (1977). (Eds.). *Personality at the crossroads: Current issues in interactional psychology.* Hillsdale, NJ: Erlbaum.

Maier, N. R. F. (1949). *Frustration: The study of behavior without a goal.* New York: McGraw-Hill.

Malamuth, N. (1981a). Rape fantasies as a function of exposure to violent-sexual stimuli. *Archives of Sexual Behavior, 10,* 33–47.

Malamuth, N. (1981b). Rape proclivity among males. *Journal of Social Issues, 37,* 138–151.

Malamuth, N. (1983). Factors associated with rape as predictors of laboratory aggression against women. *Journal of Personality and Social Psychology, 45,* 432–442.

Malamuth, N., & Check, J. (1980). Penile tumescence and perceptual responses to rape as a function of victim's perceived reactions. *Journal of Applied Social Psychology, 10,* 528–547.

Malamuth, N., & Check, J. (1981). The effects of violent-sexual movies: A field experiment. *Journal of Research in Personality, 15,* 436–446.

Malamuth, N., & Check, J. (1984). Debriefing effectiveness following exposure to pornographic rape depictions. *Journal of Sex Research, 20,* 1–13.

Malamuth, N., & Check, J. (in press). Sexual arousal to rape depictions: Individual differences. *Journal of Abnormal Psychology.*

Malamuth, N., & Donnerstein, E. (1982). The effects of aggressive-pornographic mass media stimuli. In L. Berkowitz (Ed.), *Advances in experimental social psychology* (Vol. 15, pp. 103–136). New York: Academic Press.

Malamuth, N., Feshbach, S., & Heim, M. (1980) Ethical issues and exposure to rape stimuli: A reply to Sherif. *Journal of Personality and Social Psychology, 38,* 413–415.

Malamuth, N., Haber, S., & Feshbach, S. (1980) Testing hypotheses regarding rape: Exposure to sexual violence, sex differences, and the "normality" of rape. *Journal of Research in Personality, 14,* 121–173.

Malamuth, N., Heim, M., & Feshbach, S. (1980). The sexual responsiveness of college students to rape depictions: Inhibitory and disinhibitory effects. *Journal of Personality and Social Psychology, 38,* 399–408.

Malamuth, N., & Spinner, B. (1980). Longitudinal content analysis of sexual violence in the best selling erotic magazines. *Journal of Sex Research, 16,* 226–237.

Manaster, G. J., & Perryman, T. B. (1979). Manaster-Perryman Manifest Content Early Recollection Scoring Manual. In H. A. Olson (Ed.), *Early recollections: Their use in diagnosis and psychotherapy* (pp. 347–353). Springfield, IL: Charles C Thomas.

Mandler, G., & Sarason, S. B. (1952). A study of anxiety and learning. *Journal of Abnormal and Social Psychology, 47,* 166–173.

Mann, L. (1981). The baiting crowd in episodes of threatened suicide. *Journal of Personality and Social Psychology, 41,* 703–709.

Mariotto, M. J., & Paul, G. L. (1974). A multimethod validation of the Inpatient Multidimensional Psychiatric Scale with chronically institutionalized patients. *Journal of Consulting and Clinical Psychology, 42,* 497–509.

Martens, R., & Landers, D. M. (1970). Motor performance under stress: A test of the inverted-U hypothesis. *Journal of Personality and Social Psychology, 16,* 29–37.

Martin, A. R. (1975). Karen Horney's theory in today's world. *The American Journal of Psychoanalysis, 35,* 297–302.

Maslow, A. H. (1951). Resistance to acculturation. *Journal of Social Issues, 7,* 26–29.

Maslow, A. H. (1954). *Motivation and Personality.* New York: Harper & Row.

Maslow, A. H. (1959). Psychological data and value theory. In A. H. Maslow (Ed.), *New knowledge in human values* (pp. 119–136). New York: Harper & Row.

Maslow, A. H. (1962). Lessons from the peak-experiences. *Journal of Humanistic Psychology, 2,* 9–18.

Maslow, A. H. (1966). *The psychology of science: A reconnaissance.* New York: Harper & Row.

Maslow, A. H. (1967). A theory of metamotivation: The biological rooting of the value-life. *Journal of Humanistic Psychology, 7,* 93–127.

Maslow, A. H. (1968). Toward the study of violence. In L. Ng (Ed.), *Alternatives to violence* (pp. 34–37). New York: Time-Life.

Maslow, A. H. (1969). Toward a humanistic biology. *American Psychologist, 24,* 724–735.

Maslow, A. H. (1970). *Motivation and personality* (2nd ed.). New York: Harper & Row.

Maslow, A. H. (1971). *The farther reaches of human nature.* New York: Viking Press.

Maslow, B. G. (Ed.). (1972). *Abraham H. Maslow: A memorial volume.* Monterey, CA: Brooks/Cole.

Masserman, J. H. (1943). *Behavior and neurosis.* Chicago: University of Chicago Press.

Masters, W., & Johnson, V. (1966). *Human sexual response.* Boston: Little, Brown.

Mathes, E. W. (1981). *From survival to the universe: Values and psychological well-being.* Chicago: Nelson-Hall.

Mathes, E. W., Zevon, M. A., Roter, P. M., & Joerger, S. M. (1982). Peak experience tendencies: Scale development and theory testing. *Journal of Humanistic Psychology, 22,* 92–108.

Mathews, T. (1976, March 1). Patty's defense. *Newsweek,* pp. 20–28.

Mathews, T. (1978a, December 4). The cult of death. *Newsweek,* pp. 38–53.

Mathews, T. (1978b, December 18). The sounds of death. *Newsweek,* p. 31.

Maurer, A. (1964). Did Little Hans really want to marry his mother? *Journal of Health Professions, 4,* 139–148.

May, R. (1950). *The meaning of anxiety.* New York: Ronald Press.

May, R. (1958). Contributions of existential psychotherapy. In R. May, E. Angel, & H. F. Ellenberger (Eds.) *Existence: A new dimension in psychiatry and psychology* (pp. 37–91). New York: Basic Books.

May, R., Angel, E., & Ellenberger, H. F. (Eds.). (1958). *Existence: A new dimension in psychiatry and psychology.* New York: Basic Books.

McAskie, M. (1978). Carelessness or fraud in Sir Cyril Burt's kinship data? A critique of Jensen's analysis. *American Psychologist, 33,* 496–498.

McCarty, D., Diamond, W., & Kaye, M. (1982). Alcohol, sexual arousal and the transfer of excitation. *Journal of Personality and Social Psychology, 42,* 977–988.

McCary, J. (1973). *Human Sexuality.* New York: Van Nostrand.

McClelland, D. C. (1957). *Personality.* New York: Holt, Rinehart & Winston.

McClelland, D. C. (1958). Risk taking in children with high and low need for achievement. In J. W. Atkinson (Ed.), *Motives in fantasy, action, and society* (pp. 306–321). Princeton, NJ: Van Nostrand.

McClelland, D. C. (1961). *The achieving society.* New York: Free Press.

McClelland, D. C., Atkinson, J. W., Clark, R. A., & Lowell, E. L. (1953). *The achievement motive.* New York: Appleton-Century-Crofts.

McClelland, D. C., Atkinson, J. W., Clark, R. A., &

Lowell, E. L. (1958). A scoring manual for the achievement motive. In J. W. Atkinson (Ed.), *Motives in fantasy, action, and society* (pp. 179–204). Princeton, NJ: Van Nostrand.

McClelland, D. C., Clark, R. A., Roby, T. B., & Atkinson, J. W. (1949). The effect of the need for achievement on thematic apperception. *Journal of Experimental Psychology, 37,* 242–255.

McClelland, D. C., & Steele, R. S. (1972). *Motivation workshops: A student workbook for experiential learning in human motivation.* New York: General Learning Press.

McCully, R. S. (1980). A commentary on Adolf Eichmann's Rorschach. *Journal of Personality Assessment, 44,* 311–318.

McEwan, K. L., & Devins, G. M. (1983). Is increased arousal in social anxiety noticed by others? *Journal of Abnormal Psychology, 92,* 417–421.

McGrath, J. E. (1970). *Social and psychological factors in stress.* New York: Holt, Rinehart & Winston.

McGraw-Hill Films. (1971). *Personality.* New York: CRM Educational Films Collection.

McGuire, W. (Ed.). (1974). *The Freud/Jung letters* (R. Manheim & R. F. C. Hull, Trans.). Princeton, NJ: Princeton University Press.

McGuire, W., & Hull, R. F. C. (Eds.). (1977). *C. G. Jung speaking: Interviews and encounters.* Princeton, NJ: Princeton University Press.

McIntosh, D. (1979). The empirical bearing of psychoanalytic theory. *International Journal of Psychoanalyis, 60,* 405–431.

Mead, M. (1974). On Freud's view of female psychology. In J. Strouse (Ed.), *Women and analysis: Dialogues on psychoanalytic views of femininity* (pp. 95–106). New York: Grossman.

Mead, M. (1975). *Blackberry winter: My earlier years.* New York: Pocket Books.

Meehl, P. E. (1956). Wanted—A good cookbook. *American Psychologist, 11,* 236–272.

Meltzoff, J., & Kornreich, M. (1970). *Research in psychotherapy.* New York: Atherton.

Mendelsohn, G., Weiss, D., & Feimer, N. (1982). Conceptual and empirical analysis of the typological implications of patterns of socialization and femininity. *Journal of Personality and Social Psychology, 42,* 1157–1170.

Menninger, K. (1963). *The vital balance: The life process in mental health and illness.* New York: Viking Press.

Menninger, W. C. (1948). *Psychiatry in a troubled world.* New York: Macmillan.

Merleau-Ponty, M. (1963). *The structure of behavior* (A. L. Fisher, Trans.). Boston: Beacon Press.

Merrens, M. R., & Richards, W. S. (1970). Acceptance of generalized versus "bona fide" personality interpretation. *Psychological Reports, 27,* 691–694.

Miale, F. R., & Selzer, M. (1975). *The Nuremberg mind: The psychology of the Nazi leaders.* New York: Quadrangle/New York Times.

Miley, C. H. (1969). Birth order research 1963–1967: Bibliography and index. *Journal of Individual Psychology, 25,* 64–70.

Milgram, S. (1963). Behavioral study of obedience. *Journal of Abnormal and Social Psychology, 67,* 371–378.

Milgram, S. (1965). *Obedience* (A filmed experiment). New York: New York University Film Library.

Milgram, S. (1970). The experience of living in cities. *Science, 167,* 1461–1468.

Milgram, S. (1974). *Obedience to authority.* New York: Harper & Row.

Miller, N. (1941). The frustration-aggression hypothesis. *Psychological Review, 48,* 337–342.

Millon, T. (1984). On the Renaissance of personality assessment and personality theory. *Journal of Personality Assessment, 48,* 450–466.

Mills, C. (1942). *Climate makes the man.* New York: Harper & Row.

Mirels, H. L., & Garrett, J. B. (1971). The Protestant Ethic as a personality variable. *Journal of Consulting and Clinical Psychology, 36,* 40–44.

Mischel, W. (1968). *Personality and assessment.* New York: Wiley.

Mischel, W. (1973). Toward a cognitive social learning reconceptualization of personality. *Psychological Review, 80,* 252–283.

Mischel, W. (1977). On the future of personality measurement. *American Psychologist, 32,* 246–254.

Mischel, W. (1984). Convergences and challenges in the search for consistency. *American Psychologist, 39,* 351–364.

Mischel, W., Ebbesen, E., & Zeiss, A. (1972). Cognitive and attentional mechanisms in delay of gratification. *Journal of Personality and Social Psychology, 21,* 204–218.

Mischel, W., Ebbesen, E., & Zeiss, A. (1973). Selective attention to the self: Situational and dispositional determinants. *Journal of Personality and Social Psychology, 27,* 129–142.

Mischel, W., & Peake, P. (1982). Beyond déja vu in the search for cross-situational consistency. *Psychological Review, 89,* 730–733.

Mischel, W., & Peake, P. (1983) Analyzing the construction of consistency in personality. In M. M. Page & R. Dienstbier (Eds.), *Personality—Current theory and research, 1982 Nebraska symposium on motivation* (pp. 233–262). Lincoln: University of Nebraska Press.

Mitchell, K. M., Bozarth, J. D., & Krauft, C. C. (1977). A reappraisal of the therapeutic effectiveness of accurate empathy, nonpossessive warmth and genuineness. In A. S. Gurman & A. M. Razin (Eds.), *Effective psychotherapy: A handbook of research* (pp. 482–499). New York: Pergamon Press.

Molière, J. (1928). *Le bourgeois gentilhomme.* In I. A. Gregory (Ed.), *Three last plays.* New York: G. P. Putnam. (Original work published 1670)

Monson, T., Hesley, J., & Chernick, L. (1982). Specifying when personality traits can and cannot predict behavior: An alternative to abandoning the attempt to predict single-act criteria. *Journal of Personality and Social Psychology, 43,* 385–399.

Moody, S., & Graham, V. (1978, November 26). Why? *Chicago Sunday Sun-Times,* pp. 8–10.

Moos, R. H. (1973). Conceptualizations of human environments. *American Psychologist, 28,* 652–665.

Moos, R. H. (1974). Systems for the assessment and classification of human environments: An overview. In R. H. Moos & P. M. Insel (Eds.), *Issues in social ecology* (pp. 5–28). Palo Alto, CA: National Press Books.

Moos, R. H. (1976). *The human context: Environmental determinants of behavior.* New York: Wiley.

Moos, R. H., & Brownstein, R., (1977). *Environment and utopia: A synthesis.* New York: Plenum.

Moos, R. H., & Insel, P. M. (Eds.). (1974). *Issues in social ecology.* Palo Alto, CA: National Press Books.

Morrow, L. (1984, January 9). "I spoke . . . as a brother." *Time,* pp. 26–33.

Mosak, H. H. (1969). Early recollections: Evaluation of some recent research. *Journal of Individual Psychology, 25,* 56–63.

Mosak, H. H., & Kopp, R. R. (1973). The early recollections of Adler, Freud, and Jung. *Journal of Individual Psychology, 24,* 157–166.

Moser, P. W. (1983, January). Untitled article. *Life,* pp. 110–111.

Moss, P. D., & McEvedy, C. P. (1966). An epidemic of overbreathing among schoolgirls. *British Medical Journal, 2,* 1295–1300.

Mowrer, O. H. (1947). On the dual nature of learning: A reinterpretation of "conditioning" and "problem solving." *Harvard Educational Review, 17,* 102–148.

Mullahy, P. (1948). *Oedipus: Myth and complex.* New York: Grove Press.

Mullahy, P. (Ed.). (1952). *The contributions of Harry Stack Sullivan.* New York: Science House.

Mullahy, P. (1970). *The beginnings of modern American psychiatry: The ideas of Harry Stack Sullivan.* Boston: Houghton Mifflin.

Mummendey, H., Wilk, W., & Sturm, G. (1979). Die erfassung retrospektiver Selbstbildanderungen Erwachsener mit der Adjektivbeschreibungstechnik (AGT) [Incorporating retrospective self-concept changes of adults by means of the Adjective Generation Technique]. *Bielefelder Arbeiten zur Sozialpsychologie, 48,* 1–16.

Murray, H. A. (1943). *Thematic Apperception Test manual.* Cambridge, MA: Harvard University Press.

Murray, H. A. (1962). *Explorations in personality.* New York: Science Editions. (Original work published 1938)

Murstein, B. I. (1963). *Theory and research in projective techniques: Emphasizing the TAT.* New York: Wiley.

Murstein, B. I. (Ed.). (1965). *Handbook of projective techniques.* New York: Basic Books.

Murstein, B. I. (1972). Normative written TAT responses for a college sample. *Journal of Personality Assessment, 36,* 109–147.

Musante, L., MacDougall, J., & Dembroski, T. (1984). The Type A behavior pattern and attributions for success and failure. *Personality and Social Psychology Bulletin, 10,* 544–553.

Muson, H. (1978, March). Teenage violence and the telly. *Psychology Today,* pp. 50–54.

Mussen, P., Conger, J., & Kagan, J. (1979). *Child development and personality.* New York: Harper & Row.

Myers, I. B. (1962). *Myers-Briggs Type Indicator manual.* Palo Alto, CA: Consulting Psychologists Press.

Naisbett, J. (1984). *Megatrends.* New York: Warner Books.

Nash, H. (1983, October). Thinking about thinking about the unthinkable. *Bulletin of the Atomic Scientists, 39,* 39–42.

Nay, W. R. (1979). *Multimethod clinical assessment.* New York: Gardner Press.

Needleman, H. L., Leviton, A., & Bellinger, D. (1982). Lead-associated intellectual deficit. *New England Journal of Medicine, 306,* 367.

The newest millionaire's wish. (1984, September 17). *Time,* p. 34.

Nicholls, J. G., Licht, B. G., & Pearl, R. A. (1982) Some dangers of using personality questionnaires to study personality. *Psychological Bulletin, 92,* 572–580.

Nightmare in Jonestown. (1978, December 4). *Time,* pp. 16–21.

1958 award for distinguished scientific contributions to B. F. Skinner. (1958). *American Psychologist, 13,* 735–738.

Nisbett, R. N. (1980). The trait construct in lay and professional psychology. In L. Festinger (Ed.), *Retrospections on social psychology* (pp. 92–136). New York: Oxford University Press.

Norman, W. T. (1963). Toward an adequate taxonomy of personality attributes: Replicated factor structure in peer nomination personality rat-

ings. *Journal of Abnormal and Social Psychology, 66,* 574–583.

Nova: City spaces, human places. (1982, May 16). Iowa City: KIIN Television. Nova, WGBH BOSTON, 125 Western Ave., Boston, MA 02134.

Nunnally, J. C. (1955). An investigation of some propositions of self-conception: The case of Miss Sun. *Journal of Abnormal and Social Psychology, 50,* 87–92.

Olson, H. A. (Ed.). (1979). *Early recollections: Their use in diagnosis and psychotherapy.* Springfield, IL: Charles C Thomas.

Olweus, D. (1979). The stability of aggressive reaction patterns in human males: A review. *Psychological Review, 86,* 852–875.

Osgood, C. E., Suci, G. J., & Tannenbaum, P. (1957). *The measurement of meaning.* Urbana: University of Illinois Press.

Pace, C. R. (1969). *College and University Environment Scales (CUES)* (Technical manual, 2nd ed.). Princeton, NJ: Educational Testing Service.

Pace, C. R., & Stern, G. G. (1958). An approach to the measurement of psychological characteristics of college environments. *Journal of Educational Psychology, 49,* 269–277.

Page, M. M. (Ed.). (1983). *Personality — Current theory and research, 1982 Nebraska symposium on motivation.* Lincoln: University of Nebraska Press.

Pasley, S. (1969). *The Social Readjustment Rating Scale: A study of the significance of life events in age groups ranging from college freshman to seventh grade.* Unpublished paper, Chatham College, Pittsburgh, Pennsylvania.

Patterson, C. H. (1961). The self in recent Rogerian theory. *Journal of Individual Psychology, 17,* 5–11.

Pavlov, I. P. (1927). *Conditioned reflexes* (G. V. Anrep, Trans.). London: Oxford University Press.

Peabody, D. (1966). Authoritarianism scales and response bias. *Psychological Bulletin, 65,* 11–23.

Perls, F. S. (1969). *Gestalt therapy verbatim.* Lafayette, CA: Real People Press.

Perry, H. S. (1982). *Psychiatrist of America: The life of Harry Stack Sullivan.* Cambridge, MA: Harvard University Press.

Pervin, L. A. (1985). Personality: Current controversies, issues, and directions. *Annual Review of Psychology, 36,* 83–114.

Phares, E. (1962). Perceptual threshold decrements as a function of skill and chance expectancies. *Journal of Psychology, 53,* 399–407.

Phares, E. J. (1976). *Locus of control in personality.* Morristown, NJ: General Learning Press.

Phares, E. J., & Lamiell, J. T. (1977). Personality. *Annual Review of Psychology, 28,* 113–140.

Phillips, W. M., Watkins, J. T., & Noll, G. (1974). Self-actualization, self-transcendence, and personal philosophy. *Journal of Humanistic Psychology, 14,* 53–73.

Piaget, J. (1965). *The moral judgment of the child.* New York: Free Press. (Original work published 1932)

Pogrebin, L. (1980). *Growing up free.* New York: Bantam Books.

Potkay, C. R. (1971). *The Rorschach clinician: A new research approach and its application.* New York: Grune & Stratton.

Potkay, C. R. (1973). The role of personal history data in clinical judgment: A selective focus. *Journal of Personality Assessment, 37,* 203–212.

Potkay, C. R. (1974). Using the word association test "to catch a thief." *Professional Psychology, 5,* 446–447.

Potkay, C. R. (1982, March–April). Current isues in projective and personality assessment in the schools. *School Psychology in Illinois: Newsletter of the Illinois School Psychologists Association,* pp. 9–11.

Potkay, C. R., Allen, B. P., & Merrens, M. R. (1975, September). *Adjective Generation Technique descriptions of Kohoutek: A comet that fizzled.* Paper presented at the meeting of the American Psychological Association, Chicago.

Potkay, C. R., & Merrens, M. R. (1975). Sources of male chauvinism in the TAT. *Journal of Personality Assessment, 39,* 471–479.

Potkay, C. R., Merrens, M. R., & Allen, B. P. (1979, May). *AGT descriptions of TAT figures: "Loving" females more favorable than "lonely" males.* Paper presented at the meeting of the Midwestern Psychological Association, Chicago.

Potkay, C. E., Potkay, C. R., Boynton, G., & Klingbeil, J. (1982). Perceptions of male and female comic strip characters using the Adjective Generation Technique (AGT). *Sex Roles, 8,* 185–200.

Powell, G. E. (1981). A survey of the effects of brain lesions upon personality. In H. J. Eysenck (Ed.), *A model for personality,* (pp. 65–87). New York: Springer-Verlag.

Presidential Commission on Obscenity and Pornography. (1970). *The report of the Commission on Obscenity and Pornography.* New York: Bantam.

Proshansky, H. M. (1976). Environmental psychology and the real world. *American Psychologist, 31,* 303–310.

Proshansky, H. M., Ittelson, W. H., & Rivlin, L. G. (1970). Freedom of choice and behavior in a physical setting. In H. M. Proshansky, W. H. Ittelson, & L. G. Rivlin (Eds.), *Environmental psychology* (pp. 173–183). New York: Holt, Rinehart & Winston.

Rabin, A. I. (Ed.). (1981). *Assessment with projective techniques.* New York: Springer.

Rabin, A. I., Aronoff, J., Barclay, A. M., & Zucker, R. A. (Eds.). (1981). *Further explorations in personality.* New York: Wiley.

Rahe, R. H. (1975). Life changes and near-future illness reports. In L. Levi (Ed.), *Emotions: Their parameters and measurement* (pp. 511–529). New York: Raven.

Ram Dass. (1971). *Be here now.* New York: Crown.

Rank, O. (1945). *Will therapy.* (J. Taft, Trans.). New York: Knopf.

Ravizza, K. (1977). Peak experiences in sport. *Journal of Humanistic Psychology, 17,* 35–40.

Read, P. P. (1974). *Alive: The story of Andes survivors.* Philadelphia: Lippincott.

The (real) secret of NIMH. (1982, August 7). *Science News,* pp. 92–93.

Reisman, J. M. (1966). *The development of clinical psychology.* New York: Appleton-Century-Crofts.

Revusky, S., & Garcia, J. (1970). Learned associations over long delays. In G. Bower (Ed.), *The psychology of learning and motivation* (Vol. 4, pp. 115–137). New York: Academic Press.

Reynolds, W. M., & Sundberg, N. D. (1976). Recent research trends in testing. *Journal of Personality Assessment, 40,* 228–233.

Richardson, D., Berstein, S., & Taylor, S. (1979). The effect of situational contingencies on female retaliative behavior. *Journal of Personality and Social Psychology, 37,* 2044–2048.

Ritzler, B. (1978). The Nuremberg mind revisited: A quantitative approach to Nazi Rorschachs. *Journal of Personality Assessment, 42,* 344–353.

Roazen, P. (1974). *Freud and his followers.* New York: Knopf.

Roback, A. A. (1964). *A history of American psychology* (rev. ed). New York: Collier Books.

Rogers, C. R. (1942). *Counseling and psychotherapy: Newer concepts in practice.* Boston: Houghton Mifflin.

Rogers, C. R. (1947). Some observations on the organization of personality. *American Psychologist, 2,* 358–368.

Rogers, C. R. (1954). The case of Mrs. Oak: A research analysis. In C. R. Rogers & R. F. Dymond (Eds.), *Psychotherapy and personality change* (pp. 259–348). Chicago: University of Chicago Press.

Rogers, C. R. (1957). The necessary and sufficient conditions of therapeutic personality change. *Journal of Consulting Psychology, 21,* 95–103.

Rogers, C. R. (1959). A theory of therapy, personality, and interpersonal relationships, as developed in the client-centered framework. In S. Koch (Ed.), *Psychology: A study of a science* (pp. 184–256). New York: McGraw-Hill.

Rogers, C. R. (1961). *On becoming a person: A therapist's view of psychotherapy.* Boston: Houghton Mifflin.

Rogers, C. R. (1969). *Freedom to learn: A view of what education might become.* Columbus, OH: Charles Merrill.

Rogers, C. R. (1970). *Carl Rogers on encounter groups.* New York: Harper & Row/Harrow Books.

Rogers, C. R. (1972). *Becoming partners: Marriage and its alternatives.* New York: Delacorte Press.

Rogers, C. R. (1973). My philosophy of interpersonal relationships and how it grew. *Journal of Humanistic Psychology, 13,* 3–15.

Rogers, C. R. (1974). In retrospect: Forty-six years. *American Psychologist, 29,* 115–123.

Rogers, C. R. (1975). In R. I. Evans (Ed.), *Carl Rogers: The man and his ideas.* New York: E. P. Dutton.

Rogers, C. R. (1977). *Carl Rogers on personal power.* New York: Delacorte Press.

Rogers, C. R. (1980). *A way of being.* Boston: Houghton Mifflin.

Rogers, C. R. (1983). The foundations of the person-centered approach. In T. H. Carr & H. E. Fitzgerald (Eds.), *Psychology 83/84* (pp. 227–233). Guilford, CT: Dushkin. (Reprinted from *Education,* 1979, *100,* 98–107.)

Rogers, C. R. & Dymond, R. F. (Eds.). (1954). *Psychotherapy and personality change.* Chicago: University of Chicago Press.

Rogers, R., & Prentice-Dunn, S. (1981). Deindividuation and anger-mediated interracial aggression: Unmasking regressive racism. *Journal of Personality and Social Psychology, 41,* 63–73.

Rohrbaugh, J. (1979). *Women: Psychology's puzzle.* New York: Basic Books.

Rokeach, M. (1954). The nature and meaning of dogmatism. *Psychological Review, 61,* 194–204.

Rokeach, M. (Ed.). (1960). *The open and closed mind: Investigations into the nature of belief systems and personality systems.* New York: Basic Books.

Rokeach, M. (1967). Authoritarianism scales and response bias: Comment on Peabody's paper. *Psychological Bulletin, 67,* 349–355.

Rokeach, M., & Kemp, C. G., (1960). Open and closed systems in relation to anxiety and childhood experience. In M. Rokeach (Ed.), *The open and closed mind* (pp. 347–365). New York: Basic Books.

Rokeach, M., & Restle, F. (1960). A fundamental distinction between open and closed systems. In M. Rokeach (Ed.), *The open and closed mind* (pp. 54–70). New York: Basic Books.

Roodin, P., & Hoyer, W. (1982, August). *A framework for studying moral issues in later adulthood.* Paper presented at the meeting of the American Psychological Association, Washington, DC.

Roots of Jonestown [Editorial]. (1978, December 4). *The Christian Science Monitor,* p. 32.

Rorer, L. G., & Widiger, T. A. (1983). Personality structure and assessment. *Annual Review of Psychology, 34,* 431–463.

Rorschach, H. (1951). *Psychodiagnostics: A diagnostic test based on perception* (5th ed.). (P. Lemkau & B. Kronenberg, Trans.). New York: Grune & Stratton. (Original work published 1942)

Rosch, E. (1978). Principles of categorization. In E. Rosch & B. B. Lloyd (Eds.), *Cognition and categorization.* Hillsdale, NJ: Erlbaum.

Rosenhan, D. L. (1973). On being sane in insane places. *Science, 179,* 365–369.

Rosenthal, R. (1979). The "file drawer problem" and tolerance for null results. *Psychological Bulletin, 86,* 638–641.

Ross, L. (1977). The intuitive psychologist and his shortcomings: Distortion in the attribution process. In L. Berkowitz (Ed.), *Advances in experimental social psychology* (Vol. 10, pp. 210–235). New York: Academic Press.

Rotter, J. (1954). *Social learning and clinical psychology.* New York: Prentice-Hall.

Rotter, J. (1966). Generalized expectancies for internal versus external control of reinforcement. *Psychological Monographs: General and Applied, 80* (1, Whole No. 609), 1–28.

Rotter, J. (1967). A new scale for the measurement of interpersonal trust. *Journal of Personality, 35,* 651–665.

Rotter, J. (1975). Some problems and misconceptions related to the construct of internal versus external control of reinforcement. *Journal of Consulting and Clinical Psychology, 43,* 56–67.

Rotter, J. (1982). *The development and application of social-learning theory.* New York: Praeger.

Royce, J. R., & Mos, L. P. (1981). *Humanistic psychology: Concepts and criticisms.* New York: Plenum.

Ruch, L. O., & Holmes, T. H. (1971). Scaling of life change: Comparison of direct and indirect methods. *Journal of Psychosomatic Research, 15,* 221–227.

Rushton, J., Jackson, D., & Paunonen, S. (1981). Personality: Nomothetic or idiographic? A response to Kenrick and Stringfield. *Psychological Review, 88,* 582–589.

Russell, J. A., & Ward, L. M. (1982). Environmental psychology. *Annual Review of Psychology, 33,* 651–688.

Ryan, C. (1966). *The last battle.* New York: Simon & Schuster.

Rychlak, J. R. (1968). *A philosophy of science for personality theory.* Boston: Houghton Mifflin.

Rychlak, J. F. (1976). Is a concept of "self" necessary in psychological theory? In A. Wandersman, P.

Poppen, & D. Ricks (Eds.), *Humanism and behaviorism: Dialogue and growth* (pp. 121–143). New York: Pergamon Press.

Sabatelli, R., Buck, R., & Dreyer, A. (1983). Locus of control, interpersonal trust, and nonverbal communication accuracy. *Journal of Personality and Social Psychology, 44,* 399–409.

Samelson, F. (1972). Response style: A psychologist's fallacy? *Psychological Bulletin, 78,* 13–16.

Sapir, E. (1921). *Language: An introduction to the study of speech.* New York: Harcourt, Brace.

Sarason, I. G. (1975). Anxiety and self-preoccupation. In C. D. Spielberger & I. G. Sarason (Eds.), *Stress and anxiety* (Vol. 2, pp. 27–44). New York: Wiley.

Sarason, I. G., Smith, R. E., & Diener, E. (1975). Personality research: Components of variance attributed to the person and the situation. *Journal of Personality and Social Psychology, 32,* 199–204.

Sarbin, T. (1982, August). *Metaphorical encounters of the fourth kind.* Paper presented at the meeting of the American Psychological Association, Washington, DC.

Sartre, J-P. (1956). *Being and nothingness: An essay on phenomenological ontology* (H. E. Barnes, Trans.). New York: Philosophical Library. (Original work published 1943).

Sartre, J-P. (1957). *Existentialism and human emotions* (H. E. Barnes, Trans.). New York: Philosophical Library. (Original work published 1943)

Scarr, S., Webber, P., Weinberg, R., & Wittig, M. (1981). Personality resemblance among adolescents and their parents in biologically related and adoptive families. *Journal of Personality and Social Psychology, 40,* 885–898.

Schafer, R. (1976). *A new language for psychoanalysis.* New Haven, CT: Yale University Press.

Schneiderman, W. (1983). *The reinvention of the wheel in personality research.* Unpublished paper, Marshall University, Huntington, WV.

Schoggen, P. (1963). Environmental forces in the everyday lives of children. In R. Barker (Ed.), *The stream of behavior* (pp. 42–69). New York: Appleton-Century-Crofts.

Schooler, C. (1972). Birth order effects: Not here, not now! *Psychological Bulletin, 78,* 161–175.

Schroeder, D. J., & Pendleton, M. G. (1983). The adjective generation technique: Consistency of self-description in psychiatric patients. *Journal of Personality, 51,* 631–639.

Schumer, F. (1983). *Abnormal psychology.* Lexington, MA: D. C. Heath.

Schwartz, B. (1978). *Psychology of learning and behavior.* New York: Norton.

Sears, R. R. (1942). *Studies in personality.* New York: McGraw-Hill.

Sears, R. R. (1943). *Survey of objective studies of psychoanalytic concepts* (Bulletin No. 51). New York: Social Science Research Council.

Sechrest, L., & Jackson, D. N. (1961). Social intelligence and accuracy of interpersonal predictions. *Journal of Personality, 29,* 167–182.

Seligman, M. (1970). On the generality of the laws of learning. *Psychological Review, 77,* 406–418.

Seligman, M. (1975). *Helplessness: On depression, development, and death.* San Francisco: W. H. Freeman.

Selye, H. (1978). *The stress of life* (rev. ed.). New York: McGraw-Hill.

Shakow, D. (1947). Recommended graduate training program in clinical psychology. *American Psychologist, 2,* 539–558.

Shanab, M., & Yahya, K. (1977). A behavioral study of obedience in children. *Journal of Personality and Social Psychology, 35,* 530–536.

Shanab, M., & Yahya, K. (1978). A cross-cultural study of obedience. *Bulletin of the Psychonomic Society, 11,* 267–269.

Sheldon, W. H. (1940). *The varieties of human physique: An introduction to constitutional psychology.* New York: Harper.

Sheridan, C. L., & King, R. (1972). Obedience to authority with an authentic victim. *Proceedings of the American Psychological Association Convention, 7,* 165–166.

Sherif, C. (1980). Comment of ethical issues in Malamuth, Heim, and Feshbach's "Sexual responsiveness of college students to rape depictions: Inhibitory and disinhibitory effects." *Journal of Personality and Social Psychology, 38,* 409–412.

Shirer, W. L. (1960). *The rise and fall of the Third Reich.* Greenwich, CT: Fawcett Crest.

Shlien, J. M. (1970). Phenomenology and personality. In J. T. Hart & T. M. Tomlinson (Eds.), *New directions in client-centered therapy* (pp. 95–128). Boston: Houghton Mifflin.

Shlien, J. M., & Zimring, F. M. (1970). Research directives and methods in client-centered therapy. In J. T. Hart & T. M. Tomlinson, (Eds.), *New directions in client-centered therapy* (pp. 33–57). Boston: Houghton Mifflin.

Shneidman, E. S., Farberow, N. L., & Litman, R. E. (1970). *The psychology of suicide.* New York: Science House.

Shostrom, E. L. (Narrator). (1965). *Three approaches to psychotherapy: Rogers, Perls and Ellis* [Film]. Orange, CA: Psychological Films.

Shostrom, E. L. (1966). *EITS Manual for the Personal Orientation Inventory.* San Diego, CA: Educational and Industrial Testing Service.

Shostrom, E. L. (1972). *Freedom to be: Experiencing and*

expressing your total being. New York: Bantam Books.

Signell, K. (1966). Cognitive complexity in person perception and nation perception: A developmental approach. *Journal of Personality, 34,* 517–537.

Silverman, L. (1971). An experimental technique for the study of unconscious conflict. *British Journal of Medical Psychology, 44,* 17–25.

Silverman, L. (1976). Psychoanalytic theory: "The reports of my death are greatly exaggerated." *American Psychologist, 31,* 621–637.

Simonton, O. C., & Simonton, S. (1975). Belief systems and management of the emotional aspects of malignancy. *Journal of Transpersonal Psychology, 7,* 29–48.

Singer, J. (1977). *Androgyny: Toward a new theory of sexuality.* Garden City, NY: Anchor Books.

Singer, J. L., & Singer, D. G. (1972). Personality. *Annual Review of Psychology, 23,* 375–412.

Sistrunk, F., & McDavid, J. (1971). Sex variable in conformity behavior. *Journal of Personality and Social Psychology, 17,* 200–207.

Skinner, B. F. (1948). *Walden Two.* New York: Macmillan.

Skinner, B. F. (1957). *Verbal behavior.* New York: Appleton-Century-Crofts.

Skinner, B. F. (1971). *Beyond freedom and dignity.* New York: Knopf.

Skinner, B. F. (1972a). Baby in a box. In B. F. Skinner (Ed.), *Cumulative record: A selection of papers* (3rd ed., pp. 567–573). New York: Appleton-Century-Crofts.

Skinner, B. F. (1972b). Contingency management in the classroom. In B. F. Skinner (Ed.), *Cumulative record: A selection of papers* (3rd ed., pp. 225–235). New York: Appleton-Century-Crofts.

Skinner, B. F. (1972c). Creating the creative artist. In B. F. Skinner (Ed.), *Cumulative record: A selection of papers* (3rd ed., pp. 333–344). New York: Appleton-Century-Crofts.

Skinner, B. F. (Ed.). (1972d). *Cumulative record: A selection of papers* (3rd ed.). New York: Appleton-Century-Crofts.

Skinner, B. F. (1972e). The design of cultures. In B. F. Skinner (Ed.), *Cumulative record: A selection of papers* (3rd ed., pp. 39–50). New York: Appleton-Century-Crofts.

Skinner, B. F. (1972f). Freedom and the control of men. In B. F. Skinner (Ed.), *Cumulative record: A selection of papers* (3rd ed., pp. 3–24). New York: Appleton-Century-Crofts.

Skinner, B. F. (1972g). A lecture on "having" a poem. In B. F. Skinner (Ed.), *Cumulative record: A selection of papers* (3rd ed., pp. 345–358). New York: Appleton-Century-Crofts.

Skinner, B. F. (1972h). The operational analysis of psychological terms. In B. F. Skinner (Ed.), *Cumulative record: A selection of papers* (3rd ed., pp. 370–384). New York: Appleton-Century-Crofts.

Skinner, B. F. (1972i). Reflection on a decade of teaching machines. In B. F. Skinner (Ed.), *Cumulative record: A selection of papers* (3rd ed., pp. 194–207). New York: Appleton-Century-Crofts.

Skinner, B. F. (1972j). Some relations between behavior modification and basic research. In B. F. Skinner (Ed.), *Cumulative record: A selection of papers* (3rd ed., pp. 276–282). New York: Appleton-Century-Crofts.

Skinner, B. F. (1972k). "Superstition" in the pigeon. In B. F. Skinner (Ed.), *Cumulative record: A selection of papers* (3rd ed., pp. 236–256). New York: Appleton-Century-Crofts.

Skinner, B. F. (1972l). What is psychotic behavior? In B. F. Skinner (Ed.), *Cumulative record: A selection of papers* (3rd ed., pp. 257–275). New York: Appleton-Century-Crofts.

Skinner, B. F. (1972m). Why we need teaching machines. In B. F. Skinner (Ed.), *Cumulative record: A selection of papers* (3rd ed., pp. 171–193). New York: Appleton-Century-Crofts.

Skinner, B. F. (1976a). *About behaviorism.* New York: Vintage Books.

Skinner, B. F. (1976b). *Particulars of my life.* New York: Knopf.

Skinner, B. F. (1979). *The shaping of a behaviorist.* New York: Knopf.

Skinner, B. F. (1983, September). Origins of a behaviorist. *Psychology Today,* pp. 35–41.

Smith, G. (1973). *Sex and obedience to authority.* Unpublished paper, Department of Psychology, Western Illinois University, Macomb, IL.

Smith, M. B. (1973.) On self-actualization: A transambivalent examination of a focal theme in Maslow's psychology. *Journal of Humanistic Psychology, 13,* 17–33.

Smith, M. L., & Glass, G. V. (1977). Meta-analysis of psychotherapy outcome studies. *American Psychologist, 32,* 752–760.

Smith, S. L. (1968). Extraversion and sensory threshold. *Psychophysiology, 5,* 293–299.

Snyder, M. (1974). The self-monitoring of expressive behavior. *Journal of Personality and Social Psychology, 30,* 526–537.

Snyder, M., & DeBono, K. (1984). *Appeals to image and claims about quality: Understanding the psychology of advertising.* Unpublished paper, Department of Psychology, University of Minnesota, Minneapolis, MN.

Snyder, M., & Monson, T. (1975). Persons, situations, and the control of social behavior. *Journal of Personality and Social Psychology, 32,* 637–644.

Sohn, D. (1980). Critique of Cooper's meta-analytic assessment of the findings on sex differences in conformity behavior. *Journal of Personality and Social Psychology, 39,* 1215–1221.

Solomon, R., & Wynne, L. (1953). Traumatic avoidance learning: Acquisition in normal dogs. *Psychological Monographs, 67* (354), 1–19.

Spearman, C. (1904). "General intelligence" objectively determined and measured. *American Journal of Psychology, 15,* 201–293.

Spearman, C. (1927). *Abilities of Man.* New York: Macmillan.

Speer, A. (1970). *Inside the Third Reich.* New York: Avon.

Spence, J. T. (Ed.). (1983). *Achievement and achievement motives: Psychological and sociological approaches.* San Francisco: W. H. Freeman.

Spence, K. W. (1956). *Behavior theory and conditioning.* New Haven, CT: Yale University Press.

Spence, K. W. (1958). A theory of emotionally based drive (D) and its relation to performance in simple learning situations. *American Psychologist, 13,* 131–141.

Spence, K. W. (1964). Anxiety (drive) level and performance in eyelid conditioning. *Psychological Bulletin, 61,* 129–139.

Spielberger, C. D. (Ed.). (1972). *Anxiety: Current trends in theory and research* (Vol. 1). New York: Academic Press.

Spielberger, C. D. (1975). Anxiety: State-trait-process. In C. D. Spielberger & I. G. Sarason (Eds.), *Stress and anxiety* (Vol. 1, pp. 115–143). New York: Wiley.

Spielberger, C. D., Gorsuch, R. L., & Lushene, R. E. (1970). *Manual for the State-Trait Anxiety Inventory.* Palo Alto, CA: Consulting Psychologists Press.

Spitz, R. A. (1946). Hospitalism: An inquiry into the genesis of psychotic conditions in early childhood. In A. Freud, H. Hartmann, & E. Kris (Eds.), *Psychoanalytic study of the child* (Vol. 2, pp. 53–74). New York: International Universities Press.

Spivack, G., & Levine, M. (1964). The Devereux Child Behavior Rating Scales: A study of symptom behaviors in latency age atypical children. *American Journal of Mental Deficiency, 68,* 700–717.

Standal, S. (1954). *The need for positive regard: A contribution to client-centered theory.* Unpublished doctoral dissertation, University of Chicago.

Steele, R. (1978, December 4). Life in Jonestown. *Newsweek,* pp. 62–66.

Stein, A. H., & Bailey, M. M. (1973). The socialization of achievement orientation in females. *Psychological Bulletin, 80,* 345–366.

Stein, J. (1964). *Fiddler on the roof.* New York: Pocket Books.

Stepansky, P. E. (1983). *In Freud's shadow: Adler in context.* Hillsdale, NJ: Analytic Press.

Stephenson, W. (1953). *The study of behavior.* Chicago: University of Chicago Press.

Stern, G. G. (1970). *People in context: Measuring person-environment congruence in education and industry.* New York: Wiley.

Stern, G. G., & Pace, C. R. (1958). *College Characteristics Index.* Copyright by G. G. Stern, Dept. of Psychology, Syracuse University, Syracuse, NY.

Stern, P. J. (1976). *C. G. Jung: The haunted prophet.* New York: Delta.

Stolorow, R. D., & Atwood, G. E. (1979). *Faces in a cloud: Subjectivity in personality theory.* New York: Aronson.

Strube, M., Turner, C., Cerro, D., Stevens, J., & Hinchey, F. (1984). Interpersonal aggression and the Type A coronary-prone behavior pattern: A theoretical distinction and practical implications. *Journal of Personality and Social Psychology, 47,* 839–847.

Sullivan, H. S. (1947). *Conceptions of modern psychiatry.* New York: Norton.

Sullivan, H. S. (1953). *The interpersonal theory of psychiatry* (H. S. Perry & M. L. Gawel, Eds.). New York: Norton.

Sullivan, H. S. (1954). *The psychiatric interview* (H. S. Perry & M. L. Gawel, Eds.). New York: Norton.

Sulloway, F. J. (1979). *Freud, biologist of the mind: Beyond the psychoanalytic legend.* New York: Basic Books.

Sundberg, N. D. (1961). The practice of psychological testing in clinical services in the United States. *American Psychologist, 16,* 79–83.

Sundberg, N. D. (1977). *Assessment of persons.* Englewood Cliffs, NJ: Prentice-Hall.

Sundberg, N. D., & Tyler, L. E. (1962). *Clinical psychology: An introduction to research and practice.* New York: Appleton-Century-Crofts.

Sundberg, N. D., Tyler, L. E., & Taplin, J. R. (1973). *Clinical psychology: Expanding horizons.* Englewood Cliffs, NJ: Prentice-Hall.

Suomi, S. J., Collins, M. L., Harlow, H. F., & Ruppenthal, G. C. (1976). Effects of maternal and peer separations on young monkeys. *Journal of Child Psychology and Psychiatry, 17,* 101–112.

Suomi, S. J., & Harlow, H. F. (1972). Social rehabilitation of isolate-reared monkeys. *Developmental Psychology, 6,* 487–496.

Sutich, A. J. (1968). Transpersonal psychology: An emerging force. *Journal of Humanistic Psychology, 7,* 77–78.

Suzuki, D. T. (1974). *An introduction to Zen Buddhism.* New York: Causeway.

Szasz, T. S. (1960). The myth of mental illness. *American Psychologist, 15,* 113–118.

Szasz, T. S. (1963). *Law, liberty and psychiatry.* New York: Macmillan.

Szent-Gyoergyi, A. (1974, Spring). Drive in living matter to perfect itself. *Synthesis,* pp. 12–24.

Tanner, O. (1976). *Stress.* New York: Time-Life.

Taylor, J. A. (1951). The relationship of anxiety to the conditioned eyelid response. *Journal of Experimental Psychology, 41,* 81–92.

Taylor, J. A. (1953). A personality scale of manifest anxiety. *Journal of Abnormal and Social Psychology, 48,* 285–290.

Taylor, J. A. (1956). Drive theory and manifest anxiety. *Psychological Bulletin, 53,* 303–320.

Taylor, M., & Hall, J. (1982). Psychological androgyny: Theories, methods, and conclusions. *Psychological Bulletin, 92,* 347–366.

Taylor, S. E. (1983). Adjustment to threatening events: A theory of cognitive adaptation. *American Psychologist, 38,* 1161–1173.

Tavris, C. (1976). The end of the IQ slump. *Psychology Today, 9,* 69–74.

Tedeschi, J., Smith, R., & Brown, R. (1974). A reinterpretation of research on aggression. *Psychological Bulletin, 81,* 540–562.

Teplov, B. M. (1964). Problems in the study of general types of higher nervous activity in man and animals. In J. A. Gray (Ed.), *Pavlov's typology* (pp. 3–153). New York: Pergamon Press.

Teplov, B. M., & Nebylitsyn, V. (1969). Investigation of the properties of the nervous system as an approach to the study of individual psychological differences. In M. Cole & I. Maltzman (Eds.), *A handbook of contemporary Soviet psychology* (pp. 503–530). New York: Basic Books.

Thompson, C. (1943). "Penis envy" in women. *Psychiatry, 6,* 123–125.

Thompson, G. (1968). George Alexander Kelly (1905–1967). *Journal of General Psychology, 79,* 19–24.

Thorne, F. C. (1961). *Clinical judgment: A study of clinical errors.* Brandon, VT: Journal of Clinical Psychology.

Thorne, F. C. (1967). *Integrative Psychology.* Brandon, VT: Clinical Psychology Publishing Company.

Three-Mile Island mothers' stress now seen as long-term. (1980, November 9). *Chicago Sunday Sun-Times,* p. 22.

Thurstone, L. L. (1938). Primary mental abilities. *Psychometric Monographs,* (No.1).

Tillich, P. (1952). *The courage to be.* New Haven, CT: Yale University Press.

Timnick, L. (1981, January 25). Chowchilla's kidnapped kids—Five years later. *Chicago Sunday Sun-Times,* p. 52.

Toffler, A. (1970). *Future Shock.* New York: Random House.

Tomkins, S. S., & Izard, C. E. (1965). *Affect, cognition and personality.* New York: Springer.

Tosi, D. J., & Hoffman, S. (1972). A factor analysis of the Personal Orientation Inventory. *Journal of Humanistic Psychology, 12,* 86–93.

Towson, S., & Zanna, M. (1982). Toward a situational analysis of gender differences in aggression. *Sex Roles, 8,* 903–914.

Truax, C. B., & Carkhuff, R. R. (1967). *Toward effective counseling and psychotherapy: Training and practice.* Chicago: Aldine.

Truax, C. B., & Mitchell, K. M. (1971). Research on certain therapist interpersonal skills in relation to process and outcome. In A. E. Bergin & S. L. Garfield (Eds.), *Handbook of psychotherapy and behavior change: An empirical analysis* (pp. 299–344). New York: Wiley.

Turco, R., Toon, T., Ackerman, T., Pollack, J., & Sagan, C. (1983). Nuclear winter: Global consequences of multiple nuclear explosions. *Science, 222,* 1283–1292.

Ullmann, L., & Krasner, L. (Eds.). (1965). *Case studies in behavior modification.* New York: Holt, Rinehart & Winston.

Ulrich, R. E., Stachnik, T. J., & Stainton, N.R. (1963). Student acceptance of generalized personality interpretations. *Psychological Reports, 20,* 831–834.

Unger, R. (1979). Toward a definition of sex and gender. *American Psychologist, 34,* 1085–1094.

Vacchiano, R. B., Strauss, P. S., & Hochman, L. (1969). The open and closed mind: A review of dogmatism. *Psychological Bulletin, 71,* 261–273.

Vaihinger, H. (1925). *The philosophy of "as if": A system of the theoretical, practical and religious fictions of mankind.* New York: Harcourt, Brace.

Valins, S., & Nisbett, R. (1971). *Attribution processes in the development and treatment of emotional disorders.* Morristown, NJ: General Learning Press.

van Kaam, A. (1963). Existential psychology as a comprehensive theory of personality. *Review of Existential Psychology and Psychiatry, 3,* 11–26.

van Kaam, A. (1965). Existential and humanistic psychology. *Review of Existential Psychology and Psychiatry, 5,* 291–296.

van Kaam, A. (1969). *Existential foundations of psychology.* New York: Image Books.

Vinokur, A., & Selzer, M. L. (1975). Desirable versus undesirable life events: Their relationship to stress and mental distress. *Journal of Personality and Social Psychology, 32,* 329–337.

Vockell, E. L., Felker, D. W., & Miley, C. H. (1973). Birth order literature 1967–1971: Bibliography and index. *Journal of Individual Psychology, 29,* 39–53.

Wade, T. C., & Baker, T. B. (1977). Opinions and use of psychological tests: A survey of clinical psychologists. *American Psychologist, 32,* 874–882.

Wallace, J. (1966). An abilities conception of personality: Some implications for personality measurement. *American Psychologist, 21,* 132–138.

Watkins, M. M. (1976). *Waking Dreams.* New York: Harper/Colophon Books.

Watson, D. L., & Tharp, R. G. (1977). *Self-directed behavior: Self-modification for personal adjustment* (2nd ed.). Monterey, CA: Brooks/Cole.

Watson, J. B. (1959). *Behaviorism.* Chicago: University of Chicago Press. (Original work published 1930)

Watson, J. B., & Rayner, R. (1920). Conditioned emotional reactions. *Journal of Experimental Psychology, 3,* 1–14.

Watts, A. (1961). *Psychotherapy East and West.* New York: Pantheon.

Weber, M. (1930). *The Protestant Ethic and the spirit of capitalism* (T. Parsons, Trans.). New York: Scribner. (Original work published 1904)

Weidner, G., & Griffitt, W. (1983). Rape: A sexual stigma? *Journal of Personality, 51,* 152–166.

Weinberger, D. A., Schwartz, G. E., & Davidson, R. J. (1979). Low-anxious, high-anxious and repressive coping styles: Psychometric patterns and behavioral and physiological responses to stress. *Journal of Abnormal Psychology, 88,* 369–380.

Weiner, B. (1978). Achievement strivings. In H. London & J. E. Exner, Jr. (Eds.), *Dimensions of personality* (pp. 1–36). New York: Wiley.

Weiss, B. (1983). Behavioral toxicology and environmental health science: Opportunity and challenge for psychology. *American Psychologist, 38,* 1174–1187.

Weiss, D., Mendelsohn, G., & Feimer, N. (1982). Reply to the comments of Block and Ozer. *Journal of Personality and Social Psychology, 42,* 1182–1184.

Wessman, A. E., & Ricks, D. F. (1966). *Mood and personality.* New York: Holt, Rinehart & Winston.

Wexler, D. A. & Rice, L. N. (1974). *Innovations in client-centered therapy.* New York: Wiley.

Wheeler, L. (1966). Motivation as a determinant of upward comparison. *Journal of Experimental Social Psychology,* Supplement No. 1, 27–31.

Wheeler, L., Deci, E., Reis, H., & Zuckerman, M. (1978). *Interpersonal influence.* Boston: Allyn & Bacon.

White, C., Flatley, D., & Janson, P. (1982, August). *Moral reasoning in adulthood: Increasing consistency or contextual relativism?* Paper presented at the meeting of the American Psychological Association, Washington, DC.

White, R. W. (1975). *Lives in progress: A study of the natural growth of personality* (3rd ed.). New York: Holt, Rinehart & Winston.

Why people join. (1978, December 4). *Time,* p. 27.

Wiesel, E. (1961). *Night.* New York: Pyramid Books.

Will, O. A. (1964). Introduction. In H. S. Sullivan (H. S. Perry & M. L. Gawel, Eds.), *The Psychiatric Interview* (pp. ix–xxiii). New York: Norton.

Williams, J. H. (1983). *Psychology of women: Behavior in a biosocial context* (2nd. ed). New York: Norton.

Williams, J. E., & Morland, J. (1979). Comment on Bank's "White preference in blacks: A paradigm in search of a phenomenon." *Psychological Bulletin, 86,* 28–32.

Wills, T. A. (1981). Downward comparison principles in social psychology. *Psychological Bulletin, 90,* 245–271.

Wilson, G. D. (1981). Personality and social behavior. In H. J. Eysenck (Ed.), *A model for personality* (pp. 210–245). New York: Springer-Verlag.

Wilson, S., & Barber, T. X. (1983). The fantasy prone personality: Implications for understanding imagery, hypnosis, and parapsychological phenomena. In A. Sheikh (Ed.), *Imagery: Current theory, research and application* (pp. 340–387). New York: Wiley.

Winterbottom, M. R. (1953). *The relation of need for achievement to learning experiences in independence and mastery.* Unpublished doctoral dissertation, University of Michigan, Ann Arbor. [Summarized in J. W. Atkinson (Ed.), *Motives in fantasy, action, and society* (pp. 453–478). Princeton, NJ: Van Nostrand.]

Wise, P., & Joy, S. (1982). Working mothers, sex differences, and self-esteem in college students' self-descriptions. *Sex Roles, 8,* 785–790.

Wise, P., & Potkay, C. R. (1983). The KD-S: A technique in need of validation. In M. E. Sarbaugh, *The Kinetic Drawing—School Technique.* Monograph of the Illinois School Psychologists Association, *1*(1), 71–75.

Wohlwill, J. F. (1970). The emerging discipline of environmental psychology. *American Psychologist, 25,* 303–312.

Wohlwill, J. F., & Carson, D. H. (Eds.). (1972). *Environment and the social sciences: Perspectives and applications.* Washington, DC: American Psychological Association.

Wolfe, B., & Baron, R. (1971). Laboratory aggression related to aggression in naturalistic social situations: Effects of an aggressive model on the behavior of college student and prisoner observers. *Psychonomic Science, 24,* 193–194.

Wolff, P. (1960). *The developmental psychologies of Jean Piaget and psychoanalysis* (Psychological Issues Monograph No. 5). New York: International Universities Press.

Wolman, B. B. (1981). *Contemporary theories and systems in psychology* (2nd. ed.). New York: Plenum.

Wolpe, J. (1982). *The practice of behavior therapy* (3rd ed.). New York: Pergamon Press.

Wolpe, J., & Rachman, S. (1960). Psychoanalytic evidence: A critique based on Freud's case of Little Hans. *Journal of Nervous and Mental Diseases, 131,* 135–145.

Wong, P. T. P., & Weiner, B. (1981). When people ask "why" questions, and the heuristics of attributional search. *Journal of Personality and Social Psychology, 40,* 650–663.

Woodward, K. L. (1978, December 4). How they bend minds. *Newsweek,* pp. 72–77.

Woody, R. H. (1980). *Encyclopedia of clinical assessment* (Vols. 1–2). San Francisco: Jossey-Bass.

Worchel, S., & Cooper, J. (1976). *Understanding social psychology.* Homewood, IL: Dorsey Press.

Wortis, J. (1954). *Fragments of an analysis with Freud.* New York: Charter.

WQED, Pittsburgh. (1971). *Because that's my way* [Film]. Lincoln: University of Nebraska, GPI Television Library.

Wundt, W. M. (1904). *Principles of physiological psychology* (E. B. Titchener, Trans.). London: Swan Sonnenschein. (Original work published 1874)

Wylie, R. (1974). *The self-concept: A review of methodological considerations and measuring instruments* (Vol. 1, rev. ed.). Lincoln: University of Nebraska Press.

Wylie, R. (1979). *The self-concept: Theory and research on selected topics* (Vol. 2, rev. ed.). Lincoln: University of Nebraska Press.

Young, M. (1980). Attitudes and behaviors of college students relative to oral-genital sexuality. *Archives of Sexual Behavior, 9,* 61–67.

Young, P. T. (1941). The experimental analysis of appetite. *Psychological Bulletin, 38,* 129–164.

Young, P. T. (1948). Appetite, palatability and feeding habit: A critical review. *Psychological Bulletin, 45,* 289–320.

Zajonc, R. B. & Markus, G. B. (1975). Birth order and intellectual development. *Psychological Review, 82,* 74–88.

Zillmann, D., Baron, R., & Tamborini, R. (1981). Social costs of smoking: Effects of tobacco smoke on hostile behavior. *Journal of Applied Social Psychology, 11,* 548–561.

Zillmann, D., & Bryant, J. (1982) Pornography, sexual callousness, and the trivialization of rape. *Journal of Communication, 32,* 10–21.

Zillmann, D., Bryant, J., & Carveth, R. (1981). The effect of erotica featuring sadomasochism and bestiality on motivated intermale aggression. *Personality and Social Psychology Bulletin, 7,* 153–159.

Zillmann, D., Bryant, J., Comisky, P., & Medoff, N. (1981). Excitation and hedonic valence in the effect of erotica on motivated intermale aggression. *European Journal of Social Psychology, 11,* 233–252.

Zillmann, D., Katcher, A., & Milavsky, B. (1972). Excitation transfer from physical exercise to subsequent aggressive behavior. *Journal of Experimental Social Psychology, 8,* 247–259.

Zimbardo, P. (1970). The human choice: Individuation, reason, and order versus deindividuation, impulse, and chaos. In W. Arnold & D. Levine (Eds.), *Nebraska symposium on motivation* (pp. 237–307). Lincoln: University of Nebraska Press.

Zuckerman, M. (1978). Sensation seeking. In H. London & J. E. Exner, Jr. (Eds.), *Dimensions of personality* (pp. 487–559). New York: Wiley.

Zuckerman, M. (1979). *Sensation seeking: Beyond the optimal level of arousal.* Hillsdale, NJ: Erlbaum.

Zuckerman, M. (1983). The distinction between trait and state scales is *not* arbitrary: Comments on Allen and Potkay's "On the arbitrary distinction between traits and states." *Journal of Personality and Social Psychology, 44,* 1083–1086.

Zuckerman, M., Bone, R. N., Neary, R., Mangelsdorff, D., & Brustman, B. (1972). What is the sensation seeker? Personality trait and experience correlates of the sensation-seeking scales. *Journal of Consulting and Clinical Psychology, 39,* 308–321.

Zuckerman, M., Buchsbaum, M. S., & Murphy, D. L. (1980). Sensation seeking and its biological correlates. *Psychological Bulletin, 88,* 187–214.

Zuckerman, M., Kolin, E. A., Price, L., & Zoob, I. (1964). Development of a Sensation-Seeking Scale. *Journal of Consulting Psychology, 28,* 477–482.

Zuckerman, M., & Lubin, B. (1965). *Manual for the Multiple Affect Adjective Check List.* San Diego, CA: Educational and Industrial Testing Service.

Zuckerman, M., & Wheeler, L. (1975). To dispel fantasies about the fantasy-based measure of fear of success. *Psychological Bulletin, 82,* 932–946.

Zuroff, D. (1982). Person, situation, and person-by-situation interaction components in person perception. *Journal of Personality, 50,* 1–14.

Zweig, S. (1962). Wider horizons on Freud. In G. Lauzun (Ed.), *Sigmund Freud: The man and his theories* (pp. 205–215) (P. Evans, Trans.). (Original work published 1933)

Name Index

Subject Index

These pages constitute an extension of the copyright page.

Photos

CHAPTER 1   6, Joel Gordon, Joel Gordon Photography; 11, Ken Robert Buck, Stock Boston, Inc.

CHAPTER 2   30, Ken Heyman; 38, Frank Siteman, Jeroboam, Inc.

CHAPTER 3   66, The Bettmann Archive; 80, Rose Skytta, Jeroboam, Inc.; 84, Henri Cartier Bresson, Magnum Photos, Inc.; 87, Mike Mazzaschi, Stock Boston, Inc.; 97, Abigail Heyman, Archive Pictures, Inc.

CHAPTER 4   114 and 120, The Bettmann Archive; 126, Dr. Erich Salomon, Magnum Photos, Inc.; 131, Rene Burri, Magnum Photos, Inc.; 139, Mark Antman, The Image Works, Inc.

CHAPTER 5   155, The Bettmann Archive; 165, Alan Carey, The Image Works, Inc.; 170, Photo by Stuart; 173, Bernard Pierre Wolff, Magnum Photos, Inc.; 182, Christopher S. Johnson, Stock Boston, Inc.

CHAPTER 6   189, S. Robert Pugliese, University of Connecticut; 191, Inge Morath, Magnum Photos, Inc.; 202, Albert Bandura; 206, Elliott Erwitt, Magnum Photos, Inc.; 220, Mary Ellen Mark, Archive Pictures, Inc.

CHAPTER 7   226, AP/Wide World Photos, Inc.; 229, The Bettmann Archive; 232, Greg Mancuso, Stock Boston, Inc.; 241, William Carter; 246, Peter Vandermark, Stock Boston, Inc.

CHAPTER 8   266, Brandeis University; 272, Bernard Pierre Wolff, Magnum Photos, Inc.

CHAPTER 9   297, University of London British Postgraduate Medical Federation; 301, Gilles Peress, Magnum Photos, Inc.; 311, Susan Lapides, Design Conceptions.

CHAPTER 10   331, L'Illustration, Sygma Photos; 344, Cornell Capa, Magnum Photos, Inc.; 345, University of Texas at Austin; 348, The Bettmann Archive; 357, AP/Wide World Photos, Inc.

CHAPTER 11   370, UPI/Bettmann Newsphotos; 378, David Hurn, Magnum Photos, Inc.

CHAPTER 12   402, Robert A. Baron; 404, (left) AP/Wide World Photos, Inc.; (right) Reuters/Bettmann Newsphotos; 411, Photo from "Imitation of Film-Mediated Aggressive Models," by A. Bandura, D. Ross and S. A. Ross. In *Journal of Abnormal and Social Psychology*, 1963, 66, 3–11. Copyright 1963 by the American Psychology Association. Reprinted by permission; 412, Charles Gatewood, The Image Works, Inc.

CHAPTER 13   438, Joe Kelly, Archive Pictures, Inc.; 442, Dr. Norman S. Endler; 447, Joe Pineiro, Columbia University.

CHAPTER 14   465 and 472, Joel Gordon, Joel Gordon Photography; 477, Alice Eagly; 480, Stuart Franklin, Sygma Photos, Inc.; 485, Dr. Stuart P. Taylor.

CHAPTER 15   496, UPI/Bettmann Newsphotos; 498, Frances M. Cox, Omni Photo Communications, Inc.; 502, UPI/Bettmann Newsphotos; 505, Chris Steele-Perkins, Magnum Photos, Inc.; 507, Mike Button, EKM-Nepenthe; 509, Lawrence Kohlberg; 525, Ron Cooper, EKM-Nepenthe.

CHAPTER 16   555, United Nations.

Boxes, Figures, Quotes, Tables

CHAPTER 2   46, Table 2.2 adapted from "Recent Research Trends in Testing," by W. M. Reynolds and N. D. Sundberg. In *Journal of Personality Assessment*, 1976, *40,* pp. 228–233. Copyright 1984 by The Journal of Personality Assessment, Inc. Reprinted by permission. 47, Table 2.3 adapted from "The Practice of Psychological Assessment Among School Psychologists," by D. S. Goh, C. G. Teslow, and G. B. Fuller. In *Professional Psychology*, 1981, *12,* pp. 696–706. Copyright 1981 by the American Psychological Association. Reprinted by permission. 50, Figure 2.5 adapted from *A Handbook for Clinical and Actuarial MMPI Interpretation* by H. Gilberstadt and J. Duker. Copyright 1976 by W. B. Saunders Company. Reprinted by permission. 52, Table 2.4 based on material from *Assessment of Persons* by N. D. Sundberg. Copyright 1977 by Prentice-Hall, Inc.

CHAPTER 3   89 and 90, quotes from *The Collected Works of C. G. Jung*, revised trans. R. F. C. Hull, trans. by H. G. Baynes, Bollingen Series 20. Vol. 6: *Psychological Types*. Copyright © 1971 by Princeton University Press.

CHAPTER 4   116, Table 4.1 adapted from *The Neurotic Personality of Our Time*, by K. Horney. Copyright 1937 by W. W. Norton & Company, Inc. Copyright renewed 1964 by Renate Mintz, Brigitte Swarzenski, and Marianne von Eckardt. Reprinted by permission. 122, Table 4.2 adapted from *The Interpersonal Theory of Psychiatry* by H. S. Sullivan. Copyright 1953 by The William Alanson White Psychiatric Foundation. Copyright renewed 1981 by The William Alanson White Psychiatric Foundation. Reprinted by permission.

CHAPTER 5   166 and 167, Figures 5.3, 5.4, and 5.5 adapted from *The Analysis of Behavior* by J. Holland and B. Skinner. Copyright 1961 by McGraw-Hill Book Company. Reprinted by permission. 172, Table 5.1 adapted from *Beyond Freedom and Dignity* by B. F. Skinner. Copyright 1971 by Alfred A. Knopf, Inc. Reprinted by permission. 183, Table 5.3 from "Psychology's Contemporary and All-time Notables: Student, Faculty and Chairperson Viewpoints" by S. Davis, R. Thomas, and M. Weaver. In *Bulletin of Psychonomic Society*, vol. 20, pp. 3–5. Copyright 1982 by The Psychonomic Society. Reprinted by permission.

CHAPTER 6   215 and 217, Figures 6.3, 6.4, and Table 6.1 adapted from "Microanalysis of Action and Fear Arousal as a Function of Differential Levels of Perceived Self-Efficacy," by A. Bandura, L. Reese and N. Adams. In *Journal of Personality and Social Psychology*, 1982, *43,* pp. 5–21. Copyright 1982 by the American Psychological Association. Reprinted by permission.

CHAPTER 7   228 and 229, quotes from *On Becoming A Person, A Therapist's View of Psychotherapy*, by Carl Rogers. Copyright © 1961 by Houghton-Mifflin Company. Reprinted by permission. 231, quotes from *The Foundations of the Person-Centered Approach*, by Carl Rogers. Copyright © 1983 by Carl Rogers. Reprinted by permission.

CHAPTER 8   280–282, Box 8.1 from *The Psychology of Personal Constructs* by G. Kelly. Copyright © 1955 by W. W. Norton & Company, Inc. Reprinted by permission.

CHAPTER 9   297, Figure 9.1 from *A Model for Personality* by H. J. Eysenck. Copyright © 1981 by Springer Verlag, New York. Reprinted by permission. 304–305, Box 9.2 adapted from *Personality Structure* and Measurement by H. J. Eysenck and S. B. G. Eysenck. Copyright 1969 by EDITS Publishers. **307**, Table 9.1 adapted from "A Short Questionnaire for the Measurement of Two Dimensions of Personality," by H. J. Eysenck. In Journal of Applied Psychology, 1958, 42, pp. 14–17. Copyright 1958 by the American Psychological Association. Reprinted by permission. **314**, Figures 9.3 and 9.4 adapted from Biological Bases of Individual Behavior, by H. J. Eysenck and A. Levey. Copyright 1972 by Academic Press. Reprinted by permission. **319**, Figure 9.5 based on material from Handbook for the Sixteen Personality Factor Questionnaire, by R. B. Cattell, H. W. Eber and M. M. Tatsuoka. Copyright 1970 by the Institute for Personality and Ability Testing.

CHAPTER 10   **329–330, 332, and 333**, Box 10.1, Table 10.1 and 10.2, adapted and abridged from The Authoritarian Personality, by T. W. Adorno, Else-Frenkel Brunswik, D. J. Levinson and R. N. Sanford. Copyright 1950 by the American Jewish Committee. Reprinted by permission of Harper & Row, Publishers, Inc. **334**, Figure 10.1 from Dimensions of Personality by R. C. Dillehay. Copyright © 1978 by John Wiley and Sons, Inc. Reprinted by permission. **341 and 342**, Tables 10.3 and 10.4 adapted from The Nature and Measurement of Anxiety, by R. B. Cattell. Copyright 1963 by Scientific American. Reprinted by permission. **343–344**, Box 10.2 adapted and abridged from Theories of Anxiety, by William F. Fischer. Copyright © 1971 by William F. Fischer. Reprinted by permission of Harper & Row, Publishers, Inc. **347**, Figure 10.2 from Manual for the Multiple Affect Adjective Check List by M. Zuckerman and B. Lubin. Copyright © 1965 by the Educational & Industrial Testing Services. Reprinted by permission. **352**, Figure 10.3 from "Motivational Determinants of Risk Taking Behavior," by J. W. Atkinson. In Psychological Review, 1957, 64, pp. 359–372. Copyright 1957 by the American Psychological Association. Reprinted by permission. **355**, Box 10.3 adapted from "What is the Sensation Seeker?" by M. Zuckerman, R. N. Bone, R. Neary, D. Mangelsdorff, and B. Brustman. In Journal of Consulting and Clinical Psychology, 1972, 39, pp. 308–321. Copyright 1972 by the American Psychological Association. Reprinted by permission. **358**, Table 10.6 adapted from "Sensation Seeking and its Biological Correlates," by M. Zuckerman, M. S. Buchshaum, and D. L. Murphy. In Psychological Bulletin, 1980, 88, pp. 187–214. Copyright 1980 by the American Psychological Association. Reprinted by permission.

CHAPTER 11   **384**, Table 11.1 adapted from People in Context, Measuring Person-Environment Congruence in Education and Industry, by G. C. Stern. Copyright 1970 by John Wiley & Sons, Inc. Reprinted by permission. **390**, Table 11.2 adapted from "Mount Saint Helen's Ashfall," by P. R. Adams and G. R. Adams. In American Psychologist, 1984, 39, pp. 252–260. Copyright 1984 by the American Psychological Association. Reprinted by permission. **391**, Table 11.3 reprinted with permission from the Journal of Psychosomatic Research, Vol. 11, T. H. Holmes and R. H. Rahe, "The Social Readjustment Scale." Copyright 1967, Pergamon Press, Ltd.

CHAPTER 13   **444 and 446**, Figures 13.2 and 13.3 adapted from 1982 Nebraska Symposium on Motivation, by permission of University of Nebraska Press. Copyright 1983 by the University of Nebraska Press. **453, 454, and 455**, Table 13.6 and Figures 13.4, 13.5, and 13.6 adapted from "Selective Attention to the Self: Situational and Disposi-

tional Determinants," by W. Mischel and E. Ebbesen. In Journal of Personality and Social Psychology, 1973, 27, pp. 129–142. Copyright 1973 by the American Psychological Association. Reprinted by permission. **457**, Table 13.7 adapted from "Personality Traits and the Eye of the Beholder: Crossing Some Traditional Philosophical Boundaries in the Search for Consistency in all of the People," by D. Kenrick and D. Stringfield. In Psychological Review, 1980, 87, pp. 88–104. Copyright 1980 by the American Psychological Association. Reprinted by permission.

CHAPTER 14   **465**, Figure 14.1 adapted form "Authoritarianism, Displaced Aggression, and Social Status of the Target," by R. Epstein. In Journal of Personality and Social Psychology, 1965, 2, pp. 585–588. Copyright 1965 by the American Psychological Association. Reprinted by permission. **467**, Figure 14.2 adapted from "Stress Effects on Affiliation Preferences Among Subjects Possessing the Type A Coronary-Prone Behavior Pattern," by T. Dembroski and J. MacDougall. In Journal of Personality and Social Psychology, 1978, 36, pp. 23–33. Copyright 1978 by the American Psychological Association. Reprinted by permission. **473**, Table 14.1 adapted from "Sex, Androgyny, and Approach Responses to Erotica: A New Variation on the Old Volunteer Problem," by D. Kenrick, D. Stringfield, W. Wagenhals, R. Dahl, and H. Ransdell. In Journal of Personality and Social Psychology, 1980, 38, pp. 517–524. Copyright 1980 by the American Psychological Association. Reprinted by permission. **474**, Figures 14.4 and 14.5 adapted from information appearing in the article, "Sex" by R. Athanasious, P. Shaver, and C. Travis. In Psychology Today, July 1970. **476**, Figure 14.6 adapted from "Motivation and Emotion," by C. Jazwinski and D. Byrne. In Bulletin of Psychonomic Society, 1978, 2, pp. 287–297. Copyright 1978 by the Psychonomic Society. Reprinted by permission. **477**, Table 14.2 adapted from "Sex Differences in Influenceability," by A. Eagly. In Psychological Bulletin, 1978, 85, p. 86–166. Copyright 1978 by the American Psychological Association. Reprinted by permission. **478**, Box 14.2, adapted from "Sex Variable in Conformity Behavior," by F. Sistrunk and J. McDavid. In Journal of Personality and Social Psychology, 1971, 17, pp. 200–207. Copyright 1971 by the American Psychological Association. Reprinted by permission. **481**, Table 14.3 adapted from "Sex Differences in Conformity: Surveillance by the Group as a Determinant of Male Non-Conformity," by A. Eagly, W. Wood, and L. Fishbaugh. In Journal of Personality and Social Psychology, 1981, 40, pp. 384–389. Copyright 1981 by the American Psychological Association. Reprinted by permission. **486**, Figures 14.8 and 14.9 adapted from "The Effect of Situational Contingencies on Female Retaliative Behavior," by D. Richardson, S. Berstein, and S. Taylor. In Journal of Personality and Social Psychology, 1979, 37, pp. 2044–2048. Copyright 1979 by the American Psychological Association. Reprinted by permission.

CHAPTER 15   **511–516**, quotes from "Moral Stages and Moralization," by L. Kohlberg. In T. Lickona (Ed.), Moral Development and Behavior-Theory, Research and Social Issues. Copyright © 1976 by CBS Educational and Professional Publishing. Reprinted by permission of Holt, Rinehart & Winston.

CHAPTER 16   **557**, Figure 16.1 from Sundberg/Tyler/Taplin, Clinical Psychology: Expanding Horizons, 2nd Ed., © 1973, p. 101. Reprinted by permission of Prentice-Hall, Inc., Englewood Cliffs, N.J.

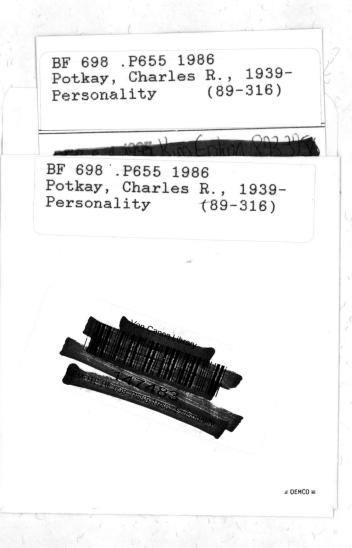